STUDIES IN WELSH EDUCATION

WELSH EDUCATIONAL STRUCTURE
AND ADMINISTRATION

1880–1925

by

LESLIE WYNNE EVANS
Reader in Education University of Wales

CARDIFF
UNIVERSITY OF WALES PRESS
1974

© LESLIE WYNNE EVANS, 1974

ISBN 0 7083 0554 7

TO
MY WIFE
MEGAN

Contents

		Page
	PREFACE	1
I	A SURVEY OF THE EVOLUTION OF WELSH EDUCATIONAL STRUCTURE AND ADMINISTRATION 1880–1925	5
II	THE CONTENTIOUS WELSH BOARD	47
III	THE CARMARTHENSHIRE INQUIRY	117
IV	THE GENESIS OF THE WELSH DEPARTMENT, BOARD OF EDUCATION	183
V	THE EXPLOSIVE REPORT	239
VI	THE WELSH DEPARTMENT, BOARD OF EDUCATION 1907–1925	307
	EPILOGUE	377
	APPENDICES at the end of each Study	
	BIBLIOGRAPHY	391
	INDEX	411

Preface

It is strange that so very little detailed research has been undertaken on what is undoubtedly the most important period in the evolution of Welsh educational structure and administration, the years 1880 to 1925. The six studies in this book attempt in some measure to supply this deficiency. They are inter-related and for that reason I may be forgiven if there appears to be occasional overlap in content. It was my intention originally to bring the story up to date, but immediately two difficulties arose. In the first place, the operation of the Records Act continues to render impracticable a close and detailed study of Welsh educational affairs in recent years. Secondly, the inclusion of such material would have made the proportions of this book quite unwieldy. But the death of Sir Owen Edwards in 1920 and the retirement of Sir Alfred T. Davies in 1925 brought to an end their partnership at the Welsh Department of the Board of Education. This seemed a convenient stopping place.[1]

Two of these studies have appeared (in much less elaborate form) in other publications: 'The Evolution of Welsh Educational Structure and Administration' in *Studies in the Government and Control of Education since* 1860, London, 1970, the first publication of the History of Education Society. 'The Genesis of the Welsh Department, Board of Education, 1906-7', a lecture delivered to the Honourable Society of Cymmrodorion at King's College, University of London in January 1970, appeared in the *Transactions of the Society*, Session 1969, Part II, 1970.

The emergence of Wales as a nation in the field of education dates from 1880. The next forty-five years was a most significant period in many ways for it witnessed a national awakening and a cultural renaissance. The first study is a survey of this evolutionary process. It does not pretend to be exhaustive or even adequate but endeavours to cover the main background and educational developments in Wales up to 1925. Other writers might have treated such a survey quite differently and given more prominence to other features, but I have merely attempted a general framework. The second study is concerned with the Central Welsh Board which was responsible for Welsh *intermediate* education or *intermediate schools*.

---

[1] Throughout this book, Owen Edwards is used instead of *Owen M. Edwards*. On 17 May 1907, (at the end of one of his first Minutes as HMCI in the Welsh Department) he crossed out the letter M, and from then on to his death he used O. E. or Owen Edwards.

Preface

The unsteady relationships between this Board and the Welsh Department of the Board of Education are discussed.

The third study deals with the impact of the Education Act of 1902 upon Wales, a legislative measure which aroused bitter controversy between Church and Chapel and more particularly between the Principality and the central government—epitomized in the Carmarthenshire Inquiry. This was a county which presented a resurgence of the old Nonconformist radical tradition at the start of this century. It posed administrative problems in the evolution of its local government politics by exhibiting its own peculiar loyalties. Its older Dissenting denominations, notably Independents, ignored the Balfour Education Act, and the county council adopted an *independent* and uncompromising attitude towards the Welsh National Council for education. It was the only Welsh county which refused membership and the whole scheme was wrecked.

The fourth study shows how the Welsh Department of the Board of Education emerged as a result of the abortive attempts to secure for Wales a major measure of administrative differentiation in educational affairs in the form of a Welsh National Council for education. The fifth study examines the cause of an unpleasant, academic quarrel between the Welsh Department and the Central Welsh Board. The final study traces the growth and development of the Welsh Department from 1907 to 1925.

The outstanding personalities in Welsh education during that period introduce themselves in each study. Some, according to their stature, were more prominent than others. One, in particular, Sir Owen Edwards almost dominates the whole scene. Almost all the material about Edwards has been extracted from his *official* memoranda and minutes at Whitehall and his massive correspondence with Sir J. Herbert Lewis. Unfortunately, during the preparation of this book I was not able, due to certain restrictions to have access to his personal diaries and private papers. It might be acclaimed without contradiction that Edwards, in addition to being one of the leading Welsh educationists of his time, was also an extremely complex personality, and in the eyes of more than one Welsh educational institution—and some of his contemporaries—the *enfant terrible*.

The bulk of the material in these studies has been drawn from original documents in the files of the Department of Education and Science now deposited in the Public Record Office, London. The papers dating from the early years of the Board of Education, which have been sorted, are also available in the same building. I have also used the Lloyd George

Preface

papers housed in the Beaverbrook Library, London, and his large collection of letters and papers deposited at the National Library of Wales.

Much important and hitherto unpublished MS material was made available to me from private sources. I am deeply grateful to Mrs. K. Idwal Jones of Penucha, Caerwys, Flintshire, for placing at my disposal the Penucha MSS which comprise the diaries, letters and private papers of her late father, Sir J. Herbert Lewis, MP. Also, by a stroke of good fortune, I was able to meet one of the sons of the late Sir Alfred T. Davies —Mr. A. Mervyn Davies, of Wilton, Connecticut, USA, who so kindly talked with me of his father and loaned me a considerable number of Sir Alfred's private papers. I am indebted to Lady Eirene White and Mr. Tristan Jones for allowing me to see some papers of their father, Dr. Thomas Jones, which are still under restriction at the National Library of Wales.

My sincere thanks are accorded to Dr. Kenneth O. Morgan, of the Queen's College, Oxford, who (apart from the second study) read the whole of the work in typescript and offered many suggestions which were adopted with advantage. Mr. David I. Allsobrook, one of my colleagues, and Mr. Owen E. Jones, HMI, carefully read the initial galley proofs. My debt to other Welsh historians is, I hope, sufficiently indicated in the footnotes and text. But for the conclusions I have drawn and any errors that undoubtedly remain, I am solely responsible.

The 'Reproductions of Crown-copyright Records in the Public Record Office' appear by permission of the Controller of HM Stationery Office, i.e. in this book, facsimiles in Appendices I and II of the fifth study. Finally, I wish to thank: University College, Cardiff, for some assistance at certain stages of my researches with grants from its research fund; Miss Phyllis M. Downie, late librarian, Department of Education and Science, and her staff at Curzon Street; the late Miss M. Forsyth, Deputy Departmental Records Officer at Elizabeth House, York Road, Waterloo, SE1 (who also arranged for files to be brought to me at Curzon Street and Waterloo); Dr. R. Brinley Jones, Director, University of Wales Press, for many kindnesses and help, and to the printers for their excellent work. My wife, who proved to be an excellent page-proof reader also indexed the whole work.

LESLIE WYNNE EVANS

University College,
Cardiff,
Saint Davids Day, 1974.

I

A SURVEY OF THE EVOLUTION OF WELSH EDUCATIONAL STRUCTURE AND ADMINISTRATION 1880–1925

APPENDICES 39

A Survey of the Evolution of Welsh Educational Structure and Administration 1880-1925

WHEN Henry Austin Bruce, 1st Lord Aberdare, sat in his study at 1 Queen's Gate, S.W., on 10 May 1880, and composed a letter to the Prime Minister, Mr. Gladstone, fresh from his Mid-Lothian campaign, he initiated a Welsh educational awakening. The burden of his letter was to impress upon the Prime Minister 'that in all the Welsh elections one subject was everywhere prominent, and that every candidate, whether successful or not, pledged himself to keep upon the government the consideration of the defective condition of intermediate and higher education in Wales'.[1] The consequences of that letter proved to be of great significance for Welsh education. Its tangible result over a short period of twenty-seven years was the creation of an educational blueprint for Wales which had no parallel in any other country in western Europe. In short, the Aberdare Report of 1881 (the fruit of the Committee set up in 1880 to inquire into the condition of intermediate and higher education in Wales and Monmouthshire) heralded the evolution of Welsh educational structure and administration which in due season brought forth many institutions of a national character. It is not without some significance that the second son of Lord Aberdare, the Hon. William Napier Bruce was inevitably to be deeply involved in almost every major aspect of the evolutionary administrative processes. No son wore his father's mantle with greater pride or distinction, and Sir Herbert Lewis rightly described him as 'a prince of civil servants'.[2]

Excluding the Welsh elementary school system which, after 1870 followed the English national pattern, Wales acquired between 1881 and 1910 a national university, a Central Welsh Board, a successful and thriving organization of intermediate and secondary schools, a National Library and National Museum, and a Welsh Department of the Board of Education. No catalogue of achievements could be more impressive for such a brief interval of time. But withal, this array of Welsh national accomplishments lacked one vital ingredient—a National Council for

---

[1] PRO Ed 91/8, File No. 1, Lord Aberdare to Gladstone.
[2] Herbert Lewis's Diary, 29th November, 1915, Penucha MSS.

A Survey of the Evolution of Welsh Educational Structure & Administration

Education. For many years, its establishment became the cherished dream of Lloyd George and his followers. Its non-fulfilment remained one of his bitter memories. Had it materialized, it would have given Wales a substantial measure of autonomy in educational affairs.

On St. Davids Day, 1921, Sir Harry Rudolph Reichel, first Principal of the University College of North Wales, Bangor, said, in his address to the Manchester Welsh Society:

> My own experience, extending now over thirty-seven years in Wales, has witnessed a Renaissance period, a time of extraordinary activity, of rapid development and reconstruction. So completely have the mental outlook and social life been transformed, that anyone who had known the Principality before the eighties, and been cut off from all communication with it ever since, would hardly recognize his surroundings if he returned to it now . . . During this brief period, a great system of secondary schools has been established, and the small and struggling College of 1872 has grown into a National University with four times as many teachers as the original college possessed students.[1]

Reichel should have gone further to include the establishment of the Welsh Department of the Board of Education in 1907 and its many-sided activities in its formative period up to 1925. He would have had a great deal to reveal.

The year 1880 is the starting point of this survey, but it is necessary as a preliminary to review some developments earlier in the century. On the educational side, before 1868, the provision of education for the children of Wales in day schools, whether at elementary or higher levels, was most inadequate apart from the Works Schools System where employers of labour provided excellent elementary schools for their populations gathered within the centres of heavy industries and coalmining.[2] The two main Voluntary Societies, within their limits, were also doing commendable work. The publication of the notorious *Reports* by the *Education Commissioners* in 1847, called in Wales the *Treachery of the Blue Books*, 'largely nullified the effect of their report through their mass indictment of the culture, social conditions, religion, and morals of the people of Wales'.[3] They did little to improve relations between England and Wales but served to unite Welshmen from one end of the country to the other, and more important still, brought into the limelight the whole question of Welsh education. The *Reports* which revealed the low state of education in the Principality merely substantiated Hugh Owen's concern when he published in 1843 his famous letter to the Welsh nation in general, and to

---

[1] H. R. Reichel, Patriotism, True and False, *The Welsh Outlook*, Newtown, 1921, pp. 104–6.
[2] Leslie Wynne Evans, *Education in Industrial Wales*, 1700–1900, Cardiff, 1971, pp. 15, ff.
[3] Kenneth O. Morgan, *Wales in British Politics*, 1868–1922, Cardiff, 1963, p. 3

A Survey of the Evolution of Welsh Educational

Nonconformists in particular, urging them to provide undenominational schools to counteract those of the Church which were spreading rapidly. He was equally concerned with the problem of providing teachers, who should be properly trained for the tasks which lay ahead.

Welshmen also realized the force of Kay-Shuttleworth's contention that there would never be any real improvement in education until Wales had a good supply of trained teachers. This implied Training Colleges in the Principality to supplement the already well known trek of Welsh pupil teachers to the Borough Road Training College in London which almost became a household name in Wales during the nineteenth century. But Wales had, long before 1870, three or four Training Colleges such as the Brecon Normal School in 1846 which had a brief life since it depended on voluntary subscriptions; Church of England colleges at Trinity, Carmarthen, and Caernarvon in 1848 and 1849 respectively,[1] and Bangor Normal College in 1858. At secondary level there were a few 'considerable boarding schools for the middle classes especially in Swansea and Cardiff' but many of the upper middle class of those towns sent their children to Bath or Clifton.[2] There was a number of old endowed grammar schools, for example, Abergavenny Grammar School; Friars' School, Bangor; Cowbridge Grammar School; Ruthin School; Queen Elizabeth's Grammar School, Carmarthen; and Christ's College, Brecon. The Llandovery Collegiate School was of much later (nineteenth century) origin, and its first Warden was the Venerable John Williams, Archdeacon of Cardigan, who had for over twenty years been Rector of Edinburgh Academy, and if Sir Walter Scott can be believed 'he was a heaven born teacher and the greatest schoolmaster in Europe'![3]

Only four secondary schools were available for girls, Dr. Williams's school, Dolgellau, the Howells schools at Denbigh and Llandaff, and at Carmarthen. Finally, on the higher education side, the Presbyterian and Congregational Fund Boards in London, maintained from 1704 a 'Welsh Academy' at Carmarthen, which later became the Presbyterian (Unitarian) College and a Theological College, the oldest institution of higher education in Wales.[4] The Anglican college at Lampeter and other denominational colleges were of much later date. At the base, there was one pure Welsh educational institution which preserved the Welsh language—the Sunday school. Everyone who wished to do so attended

---

[1] The college at Caernarvon moved to Bangor in 1894, and named St. Mary's.

[2] *Report of Schools Inquiry Commission, vol. VIII, Report* by H. M. Bompas, p. 3. The passing of the Endowed Schools Act in 1869, a measure which though it had but little effect upon the mere statistics of Welsh education exerted important influences in other ways.

[3] *Welsh in Education and Life*, Board of Education, HMSO, 1927, p. 62.

[4] J. E. Lloyd (ed.) *History of Carmarthenshire*, vol. II, Cardiff, 1939. p. 240.

this school from the cradle to the grave, and well after the Education Act of 1870 and the introduction of compulsory education by Mundella in 1880, Sunday schools were far more popular than day schools.[1] In fact, only the Sunday schools remained a truly Welsh institution, for the system of Welsh intermediate schools after 1889 was modelled on continental lines (the *Real-schulen* of Prussia) or on the older English endowed schools, and the University of Wales on the Queen's University of Ireland and London University.[2]

Politically, the year 1868 was of great significance for Welsh education. Briefly, the triumphant elections of 1868 in Wales after the extension of the franchise in Disraeli's Reform Act of 1867, 'were widely acclaimed as symbolizing the awakening of the Welsh nation'.[3] This was the time when Nonconformity and political radicalism became synonymous, engendering consciousness of nationhood, particularly in the field of higher education after 1880. For the first time Wales had at Westminster a band of Liberal MPs which in the nineties grew into a vigorous Welsh Parliamentary Party with the two stars Tom Ellis and Lloyd George at the centre. In this same context tribute should be paid to the English friends of Wales in the evolution of the Welsh educational system, such as Gladstone, Lord Spencer, James Bryce and his friend W. T. Warry (one of the Principal Officers of the Charity Commissioners and Secretary to the Aberdare Departmental Committee). Among those in the House of Commons who played a major part were A. J. Mundella, Sir William Hart-Dyke, A. H. Dyke Acland (a close friend of Tom Ellis), and Augustine Birrell, briefly President of the Board of Education—not forgetting two inspectors of the Board who knew Wales so thoroughly—A. G. Legard and Thomas Darlington, the latter being fluent in Welsh. All these people are more than mere names to any student of Welsh education.

Before considering the Aberdare Report of 1881 reference must be made to the Education Act of 1870 and the establishment of the University College of Wales, Aberystwyth, in October 1872. Legislatively, Wales was merely part of the English elementary school pattern which emerged from Forster's Act, but the main features in Wales were the controversies which arose with regard to Church National schools in 'single school' areas where such schools catered for a Nonconformist community, and the question of religious instruction which again raised its head after the Balfour Act of 1902 and the Welsh Defaulting Authorities in 1904. But

[1] Leslie Wynne Evans, 'Voluntary education in the industrial areas of Wales before 1870', *NLWJ*, vol. XLV, No. 4.
[2] D. Emrys Evans, *The University of Wales, A Historical Sketch*, Cardiff, 1953, p. 15.
[3] Kenneth O. Morgan, op. cit., p. 28.

the opening of the college at Aberystwyth was the spearhead of a national campaign for higher education and became a distinctively Welsh question in the House of Commons evoking 'sympathetic response from both political parties'.[1] This led to the establishment of the Departmental Committee of 1880 under the chairmanship of Lord Aberdare which inquired into the defective condition of intermediate and higher education in Wales.

The population of Wales in 1871 was just under one and a half million and the funds for establishing and maintaining the Aberystwyth college were collected from all over Wales and many English cities, including Manchester and Liverpool, in a campaign organized by Sir Hugh Owen and others. Even a University Sunday was set apart for collections from the Welsh Nonconformist Chapels.[2] The monetary details are fascinating: nearly £9,000 was raised in three years: 100,000 persons gave sums under 2*s*. 6*d*.; 5,000 exactly 2*s*. 6*d*. each; 4,000 gave over 2*s*. 6*d*.; in later years only seven persons had given sums of £1,000, and seven persons from £500 to £1,000.[3] Right up to 1882 the college depended on voluntary subscriptions for its existence. Two Welsh MPs, Henry Richard and Osborne Morgan failed to persuade Gladstone to sanction government subvention because 'it would raise the religious issue, and would commit the State to a new principle in aiding colleges from the exchequer on the basis of their teaching only "an undenominational education" '.[4] But the college opened in 1872 with twenty-five students. By 1900 there were 1,310 students undergoing courses at the *three* constituent colleges of the University of Wales. What accounted for the rapid rise in student numbers by 1900? How did Wales obtain three constituent colleges between 1872 and 1884, and a full-blown University of Wales in 1893? These are the questions which must be considered in order to follow the remarkable and rapid developments that took place in Welsh higher education in the brief span of twenty years, from the Aberdare Report of 1881 to the Education Act of 1902, which covers the first phase in the evolution of Welsh educational structure and administration. The second extends from 1902 up to, and including the creation of the Welsh Department of the Board of Education in 1907. The third from 1907 to the publication of the Bruce Report on the reorganization of secondary education in Wales, in 1920, and the end of the first phase of the Welsh Department in 1925.

---

[1] Kenneth O. Morgan, op. cit., p. 46.

[2] *Report of the Committee appointed to Inquire into the Condition of Intermediate and Higher Education in Wales and Monmouthshire*, (c. 3047), 1881 (*Aberdare Report*), *Vol. II*, evidence of Hugh Owen, pp. 12–15. Also *Parl. Deb.*, 4th *Vol. Session* 1889, p. 126; pp. 153–4.

[3] K. Viriamu Jones, *Life of J. Viriamu Jones*, London, 1921, p. 99.

[4] Kenneth O. Morgan, op. cit., p. 47.

Structure and Administration 1880-1925

I

The development of Welsh education shows that history is no respecter of logic. Wales, like England, had training colleges before it acquired a national system of elementary schools, and university colleges before secondary schools. In point of fact, Wales was in the singular position of building its educational system from the top instead of from the bottom.[1] Long before 1881 much had been written on Welsh higher education and many meetings had been held by leading Welshmen in London and elsewhere. One of the first colleges for higher education in Wales *which granted degrees*, was Saint Davids College, Lampeter, founded by Bishop Thomas Burgess in 1822 and incorporated by Royal Charter in 1828 'for the reception and education of persons destined for Holy Orders'. For special reasons, Lampeter was never merged into the Welsh University until 1971 when arrangements were completed for its incorporation as a constituent institution of the University after a period of sponsorship by University College, Cardiff.[2]

Strange to relate, the Welsh University movement was initiated by a body of Welsh clergy ministering in England.[3] In 1852 they petitioned Parliament for 'a University founded on broad and liberal principles to meet the needs of the Welsh people, churchmen or dissenters'.[4] There were other moves, for example, in 1853, when B. T. Williams, a young Glasgow graduate who later became a QC, and MP for Carmarthen in 1878, proposed in a pamphlet—*The Desirableness of a University for Wales*—the idea of a unitary University in one place on the Scottish plan. In 1854, Sir Hugh Owen at a London meeting proposed a Welsh University on the model of the Queen's Colleges in Ireland, run on unsectarian lines. The Crimean War intervened, but in 1862, 1863 and afterwards, further meetings led to the opening of the University College of Wales, Aberystwyth, which many thought would become the national university, but this was not to be.[5] Although the Welsh people were in full accord with the establishment of a degree-giving university in Wales, and Owen in his evidence to the Aberdare Committee in 1880 expressed the opinion 'that

---

[1] *Parl. Deb.*, op. cit., 1889, p. 122, Stuart Rendel moving the second reading of the *Intermediate Education (Wales) Bill*, 15 May.

[2] PRO Ed 91/8, Memorial from Francis John Jayne, Principal, St. David's College, Lampeter to Gladstone, 19 May 1880. *Calendar, University of Wales*, 1971. It should be remembered that Carmarthen Presbyterian College was the *first* to grant degrees—the B.D. of London University, given by Royal Charter in 1847.

[3] *Report of the Association of Welsh Clergy in the West Riding*, 1854, p. 5. This Association was formed in the West Riding in 1821. It was composed of disgruntled clerics who had left Wales rather than tolerate a system which promoted strangers to all the lucrative livings in preference to native clergy, many of whom were men of outstanding academic ability.

[4] *Report of the Association of Welsh Clergy*, op. cit.

[5] D. Emrys Evans, op. cit., p. 12.

the educational machinery of Wales would be incomplete unless elementary, intermediate and higher education culminated in academic distinction',[1] there were others opposed to the proposal, including Owen Owen, Oswestry, Dean Edwards of Bangor, Dr. Vance Smith (a Unitarian) of the Presbyterian College, Carmarthen, and Richard Davies, MP for Anglesey. Also, almost all the headmasters of the Welsh grammar schools disapproved.[2] Owen Owen, at that time headmaster of the Willow Street Academy at Oswestry (and later of Oswestry High School) regarded Jesus College, Oxford 'as the apex of the whole system of Welsh secondary education . . . Jesus College has been regarded for nearly three centuries as the national college of Wales'.[3] Dean Edwards, Vance Smith and Richard Davies were doubtful as to whether the Principality could furnish 'material enough to support a Welsh university' and questioned 'the inexpediency of multiplying degree-giving bodies'. They acknowledged that Oxford and Cambridge were beyond the reach of the main body of poor students and ventured the opinion 'that London and Victoria (Manchester) universities could sufficiently meet the requirements of this class in Wales'.[4] The headmasters argued that a Welsh university would be 'of a lower and narrower type, with none of the literary prestige and the varied and educating social advantages of the ancient seats of learning'.[5]

There was little purpose in having a university or colleges unless students were forthcoming above elementary level. This criticism was levelled against the University College at Aberystwyth at the Aberdare Inquiry of 1880, and was, of course due to the absence of a Welsh secondary school system. There was a similar lack of secondary education in many parts of England where the Endowed School reform was an issue at this time. In Wales, several people had drawn attention to this situation including the Rev. D. Lewis Lloyd, headmaster of Friars' school, Bangor, in his pamphlet published in 1876.[6] Lloyd was concerned that the education of the working classes ended with the public elementary

---

[1] *Aberdare Report*, op. cit., Vol. 1, p. xxxiii.

[2] Ibid.

[3] Ibid., Vol. II, p. 387, ff. Owen Owen was speaking years before the Welsh Intermediate Education Act of 1889, which created intermediate schools to feed the Welsh university colleges. In 1896, Owen, who became Chief Inspector of the new Central Welsh Board, was virtually in command of intermediate education. In his evidence to the Aberdare Committee, he proposed a novel way of raising revenue for providing exhibitions to Oxford and Cambridge—for pupils of the older Welsh grammar schools—including his own. He believed in 'a complete system of *result fees*' whereby the government could allow 5/- for each boy who passed in certain subjects, e.g. arithmetic, English grammar, orthography, English history, geography and writing. It is tempting to postulate whether his idea was inherent in the Central Welsh Board's mania for examinations and examination fees!

[4] Ibid., Vol. 1.

[5] Ibid.

[6] D. Lewis Lloyd, *The Missing Link in Education in Wales*, Bangor, 1876. Lloyd was one of the witnesses at the Inquiry into Intermediate and Higher Education in Wales and Monmouthshire, and after being headmaster of Friars' School, Bangor, became headmaster of Dolgellau Grammar School and Christ's College, Brecon, became Bishop of Bangor.

school and that 'a vast amount of natural ability existed among the artisan and working classes which was wasted'.[1] He suggested some remedies including schemes of scholarships to be established all over Wales. In 1879, H. Hussey Vivian of Swansea and MP for Glamorgan, brought the attention of the House of Commons to the deficiencies of Welsh higher education. While Ireland had 1,634 students (1 to 3,121 of the population), and Scotland an impressive 4,000 (1 to 840), the total number of Welsh students enjoying higher education of any kind at Jesus College, Oxford, at Saint Davids College, Lampeter and at the newly-fledged college at Aberystwyth was a mere 189, and secondary education was almost non-existent. The twenty-seven endowed Welsh grammar schools were largely situated afar from the large urban centres swollen by industrial expansion. These schools shared endowments of £6,531 annually and their pupils numbered less than 4,000. The debate 'made Welsh higher education a political issue for the first time' and when Gladstone returned to power he acted quickly.[2] The letters from Gladstone and Lord Spencer to Lord Aberdare (who had proposed an Inquiry), and from Bryce and Mundella to Sir Hugh Owen and others between 10 May and 25 August 1880, describe in detail the establishment of the Aberdare Departmental Committee on intermediate and higher education in Wales.[3]

The Inquiry was completed in a short space of time and the *Report* appeared within a year, on 18 August, 1881. This *Report* was hailed in the Principality as the Welsh educational charter. It dealt with the educational requirements under four headings:

1. The provision needed for intermediate education.
2. The establishment of provincial colleges.
3. The expediency of creating a degree-giving University in Wales.
4. The sources from which the necessary funds might be obtained.

In Chapter IV of the *Report* due attention was paid to the distinct nationality of Wales:

> 'that system of education is most desirable for Wales which while preserving the national type, improves and elevates it, and at the same time gives opportunity for the development of any literary tastes or intellectual aptitudes which may be characteristic of the nation ... this is, in our opinion, a reason for securing within the limits of Wales itself a system of intermediate and higher education in harmony with the distinctive pecularities of the country'.[4]

Mention was also made of the deep religious convictions and the zeal for education of the Welsh people, and one witness gave the astounding

---

[1] Ibid., p. 5, ff.
[2] *Parl. Deb.*, 3rd., *vol. cclxvii*, pp. 1141 ff. Kenneth O. Morgan, op. cit., p. 48.
[3] PRO Ed 91/8, File I, Preliminaries to the Aberdare Report, 1880.
[4] *Aberdare Report*, op. cit., p. xxiv. ibid., pp. xlvi–vii.

testimony that in 1875 the Welsh people spent no less than £100,000 on Welsh literature of all kinds.[1] Even Hussey Vivian on the night of 14 May, 1889 (the night previous to the second reading of the Intermediate Education [Wales], Bill), in the debate on the Established Church in Wales, stated in his speech that 'the Welsh Nonconformists have built their own places of worship and maintain them by expending £300,000 and £400,000 annually'.[2] On the schools' side the *Report* found that the total number of boys in endowed grammar schools, proprietary schools and private schools was 4,036, and maintained that out of a total population of 1,570,000 Wales was entitled to accommodation for 15,700 pupils on a basis of 10 per 1,000.[3]

The *Report* recommended the creation of a new system of intermediate schools and the establishment of two colleges, one in south Wales and one in the north, at Aberystwyth, Bangor or Caernarvon, with a grant of £4,000 a year each.[4] Saint Davids College, Lampeter was to be affiliated to them.[5] No recommendation was made for Jesus College, Oxford, nor for the teaching of Welsh.[6] It is significant to note that although the *Report* acknowledged separate treatment for Wales in the field of higher education, it did not mention a national body or Council of Education for Wales. It will be seen that this matter reappears more than once before 1907. Nevertheless, the Welsh educational structure for the next twenty years emerged from the recommendations of this *Report*.

Expeditiousness was again the keynote in the implementation of the *Report's* recommendations and strangely enough the order was: (i) the establishment of two University Colleges in 1883 and 1884;[7] (ii) the Welsh Intermediate Education Act of 1889 to set up intermediate schools, and (iii) the Royal Charter of incorporation as the University of Wales in 1893. Stranger still, the Welsh intermediate schools appeared *after* the creation of the Welsh University. A tremendous amount of heat and jealousy was engendered in Wales over the location of the two new colleges, for Aberystwyth was considered too remote to serve the interests of north Wales. The south Wales contenders were Swansea and Cardiff who presented imposing memorials setting forth their claims. More humble petitioners had submitted claims for towns like Bridgend, on the grounds that 'Cardiff and Swansea being shipping ports, had temptations to

---

[1] Ibid., p. xvi. Also: *Parl. Deb.*, 4*th Vol. Session*, 1889, p. 130.
[2] *Parl. Deb.*, ibid., pp. 105–6.
[3] *Aberdare Report*, op. cit., p. xvi. Also *Parl. Deb.*, ibid., p. 124.
[4] Ibid., p. lxvi.
[5] Ibid., p. lxviii.
[6] Ibid., p. lxix.
[7] See Appendices I and II.

immorality'. Three arbitrators were appointed—Lord Carlingford, A. J. Mundella, and Sir Frederick Bramwell—and Cardiff won the day.[1] The same men selected Bangor from among thirteen applications in north Wales.[2] University College of South Wales and Monmouthshire was opened at Cardiff in 1883, the first Principal being John Viriamu Jones, then aged 27, son of a Welsh Congregational minister. Formerly Principal and professor of physics and mathematics at Firth College (afterwards University), Sheffield, he was a close friend of Mundella who was MP for the Brightside division of the city and a moving spirit in Welsh educational development on many fronts in subsequent years.[3] University College of North Wales, Bangor, opened in 1884 with H. R. Reichel as Principal.[4]

Here was a dilemma! This brought into question the position of Aberystwyth which had been awarded a grant of £4,000 in 1882 as the only existing college in Wales.[5] Mundella[6], Vice-President of the Council in Gladstone's Second Ministry, had to overcome the opposition of some of his colleagues to the recommended grant of £8,000 a year to two new Welsh colleges, and this was only approved in 1883 'with the greatest difficulty and by Gladstone's imperative decision'.[7] With half this sum earmarked for Cardiff in the same year and the other half for Bangor in 1884, was the *Alma Mater* at Aberystwyth to be summarily dismissed? But that college had penetrated too deeply into the affections of the Welsh people to be the object of such treatment. Numerous controversies and objections were swept aside and Mundella once more extracted a further grant of £2,500 for the college. This was raised to £4,000 in 1885 and in 1890 the Salisbury administration granted Aberystwyth its charter as a University College, according it equal status with Cardiff and Bangor.[8] Instead therefore of the two University Colleges recommended by the *Aberdare Report*, Wales secured three in less than a decade.

Here, it would not be amiss to digress a little—to dispel any misgivings English people might entertain regarding the temperance inclinations of the Welsh. Paradoxically, notwithstanding the fact that Wales secured an Act in 1881 prohibiting the sale of intoxicating liquors on Sundays, two of her University Colleges started life in hotels, and, moreover, after the

[1] PRO Ed 91/8; K. Viriamu Jones, op. cit., p. 103.
[2] PRO Ed 91/8; D. Emrys Evans, op. cit., p. 33.
[3] K. Viriamu Jones, op. cit., p. 50.
[4] D. Emrys Evans, op. cit.
[5] PRO Ed 91/8.
[6] W. H. G. Armytage, *A. J. Mundella, 1825–1897: the Liberal Background to the Labour Movement* 1951. p. 207: 'Appointed to office for the first time in 1880, saw the reform of intermediate education in Wales as an opportunity for trying out schemes which could later be applied to England'.
[7] Ibid.
[8] Kenneth O. Morgan, op. cit., p. 52. See Appendices III and IV.

A Survey of The Evolution of Welsh Educational

passing of the Local Taxation (Customs and Excise) Act of 1890, the appropriation of 'whisky money' (commonly called the Goschen Fund) with such alacrity by the Welsh county authorities expedited the completion of the system of Welsh intermediate schools.[1] Again, the Central Welsh Board was conceived and born at the Raven Hotel, Shrewsbury, the Welsh academic capital. Even today many university meetings are held in similar hostelries in the same town, whilst innumerable appointments to Chairs in the University of Wales have been filled at the Great Western Hotel, Paddington.

Once established, where were the students to come from for the colleges? Of the 313 students enrolled at Aberystwyth between 1872 and 1880, seventy were under sixteen years of age and many returned home after one or two terms.[2] At Cardiff, Viriamu Jones was faced with the same problem, for entrance requirements were meagre and professors had to impart elementary instruction. He was more than ever convinced of the urgent need to develop intermediate education. On the other hand, headmasters of grammar and proprietary schools in south Wales were hostile to what they regarded as a rival institution. Meeting at Shrewsbury in 1885 to form a provisional committee for the protection of the old endowed schools, and to watch the progress of the Intermediate Bill for Wales due to come before Parliament, they called for an admission age of seventeen and an entrance examination which would 'effectually protect such colleges from the necessity of undertaking elementary instruction'.[3] But the fears of competition were largely illusory, as the majority of students entering the Welsh colleges in the 1880s could have had no opportunity of secondary education.

From 1882 to 1889 Mundella proved to be the fairy godmother of Welsh intermediate education. His work throughout was prosecuted in the spirit of a letter which he wrote to Viriamu Jones in 1893:

> 'I am well satisfied with the progress of education in Wales. My initiative is working like a little leaven, and I hope when Wales has worked out its own salvation, it will have the effect of leavening the larger and more inert mass of Englishmen. I always desired to see Wales become a model for our national system, and I am increasingly hopeful that it will gradually become so'.[4]

But at first there were disappointments. Bills to promote Welsh intermediate education introduced by Mundella in 1882, 1883 and 1885

---

[1] *Report of the Departmental Committee on the Organization of Secondary Education in Wales* (*Bruce Report*), HMSO, 1920, p. 17. Also, W. N. Bruce, *The Welsh Intermediate Education Act, 1889, Its Origin and Working*, Department of Education, Committee of Council, Vol. 1, p. 13.
[2] D. Emrys Evans, op. cit., p. 24. David Williams, *Thomas Francis Roberts*, Cardiff, 1961, pp. 13–19.
[3] K. Viriamu Jones, op. cit., pp. 202–3.
[4] Ibid.

Structure and Administration 1880–1925

proved abortive. Two others were mooted in 1887 and 1888 but neither was discussed. One of the major stumbling blocks was the question as to how intermediate schools should be administered, but with the passing of the Local Government Act of 1888 it could be proposed that the new county councils should become the local education authorities.[1]

The parliamentary debates for the session 1889 cover many points in Welsh educational history relating to secondary schools.[2] It fell to Stuart Rendel, MP for Montgomeryshire, who was successful in a draw for private members' Bills, to conduct the measure for Welsh intermediate education through its second reading in the Commons on 15 May, 1889.[3] He had worked in complete harmony with Tom Ellis, MP for Merioneth, and other English MPs such as Gladstone, Mundella, Hart-Dyke and A. H. Dyke Acland to bring it to this stage. Rendel pleaded for the 'completion of the missing link' and an educational ladder from elementary school to university by establishing a system of intermediate schools, undenominational in character and administered by the new county councils which would have powers to levy a half-penny rate backed by an equivalent Treasury grant. The Bill also provided for a National Council of Education for Wales.[4] But before the Act was passed many mutilations were inevitable. The proposed National Council was deleted, thus perpetuating the powers of the Charity Commissioners, whilst administrative responsibilities were ceded to local quasi-representative authorities instead of the county councils.[5] The Act received Royal Assent on 12 August, 1889. At the end of the same month the Technical Instruction Act was passed.[6]

The quasi-representative authorities set up by the Welsh Intermediate Education Act were designated joint education committees representing each county council and county borough. The Charity Commissioners had the right to be represented at any meetings of such committees by an Assistant Commissioner. It was the duty of the joint committees to submit to the Charity Commissioners a scheme or schemes for intermediate and technical education in their localities. The Charity Commissioners in turn

[1] For a full statement on these Bills see J. R. Webster, 'The Welsh Intermediate Education Act of 1889', *Welsh History Review*, 1969, Vol. 4, No. 3.

[2] *Parl. Deb.*, 3rd Ser., vol. cccxxxvi, p. 121 ff.

[3] *Young Wales*, February, 1902, Lord Rendel discusses his Welsh Intermediate Education Act, 1889, and mentions that Sir William Hart-Dyke claimed paternity for the Bill. All Hart-Dyke did was to get the measure drafted by government draftsmen, and did everything he could to get the Bill through parliament.

[4] *Parl. Deb.*, 3rd Ser., vol. cccxxxvi, op. cit., Also, T. Ellis and Ellis Griffith, *Intermediate and Technical Education (Wales)*, the National Association for the Promotion of Technical and Secondary Education, London, 1889.

[5] Ibid., p. 13, ff.

[6] 30 August 1889.

submitted the schemes to the Education Department at Whitehall. Thereafter they were laid before parliament and approved by the Queen in Council. The Charity Commissioners were required to prepare and present an annual report to both Houses, on proceedings under the Act which was to be construed as one with the Endowed Schools Acts of 1869, 1873 and 1874, and cited with these as the Endowed Schools Acts 1869–89. In this guise the Welsh Intermediate Education Act came into operation on 1 November, 1889.[1]

Two other Acts were also passed which had a direct bearing on Welsh secondary education. The Technical Instruction Act (already referred to), applied to Wales and Monmouthshire as well as to England, and gave to county councils, county boroughs and urban sanitary authorities the power to levy a rate of 1d in the £, or twice the amount that could be raised under the Welsh Intermediate Education Act. The Local Taxation (Customs and Excise) Act, 1890, made available certain imperial funds for educational purposes at the discretion of county councils, provided that in Wales and Monmouthshire these funds, if devoted to education, might be applied under either the Technical Instruction Act or the Welsh Intermediate Education Act, as the county council might prefer. Without the aid afforded from this source, the 'Welsh system of secondary schools would have been very far from the degree of completeness which it had attained'.[2]

The Welsh people responded to the Welsh Intermediate Education Act with few signs of hesitation. Within the first two months, the joint education committees were at work in four counties and before six months had elapsed, all sixteen committees, including the county boroughs of Cardiff, Newport and Swansea were similarly engaged. Between 1890 and 1892, ten conferences of the committees were held, three for North Wales and the remainder covering the Principality, under the chairmanship, first of A. H. D. Acland, MP (also chairman of the Caernarvonshire joint education committee), and afterwards A. C. Humphreys-Owen, MP.[3] The Charity Commissioners were represented at all these meetings by W. N. Bruce.[4]

Most of the preliminary work involved ascertaining the requirements and wishes of the population within each respective area by issuing

---

[1] *The Welsh Intermediate Education Act, Its Origin, etc.*, op. cit., pp. 10, ff.
[2] Ibid.
[3] *Report of Proceedings, Joint Education Committees of Wales and Monmouthshire*, 1890–92.
[4] R. L. Morant succeeded Bruce as the Board of Education's representative at meetings of the Central Welsh Board and its executive committee, prior to his appointment as Permanent Secretary to the Board of Education in 1903.

printed questions to public bodies, receiving deputations and holding public inquiries in the county towns. The principal subjects discussed were the treatment of endowments; the constitution, functions and administrative area of governing bodies; the appointment and dismissal of assistant teachers; the problem of thinly populated rural districts; the education of girls, co-education, tuition fees, religious instruction; the teaching of Welsh and manual instruction. Finally, the setting up of an all-important body, a Welsh Central Board, had to be considered.[1]

When considering proposals for the type of intermediate school that Wales needed under the Welsh Intermediate Education Act, the policy adopted by the Joint Education Committees was not one based on a definition of education which emphasized classical and literary training so admirably given in the large public and grammar schools and which naturally led on to the university. They favoured a school policy which was broader and more in accord with Welsh culture and society. The position of the already existing grammar schools called for careful consideration because the Act gave the Joint Education Committees jurisdiction over educational endowments applied within their counties. This definition included large and small boarding schools which attracted pupils from very wide territorial limits. It was decided to adopt the *existing* grammar schools, so far as possible, as the intermediate or county schools for their respective areas.[2]

Principal Reichel, a member of the Joint Education Committee who had some share in selecting the general lines of the system on which the *new* intermediate schools were based gave his views in a speech at Newtown intermediate school in 1896. He argued that two courses were open to the committee: whether to establish a small number of schools of the grammar type enlarged on the science side so as to meet modern developments, available to the greater part of the population as one or two large 'comprehensive' boarding schools in each county; or to accept the principle that the great bulk of the population ought to be within reach of smaller intermediate schools in every town. There was much to be said in favour of the former plan. It was the more cautious and the more easily worked, being nothing more than the adoption and completion of a system already in partial operation. If this was accepted Reichel was afraid that it gave up once for all the idea of a secondary system open to the whole population (such as prevailed in Switzerland and Germany) and accepting the view that secondary education should be confined to preparing for the learned

[1] *Report of Proceedings, Joint Education Committees*, op. cit.
[2] *Ibid.*

A Survey of The Evolution of Welsh Educational

professions.[1] This view the committee declined to accept. They determined to look rather to the continent than to England for their model, and it seemed that the Welsh intermediate school was to be fashioned on the *Secundar-schulen* of Zurich and the *Bürger* and *Real-schulen* of Prussia.[2] They deliberately chose the second alternative, a large number of day schools instead of a small number of boarding schools. But in the most rural parts of Wales pupils still had to travel by train or buses to their nearest school or had to be in lodgings during the school week.[3]

But, for special reasons, certain endowed grammar schools with a larger boarding element coupled with their non-local character, remained outside county organizations, for example, Christ's College, Brecon, and Llandovery Collegiate School. The grammar schools at Cowbridge, Ruthin, and the Howells school for girls at Denbigh, although included in the schemes for their respective counties, were subsequently omitted due to opposition raised to those schemes in parliament. The Howells girls school, Llandaff, though to some extent independent of the county organization, was examined and inspected by the Central Welsh Board.[4]

Building a large number of small schools was a costly business but was borne gladly by the Welsh people. A large central intermediate school would never have appealed to the farmer and village artisan, but the district school was successful. It might be argued that a Higher Grade department in the elementary school would in many places have done all that an intermediate school could do,—especially when some parents merely sent their children to school for one or two years and sometimes, for what they called 'chwarter o ysgol',[5]—but this would never have caught the imagination of the Welsh people.[6] Before 1944 it was a great

---

[1] *Young Wales*, vol. II, No. 23, November 1896, p. 254.

[2] *Report of Schools Inquiry Commission*, 1867, vol. 1, pp. 78–84: Schools of the Second and Third Grade. Schools of Second Grade cease at about 16. After that the boys are not supposed to go to universities but to employments or special preparation for employment. Prepares youths for business, some professions, manufactures, army and civil service; sons of farmers and richer shopkeepers. They learn Latin, more science and mathematics. These schools are *Real-schulen* of Prussia. Schools of Third Grade—most urgent need for these, pupils up to 14 or 15. It is just here that the endowed schools appear to fail, while nothing else takes their place. They are for children of small shopkeepers, artisans and smaller farmers. Organisation of school: lower, boys 6–7 to 12; examined in 3 Rs and geography, etc., for Upper Division. Then they study English, Modern Languages and Political Economy or Latin; algebra, geometry, botany, physics and chemistry, drawing. These schools would correspond to the *Secundar-schulen* of Zurich and the *Bürger-schulen* of Prussia. Choice of curriculum for all, plenty of flexibility. Boys of 14 should be able to quit at end of current half-year.

[3] Schools especially at Cardiganshire, Merioneth and parts of Carmarthenshire, etc.

[4] Other schools such as Abergavenny, and the Jones Foundation schools at Monmouth and Pontypool, although outside their county schemes, were related to them by means of county scholarships and representation by the county councils.

[5] A term or a 'quarter' of school, used in Cardiganshire by farmers when their children were sent to the intermediate schools, as a 'finishing school' after elementary school.

[6] One or two facts show how real and effective were the contacts between the intermediate and the elementary schools in Wales. In 1899, of the 7,390 pupils in the 92 intermediate schools, no fewer than 5,003 proceeded direct from public elementary schools and 420 from Higher Grade schools. The total number of girls in endowed secondary schools in Wales in 1880 was 263; in 1899 there were 3,513 in schools regulated by schemes under the Welsh Act, and 174 in other endowed secondary schools—a total of 3,687 girls. *Young Wales*, August, 1900.

thrill for Welsh working class parents to boast that one or more of their children had been to the county school, whether it was for a couple of years or up to the time when they took the Higher School Certificate examination, and went on to take a degree at a Welsh University College or elsewhere.

The Joint Committees were determined that the new schools *should not follow the old grammar school traditions*. They hoped to bring secondary education to the door of every cottage, and cater, if possible for every type of child, academic or otherwise. It was the principle of adapting the school to local conditions, and it was Reichel who again said 'that Welsh intermediate schools enjoyed an advantage which the English schools lacked in 1896. They had an organized body and the legislature had provided machinery for testing the efficiency of the schools and for working out schemes of work—the Central Welsh Board. It will need to construct a system of examination and inspection for the new schools *adapted to their special needs*'.[1] But five years later, ominously, A. C. Humphreys-Owen, chairman of the Central Welsh Board, was of the opinion that 'the schools were giving real secondary or intermediate education of the same range and high standards as that obtained *in the old grammar schools*'.[2]

The first county scheme to be established was that of Caernarvonshire in 1893; the last, that of Glamorgan in 1896. When all schemes had been completed and approved, the real executive work remained to be done. Schools had to be located at convenient centres for each district, sites negotiated and buildings erected. In many areas, temporary accommodation was inevitable for many schools—in halls, chapel vestries, or improvised huts; new teachers were needed, and before 1900 it was difficult to secure well-qualified staff.[3] Yet, by 1898, eighty-eight new schools had been opened in addition to the establishment of over sixty new local governing bodies and sixteen county bodies each operating a county scheme.[4] By the end of 1903 there were ninety-six intermediate schools (of which seventeen were old schools and seventy-nine new) with a total of 8,789 pupils. In 1910, this number had expanded to 13,729.[5] To co-ordinate this new system of intermediate education, the Central Welsh Board was created in 1896, with responsibility for the inspection and examination of all intermediate schools. Owen Owen, headmaster

---

[1] *Young Wales*, November, 1896.
[2] Ibid, January, 1901.
[3] Out of eighty-eight schools inspected in 1898, as many as forty-nine were housed in permanent buildings.
[4] Percy E. Watkins, *A Welshman Remembers*, Cardiff, 1944. p. 85.
[5] *Report of the Board of Education, Welsh Department*, 1911.

A Survey of The Evolution of Welsh Educational

of Oswestry High School became the first Chief Inspector of the Board, to the disappointment (according to many Welshmen) of Owen M. Edwards of Lincoln College, Oxford, who was, some ten years later appointed Chief Inspector of Education for Wales at the newly formed Welsh Department of the Board of Education.[1]

The primary object of the plan to establish a Central Welsh Board (whose scheme was designed, adopted and sent to the Charity Commissioners by all the joint education committees) was to set up a Welsh body capable of undertaking the supervision required by the Treasury. This would avert the risk, incidental to the acceptance of state aid, that a rigid educational code might be imposed on the new schools by an authority unfamiliar with the peculiar local needs and circumstances of the Welsh county areas. There had arisen initial difficulties in 1891, when Sir John Goschen, then Chancellor of the Exchequer, felt that the proposal implied a large surrender of responsibility by the Treasury to a Welsh body naturally interested in the success of the schools. Eventually, the regulations under which the Treasury grant was awarded were issued in 1892, and four years elapsed before they were approved. The difficulty indicated by Goschen was overcome by interposing the Charity Commissioners between the Treasury and the Central Welsh Board. In this way, Wales obtained the freedom to plan and guide its own educational development, while the Treasury obtained, through the department charged with the administration of the Intermediate Education Act, a guarantee that the conditions of state aid imposed by parliament were fulfilled.[2]

The constitution of the Central Welsh Board as set out in its scheme, comprised two Bodies: a Board consisting of eighty members, and an executive committee of fifteen members chosen from the Board. The Board was composed of three *ex officio* members (the Principals of three Welsh University Colleges), seventy-one representative and six co-optative members, made up thus: representative members of county councils, twenty-one; county governing bodies under schemes, twenty-six; headmasters and headmistresses of intermediate schools, five; certificated teachers of elementary schools, five; university bodies, fourteen. The executive committee was elected by the Board and members of both bodies held office for three years.[3] The funds administered by the scheme

---

[1] Percy E. Watkins, op. cit., A detailed account of the appointment is given on pp. 38, ff. Watkins is hardly fair to Edwards, for in the light of new evidence laid bare in the files of the Board of Education, it could scarcely be said that Edwards harboured a perpetual grudge against either Owen or the Central Welsh Board. See Studies Nos. 2 and 6.

[2] *The Welsh Intermediate Education Act, Its Origin*, etc., op. cit., p. 28.

[3] Ibid.

were: a uniform annual contribution to be paid by the county governing body of each county and county boroughs, being not more than five per cent of its total revenue for the preceding year; by the share of the county in the Exchequer contribution, known as 'whisky money'; an annual grant from the Treasury of £500;[1] any donations or endowments received thereafter.[2]

It is important to emphasize and clarify what were the precise functions of the Central Welsh Board, for in certain dealings with the Welsh Department of the Board of Education after 1907, constant reference was made to what they termed 'their autonomy'. No. 4 of the Treasury Regulations stated:

'For the purpose of ascertaining whether these conditions (i.e. those governing payment of the Treasury Grant) are fulfilled, there shall be an annual examination and inspection of the school. Such examination and inspection may be conducted by a Central Welsh Board, established by scheme under the Act, provided that such scheme is approved by the Treasury. The results of such examination and inspection shall be reported to the Charity Commissioners; and the Charity Commissioners will make such inquiry, and, in the case of need, such further examination and inspection as they think necessary'.[3]

It was quite clear, what, in the matter of inspection and examination, the functions of the Central Welsh Board were, viz., (a) They *may*—the power was permissive only—under the Treasury Regulations, examine and inspect the intermediate schools, but merely for the purpose of the award of the Treasury grant; (b) They *shall* report to the Charity Commissioners—not to the Treasury direct. But the Treasury Regulations were liable to change, for the 1889 Act stated that the Treasury might vary or revoke their regulations. In fact they were varied in 1909 by substituting in them 'the Board of Education' for 'the Charity Commissioners'. Therefore, for the purposes even of the Treasury grant (which formed only a fractional part of the grants voted by Parliament in aid of Welsh secondary education, and for the administration of which the Board of Education was responsible to Parliament) the Central Welsh Board had to report to the Board of Education, and that was all they could do. They had no power to follow up their own reports or to take any action upon them; they could take no steps to improve the staffing or equipment of any intermediate school; endowments were outside their purview; time-tables and syllabi could not be modified or improved by them; they never had a full-time inspector of art, music,

---

[1] Made in recognition of the fact that the Central Welsh Board relieved the Treasury of the duty of providing examinations and inspection.
[2] *The Welsh Intermediate Education Act, It's Origin*, ibid. supra.
[3] Ibid, Appendix A.

A Survey of The Evolution of Welsh Educational

handicraft, domestic subjects or physical training. Curricula in intermediate schools were controlled by the local governing bodies.

In the matter of examinations a distinction should be made between their examination for the purposes of the Treasury grant—what they were originally created, as an agent, to do—and their examinations for certificates. The scheme provided that 'the examinations need not be the same for all schools, but regard shall be had by the examiners to the teaching in each school as provided by the governors'.[1] Even regarding their own examinations, the Central Welsh Board were subject to the control of the Secondary Schools Examination Council, who carefully watched the Board's schedules and standard of marking. Without the approval of this Council the Board's certificates were of no value. The definition of intermediate education in Section 17 of the Act described a course of education which did not consist chiefly of elementary education in reading, writing and arithmetic, but which included instruction in 'Latin, Greek, the Welsh and English language and literature, Modern languages, Mathematics, Natural and Applied Science, or in some of such studies, and generally in the higher branches of knowledge'.[2] Technical education was defined as including instruction in 'any of the branches of science and art with respect to which grants are for the time being made by the Department of Science and Art; the use of tools and modelling in clay, wood, or other material; Commercial Arithmetic, Commercial Geography, Book-keeping and Shorthand; any other subject applicable to the purposes of agriculture, industries, trade or commercial life and practice, which may be specified in a scheme, or proposals for a scheme, of a joint education committee as a form of instruction *suited to the needs of the district*, but it shall not include teaching the practice of any trade, or industry, or employment'.[3]

But a wide discretion was left to school governors to arrange a suitable curriculum which was drawn up from a list of obligatory subjects (those which every pupil who went through an ordinary school course were expected to take) and a supplementary list, from which additional subjects might be selected. History, Geography, Drawing, Vocal Music, Drill, Cookery and Needlework figured in the obligatory curriculum (in addition to Latin,) etc., mentioned before. It was strange to find that Welsh

---

[1] Ibid., p. 30.
[2] PRO Ed 13/5. This was based on Section 20 of the Education (Scotland) Act of 1878. Also *The Welsh Intermediate Education Act, Its Origin*, etc., op. cit.
[3] Ibid. This is an important forerunner when compared with Morant's Secondary Regulations for English maintained Secondary Schools. See:
 (i) *Regulations for Secondary Schools*, 30th June, 1904, pp. 17–18;
 (ii) *Board of Education, Report for the Year* 1905–6, pp. 52, 55, 61. *Conditions in The Schools;*
 (iii) *Regulations for Secondary Schools*, 30th June, 1907, pp. v–viii.

grammar, composition and literature were relegated to the supplementary list which included Greek, Agriculture, Navigation and Laundrywork! Religious Instruction, an obligatory subject, was given 'in accordance with the principles of the Christian Faith . . . and no religious catechism or religious formulary which is distinctive of any particular denomination shall be taught to day-scholars'.[1]

It would appear that 'the Welsh Intermediate Education Act afforded another valuable precedent for separate legislation for Wales including Monmouthshire. Educationally, socially, and administratively it was one of the most impressive memorials of the political awakening of Wales'.[2] In 1898, D. R. Fearon, Secretary to the Charity Commissioners, speaking at the Keighley Institute, Yorkshire, of developments in Welsh intermediate and technical education, ventured to suggest 'that no educational reform more remarkable than this has ever been accomplished in any European country'.[3] What England had failed to accomplish in the 1860s, and was not to achieve until 1902, Wales accomplished, with the help of English reformers, in the 1890s. There were, of course, no powerful independent schools in Wales to organize opposition to the development of a national system of secondary education and which, in effect, postponed its establishment in England for forty years. When the time arrived to establish a secondary system in England it was guided by men who had gained invaluable experience in similar matters in Wales. A. H. D. Acland organized secondary education in the West Riding precisely as he had done earlier in Caernarvonshire. Others, like W. N. Bruce, Robert L. Morant, and particularly J. W. Headlam, A. G. Legard, and Thomas Darlington—the latter three being senior inspectors of the Board of Education—knew Wales and the Welsh secondary system thoroughly.[4] It could really be said that the success of the Welsh Intermediate Act was firmly founded on the ruins of English attempts at secondary reform in the 1869–74 period.[5]

During the 1890s there was also some development in technical education on lines similar to England, which greatly extended opportunities for

---

[1] Ibid.
[2] Kenneth O. Morgan, op. cit., p. 102.
[3] Percy E. Watkins, op. cit., p. 58.
[4] Ibid. Watkins makes an interesting comparison between Wales and Yorkshire, where he spent some years as clerk to the West Riding Education Committee. When the new secondary schools were being built in Yorkshire 'there was an entire absence of any reference to the provision of voluntary subscriptions towards the building funds. The people asked 'How much money can we get from the County Authority', and the County Authority asked 'How much can we get from the Board of Education' . . . To one like myself who had taken part in a house to house collection for our new school and was never given a refusal . . . the omission of all reference to voluntary subscriptions on the part of great wealth was rather striking. These men, however, were perfectly willing to be *rated* for their new secondary schools, after they had become entirely satisfied that every available penny from outside sources had been obtained'. (pp. 83–4).
[5] David Allsobrook, The Reform of the Endowed Schools: the work of the Northamptonshire Educational Society 1854–1874. *History of Education*, vol. 2, No. 1. January, 1973.

A Survey of The Evolution of Welsh Educational

technical training, at the time intermediate schools were being established. Viriamu Jones saw that his University College at Cardiff could become a centre for developments in technical education and was anxious that all sections of manual workers should understand the importance of such training. He realized that by co-operating with the College, the contiguous industrialized counties and urban centres might be able to provide facilities for efficient teaching on a comprehensive scale. In 1889, the Cardiff Technical Instruction Committee was formed, and Glamorgan and Monmouthshire county councils formed similar committees. Jones planned Mining and Metallurgical Departments in his College where seven or eight hundred evening students attended. Large numbers of night schools for young colliers also flourished in Glamorgan and Monmouthshire. By 1892, technical classes had been established throughout south Wales. Quarrymen in north Wales were known to tramp sixteen miles after a day's work to learn mathematics, and colliers in south Wales, many 60 years of age, trudged to lectures on geology and mining. In February 1895, the Cardiff Technical School was providing fifty different courses in science and art, and had 2,600 students whose work was annually examined by government examiners.[1]

No account of the development of Welsh education can evade the problem of the Welsh language and its survival. Paradoxically, with the development of Welsh elementary and secondary education, the Welsh language became neglected and was in danger of elimination in the densely populated industrial areas. In the latter half of the nineteenth century many Welsh people were convinced that the only way to get on in the world was to learn English at the expense of the vernacular. We must again salute one of the wisest educationists of the nineteenth century, Kay-Shuttleworth. He foresaw the problem in 1849 when he instructed an inspector of National schools, the Rev. H. Longueville Jones, to carry out a bilingual policy in the schools and training colleges of Wales. It is perhaps idle to speculate what the consequences to the education and language of Wales would have been, had Kay-Shuttleworth's policy been pursued over the years.[2] It was extremely unfortunate for Wales that he had to resign his post nine months later on grounds of ill-health. Again, it is strange that the leading Welshmen who agitated for a Welsh University were prepared to advocate the natural right of the Welsh language to a place in Welsh education, and yet to advance the view that a better system of education might hasten its disappearance as a necessary pre-

[1] K. Viriamu Jones, op. cit., p. 152 ff.
[2] *Welsh in Education and Life*, op. cit., p. 60.

Structure and Administration 1880-1925

liminary to the due progress of the people.[1] As late as 1888 the Cross Commission threw out the first life-line and recognized Welsh as a grant-earning subject under the Elementary Code (mainly through the efforts of Dan Isaac Davies, HMI) on an equal footing with other languages.[2] The Central Welsh Board and the Welsh intermediate schools paid scant attention to the teaching of Welsh until the years immediately preceding the outbreak of the first World War. Welsh parents and headmasters of the intermediate schools pressed the pupils to learn French (which was also an easier mark-getting examination subject) and it was little wonder that the Board was often dubbed the Central French Board. This state of affairs the new officials of the Welsh Department were determined to amend after 1907.[3]

The third and final recommendation of the *Aberdare Report*, and the crown of the structure of the Welsh system of secondary and higher education brought into being after 1881 was a degree-awarding University of Wales. In the movement to this end, familiar names are again prominent, Viriamu Jones, Lord Aberdare, Lord Rendel, A. H. D. Acland, and Sir H. Isambard Owen. The latter, a distinguished physician practising in London and who later left his mark on more than one English university, was responsible for drafting the charter of the University of Wales.[4] This movement was not without its problems, for there were rival opinions regarding the type of university most suitable. Many meetings were inevitable, but the crucial one, held in Shrewsbury in 1891 decided two important issues: (a) it was to be a teaching, in preference to an examining university, conferring degrees on its own students with residential qualifications, and (b) the federal principle was adopted, and the three University Colleges became constituent colleges of the University of Wales. The new University received the Royal Charter of incorporation on 20 November, 1893.[5]

---

[1] D. Emrys Evans, op. cit., p. 15.

[2] *Third Report of the Commissioners of Inquiry into the Elementary Education Acts*, 1887 (c. 5158), Vol. iii. Also *Final Report*, ibid., 1888 (c. 5485), pp. 144-5. Also: W. R. Jones, *Bilingualism in Welsh Education*. Cardiff, 1966. Part I, pp. 3-44 deals with the historical background of the bilingual movement in Welsh Education.

[3] See Study No. 6.

[4] Isambard Owen's father was the chief architect of the Great Western Railway with the famous engineer Isambard Kingdom Brunel, who was Owen's godparent. In addition to his work in connection with the University of Wales, Owen became Principal of Armstrong College, Newcastle upon Tyne, 1904-9, and was responsible for the reconstitution of the Durham Colleges culminating in the passing of the University of Durham Act in 1908. He left to become Vice-Chancellor of Bristol University in 1909, where he reorganized and redrafted its Charter, and also took a leading part in the establishment of the National Library and National Museum of Wales.

[5] D. Emrys Evans, op. cit., p. 41. 'The Future of the University of Wales', *Triban*, Vol. II, No. 4, 1962

II

The brief quinquennium 1902-7 in the evolution of Welsh educational structure and administration was, in many ways, both contentious and significant. Documentary sources relating to Welsh educational matters become prolific after 1902, and the events were centred mainly on the efforts of one dominating personality. These years might be aptly described as the Lloyd Georgian phase in Welsh education. They were years of unsuccessful attempts to achieve, rather than years of achievement, when religion and politics perhaps became too involved in important educational deliberations. During this period, secondary education was not the main concern in Wales. The two burning issues were religious controversy leading to the 'Welsh Revolt' and a renewed demand for autonomy in the form of a Welsh National Council for Education. Neither issue was fought to a successful conclusion, but in lieu of the latter, there was a good measure of administrative compensation with the establishment of the Welsh Department of the Board of Education in December 1906.[1]

The religious issue had, of course been actual since the Act of 1870, if not before. Wales was mainly Nonconformist and there had been bickerings and animosity between National and British schools before the establishment of the dual system of Church and Board schools. When the Forster Bill was under discussion, Welsh Nonconformist leaders made their position clear at a meeting held in Aberystwyth in January 1870. Their decision was for permissive Biblical instruction, and denominational teaching outside school hours, a view put to Gladstone and Forster by a deputation in March, and which was reflected in the Cowper-Temple Clause eventually adopted.[2] After 1870 Wales proved a fertile ground for the establishment of School Boards. In 1897 there were 326, and by 1902, 379 such Boards. During these years the dominance of voluntary schools diminished, and 'churchmen noted with alarm the growing tendency of Welsh School Boards to favour an entirely secular system of instruction'.[3] It would be tiresome and too long a narrative to unravel the religious disputations between Lloyd George, the Welsh Bishops, and the government. But from the Welsh point of view the religious issue and the desire for national autonomy were closely inter-linked.

At the risk of having to mention what is treated in more detail in a later study,[4] a brief reference to the 'Welsh Revolt' has to be fitted into

[1] See Study No. 4 and No. 5.
[2] T. Gwynn Jones, *Cofiant Thomas Gee*, Denbigh, 1913, p. 309.
[3] Kenneth O. Morgan, op. cit., p. 183.
[4] See Study No. 3.

Structure and Administration 1880–1925

the picture at this juncture. In prosecuting the Welsh cause in the Commons during the debates on Balfour's Bill in 1902, Lloyd George worked out a clever strategy and perhaps his greatest memorial was its failure. He secured a significant amendment, moved at his instigation by the chairman of the Welsh Parliamentary Party, Sir Alfred Thomas, transferring the powers of Welsh local authorities under the 1889 Act to the new local education authorities constituted by Balfour's Bill.[1] The point was, that Section 17, Clause 5, of the Bill provided for the setting up of a Joint Education Committee covering a combination of counties and county boroughs, and Lloyd George saw here an opportunity to create a National Council of Education for Wales. This was also a way of drawing county councils into opposition to the religious provisions of the Bill, and he emphasized that they should operate the measures envisaged, only on certain important conditions, i.e. that voluntary schools be brought under public control, religious tests for pupil-teachers be abolished, and the 'Colonial Compromise' offered in relation to denominational instruction.[2] If these conditions were not satisfied, Nonconformists were to refuse to pay rates for educational purposes. Lloyd George's motto was 'No control, no cash', and this was the genesis of what came to be known as the 'Welsh Revolt'.[3] The result of this opposition was that Sir William Anson was compelled to present to Parliament the Education (Local Authority) Default Bill, empowering the Board of Education to administer the Act of 1902 when a local education authority failed to comply. This became known as the 'Coercion of Wales Bill' and was operated on more than one occasion.[4]

There was a more hopeful development on the question of a National Council when, in 1903, Anson proposed a Joint Board of Welsh county councils for educational purposes. Between 1903 and 1905 a succession of conferences and meetings sought some agreement among Welsh LEAs as to the powers of such a Council and how it could function within the parliamentary system of the United Kingdom. Model schemes were actually drawn up by the Board of Education, but with the fall of the Unionist government at the end of 1905, the plans lapsed. That was the phase of external negotiation. In the new Liberal Administration with Lloyd George in the Cabinet, there was a direct approach to the question. Birrell's Education Bill provided in Part IV for a National Council of

---

[1] Kenneth O. Morgan, op. cit., p. 186.
[2] In many of the Colonies, undenominational instruction based on simple Bible teaching was reinforced by denominational right of entry one or more days per week.
[3] Kenneth O. Morgan, op. cit., pp. 187–8.
[4] Kenneth O. Morgan, op. cit., p. 195. PRO Ed 24/577, *Confidential Memorandum on the Defaulting Authorities Bill*, 25 June 1904.

29

Education for Wales, but the Bill, heavily amended by the Lords, including the deletion of Part IV, was withdrawn by the Prime Minister, Campbell-Bannerman, on 20th December 1906. Meanwhile, the first mention of some kind of administrative differentiation for Wales occurred on 12th December, when, in the closing stages of the debate on Birrell's Bill, Llewelyn Williams, MP for Carmarthen, stated in his speech that he hoped that since Part IV had been deleted, that the government, by an administrative Act which would not require the sanction of the Lords, would be able *to establish a subordinate branch of the Board of Education in Wales*.[1] But this suggestion was never pursued, for a week later, on 19 December, the first correct parliamentary reference to the Welsh Department was made by Sir Alfred Thomas, MP for Glamorgan East who said that 'the Minister of Education was about to reorganize the Office and to set up a Welsh Department in the Board of Education'. He recognised that this proposal was a great advance towards securing autonomy in educational matters for Wales.[2]

III

The establishment of the Welsh Department at the end of December 1906 was one of Birrell's last acts before leaving the Board of Education for another post in Ireland. The Permanent Secretary of the Board, R. L. Morant lost no time in giving effect to the decision of the Cabinet, in a strictly *Confidential Memorandum on Office Administration* which stated that 'the degree of separation had not yet been precisely determined'.[3] The two chief posts in the new Department, that of Permanent Secretary and Chief Inspector of Education for Wales, were offered to, and accepted by A. T. Davies (a Liverpool solicitor) and Owen M. Edwards, of Lincoln College, Oxford, respectively. In its initial stages the new Department took charge of elementary and secondary education, and later, with the completion of new buildings in Whitehall, it became responsible for technical education, schools of art, further education and training colleges.[4] The creation of this Department inevitably involved a certain measure of administrative dichotomy. On the one hand, it functioned as an integral part of the Board of Education which meant that the resources of the Board in administrative ability and specialized expertise were at its disposal, including inspectorial aspects. The Welsh Department also naturally had to develop administrative relationships

---

[1] *Parl. Deb.*, 4*th Ser.*, *vol. clvii*, 1906, cs. 499–51.
[2] Ibid. *vol. ccxvii*, c. 1775.
[3] PRO Ed 23/216 F, No. 3, *Confidential Memorandum*, R. L. Morant, January 1907, pp. 6–7.
[4] PRO Ed 24/581, PRO Ed 24/580.

Structure and Administration 1880–1925

with the Welsh LEAs and the Central Welsh Board. On the other hand, the new Permanent Secretary and Chief Inspector had to initiate developments *de novo* in the administrative pattern of the Welsh side of educational matters. There was a separately organized Welsh inspectorate, and 'the soundness of this conception is shown by its survival, unchanged in structure, and justified in practice over a period of sixty years'.[1] Owen Edwards built up carefully over a period of years a body of Welsh-speaking inspectors[2], and in 1909 had submitted to the President of the Board a survey of the responsibilities attached to his own post and the work being done by the Department in Wales.[3]

The broad picture of the years 1907 to 1925 was one of evolution rather than revolution, but this period was characterized by more than one interesting event, including a major rebellion on the part of the Central Welsh Board.[4] Having reorganized the inspectorate, other important matters requiring attention were the Welsh language, reform of the Central Welsh Board system, the curricula and organization of training colleges, and the extension of technical and further education. From the outset, Edwards paid particular attention to the Welsh language in the schools of Wales. In the first *Report* of the Welsh Department in 1908, it was stated that:

> 'the outstanding feature of the year in connection with the work of the Board in Wales has been the definite recognition of the Welsh language and literature in the curricula of elementary and secondary schools, and Training Colleges of the Principality... In the Code for 1907, as also in the Regulations for Secondary Schools and for Training Colleges in Wales for that year, the teaching of Welsh was fully and definitely recognized'.[5]

In 1909 Edwards was able to report that 'the introduction of Welsh to elementary schools, secondary schools and training colleges has already begun to react on, and give new vigour to the three great educational institutions that stand outside the Board's purview, i.e. the Sunday school, the Literary Meetings, and the Eisteddfod'.[6] He also added that in administering the Code:

> 'It has some special aims ... e.g. to deal wisely and efficiently with the distinct problem of Welsh education—the bilingual problem. It has changed a "bilingual difficulty" into a bilingual opportunity. In most elementary schools children get the

---

[1] Ministry of Education, *Education*, 1900–1950, HMSO, 1951, p. 115.
[2] PRO Ed 23/145, 23/146, 23/147, 23/148.
[3] PRO Ed 24/584.
[4] See Study No. 6.
[5] *Report of the Board of Education*, 1907–08, Cd. 4566, p. 13.
[6] PRO Ed 24/584, Edwards to the President: Memorandum on the Work of the Welsh Department, 27 November 1909, p. 7.

educational advantage that comes from a knowledge of two languages. The utilization of Welsh dates much further back than the establishing of the Welsh Department; but it was the Department that made universal—where LEAs desire it—an efficient and logical system of bilingual teaching, varying according to whether the district is Welsh-speaking, bilingual, or English-speaking. The problem is important to other parts of the Empire, and the experience of the Welsh Department has been of much value to such parts as Mauritius and Cape Colony'.[1]

Edwards also emphasized the importance in the same Code, of relating the education of the Welsh child to his own environment, traditions, and way of life—rather than to an English background.

In the field of elementary education the old bitterness over the voluntary schools engendered by the settlement in the Act of 1902 was diminishing very slowly. Here, the Welsh Department was able to encourage LEAs to erect new council schools in many districts hitherto served only by the Church of England, so remedying a long-standing grievance. But this could not always be done, disputes between school managers and LEAs continued, and the Department's decisions in accordance with the law and current policy were not always accepted with equally good grace by both sides.[2]

It was in secondary education that the problem of relations with the Central Welsh Board arose. From 1907 this Board became hostile to the Welsh Department, both for historical reasons, and also because Edwards became critical of the multiplicity and rigidity of their examinations, and was also concerned about the uniform character of the Welsh intermediate schools. He was also disappointed, that in their evolution, the schools had become so similar to the older English grammar schools and had neglected the teaching of Welsh. Also, unfortunately for the Central Welsh Board, the Board of Education paid their grants after 1902, and also shared the inspection of the intermediate schools for grant purposes. This led to the burning question of dual inspection,[3] which contributed in no mean measure to the mounting tide of enmity which developed between the two Boards after 1907. This, along with the contents of the explosive *Report* of 1909, brought matters to a head and into the open. Several years later, after the tumult died down, a compromise was reached regarding dual inspection, but the Welsh Department refused to withdraw from the position of advising the Central Welsh Board on its functions.

[2] Ibid. p. 2.
[3] Ministry of Education, ibid., pp. 115 ff.
[4] See Study No. 2.

Structure and Administration 1880–1925

During World War I, a Royal Commission was appointed, presided over by Lord Haldane, which enquired between 1916–18 'Into the organization and work of the University and its three constituent Colleges, and into the relations of the University to those Colleges and to other institutions in Wales providing education of a post-secondary nature, and to consider in what respects the present organization of University Education in Wales can be improved, and what changes, if any, are desirable in the constitution, functions and powers of the University and its three Colleges'.[1] Welsh people had hoped that the University would become the symbol of national unity, but after twenty years' experience, the Commission was told that 'the Welsh Colleges were very far from exhausting their possibilities for good for the people of Wales ... Of late years the people had undoubtedly lost touch with the Colleges just as the Colleges had lost touch with the people'.[2] In his evidence, Sir Isambard Owen was quite convinced that the educational policy of the University had not been 'adequately brought into consonance with the mental needs of Welsh students'.[3] Reforms in both contexts were recommended and incorporated in the Charter of the re-constituted University. The University Court was re-modelled to include substantial representation from the Welsh county councils, which had become so important after the Education Act of 1902, and also representation of other institutions, including, for example, the National Library and National Museum, the Honourable Society of Cymmrodorion, and Welsh MPs.

A smaller executive, known as the University Council was to be established to ensure that effect was given to the policy of the Court; an Academic Board to replace the unwieldy University Senate, and the establishment of a University College of Medicine.[4] The special needs of Wales in the fields of Welsh history, literature and Music were recognised by the formation of the Board of Celtic Studies and the National Council of Music. Finally, it recommended the creation of another University College at Swansea which was founded in 1920. Thus the re-constituted University of Wales, still organized on the federal principle, now involved four constituent Colleges.[5]

The re-constitution of the University, and the passage of the Education Act of 1918, necessitated a fresh inquiry into the organization of Welsh secondary education. In 1919, a Departmental Committee was appointed

---

[1] *Royal Commission on University Education in Wales: Three Volumes*, 1916–1918, Cd. 8507, 8993, 8991, HMSO, 1918.
[2] Ibid., *Final Report of the Commissioners, February* 1918, Part 2, p. 24.
[3] Ibid., *Vol. 1, Minutes of Evidence*, 30 November 1916, p. 259.
[4] Ibid., *Final Report of the Commissioners*, Part 3, pp. 60 ff.
[5] Ibid.

A Survey of The Evolution of Welsh Educational

by the President of the Board of Education, under the chairmanship of the Hon. W. N. Bruce, 'To inquire into the organization of Secondary Education in Wales, and to advise how it may be consolidated and co-ordinated with other branches of education *with a view to the establishment of a national system of public education in Wales*, regard being had to the provisions of the Education Act, 1918, and to the recommendations of the Royal Commission on University education in Wales'.[1] This Inquiry had a direct relation to the proposal made by William George of Criccieth, at a conference held at Llandrindod in May, 1915.[2]

The first section of the *Report* dealt with the background history of Welsh secondary education, including a long discussion on the administrative and examinational functions of the Central Welsh Board. It showed how the new administrative changes brought about by the Education Act of 1902 and the creation of the Welsh Department of the Board of Education in 1906 demanded radical changes in the relationships between the Central Welsh Board, the Welsh Department and the LEAs. These were mainly concerned with the new situation where the intermediate schools were controlled by the Central Welsh Board, and the new municipal secondary schools established under the 1902 Act were under the jurisdiction of the Welsh Department and the LEAs.[3] Questions of new financial arrangements under the Education Act of 1918 were also involved, together with the matter of dual inspection of secondary schools,[4] a problem which was not solved, but a compromising situation was eventually agreed to in 1925, because the Central Welsh Board were still confident that a Welsh National Council for Education might be established.[5]

A large part of the *Report* re-examined the possible exhumation of the National Council which was buried with the education Bill of 1906.[6] It

---

[1] *Report of the Departmental Committee*, 1920, op. cit.,

[2] See Study No. 2.

[3] Ibid.

[4] *Report of the Departmental Committee*, 1920, op. cit., pp. 109-110: County Schemes should be radically reconstructed, 'and the relation of intermediate and municipal secondary schools towards the LEAs should be assimilated. The provisions of the County Schemes which constituted the County Fund should be abrogated, and the ½d. rate, the Exchequer contribution, and the Board of Education grant, put at the disposal of the LEA on the same footing as they would be if they were levied or received by the Authority for the purposes of the Education Act, 1918. It was essential to unity of policy in the administration of secondary schools that all those which were in effect maintained by the LEA, in the sense that they could not pay their way without the Authority's aid, should have a common system of finance.'

The Central Welsh Board, due to mounting costs of secondary education, found it impossible to manage on the existing financial arrangements under their original Scheme, and had applied for more aid from the LEAs. But by 1925, a system of joint and unified inspection of secondary schools by the two Boards was effected, together with a change in the method of providing income for the Welsh Board. A direct annual Treasury Grant was to be paid to the Welsh Board, of an amount equivalent to the total amount of the statutory contributions made in each year by the LEAs of Wales and Mon. under Section 42 of the Education Act, 1918. (*Board of Education, Welsh Department, Annual Report for* 1925, *Appendix II, p.* 10). Also, see Study No. VI.

[5] Ibid., Appendix I, p. 6.

[6] *Report of the Departmental Committee*, 1920, op. cit., pp. 86-106.

34

came to a decision that it was desirable that the National Council should be established, and described in considerable detail its constitution and functions. The Council was to be composed of 120 members, the majority to be drawn from the LEAs, and the remainder from the University bodies, teachers of various types, and other bodies concerned with education. All branches of education were to be within its purview, including the University. The Council should replace the University Court, and the Central Welsh Board. The functions of the Council were designated as 'advisory, deliberative and administrative'. It was to be 'the crown of a national system in Wales, embracing all aspects of education from top to bottom',[1] in short, a Welsh educational pantechnicon. It would discuss schemes submitted by LEAs under the Education Act, 1918, and regulations of the Board of Education for the distribution and administration of state grants; the Minister would consult it on other matters from time to time; it should be entitled to submit to the Minister its opinions and recommendations upon any other matters, and it should advise LEAs on matters submitted by them whether singly or jointly.[2]

Administratively, it would deal with functions delegated to it by the Minister, and a beginning should be made with the framing and administration of regulations for secondary schools, and the handing over to the Council the aggregate sum voted by parliament for secondary schools, with the duty of making and administering regulations for its distribution. It should collect and circulate information on educational subjects, and also be responsible for the organization and conduct of school examinations. Finally, it was to participate in the selection of a unified inspectorate for Wales.[3] The ordinary expenses of the Council as an advisory body was to be covered by a block grant from the State, and the administrative outlay, by transferring to the Council the equivalent of the $\frac{1}{2}d.$ rate paid by the Treasury under the Welsh Intermediate Education Act (which was to be repealed) to the several LEAs for distribution under the county schemes.[4]

But the National Council never materialized. It was too elaborate, too comprehensive, and perhaps too revolutionary in conception for the mood of Wales in the years following the end of World War I. Moreover, the Board of Education and the University had adopted a cool and negative attitude, the former preferring, through the Welsh Department,

[1] *Report of the Departmental Committee*, 1920, op. cit., p. 87.
[2] Ibid. p. 114.
[3] Ibid. p. 115.
[4] Ibid. pp. 104–6.

to continue its influence and guidance from Whitehall, and the latter determined to identify itself with purely academic than national responsibilities. In addition, the LEAs were becoming more important, were growing in stature and influence, and could exercise considerable power in educational affairs, especially through the Federation of Welsh Educational Committees.[1] This body might have contained the germ of a really constructive executive body—with some basis to call itself national —which could unite the LEAs into one single LEA for Wales, giving it a national character. This would seem to be a far better arrangement than an agglomeration of the thirty independent local authorities of Wales, each one of them remaining a law unto itself, which the National Council envisaged.[2] But the Welsh LEAs were not prepared to surrender any substantial measure of their autonomy, even for the sake of a national system of education. Wales had to wait until 1948 for a truly democratic national body, the Welsh Joint Education Committee (W.J.E.C.) which absorbed the Central Welsh Board, the two Advisory Councils on Technical Education, and the Federation of Welsh Education Committees. The W.J.E.C. was also endowed with additional executive and advisory powers in the field of Welsh education.[3]

*   *   *

The *Aberdare Report* of 1881 which inaugurated a national movement for education in Wales, and prepared the ground for forty-five glorious years of real achievement in the fields of secondary and university education by the creation of an 'autonomous' body in the form of a Central Welsh Board with its system of intermediate schools, and the structuring and establishment of a national university. To many Welshmen, these achievements were merely desirable preliminaries to a unified national system of education, which was to be crowned by the formation of a Welsh National Council for Education responsible for both academic and administrative functions within the Principality—complete Welsh educational devolution.

Unfortunately, the translation of this national aspiration into reality was impaired by administrative and political impediments. At the turn of the century, further educational legislation produced fundamental changes in the administration of education. This was of particular significance in the evolution of a Welsh national system. The establishment of the Board of Education in 1899 and the Education Act of 1902 gave

---

[1] Sir Ben Bowen Thomas, 'The Welsh Department, Ministry of Education, 1907–1957', *Trans. Hon. Soc. Cymm.*, 1958, p. 35.

[2] Percy E. Watkins, op. cit., p. 64.

[3] *Trans. Hon. Cymm. Soc.*, op. cit., p. 36.

rise to a strange situation in Welsh secondary education, whereby the working of the Welsh Intermediate Education Act of 1889 through the Central Welsh Board with its system of intermediate schools, had to function thereafter (a) under the jurisdiction of the Board of Education (and after 1906, the Welsh Department of that Board), and (b) side by side with another developing system of Welsh municipal secondary schools established by the Welsh LEAs under the Act of 1902, and administered directly by the Board of Education.

This situation might have been resolved by either the Central Welsh Board being delegated responsibility for both types of secondary school, or by the establishment of a Welsh National Council for Education which would absorb the Central Welsh Board and its school system along with the newer schools opened by the LEAs. But the Board of Education were not prepared to surrender jurisdiction over the newer schools. On the political side, the failure to establish a National Council, mainly due to the joint hostility of Anson and Morant at the Board of Education on the one hand, and the complete mis-handling of the parliamentary procedure by Lloyd George and the opposition of Lord Cawdor in the House of Lords on the other, was a bitter blow to Welsh educationists. But even before the parliamentary phase of the National Council in 1906, the attempts made to secure it by means of a long period of external negotiation, led by Lloyd George between 1903 and 1905 was not successful because Wales was neither ready nor were the Welsh LEAs unanimous in their desire for a national body.[1]

The small offering of administrative differentiation in educational affairs for Wales in the form of a Welsh Department of the Board of Education was in lieu of the fate of the National Council in the withdrawn education Bill of December 1906.[2] This gesture merely served to postpone indefinitely any hope for a unified system of Welsh education. Instead, dichotomy raised its head on many fronts: the Welsh Department of the Board of Education and the Central Welsh Board; two separate Chief Inspectors; dual inspection of secondary schools; duality of secondary schools; multifarious relationships between the LEAs, the Central Welsh Board and the Welsh Department, and worst of all, the unpleasant and inimical relationships which developed after 1907 between the Welsh Board and the Board of Education.[3]

On the academic side, the Central Welsh Board had evolved a system of intermediate schools modelled on continental and the older English

[1] See Study No. IV.
[2] Ibid.
[3] See Studies No. II and VI.

A Survey of The Evolution of Welsh Educational

endowed establishments, and the curricula and examination system of the Welsh schools were at variance with the ideas of the original founders who designed the County Schemes. They also clashed with the cherished ideas of the Chief Inspector of Education for Wales at the Welsh Department. This led to open guerrilla warfare between the two Boards, when the Chief Inspector at the Welsh Department severely criticized the alien nature an uniformity of the Central Welsh Board system and pleaded for differentiation of schools with a more liberal and vocational curriculum more in keeping with the needs of the majority of Welsh secondary school pupils. It was a long and largely inconclusive struggle, but the Welsh Department managed to secure many, long overdue, reforms.[1]

During the period leading up to, and including the first World War, it became evident that the structure and administration of Welsh education both at secondary and university levels needed re-examination and reform. The *Royal Commission on University Education in Wales*, 1916–18 brought new changes in the administration of the university and also infused new life into its academic content. Likewise, the *Report of the Departmental Committee* in 1920 sought to clear up the anomalies of past legislation, and also to bring the secondary schools into line with modern developments—'its comprehensive criticism of the disorganization of the Welsh secondary education system, with its recommendation that the Intermediate Education Act of 1889 should be repealed, formed a depressing commentary on the outcome of the national movement for education'.[2] The Report also embodied another bold, but unsuccessful attempt to secure a National Council for Education.

In its educational awakening, although Wales achieved a great deal, it never realized the goal of its desire—the co-ordination of all branches of education. Legislative difficulties and political vicissitudes were not solely to blame. The real enemy to educational unity came from within the Principality—the LEAs, who jealously guarded and relished their individual sovereignty.[3]

[4] See Study No. VI.
[1] Kenneth O. Morgan, op. cit., p. 294.
[2] See Study No. IV.

APPENDICES

I   NAMES OF DEPUTATION TO A. J. MUNDELLA

II MEMORIAL PRESENTED TO LORD PRESIDENT OF THE COUNCIL

III MEMORIAL CONSIDERED BY THE TREASURY

IV TREASURY'S REPLY TO THE LORD PRESIDENT

APPENDIX I

A Deputation, consisting of the following Noblemen and Gentlemen, was received by Mr. Mundella at the Council Office on 19 June 1882:

His Grace the Duke of Westminster, K.G.	Stuart Rendel, Esq., MP
Right Hon. the Earl of Jersey	M. Lloyd, Esq., MP
Right Rev. the Bishop of Bangor	E. H. Carbutt, Esq., MP
Right Rev. the Bishop of St. Asaph	Richard Davies, Esq., MP
Right Hon. Lord Aberdare	Capt. Verney, R.N.
Right Hon. Lord Penrhyn	Lewis Morris, Esq.
Right Hon. Lord Dynevor	W. Rathbone, Esq., MP
Lord Kensington, MP	Ven. Archdeacon Griffiths
Lord Emlyn, MP	Rev. D. Evans, MA, Gelligaer
Right Hon. G. O. Morgan, MP	Lewis Angell, Esq.,
Sir H. Hussey Vivian, Bart., MP	W. Fuller Maitland, Esq., MP
Sir R. A. Cunliffe, Bart., MP	Stephen Evans, Esq.,
L. P. Pugh, Esq., MP	Abel Simner, Esq., and
W. R. H. Powell, Esq., MP	T. J. Thomas, Esq., CC
Henry Richard, Esq., MP	

PRO Ed. 91/8

APPENDIX II[1]

The Deputation left a Memorial of which the following is a copy:
"MEMORIAL to the Lord President of the Council, presented by a Deputation consisting of Peers residing in Wales, Members of Parliament representing Welsh Constituencies, and the Council of the University College of Wales".

In the first place we desire to express our satisfaction with the announcement in the Queen's Speech at the opening of this Session, that a Bill providing for 'Improved Education in Wales' would be presented to Parliament; and with the assurance given by the Lord President and the Vice President that such a Bill had been prepared.

We are too well aware of the obstacles which have prevented the introduction of this Bill, to impute the delay in the fulfilment of their pledge to any indifference or lukewarmness on the part of Her Majesty's Government.

If the introduction of such a Bill in the House of Commons and its successful prosecution there, were dependent upon the unanimous support of Welsh Representatives, we believe that such unanimity would not be wanting.

We are, however, well aware that a Measure dealing with Endowments, Local Rating, and the constitution of Local Bodies for the promotion of Intermediate Education in accordance with the recommendation of the Departmental Committee, could not, although receiving the unanimous support of Welsh Members, be expected to pass through either House of Parliament without exciting considerable discussion for which time and opportunity must be found.

We are therefore not unprepared to hear that in the present state of public Business, Her Majesty's Government are unable to hold out any hope of prosecuting their Measure during the present Session. But we must not the less express our deep regret at this delay, and our conviction of the disappointment it will cause to the people of Wales, whose sense of the great deficiencies in the provision of Intermediate and Higher Education in Wales had been painfully excited by the Inquiry held by the Departmental Committee; who had warmly approved of the Report of that Committee as a whole; and who had received, with intense satisfaction, the promise of the Government to deal with the subject during the Session.

While therefore we earnestly desire that the Government should have an opportunity of stating their views on the whole subject of Welsh Education and of explaining the measures they are prepared to recommend for its improvement, we have felt it our duty to consider whether, and to what extent, it might be in the power to give effect to some of the recommendations of the Departmental Committee without the aid of actual legislation, and without interfering with the larger and complete scheme, which could only be carried with the sanction of Parliament.

And it appeared to us that no sufficient reasons existed why immediate effect should not be given to those of the Government's intended proposals which would not have been included in their Bill.

Among these we are probably right in assuming the following subjects:

First, The assistance proposed to be given to Higher Education through Colleges:
On this subject, the Departmental Committee said (p. LXVI) "We recommend that, towards the maintenance of the Colleges, recourse shall be had to a Parliamentary Grant. In no other way, indeed, so far as we can see, will it be possible to maintain them. The Committee showed that such institutions could, in no instance, be made self-supporting; that it had been proved to them, on the best evidence, that not more

[1] PRO Ed 91/8: Letters and papers, 1882-3.

than one-third of the yearly expenditure could be derived from the fees of the students; and that at the College at Aberystwith, that source of supply did not contribute more than one-fourth of the cost of maintenance. They suggested the establishment of two Colleges, one for each division of Wales; and, referring to the Grant of £100,000 for building the Queen's Colleges in Ireland, and that of £140,000 towards the new Colleges of Glasgow, they proposed that the Government should make a grant, the amount of which they did not specify, to meet local contributions raised voluntarily or by way of rate. In like manner, while recalling the fact that for the year 1881–2, £25,836 had been voted towards the maintenance of the Universities and Colleges of Ireland, and £18,992 towards that of the Scottish Universities, they suggested that a yearly grant of £4,000 should be made to each of the Welsh Colleges.

We have no hesitation in expressing our conviction that an announcement of the intention of the Government on this subject would have the immediate effect of raising such contributions in Wales as would ensure the establishment of the two suggested Colleges.

In the meantime, we venture strongly to urge that such Grant as the Government shall decide upon recommending to any College, should be enjoyed by that of Aberystwith until the establishment of the other two Colleges.

Nearly £30,000 have been expended on the Buildings, Library, Museum, Laboratories, and furnishing of the College of Aberystwith; and it would be much to be regretted that its remaining Endowment of about £10,000, which might be applied to so many useful purposes, should be dissipated in meeting the annual expenses of the College.

Second, The Departmental Committee made several suggestions for the better application of Endowments which might be dealt with under the existing Acts, or otherwise, without the aid of fresh legislation. As instances of these we would direct attention to the Howell Charity with its Endowment of £6,500 a year; to the Betton Charity of £4,950 a year, of which £725 are frittered away in petty grants to Denominational Schools, although it is beyond question mainly an undenominational Endowment; to Wells' Charity at Cardiff; and to the Capital sum of £20,000, part of the Meyrick Endowment, which by an agreement between the Oxford University Commissioners and the Charity Commissioners, is to be dealt with by a Scheme, under the Endowed Schools Act, for the benefit of education in Wales.

These are the principal, although only a few, of the Endowments which could and should, with the least possible delay, be applied in various ways towards the advancement of the objects which the Government, no less than ourselves, have at heart.[1]

Third, We should also recommend to the attention of the Education Department the expediency of promoting the establishment of advanced Elementary Schools for Boys and Girls in places where—to employ the language of the Report—'there is a considerable population requiring education superior to that which can be provided in an ordinary Elementary School, but unable to avail themselves of a Higher School'.[2]

---

[1] Similar re-apportioning of endowments to that suggested by Schools Inquiry Commission, 1867.

[2] These 'advanced elementary schools' are similar to third-grade schools of Schools Inquiry Commission and to Sandford's recommendations concerning West-Midlands Schools with 'higher tops'. 'The sum of what I have to say is this: that what we require is a class of public schools for secondary instruction, answering to those which we have for primary instruction. That whether these schools be created by remodelling the old Grammar Schools, or by developing the elementary school system, or by establishing them on the proprietary basis, care should be taken to make them really schools of higher instruction ... they should supplement and carry forward the work of the primary schools ... there should be county boards to serve as educational councils in each county, for the double purpose of treating a local interest in education and supervising the different institutions. *Schools Inquiry Commission, Vol. II.* From Rev. H. Sandford, HM Inspector of Schools, 3 Sept., 1866: Correspondence addressed to Commissioners, pp. 106–119.

Structure and Administration 1880–1925

By the adoption of these and possibly of other measures which may occur to your Lordships, much may be done to allay disappointment, to utilise existing funds and Institutions and to provide for the education of large numbers of the people of Wales. And we believe that such preliminary steps would tend to facilitate the passage through Parliament of the larger measures prepared by Government, by defining more accurately than can at present be done the amount of provision required fully to supply the educational deficiency after all existing means have been applied and exhausted.

APPENDIX III

MEMORIAL sent to the Treasury for consideration:

Education Department,
14 July 1882

Sir,

I am directed to forward for the consideration of the Treasury the enclosed copy of a Memorial, recently placed in the hands of the Lords of the Committee of Council on Education by an influential deputation, who waited upon them to urge that immediate steps should be taken by the Government in furtherance of the recommendations of the Departmental Committee on Intermediate and Higher Education in Wales.

In the present state of public business it is, of course, impossible to deal this Session with any of the recommendations of the Committee which require legislation. But My Lords are of opinion that it would be advisable to take advantage of the present interest in the subject which is felt among the Welsh Members of both Houses, and throughout the Principality, and to give effect to the wish expressed in the Memorial, and strongly advocated by the Deputation, that a Public Grant should be made in aid of the expenses of two Colleges in North and South Wales respectively; a commencement being made at once, by a Grant in aid to the University College at Aberystwith, for the current financial year.

My Lords believe that this Institution is, even with its present limited means, doing very valuable work, and as it is likely that, though recommended by the Committee for recognition as the College for North Wales, it will not be continued at Aberystwith. They think that the opportunities for higher education which are now afforded there, should not be allowed to cease in consequence of the probable failure of contributions for its support during the period which must elapse before the question of the future site of the College is determined.

I am, therefore, directed to request that you will invite the favourable consideration of the Treasury to the proposal that a Vote of £2,000 should be submitted to Parliament this Session in aid of the University College at Aberystwith for the remainder of the current financial year.

This would be one-half of a Vote of £4,000, which My Lords think should be taken for Aberystwith in 1883–4 and thereafter yearly for each of the Colleges for North and South Wales respectively.

In proposing the Vote for Aberystwith, notice should be given that it would not be continued beyond 31 March 1884, unless by that time the two projected Colleges had been started, or satisfactory progress made towards their establishment, and a Scheme submitted and approved for their management and maintenance.

P.H.A.

PRO Ed. 91/8

APPENDIX IV

Treasury's reply to the Right Hon. A. J. Mundella, MP.

Treasury Chambers,
22 July 1882

Sir,

I have laid before the Lords Commissioners of Her Majesty's Treasury Sir F. Sandford's letter of the 14th instant covering a Memorial presented to the Lord President by persons interested in Education in Wales.

I am to state, for the information of the Lords of the Committee of Privy Council on Education, that, in the circumstances represented in that letter and its enclosure, My Lords will consent to ask Parliament, in the present Session to Vote a sum of £2,000 as a Grant in aid of the Aberystwith College.

With reference to the recommendation that a grant of £4,000 a year should be made to each of two Welsh Colleges, I am to state that My Lords must reserve generally the question of the continuance of the Grant; and notice should be given to those interested that in no case would it be continued beyond the 31st of March 1884 unless by that time the two projected Colleges had been started or satisfactory progress made towards their establishment and a Scheme submitted and approved for their management and maintenance.

My Lords think that this grant in aid had better be paid direct by the Treasury which in that case would be the accounting Department; and for this purpose I am to request you to inform My Lords of the names of the persons at Aberystwith to whom correspondence should be addressed, and to whose orders money should be made payable. They would also be glad to receive a copy of the last years accounts of the College.

I have the honour to be,
Sir,
Your obedient Servant,
Leonard Courtney, MP.

PRO Ed 91/8.

II

THE CONTENTIOUS WELSH BOARD

INTRODUCTION	48
I END OF THE FIRST QUINQUENNIUM	50
II DUAL INSPECTION	58
III PROCEDURAL IRREGULARITIES	79
IV PUPIL TEACHERS AND BURSARS	89
V THE JOLLIFFE CASE	97
VI DEFALCATION: END OF AN ERA	102
APPENDICES	109

The Contentious Welsh Board

THE Central Welsh Board, a representative Welsh body for secondary education, constituted by Scheme under the Welsh Intermediate Education Act, 1889,[1] upon a joint application from the sixteen Welsh counties and county boroughs, was approved by the Queen in Council on 13 May 1896. The Scheme incorporated the duties and functions of the Board which were administrative, examinational and inspectorial with regard to the new intermediate schools established in Wales up to the Education Act of 1902.[2] The Board enjoyed the privilege of being the only pseudo-autonomous educational body within the Principality, so far as secondary education was concerned.

It seemed that Wales had at last achieved the basis of a national system of secondary education with its own administrative machinery, which could play an important part not only in providing students for Welsh higher education, but also preparing the less-academic pupils for their role in Welsh society. But subsequent happenings interfered with its primary function, affected its behaviour, and encouraged the adoption of a contentious attitude towards the Welsh Department of the Board of Education between 1907 and 1925.[3]

This Study is an attempt to assess the relationships between the Central Welsh Board and the central government, which was represented by the Welsh Department. During its formative years from 1896 to 1902, the Central Welsh Board had settled down in real earnest to the task of organizing its work and putting into operation its examinational and inspectorial responsibilities, and in this respect received the fullest co-operation and sympathetic consideration by the Board of Education.[4] But at the turn of the century, several events profoundly affected the Central Welsh Board's attitude towards Whitehall. Apparently, the first taste of 'autonomy' had whetted its appetite for more, which might have been justifiably regarded as a healthy portent in a young and developing Body lusting for more power and responsibilities.

---

[1] 52 *and* 53 *Vict.*, c. 40. See Study No. I for its functions.

[2] By 1903 there were 96 intermediate schools in Wales with 8,789 pupils.

[3] Intermediate or county schools, i.e. a school between the elementary school and the university, was the term used in the greater part of Wales up to the 1944 Act. 'Secondary' Schools was an English intrusion. The first-grade pseudo-Welsh public schools according to the Taunton classification were few in number and therefore just stood apart from the national system.

[4] PRO Ed 35/3406, 35/3407

The Contentious Welsh Board

The first event which provided a loop-hole for the extension of the Central Welsh Board's powers was the passing of the Board of Education Act of 1899.[1] Secondly, Part II of the Education Act of 1902 gave powers to local education authorities to establish another kind of secondary school—the municipal—with more favourable grants, paid, not under the Welsh Scheme of 1896 (which came directly from the Treasury) but by the Board of Education, supplemented by money from the local rates. This new development, which engendered suspicion and jealousy, did not altogether meet with the approval of the Central Welsh Board. Thirdly, the rejection of the proposed Welsh National Council for Education in December 1906 (which, if it had come into being would have meant the extinction of the Central Welsh Board) gave the Board new hope that it might be regarded as its natural successor. But the unkindest cut of all was the establishment of the Welsh Department of the Board of Education at the end of the same year, which gave rise to dual inspection. This was regarded by the Central Welsh Board as a rival institution and an attempt to undermine its status and prestige, and provoked open hostility between the two bodies from 1907 to 1925, with several abortive attempts by the Central Welsh Board to assume full inspectorial control over *all* secondary schools in Wales, both intermediate and municipal.

Other developments were inevitable when the Welsh Department began its work in April 1907. This meant not only administering Welsh education from South Kensington, backed by experts who could be called upon from other departments of the Board of Education, but also an attempt (at the express request of McKenna, President of the Board) to build up harmonious relationships with the Central Welsh Board, a proud, *national* body with a different background.[2] This Board with its headquarters in Cardiff, had a small, overworked office staff and a tireless and meticulous Chief Inspector, Owen Owen. He was responsible for the overall administration (both office and academic) and had only one assistant inspector, W. Hammond Robinson, to cover the whole of Wales.[3]

Efforts to achieve amicable relationships were hampered by unfortunate clashes between civil service protocol at Whitehall—with its traditional emphasis on correct official procedures, which the new chief officials at the Welsh Department, A. T. Davies and Owen Edwards had to observe in the course of their duties—and the somewhat domestic office procedure

---

[1] 62 *and* 63 *Vict., c.* 33, *Section* 3 (1).
[2] See Study No. 4.
[3] PRO Ed 35/3407. The Central Welsh Board also used two or three part-time inspectors for short periods during the year; Headlam of King's College, Cambridge, and Bell, of Balliol College, Oxford.

which existed at the Central Welsh Board's office in Cardiff. A typical example is cited later on regarding the simple matter of correspondence and the issuing of regulations. On the academic side acute differences arose between the Welsh Department and the Central Welsh Board on important matters of examinations and curricula which came to a head in the explosive *Report* of 1909.[1] This was inevitable when the Chief Inspector for education in Wales, Owen Edwards, who had a remarkably flexible mind in educational matters, and whose ideas regarding curricula and examinations confounded both the academic and lay members of the Central Welsh Board, by his constant attacks on the rigidity and multiplicity of examinations within the system of that Board. Edwards was perhaps the central figure during the most controversial period 1907–1915, and suffered more than one indignity and personal attack from members of the Central Welsh Board for pursuing an enlightened policy which demanded radical changes. On other matters, endless deputations were sent from the Central Welsh Board to Whitehall, which usually produced negative results, while the Jolliffe case, and the defalcations on the part of the clerical staff in Cardiff, which led to the Assize proceedings, considerably embarrassed the Welsh Board in the eyes of the Welsh nation, and could have been the subject of harsh action on the part of the Board of Education had they been so disposed.

These are the main controversial issues which appear prominent in the official records. They were not conducive to healthy relationships between the Welsh Department and the Central Welsh Board—and eclipsed the more salutary and fruitful aspects of the work of both bodies. The Department were steadily evolving an educational programme and development *de novo* which proved to be of the greatest benefit to Wales, whilst the Board were doing so well the task for which they were originally intended, i.e. administering, examining and inspecting the Welsh intermediate schools. It was most regrettable that the years of incompatibility intervened and disrupted so much of the constructive work of both bodies. Had wiser counsels prevailed, a vast amount of distrust and misunderstanding could have been averted.

I END OF THE FIRST QUINQUENNIUM

Less than five years after its establishment, Owen Owen,[2] Chief Inspector of the Central Welsh Board, had to write to the Board of Education

---

[1] See Study No. 5.

[2] Owen Owen, 1850–1920. Educated at Botwnnog Grammar school (with his cousin, Bishop John Owen of St. David's) and Jesus College, Oxford; graduated in Classics, became Headmaster of Oswestry Academy (later High School) which attracted pupils from all parts of Wales. Appointed Chief Inspector, Central Welsh Board, 18 February, 1897.

regarding the Welsh Board's financial situation. The executive committee of that Board found, on examining the accounts for the financial year ended on 31 March 1902 that the additional work which had devolved upon the Board in various directions had not been accompanied by an increase in income, and that no such increase was probable in the immediate future. It had become necessary to devise ways and means of reducing the costs of the Board's work, and in view of the increased amount of inspection provided by the Board, the committee had considered that such reduction would be best met by less expenditure on examinations.[1]

The committee had proposed, with the sanction of the Board of Education, the discontinuance of oral examinations in the lower forms of the schools, the written examination in the case of all work below the Junior Certificate standard, and the practical science examinations for all pupils below that of the Honours Certificate standard.[2] The Board of Education was asked to consider these proposals, for their decision would affect the draft regulations and schedules of the Central Welsh Board for 1903.[3]

Having considered the application, Casson (legal assistant) did not think that Owen's proposals involved any amendment of the Treasury regulations, and Bruce informed the Welsh Board that in view of the fact that important questions relating to the examination of schools were under consideration by the Board of Education, any final pronouncement upon the proposals of the Central Welsh Board would at that time be inopportune, but the Board of Education would not raise any objection to the regulations and schedules of the Central Welsh Board for 1903 being framed experimentally on the suggested lines.[4] This interim arrangement was followed up by the Board of Education after careful analysis of the requirements of the Central Welsh Board. The estimated costs were submitted and showed that the whole expense of inspection, examination, administration and office accommodation for 1903-4 would be £3,920. 8. 2; for 1904-5, £4,919. 5. 3; and for 1907-8, £5,363. 3. 3.[5] Bruce told the Central Welsh Board that he was satisfied that further funds were necessary for the efficient discharge of their duties, and requested the Welsh Board to make an application to the Treasury. This would have the full support of the Board of Education.[6]

[1] PRO Ed 35/3406, Owen to Board of Education, 5 April 1902.
[2] Note the proliferation of examinations of the Central Welsh Board at this early stage!
[3] PRO Ed 35/3406
[4] Ibid., Minute from Casson to Lefroy, 7 April. Minute from Casson to Bruce, 8 April. Board of Education to Central Welsh Board, 10 April.
[5] PRO Ed 35/3407. See Appendix I to this study.
[6] Ibid., Board of Education to Central Welsh Board, 16 June 1903.

Accordingly, A. C. Humphreys-Owen and Professor Edward Anwyl,[1] chairman and vice-chairman respectively of the Central Welsh Board sent a long letter to the Treasury, including a historical survey of the Board and explaining in detail its functions and growing responsibilities since 1897. It was stressed that the Board's work had assumed dimensions which were unforeseen when its constitution was fixed and its finances arranged for. The number of schools had increased from eighty-eight to ninety-six, and the number of pupils from 6,427 to 8,789, i.e. over thirty per cent. In addition to this, the importance of the examinations had become greater. The certificates of the Welsh Board were accepted by the Board of Education and by an increasing number of professional bodies as equivalent to their own. The inspectorial demands were expanding, for when the work of the Board began, one visit a year by one inspector was regarded as sufficient, but owing to the growth of the schools and of the curricula followed in them, two or three part-time inspectors were now required for a complete inspection. Humphreys-Owen was of the opinion that the salaries of the officials and clerical staff were due for review and also made a strong case for the appointment of a woman inspector. Anwyl said that the Board had postponed applying for an increased grant as long as they could, and they had called for the full five per cent authorized by the Scheme on the educational income of the county councils. They had also charged the maximum capitation fee of 2/6 per pupil examined, a payment of 10/- for each Honours Certificate, 7/6 for each Senior, and 5/- for each Junior Certificate candidate, 'an impost which had caused much dissatisfaction'. They had been compelled to reduce the amount of examination work, the amount of payment to examiners, thus losing some of the best qualified, and the work devolving on the office staff was causing overstrain.[2] The Board of Education apparently approved of this array of examinations which did not include several other oral and practical examinations held annually almost at every stage in the schools. The obvious economic, and, certainly, educational course would have been to stream-line the whole examination system of the Welsh Board, by conducting examinations only at the ages of around sixteen and eighteen. This would have relieved considerably the overstrain of both schoolteachers and office staff. The effect on the pupils was far worse. The members of the Central Welsh Board devoted considerable time at half-yearly meetings to express concern on the

---

[1] Sir Edward Anwyl (knighted 1911), 1866–1914. Celtic scholar; educated King's School, Chester, Oriel and Mansfield Colleges, Oxford. Appointed Professor of Welsh at the University College of Wales, Aberystwyth in 1892 at 26 years of age. Became chairman of the Central Welsh Board and appointed first Principal of Caerleon Training College in 1913, but died before taking up the appointment.

[2] PRO Ed 35/3407, Central Welsh Board to Treasury, 11 August 1903.

The Contentious Welsh Board

effects of overstrain upon pupils 'whose strength was not equal to the task of over-study' and yet nothing had been done to mitigate the evils of their examination system.[1]

On 1 May 1903 the Parliamentary Secretary of the Board of Education had received a deputation from the executive committee of the Central Welsh Board to discuss matters relating to the finances of that Board raised in Humphreys-Owen's letter.[2] It was submitted that by Clause 2(b) of Scheme, the Treasury contribution was £500 or one half of the expenses incurred by the Central Welsh Board in respect of the examination and inspection of intermediate schools whichever should be least. The delegates ventured to regard this as some indication that when the Scheme was framed, it was contemplated that such expenses might be shared equally between the Board and the Treasury. It was hoped that the estimate showing the need for an additional grant of £1,000 rising to £1,500 might receive the support of the Board of Education and the careful attention of the Lords of HM Treasury.[3] But the Treasury passed Humphreys-Owen's letter to the Board of Education with a request for their observations on the proposed increase of grant.[4] This was precisely what Bruce hoped they would do.

So far, the Central Welsh Board was getting on well with the Board of Education. Morant in particular, was most anxious that their cause should succeed, and informed Bruce that although Mr. Heath of the Treasury came to see him about the Welsh Board letter, and was 'prepared to refuse a single penny'—after being informed of the full history of the matter he 'was prepared to consider favourably whatever we now say'. Morant went a step further and said 'I think we could make more clear than the Central Welsh Board has done, the greatly increased complexity of its task. But I told Mr. Heath that in pressing the Welsh Board's demands we must not be taken to preclude ourselves from making demands very soon for improved Board of Education inspection arrangements in Wales as in the rest of England'.[5]

Bruce was entrusted with the task of drafting a reply to the Treasury, and as usual when involved in any important decision regarding Welsh education, was most concerned to make out a strong and logical case. He discussed the whole question of the Central Welsh Board, particularly

---

[1] NLW Deposit No. 88B: Board of Education, Minutes of the Central Welsh Board, 5 October 1908–22 October 1915, J. L. Casson, Minutes for 20 May 1909. *South Wales Daily News*, 21 May.
[2] PRO Ed ibid. supra.
[3] Ibid.
[4] Ibid., Treasury to Board of Education, 17 October. Minute from Murray to Bray, 19 October.
[5] PRO Ed 35/3407, Minute from Morant to Bruce, 19 October.

the inspection side, with Morant before framing his reply.[1] Bruce, above any one else, either in Wales or Whitehall, knew most about the Welsh Board and their problems at the end of the first quinquennium. His case for the Board was carefully worded, since he was well aware that a great deal depended on his letter. He strongly commended, on behalf of the Board of Education, to the favourable consideration of Their Lordships, the application of the Central Welsh Board for an increase of the grant of £500 a year towards the cost of examination and inspection of Welsh intermediate schools, a task which that Board had conducted since 1897, and which the State would otherwise have had to discharge. The local authorities for intermediate education in Wales regarded the discharge of this duty as in the nature also of a privilege, and had accordingly been content to bear much the larger share of the cost, the whole of which would otherwise presumably have fallen on the national exchequer.[2] Speaking of the work done by the schools, Bruce made the point (which might have been quite legitimate during those early years of the Central Welsh Board, but later, after the setting up of the Welsh Department, this was challenged vigorously by Owen Edwards) that 'from an educational point of view, the Central Welsh Board by creating a system of certificates of attainment issued to the pupils, *had relieved the schools from the evil effects of the multiplicity of examinations* which were so frequently evident in schools of a similar class in England. It had also been secured that the examination of the schools should be conducted *with a satisfactory knowledge of the character and aims of each school, and with due regard to the liberty of the school to choose its own curriculum.*[3]

Bruce was also concerned about the inspectorial efficiency and stressed that this important educational service required adequate staff who could ensure that the schools were maintaining and improving their standards, and this meant, of course, adequate funds for the purpose. The most important feature of this first quinquennium in the Welsh intermediate schools was their growth in numbers, pupils, curricula and staff, 'most of the Welsh schools were now similar in these respects to English schools, for the inspection of which, under the Board of Education Act, 1899, the Board of Education would employ three or four full-time inspectors, while the Central Welsh Board could, as a rule, only employ a

---

[1] Ibid., Minute from Bruce to Morant, 20 October.
[2] Scores of Welsh intermediate schools were built by public subscription and in many instances free sites were provided.
[3] Bruce was obviously out of touch with the Welsh schools at this time. These matters were considered to be of prime importance when the schools were established. But Owen Edwards knew otherwise. See next Section on Dual Inspection.

single inspector for each school'.[1] Moreover, the Welsh local authorities were contributing to the expenses of the Central Welsh Board the full amount sanctioned by their respective schemes, and unless further aid was forthcoming, that Board would either become bankrupt and stop work, or work to a lower standard of efficiency. In the former case, the Board of Education would be compelled to make arrangements for the inspection of the Welsh schools, and for this purpose would require an increase of staff involving a far greater expenditure than was being asked from the Treasury by the Central Welsh Board. In the latter case, the Board of Education could hardly give Their Lordships that guarantee of the efficiency of the system for testing the eligibility of schools for the Treasury grant which was implied in the present arrangement; so that in either case it appeared inevitable that, unless more funds were available, the examination and inspection of the Welsh schools would cost more to the national exchequer than hitherto. It appeared, therefore, to the Board of Education, that a substantial addition to the grant would be money more than well spent.[2]

Owen's initial letter to the Board of Education was producing extremely favourable developments, for not only was the Board committing itself to a substantial financial award to the Central Welsh Board, but also the reply of the Board of Education to a subsequent letter from the Treasury ensured that the Central Welsh Board, in all its aspects, administrative, examination and inspection, was to be placed on a more liberal and secure footing for the future. But commendation, fortified with detailed estimates was not enough for the Treasury. A further letter to the Board of Education required additional particulars (a) how could a detailed case be made out for increased expenditure in future years? (b) could any increases in the reviewed salaries be made more gradual? (c) the Treasury had only contemplated a grant for inspection and examination—why did the Board of Education include administrative and office accommodation?[3] The answers supplied by Bruce were again logical. It was explained that the Central Welsh Board had, in order to save themselves from getting into further debt, reduced their expenditure below what was in fact necessary for due efficiency. The claim for an increased grant was therefore based not solely on the ground of inevitable increase of expenditure after 1903–4, but also on the ground that the expenditure in the past had been less than it probably should have been, considering

---

[1] PRO Ed ibid. supra, Minute from Morant to Bruce, 8 November. Board of Education to Treasury, 9 November.
[2] PRO Ed 35/3407, ibid.
[3] Ibid., Treasury to Board of Education, 20 November. Minute from Bruce to Casson, 23 November.

The Contentious Welsh Board

the nature and importance of the duties which the Central Welsh Board had to perform. The Board of Education also regarded the increases for 1907-8 as fair and reasonable in view of the fact that proper clerical staff would be required; perhaps additional inspectors would have to be appointed; and that the work of inspection and examination could not be conducted efficiently without proper office accommodation.[1]

There followed yet another detailed analysis of the financial requirements of the Central Welsh Board and, in particular, their needs for the following years. But eventually, on 14 December the Treasury informed the Board of Education that they were sending a formal letter to the Central Welsh Board with details of the proposed increase of grant.[2] It stated that while the Treasury could not support the request for an additional grant of £1,000 rising gradually to £1,500 by estimates of expenditure for the years 1904-5 and 1907-8, they did agree that some increase in expenditure beyond that of 1903-4 was justified. They considered that the immediate increases provided for in the estimate for 1904-5 (especially the proposed increments of salary for the Chief Inspector and Assistant Inspector) went beyond the necessities of the case. They did not wish to criticize too much the expenses of the Welsh Board, but in their opinion, the salary of the Chief Inspector should rise from £600 to £800 by £25 a year, while the salary of assistant inspector was at too high a maximum at £600 a year. However, the Treasury maintained that that was the business of the Central Welsh Board, and accordingly they were prepared to ask parliament to increase the present grant of £500 a year by £700 to £1,200, on the estimates for 1904-5. The Central Welsh Board were advised that it was not the practice to make grants-in-aid subject to progressive increase year by year and 'My Lords will not be able to increase the grant beyond £1200 in the years after 1904-5. They request therefore that the Welsh Board will take note of this intimation with a view to adjusting its expenditure in future years in accordance therewith'.[3]

But the Central Welsh Board nearly lost their increase of £700. On 19 December 1903, a few days after the increased grant had been sanctioned, Casson discovered a technical hitch, that 'the only contribution from the Treasury which is specifically made an endowment under the Central Welsh Board is a contribution which cannot exceed £500. The question arises whether anything should be done to make the additional £700 also subject to the Scheme. I submit that the additional £700 may

[1] Ibid., Board of Education to Treasury, 2 December. Minute from Bruce to Morant, 28 November.
[2] PRO Ed 35/3407, Treasury to Board of Education, 14 December.
[3] Ibid., Treasury to Central Welsh Board, 14 December.

be regarded *as an additional donation or endowment* for the general purposes of the Scheme (within the meaning of Clause 17 of the Scheme) and that we need not do anything'.[1] Bruce was extremely ruffled by this interruption to all his good works and directed that no action should be taken,[2] but in December 1904, when the grant again came up for payment, Casson's minute proved obstructive and led to a whole chain of new events and correspondence with the Treasury. This new development is relevant since the whole financial stability and future work of the Central Welsh Board were in the balance. Briefly, the position was, that it seemed necessary to amend the Central Welsh Board Scheme in order to empower the Treasury to make an increased *grant*. Rather than get involved in a complicated legal situation (which Bruce maintained could last for several years) it was decided to persuade the Treasury to adopt Casson's ingenious suggestion to look upon the increase of £700 as an additional donation or endowment. Bruce, with Morant's approval, advised the Treasury that the Board of Education thought it very undesirable that an amendment of the Central Welsh Board Scheme should be undertaken if it could possibly be avoided, and that 'it appeared to the Board of Education that upon the strict interpretation of Scheme as approved by Her late Majesty in Council, any yearly contribution which HM Treasury think well to make to the Central Welsh Board over and above the annual contribution of £500 may properly be regarded as an additional donation or endowment within the meaning of Clause 2 (6) and (17) ... but I am to add that, should Their Lordships think otherwise, the Board of Education would be prepared to take the necessary steps in the matter'.[3]

The Treasury paid up with some reluctance but were 'still disposed to think that their payment of £1,200 to the Welsh Board might at some future time be criticized on the grounds of the terms of Clause 2 of Scheme as it now stood. They would not, in the circumstances, press for its being amended forthwith, and would be content if steps were taken to that end when a convenient opportunity presented itself'.[4] Bruce informed the Central Welsh Board of this decision and in reply the Board 'urgently hoped that if an Amending Scheme was found to be necessary that it would become law before the end of the next financial year.[5]

---

[1] Ibid., Minute from Casson to Bruce, 19 December.
[2] Ibid., Minute from Bruce to Casson, 21 December.
[3] PRO Ed 35/3407, Minute from Lefroy to Bruce, 1 December 1904. Minute from Casson to Bruce, and from Pease to Morant, 5 December. Board of Education to Treasury, 10 December.
[4] Ibid., Treasury to Board of Education, 22 December.
[5] Ibid., Central Welsh Board to Board of Education, 24 December.

The Contentious Welsh Board

II DUAL INSPECTION

During the years 1903 to 1906 when negotiations were afoot in Wales and parliament for the establishment of a Welsh National Council for Education, the position of the Central Welsh Board in relation to such Council, if formed, was indeterminate. Most people were of the opinion that the Board might become the nucleus of the National Council with very substantial powers over the whole field of Welsh education. But the rejection of Part IV of the Education Bill of 1906 by the Lords, which provided for a National Council, and the eventual withdrawal of the Bill by the Commons, setting up the Welsh Department of the Board of Education, raised special problems for the Central Welsh Board, not the least of which was the question of dual inspection of secondary schools. The Central Welsh Board were not slow to act. A few weeks after the Welsh Department started on its work, the trouble began. Anwyl wrote to the Board of Education with reference to those schools which were aided or maintained under Part II of the Education Act, 1902, but which did not come within the scope of the Central Welsh Board Scheme. The executive committee of the Board drew the attention of the Board of Education to a resolution which had been passed on 17 May 1907, 'that an application be made to the Board of Education for an amending scheme enabling the Welsh Board to undertake at the request of a local education authority the inspection and examination of *any* secondary school in Wales and Monmouthshire, aided or maintained under Part II of the Education Act, 1902'.[1]

The Central Welsh Board sent a deputation to McKenna, President of the Board of Education, on the matter of inspection. It was to seek powers for the Central Welsh Board to have sole responsibility for inspecting their intermediate schools, without interference by the Chief Inspector of Education for Wales, Owen Edwards. This was the first stage of the Central Welsh Board's attempts to achieve 'practical autonomy' of inspection of their schools. The deputation was introduced by Sir Alfred Thomas, MP, in a rambling speech, in which, for his own purposes, he did not lament the rejection of the Welsh National Council for Education,' because 'he, and other members of the Central Welsh Board wanted to assure the President, at that moment, that Wales already possessed such a Council in the Central Welsh Board'.[2] Anwyl, speaker for the deputation, showed how unanimous that Board were in their demand for having the

[1] PRO Ed 35/3406, Central Welsh Board to Board of Education, 4 June, 1907. The same request was made on 13 January, 1908.
[2] At the deputation, the President was accompanied by Davies, Edwards, Casson, and H. J. R. Murray of the Treasury. 12 members of the executive committee of the Central Welsh Board attended, led by Anwyl, and including Owen Owen, C.I.

inspection of the Welsh intermediate schools entrusted entirely to them, in order to get rid of dual inspection. He reminded the President of his promise at the time of the establishment of the Welsh Department, that he had no intention of destroying the Central Welsh Board, and now, by the simple expedient of granting them 'practical autonomy' in the inspection of their intermediate schools the President could eliminate dual inspection. Anwyl assured the President that the Board of Education, through the Welsh Department, would still inspect the work of the Central Welsh Board, i.e. Anwyl had no desire to remove his Board from the ultimate control of the Board of Education in the matter of inspection. In other matters there was no reason why there should not be the closest liaison between the two Boards, since Edwards, the Chief Inspector for Wales, attended all the meetings of the Welsh Board and had access to all the reports on subsidiary and triennial inspections regarding the intermediate schools.[1]

Anwyl again emphasized the dangers of the overlapping of inspection by both Boards. It was his contention that it would not be in the best interests of Welsh education that two different sets of inspectors should report on schools, as it might give rise to the risk of conflict and irritation on the part of headmasters and teachers. His reasons for delegating complete inspectorial control to the Central Welsh Board were, that, when it was established, its work was regulated by Treasury regulations for the Treasury grant, in the distinct hope that Wales would receive a considerable measure of autonomy in secondary education; Wales was most anxious to preserve any self-government that was accorded to it; the Welsh Board desired inspection in its own hands because it was their duty to examine the schools; and, if Wales was entrusted with the work of inspection, there would be continued enthusiasm for secondary education.[2]

In his reply, the President affirmed that he had no intention of destroying the Central Welsh Board, but was anxious to secure its position, and they should take no notice of what appeared in ill-informed Welsh newspapers. He was in complete agreement that dual inspection should cease for the reasons recited by Anwyl—on its effects on the intermediate schools in Wales; the statutory position of the Welsh Board was fairly strong but not *impregnable* and they had nothing to fear without an amending Act of Parliament, which was unlikely. McKenna came to the all-important issue at once, namely, how far the work of the Central Welsh Board

---

[1] PRO Ed 3415 B, Transcript of Deputation from the Central Welsh Board to the Rt. Hon. Reginald McKenna, MP, President of the Board of Education, 7 June 1907, from shorthand notes of Messrs. G. Moore & Co., Parliament Chambers, Westminster, S.W. pp. 3–8.
[2] Ibid., pp. 8–11.

could cover the *whole field of inspection of secondary schools*. Here, he was in real difficulty because he was speaking for the Welsh Department of the Board of Education. The parliamentary grants for 1907–8 (and he was not referring to the Treasury grant administered through the Central Welsh Board) i.e. for the current year, for secondary schools and pupil-teacher centres in Wales, were estimated at no less than £48,000 or exactly twice as much as the Treasury grant. Of the whole amount of about £72,000 provided by parliament for the purposes of secondary education in Wales, whether on the estimates or through the Treasury grants, no less than two-thirds were voted on the estimates and had to be *directly administered* by the Welsh Department, although the Treasury grant also had to be *indirectly* administered by that Department. Therefore, the Welsh Department could not wash its hands of secondary education in Wales, cutting it out of the educational system and saying, 'Well, we will hand that over to the Central Welsh Board. It could not be done for the very simple reason that the House of Commons would not let them do it, because he was answerable to that House for the expenditure of parliamentary grants'[1] There were further long discussions on both sides, Owen, J. E. Powell (Wrexham), and Lewis Morgan (Cardiff) bolstering up the points put forward by Anwyl, but the question of dual inspection proved too complicated, and although direct questions were asked, no specific answers were possible. What Anwyl really wanted was jurisdiction over all Welsh intermediate schools, which were answerable to the Welsh Department through their Chief Inspector, Owen Edwards. The President called this 'practical autonomy coupled with the inspection of the Central Welsh Board by the Board of Education', and said that this would be completely acceptable to him provided it was understood that he was to look to the Chief Inspector of the Welsh Department who was paid by Parliament, and that he was to have the responsibility—but he admitted that that was not quite bearing out the words 'practical autonomy'.[2]

Compromise without autonomy was the President's solution. He recommended that the two Chief Inspectors should agree together as to how the field should be covered in terms of inspection, but that Owen Edwards should answer to him for the efficiency of the secondary schools in Wales. But this did not mean that dual inspection would cease, for Lord Stanley of Alderley, another member of the deputation, said that (a) the Board of Education, which was responsible for the parliamentary grants must retain the supreme control, and the power of performing

---

[1] PRO Ed 3415 B, Transcript of Proceedings of Deputation, ibid., pp. 11–13.
[2] Ibid., p. 14.

The Contentious Welsh Board

anything which it wanted to perform for the purpose of parliamentary control; (b) he thought, personally, that if the Board of Education thought fit to direct their Chief Inspector to carry out the inspection—which might be called a dual inspection—they would have a perfect right to do so; and (c) that the two inspectors would be able to consult together and come to some agreement. Lord Stanley made another point of considerable importance—that the county boroughs in Wales were also starting new *municipal schools*, and that he could see very well that the Central Welsh Board could not cover the whole work in Wales.[1] This matter was to provide another opportunity later on for the Central Welsh Board to try to lure the municipal schools into its fold.[2]

During the course of the year Edwards came to a satisfactory arrangement with the Central Welsh Board regarding inspection[3] and for the purposes of the Regulations of the Board of Education, had confined his own visits to the triennial inspections of the intermediate schools, thus leaving a free hand to the Welsh Board's inspectors to deal with subsidiary inspections. This mutual understanding was acceptable to Owen only as a preliminary to further independence, but for the time being it ensured no overlap of visits, and suited Edwards's policy that every school should be seen once a year.[4] But in January 1908 the Board of Education were reminded of the resolution sent to them (in the letter of 4 June 1907) of the desire to have an Amending Scheme to enable the Welsh Board to undertake, at the request of a local education authority the inspection and examination of *any secondary school* in Wales and Monmouthshire. This was the second stage in their attempt to expand their powers. However, the Board of Education were not prepared to consider any such proposal at that time, and, ignoring the matter of inspection, the Welsh Board were informed that 'in view of the existing uncertainty as to the effects of the Regulations which will in future govern the payment of the Board's grant to secondary schools, the present is not a suitable or convenient time to consider *a proposal for the extension of the powers of the Central Welsh Board in the direction indicated*'.[5]

When this letter was discussed at the Welsh Board's meeting at Shrewsbury in February, Anwyl spoke in bitter terms and accused the Board of

---

[1] Ibid.

[2] Ibid., Lewis Morgan, chairman of the Cardiff Local Education Authority, said that they were building two new municipal secondary schools in Cardiff (Canton and Howard Gardens) and asked if they would come under the C.W.B. The President replied that they could not extend the powers of the C.W.B. without altering Scheme.

[3] PRO Ed 35/3406, Minute from Davies to President, 24 January, 1908.

[4] PRO Ed 35/3406, Minute from Edwards to Casson, 24 April.

[5] Ibid., Central Welsh Board to Board of Education, 13 January, 1908. Minute from Casson to Davies, 17 January. Minute from President to Davies, 1 February. Board of Education to Central Welsh Board, 7 February.

Education of having 'let the matter slide for a long time, and such a small concession could easily be given'.[1] But Edwards reminded him that with regard to his remark, the President undoubtedly understood that the Welsh Board had, after his answer to their deputation, withdrawn this request, and the municipal schools were developing on lines quite different from those of the intermediate schools. It would also be regrettable at that moment to bring the municipal schools into the examination system of the Welsh Board, a system which was not suitable to them, and they were on the eve of important changes. Edwards was also assured by the representative of the headmasters of the intermediate schools they agreed with the view taken by the Board of Education. Further, Edwards was convinced that 'in this particular, *as in all others*, the chief aim of the Central Welsh Board was to extend its own power. The Board of Education has taken, and must take, a wider view of the situation.'[2]

In order to get a clear picture of the inspectorial activities of the Central Welsh Board, Casson had been directed to prepare a memorandum 'as to the period within which the inspections of the Central Welsh Board for the purposes of the Treasury grant should take place'.[3] Briefly, it meant that every intermediate school had to be examined and inspected as soon as possible after 30 June in any school year, and its inspection should be concluded not later than the examinations. It was observed, however, that the Central Welsh Board were inspecting their schools much earlier—in November and December—so that it was impossible for that Board to say that the conditions upon which the payment of the Treasury grant depended, had been fulfilled throughout the school year. The Board of Education held the view that the inspections should be made between 1 March and the end of July, but this might interfere with the arrangements which Edwards had made for his own inspections.[4] But Edwards was able to assure the Board of Education that the newly proposed dates, from his point of view, would be easier to work, and he also suggested that they should insist on more serviceable reports from the Central Welsh Board, since such reports would refer to the condition of the schools at the latter part of the session.[5] Casson feared that this would be strongly opposed by Anwyl, and would lead to further deterioration of relationships with the Board of Education.[6] Davies, however, was bent on a more rational system of inspection, and suggested a 'carefully worded and very

[1] Ibid., Minute from Edwards to Casson, 22 February, seen by Davies, 25 February.
[2] Ibid.
[3] Ibid., Memorandum on Welsh Intermediate Education, J. L. Casson, 9 March.
[4] PRO Ed 35/3406, Memorandum, op. cit., 9 March.
[5] Ibid., Minute from Edwards to Casson, 16 March.
[6] Ibid., Minute from Casson to Davies, 19 March.

The Contentious Welsh Board

moderately toned letter' to Owen with an invitation to confer on the matter.[1] The subject was to be brought up again in January 1909, but the anticipated antagonism did not appear, the Board of Education's observations were not taken seriously, and Anwyl promised that the matter would be adjusted.[2]

In April 1908, after the inspections episode, Davies forewarned the President that the case raised the rather delicate question of the relations of the Board of Education, and more particularly of the Welsh Department, with the Welsh Board 'a statutory Body of which you will necessarily hear not a little in course of time, and therefore calls for careful consideration'.[3] Davies knew that the Central Welsh Board were very sensitive both of their functions and jurisdiction, and were determined to extend their powers in any direction they could. He was also very disturbed regarding the administrative relationships between the Welsh Board and his Department. These were both wasteful and extravagant, and he proposed to investigate them later. As to the irregular practice of holding inspections at an early date in the school year, which 'the Board of Education had tacitly allowed for the past few years ... they should not wink at the present state of things, and would not be dismayed if the Central Welsh Board raised a certain amount of pother over their action'.[4]

On 4 May, the Central Welsh Board asked the Board of Education's permission to examine and inspect the school at Mountain Ash, Glamorgan.[5] This school had just been established as a municipal school, but was intended to become an intermediate school. The Board replied that an amendment of the Glamorgan county scheme would take some time, and in the circumstances 'no occasion arose for inspection by the Central Welsh Board, but that as its pupils would suffer hardship if not examined by that Board, and in the very exceptional circumstances of the case, if the Central Welsh Board were prepared to examine the school, and the school was prepared to pay the full cost of such examination, the Board of Education on their part would *originate no objection* to the adoption of this course'.[6]

June was a critical month for further straining of relationships between the Board of Education and the Central Welsh Board. This was caused by

---

[1] Ibid., Minute from Davies to Casson, 14 April. Minute from Casson to Edwards, 22 April. Board of Education to Central Welsh Board, 21 April.
[2] Ibid., Minute from Davies to Edwards, 2 February, 1909, Edwards to Davies, 8 February. Casson had been appointed by the President to attend all meetings of the C.W.B. with Edwards.
[3] PRO Ed ibid. supra, Minute from Davies to President, 27 April.
[4] Ibid.
[5] Ibid., Central Welsh Board to Board of Education, 4 May.
[6] PRO Ed 35/3406, Board of Education to Central Welsh Board, 7 May.

The Contentious Welsh Board

the revision of administrative procedures by the Board of Education, (which is discussed later); the burning question of dual inspection; and the outright demand by the Central Welsh Board at this stage for complete autonomy in the inspection of all Welsh secondary schools.

An important meeting of the Central Welsh Board at Cardiff on 9 July[1] had discussed these issues. Edwards, reporting to Davies at some length, said that Davies's letter to Anwyl offering a conference was not read until that Board had resolved to fight the Welsh Department. The members also seemed ignorant of such points as (a) Treasury money was not paid through the Central Welsh Board, but directly; (b) the Central Welsh Board's statutory powers extended to inspection and examination in order to report for Treasury grant alone—the Central Welsh Board had never (and never would be) allowed to inspect for the secondary grant, or to interfere with the education of Pupil Teachers or Bursars. Anwyl maintained that the new administrative arrangements would endanger the harmony in inspection established that year after so much misunderstanding and so many difficulties. Edwards could re-assure Davies that his inspection arrangements with the Central Welsh Board (who were quite pleased with them) would not be affected in the least. He did not wish to curtail their inspection, and everything could be adjusted between himself and Owen. But Edwards made a striking observation in postscript: 'The Central Welsh Board are afraid we are trying to punish them for misleading Wales into rejecting McKenna's magnificent offer of autonomy in Welsh secondary education, (equivalent grant and Welsh Regulations) I wonder whether it will not be possible to get this offer made again'?[2] After just eighteen months in office, Edwards could speak of his two great disappointments 'the rejection by Wales,—misled by men who ought to have known better—of the autonomy offered by Mr. McKenna, and the hostility of the Central Welsh Board, and especially that revolt in Parliament.[3] We are really aiming at getting as much power for the Central Welsh Board as is consistent with the thorough efficiency of the Welsh system of education. If they tried to meet us, so as to avoid misunderstanding, all would go well'.[4]

A deputation from the Central Welsh Board, accompanied by several Welsh MPs attended at the House of Commons on 28 July and was

[1] PRO Ed 35/3415B, Minute from Edwards to Davies, 10 July.
[2] Ibid.
[3] The 'revolt' of 13 Welsh Members in the House was a protest against Runciman's reception of the Central Welsh Board deputation on 28 July. The Members were: Ellis Davies, Clement Edward, Ellis Griffith, Ivor Guest, Keir Hardie, Edward Hemmerde, Howell Idris, Thomas Richards, Sidney Robinson, Walter Roch, D. A. Thomas, John Williams and Llewelyn Williams.
[4] Edwards to Herbert Lewis, 4 October, Penucha MSS.

The Contentious Welsh Board

received by the Rt. Hon. Walter Runciman, MP, President of the Board of Education. A. T. Davies, Owen Edwards, Casson and Murray represented the Board of Education; the members from the Central Welsh Board were Anwyl, Owen, Lord Stanley, Sir John Rhys, J. E. Powell, Charles Lloyd, Tom John and Miss Collin; the MPs were Sir D. Brynmor Jones, Sir Frank Edwards, Ellis Griffith, John Williams, D. A. Thomas, J. Lloyd Morgan, William Jones, Sidney Robinson, Ellis Davies and J. Herbert Lewis. Sir Herbert Roberts introduced the deputation and the speakers were Anwyl, Lord Stanley, Powell and Rhys. With regard to dual inspection, Anwyl said that Wales wanted unity of control in secondary education; the Central Welsh Board should have complete autonomy, subject only to Imperial control in financial matters; they should have the right to inspect all the secondary schools, and should be expressly mentioned in the Board of Education's Regulations as the proper Body to inspect the Welsh schools.[1] Lord Stanley maintained that under the Board of Education Act, 1899, the Central Welsh Board was made the proper Body to inspect intermediate schools, dual inspection should cease, and the Welsh Board alone should inspect. The Regulations should give power to the Board of Education to use the Central Welsh Board's inspectors for the purposes of the secondary school grants. Powell, supporting, demanded that the Welsh Board should be in complete control. Rhys, speaking 'from the educational point of view,' asked for autonomy and freedom for Wales, adding 'that the attitude taken by the Board of Education led to harmful discussions in the newspapers'.[2]

The President, in his reply, spoke of the value of the Central Welsh Board to Welsh secondary education, and no one wanted to deprive it of any powers. He could only re-iterate what had been said by his predecessor, Mr. McKenna, that the Minister responsible for the administration of the Board of Education's grants must be responsible directly to Parliament. Autonomy for Wales in this matter had to be made subject to Parliamentary control. He reminded the deputation of the arrangements already made between the Chief Inspector for Wales and the Chief Inspector for the Central Welsh Board, and also a resolution of that Board of November 1907 giving qualified approval to those arrangements, in addition to another resolution of 15 May 1908 which recorded that a fairly satisfactory arrangement had been arrived at. The arrangements provided that when a school had its triennial inspection by the Central Welsh Board, it should be visited only by the Chief Inspector for Wales,

---

[1] PRO Ed 35/3415B, Deputation from the Central Welsh Board to Board of Education, 28 July pp. 1–2.
[2] Ibid., pp. 2–3.

and that in the case of schools undergoing subsidiary inspection, care would be taken that any visit by HMI should not be held about the same time. Moreover, the Regulations for 1908 provided that the schools had to be open at all times to inspection by the Board of Education. If these arrangements could be improved, he would endeavour to effect this, but any arrangements made should be adhered to in good faith by both parties, and not re-opened year by year.[1] Runciman advised the deputation that they should choose a few of their members to remain in London to discuss the main points raised that day in order that some permanent agreement might be arrived at, bearing in mind, of course, the statutory limits within which both parties had to work.

The following day, Davies and Edwards with other officials of the Board of Education conferred with members of the deputation on matters which were to be placed before the Central Welsh Board. The deputation insisted that both questions of revised administrative procedures and autonomy of inspection should be considered together.[2] Regarding autonomy of inspection, Davies refused to commit himself until the President had come to a decision, but was prepared to consider further reduction of dual inspection. With reference to the new administrative procedures which were discussed in detail, he promised to put their views before the President, and they would hear from him later in the year. During the following weeks, Edwards, Murray, Casson and Hobhouse were devising plans to reduce dual inspection, but the legal position proved unassailable.[3] Casson could only confirm the view, eventually adopted by the Board of Education, that while the Central Welsh Board had full power (a) to inspect schools for the purpose of the Treasury grant, and (b) to inspect such of the schools as were desirous of inspection under section 3 of the Board of Education Act, 1899, the Board of Education had full power to inspect the schools under the Regulations for Secondary Schools (Wales) 1908, for the purpose of the Board's grants, and that their inspection could take such form as they thought desirable.[4]

Edwards had some pertinent comments to make on the situation. He was afraid that the prominent supporters of the Central Welsh Board had a plan for ousting the Board of Education's inspectors from the Welsh intermediate schools. Its success was based on two popular cries, both mistaken and both assiduously nursed by those who ought to have known

[1] PRO Ed 35/3415B, Deputation from Central Welsh Board, op. cit., pp. 3–6.
[2] Ibid., Minute from Davies to President, 29 July.
[3] Ibid., Memorandum on the legal position of the Powers of the Board of Education and the Central Welsh Board respectively as to inspection of Welsh Intermediate Schools, 22 July by J. L. Casson, pp. 4–5 Also see Appendix IV.
[4] Ibid.

better. The first was a notion that the Central Welsh Board was a national institution, and the Board of Education an anti-national one. The truth was that the Board of Education had done much to develop the national literature of Wales—the Central Welsh Board, nothing. The second was based on the plea that the headmasters were groaning under the tyranny of double inspection. Edwards dismissed this as a purely manufactured grievance, stating that he had seen nearly one-half of the intermediate schoolmasters in Wales, and that far from resenting the visits of HMIs, they welcomed them. The unreality of the cry was seen in the case of Portmadoc.[1] In the last year that school was not dually inspected at all; it was inspected by the Central Welsh Board only, but the governors of the school were apparently unaware of that fact.[2]

The matter was serious enough to refer it to the President on his return after the summer recess. The best thing Edwards could think of was to arrange to meet the local education authority or the school governors and discuss the matter with them. Then he made some very striking observations—that the success of this plan (to oust HMIs) would be a grave misfortune to Welsh education, since it would make the unity and harmonious working of the Welsh system impossible because an important part of the Welsh 'ladder' was removed from the sight of the Board of Education, and only disconnected fragments could be seen by the Board's inspectors; also, by the late democratizing policy of the Board of Education, the intermediate schools had become open to all, and they were closer to the elementary schools. In Wales, the Central Welsh Board demanded that the elementary and secondary schools should be guided by two different Boards. With regard to intending teachers and inspection, Edwards was highly critical of the Central Welsh Board, for the pupil teachers and bursars came to the training colleges from the intermediate schools equipped with the wrong subjects and lacked proper guidance. Inspection would be reduced to an absurdity, for the Welsh schools would be inspected and guided by one man, expert advice would be impossible, and the Central Welsh Board could not advise on special subjects like Agriculture, Manual Work, Physical Training and Music. He earnestly hoped that other governors would not follow suit and pass the same resolution.[3]

Only a few schools passed similar resolutions between the end of July and December, copies of which were sent to the two Boards. They were

---

[1] Resolution passed by the school governors that dual inspection should cease, copy sent to Board of Ed. and C.W.B., 17 July.
[2] PRO Ed ibid. supra, Minute from Edwards to Davies, 30 July.
[3] PRO Ed 35/3415B, Minute from Edwards to Hobhouse, 15 August, 1908.

The Contentious Welsh Board

Caernarvon, Denbigh, Pontywaun (Monmouthshire), Llanelli, Llandysul, Llandeilo, Builth Wells, Aberystwyth, and the local education authorities of Montgomeryshire, Cardiganshire, and Caernarvonshire.[1] Davies, in the meantime, had told the Central Welsh Board that the Board of Education had decided to reduce dual inspection to a minimum, and that in the school year just ended 'such inspection had ceased in very nearly one-half of Wales, and arrangements would be made as soon as practicable to effect a still further diminution, but as to the request that the Welsh Board's inspection should be specifically mentioned in the Regulations of the Board of Education, this raised complex issues which would have to be considered by the Treasury'.[2] This assurance of better relationships between the two Boards gave satisfaction to Anwyl and Owen, but they were still adamant that specific reference should be made in the Regulations to 'the place which the State has accorded to the Central Welsh Board in the administration of Welsh education' and looked forward to a final decision on the matter.[3] But Edwards declared that 'their re-iterated demand for the reduction of duality of inspection to a minimum should have a re-iterated answer—that the Chief Inspector for Wales was charged with the duty of carrying that out, as soon as possible, and whenever practicable'.[4]

In February 1909 the Central Welsh Board again asked for an assurance regarding the inclusion in the Regulations of a specific reference to their inspection duties 'in order to place beyond the reach of any future misunderstanding the relations of that Board with the Board of Education'.[5] Davies, writing to the President, said that the time for giving their reply promised in a former letter, had now arrived. But he was now determined to furnish all the particulars from the constitutional, educational and administrative aspects. He said that from the constitutional point of view, the Central Welsh Board had no power to inspect schools other than intermediate, for the purpose of the Treasury grant. The proviso in the Act of 1899 only recognized the Central Welsh Board as the proper organization for the inspection of any such secondary schools 'as may be desirous of inspection under that section'. This was a very different thing

---

[1] Ibid., correspondence to Board of Education from the schools and LEAs concerned.

[2] Ibid., Board of Education to Central Welsh Board, 7 August. In answer to a question in the House of Commons by Sir Herbert Roberts, the President of the Board of Education said 'that there would be a further diminution of the inspections in the present school year, and those inspections would be restricted to the bursars in some counties, who were being taught in the secondary schools, and that he intended to make as much use as possible of the Central Welsh Board rather than cover the ground twice over, although that might be necessary in some cases'. 30 July, 1908.

[3] Ibid., Central Welsh Board to Board of Education, 9 October.

[4] Ibid., Minute from Edwards to Davies, 15 October.

[5] Board of Education, Minutes of the Central Welsh Board, 15 February 1909. Central Welsh Board to Board of Education, 23 February.

The Contentious Welsh Board

to that wider meaning which that Board evidently read into those words when they talked about 'the place which the State has accorded to them in the administration of Welsh secondary education'. That Board now wanted the same authority in regard to the Board of Education's 'S' grants as they occupied in regard to the Treasury grant. The Central Welsh Board were never, by Scheme, Act or Regulation constituted the Authority to inspect or examine schools for the purposes of the Board of Education's *secondary* school grants, although the Board went some considerable way in the direction of recognizing the Central Welsh Board's inspections for such purposes, when, in 1908, HMIs, with the exception of the Chief Inspector for Wales, were withdrawn from one-half of the intermediate schools in Wales.[1]

On the educational side, Davies could only cite the opinion of his Chief Inspector, and the crux of this matter was the dominating influence of the Central Welsh Board through their highly centralized and rigid examination system. That Board worshipped examination results, and the sole purpose of the school was to participate in the examination race without regard to a liberal curriculum or the environment of the pupil. The work in the schools was geared to the wants of a few who went on to university, without regard to the needs of intending teachers in such subjects as Welsh, English literature, geography, history, drawing and singing. It went without saying 'that apart from the constitutional difficulty, this condition of things would be likely rather to be accentuated than mitigated by any more express recognition of the Central Welsh Board in the Board of Education's Regulations, with correspondingly bad educational results'.[2]

Regarding the administrative aspect, he reminded the President of what happened the previous year when the Welsh Department, in view of the application to Wales of the English secondary schools Regulations, found itself obliged to revise the administrative procedure.[3] If they encouraged administrative recognition to the Central Welsh Board as well, 'it would not be long before the President of the Board of Education would be told that dual administration was just as much evil as dual inspection, and that as the Board of Education had put an end to one, it ought to remove the other. If that were done, control for the distribution of some £70,000 annually would at once virtually pass from Whitehall to Cardiff'.[4] Davies could envisage no limit to this grasping for power, for every concession

---

[1] PRO Ed 35/3415B, Minute from Davies to President, 21 March.
[2] Ibid.
[3] See 'Procedural Irregularities' in this Study.
[4] PRO Ed 35/3415B, Davies to President, ibid.

to the Central Welsh Board was apt to form the jumping off ground for further efforts to secure that practical autonomy which Anwyl sought with McKenna, which meant constituting that Board as the authority for controlling Welsh secondary education. He contended that if it was right that this jurisdiction should be extended, and that Wales should be given the practical autonomy which the Central Welsh Board frankly asked for, then he thought it should be conceded deliberately and directly, and not by the process of annual concession.[1]

Another issue which had been discussed by Edwards with the Central Welsh Board, Davies, and the President caused some disquiet for the Welsh Department. It was the question of the brevity of the *Reports* sent to the Board of Education by the Welsh Board on the results of their full (triennial) inspection of intermediate schools. Edwards described them as meagre and superficial, extending to only three or four pages, whereas a full inspection *Report* by the Welsh Department of the Board of Education was twenty pages or more. Owen argued that it was his practice to put in their *Reports* only what was actually necessary, and suggested that a *Report* of twenty pages 'would drown the really important points',[2] but Edwards maintained that a *Report* should present a complete picture of the school as a whole. Owen's assistant inspector, Hammond Robinson, supported Edwards in this, and stated that Mr. Lefroy of the Board of Education, when he attended meetings of the Central Welsh Board some years previously, used the same phrase as Edwards, and it was decided to refer the matter to a sub-committee for report.[3]

In the meantime, the President had decided that the Central Welsh Board should not have practical autonomy, and also that no reference was to be made to inspection in the Board's Regulations for 1909. A letter to this effect was drafted but not sent. On reflection, the President conceded that a 'slight reference' might be included in the Prefatory memorandum to the secondary school Regulations, to the effect that 'the Board of Education wish to utilise the Central Welsh Board inspection so far as the responsibility of the Board of Education for the administration of the monies voted by Parliament permits'.[4] At the next meeting of the Central Welsh Board, Anwyl jubilantly announced that the Board of Education had, for the first time, given express recognition to the Central Welsh Board in their Regulations.[5]

[1] Ibid.
[2] Board of Education, Minutes of Central Welsh Board, 19 February, 1909.
[3] Ibid.
[4] PRO Ed ibid. supra, Minute from President to Davies, 9 June.
[5] Board of Education, Minutes of executive committee of the Central Welsh Board, 16 July. Board of Education to Central Welsh Board, 15 June.

The Contentious Welsh Board

During the next three years 1910–1913 other attempts were made by the Welsh Board to amend their Scheme to include the inspection and examination of *the municipal secondary schools*. In February 1910, Ald. D. H. Williams (Glamorgan) proposed that this type of school should be examined by the Central Welsh Board, and mentioned that Cowbridge Girls' intermediate school would, under the county scheme then in progress, shortly become a municipal school.[1] Further meetings of the Welsh Board pressed forward with the amendment, and in November a formal resolution was passed authorizing the chairman to sign the application, which was to be in a limited form, on the proposal of T. Mansel Franklen. But Casson warned them that an application of that kind was unlikely to meet with the approval of the Board of Education.[2] His warning went unheeded, and in February 1911 a formal application for an amending Scheme was sent to Whitehall (a) to extend the powers of the Central Welsh Board to undertake, at the request of a local education authority the inspection and examination of municipal secondary schools, and (b) to give Merthyr Tydfil, which had recently achieved county borough status, representatives on the Central Welsh Board.[3] The Legal Branch of the Board of Education declined to accept the limited application. But the Central Welsh Board passed a fresh resolution, and although about fifty members were present at the meeting, all but seven had left before the resolution was passed, and as twenty-one formed a quorum, the legal branch at first refused to act on the resolution.[4]

Nevertheless, as the submission of the application was only a technical matter, the question was taken up by the Board of Education on its merits. A draft letter was referred to the President, and the Central Welsh Board were informed on 26 October that the inclusion in any amending Scheme of powers enabling them on the application of any local education authority to inspect and examine municipal secondary schools could not be granted for two reasons, (a) the schools would be subjected to dual inspection, and (b) there would be a tendency for all the secondary schools of Wales to follow one uniform type. Surprisingly, this letter was only read and noted—the two points were not discussed—at the October meeting of the Executive Committee of the Central Welsh Board.[5] In November, at a full meeting, the Board succeeded in passing a valid resolution for amending their Scheme. The letter of

---

[1] Board of Education, Minutes, ibid. supra, 18 February, 1910.
[2] Ibid., 26 May. ibid., 18 November. PRO Ed 35/3409, Minute from Casson to Legal Branch, 28 May.
[3] Board of Education, Minutes, ibid., 8 February, 1911.
[4] Ibid., 19 May. PRO Ed ibid. supra, Minute from Casson to Legal Branch, 20 June.
[5] Ibid., 27 October. PRO Ed 35/3408, Minute from Davies to President, 24 October. Board of Education to Central Welsh Board, 26 October.

The Contentious Welsh Board

26 October was received at first without comment, but subsequently Tom John (Rhondda) objected to 'taking the letter lying down' and it was referred to the executive committee to renew the application, but again the two points were not discussed.[1]

Notwithstanding the Board of Education's letter of 26 October 1911, the Central Welsh Board decided to renew their application for an amended Scheme (which did not include the desired extension of powers) at the Executive Committee in May 1912. But in the meantime, Glamorgan local education authority, (at the instigation of Tom John, who was devoting his energies to a revival of the agitation to extend the examinations of the Central Welsh Board to municipal secondary schools and was also one of the governors of the newly established Maesteg municipal school), had unsuccessfully applied to the Board of Education to have this school examined by the Welsh Board.[2] John and his fellow-members were oblivious of the fact that the rejected amended Scheme applied to this or any other municipal secondary school, and they discussed it 'as if no such request had been made, and no such reply had been given' until Casson drew attention to the fact.[3] Lord Sheffield, (Penrhos, Holyhead) vice-chairman, then obtained and read the letter, and tried to discourage the committee from pressing the matter. But Ald. Williams and others, hotly opposed this, and it was resolved to approach the Board of Education again—on the new factor which had arisen—that a local education authority had now *applied* that the powers in question should be conferred on the Central Welsh Board. Casson mentioned that again the two points were not discussed.[4]

The celebrated 'Thus Far' meeting of the full Central Welsh Board was held at Llandrindod on 17 May. A resolution approving a draft amending Scheme to include the representatives of Merthyr Tydfil on the Board was passed, Ald. Williams regretting the exclusion of the desired powers from the draft. This incited Tom John to make a violent speech attacking the Welsh Department. He moved the re-affirmation of the desire of the Board to inspect and examine municipal secondary schools, and demanded that every new school that wished to come under the Board should be given the opportunity. The success of their schools was recognized, yet they were told by the Board of Education 'Thus far shalt thou go and no further'. He denounced the Welsh Department, saying that 'the Central Welsh Board had never had any trouble with the Board of

[1] Board of Education, Minutes of Central Welsh Board, op. cit., 17 November, 1911.
[2] Ibid., Edwards to Davies, 5 May, 1912.
[3] Ibid., note by Casson, 8 May.
[4] Ibid.

Education until that Department arrived, and there seemed to be an underlying spirit of objection to the Welsh Board's schools'.[1] He was supported by Ald. Williams, Principal T. F. Roberts, (Aberystwyth) and Ald. Hopkin Morgan, (Neath) the latter proposing the inevitable deputation to the Board of Education, should their request be again rejected.[2]

At the meeting, Owen Edwards was compelled to challenge the allegations 'in case his silence should be misunderstood'.[3] He said that Tom John had made a statement—not by any means for the first time—that the Welsh Department had some kind of strange and inexplicable antipathy towards the Welsh intermediate schools. Anyone from Glamorgan or Monmouthshire could prove that the Board of Education had been fighting battles of intermediate schools against municipal schools. The Board of Education were against the building of municipal schools in close proximity to intermediate schools, and had always shown the greatest favour to the latter. But he protested that the municipal schools should be regarded as being outside the Welsh system—they were as national in character as any of the schools in Wales, and Welsh was taught, and taught thoroughly in every one of them. The Board of Education did not sanction the Mountain Ash school, but they did not object, because Mountain Ash should have been long ago an intermediate school—but it had never been proposed that Maesteg should be an intermediate school. It would be perfectly easy for Glamorgan to get this school in—the counties had their own remedy. If local education authorities preferred to establish schools outside their systems, he did not think that the Board of Education should step in and bring about another change. It was not a question of the Central Welsh Board against the Board of Education, but of the policy of local education authorities.[4]

In October, a copy of the resolution passed on 17 May was sent to the Board of Education, without comment or reply to the two questions referred to.[5] The Board replied, stating that 'they could see no reason for modifying the views expressed therein'.[6] This reply was read to the Central Welsh Board in November, and it was resolved to send a deputation to Whitehall, which should also include representatives of the local education

---

[1] Ibid., 19 May. *South Wales Daily News*, 18 May.
[2] Minutes, ibid supra, 17 May, Minutes by Edwards.
[3] *South Wales Daily News*, ibid. supra.
[4] Board of Education, Minutes, op. cit., Edwards said that to influence non-intermediate schools to take the Central Welsh Board examinations was part of a definite plot to capture the whole of Welsh education. The LEAs would be asked to get power to request the Central Welsh Board to examine municipal schools: then pressure would be brought upon them. *South Wales Daily News*, ibid.
[5] PRO Ed 35/3408, Central Welsh Board to Board of Education 23 October.
[6] Ibid., Board of Education to Central Welsh Board, 6 November.

The Contentious Welsh Board

authorities affected.[1] It was a strange delegation which met at a lunch-hour in Whitehall—on an ill-chosen day and year—13 February 1913, confronted by yet another President of the Board, the Rt. Hon. J. A. Pease, MP. The Central Welsh Board's delegates were to be accompanied by representatives from the Glamorgan, Monmouthshire, Denbighshire, Swansea, and Cardiff LEAs. But Denbighshire and Monmouthshire had no municipal secondary schools, and their representatives had no business to be there. Swansea had declined, Cardiff's envoy had to leave almost as soon as he arrived, and Merthyr Tydfil had not even been invited. Owen Edwards was absent because of a 'serious family bereavement'.[2]

The officials at the Board of Education had prepared a brief for the President. The schools which would be affected by any extension of the Central Welsh Board's powers, were set out in a table: Cowbridge Girls'; Maesteg, (Glamorgan); Ferndale, (Rhondda); Canton Boys' and Girls', and Howard Gardens Boys' and Girls', in Cardiff county borough; the municipal secondary schools for Boys and Girls in Swansea county borough, and Cyfarthfa Castle municipal secondary school for Boys in Merthyr Tydfil county borough.[3] A memorandum on inspection was prepared by Edwards; another on the general situation by Davies, and numerous other tables and details. Casson, as ever, had made a neat appraisal of the position. Since the request was for extension of powers of inspection and examination, the main bone of contention was dual inspection, and he reviewed past history on this problem, observing the arrangements arrived at between the two Chief Inspectors. Municipal schools were the province of the Board of Education only, and the Central Welsh Board's case for exclusive inspection of intermediate schools did not help them as regards the non-intermediate ones. He condemned the examination system of the Welsh Board because it produced certificates—the Junior certificate was useless and should be abolished.[4] But the Welsh Board attached too much importance to the Senior certificate, and large numbers of intending teachers, owing to its nature, failed to qualify for Training Colleges. There was no need to extend the evils of this system to the municipal schools. The Scheme setting up the Central Welsh Board was agreed to by all the Welsh authorities, but in this case, Swansea, Cardiff, and Merthyr Tydfil objected to the Central Welsh Board system, and beyond Glamorgan and possibly Monmouthshire, the Board of

---

[1] Board of Education, Minutes, op. cit., 15 November.
[2] PRO Ed ibid. supra, Minute from Davies to President, 2 February 1913.
[3] See Appendix III to this Study.
[4] The Central Welsh Board received an income of nearly £1,400 p.a. from these certificates. Board of Education, Minutes of the Central Welsh Board, op. cit.

The Contentious Welsh Board

Education had no knowledge that any other county desired the extension of powers, and 'seeing that the Central Welsh Board is the creature of the county and county borough authorities, it would seem to be only fair and right if the Board of Education were to decline to confer these additional powers on the Central Welsh Board, except *at the unanimous request of all the county and county borough authorities*'.[1]

Edwards was convinced that a reversal of the previous decisions of the Board of Education with regard to this request would be a calamity to Welsh education. Cardiff and Swansea refused to let the Central Welsh Board have anything to do with their municipal secondary schools, and the chairman of the Merthyr Tydfil education committee, said, at the opening of the Cyfarthfa Castle school, that it was fortunate in being free, and not under the Regulations of the Central Welsh Board. The other two schools in Glamorgan, already referred to, were, unfortunately, under the influence of Ald. Williams and Tom John. But the situation was not without its merits, for the two types of schools gave variety in the system of education—the municipal secondary schools were developing new ideas on practical lines. It was quite possible that if the request was granted, several intermediate schools would disappear due to the differences in school fees. Edwards opted for continued harmonious collaboration with the Central Welsh Board, 'we can only do this on the principle of *quieta non movere*—"let sleeping dogs alone". They are trying to awake a very dangerous old dog'.[2]

The memorandum prepared by Davies for the President was a summary of the previous points, but the fact that the powers sought by the Central Welsh Board were merely permissive, i.e. that they could inspect municipal secondary schools only if the LEA desired it, really incensed the Permanent Secretary. The answer to that plea was two-fold, that the Board of Education were not in the habit of granting even permissive powers unless they were desirable and were desired. But the 'ideals' of the Central Welsh Board conflicted very seriously with the Welsh Department, the English (S) side of the Board of Education, the Consultative Committee, and the LEAs which administered the municipal secondary schools. The Central Welsh Board might be a national body, but it suffered, unfortunately, on its educational side, from being the cockpit in which the political subject of Welsh Nationalism was often fought out, for lack of a better arena. Moreover, he had been given to understand that the

---

[3] PRO Ed 35/3408, Minute from Casson to Davies, 3 February, 1913.
[4] Ibid., Minute from Edwards to Davies, 30 January, 1913.

resolution in favour of this proposal had not been, by any means, unanimous, and if that was so, it could be pressed at the interview.[1]

The deputation was introduced to the President by J. Hugh Edwards, MP for Mid-Glamorgan, (and later, Lloyd George's biographer), and those chosen to speak were Anwyl, Dr. T. H. Morris and Ald. D. H. Williams, (Glamorgan); Ald. S. N. Jones, (Monmouthshire) and J. E. Powell, (Denbighshire)—the last two being mere appendages.[2] Anwyl resurrected his speech of past deputations, with the additional prayer that the Central Welsh Board should inspect and examine municipal secondary schools on a permissive basis. He argued that since his Board had been allowed this with regard to endowed schools under the Welsh Scheme, he saw no reason why it should not be extended to the new secondary schools established by LEAs under the Education Act, 1902. He wanted LEAs to have the freedom to choose between the Central Welsh Board and the Board of Education. Dr. Morris, following, mentioned that one endowed school in Glamorgan, the Howells' school for Girls at Llandaff, which was practically outside the Scheme, was being examined by the Welsh Board, and he hoped that this practice could be extended to other secondary schools outside, namely, Maesteg, Cowbridge Girls' and Ferndale (Rhondda). Ald. Williams strongly supported this, and made a great issue of the disadvantages of the municipal secondary schools inspected by the Board of Education. He maintained that pupils had to go outside Wales for any certificate of proficiency—apart from the matriculation examination of the University of Wales—and where the fees for such external examinations were much higher than those of the Welsh Board. He extolled the virtues of the intermediate schools with their differentiated schemes of work, their freedom and elasticity. He instanced the schools at Mountain Ash and Maesteg which had come under the wing of the Welsh Board (Mountain Ash for examination only) because before, the pupils at Maesteg had gone to Bridgend or Port Talbot in order to get the certificate of the Central Welsh Board. S. N. Jones deplored the poor education provided in the endowed schools —at the Monmouth and West Monmouth Grammar schools, and the King Henry Grammar school, Abergavenny—as compared with the intermediate schools in Monmouthshire. He also stated, quite incorrectly, that the Cardiff representative, F. J. Beavan (Deputy Lord Mayor), who had left the room, was of the same opinion as the Glamorgan speakers.

---

[1] Board of Education: Minutes of Central Welsh Board, op. cit., 17 May 1912. J. Trefor Owen, Headmaster of Swansea Grammar School, who was present at the meeting, told Owen Edwards that only 27 out of 60 voted!

[2] PRO Ed 35/3408, Minutes of Proceedings at a deputation from the Central Welsh Board to the President of the Board of Education, 13 February 1913.

The Contentious Welsh Board

Powell was present apparently to provide a boring and colourless historical interlude on the failure of Wales to establish a Welsh National Council for Education, and said, in his ignorance, that all the Welsh counties had joined in the attempt.[1]

The President, dealt firmly but fairly with the deputation. Having annointed the Central Welsh Board with the traditional words of praise and appreciation of their work, he came straight to the point and did not mince his words. He said that the Glamorgan delegates had spoken very strongly in favour of this alteration, and only asked that it should be permissive, and wanted to come under the jurisdiction of the Central Welsh Board. But, apart from Glamorgan, it was extraordinary that all the other municipal secondary schools at Cardiff, Swansea and Merthyr Tydfil, all county boroughs, which would comprise at least 2,500 pupils (including Ferndale, Rhondda), were indifferent, and not very keen to associate themselves with the inspection provided by the Welsh Board. If the delegation induced those schools to come under the control of the Welsh Board, and they were not willing, he could foresee the possibility of friction. He was most anxious that if the Board of Education responded to an appeal of this kind, *there should be a general demand*, and not a piece-meal movement. But there was no unanimity, and not even much interest from the direction of the municipal schools. In addition, there was more variety of curricula and practical bias in the municipal schools than in the intermediate, and if the pupils did not wish to have the hall-mark of the Central Welsh Board certificate, he did not see any reason to urge them to do so.[2]

Another important point was that the Central Welsh Board examination system was of little advantage to those who wished to become teachers. In fact, a high percentage of intending teachers failed in that examination. The President then alluded to the fact that the Central Welsh Board had taken no notice of two important questions which had been put to them as far back as 26 October 1911, with reference to dual inspection and uniformity in education, which the Board of Education considered undesirable. He concluded that the Welsh Board did not consider them of sufficient importance for discussion at their meetings, and yet they deemed it necessary to be uproarious at a certain meeting, and also to waste time sending deputations to London. Finally, he brought forth the impregnable argument of parliamentary responsibility, and drew their attention to the fact that the Board of Education had the undeniable

[1] PRO Ed 35/3408, Minutes of Proceedings of deputation, op. cit.
[2] Ibid.

right to inspect both the municipal and intermediate schools. Anwyl made a weak and unimpressionable effort to apologize on behalf of the Central Welsh Board for being so remiss in replying to the questions, and admitted that the problem of dual inspection had, through friendly conferences with the Chief Inspector for Wales, been practically solved in practice.[1]

Beavan, Deputy Lord Mayor of Cardiff, wrote to the President apologizing for having to leave the meeting, and intimated that his council had decided not to join the deputation, which meant objection to the Central Welsh Board.[2] Further letters were sent to the President by Anwyl and Williams referring to details they had omitted to mention at the deputation. They even invited him to a conference at Colwyn Bay on 16 May which was held to discuss the organization of Welsh secondary education, but the date was inconvenient.[3] On another fateful day, 13 May, came the President's inevitable reply to the Central Welsh Board's deputation—'that after careful consideration of all the circumstances, the President regretted that he could not accede to their request'.[4]

In June, T. Mansel Franklen, Clerk to the Glamorgan County Council informed the Swansea local education authority that Glamorgan had been endeavouring to induce the Board of Education to allow certain municipal schools in that county to be examined by the Central Welsh Board—*schools which had been established under the Welsh Intermediate Education Act!*[5] Franklen stated that they had been refused permission, and desired to know Swansea's position. Replying, that authority said that it was definitely opposed 'to any proposal that may lead to the Central Welsh Board examining its municipal schools', and a copy of this letter was sent to the Board of Education.[6]

There were no violent reactions to the President's decision, but considerable disappointment was expressed at the Colwyn Bay meeting. The usual storm-birds raised their voices including Ald. Williams, Ald. Hopkin Morgan, Tom John and J. E. Powell. Morgan called it a 'decided snub to the Central Welsh Board' and said that they expected no other answer because the deputation was weak, only Maesteg had supported it, and the county boroughs had stood aloof. Powell called for a National

---

[1] PRO Ed 35/3408, Minutes of Proceedings of deputation, op. cit.
[2] Ibid., Beavan to Board of Education, 14 February, 1913.
[3] Ibid., Anwyl to President, 1 May.
[4] Ibid., Board of Education to Central Welsh Board, 13 May.
[5] Ibid., Franklen to Swansea LEA, 3 June. Note Franklen's error! He obviously meant the Education Act, 1902.
[6] ibid., Swansea county borough to Franklen, and Board of Education, 25 June.

Council of Education for Wales as the only solution.[1] This marked the end of the attempts by the Central Welsh Board for the time being to acquire substantial extension of powers in the inspectorial and examination fields.

III PROCEDURAL IRREGULARITIES

The administrative machinery of the Central Welsh Board was set in motion before the creation of the Board of Education and its offspring the Welsh Department. Certain methods of administrative procedure between both Boards had become well-established and accepted in the intervening years between 1900–8. But the channels of communication, however satisfactory and effective from the Central Welsh Board's standpoint, led to waste of money, time and effort, and worst of all, produced irregularities of a somewhat serious nature in correspondence between the Board of Education and the Welsh intermediate schools. This aspect of the Central Welsh Board's work, and its overhaul by the Board of Education, caused yet another unpleasant relationship, which, however, was not entirely the fault of the Welsh Board.

The administrative procedure initiated by the Board of Education arose out of the peculiar circumstances of the time. During 1899, 1900 and the early part of 1901, correspondence passed between the Board of Education and the Central Welsh Board on the subject of a revised system of grants to Welsh intermediate schools, and in July 1901 when batches of applications and schemes of work were sent for the Board's approval from the Central Welsh Board, the Board's criticisms of the schemes were included in a *single letter* addressed to the Central Welsh Board. This practice of the Board of Education corresponding with the Central Welsh Board instead of with the schools direct, on all matters arising under the Secondary Schools Regulations continued until 1908.[2] The applications referred to were submitted on forms similar to those used in England, but printed by the Central Welsh Board. There were other, less important matters of office procedure which, unfortunately, the Central Welsh Board had come to regard as falling legitimately within their own jurisdiction, and no objection appeared to have been raised by the Board of Education to these matters until Casson discovered certain irregularities.

In February 1908 Casson and Sykes (an assistant secretary) had been considering better methods of conducting correspondence between

[1] *Liverpool Daily Post and Mercury*, 17 May.
[2] PRO Ed 35/3415B, Memorandum prepared by Casson for Davies, 5 May 1908.

Whitehall and Cardiff, in order to avoid different practices as regards intermediate and other schools.[1] On going through the Board of Education's files informally, Casson came across copies of letters which had passed between the Central Welsh Board and Merthyr Tydfil intermediate school governors—which indicated a further reason for terminating the system of corresponding with the intermediate schools through the Central Welsh Board. He discovered that the Chief Inspector, Owen Owen, had acted in an extremely unconstitutional manner. Referring to a letter of the 15 November 1907 which Owen had written to the clerk of the governors of Merthyr Tydfil intermediate school, Casson observed that excepting the words 'of Education' which had been inserted in a certain paragraph, the letter was identical with a letter written from the Board of Education to the Central Welsh Board.[2] In other words, the Central Welsh Board, instead of forwarding to the school a copy of the Board of Education's letter to them, issued the letter as their own. The result was most misleading, and made the school think that the views and requirements of the Board of Education were those of the Central Welsh Board. If, as was probably the case, the Central Welsh Board adopted the same practice with regard to all schools, Casson thought that it should be stopped.[3] Davies sent to Merthyr Tydfil for a copy of the letter referred to—which the chairman of the governors had alluded to at a deputation with regard to the school buildings, and had been sent from the Central Welsh Board.[4]

Davies discussed this matter with the President (McKenna), who, however, was on the point of leaving the Board of Education. In order to equip the incoming President (Runciman) with all the information, Casson was instructed to prepare a memorandum on office procedure, with regard to correspondence with intermediate schools under the Regulations for Secondary Schools (Wales).[5] All matters with reference to this subject were to be thoroughly investigated, for example, the advantages and disadvantages of the existing procedure and suggestions as to the future. Definite examples, facts and figures, and other relevant points were to be included in order to show how the system could work more economically. Davies emphasized that 'the whole matter raised

---

[1] Ibid., Minute from Casson to Davies, 2 February. The Board of Education corresponded directly with the municipal secondary schools.

[2] Ibid., Central Welsh Board to Stephens, Clerk to the Governors, Merthyr Tydfil Intermediate school, 15 November 1907.

[3] Ibid., Minute from Casson to Davies, 21 February, 1908.

[4] Ibid., Board of Education to Ald. E. Morrell, Merthyr Tydfil, 10 February. It transpired that several letters had been sent by Owen to Merthyr Tydfil between June and November, 1907.

[5] PRO Ed 35/3415B, Memorandum, op. cit.

questions of policy of the highest importance, and therefore the document could not be too carefully drawn or well-supported by evidence'.[1]

Casson and Sykes produced a comprehensive statement by 5 May. Their task was more difficult and complex than anyone had imagined, for it involved the consideration of all aspects of administrative procedure covering a whole series of subjects. But the complete machinery had to be overhauled from top to bottom, all the dead wood removed, and a new stream-lined structure evolved. The new system, once in operation, was to inculcate administrative and economic efficiency in the Welsh Department and the Central Welsh Board, but was not to be relished by the latter. The main issues involved in the re-organization of procedural methods, hinged on Pupil Teacher Centres and correspondence with schools. The Regulations issued in 1903 which dealt with the training of pupil-teachers in centres attached to secondary schools, was administered by the Elementary Branch of the Board of Education. The majority of the LEAs in Wales had adopted the new Regulations, and sent their pupil-teachers to the secondary school Pupil Teacher Centres as half-time pupils, and the necessary Returns of the Centres were sent, not through the Central Welsh Board, but directly to the Board of Education. Therefore, there was duplication of effort here, where the Board of Education dealt with the Centres direct, but through the Central Welsh Board for the secondary schools. In February 1907 however, when the Welsh Department was announced, the division of the Board which dealt with Pupil Teacher work was amalgamated—so far as England was concerned —and Centres attached to secondary schools became part of the secondary school. This arrangement enabled the Board of Education to obtain all the information on a single form from the secondary schools. But in Wales, all dealings between the Board of Education and the secondary schools continued to be conducted through the Central Welsh Board.[2]

The educational disadvantage was the separate treatment of the secondary school and the Pupil Teacher Centre which formed an integral part of that school. In view of the statutory powers of inspection and examination vested in the Central Welsh Board and their right to be kept in touch with the Board of Education's dealings with the intermediate schools, the practice of corresponding through the Central Welsh Board ensured this, but did not apply to the Pupil Teacher Centres in such schools. It appeared to be the practice that 'the Central Welsh Board merely copied out any letter from the Board of Education and issued it

[1] Ibid., Minute from Davies to Casson, 15 April 1908.
[2] Ibid., Memorandum, op. cit., pp. 8–9.

to the school concerned *as their own letter*.[1] The example of the letter to Merthyr Tydfil was cited, which apart from a change of date and two words, was a replica of the one issued to that Board by the Board of Education. The effect of this procedure on the schools was obvious. The governors of the Merthyr Tydfil school enquired what powers the Central Welsh Board possessed to enforce certain requirements. The course adopted by the Central Welsh Board gave the impression to schools that it was that Board which they had to satisfy and not the Board of Education. Some schools actually referred, in their accounts, to the Board of Education grants as the Central Welsh Board grants. It naturally followed that the Board of Education and their inspectors were not in such close touch with the schools as was desirable. The Central Welsh Board in corresponding with the schools were, in fact, merely the agents of the Board of Education, for they offered no observations of their own. The proper course was for the Board of Education to correspond directly with all the secondary schools, whether intermediate or municipal. There was, in addition, no necessity of such close vigilance on the schools by the Central Welsh Board since the establishment of the Welsh Department, whose Chief Inspector was in close touch with that Board.[2]

The administrative disadvantages were clear. There was no ground for the Central Welsh Board to use forms printed by themselves for the intermediate schools. A single form should be used, as in England, when intermediate schools had Pupil Teacher Centres—instead of two forms as used by the Central Welsh Board. This duplication meant a great deal of extra work for Welsh headmasters and much inconvenience at the Board of Education. Besides, it meant considerably more expense, for the cost of printing forms by the Board of Education for the dozen or so municipal schools in Wales was almost as great as the cost of printing for all the Welsh secondary schools, about 110 in number. The large cost of the Central Welsh Board's printing bill raised the question as to whether they had power to expend this part of their income on printing. Moreover, correspondence which passed through several hands meant delays and loss of efficiency as was evidenced in certain situations at Llangefni, Carmarthen and Rhyl intermediate schools.[3]

The proper and most economic solution would be 'to assimilate the procedure of the Welsh Department to that existing in England'. Adopting the English procedure would remove all the educational and administrative

---

[1] PRO Ed 35/3415B, Memorandum, op. cit., p. 10.
[2] Ibid., p. 11.
[3] Ibid., Deputation from the Central Welsh Board to the President, 13 July 1908. PRO Ed ibid. supra p. 13.

disadvantages, but it was envisaged that the Central Welsh Board might not be enthusiastic for this change, and also the LEAs, whose servants the Pupil Teachers were, would not look with favour upon such an arrangement. It was recommended that in future the Board of Education should correspond directly with all schools, intermediate or municipal, on all matters relating to the schools, including Pupil Teacher Centres, and that the secondary school and Pupil Teacher Centre should be treated as a single institution as in England. All letters of importance, and matters relating to curricula, time tables, etc., could still be available to the Central Welsh Board, but all forms relating to intermediate schools would be printed and issued by the Board of Education.[1]

The new President's introduction to the Central Welsh Board by Davies, was somewhat harsh. Davies spared nothing in denouncing its methods of administration and conduct, and begged the President to make a quick decision in order (a) that the Welsh Department might know how to frame its procedure, and (b) to consider the format of the numerous forms required for issue to the Welsh intermediate schools under the Secondary Regulations (Wales). As matters stood, the Central Welsh Board had shown beyond doubt that their methods were unbusinesslike, wasteful, and hampered the work of the Welsh Department in dealing with the secondary schools of Wales. He warned the President that the Central Welsh Board were very jealous of their position and prerogatives, and would view unfavourably any move to diminish their prestige and influence. The Welsh Board existed to perform their statutory duties, and the proposed change would relieve that Board of the drudgery of a great deal of administrative work which could be performed far more expeditiously by the Board of Education corresponding directly with the schools. Davies had been shocked by the waste of public money involved in the existing procedure, and had sought, by private talks with Owen, to effect economies, but his suggestions had been received with coldness. The dignity and prestige of the Board of Education, as the supreme authority under Parliament, became seriously impaired when tricks and 'doctored' methods were employed with regard to the Board's letters, as in the case of Merthyr Tydfil, and in the course of 30 years' experience of public life he could say frankly that he had never known official communications from a responsible public body dealt with in the highly reprehensible way in which that letter had been treated. He advised the President to recommend that the new Regulations for Secondary Schools in England be applied to Wales, and that the administrative procedure

[1] PRO Ed 35/3415B, Memorandum, op. cit., p. 15.

relative to all secondary schools in Wales, whether intermediate or not, should be assimilated. Davies sent the President a draft letter for transmission to the Central Welsh Board.[1] Runciman's reply was brief, 'I agree to the principle. Modify the letter'.[2]

The letter which finally arrived in Cardiff was innocuous enough, and the reasons given for the administrative changes were irrefutable in the circumstances. It comprised the main reasons for revising the administrative procedure between the two Boards on the basis of wastage of time, effort, money, duplication of work and unnecessary form-filling. It also referred to the new proposal regarding the setting up of Pupil Teacher Centres in secondary schools, and the uniformity of procedure respecting the direct correspondence to schools by the Board of Education. The schools were to be informed of the new procedure at an early date.[3]

All this was agreed to, and done (together with the printing of the new Regulations for the schools) by the Board of Education without any prior consultation with the Central Welsh Board. Four days after the letter was sent to Cardiff, the printed Regulations were ready for issue to the Welsh secondary schools of both types.[4] The reaction by Owen was almost immediate (for a week-end intervened). On 23 June, Owen sent a telegram to Davies, confirmed by letter of the same date, protesting that the Central Welsh Board should have had an opportunity of expressing their views on the subject of the letter, and trusted that 'pending a further communication from this Board, no action will be taken affecting the procedure which has been followed for the past seven years'.[5] Davies replied immediately, enclosing printed copies of the new Regulations and procedure which had been sent to the schools the previous day. He regretted that this had been done prior to the receipt of the telegram, but the matter was urgent in view of the large amount of correspondence expected from the schools.[6]

In the meantime, Casson was arranging matters with the chief Officials regarding which letters of importance should be sent to the Welsh Board

[1] Ibid., Minute from Davies to President, 3 June, 1908.

[2] Ibid., Minute from President to Davies, 17 June.

[3] PRO Ed 35/3415B, Board of Education to Central Welsh Board, 19 June: The letter stated 'The Board of Education, (simultaneously with the preparation of the Regulations for Secondary Schools and the Regulations for the Preliminary Education of Elementary School Teachers which would come into force in Wales on 1 August), had found it necessary to consider how far the administrative machinery hitherto in use, (and relating particularly to the conduct of correspondence with the Board of Education, and the payment of the latter's grants to schools), was suited to the conditions which would be set up by the application to Wales of the scale of grants and conditions of payments which came into operation in 1907 in England in respect of secondary schools, and by the changes introduced into the Regulations for the Preliminary education of Elementary School Teachers'.

[4] Ibid.

[5] Ibid., Central Welsh Board to Board of Education, 23 June.

[6] Ibid., Board of Education to Central Welsh Board, 24 June.

under the new procedure. It was decided to send copies of every Report of HMI issued to schools; matters dealing with curricula, school premises and accommodation; and official letters dealing with the functions of the Central Welsh Board.[1] The clerks concerned were told that as from 23 June all correspondence under S Regulations were to go direct to the intermediate schools, and all forms for such schools were to be printed and issued from the office; grants would not be paid through the Central Welsh Board from then onwards.[2] When all the orders had been given, Davies and the President thought it prudent to invite Owen, the chairman and vice-chairman of the Central Welsh Board to London for a discussion on the revised procedure, and a date was fixed for a meeting at the House of Commons on 13 July.[3]

Before the deputation's visit to London, Edwards had furnished Davies with a full report of an executive committee meeting of the Central Welsh Board at Cardiff on 9 July. That Board decided to meet again in Shrewsbury on 16 July 'after having been supplied by their officials with a summary of the history of the relations between the Board of Education and themselves in the past, and to summon the whole Central Welsh Board to a meeting on 24 July to consider the situation'.[4] But the main part of the meeting was devoted to a scathing attack on the Board of Education for instituting the administrative changes without consulting the Welsh Board, and according to Owen, Anwyl and Tom John, this meant a considerable undermining of the power and prestige of that Board. Others, like Lord Stanley and Edward Thomas (Cochfarf) advised moving cautiously by discussing the situation with the President of the Board.[5]

Only Owen and Anwyl came to meet the President, who was accompanied by Davies, Edwards and Casson. Runciman wasted no time in broaching the subject of the new methods of procedure, and his frankness at times bordered on impatience. He was given to understand that the Central Welsh Board were displeased with his recent action, and he thought it best that a talk about the matter would have beneficial results.

[1] Ibid., Minute from Casson to Davies and Edwards, 24 June.
[2] PRO Ed 35/3415B, Casson to Hobhouse and all Departments, 22 and 24 June.
[3] Ibid., Board of Education to Central Welsh Board, 4 July. Minute from Davies to President, 9 July.
[4] Board of Education, Minutes of C.W.B., op. cit., 10 July.
[5] PRO Ed ibid. supra. Minute from Edwards to Davies: Edwards said 'that the Central Welsh Board, by stalking in the borrowed clothes of the Board of Education, had been able to force their will upon the headmasters and the LEAs—some of which were at that time on the verge of rebellion against the C.W.B. The prestige of the B. of Ed. was at stake because they were not sure whether their letters had been communicated as written; the LEAs did not know that they had been in communication with the Board of Education, and the schools had asked him which Board, in case of disagreement, was to be obeyed. He hoped the action taken by the President would be strictly carried out, and the Central Welsh Board should make their authority felt, not by impersonating the Board of Education, but by doing their own legitimate work well, i.e. of inspecting and examining the intermediate schools'.

Whereupon Anwyl interrupted and said incautiously, that they had merely come as a courtesy; that the Central Welsh Board had not yet discussed the circular to the schools, and therefore they had no power to discuss the matter. This rebuff annoyed the President, who retorted that in that case they should be listeners and he the speaker. Anwyl again interjected to say that Owen and himself should have been given an explanation of the Board of Education's recent action. This time, the President said quite forthrightly that the Board had no apology to make, and that if they could not discuss the matter, he could not.[1]

Owen, who had committed the indiscretions and was the root-cause of the change of procedure, added fuel to the fire by maintaining that a practice which had existed for seven years should not have been terminated so abruptly without consultation, and if the relations between the two Boards were to be harmonious, they should be consulted on all matters. In this he was supported by Anwyl, but the President attacked unmercifully and referred to the Merthyr Tydfil letters, and the wasteful methods which had prevailed in the past. Anwyl admitted that the system could be improved, but not swept away, and Owen feared a collision between the two Boards if schools were in direct correspondence with the Board of Education. The President made it plain that the Board of Education could not allow the Central Welsh Board to be judges of the Board of Education's decisions, but Owen again lamented that the Central Welsh Board could no longer print their own forms. The rest of the arguments centred on the points made by Casson in his memorandum, regarding Pupil Teacher Centres and economies in administration, the President closing the interview by suggesting that a conference with the chief officials of the Welsh Department could resolve the matter in an afternoon. The deputation could rest assured that he was the last person who wished to interfere with the statutory duties of the Central Welsh Board, and he had no desire to disturb the amicable arrangements which had been made already in the field of dual inspection.[2]

On 21 July, Ellis Griffith, MP (Anglesey) put several questions to the President of the Board of Education in the House of Commons. He wanted to know (a) if the Board of Education proposed depriving the Central Welsh Board of any, and which, of the powers hitherto exercised by it over secondary schools in Wales, and (b) whether the Board of Education proposed to deprive the Central Welsh Board of any of the statutory powers conferred upon it by the Welsh Intermediate Education

[1] PRO Ed ibid. supra, Transcript of deputation by Casson, 14 July.
[2] PRO Ed 35/3415B, Transcript of deputation, op. cit.

Act, 1889. The President gave a negative reply to both questions. Griffith also asked whether the Board of Education wished to deprive the Central Welsh Board of powers with regard to the distribution of the Welsh secondary school grants, and with regard to its position as intermediary for the purpose of communication between the Board of Education and the Welsh secondary schools. McKenna replied to these questions, and explained that the secondary school grants in Wales had hitherto been paid through the Central Welsh Board, although the Treasury grant was always paid direct, but that body had no power of discretion as to the allocation of the secondary grants as between particular schools. With regard to the correspondence, he said that the new procedure was initiated on grounds of efficiency and economy.[1]

In Wales, Glamorgan, on the motion of Ald. D. H. Williams (arch-enemy of the Welsh Department), quickly came to the aid of the Central Welsh Board, and sent a copy of a resolution (passed at the county council meeting on 21 July) to the Board of Education, expressing its complete satisfaction 'whereby in the past seven years the Central Welsh Board was its channel of communication with the Board of Education' and deprecated the discontinuance of the procedure by the Board of Education without previous conference with the Central Welsh Board. The letter also trusted that the Board would confer with the Central Welsh Board on the administrative relations between the two Boards.[2] The Welsh press spoke of 'strong protests by Glamorgan' and the Board of Education's 'alleged plot'.[3] Ald. Williams claimed that the action of the Board of Education 'was the beginning of a process to extinguish the Central Welsh Board, which had rendered incalculable service to secondary education, and the Hon. W. N. Bruce, who had given autonomy in Welsh education through the Central Welsh Board, was a man who understood secondary education in Wales better than any one in Whitehall or anywhere else'. Ald. John Morgan, chairman of the county education committee, referred to the action of the Board of Education as an attempt to capture the Central Welsh Board as a preliminary canter to its elimination.[4]

The next step was the inevitable deputation to the Board of Education, which has already been referred to in connection with dual inspection. The new administrative procedures was the second point raised by that

---

[1] Questions and Answers, House of Commons, 21 July. In a supplementary question, Griffith asked 'if there had been any recent change in the relations between the Board of Education and the Central Welsh Board', to which he got the apt reply from Runciman 'only a change in the channel through which communications pass'.
[2] PRO Ed ibid. supra, Glamorgan County Council to Board of Education, 24 July.
[3] *South Wales Daily News; Western Mail*, 22 July.
[4] *South Wales Daily News; Western Mail*, op. cit.

The Contentious Welsh Board

deputation, and is now dealt with here. On this matter, the delegates who met the President on 28 July, were told that they 'were rather making a storm in a teacup about it'. Runciman could not defend the former practice, and the question of correspondence and of forms was a matter that he and the deputation should not be troubled with. He was anxious that a harmonious arrangement should be achieved by the representatives of the Central Welsh Board and the officials of the Welsh Department conferring together—as he had informed Owen and Anwyl when they came to see him on 13 July.[1]

This meeting was arranged for the following day. Anwyl, Owen, Powell, Charles Lloyd, W. C. Griffiths, and W. Hammond Robinson, met Davies Edwards, Casson, and Hobhouse. The Welsh Board members were introduced by Sir Herbert Roberts (later 1st Baron Clwyd). Roberts hoped that any agreement reached would be accepted later by a full meeting of the Central Welsh Board, but the ever impetuous Powell was not prepared to admit that agreement would be possible that day. Davies outlined the circumstances which gave rise to Circular 11 (Wales), and repeated the reasons for suspending the old methods of procedure. Owen tried unsuccessfully to persuade the Welsh Department to revert to a partial form of the previous procedure, for example, that his Board should continue to print the forms, and that the Welsh Department should inform him of any decisions before they were sent to the schools. But in spite of strong support by Roberts, Anwyl and Robinson, Davies was adamant. He said that the President would not countenance any reversion to the old system. Proposals were submitted which could be considered by the Central Welsh Board, one of the most important being, that in really important matters the Central Welsh Board should be given an opportunity of expressing *their* views before a decision was communicated to the schools, but Davies emphasized that nothing could prevent the Board of Education from exercising their right finally to decide as to what their requirements under their own Regulations should be. Finally, it was agreed that the proposals read by Davies should be sent to the Central Welsh Board for consideration, on the understanding that the document was not to be released to the press. Before taking their leave, the delegates (as mentioned in section II of this Study) re-affirmed their decision not to consider any letter from the Board of Education relating to the new procedure, unless it was accompanied by proposals for the modification of the system of dual inspection.[2]

[1] PRO Ed. 35/3415B, Deputation from the Central Welsh Board, op. cit. 28 July.
[2] PRO Ed 35/3415B, Notes of Interview between the Permanent Secretary, Welsh Department and a Deputation from the Central Welsh Board, 29 July.

The Contentious Welsh Board

The outcome was a very modest compromise. The Central Welsh Board were furnished with the proposals on a memorandum which was designed to reduce dual correspondence to a minimum, as well as keeping that Board in the closest touch with the schools and the Board of Education. Regarding time tables, curricula, and other minutiae, it substantially ensured that retention of former practice which the Board of Education knew that the Central Welsh Board so ardently desired.[1]

IV PUPIL TEACHERS AND BURSARS

To the Central Welsh Board, the word 'intermediate' which described their schools and the education provided in them, meant one thing only—institutions set up by the Welsh Intermediate Education Act, 1889, to bridge the gap between elementary schools and university. Both Chairman and Chief Inspector of the Board symbolized the academic 'establishment'. Anwyl was Celtic scholar and university don; Owen, an Oxford graduate in Classics, and former headmaster of a traditional English grammar school. The Welsh intermediate schools were fashioned in this tradition of narrow scholasticism, were pedestrian and pedantic to a high degree, and almost completely divorced from their native environment. Such schools should have been geared to the fabric of the society which they served, so that they could devise a philosophy of their own to match the national needs of Wales. One writer has described the provision of education in a coastal town of south Cardiganshire: 'The syllabus is one which might be found in any secondary school in Britain; it is unrelated to purely local or specifically Welsh needs... The results of such education is to add prestige to distant affairs, and to alienate boys and girls from the local culture'.[2] In short, the schools were organized essentially for examinations and university entrance. The highly vulnerable aspect of this system was its inability and inaction in providing other essential facilities, and to design courses appropriate for pupils who wished to enter Training Colleges to become elementary schoolteachers. This circumscribed policy of the Board created conflicting situations between itself and the Welsh Department of the Board of Education up to Anwyl's death in 1914, and Owen's retirement in the following year.

In March 1908 the Welsh Board began exploring the possibilities of adapting their examinations to the specific needs of intending teachers in elementary schools, and desired to discuss this matter, in its preliminary

[1] PRO Ed ibid. supra, Board of Education to Central Welsh Board, 7 August.
[2] R. Brinley Jones, (Ed.), *Anatomy of Wales*, Gwerin Publications, 1972, p. 167.

stage, at a conference with the Board of Education.[1] This subject was of the utmost importance to Welsh education at that time, and the Welsh Department and the University of Wales had already been discussing the matter on informal lines, mainly through the efforts of Edwards, who was also in close touch with the Welsh Training Colleges.[2] There was need for closer liaison in academic content between the Central Welsh Board and the Welsh University Colleges, for large numbers of pupils from the intermediate schools who looked to the teaching profession, preferred to enter the day-training departments of those colleges. Edwards was also acquainted with the work of his colleagues at the Board of Education who were responsible for the inspection of the English Training Colleges. Principal Roberts of Aberystwyth had already arranged that the college Senate should meet representatives of the Welsh Headmasters Association, and the Central Welsh Board were annoyed because the Senate had refused to move through them, and that was possibly the reason why the Board wished to meet the Welsh Department so soon.[3]

Before convening the conference with the Central Welsh Board, Edwards wanted time to discuss the curricula of the Welsh intermediate schools, and the extent to which they could be adapted to the requirements of intending teachers. He was not a little apprehensive also, that the Central Welsh Board might propose some extension of power which the Welsh Department had not visualized, and, moreover, he did not know the President's policy. It was arranged that the two Chief Inspectors should have preliminary discussions to define the limits of the proposed conference.[4] Owen revealed that the Central Welsh Board wanted to know what the Welsh Department considered to be a model curriculum for pupil teachers and bursars in the intermediate schools, who intended to become elementary school-teachers; what standards the Board of Education would accept in each subject, and the combination of Central Welsh Board subjects equivalent to the Board of Education's Preliminary Examination

---

[1] Ibid., Central Welsh Board to Board of Education, 4 March. But as far back as January 1902, Humphreys-Owen argued that there should be co-operation between the primary and secondary teachers. In the meantime, in addition to the automatic passage transfer of pupils from the elementary to the intermediate schools, the latter are beginning to be used for the purpose of giving a literary and scientific training to probationer pupil teachers. Under this arrangement, while the pupil teachers get this professional training from the elementary teachers, those teachers are relieved of the duty of giving them literary and scientific instruction by the entry of the pupils for part of their time of apprenticeship into the intermediate schools. Different schemes have been adopted for this purpose: 'the teaching which the pupils receive in the intermediate schools must consist of complete courses. It would be fatal to the complete education of the probationers, not less than to the organisation of the school, if their attendance at the lessons in the subjects which they take are not continuous'. *Young Wales*, January, 1902.

[2] Edwards had already seen Principal Griffiths, and the Professors of English and History, (Harold Littledale and Herbert Bruce) at the University College, Cardiff; Principal Roberts and the Professors of English and History, (J. W. H. Atkins and Edward Edwards—Owen Edwards's brother) at the University College of Wales, Aberystwyth, and was about to go to the University College of North Wales, Bangor, for the same purpose.

[3] PRO Ed 35/3415B, Minute from Davies to Edwards, and Edwards to Davies, 21 March.

[4] Ibid., Minute from Sykes to Casson, 23 March.

The Contentious Welsh Board

for intending teachers. This was difficult to resolve because of the rigidity and inflexibility of the Central Welsh Board's Senior Certificate. But the Board of Education would certainly require the subjects as set out in their Code—but not too many—for the Board of Education would object to any scheme of work for pupil-teachers taking the Senior Certificate if it meant no time for general reading, and this matter required serious discussion. Regarding standards, that was a matter for the Pupil Teacher Regulations Committee or the Examinations Committee of the Board of Education. The Central Welsh Board had already met Messrs. Mayor, Barnett, Chambers and Pelham on the English (Training Colleges) side, but the latter were not satisfied with the conditions suggested to them, and asked for a three-cornered conference composed of the English P.T. Department, the Welsh Department and the Central Welsh Board.[1]

After considerable discussion at the conference on 1 May, the results were inconclusive, just because of the reluctance of the Central Welsh Board to modify the requirements of their Senior Certificate for intending teachers. That certificate, seemingly, was sacrosanct. Owen suggested it might be possible to arrange for a preliminary examination for the certificate to be recognized for prospective teachers, rather like the Board of Education's Examination for English pupil teachers. This would involve parallel classes of pupils working for the two examinations in the intermediate schools, but it was generally agreed that this arrangement would be unsatisfactory.[2] The real truth of the matter was, of course, that as compared with the Board of Education's Preliminary Examination for the elementary teacher's certificate, the Central Welsh Board Senior Certificate was too difficult for intending elementary schoolteachers, and there was a very high rate of failures in Wales every year. In February 1909 the Central Welsh Board once more tried to frame a qualification of entry to Training Colleges for elementary teachers and sought another interview. But the Board of Education, on realizing that this further proposal merely meant a re-arrangement of the Senior Certificate, took no further steps in the matter. It meant that candidates had to have six subjects endorsed on the Senior Certificate, and also an alternative syllabus in English; Welsh as an optional subject, and certificates of proficiency in penmanship, vocal music, drawing, and needlework.[3] The Central Welsh Board could not refrain from proliferating

[1] Ibid., Minute from Edwards to Casson, 10 April.
[2] PRO Ed 35/3415B, Minute from Pelham to Mayor re Deputation from the Central Welsh Board to the Board of Education, 4 May.
[3] Ibid., Central Welsh Board to Board of Education, Memorandum on curricula for Primary Teachers 2 February 1909.

examinations, and no solution seemed to be in sight for the poor Welsh pupil teacher!

But the problem still remained, and Edwards was to refer to it time and again in the following years. It was on his suggestion that pupil teachers should have a good grounding in Penmanship, Arithmetic, Music, Drawing and Needlework, as well as History, English literature, Geography, and Welsh. These were the subjects to be taken in the years leading up to the Senior Certificate (providing a broad general education for the future elementary schoolteacher), and the certificate should accordingly, be adapted for this purpose. To Edwards, intending elementary schoolteachers should continue to have the good teaching and background which they were accustomed to in the elementary schools, and should have the opportunity of working at subjects in the intermediate schools which would stand them in good stead when they entered Training Colleges—but the examinations of the Central Welsh Board did not provide this kind of education. One of the advantages gained from the uproar of the explosive *Report* of 1909 was that Edwards was able to explain *in detail* his criticisms against the Central Welsh Board system of examinations, certificates, and quality of teaching provided in the Welsh intermediate schools, particularly with reference to the training of future teachers at both elementary and secondary levels.

The teaching of English was extremely bad, and the Board of Education had given the Central Welsh Board an alternative syllabus for its teaching on newer and better lines. That syllabus alone would the Board of Education accept as qualifying for entrance to a Training College. But this syllabus had been strenuously opposed by one of the members of the Central Welsh Board, Mr. Edgar Jones, headmaster of Barry intermediate school—and the author of the attack on the Board of Education's *Report* for 1909.[1] Edwards declared 'we say persistently, what we say this year is only a repetition of what we said last year, that the teaching of English in Wales—though often painstaking and conscientious—is on antiquated, uneconomical and ineffective lines. We realize this when the pupils come to the Training Colleges and, unfortunately, still more so when they begin to teach English in elementary schools ... Edgar Jones is a good and inspiring teacher of English, but he is conservative to a degree, and he offers the most strenuous opposition at the Central Welsh Board to the kind of English teaching which is demanded by the Board of Education, from that Board, in the examination equivalent to the Preliminary

[1] PRO Ed 24/588, Reply by Owen Edwards to Edgar Jones, 18 November 1910.

Examination for the Certificate'.[1] The same could be said for the teaching of history, whilst the teaching of music and physical training was either non-existent or at a very low ebb.

It was both ridiculous and unfair that entrance into the teaching profession was much more difficult in Wales than in England. In England pupils were presented for the easier Government Examination, the Preliminary Examination of the Board of Education. In Wales, the training of intending teachers in elementary schools was made as hard as possible through the only door—the Central Welsh Board. The pupil teachers and bursars, an important class of intermediate school pupils, were sacrificed to a system. The scheme of Bursarship and Student-Teachership, which was intended to unite the advantages of the old Pupil Teacher system with those of a good secondary education, and to provide guidance in that wide general reading that was so essential to a teacher, was in danger of failure in Wales, while it was most successful in other parts of the kingdom. It was most unfortunate that Welsh children, so well adapted to the teaching profession were made subservient to a rigid examination system. Intending teachers were required to take the Central Welsh Board Senior examination as the only one qualifying them to become student teachers or for entering a Training College.[2]

Fourteen Welsh LEAs applied during the months June–August 1910 for the recognition of 153 ex-Bursars as Student Teachers. This was on condition that they qualified by means of the 1910 Senior examination of the Central Welsh Board. Of these, 89 failed on the results of that examination. In Anglesey, 15 out of 19 failed; in Breconshire, 2 out of 2; in Carmarthenshire, 21 out of 28; in Glamorgan, 27 out of 48; in Pembrokeshire (including the borough of Pembroke) 14 out of 20. It is interesting to compare these results with those in the Rhondda (Glamorgan) and Swansea, where pupils did not take the Central Welsh Board's examinations. In the Rhondda, all the pupils who had been Bursars in 1909–10 qualified as Student-Teachers. In Swansea, out of 50 ex-bursars whose names were submitted in June 1910, before the results of the Preliminary Examination for the certificate—the Oxford Senior Locals and the London School Leaving Examinations were announced—as many as 48 qualified by examination for recognition as Student-Teachers from 1910. It must be remembered that the results Edwards quoted occurred among selected pupils, who had been sifted out before they were accepted. While sympathizing with the desire to maintain high standards, the Board of

[1] Ibid.
[2] PRO Ed 35/3415B, Minute from Pelham to Mayor, op. cit. Edwards to J. Herbert Lewis, 10 April 1909, Penucha MSS.

Education were forced to the conclusion that there had been a lack of adaptation on the part of the Central Welsh Board that would have very serious consequences. Injustice was done to the pupils, many of whom were too poor to remain at school for another year. The fact that 48 out of 50 passed in Swansea as against 27 in Glamorgan out of the 48 who tried to enter the profession through the Central Welsh Board examinations could not be attributed entirely to any greater intelligence of Swansea pupils, or to any superiority of educational advantages at Swansea. It was a sad outlook that the supply of trained elementary schoolteachers could not be maintained.[1]

When the Central Welsh Board met at Shrewsbury in November, Professor C. Bryner Jones, Aberystwyth, (in the absence of J. H. Davies, Registrar of the University College of Wales, Aberystwyth) moved the appointment of an independent committee 'to consider the curricula, organization and work of the intermediate schools, and the working of the Central Welsh Board system, and to report to the next meeting of the Board'.[2] Jones strongly denied that his action was an indictment of the Board's work and stated that it was a constant complaint at the University Colleges that students coming to them from the intermediate schools were badly prepared in certain subjects. His motion was seconded by Mrs. Coltman Rogers (Radnorshire), but strongly opposed by Dr. Aaron Davies (Glamorgan), who claimed it would be a vote of censure on themselves, the schoolteachers, the Inspectors, and the whole scheme. Understandably, the motion was defeated by 40 to 2.[3]

One of the pitiful features of the Central Welsh Board was the fact that special committees appointed to deal with important matters never met and never reported. This complaint was voiced on more than one occasion by J. H. Davies, Bryner Jones, Mrs. Coltman Rogers and Owen Edwards. For example, special committees had been set up to discuss and report on the teaching of agriculture, music, physical training, and the question of homework.[4] Edwards, backed by the Principals of the University Colleges, especially Roberts and Reichel, complained of inaction on the part of Owen, with reference to the teaching of music and physical training, both subjects of vital concern to intending teachers. It was

---

[1] PRO Ed 24/588, Report made by the Chief Inspector for Wales of the Board of Education to the President of the Board, on the Statement of the Central Welsh Board with reference to the Report of the Board of Education made in pursuance of Section 15 of the Welsh Intermediate Education Act, 1889, on the Proceedings under that Act in the year 1909, pp. 7–8, 3 January 1911. (Of 631 assistant teachers on the staffs of Welsh intermediate schools on 31 January 1909, only 74 had been trained for secondary school teaching. 401 had received no training at all).

[2] Board of Education, Minutes of Central Welsh Board, op. cit., 17 November 1911.

[3] *Manchester Guardian*, 18 November 1911.

[4] Board of Education, Minutes of Central Welsh Board, op. cit., 1911–1912.

The Contentious Welsh Board

revealed that army drill-sergeants taught physical exercises to girls in the intermediate schools at Welshpool, Abergele and Swansea![1] They recommended that expert inspection be provided for music and physical training, urged the appointment of teachers in those subjects, and deplored the fact that Owen and Hammond Robinson 'thought they knew everything about these subjects'.[2] It was decided to impress upon the Association of Headmasters the importance of including those subjects in the schools for prospective teachers.[3]

At this time also, a constantly recurring theme in the deliberations of the Central Welsh Board was the 'failure of Bursars'. Edwards produced the evidence, followed, as usual, by pertinent comment, at a meeting of the Board in February 1912. He showed that a great proportion of those who took the Central Welsh Board Senior examination—773 out of 1773—were intending teachers, and of those, 33.6 per cent failed to qualify, i.e. between one-third and one-half of the bursars failed. The Bursar system was being destroyed in Wales, while it succeeded in centres like Swansea, Rhondda and Merthyr. Edwards was asked why this was so, and in reply said 'because the Central Welsh Board does not guide the education of those places'.[4] He again repeated that the Board's examinations were too difficult for the majority of intending teachers, and the Central Welsh Board were unwilling to recognize any other examination. There were four damaging consequences to this policy, (a) the financial loss on the failure of Bursars was so great that many LEAs contemplated terminating the system; (b) the shortage of teachers was already telling on the schools, for only 246 out of 733 had been allowed to pass in 1911; (c) the newly-built Training Colleges, all quite necessary, would be unable to pay their way, and (d) poorer material from England would have to be introduced into the teaching staffs of Wales—those who had passed the easier examination—while Welsh pupils had been cut out of the profession. Owen meekly suggested pressing the headmasters to arrange the subjects in such a way that more pupils would be able to pass, and also to urge them to select future Bursars. To this, Edwards's tart reply was 'they meant to stick to their crystallized examination system, whatever injury happened to the pupils, the schools, or the colleges'.[5] Lord Sheffield, for once, agreed with Edwards, and remarked that Owen's suggestions 'would only touch the fringe of the difficulty'.[6] Then came the fight!

[1] Ibid., 15 December 1911, 9 February, 1912.
[2] Ibid., 5 May 1912.
[3] Ibid.
[4] Ibid., 9 February, 1912.
[5] Ibid., 13 February, 1912.
[6] Ibid.

Would the Central Welsh Board recognize other examinations? Tom John, smelling danger, moved the postponement of the subject, but eventually it was carried that the suggestion made by Owen be approved, and that if headmasters thought that the pupils could not pass the Central Welsh Board Senior examination, *they should be presented for the government examination*—the Preliminary Examination for the elementary teachers' Certificate. 'This', cried Edwards, 'was a great triumph'![1]

But at a subsequent meeting of the Board in May, Edwards protested that the minutes of the previous meeting were inaccurate and misleading. It was stated that the suggestions to headmasters made by Owen would be enough to meet the difficulty, while it had been passed that the weaker candidates should take the Board of Education's Preliminary examination. Eventually, this was righted, but it was disclosed that Owen, in the meantime had prepared a draft circular on the Training of Teachers to give effect to the erroneous resolution read in the minutes! It contained a strange and absurd suggestion—that pupils *'who shall have been presented once for a Senior Certificate* and whose marks showed that they were not likely to succeed, might be recommended to take the Preliminary examination of the Board of Education'.[2] Edwards contradicted this clause, saying that what was passed was 'if a headmaster thought a pupil would not be able to pass the Senior Certificate, the pupil should be presented for the Preliminary examination'. He strongly deprecated that a pupil should be presented for the Senior Certificate *before* being presented for the other. Owen had to withdraw his circular and promised to amend it in time for the next meeting.[3] By that time, the offending clause had been deleted.[4] His amended draft circular containing the blessing of the Central Welsh Board on the proposed government examination for the weaker candidates, provoked a question from Mrs. Coltman Rogers, who wanted to know if this was to be the Board's solution to the question of failing Bursars. On receiving no reply, Mr. Coltman Rogers came to his wife's rescue and made a fiery speech denouncing Anwyl and the executive committee, on the score that when questions were asked, no one got replies. He described the whole proceedings of the Central Welsh Board as a complete farce! Anwyl explained that the object of the circular was 'to encourage weak pupils to take an easier examination and this demonstrated the disinterestedness of the executive committee'![5] It was remark-

[1] Board of Education, Minutes of the Central Welsh Board, op. cit., 13 February.
[2] Ibid.
[3] Ibid., 3 May.
[4] Ibid., 17 May.
[5] Ibid.

able and regrettable that there was not a single soul among the members of the Central Welsh Board who could arise to censure the Board's inability to adapt its own examination requirements for the weaker vessels.

V THE JOLLIFFE CASE

'The most laudatory passage in the explosive *Report* of 1909 on the work of the intermediate schools was in mathematics ... though we have, at the Board of Education, several voluminous letters from the Chief Examiner in mathematics to the Central Welsh Board protesting against their methods of administering their examinations'.[1] Thus wrote Edwards on 18 November 1910. The chief examiner was A. E. Jolliffe, of Corpus Christi College, Oxford, described by Edwards as 'an excellent tutor and conscientious examiner'.[2] Jolliffe had written to the Central Welsh Board in December 1909 complaining, in very strong language, about the administrative side of their examinations. This complaint was considered at a meeting of the Board in order to see whether the language used by Jolliffe was justifiable. No action was taken, and Casson made the observation 'that the discussion was evidently undertaken merely to whitewash the office in Cardiff, and with no intention of taking action'.[3]

Jolliffe, however, took action, and addressed his complaint to the Board of Education.[4] He affirmed that, although the conduct of the whole examination was admirable, the business side of it was grossly mismanaged. The substance of his complaint was a matter connected with the Central Welsh Board examination, Stage I, Honours Mathematics, in 1909, when he discovered, after the results had been printed and published, that some half-dozen candidates who should have passed at this Stage, had failed, because his instructions had been disregarded. All the other complaints stemmed from this one fact. Apparently, Jolliffe had sent his instructions to the Central Welsh Board in a separate envelope, endorsed in red ink 'urgent and important' but the Board denied all knowledge of having received them. Hammond Robinson and Anwyl promised that due consideration would be given to his concern regarding the unsuccessful candidates.

Davies, at the Welsh Department, taking a more serious view of the matter, asked Jolliffe to send him, set out seriatim, the various charges

---

[1] PRO Ed 24/588, Reply to criticisms by Edgar Jones, op. cit.
[2] Ibid., Minute from Edwards to Davies, 29 January 1910.
[3] Board of Education, Minutes of Central Welsh Board, op. cit., 10 December 1909.
[4] PRO Ed 35/3408, Jolliffe to Board of Education, 20 December.

which he wished to prefer against the Central Welsh Board, their executive committee and their officials, for submission to that Board.[1] This request produced a voluminous reply from Jolliffe. He expressed concern that a number of candidates had failed because the Central Welsh Board had ignored his instructions, which had to be specially drawn up as a result of changes in the examination in 1909 because in the previous year the percentage of distinctions in mathematics was higher than in any other subject. The Welsh Board, instead of being gratified that mathematics was in such a flourishing condition in Wales, had asked him to make the papers more difficult so that this should not happen again. Jolliffe had worked out another system of allocating marks which was quite orthodox, (and which he had used with other examining bodies,) to pass the six candidates, but, to his annoyance, the Board, on the excuse of not having received his instructions, decided to fail them. The rest of his letter was a scathing condemnation of the office administration at Cardiff; that no examiners meetings were being held, and that no heed was paid to his correspondence regarding examinations. In 1909 he did not receive the packet containing the examination papers and very often his assistant examiners received information and question papers without his previous knowledge.[2]

This letter was passed on to Edwards, who was asked to report about what happened at the Welsh Board's meeting when the Jolliffe matter was discussed. He was also asked for his views on the Board's methods of conducting examinations both from the administrative and educational standpoint,[3] Before dealing with these matters it should be noted that Jolliffe derived no satisfaction from his tirade, and this could be attributed entirely to Edwards's benevolent attitude towards the Central Welsh Board. But this did not mean that the Jolliffe case was laid on the table at the Welsh Department. On the contrary, it served a very useful purpose both for Davies and Edwards.

In his report of the reaction of the Central Welsh Board to Jolliffe's complaint, Edwards said that the correspondence between Jolliffe and the clerk to the Board was read at the meeting, and the committee was divided between (a) leaving the matter un-noticed, and (b) passing a vote of censure on Jolliffe for the intemperate character of his communications. The former course was adopted. It was revealed that Jolliffe did not receive his papers because by 'a very natural inadvertance' his packet was addressed to Corpus Christi College, Cambridge, instead of Oxford. Also,

[1] Ibid., Board of Education to Jolliffe, 23 December.
[2] PRO Ed 35/3408, Jolliffe to Board of Education, 3 January 1910.
[3] Ibid., Minute from Davies to Edwards, 17 January. Sykes to Casson, 4 January.

The Contentious Welsh Board

during the summer, Jolliffe was undoubtedly overworked, and the tone of his correspondence was unfortunate, words like 'abominable' and 'damnable' being used to describe the administrative methods of the Board.[1]

The Jolliffe case focussed attention on the examination system of the Central Welsh Board, regarding which, Edwards had some very strong views. He said there was a great deal to commend and much to condemn, for that Board's system had made organization easy and tyranny all-powerful. Its examinations were rigid, uniform, and ignored the right of every school to develop its individual character and choose its own subjects. Welsh education had become an arena of competition for certificates, and subjects like Geography, Music, Physical Training and Manual Work were considered a waste of time. Instead of testing what an average pupil could do during his school career, it aimed at guiding and testing the top of the school, and Jolliffe undoubtedly touched a weak point in that respect. One important result of this was the inability to cater for those who did not require high academic qualifications, like elementary schoolteachers. There was no doubt that the standard of work demanded was high, and justly so, but by insisting on this, and cherishing a good name among examining bodies, however, the Central Welsh Board were inflicting severe tests on Welsh pupils.[2]

The academic administration of the Board had pronounced weaknesses. The arrangements for the marking of examination scripts were disorganized, and it was almost impossible to get their results out at a reasonable time. They were fond of appointing well known men, rather than experts, as examiners. They found difficulties with regard to standards of marking, and the examiners varied greatly—'some marked wildly and reported foolishly'. There was considerable confusion regarding reports, and the Central Welsh Board 'did not know their own mind whether the report is theirs or that of the examiner; sometimes they change it without reference to the examiner, and at other times, they get out of trouble by regarding it as the examiner's'.[3] Anwyl often interfered, and demanded a high standard in subjects like Latin and Greek, and left the other subjects alone. Owen, who was both Chief Inspector and Chief Examiner, along with his clerk, were hopelessly overworked, and the former was 'driven most unmercifully by Anwyl, who thought that everybody had his own physical strength and love of travelling'.[4]

[1] Ibid., Minute from Edwards to Davies, 29 January.
[2] Ibid.
[3] PRO Ed 35/3408, Minute from Edwards to Davies, 29 January, 1910.
[4] Anwyl died at the early age of 48.

The Contentious Welsh Board

With reference to Jolliffe's letter, Edwards proposed three alternatives, (a) submitting it to the Central Welsh Board for their observations. This might, of course, contest the right of the Board of Education to interfere, but Edwards thought the Central Welsh Board would regard it as a friendly act; (b) refer it to himself, with instructions to inquire, and sending it to Owen to discuss with him the Board's methods of administration; and (c) to tell Jolliffe that Edwards had been asked to watch and report. Edwards concluded by saying that 'there may be flaws in the Central Welsh Board system: there is no doubt, I think, that Mr. Jolliffe has acted unwisely and precipitately'.[1]

But Davies did not accept that they should not be justified in taking action upon Jolliffe's complaints. After discussing the situation with Casson, it seemed fairly clear that the Board of Education had, in more than one direction, jurisdiction, or at any rate, the power to intervene, for more than one reason: (a) the Central Welsh Board being established under the Endowed Schools and Charitable Trusts Acts, was subject to the jurisdiction of the Board of Education as successors of the Charity Commissioners, and 'that aspect of our powers is one of which it would be very convenient and salutary to make the Central Welsh Board and its officers thoroughly aware, as they are apt to display profound ignorance that the Board of Education have any such jurisdiction over them'; (b) it was on the implied assumption that the Central Welsh Board conducted their examinations properly that the Board of Education recognized the Central Welsh Board certificates, but in this respect that Board were '*sans peur et sans reproche*', and 'a breath of suspicion that irregularities occur which affect their examination results might have very unpleasant consequences for our Central Welsh Board friends, if the Board of Education chose to be nasty over this matter'.[2] Moreover, a hint to the Treasury would cause that Department to take action, since the government paid £1,200 a year to the Central Welsh Board for its administrative expenses, and many thousands of pounds a year to the schools on the result of their reports.[3]

The Jolliffe case which had disclosed yet another shortcoming in the administrative machine of the Central Welsh Board, however, was turned to good account by the Board of Education, through the sharp legal mind of Davies. He showed that the Welsh Board were not only tributary to the Board of Education but also this new disclosure might make them less

---

[1] PRO Ed supra ibid.
[2] Ibid., Minute from Davies to Edwards, 1 February.
[3] Ibid.

The Contentious Welsh Board

eager to snap their fingers at Whitehall in future. At the same time he saw an opportunity of impressing upon the Welsh Board (as the President had intimated more than once) that the Welsh Department were anxious to befriend them, and to increase and not diminish their influence and prestige, although they might not believe this. It was arranged that a private, semi-official letter be sent to Anwyl, stating that the Board of Education contemplated investigating the serious complaints made by Jolliffe, and that Edwards and Casson should confer privately with Owen. This arrangement would also enable those persons to thoroughly overhaul the Central Welsh Board examination procedure.[1]

The letter was diplomatic but firm in tone. Davies stated that in the interests of the Central Welsh Board it would be highly undesirable that the subject of Jolliffe's complaints should become a matter of public discussion which might undermine confidence in that Board. He expressed the hope that 'if as a result of the investigation made by Edwards and Casson, and also their private talk with Owen, the existing methods of conducting the Central Welsh Board's examinations appeared to be capable of improvement, that the necessary steps to that end would at once, and without the need for the exercise of any pressure from the Board of Education, be devised and adopted so as to relieve the Board of Education of the necessity to take action, or of having to inform the Treasury of the matter'.[2] Anwyl's reply was patronizing and docile, assuring Davies that great care would be taken in future with regard to the points raised.[3]

Edwards met all the officials of the Central Welsh Board—Anwyl, Owen, Robinson, and the clerk, Crynant Griffiths. Owen had prepared a memorandum and all the matters raised by Jolliffe were carefully considered. In his final report, Edwards was able to say that, of its kind, the examination system of the Central Welsh Board was as perfect as it could be, although he, personally, thought it was all wrong, and was 'an examination mill, but all its cog-wheels go regularly and well'.[4] Jolliffe was informed of the Board of Education's decision,[5] but he continued corresponding without avail until the end of May. No further action was taken by the Board of Education.[6]

---

[1] PRO Ed 35/3408, Minute from Davies to Edwards, ibid.; Davies to Casson, 31 January.
[2] Ibid., Davies to Anwyl, 14 February.
[3] Ibid., Anwyl to Davies, 15 February.
[4] Ibid., Minute from Edwards to Casson, 8 April.
[5] Ibid., Board of Education to Jolliffe, 25 April.
[6] Ibid., Minutes from Casson to Davies, 9 May; Davies to Casson, 1 June.

The Contentious Welsh Board

This was an incident which might have created a furore in Wales, had the facts set out in Jolliffe's letters been disclosed. It cannot be denied that Jolliffe, a person of high integrity and scholarship (respected by Edwards who had just left Lincoln College, Oxford, for his new post at the Welsh Department) and who had been chief examiner in mathematics to the Central Welsh Board for four years, was slighted, and indeed, rebuffed. The Central Welsh Board were spared embarrassment of national dimension by the kindly intervention of Owen Edwards.

VI DEFALCATION: END OF AN ERA

On 4 August 1914 when Britain declared war on Germany, and Lord Grey made his famous speech containing the phrase that 'the lights were going out all over Europe', Questions were being asked in the House of Commons about the waning lights in the affairs of the Central Welsh Board who had suffered humiliation in the eyes of the Welsh nation as a result of defalcations on the part of the administrative staff at its Cardiff office. The year 1914 was, in many ways, one of misfortune for the Central Welsh Board. In addition to the declaration of war, the defalcations, the dejected deputation to the Board of Education on 23 July which terminated any hope of extension of powers for the Welsh Board in the future, there were other set-backs. The death of the chairman, Sir Edward Anwyl, on 8 August, and the impending retirement of the Chief Inspector, Owen Owen, brought to an end an era in the history of Welsh secondary education.

On 30 January 1914 the chairman of the Central Welsh Board revealed that the clerk to the Board, W. Crynant Griffiths was a debtor to the Board in a very considerable sum, and that two assistant clerks, Messrs. Charles W. Seymour and David Williams were also involved. From statements made by the chief inspector, Owen Owen, and the solicitor to the Board, Mr. George David, it appeared that the amount unaccounted for was about £1,940.[1] This led to their trial before Mr. Justice Atkin, at the Glamorgan Assizes at Swansea on 21 July, and their subsequent imprisonment.[2] When the deficiencies were discovered, it was disclosed (a) that such irregularities had been going on since 1905; (b) that the Board's auditors were greatly to blame; (c) that the finance committee of the Board did not meet regularly, and rarely called for the office books;

---

[1] Board of Education, Minutes of Central Welsh Board, op. cit., 3 February 1914.
[2] *Cambria Daily Leader*, 21 July. *South Wales Daily News*, 24 July.

and (d) the office administration, on Owen's admission, had been 'at sixes and sevens'.[1]

Several days before the trial, Ormsby-Gore, MP, Denbigh District, had asked Questions in the House as to the relationship of the Central Welsh Board and the Board of Education, particularly regarding the financial control held by Whitehall, but Pease, the President of the Board, refused any answers since the matter was sub-judice. Ormsby-Gore said he would raise the matter again after the Assizes.[2] The Welsh press came out in force against the lax administration of the Board. *The South Wales Daily News* spoke of 'the gravity of the scandal ... the Board is the first national institution that Wales has had for centuries ... and should be a model institution in every respect, an example of what Wales can do when entrusted with the responsibility of self-government'. Llewelyn Williams, KC, MP, who defended Griffiths, called it 'a Central Board without a centre'.[3] True to his promise, Ormsby-Gore, along with Lord Ninian Crichton-Stuart, MP, Cardiff, raised Questions in the House as to whether the Board of Education proposed to take any steps to put the affairs of the Central Welsh Board in order, but the President could not promise action until that Board had considered the situation, and themselves taken action.[4] In the lobby of the House of Commons, Welsh MPs were particularly voluble, and had very definite views about the future. There was consensus of opinion among them that the Welsh Party would have nothing to do with any new scheme which did not make the Central Welsh Board a thoroughly representative body which could bring it into intimate relations with other educational movements in Wales. Dual inspection should go, and the powers of the Welsh Department over intermediate education should be strictly defined. Above all, the Central Welsh Board should be made a business-like body, so that there should be no more of the criticisms which Llewelyn Williams so rightly made at Swansea.[5]

The Central Welsh Board had already taken action before the trial, and the offending clerks had been dismissed.[6] After the trial, it remained to reorganize the office, appoint new clerks, and also a new chief inspector, since Owen was due to retire the following year. But during the week of

---

[1] *South Wales Daily News*, ibid., Minutes Central Welsh Board, op. cit., 24 February. Mr. Propert, the Local Government Board auditor who had been called to a special meeting of the executive committee, stated that 'the methods of the Central Welsh Board as regards finance were far below those of any public body which had come under his audit'.

[2] *Western Mail*, 24 July.

[3] *South Wales Daily News*, ibid.

[4] Questions and Answers, House of Commons, 27 July, 4 August.

[5] *Western Mail*, ibid.

[6] Board of Education, Minutes of Central Welsh Board op. cit., 3 February.

the trial, a deputation had waited on Davies at the Welsh Department, consisting of Ald. Williams, Glamorgan, and Ald. David Evans, Carmarthen. The purpose was to discuss certain amendments to the Welsh Scheme, which included a proposed superannuation fund for the officers of the Welsh Board, the delegation of power to examine pupils who had left the intermediate schools, and power to examine all secondary schools in Wales and Monmouthshire. They got short shrift from Davies, who refused to concede a single point on the grounds that they were 'patching amendments' and also involved organic changes in the constitution of the Central Welsh Board. He said they could not close their eyes to the fact that proceedings were that day going on in Swansea—'the ultimate results of which might have an important bearing on the whole matter, and the time was particularly inopportune for asking the Board of Education to consider what they required'.[1] He advised 'them to get their finances and administration into proper order after they emerged from their present sea of troubles, and to give serious thought to the elimination of unnecessary examinations. When those matters had been resolved, the Central Welsh Board would be in a more favourable position to approach the Board of Education with regard to the matters they had discussed that day'.[2] At the September meeting of the Board, the chairman, Lord Sheffield, after paying tribute to the late chairman, proposed that the amendments rejected by the Board of Education should be postponed for further consideration for a year, by which time the war might be over![3]

The reorganization of the Cardiff office involved major changes. After the dismissal of Griffiths, Owen was appointed acting clerk[4] and two other clerks, including a financial clerk were to be appointed.[5] Later, a reorganization committee was formed to deal with all appointments, and in November it was recommended that Owen be appointed 'Clerk of the Board and Superintendent of Examinations' at a salary of £500, and that Mr. Myrddin Evans, an assistant clerk appointed in 1912, be made chief assistant clerk at a salary of £170 rising to £200.[6] Owen relinquished his duties as Chief Inspector on 31 July 1915, but was retained as Superintendent of Examinations at a salary of £800 a year, minus his pension of

[1] PRO Ed 35/3408, *Board of Education (Welsh Department) and Central Welsh Board: Notes of Interview with Deputation at the Board of Education on* 23 *July* 1914, W. H. Fawkes, 24 July.
[2] Ibid.
[3] Board of Education, Minutes of Central Welsh Board, op. cit., 23 September, 1914.
[4] Ibid., 3 February 1914.
[5] Ibid., 27 April.
[6] Ibid., 24 November.

The Contentious Welsh Board

£200.[1] On 7 May Mr. William Edwards, MA, HMI, Merthyr Tydfil, was appointed temporary Chief Inspector, and later Myrddin Evans was appointed Clerk to the Board.[2]

Two further matters of some importance should be mentioned. Firstly, a Consultative Committee had been set up by the Board of Education in December 1911, to consider examinations in secondary schools. It recommended an overhaul of the existing number of external examinations, whereby only two examinations should be taken: (a) the first, around the age of 16 which tested the results of a general course of work; and (b) the second, for those who stayed at school till 18 or 19 years of age, who should be examined in courses of a more specialized nature.[3] This meant the abolition of the Junior Certificate examination, and the Welsh Department had written to the Central Welsh Board regarding this proposed change. Once more, this was regarded by that Board as another interference by the Board of Education. At a meeting of the Welsh Board in November, Ald. Morgan Thomas, Cardiff, protested that this proposal had come from London since the controlling authority for secondary schools in Wales was the Central Welsh Board. Edwards, declaring that Thomas was under a misapprehension on that matter, explained that the Welsh Department had no intention of ignoring the Welsh Board, and maintained, that if that Board accepted the proposal it would be a step in the right direction for its future.[4]

Secondly, an important conference of members of LEAs, local governing bodies, and the Welsh County Schools Association was held at Llandrindod in May 1915 to consider the question of the Junior Certificate, and the Welsh secondary education system generally. After long discussions it was evident that there would be no unanimity on the question of eliminating the Junior Certificate, and the matter was deferred until after the war.[5] But a significant resolution was passed at that meeting by Mr. William George of Criccieth (brother of Lloyd George) and a new member of the Central Welsh Board. He proposed 'that the Central Welsh Board would welcome a competent public inquiry under government sanction into the conditions of all grades of education in Wales... but in view of the conditions then prevailing... it should be postponed until

---

[1] This was a gesture on the part of the Board, since the Board of Education could not approve a superannuation scheme. (Minutes of Central Welsh Board, 20 April 1915).

[2] Ibid., 31 May, 25 October.

[3] PRO Ed 35/3408, *Circular Letter from L. A. Selby-Bigge, Board of Education, to Universities*, December 1912.

[4] Board of Education, Minutes of Central Welsh Board, op. cit., 24 November. *Western Mail*, 21 November.

[5] *Manchester Guardian*, 22 May 1915; *Western Mail*, 21 May.

after the war'.[1] He also wanted to establish a special committee of the Central Welsh Board to consider the prevailing state of intermediate and secondary education in Wales to prepare proposals to be submitted to that Board before the institution of the inquiry.

But the condition of intermediate and secondary education in Wales was to become the subject of a much more comprehensive inquiry. On 12 July 1919, H. A. L. Fisher, President of the Board of Education, set up a Departmental Committee under the chairmanship of the Hon. W. N. Bruce, to make recommendations for the re-organization of Welsh secondary education. The Welsh members of the committee included Principal J. H. Davies, Sir Owen Edwards and Mr. William George.[2]

* * * * *

It would hardly be true to say that the Central Welsh Board had justified the hopes of its founders. This was the verdict of the Departmental Committee which reported on Welsh secondary education in 1920. The Board had become a large, cumbersome, deliberative assembly, leaving the most important issues to be resolved by a small executive committee where academics predominated, while its special functions of examining and inspecting, though relevant to the minority of pupils proceeding to university and professional callings, neglected the needs of the majority who were to become the future citizens of Wales. The latter should have had opportunities in the Welsh intermediate schools to equip themselves with a sound general education based on their own language, literature, history, geography and the arts, along with facilities to develop practical skills which would have enriched the Welsh environment. Many others, had they been armed with this broader knowledge, would have found it less difficult to enter the new Training Colleges to prepare themselves for the teaching profession, and later on to become the leaders of Welsh life in the communities in which they served. This was the great vision—and mission—which Owen Edwards, in his thirteen brief years at the Welsh Department worked for in Welsh education.

Regarding the schools, it was a circumstance of history that there prevailed in Wales three kinds of secondary institutions, the intermediate, municipal and schools of the Public School endowed and proprietary types.[3] The twelve municipal secondary schools of that time, established

[2] *Manchester Guardian*, ibid.
[3] *Report of the Departmental Committee*, 1920, op. cit. See Study No. 1 for its recommendations.
[1] Public School type: Christ's College, Brecon, and Llandovery. Endowed schools: Monmouth Grammar School, Howell's at Denbigh and Llandaff, Ruthin Grammar School. Proprietary schools, e.g. Rydal Mount, Colwyn Bay.

The Contentious Welsh Board

and virtually controlled by LEAs—the county boroughs of Cardiff, Swansea, Merthyr Tydfil and the county of Glamorgan—'were more democratic in their government, with their lower fees, less academic bias, and freedom from examination burdens than the intermediate schools'.[1] But after the first world war there were fewer distinctions between these two types because the Central Welsh Board had started to reform itself and had introduced broader and more flexible courses particularly in practical work and other aesthetic examination subjects. In view of this, it would have been far wiser if the Board of Education had allowed the Central Welsh Board *all* the inspection which they had desired many years before. It was refused because only one of the four LEAs had shown any enthusiasm, for reasons already discussed in this Study. In the event, at the end of 1926 the system of joint and unified inspection of secondary schools by the two Boards was brought into operation.[2]

[1] Report, Board of Education (Welsh Department), 1913, p. 7.
[2] See Study No. 6.

APPENDICES

I ESTIMATES OF INCREASED GRANTS 1903–1908

II SECONDARY SCHOOLS, WALES, TABLES:
Table 1 Grants from Board of Education

Table 2 Number of Boarders and Day Scholars in Welsh Intermediate Schools in 1910–11

Table 3 (a) Number of Pupils in Welsh Intermediate Schools

Table 3 (b) Number of pupils in Welsh Municipal Secondary Schools

III LIST OF SECONDARY SCHOOLS IN WALES MAINTAINED UNDER PART II OF THE EDUCATION ACT 1902

IV MEMORANDUM ON POWERS OF BOARD OF EDUCATION AND CENTRAL WELSH BOARD RESPECTIVELY AS TO THE INSPECTION OF WELSH INTERMEDIATE SCHOOLS

APPENDIX I

CENTRAL WELSH BOARD

Estimates of Increased Grant

Particulars	Present Cost (Estimate 1903–1904)	Cost 1904–1905	Remarks	Cost (1907–1908)	Addition 1904–1905	Addition for 1907–1908
I. Inspection						
Chief Inspector	600 0 0	800 0 0		800 0 0	200 0 0	200 0 0
Second Inspector	300 0 0	450 0 0	Annual Increments of £50	600 0 0	150 0 0	300 0 0
P Lady Inspector / Temporary Inspector	} – – – } 125 0 0	} 200 0 0 } 75 0 0	Annual Increments of £50	} 350 0 0 } 75 0 0	} 150 0 0	} 300 0 0
Expenses of Inspection	349 2 11	440 0 0		440 0 0	90 17 1	90 17 1
	£1,374 2 11	1,965 0 0		£2,265 0 0	590 17 1	890 17 1
II. Examination						
Fees to Examiners	£1,879 19 3	2,079 19 3		£2,079 19 3	200 0 0	200 0 0
III. Administration						
Clerk	200 0 0	225 0 0	Annual Increments of £25	300 0 0	25 0 0	100 0 0
Senior Assistant Clerk	110 10 0	117 0 0	Annual Increments	120 0 0	6 10 0	9 10 0
Typist	84 10 0	91 0 0	Annual Increments of £6.10	104 0 0	6 10 0	19 10 0
(1) Assistant Clerk	65 0 0	96 0 0	Annual Increments of £12	120 0 0	31 0 0	55 0 0
(2) Assistant Clerk	} 52 0 0 27 0 0	72 16 0	Annual Increments of £7.16	96 4 0	20 16 0	44 4 0
General Clerk	} 40 0 0	85 10 0	Annual Increments of £7.10	91 0 0	18 4 0	23 14 0
	£579 6 0	687 6 0		£831 4 0	108 0 0	251 18 0
IV. Office Accommodation	87 0 0	187 0 0		187 0 0	100 0 0	100 0 0
Totals	£3,920 8 2	4,919 5 3		£5,363 3 3	998 17 1	1,442 15 0

PRO Ed. 35/3407

APPENDIX II

WALES

TABLE 1

GRANTS FROM BOARD OF EDUCATION (In respect of School Year)

School Year	Under Regulations for Secondary Schools					Under P.T. etc. Regulations	TOTAL	Grant from Treasury
	Welsh Intermediate Schools	Other Endowed Schools	Council Schools	Roman Catholic Schools	Total			
	£	£	£	£	£	£	£	£
1905–6	—	—	—	—	21444	14874	36318	22403
1906–7	—	—	—	—	31090	16070	47160	22949
1907–8	42402	825	6825	112	50165	15310	65475	23694
1908–9	60458	2021	9537	97	72114	12833	84947	24413
1909–10	61112	2154	9600	109	72975	8477	81452	24849
1910–11	60299	2265	9363	103	72030	8479	80509	25423
1911–12*	58611	2361	9697	133	70802*	8834*	79636*	25274

*The figures for 1911–12 are subject to correction but agree very nearly with the estimate.

PRO Ed. 3408

APPENDIX II—*continued*

WALES

Secondary Schools.

Table 2.—Number of Boarders and Day Scholars in Welsh Intermediate Schools in 1910–11.

	Boarders	Day Scholars	Total
In 95 Schools on the Grant List (on 31 January 1911)	307	12,022	12,329
In 1 School not on the Grant List (in October 1910)	70	126	196
96 Schools Total	377	12,148	12,525

Table 3 (a)—Number of Pupils in Welsh Intermediate Schools.

Year	Schools on the Grant List — Number of Schools	Number of Pupils*	Schools not on the Grant List — Number of Schools	Number of Pupils†	Total — Number of Schools	Number of Pupils
1	2	2	4	5	6	7
1905–06	83	9,394	12	1,171	95	10,565
1906–07	84	10,276	11	1,178	95	11,454
1907–08	92	11,461	4	550	96	12,011
1908–09	94	12,471	2	416	96	12,887
1909–10	95	12,571	1	198	96	12,769
1910–11	95	12,329	1	196	96	12,525
1911–12	95	12,277	1	198	96	12,475

Table 3 (b)—Number of Pupils in Municipal Secondary Schools.

Year	Number of Schools	Number of Pupils*
1905–06	2	969
1906–07	4	1,568
1907–08	8	2,154
1908–09	8	2,046
1909–10	8	2,031
1910–11	8	1,983
1911–12	9	2,107

*The figures for the first 3 years relate to 30th June, and were supplied by the Schools themselves: those for subsequent years relate to 31st January and were extracted from particulars given in the Admission Register.

†These figures relate to the 1st October and are taken from the Reports of the Central Welsh Board.

PRO Ed 3408

APPENDIX III

LIST of Secondary Schools in Wales and Monmouthshire maintained under Part II of the Education Act 1902

County or County Borough	Name of School	Responsible Body	Tuition Fee	Number of Pupils on 1 Oct. 1912 Boys	Girls	Total
Glamorgan County	*Cowbridge County School for Girls	*	£6	–	73	73
	Ferndale Secondary School	Rhondda U.D.C.	Nil	96	171	267
	Maesteg Secondary School	Glamorgan Cty. Cl.	£4.10	55	51	106
Cardiff Cty. Borough	Cardiff Canton Municipal Sec. Sch. (Boys)	Cardiff County Borough Council	** 6d a week to £9 per annum	260	–	260
	,, (Girls)	,,	,,		261	261
	Cardiff Howard Gardens Municipal Sec. Sch. (Boys)	,,	,,	331		331
	,, ,, (Girls)	,,	,,		318	318
Swansea County Borough	Swansea Municipal Sec. Sch. (Boys)	Swansea County Borough Council	1/– a week	313		313
	,, ,, (Girls)	,,	,,		266	266
Merthyr Tydfil Cty. Borough	Cyfarthfa Castle Municipal Sec. Sch. (Boys)	Merthyr Tydfil Co. Borough Cl.	Nil	–	–	–
	,, (Girls)	,,	,,	–	–	–

*Cowbridge Girls' School under the new Glamorgan County Scheme approved 16th December 1912 ceases to be an Intermediate School and is in process of being transformed into a Municipal Secondary School controlled by the County Council. Under the same scheme the Mountain Ash County Secondary School which has hitherto been maintained under Part II of the Education Act 1902 will become an Intermediate School.

**The fee at these schools is 6d a week for all pupils whose parents are resident in or ratepayers of Cardiff and sign an undertaking to keep the children in school for the whole year. If the undertaking is not signed the fee is £2 per term.
For pupils whose parents are neither resident in nor ratepayers of Cardiff the fee is £2 per term if the undertaking is signed and £3 per term if it is not signed.

PRO Ed 3408

APPENDIX IV

Powers of the Board of Education and the Central Welsh Board respectively as to inspection of Welsh Intermediate Schools.

(1) It is desirable to obtain a decision as to the power of the Board of Education to inspect Welsh Intermediate Schools for the purpose of Grants under the Regulations for Secondary Schools (Wales) 1908–9.

(2) The Central Welsh Board maintains that it has the duty and responsibility of inspecting Schools established under the Welsh Intermediate Education Act of 1889, in accordance with the provisions of the Board of Education Act of 1899, as well as under its own scheme for the award of the Treasury Grant for the following reasons:

i. The only inspection of schools supplying Secondary Education which the Board of Education is empowered to make is that authorised by Parliament in Section 3 of the Board of Education Act of 1899, and under Section 3 of that Act the Central Welsh Board is the proper organisation for the inspection of Schools established by Scheme under the Welsh Intermediate Education Act of 1889.

ii. In assigning Parliamentary Grants in aid of Secondary Education the inspection of all Schools receiving such grants is conditioned by the provisions of the Board of Education Act, Section 3, and the provisions of this Clause govern all references to inspection in the Regulations of the Board of Education.

iii. Schools applying for and receiving recognition as Secondary Schools, so as to qualify for the receipt of the Parliamentary Grants in question, are held to have applied for inspection under the Board of Education Act 1899.

iv. It is by virtue of Section 3 of the Board of Education Act for 1899, and under the conditions prescribed by that Clause, that the Board of Education itself is empowered to inspect Schools supplying Secondary Education.

(3) It is quite true that it is for the Central Welsh Board to conduct an inspection of a Welsh Intermediate School under Section 3 of the Board of Education Act 1899, but the Board of Education consider that they have full power to make such inspection, whether an ordinary or a "Full" inspection, of any such School, as they think proper or necessary for the purpose of grants under the Secondary School Regulations.

(4) Prior to the Board of Education Act 1899, grants were not paid for Secondary Education generally but only for Science and Art. These grants were conditional on inspection of the Science and Art Classes. There was no power to inspect a School as a whole.

(5) The Board of Education Act 1899 Section 3 gave to the Board of Education power to inspect on terms to be fixed by the Board with the consent of the Treasury, a School as a whole if the School desired to be so inspected and it was provided that in the case of Welsh Intermediate Schools the Central Welsh Board "shall be recognised as the proper organisation for the inspection of any such Schools as may be desirous of inspection under this Section".

(6) The Board of Education "Directory" for 1901–2 which governed the administration of "the sum of money annually granted by Parliament for instruction in Science and Art," provided that any Secondary Day School submitting a Scheme of instruction in Science and applying for and receiving recognition for grants "will be held to have applied for Inspection under the Board of Education Act 1899 and will accordingly be inspected at such periods as the Board shall determine" but, as such Inspection related to the School as a whole, and the Board's grants were for Science the Directory went on to provide that "The inspection of the Science course will not be confined to

The Contentious Welsh Board

the periodical inspection above mentioned, and the School must at all times during the hours of instruction be open to the Officers of the Board". The result was that for the periodical inspection of the School as a whole the Central Welsh Board became the inspecting body, but that any inspection of the Science course, as distinguished from the periodical inspection, was to be made by the Board of Education.

(7) The Board of Education's Regulations for Secondary Schools 1904—5 placed the administration of grants to Secondary Schools on a wider basis and the work of the whole School now came within the purview of the Board and grants became payable for general Secondary instruction given through an approved course as distinguished from a Scheme of instruction in Science. It therefore became necessary for the Board of Education to expand the scope of their inspection from the inspection of the Science Course to inspection of the whole of the course. The Regulations for that year omitted the provision contained in the Directory for 1901-2 that a School applying for grants shall be held to have applied for inspection under the Board of Education Act 1899 and provided instead (Art: 31) that the School must be open at all times to inspection by the Board and that "any School applying for and receiving recognition under these Regulations in respect of any of its work will be liable to inspection of the School as a whole and will be inspected accordingly (without charge) at such periods as the Board shall determine". A similar clause appeared in the Board's Regulations up to and including the Regulations for 1907-8 (Wales). The result of the clause was that all inspections (periodical or otherwise) made for the purposes of the Board's grant were to be made under the Regulations themselves and none were to be made under the Board of Education Act 1899.

(8) The Clause in question does not however, appear in the Regulations for Secondary Schools (Wales) 1908-9 and these Regulations merely provide (Art: 27) that "The School . . . must be open at all times to inspection by the Board".

(9) Up till the present the Board of Education have not conducted "periodical" inspections of Welsh Intermediate Schools and it is by no means certain that they will deem it necessary or wish to conduct such inspections of these Schools, but the Schools have at all times been open to and visited by the Board's Inspectors for the purposes of the Board's grants.

(10) The view the Board of Education take and wish to have confirmed is that while the Central Welsh Board have full power (a) to inspect the Schools for the purpose of the Treasury Grant and (b) to inspect such of the Schools as may be desirous of inspection under Section 3 of the Board of Education Act 1899, the Board of Education have full power to inspect the Schools under the Regulations for Secondary Schools (Wales) 1908 for the purposes of the Board's Grant, and that their inspection may take such form as they may deem desirable.

J. L. Casson.
22nd July 1908.

PRO Ed. 3415B

III

THE CARMARTHENSHIRE INQUIRY

INTRODUCTION		118
I RECALCITRANT CARMARTHENSHIRE		118
II WELSH COUNTY POLICIES		137
III INSTITUTION OF THE INQUIRY		143
IV THE INQUIRY AND RESULT		159
APPENDICES		173

The Carmarthenshire Inquiry

THE major political and educational landmark during the turbulent years of the administration of the 1902 Education Act in Wales—from 1903 to the fall of the Unionist government in December 1905—was the Carmarthenshire Inquiry.[1] It was not only an integral part of, but was the most significant event in the 'Welsh Revolt', a term which expressed the militant attitude of the Welsh nation towards Balfour's Act. Whilst almost all of the Welsh local education authorities had proceeded to administer the Act in an illegal manner, Carmarthenshire was selected by the Board of Education as the best example of a local education authority which had openly defied the Act by passing illegal resolutions. The Public Inquiry was instituted as a test case, which, if proven, could lead to the issue of an Order and, if necessary, *mandamus* proceedings under Section 16 of the Act, against the county council.[2]

I RECALCITRANT CARMARTHENSHIRE

On 17 January 1903, just a month after the passing of the Education Act of 1902[3] Lloyd George issued his famous manifesto to the Welsh people enjoining them to administer the Act only under certain important conditions, one of which was that voluntary or non-provided schools should be brought under full public control. This manifesto marked 'the genesis of what came to be called the "Welsh Revolt" '. But on 1 October 1902, the Carmarthenshire county council had already passed a resolution 'that in view of the refusal of the government to safeguard public interests by adequate control over so-called voluntary schools thrown by the Education Bill on the local rates in addition to Imperial grants, this Council, as one of the authorities to be charged with the administration of the Bill, desires to inform the government respectfully and plainly that unless the Bill provides satisfactory public control over all rate-aided schools we will not carry out the provisions of the Bill in and for the County of Carmarthenshire'.[4] Thus, in unmistakably forthright terms (before the Bill became the Education Act), did Carmarthenshire, stick

---

[1] It should be noted that the Public Inquiry was for Carmarthenshire County Council and not for Carmarthen Town Council as stated in Kenneth O. Morgan's *Wales in British Politics* 1868–1922, p. 192.

[2] *Mandamus* is a discretionary writ grantable by the King's Bench Division of the High Court of Justice to enforce the performance of a public duty which cannot be enforced by action.

[3] 2 Edw. 7, c. 42, received Royal Assent on 18 December 1902.

[4] PRO Ed 111/254, Index to Documents referred to in Instructions, Document IX, Chronological Summary, Carmarthenshire; PRO Ed 24/578, Revised notes on Wales, 27 June 1904.

The Carmarthenshire Inquiry

its neck right out to proclaim its belligerent attitude. This was uncompromisingly put into practice in subsequent months and forced the Board of Education to take steps to institute the one and only Public Inquiry in Wales into the actions of the most rebellious and recalcitrant local education authority of the Welsh Revolt, which led eventually to the passing of the Education (Local Authority) Default Act on 15 August 1904.

This attitude of Carmarthenshire, obstinately clinging to its illegal resolutions, can be traced back to a religious and educational background so spectacular that no other Welsh shire could rival. The county produced two of the greatest personalities in the history of Welsh religion, politics and journalism in the nineteenth century—Rev. David Rees (1801-1869), pastor of the Independent church at Capel Als, Llanelli, and David Owen (Brutus), (1794-1866) in turn a Baptist, Independent and Churchman. Rees was editor of the Independent *Y Diwygiwr* (Revivalist), and Owen of the Established Church's *Yr Haul* (The Sun), and for over thirty years both publications championed the opposing tendencies for which they stood, Church rates, Disestablishment, Rebecca and education.[1] Rees spent his lifetime in Llanelli, and was devoted to the spreading of Independency and the moulding of its political and other opinions.

As far as Nonconformity was concerned, Carmarthenshire was a citadel of the Independent denomination and whole areas of the county, from the Dissenting standpoint were almost exclusively Independent. There were also in less profusion Baptists and Methodists and one or two small nests of Unitarians and all of these of course, helped the followers of Rees. But in political affairs and West Wales Dissent, the Independents were the most conspicuous opponents of *Eglwys Loegr* (Established Church in Wales), and of the oligarchic system of politics which went with it.[2] Even by the beginning of the twentieth century this opposition was still smouldering and was set alight by Balfour's Act. To fight '*ysgolion Eglwys Lloegr*' (Established Church Schools in Wales) presented a real challenge.

In the educational world Carmarthenshire was unique. There is only need to mention men like the Rev. Griffith Jones (1683-1761), (a Churchman) and his Welsh Circulating Schools, and the Rev. Thomas Charles, (1755-1814), architect of the Welsh Calvinistic Methodist denomination

---

[1] Iorwerth Jones, *David Rees Y Cynhyrfwr*, Gwasg John Penry, Abertawe, 1971, pp. 69, ff.
R. Tudur Jones, *Hanes Annibynwyr Cymru*, Gwasg John Penry, Abertawe, 1966, pp. 210, ff.

[2] The '*Religious Census*' of 1851 records only attendances at services on a particular Sunday. For 1861, Dr. Thomas Rees gives the total of Independents in Carmarthenshire as 15,674, and Baptists 8,546 but in 1905, the statistics submitted to the *Royal Commission on the Church in Wales*, gave Carmarthenshire Independents a membership of 28,813, while the Baptists were 18,160.

and his Welsh Sunday School movement—men born in the county—who produced a literate nation when secular day schools were unimportant. Nor must it be forgotten that William Williams, a Llanpumsaint boy who went to the Church school with David Owen, became MP for Coventry and along with Joseph Hume became the most radical member of the House of Commons. He proposed that a Welsh Education Inquiry be set up, which produced the Blue Books of 1847. In Carmarthen a theological College had been in existence since 1704 (Presbyterian College), which produced preachers of every denomination and quite a number of postulants for Holy Orders—long before the vision of Bishop Burgess and his Anglican college at Lampeter. These preachers were acknowledged to be of very broad theological outlook, highly individualistic, a detachment from the herd, which proved of the utmost value in the development of religious thought in this part of Wales.[1]

But the most significant contribution of Carmarthenshire was, what might be called the principle of *local tradition in education*, whereby numbers of dissenting 'quasi-secondary' schools, widely distributed, cheap to run and very effective were established by private enterprise.[2] The attitude of West Wales Dissent, and in particular, Carmarthenshire Dissent, in the controversies on public education of the nineteenth century and right on to 1906 cannot be understood apart from this tradition of local seminaries. Many a Dissenter held that education like religion should be a private and voluntary concern, and brooked no interference from Church or State.[3] Finally, *and most important of all, it must be remembered that in the field of elementary schooling, Carmarthenshire was the amphitheatre of the Voluntaryist Movement in Wales*. Rees was the leader and was helped by the Rev. Joshua Lewis, minister of Henllan Amgoed Independent church. Many school-building programmes were drawn up, and whilst the Report of the British and Foreign School Society shows only ten British Schools in Carmarthenshire for 1854, it had thirty-two voluntarily-provided 'Dissenting Schools', of which sixteen belonged to the Independents. This movement collapsed through lack of money, and many 'Dissenting Schools' went over to the British and Foreign School Society. Right up to 1879, when he died, Joshua Lewis was still a voluntaryist—the Act of 1870 meant nothing to him.[4]

[1] J. E. Lloyd (ed.) *History of Carmarthenshire*, vol. 2, Cardiff, 1939, pp. 222, ff.

[2] G. Dyfnallt Owen, *Ysgolion a Cholegau yr Annibynwyr*, Abertawe, 1939, gives a full account of these schools. Also, R. T. Jenkins, 'Academiau yr Annibynwyr yng Nghymru', *Y Llenor*, 1939.

[3] The alarm caused in the minds of Nonconformists by the education clauses of Graham's Factory Act of 1843 deepened this feeling.

[4] J. E. Lloyd, op. cit. p. 244.

The Carmarthenshire Inquiry

The Independent denomination and its ministers were well represented on Carmarthenshire county council after the Local Government Act of 1888. In May 1903 the Rev. Thomas Johns, an alderman of the Carmarthenshire county council and minister of Capel Als Independent Chapel, Llanelli, (one of the largest Nonconformist chapels in Wales) and successor in the pastorate to the redoubtable Rev. David Rees,[1] had proposed a notice of motion at a meeting of the county council 'that we recommend the council not to spend more money on denominational schools than the *special grant* received from the government unless the control of the schools be given to the council'.[2] This proposition prompted Col. W. Lewes, another member of the county council and chairman of the Carmarthenshire Conservative and Liberal Unionist Association, to write to the Board of Education on 19 May to enquire whether the notice of motion, if carried, would be legal or not, as he was advised that a county council had no power to make any distinction in the treatment of schools. Further, he required to know, should the motion be adopted 'what the penalty, if illegal, would be'.[3]

This letter precipitated a course of events which eventually led to the public inquiry which was set up by the Law Officers of the Crown on behalf of the Board of Education into the illegalities of the Carmarthenshire county council with regard to the implementation of the Education Act of 1902.[4] When the letter arrived at the Board of Education the officials were extremely cautious in framing a reply, maintaining 'that the Welsh policy will certainly raise difficult questions and the less we commit ourselves beforehand with regard to them, the better . . . I am doubtful therefore whether we should not confine ourselves to the first paragraph of his proposed letter, and say nothing about the terms of the Resolution'.[5] The first draft reply referred to Section 7(1) of the 1902 Act 'that the local education authority shall maintain and keep efficient all public elementary schools within their area which are necessary'. This draft also mentioned enforcement by *mandamus* (section 16 of the Act) if the local education authority failed to discharge its duty. It also stated that the Board of Education were not prepared to offer any opinion with regard 'to the terms of the notice of motion quoted in your letter, since it does not seem

---

[1] Rev. Gwilym Rees, *Cofiant y Parch. Thomas Johns, D.D.*, Llanelli, 1929, pp. 151–2. Johns had been a member of the county council since its inception.

[2] PRO Ed 111/252, Col. W. Lewes, J.P., D.L., of Llysnewydd, Llandysul, to Board of Education 19 May, 1903.

[3] Ibid.

[4] The 'appointed day' for Carmarthenshire was 30 September, 1903.

[5] PRO Ed, ibid., Minute from Mayor to Hoare and Lindsell, 26 May, 1903.

clear what its effects would be'.[1] The final draft was brief and couched in more guarded words 'that the Board could not offer any opinion on the legality or the effect of a resolution which has not been adopted by the county council'.[2]

A meeting of the Carmarthenshire education committee was held on 19 June, whose members 'had been appointed before party spirit ran so high, and contained moderate men and whose chairman was the Rev. David Eleazer Jones, a Nonconformist minister of Carmarthen who had entered into negotiations with Bishop Owen of St. Davids.[3] The Rev. John's motion that only the parliamentary grants should be spent on voluntary schools was *rejected* by fourteen votes to six.[4] Another member of the education committee and county council, Ben Evans, of Nantgaredig, who was 'desirous of administering the Act alike to non-provided and provided schools' wrote to the Board of Education requesting answers to three questions before the meeting of the county council on 22 July: (a) would the county lose any portion of the government grant if the motion were carried; (b) are the total government grants under the Education Act of 1902 sufficient to maintain the non-provided schools at the level they were previous to that Act without any rate-aid; and (c) how many counties (if any) in England and Wales have already adopted a similar course to the Carmarthenshire motion.[5] In reply, the Board of Education referred Evans to a question asked in the House of Commons —a Question which had a significant background.[6]

Apparently, J. W. Nicholas, clerk to the Carmarthenshire county council and close friend of Bishop Owen (whose Palace was at Abergwili, near Carmarthen) was not a little concerned about the illegal course which his council proposed to follow. He confided his apprehension to the Bishop, who was no lover of the Lloyd George policy of 'no control, no cash'. Bishop Owen persuaded Morant to arrange that A. S. T. Griffith-Boscawen, MP, should ask a Question in Parliament on 8 July, and that Sir William Anson, Parliamentary Secretary to the Board of Education should answer it. Morant even composed the Question (regarding resolutions adopted by Welsh county councils as to the treatment of voluntary schools) and the answer: 'My attention has been called to the resolutions mentioned; it is the duty of every county council to maintain

---

[1] Ibid.
[2] Ibid., Minute from Mayor to Lindsell, 27 May.
[3] Eluned E. Owen, *The Later Life of Bishop Owen*, Llandysul, 1961, p. 47.
[4] PRO Ed 24/578, *Confidential Memorandum on the Educational Situation in Wales*, (*Revised*), 27 June 1904.
[5] PRO Ed 111/252, Evans to Board of Education, 13 July 1903.
[6] Ibid. Board of Education to Evans, 17 July.

The Carmarthenshire Inquiry

and keep efficient all public elementary schools within their area. The rate and the government grant together constitute the fund at the disposal of a county council for this purpose. The standard of efficiency at which all public elementary schools are maintained must be alike unless special educational reasons can be shown for a distinction. The action proposed in the resolutions would therefore be in contravention of the Act'.[1]

But the effect so carefully staged by Morant and Bishop Owen was completely spoilt by Lloyd George. He pounced on the word 'special' and said that 'Anson had answered a question, prompted by a Welsh Bishop. He had said that the resolutions of the county councils to contribute nothing but the government grants to the voluntary schools were in contravention of the Act. It was not so, for the councils had special reasons for declaring that they could not recognize the same level of efficiency in schools which were not under their control, and would decline to squander public money on them. That was the situation which the government had to face. What was the government going to do'?[2] The government had no solution and even Morant was baffled. Carmarthenshire was not only an obstinate, independent council which arrogantly flouted the Act of 1902, but was also unafraid of an exposure to the world, of its illegal actions in a public inquiry. Withal, it formed part of a diocese whose Bishop resided within its terrain and whose fertile brain produced a solution where others in high government places had failed. For Bishop Owen had a pistol in his ecclesiastical armoury which was to be fired after the public inquiry. This was the 'Pistol Bill' devised by the Bishop with the help of his friend Lord Cawdor and camouflaged as the Education (Local Authority) Default Bill.[3]

The action by the Carmarthenshire education committee of rejecting the motion put forward by the Rev. T. Johns, that only Imperial grants be spent on voluntary schools was taken after the national convention held at Cardiff on 3 June when Lloyd George and the Welsh members of parliament had advocated outright resistance to the Act. But the great day for the Nonconformists was 22 July 1903 when the Carmarthenshire county council met to discuss the report of the education committee. Some days before this meeting Lloyd George himself had come down to

---

[1] PRO Ed 111/252, Minute from Mayor to Lindsell, 16 July; Minute from Lindsell to Reid, 17 July, referring to No. 88 in House of Commons Question File: 'Whether his attention had been called to the resolutions of certain county councils whereby it was proposed to contribute nothing but the government grants to the maintenance of the voluntary schools within their area and to apply the produce of a county rate levied for educational purposes over the entire county towards the support of council schools only, and what steps he proposed to take'.

[2] Eluned E. Owen, op. cit.

[3] Ibid., p. 50, ff. *Daily News*, 27 April 1904 'The Coercion of Wales Bill', and known in Wales as *Y Mesur Gormes*.

Carmarthen to stiffen up the county councillors, and Nicholas had been inundated with letters, memoranda and resolutions from sources like the Union of Welsh Independents, their monthly and quarterly meetings, together with similar propaganda from the Baptists and Methodists. They called upon the county council 'to unite with the other Welsh councils to establish a national system of education based on the conditions laid down by Lloyd George at Cardiff'.[1]

The streets of Carmarthen were crowded with people from all over the county. They filled the Guildhall, sat among the council members and caused considerable uproar when Professor D. E. Jones, of the Presbyterian College, chairman of the education committee, had, at the end of his report proposed the rejection of Rev. Johns's motion. He was seconded by Mr. Gwilym Evans of Llanelli. A great deal of commotion was caused until Rev. Johns silenced the meeting and proposed that the education committee's report be adopted with the exception of his motion. At this point, Dr. R. L. Thomas, St. Clears and Lord Cawdor were in a heated argument as to whether the education committee's report should be adopted or rejected, but Mr. John Lloyd, Penybanc asked, as a way out of the difficulty that the full council should now consider a proposal by the Rev. William Thomas, Whitland (which had already been discussed that morning by the Liberal councillors) 'that this council decline for the present to apply any rates to the support of schools which are not provided by or are not under the full control of the council'. When the chairman, Mr. Gwynne Hughes, was about to put this to the meeting, Lord Cawdor again spoke threateningly but was immediately shouted down. The council rejected the report of the education committee and adopted the Rev. Thomas's proposal by thirty-eight votes to thirteen and a large number of the education committee who had rejected Rev. Johns's motion now voted for this. The Rev. J. Towyn Jones thanked the council on behalf of the many large Nonconformist deputations that were congregated outside the Guildhall.[2]

Subsequent events showed how Carmarthenshire prosecuted its policy of non-interference with voluntary schools. On 28 July, Nicholas wrote to the Local Government Board stating that a resolution had been passed by his council 'declining for the present to apply any rates to the support of schools which are not provided by or are not under the full control of the council'. He went on to say that in Carmarthenshire there were a large

---

[1] PRO Ed 24/578, *The Educational Situation in Wales*, op. cit. p. 3. Also, *Y Tyst*, 29 July 1903; *Seren Cymru*, 29 July 1903.
[2] *Y Tyst*, ibid.

The Carmarthenshire Inquiry

number of parishes that contained only voluntary schools and that the rate for elementary education purposes in the county would be 8*d*. The council proposed levying this rate only upon the parishes served by council schools. But Nicholas advised that in his opinion the rate for elementary education purposes 'forming as it does, part of the county rate, must be levied upon all the parishes of the county, except parishes that form part of an autonomous area under Part III of the Act'. He requested 'a decision upon this question as the matter was urgent and important'.[1] In reply, the Local Government Board said that they were 'not aware of any statutory or other authority empowering the county council of Carmarthenshire to exempt from county contributions levied by them to meet their expenses as a local education authority in the execution of Part III of the Education Act, 1902, any parish within the area for which they act, which is not served by a public elementary school provided by the council or transferred to them from a school board'. Furthermore, Nicholas was informed 'that Section 7 of the Act imposed on the local education authority the duty of maintaining and of keeping efficient all public elementary schools within their area which are necessary'.[2]

On 13 August the education committee recommended the raising of a loan to be applied only to provided (council) schools, and on the 16 September this recommendation was adopted by the county council who resolved (a) that nothing should be borrowed for voluntary schools, and (b) that no managers be appointed for such schools.[3] During the same month, and as the appointed day drew nearer, Col. Lewes once more wrote to the Board of Education asking what could be done to treat all schools alike, and another perplexed county magistrate, Charles P. Lewis, of Llandingat, Llandovery, also wrote asking that the Board should enlighten magistrates as to their powers and duties under the 1902 Act, and at the same time expressed his disapproval of the proposed illegal treatment of voluntary schools in the county. His particular problem concerned his position as a magistrate, for at the Court of Petty Sessions he would be asked by the Overseers of the parishes 'to sign the Rate Book for the Poor Rates which would include this particular school rate which is intended to support one class of schools only ... We, as magistrates, are sworn to carry out the law and to make rates according to that law, but I am not aware that there is any case on record where magistrates have ever been asked *to sign and legalise an illegal rate*'. He wanted to

---

[1] PRO Ed 111/252, Nicholas to Local Government Board, 28 July, 1903.
[2] PRO Ed 111/252, Kershaw (Local Government Board) to Nicholas; Kershaw to Board of Education, 10 August; copy seen by Mayor, Schuster and Lindsell.
[3] PRO Ed 24/578, *The Educational Situation in Wales*, op. cit.

know: (a) whether the Overseers have not the right to refuse to apply for a rate, a portion of which they know, or in any case ought to know is illegal; (b) whether we, as magistrates, have not the power to refuse to sign such a rate, which we know on the face of it to be illegal and made not according to the provisions of the Act; and (c) whether, if we have such power, we would not be absolutely justified in refusing to sign such a rate, as by so doing, we would be directly and knowingly conniving at, and assisting the county council to carry out a resolution and to levy a rate which the members, or rather, the majority of them must know is in direct contravention thereof.[1]

In reply to Lewes, the Board of Education gave him the same answer that they gave in July to Lord Braybrooke regarding a similar situation with the Cambridgeshire county council.[2] It was to the effect that the Board could not undertake to correspond with individual members of a local education authority as regards the possible consequences of a course of action which might be contemplated by that authority, but would give careful consideration to any representation that might be made to them to the effect that the local education authority had failed in a particular case to fulfil any of their duties under the Elementary Education Acts, 1870 to 1900 or the Education Act, 1902.[3] A similar answer was sent to Charles P. Lewis with the addition that 'the Board of Education had no authority to answer the questions raised in his letter'.[4]

Pursuing its policy of non-interference with voluntary schools, the county council resolved on 28 October 'that during the current quarter so much grant only shall be paid to each voluntary school as is received from the Board of Education in respect of such school'.[5] During September, Nicholas was writing constantly to Bishop Owen deploring the illegal actions of his council 'who seemed resolved to do nothing unless pulled up by the Board of Education ... I might be able to pay salaries for three months but no longer. Assuming I was permitted to administer the new Aid Grant as I thought fit, I might possibly be able to postpone a crisis until March, 1904 and possibly later'.[6] Again, on 29 October he had only

---

[1] PRO Ed 111/252, Lewes to Board of Education, 5 September; Charles P. Lewis to Board of Education 22 September.

[2] Ibid., Minute from Mayor to Lindsell and from Lindsell to Mayor, 8 September. On 30 July, 1903, Cambridgeshire county council had passed a similar resolution to Carmarthenshire. Cambridgeshire had 106 voluntary schools and 29 council schools, and A. Macmorran, K.C., had opined that that county council's action was illegal.

[3] PRO Ed 111/252, Minute and draft letter from Mayor to Lindsell for Lewes, 7 September.

[4] Ibid., Minute from Mayor to Reid, 28 September. Minute and draft letter from Mayor to Mackail for Charles P. Lewis, 29 September.

[5] Ibid., Nicholas to Board of Education, 13 November.

[6] Eluned E. Owen, op. cit.,

bad news to report, 'I am to give the voluntary schools only the grants in instalments of grants as received'.[1]

Morant, of course, was kept well-informed of developments in the county by the Bishop, and promised to expedite the payments of the Aid Grant as soon as they became due in order to lessen any embarrassment to the voluntary schools. But in accordance with the resolution of 28 October, no money except parliamentary grants was sent to the voluntary schools; no notice was taken of their requests for information, for example, as to the appointment of teachers, teachers' salaries, or other demands for coal, or money for school materials—beyond a letter from the county clerk conveying the last resolution and saying that all grants would be forwarded to managers as soon as the council received them from Whitehall. Apart from this 'the council declines to interfere with the management of the voluntary schools within its area'.[2] Numerous complaints came to the Board of Education from the managers of voluntary schools and in every case the Board wrote to the council asking what steps were being taken to maintain and keep efficient the following voluntary schools in the county: Newcastle Emlyn, Laugharne, Llanfynydd, Llanedi, Tycroes, Old Llanedi, Hendy, Llanybri, Llandefeilog[3] and Llanllwni.[4] All Nicholas could do was to refer the Board to the resolution, adding that 'the grants only are being forwarded to each voluntary school as received'.[5]

But the Board of Education, although ever watchful of the worsening situation, were, even at this juncture, cautious enough to maintain a rational attitude towards the actions of the county council. Morant had by this time issued definite instructions that from now on (since the Correspondent of the voluntary school at Cenarth had sent in another complaint) all further complaints should be referred to him and kept in a special 'Preferential Treatment' file.[6] Another letter from the Ferryside National School showed that the school was just able to carry on its work efficiently in spite of the attitude of the county council.[7] The position to date was, that from the appointed day to the beginning of December, most of the voluntary schools—provided the parliamentary grant was paid on time—were just able to manage, even though they had to do

---

[1] Ibid.
[2] PRO Ed 24/578, op. cit.
[3] PRO Ed 111/252, Carmarthenshire County Council to Board of Education, 15 November.
[4] Ibid., Minute from Schuster to Norris, 7 December.
[5] Ibid., Carmarthenshire county council to Board of Education, ibid. supra.
[6] PRO Ed 111/252, Note to Mayor with previous correspondence re Preferential Treatment in temporary file.
[7] Ibid., Minute from Mayor to Lindsell and Mackail, 19 November.

The Carmarthenshire Inquiry

so on a shoe-string. The Board were prepared to wait a little longer until more complaints arrived, or the position of some school became untenable, or an unfavourable report was sent by HM Inspector that there had been a definite failure to maintain and keep efficient. But there was undoubtedly some activity abroad in the legal department of the Board, for Mayor had suggested that the Law Officers might just as well furnish their opinion and said that 'until that is received I do not think anything would be gained by writing further to the Carmarthenshire local education authority'.[1]

The Board were very concerned about the financial straits of the voluntary schools and were anxious to make matters as easy as possible, e.g. in the payment of grants as soon as they fell due. Upon Anson's direction, letters were written to the nine schools which had lodged complaints with the Board, asking (a) for statements showing the amount of money received by the managers from the county council, (b) the estimated expenditure for school purposes during the six months from 30 September 1903 to 1 April 1904. The estimate should set out full details of the anticipated charges, distinguishing, in the case of teachers' salaries, the actual dates on which the instalments would fall due.[2] The Board conducted a survey of all the voluntary schools in Carmarthenshire, calculated the amounts already paid to the county council and made a statement of amounts payable before 20 April.[3] Furthermore HM Inspector in each case was circulated and directed to visit every voluntary school in order to ascertain (a) whether the school was still being conducted, (b) whether there were any indications of failing efficiency owing to lack of funds, and (c) whether in the Inspector's opinion the school was being maintained in efficiency. The Inspectors were to be particularly careful about their work and were informed by the Board that 'the visit should be paid as an ordinary visit, without notice; great care was to be taken to divest it of any special character; and, though complaints either from managers or teachers should be carefully noted, they should not be invited'. Finally, the Inspectors were told that their reports would be treated as confidential 'at any rate until the Board have made a further communication to you on the subject'.[4] Lindsell remarked that he agreed with all this procedure but doubted if they should get anything tangible *to act upon as yet*. It seemed to him, however, 'that the payments of the grants to managers, without obtaining vouchers as to their expenditure

[1] Ibid.
[2] Ibid., Minute from Schuster to Lindsell, 4 December.
[3] Ibid., Minute from Schuster to Sheppard, 5 December.
[4] PRO Ed 111/252, Minute from Schuster to HM Inspectors, 7 December.

The Carmarthenshire Inquiry

will land the local education authority in serious difficulties with the auditors'.[1] Lindsell was obviously unaware that the county council Treasurer was in fact most meticulous in the matter of getting receipts from every voluntary school when a grant was paid.

In the meantime, however, the plight of the voluntary schools was becoming worse. In some schools new teachers were required but the council refused to consent to their appointment. No representative managers had been appointed and no demands were made by the council for the repair and improvement of school buildings although all the voluntary schools had been surveyed during the autumn by an architect, and his report circulated to members of the county council. By the end of December many schools were in difficulties in one way or another—teachers' salaries in arrears and school materials in short supply or not forthcoming. In so far as this had not been the case in any particular school, it was probably due to managers and other supporters having voluntarily taken upon themselves the burdens of maintenance. The parliamentary grants under the 1902 Act were, in Carmarthenshire, practically equivalent to the amount spent on voluntary schools in the last respective school years under the old system (before the appointed day) upon that part of school maintenance for which the local education authority would in future be responsible.[2] But owing, no doubt, to the facts that (a) parliamentary grants were paid over by the local education authority at too wide intervals of time to enable the managers to meet liabilities such as teachers' salaries which accrued monthly; (b) while some schools gained upon the calculation mentioned, and the aggregate amounts were nearly equivalent, a large number lost (23 gained, 37 lost); (c) many of the schools had been in recent years practising the most rigid economies and had needed increased maintenance and the observance of a higher standard of efficiency, the general result was that the majority of the voluntary schools were not being efficiently maintained by the county council.[3]

At this point in the narrative, an interesting episode appears in the Board of Education correspondence. It involved the Dynevor Castle estate, Lord Dynevor and the county council. On 21 December, Lewis Bishop, solicitor, of Llandeilo—Lord Dynevor's estate agent—wrote to Lord Londonderry, President of the Board, to the effect that the county council required a site for a new council school on the Castle estate.

[1] Ibid., Minute from Lindsell to Schuster, 5 December.
[2] PRO Ed 24/578, op. cit., p. 4.
[3] Ibid.

The Carmarthenshire Inquiry

Bishop pointed out that the county council had refused to levy a rate or apply any portion of the rates being levied, towards the support of the voluntary schools in that county. He went on to say that 'the council now require a site for a new school and have applied to Lord Dynevor, and on his behalf I have refused to supply such site—and no other landowner has any available site. I stated that my reason for so doing is that the council are not carrying out the 1902 Act. The council now threaten, under the Lands Clauses Acts to compel Lord Dynevor to sell a site. His Lordship considers it will be a great hardship on the ratepayers who are supporters of voluntary schools and receive no benefit under the Act, if he assists in further encumbering the rates by the erection of a new school. And trusts your Lordship will kindly advise whether or no Lord Dynevor can be compelled, under the circumstances, to provide a site for such proposed new school'.[1]

Understandably, the letter caused a flutter at the Board and was studied by the chief officials, including Morant, who instructed Lindsell to prepare a brief memorandum for consideration by the President.[2] The Board requested further information before the letter could be answered. They asked Bishop (a) in what locality the local education authority proposed to build the new school, and for what area was there a numerical deficiency of school accommodation; (b) had the local education authority (under sub-section (1) of section 8 of the Education Act, 1902) given public notice of their intention to provide a new school; (c) had the local education authority, in accordance with section 70 (2) (a) and (b) of the Elementary Education Act of 1870, published or served notices for the purpose of putting into force the provisions of the Lands Clauses Act, and if any of these notices had been published, the Board required copies of them.[3] In his reply, Bishop informed the Board that the new school was intended for deficiency of accommodation in the urban district of Ammanford (formerly part of the Llandybie School District) but no public notice had been given nor notices of intent to enforce the provisions of the Lands Clauses Act had been issued.[4]

But the officials of the Board of Education, were, by a strange circumstance, hoist with their own petard. There was really no reason why Bishop's initial letter should have produced such an impact on the Board were it not for the fact that Carmarthenshire was by this time embarked

---

[1] PRO Ed 111/252, Bishop to President, Board of Education, 21 December.
[2] Ibid., Letter passed to Norris, Lindsell and Morant, 22 December. Minute from Morant to Lindsell, 23 December.
[3] Ibid., Minute and draft letter from Hills to Lindsell, 6 January 1904; letter sent 9 January.
[4] Ibid., Bishop to Board of Education, 23 January.

The Carmarthenshire Inquiry

upon a policy of illegality. The Board's officials had, unfortunately, overlooked or forgotten an earlier move on their part. Almost two years earlier, the Board had taken the initiative in the matter of providing a new school for an area which was, before 30 September 1903, part of the Llandybie United District School Board. In December 1903 the Dynevor situation was an embarrassment to the Board because of the no-rate policy of the county council.[1] In fact, on 1 February 1902, the Board of Education had written to the Llandybie School Board pressing them to provide more school accommodation, and on 8 August had sanctioned the use of Ebenezer vestry at Ammanford as a temporary measure for one year. On 16 September, the Board of Education was asked by the Clerk of the School Board to extend the use of the vestry, for 'the Llandybie School Board are in treaty for the purchase of a site for a new school at Ammanford, *and it is hoped that the new local education authority* (i.e. the Carmarthenshire county council) will be able to proceed with its erection very shortly'.[2] The Board of Education, replying on the 26 September, consented to the use of the vestry for a further period of one year 'from the date of this letter' and requested a site-plan of the new school 'without delay, for approval'.[3]

The Board of Education were now clarifying their position. Hills explained that 'as the local education authority have not, to judge from Mr. Bishop's second letter, complied with the provisions of section 20 (2) (a) of the Elementary Education Act, 1870, they cannot, in any case, obtain a provisional order during the current year. We may hope *that before next year the local education authority may be carrying out its obligations under the Act of* 1902'. Hills added that 'at the same time, in view of the fact that the Board of Education have recognised the necessity for more school accommodation, it scarcely appears possible that they should at any time exercise their discretion to refuse to make a provisional order on the grounds suggested by Mr. Bishop'.[4] Considering the sort of reply that should be sent to Bishop, the Board of Education made a clean breast of its past action in initiating the new school. At the same time, in spite of the attitude of Carmarthenshire to the Act of 1902, they wrote: 'In reply to your letter of 21 December, I am directed to point out that if the county council have not complied with the provisions of section 20 (2) (a) of the Elementary Education Act, 1870, it will not be possible for them to take any action with a view to putting into force the

---
[1] PRO Ed 111/252, Minute from Hills to Lindsell and Morant, 9 February, 1904.
[2] Ibid., Minute from Lindsell to Hills, 10 February.
[3] Ibid.
[4] Ibid.

provisions of the Lands Clauses Acts, until, at the earliest, October of this year. Under the circumstances, therefore, it does not appear necessary for the Board to express an opinion upon the merits of the objection which Lord Dynevor takes to the exercise by the county council of compulsory powers under the said Acts. I am, however, to add that the Board have for some time past been urging upon the late School Board the desirability of providing increased school accommodation in Ammanford urban district'.[1]

Before being sent off on 18 February the letter had to be approved by Morant, Anson and Londonderry. Morant, in a Minute to Anson was obviously pro-Dynevor: 'Would you kindly advise the President on this matter. It is no doubt singularly aggravating to a landowner to be threatened that his land will be compulsorily taken from him by an authority which is failing to administer the law in its integrity. Fortunately, this will not be the case during the present year. I do not see that we can answer in any other manner than that proposed by Mr. Hills as amended by Mr. Lindsell'.[2] Anson accepted the situation nonchalantly, was thankful that time was on their side, and told Londonderry 'If we have, for some time past, continued to urge the late School Board of this District to provide fresh school accommodation, I do not see how we can refuse, when the time comes, to render an order under section 20 (5) of the Act of 1870, in favour of the new local education authority. The requirements of that section, and of section 8 of the Act of 1902, will have to be satisfied, so that the matter will not come before us for 10 months. By that time we may hope that the local education authority may be doing its duty by all its schools'.[3] Londonderry, hoping that time would be on his side, made the brief comment—'I think the proposed answer should meet the question for the present'.[4]

To return to the situation of the voluntary schools in December 1903. It has already been seen that the managers of many schools had drawn the attention of the Board of Education to the attitude adopted by the council with regard to the fulfilment of their duties under the 1902 Act. At this stage, the Board were also concerned about the legality of certain methods of payment to such schools in Glamorgan and Carmarthenshire.

---

[1] Ibid., Draft letter from Hills to Bishop, 9 February, sent on 17 February. The original draft of the last paragraph of this letter ran: 'I am, however, to state that, subject to any further consideration which might arise at the time, the Board have grave doubts whether they would be justified in refusing assistance to the local education authority in the measures they are taking to provide school accommodation in Ammanford urban district upon the grounds suggested in your letter of 23 January'. R. P. Hills, amended by Lindsell.

[2] PRO Ed 111/252, Minute from Morant to Anson, 11 February.

[3] Ibid., Minute from Anson to Londonderry, 13 February.

[4] Ibid., Minute from Londonderry to Anson, 15 February.

The Carmarthenshire Inquiry

Schuster had prepared a long statement on this question. It was pointed out that in the case of Glamorgan the county clerk had addressed a letter to the managers of voluntary schools explaining at length their duties with regard to repairs and improvements, which the council—as a result of their architect's report—deemed necessary under section 7 (1) (d) of the 1902 Act.[1] It also detailed the manner in which the grant would be paid to the managers: 'subject to the remedy of the deficiencies of school premises, the council will, during the remainder of the financial year ending on 31 March 1904, provide as a fund for school requisites, one-half of the total amount applied in your school for such purposes during the last year of which the accounts were reported by you to the county council ... and with regard to section 18 (5) of the Act, managers should keep proper accounts of the money and preserve all vouchers relating thereto for production at audit ... with regard to the payment of teachers, the council intends for the present to pay monthly one-twelfth of the fixed salaries paid them on 30 September 1902, by cheque direct from the county offices'.[2]

In the case of Carmarthenshire, the county council announced their intention of handing over to the managers of each school the amount received in parliamentary grants on account of that school. In a specific case which was brought to the notice of the Board, this intention was intimated in the following terms[3]: 'I am directed to convey to you the following resolution which was passed by this council on 28 October:— "that during the current quarter so much grant only shall be paid to each voluntary school as is received from the Board of Education in respect of such school". In accordance therewith, I beg to inform you that I shall forward to you on behalf of your managers all grants or instalments of grants as soon as received by this council from the Board of Education. Beyond this, the council declines to interfere with the management of the voluntary schools within its area'. In accordance apparently with the intention stated in the above letter, the following letter was sent by the County Treasurer to the Correspondent of the school:

---

[1] 'The managers of the school shall provide the school house free of charge except for the teacher's dwelling-house, if any, to the local education authority for use as a public elementary school and shall out of funds provided by them, keep the school house in good repair, and make such alterations and improvements in the buildings as may be reasonably required by the local education authority'.

[2] PRO Ed 111/252, Minute from Schuster to Lindsell and Norris, 7 December. Section 18 (5) of the Act of 1902 stated: Where any receipts or payments of money under this Act are entrusted by the local education authority to any education committee established under this Act or to the managers of any public elementary school, the accounts of those receipts and payments shall be accounts of the local education authority, but the auditor of those accounts shall have the same powers with respect to managers as he would have if the managers were officers of the local education authority'.

[3] PRO Ed ibid. supra.

The Carmarthenshire Inquiry

County Treasurer's Office
Shire Hall
Carmarthen
13 November 1903

Dear Sir,
Herewith please find cheque value £41, being the amount of grants received from the Treasury on account of St. Thomas's Ferryside school from the 30 September to the 6 November 1903 inclusive. Please return me the enclosed form of receipt duly stamped and receipted by first post.

Yours faithfully,
R. Peel Price.

The following was the form of receipt:

Non-Provided School, No. 151.
Received this.................. day of.. 1903 from the Treasurer of the Carmarthenshire County Council the sum of forty one pounds (£41) being the amount of grant received from the Treasury on account of St. Thomas's Ferryside National School from the 30 September to the 6 November, 1903, inclusive.

Schuster included these details which were to be incorporated in a letter from the Board of Education to the Local Government Board, with the request that the latter Board should advise the Board of Education as to the legality of such methods of payments as those contemplated in the Glamorgan case and those actually carried out in the Carmarthenshire case, with special regard to the provisions of section 18 (5) of the Education Act, 1902. The Board of Education also desired an opinion on the view which would be adopted by the District Auditor with respect to such cases.[1] Lindsell had some pertinent remarks to make on Schuster's letter. It seemed to Lindsell that the Glamorgan county council had made no such distinct announcement of their intention to break the law as the Carmarthenshire county council had done. The line which Glamorgan proposed to adopt seemed rather obscure, but so far as he could see, did not amount to a pronouncement that they would limit their payments to the grants earned by the school, to the exclusion of any assistance from the rates. Carmarthenshire, on the other hand, had made a distinct declaration of proceeding in an illegal manner, i.e. of merely transmitting the grants to the managers, and refusing to have anything to do with the control or the maintenance of the school.[2] Nevertheless, the reply received from the Local Government Board was rather surprising, 'with reference to the method of making payments to the managers of voluntary schools

---

[1] PRO Ed 111/252, Draft letter from Board of Education to Local Government Board, 7 December. Final draft seen and approved by Anson, 12 December.
[2] Ibid., Minute from Lindsell to Schuster, 10 December.

The Carmarthenshire Inquiry

proposed to be adopted by the county councils of Glamorgan and Carmarthenshire, as at present advised, it does not seem to the Board to be likely that the proceedings indicated in your letter would give the District Auditor an opportunity for intervention'.[1]

On 1 February, Anson had settled the draft of an important and comprehensive letter to be sent to Carmarthenshire county council.[2] Since the middle of November, 1903, in addition to those voluntary schools, already mentioned earlier, which had complained to the Board of Education, Anson stated that 'he was directed by the Board of Education to call the attention of your Council to the letters addressed respectively by the Board to your Council with regard to the following voluntary schools: Cil-y-cwm, Tremoilet, Golden Grove, Cwm Amman, Llanddowror, Rhandirmwyn, Llangennech, Llanllwni, Mothfai (Myddfai), Pembrey and St. Clears'. Anson also referred to the county council's letter addressed to the Board on 13 November and to the letters of complaint from the other nine voluntary schools. In addition to all these schools, other letters were coming to the Board almost daily, the more recent ones being from Ferryside, Llansaint and Llanddeusant. Then followed the full blast of official accusations against the Carmarthenshire county council. Anson, on behalf of the Board of Education, maintained that it appeared from the above correspondence that the county council had in many cases refused or failed (a) to provide voluntary schools with fuel and other articles necessary for their maintenance, or to pay teachers' salaries as they fell due, or to furnish money sufficient for these purposes; (b) to give managers of voluntary schools necessary directions for carrying on the secular instruction under the control of the council; (c) to appoint a person to represent the council on the body of managers of a voluntary school. The Board observed that such conduct would violate the provisions of sections 6 (2) and 7 (1) of the Education Act, 1902, and would constitute a very serious situation. Anson requested that the county council should give earnest consideration to the subject of his letter and desired an early answer to the Board. Finally, he regretted that the Board of Education 'must now contemplate the necessity of an inquiry into the matters complained of'.[3]

Nicholas placed this letter before the Carmarthenshire county council at their meeting on 5 February. The council, unimpressed and undeterred, resolved 'that the letter from the Board of Education, dated 1 February,

---

[1] Ibid., Local Government Board to Board of Education, 21 December.
[2] Ibid., Minute from Hills to Norris, 1 February, 1904.
[3] PRO Ed 111/252, Board of Education to Carmarthenshire county council, 1 February.

The Carmarthenshire Inquiry

1904, be laid on the table until after the county council elections'.[1] Col. Lewes, on behalf of the county Conservative and Liberal Unionist Association, sent a message to the Board of Education 'that the Association passed the following resolution unanimously at their meeting held at Carmarthen on 20 February, "this meeting fervently hopes that action and prompt measures be taken to prevent the illegal resistance to the Education Act now offered by the Welsh County and District Councils" '.[2]

The Board of Education had no alternative but to set in motion the machinery necessary for an inquiry. Two letters were written, one to the Carmarthenshire county council stating that the Board had decided 'to shortly hold a Public Inquiry into the matters alluded to in their letter of 1 February. Formal notice of the inquiry containing particulars of the date and place will be sent at an early date'. The second letter, sent to the Rev. Charles Gilbert Brown, Principal of Trinity College, Carmarthen, and hon. sec. of the St. Davids Diocesan Association of Schools, referred to complaints made to the Board of Education of the failure 'of the local education authority of the administrative county of Carmarthenshire' to fulfil certain of their duties under the Education Act of 1902, towards voluntary schools, and the Board desired to inform him that a public inquiry would be held, and formal notice of such inquiry and the date and place thereof would be sent to his Association as soon as possible.[3]

The National Society were not slow to associate themselves with the action of the Board of Education. On 5 March, Canon Brownrigg, the secretary, wrote to the Board saying that he had observed in the newspapers of the proposed Inquiry in Carmarthenshire, and since (a) the great majority of the non-provided schools in the county were in union with the National Society, the Society would like to be represented at the Inquiry, (b) the Society had already been in communication with all the voluntary schools, and at the request of the managers were taking all steps to ensure that the case of the voluntary schools would be fully represented, he requested the Board of Education to furnish the Society with a formal notice of the Inquiry, copies of any correspondence between the Board, the local education authority and the schools, and a statement showing what grants due to voluntary schools had been paid to the local education authority during the half-year ended 31 March, 1904.[4] The Board replied on 8 March enclosing all the information asked for.[5]

[1] Ibid., Carmarthenshire county council to Board of Education, 5 February.
[2] Ibid., Lewes to Board of Education, 22 February.
[3] Ibid., Minute from Hills to Lindsell and Poores, 26 February.
[4] PRO Ed 111/252, National Society to Board of Education, 5 March.
[5] Ibid., Board of Education to National Society, 8 March. Minute from Hills to Lindsell, 8 March. Minute from Hills to Norris and Poores, 9 and 15 March.

II WELSH COUNTY POLICIES

For the purposes of the Education Act, 1902, the council of every county and of every county borough became the local education authority: 'provided that the council of a borough with a population of over 10,000 or of an urban district with a population of over 20,000, shall as respects that borough or district, be the local education authority for the purpose of Part III of the Act, and for that purpose as respects that borough or district, the expression "local education authority" means the council of that borough or district'.[1] Part III of the Act dealt with elementary education: 'the local education authority shall throughout their area have the powers and duties of a school board and school attendance committee under the Elementary Education Acts 1870 to 1900 and any other Acts including local Acts, *and shall also be responsible for and have the control of all secular instruction in public elementary schools not provided by them*, and school boards and attendance committees shall be abolished'.[2] All public elementary schools not provided by the local education authority shall, in place of the existing managers, have a body of managers consisting of a number of foundation managers not exceeding four appointed as provided by this Act.[3]

The Act of 1902 further stated that '*the local education authority shall maintain and keep efficient all public elementary schools within their area which are necessary and have the control of all expenditure required for that purpose*, other than expenditure for which, under the Act, provision is to be made by the managers; but in the case of a school *not provided by them*, only so long as the following conditions and provisions are complied with (a) managers to obey the local education authority as to secular instruction, (b) the local education authority shall have power to inspect the school, (c) the consent of the local education authority shall be required to appoint teachers and pupil teachers, and (d) managers were to be responsible for school improvements and repairs, etc.'[4] There were other stipulations referred to by Schuster in his case for the Board of Education.[5] The conditions contained in Part III have already arisen and have an intimate connection with the attitude of the Welsh LEAs towards the working of the 1902 Act after the 'appointed day', which, for many of them was 30 September 1903.

---

[1] 2 Edw. 7, c. 42. *An Act to make further provision with respect to Education in England and Wales*, 18 *December*, 1902, Part I (1). The italicized words are relevant to the theme of this study.

[2] Ibid., Part III, Section 5.

[3] Ibid., Part III, Section 6 (2).

[4] 1902 *Education Act*, op. cit., Part III, Section 7 (1), (a) to (d).

[5] The details included here are for the convenience of those readers who do not wish to be bothered to refer to the actual texts of Education Acts.

The Carmarthenshire Inquiry

The Welsh opposition to the implementation of Part III of the Education Act hinged on the fact that the distinction between Board and Voluntary schools disappeared, and henceforth, apart from the parliamentary grants, all schools were to be financed from the rates. It has already been shown that Carmarthenshire had made its position quite clear in October 1902, before the passing of the Act, that it would not operate the Act unless the Bill then before Parliament provided full public control over all rate-aided schools. The failure of the Act to do this determined the future actions of the county council—nothing less than a rigid discrimination between council and voluntary schools.

Lloyd George was the central figure of Welsh opposition to the Act. Between January and May 1903, the crucial months after the passing of the Act, he was devising ways and means of frustrating and embarrassing the government to implement it in Wales. By the end of December 1902, eleven Welsh county councils had passed 'no rate' resolutions, and declared that they would not administer the Act. But Lloyd George, in his manifesto of 17 January 1903 declared that 'refusal to administer the Act would neglect the great opportunity afforded by Sir Alfred Thomas's sub-clause. The Education Act should be operated, but on certain important conditions. Voluntary schools should be brought under public control, religious tests for pupil teachers should be abolished, and the "Colonial Compromise" should be offered over denominational instruction. Only if these terms were refused, should Nonconformists refuse to pay rates'.[1]

It would only be fair to say that Lloyd George, and surprisingly enough, 'his greatest adversary, the Bishop of St. Asaph' made two honest attempts to reconcile popular control with religious education in the form of a compromise or concordat, but both schemes failed.[2] Before the county council elections in March 1904, Lloyd George and other Welsh members of parliament campaigned throughout Wales invoking opposition to the Act, and 'the results were brilliantly successful . . . in place of 543 Progressives and 252 Sectarians, the thirteen Welsh councils now comprised 639 Progressives and 157 Sectarians. The Liberal triumph was complete and overwhelming . . . and from now on the real conflict began between the Board of Education and the Welsh county councils'.[3]

---

[1] Kenneth O. Morgan, op. cit., p. 187, ff., p. 186: 'It was Lloyd George who inspired a significant amendment concerning Wales, when on 12 November 1902, at his instigation, Sir Alfred Thomas, Chairman of the Welsh Party, moved to transfer the powers of the local authorities in Wales under the 1889 Act to the new LEAs constituted under Balfour's Bill. By using the county councils, Lloyd George had a powerful weapon to operate his opposition to the 1902 Act'.

[2] Herbert Lewis's Diary, 3 February, 1903, Penucha MSS. PRO Ed 24/576, *Confidential Memorandum on Proposals towards an Interim Concordat in Wales*, 28 January 1904.

[3] Kenneth O. Morgan, op. cit., p. 191. Also, Herbert Lewis's Diary, 24 February; 11 March, 1904; Lewis to Morant, 11 March, 1904; Morant to Lewis, 13 March, 1904; Lloyd George to Lewis, 16 March, 1904, Penucha MSS.

The Carmarthenshire Inquiry

To return to the situation in 1903, Lloyd George's conditions for the operation of the Act were ignored by the government. The genesis and progress of the 'no rate' movement in Wales—quite different from the passive resistance movement in England—showed that the Principality was determined to follow a course peculiar to itself owing to the Welsh device of declining to hand over to the managers of voluntary schools any money beyond the ordinary parliamentary grants. The ostensible policy of the Welsh Party, through the county councils, was to use all the powers in the Act to make the position of the voluntary school manager untenable and worthless, while at the same time *refusing to spend any money from the rates* on voluntary schools.[1] In other words, the Welsh Party asserted that the parliamentary grants were sufficient for the needs of voluntary schools.

The policies of the Welsh county councils in administering the Act under these terms varied considerably. In January 1904, Anson called for a survey of the conditions and degrees of implementation of the Act in Wales,[2] (revised in June, after the Carmarthenshire Inquiry and the introduction of the Default Bill).[3] It was revealed that of the 29 local education authorities in Wales (Bangor borough having relinquished its powers to Caernarvonshire county council) the Act was in operation among 17. Carmarthenshire had 62 voluntary schools and the appointed day was 30 September 1903. This authority was hostile both in motive and results. A 'no rate' resolution was passed in July 1903 and a 'grant only' resolution on 28 October. In accordance with this last resolution, no money was sent to voluntary schools except the grants from Whitehall, no notice was taken of their requests for information, requisitions for coal, or teachers' salaries, etc., except a letter from the county council conveying the 'no rate' resolution. The same sort of reply was sent to all protests and inquiries by the Board of Education.[4]

In Merioneth there were 27 voluntary schools, and the appointed day 30 September. This authority was hostile in practically the same way as

---

[1] PRO Ed 24/577, *Confidential Memorandum on the Defaulting Authorities Bill:* suggesting points which may be useful to justify this Bill now before Parliament, R. P. Hills to Morant, 25 June 1904. PRO Ed 23/218.49: Board of Education to the Treasury, 8 October 1904:—'Mr. R. P. Hills is one of the Barristers temporarily employed at the rate of one guinea a working day, in connection with the inauguration of the Education Act, 1902. Date of employment: 1 October 1904—11 April 1906. In normal conditions this rate of remuneration has proved to be adequate for this class of officer; but, owing to the difficulties that have arisen in certain localities (i.e. defaulting authorities, the majority of which were in Wales, but, there were some in England) in the administration of the Act, work of an exceptionally responsible kind has gradually devolved on Mr. Hills, and he can no longer be considered to be adequately compensated by payment on this scale. The work in question is of a special and delicate legal character, requiring the constant attention of one and the same officer, and it could not, without serious disadvantage be transferred to a member of the ordinary staff'. The Board recommended a higher rate of pay.

[2] PRO Ed 111/254, Minute to Anson on the State of Wales, 23 January, 1904.

[3] PRO Ed 24/578, op. cit.

[4] PRO Ed ibid. supra, Minute to Anson.

Carmarthenshire, passing a 'no rate' resolution on 4 June and reiterated on 3 December. In reply to all claims for payment of salaries and other maintenance costs by voluntary schools, the county council sent out a letter in the terms of the 'no rate' resolution. On 3 December the council resolved to pay the grants only. The replies of the council to the Board of Education were similar in character to their replies to the managers of voluntary schools. Glamorgan had 81 voluntary schools and the appointed day was 30 September. The council were hostile in motive and, to a certain extent, in results.[1] They pretended to pay over sums that were required for school requisites and also teachers' salaries, but (a) they apparently refused the sums for school requisites in the case of those schools whose managers did not give an undertaking from some responsible person that the sum sent should be spread over the six winter months, and that no further sum should be asked for from the council; (b) the teachers' salaries were paid direct to the teachers, and assessed on the old basis of 1902; the council refused to give consent to the appointment of teachers, or any information about the maintenance of voluntary schools.[2]

The situation in Caernarvonshire was rather different, due no doubt to the influence of Lloyd George who had urged the county council not to display any untoward or outward signs of evasion nor pursue any action of outright illegality. Although this authority had not passed a 'no rate' resolution this did not mean that it was non-hostile. It was Lloyd George's intention (as he had hoped all other councils would do) that Caernarvonshire should pretend to behave with strict legality, and maintained that voluntary schools could be kept efficient out of parliamentary grants alone. It appeared, from the information available, that the council paid the teachers' salaries, and also provided for school requisites. But a resolution was passed on 17 December that no more salaries would be honoured until repairs ordered by the council's surveyor had been carried out by the managers. The council also resolved that they would not allow diocesan inspection or examination to be effected in voluntary schools except out of school hours. Private information also suggested that the Caernarvonshire policy was to pay salaries without regard to the sources from which the fund came, but this policy was never admitted publicly.[3]

Montgomery, Brecon and Radnor had 66, 45, and 40 voluntary schools respectively. The Montgomery policy was almost the same as that of

[1] PRO Ed 24/578, op. cit.: it was stated 'that the attitude of the Glamorgan Council was evasive and peculiar'.
[2] PRO Ed 24/578, op. cit.; 111/254, op. cit.
[3] PRO Ed 24/578, op. cit.

The Carmarthenshire Inquiry

Caernarvonshire. No complaints had arisen with regard to deficiency of salaries or school requisites although a 'no rate' resolution was passed on 20 October. But Brecon and Radnor were quite different—until the county council elections in March. They had passed no hostile resolutions and were amenable to the levying of rates for voluntary schools. But after the March elections, both counties went 'Progressive', became recalcitrant, and imitated Caernarvonshire. Building and repair demands were made on voluntary school managers, with the threat, that in default, all maintenance grants would be withheld.[1]

For the other Welsh counties, Anglesey, Denbigh, Flint, Cardigan, Pembroke and Monmouth, together with the borough of Newport, the county boroughs of Cardiff, and Swansea, and the urban district councils of Llanelli, Merthyr Tydfil and Abertillery, there was no information at this time (January). There remained the smaller or 'Part III authorities' such as the boroughs of Carmarthen, Pembroke, Neath and Wrexham, and the urban district councils of Mountain Ash, Pontypridd, Rhondda, Aberdare, Barry and Ebbw Vale. The case of Carmarthen borough was particularly interesting and strange, with three voluntary schools (the appointed day, 1 June 1903)—the administrative centre of the most hostile of Welsh county councils—and the town in which the Inquiry was held. This borough was non-hostile from the outset, gave rate-aid to all schools and administered the Act without discrimination against voluntary schools. There was no information at this time about Pembroke and Neath, apart from the fact that they had not passed a 'no rate' resolution, whilst Wrexham's position was almost the same as Aberdare. Mountain Ash, Pontypridd, Rhondda and Aberdare had passed 'no rate' resolutions and only helped the voluntary schools on certain conditions. In the case of Barry, a compromise was being arranged by which the council would have some hand in the appointment of teachers, but this compromise was not likely to be approved by the extreme party among the Nonconformists.[2]

So much for the policies of the individual Welsh authorities. Nationally, there were two distinct policies—Carmarthenshire and Caernarvonshire.

---

[1] Ibid.

[2] PRO Ed 24/578, op. cit.; 111/254, op. cit. At the end of June 1904, Denbighshire, appointed day, 1 June, 1904, was hostile; Anglesey, appointed day 1 June 1904, passed 'no rate' resolution, but no developments to this date. Newport borough and Flintshire passed 'no rate' resolutions and followed the Caernarvon policy. Pembrokeshire passed a 'no rate' resolution 3 November 1903 and was hostile. Monmouthshire passed a 'no rate' resolution and gave no rate aid to voluntary schools apart from £1,200 out of grants received from the Agricultural Rates Act. Cardiganshire was in a peculiar situation—it was operating Part II of the Act but had postponed Part III in order to avoid strife, but were hostile. The Act was not yet in operation among the Cardiff and Swansea county boroughs, but both were hostile.

The boroughs of Pembroke and Neath, and the urban district council of Abertillery were non-hostile. Merthyr Tydfil imitated Caernarvonshire and was hostile. Llanelli urban district council had passed a 'no rate' resolution in November 1903, the appointed day was 1 June 1904 but no developments as yet.

The Carmarthenshire Inquiry

The only common element in both policies was the refusal to give rate aid to voluntary schools. They employed the parliamentary grants only, for the maintenance of such schools. The Carmarthenshire policy was that which reached its extreme form in that county, when the council, after passing a 'no rate' resolution followed it up defiantly by adopting illegal resolutions, and withheld subsidies from voluntary schools until the grants were received from the government. In essence, the council disclaimed all responsibility for, and all control of voluntary schools, as we have seen earlier. Managers who wrote to the council asking what books they should use were told in effect that the council did not care. Teachers who wrote for their salaries were referred to the managers. The parliamentary grants were regarded as a separate fund earmarked for each voluntary school which earned them, and were handed over to that school when they came from Whitehall, without any directive as to how they were to be applied. The other authorities which pursued this policy, Merionethshire, Rhondda, Mountain Ash, and Pontypridd, were particularly anxious that they should incur no legal liability to teachers, lest they should be sued for salaries. They therefore did all they could to avoid any assumption of control or responsibility.[1]

In contrast with Carmarthenshire, Caernarvonshire and the other councils which emulated its policy, maintained strict control over voluntary schools from the outset, and the managers were completely ignored. The council took everything into its own hands, chose books, bought school requisites, advertised for, and appointed teachers, and fixed the teachers' salaries. The council corresponded directly with the teachers, who were informed that they were the servants of the local education authority and not the managers. On the financial side, all grants received from the government which were earned by the voluntary schools were pooled, and regarded as a common fund for their upkeep. The council also used their credit with tradesmen to supply goods and coal, and by means of bulk-buying could save an appreciable amount of money.[2]

The smaller local education authorities such as the boroughs of Carmarthen and Pembroke adopted a policy which could only be described as being clandestine. Such small ancient boroughs, were rarely enmeshed in violent regional or national political and religious upheavals. They were also less well off, were more tolerant in their attitude towards minority groups, coupled with a desire to await events, and less anxious

[1] PRO Ed 24/578, op. cit.
[2] PRO Ed 24/577, op. cit., p. 4.

to force any question to an issue. Carmarthen town almost unaffected by the heat of the March county council elections, went on quietly pursuing its policy of subsidizing any deficit that might arise from the pure parliamentary grants from the rates, without apparently incurring any displeasure from the local Nonconformists.

The Board of Education kept their hands strictly off Caernarvonshire, since no direct complaints of failure to maintain and keep efficient had come from that area, and the government were hearing and seeing more than enough of Lloyd George at this period, without over-indulging themselves in his constituency. But Carmarthenshire was a different proposition. The county council had landed itself in a situation which the Board of Education could no longer ignore, and consequently was selected as the clearest evidence of illegal behaviour which warranted a public inquiry.

III INSTITUTION OF THE INQUIRY

On 6 February 1904, Morant addressed a letter to the Secretary, HM Treasury, on behalf of the Board of Education, requesting that the Lords Commissioners of HM Treasury 'should instruct the solicitor of the Treasury to advise upon the procedure which this Board should take under section 16 of the Education Act, 1902, with a view to making, and ultimately enforcing an Order under that section. I am to request that the accompanying papers be submitted to the solicitor of the Treasury for that purpose',[1] This was done on 8 February[2] enclosing the correspondence between the Board of Education and the Carmarthenshire county council, regarding the council's treatment of voluntary schools, and also a copy of a long Minute to Anson on 'The state of Wales'.[3] On 17 February, a further letter[4] was sent to the Treasury, enclosing a copy of the letter received by the Board from the Carmarthenshire county council declaring 'that the letter received from the Board of Education dated 1 February, be laid on the table until after the county council elections'.[5] The following documents were also enclosed:

1. Copy of the Opinion of Sir Hugh Owen regarding the relations of the local education authority towards teachers employed in voluntary schools, dated 4 September 1903.[6]

---

[1] PRO Ed 111/254, Part IA, Morant to Treasury, 6 February.
[2] Ibid., G. H. Murray, Treasury Chambers to Treasury Solicitor, 8 February.
[3] PRO Ed 111/254, Minute to Anson, op. cit.
[4] Ibid., Board of Education to Treasury Solicitor, 17 February.
[5] PRO Ed 111/252, Carmarthenshire County Council to Board of Education, 5 February.
[6] PRO Ed 111/254, Index to Further Papers received from Board of Education, 17 February, p. 16.

The Carmarthenshire Inquiry

2. Copy of the Cambridgeshire Case and Opinion, dated 2 February 1904.[1]
3. Copy of the Case of the Board of Education, drawn up by Claude Schuster for consideration by the Law Officers of the Crown and their Opinion, dated 16 November 1903.[2]
4. Copy of the Case of the National Society and Opinion, dated 12 December 1903.[3]

The production of these legal documents by the Board of Education indicated that behind the mass of correspondence between the Board, Carmarthenshire county council, and the voluntary schools in that county, the Board had all their ammunition ready in case they would have to resort to some action against the county council in the not too distant future. The dates on the documents show that the Board had sought counsels' opinion long before the threat of a public inquiry. Sir Hugh Owen's opinion reached the Board at the beginning of September 1903 and the Law Officers of the Crown had opined for the Board by the middle of November. The National Society had briefed three learned counsel, Edward Clarke, W. O. Danckwerts and G. Edwardes Jones (the last named representing the Society at the public inquiry) and their opinion was ready by 12 December. The Cambridgeshire Case and Opinion of Alexander Macmorran, KC, was dated 2 February 1904. This was produced as an example of an English county which endeavoured to employ certain devices in order to evade their duty to use rates for subsidizing any deficit for the maintenance of voluntary schools. Macmorran ruled that all such devious devices and techniques contemplated by that county council were illegal.

Sir Hugh Owen's Opinion as to the relations of the local education authority towards the teachers employed in voluntary schools was brief and clear. In his view there was no provision in the Act of 1902 that the appointments of teachers in voluntary schools should be determined on the appointed day under the Act, neither was there anything in the Act from which it was to be inferred that it was the intention that the appointments of the thousands of teachers in such schools should be determined by the mere fact of the Act coming into operation.[4] Therefore the teachers in the voluntary schools should continue in their posts unless (a) their appointments came to an end by a notice in their terms of agreement,

---

[1] Ibid.
[2] Ibid., Index to Documents, op. cit., Documents XI, XII.
[3] Ibid., Index to Further Papers, ibid. supra, p. 1 (b).
[4] PRO Ed 111/254, Opinion of Sir Hugh Owen, Further Papers, op. cit.

The Carmarthenshire Inquiry

(b) they were dismissed on grounds of grave misconduct, or (c) the consent of the local education authority had been given. With respect to the liabilities of the local education authority, it devolved on the authority from the appointed day to pay the salaries of the teachers or to provide the managers with the necessary money for the payment of such salaries. But under section 7 of the 1902 Act, the local education authority had control over all expenditure necessary for maintaining and keeping efficient all the public elementary schools within their area. They could, therefore regulate the salaries of the teachers and they could give directions with respect to the number and educational qualifications of the teachers to be employed for secular instruction. Owen thought 'that the exercise of these powers must be regarded as subject to the determination of the appointments of the teachers serving in a school on the appointed day, if the arrangements which the council direct shall be carried out are not accepted by the teachers, and the teachers do not voluntarily resign'.[1] The view of the Board of Education was that all teachers in voluntary schools should be asked to resign by the local education authority and then re-appointed in a formal way, *if the teachers so desired*. In fact, this was attempted in Carmarthenshire after the result of the inquiry was known, but caused tremendous friction between the managers and the county council since it could not be guaranteed that salaries would be higher or reduced, as will be seen later.

As early as 30 July 1903 the Cambridgeshire county council (which had 106 voluntary schools and only 29 council schools) had passed a resolution 'that it be an instruction to the education committee not to recommend any expenditure out of the county rate towards the maintenance of non-provided schools so long as the majority of the managers are privately appointed, or any religious test for teachers is required, or any denominational teaching is given by paid teachers'.[2] The majority of the schools were non-provided, the managers privately elected, and religious tests imposed in addition to denominational teaching within the meaning of the resolution. After considering the resolution, the education committee referred the matter to a sub-committee. In brief, the report of the sub-committee recommended the keeping of two accounts, one for general purposes (Section A), and one for the maintenance of non-provided schools (Section B). The grants received for voluntary schools were to be distributed to each school in proportion to the average attendance, and the aggregate of the sums so arrived at in respect of voluntary schools were

---
[1] Ibid.
[2] Ibid., Case and Opinion of Macmorran, Further Papers, op. cit.

to be credited to Section B and the balance to Section A. Also the proceeds of any rate for elementary education were to be credited to Section A (whereupon the clerk advised that it would be illegal to carry out this resolution), and that in the event of a sum of money being raised by loan, so much of the loan be paid to Section B as is calculated to represent the amount of the unpaid grants accruing due for voluntary schools. The clerk again maintained that this was illegal, and that the Local Government Board would not sanction any loan in the face of such a resolution.[1]

The report of the sub-committee was rejected by the education committee, and that committee reported to the council the opinion that the 'instruction' contained in the resolution could not be carried out. Macmorran, in his Opinion, was quite categorical, and stated that the 'Instruction' was not consistent with the powers and duties of the county council as the local education authority under the Act of 1902; that all the public elementary schools of the county be maintained out of county rates, in addition to parliamentary grants; that refusal to do this by the county council would be contrary to Act of Parliament, and would lead to action on the part of the Board of Education under section 16.[2]

Regarding Carmarthenshire, the case for the Board of Education was considered by the Law Officers of the Crown, Messrs. R. B. Finlay and Edward Carson, and their Opinion was transmitted to the Board on 16 November 1903.[3] Schuster, as usual, had set out the case with extreme clarity and in great detail. The Board desired to be advised as to the methods which could in law be adopted, having regard to the action of certain local education authorities in Wales who had, by various means, declined to fulfil the obligations imposed upon them by the Education Act 1902, with reference to the maintenance of voluntary schools. There followed a long recital of the provisions of the Act which were relative to the matter, section 5, section 6 (2), section 7 (1), section 10, and section 18 (1).[4]

Wales and Monmouthshire, which for this purpose were treated together, comprised the following local education authorities, namely 13 counties, 3 county boroughs, 5 boroughs, and 9 urban districts. Of these, the Board of Education were aware that all the county councils, with the exception of Brecon and Radnor, and possibly Monmouth and Glamorgan,[5] all the boroughs except Carmarthen and Wrexham, and all

[1] PRO Ed 111/254, Case and Opinion of Mr. Macmorran, K.C.
[2] Ibid.
[3] Ibid., Index to Documents, op. cit. Documents XI, XII.
[4] These provisions have been set out earlier.
[5] Brecon and Radnor, Monmouthshire and Glamorgan became hostile after March, 1904.

The Carmarthenshire Inquiry

the urban districts except Barry[1] had in one form or another, intimated their intention of refusing to apply any monies derived from rates to the maintenance of voluntary schools in their respective areas. At the time Schuster was compiling his case, the Act was in operation in Wales in 7 counties (including Brecon and Radnor), 3 boroughs, namely Carmarthen, Pembroke and Wrexham, and in 5 urban districts, namely Aberdare, Barry, Mountain Ash, Pontypridd, and Rhondda. The forms in which the intention to refuse to apply the rates had been intimated differed in the different counties, but all were basically the same as Carmarthenshire, i.e. that no voluntary schools should receive rate aid unless they were under the full control of the county council, and the policies adopted by the Welsh LEAs included in Schuster's document have already been discussed. The rest of the case consisted of detailed references to the illegal actions of Carmarthenshire county council already considered in Part I of this study.

Schuster submitted that whatever remedy might exist against the LEA which had refused rate aid, it was not necessary for the Board to wait until the actual consequences of that refusal had become apparent and the voluntary school had been closed, but that it was open to the Board to act as soon as it became obvious that the LEA were failing in their duty. He stated that 'the Board were not anxious to move in the matter, and in order to obviate the necessity of so doing for as long a period as possible, the payments of grants had been accelerated, in the hope that the LEAs concerned would pay over the money as soon as it came into their hands, and so enable the managers to carry on, at any rate, for some little time longer'.[2] But as a matter of fact, cases had already arisen in Carmarthenshire where voluntary schools were losing efficiency owing to definite action on the part of the LEA, for example, Cwmamman national school applied to the LEA on 5 October 1903 for school equipment including school registers which were urgently needed, but the council had written saying that they had as yet 'made no regulations for the maintenance of voluntary schools in their school area'.[3]

Again, in the matter of teachers' salaries, similar circumstances might arise, and indeed become more acute, as Schuster pointed out, if the LEA, in the first few months after the appointed day did not distribute the Imperial grants promptly. The Board of Education, under the 1902

---

[1] Wrexham later became hostile, but the boroughs of Carmarthen, Pembroke and Neath, and the urban districts of Ebbw Vale and Abertillery remained non-hostile and maintained voluntary schools.

[2] PRO Ed 111/254, Index to Documents, op. cit., Document XI.

[3] Ibid.: Rev. E. A. Davies, School Correspondent to Carmarthenshire County Council, 5 October 1903 County Council to Davies, 7 October.

The Carmarthenshire Inquiry

Act, had no authority to pay such grants directly to the managers, and, as matters stood, the LEA was a mere conduit pipe between the Board and the voluntary schools. In the matter of grants being paid promptly to school managers by the LEA, Schuster raised the same point discussed by Counsel for the National Society regarding Section 18 of the Elementary Education Act, 1870, which if it had remained unrepealed would have enabled the Board 'to proceed accordingly'.[1] But it remained for the Board, under the Act of 1902, to compel the LEA to fulfil their duty by issuing an Order after holding a public inquiry. If the Order was disregarded, it could be enforced by *mandamus*.[2]

The Board of Education therefore, asked the Law Officers of the Crown to advise them whether, in the Law Officers' Opinion:

1. this or any other steps are open to the Board of Education or to members of the public by which a local education authority which has made default in its duty to maintain and keep efficient a voluntary school can be compelled to do its duty:

2. whether, having regard to the provisions of section 7 (4), it will be the duty of the Board of Education to withhold the grant in the case of a voluntary school which, owing to the default of the local education authority, does not comply with the remaining provisions of section 7, although it is maintained by the assistance of a parliamentary grant and by voluntary effort, and kept reasonably efficient:

3. whether the procedure provided by section 16 of the Education Act 1902, can be put into action as soon as the local education authority concerned has intimated its intention to disregard the law; or whether such action can be taken upon the commission of any overt act of neglect, as, for example, the failure to pay a teacher's salary when due, or to provide fuel necessary for the daily use of the school; or whether it is necessary to wait until the school has been pronounced inefficient in consequence of the failure of the local education authority to maintain it:

---

[1] If the last paragraph of Section 18 of the Education Act, 1870, had remained unrepealed, it might have been open to the Board of Education to declare the LEA in default and to have 'proceeded accordingly', i.e. they might have appointed fresh members of the LEA to perform the duties that had been neglected, in accordance with the provisions of Section 63 of that Act. This procedure being inapplicable to county boroughs and urban district councils, had disappeared, and by Section 16 of the Act of 1902, it was provided that 'if the LEA fail to fulfil any of their duties under the Elementary Education Acts, 1870 to 1900, or this Act, or fail to provide such additional public school accommodation within the meaning of the Elementary Education Act, 1870, as is, in the opinion of the Board of Education necessary in any part of their area, the Board of Education may, after holding a public inquiry, make such order as they think necessary or proper for the purpose of compelling the authority to fulfil their duty, and any such Order may be enforced by *mandamus*'.

[2] PRO Ed 111/254, Document XI.

The Carmarthenshire Inquiry

4. whether, as the measures preliminary to that procedure, any other steps are necessary beyond the following, namely:—
   (a) Report by one of the Board's Inspectors that a school is not being maintained and kept efficient in accordance with section 7.
   (b) Local inquiry.
   (c) Order.
   (d) Motion for *mandamus*.
5. Generally the Case.[1]

The Law Officers' Opinion fitted the illegal actions of Carmarthenshire county council like a glove. They stated that the Board of Education, after public inquiry could issue an Order under section 16, and if necessary could be enforced by *mandamus*. But this procedure should not be adopted upon a mere intimation by a local education authority of its intention to disregard the law—*it was necessary for this purpose that the law should in fact have been disregarded.* The procedure could be adopted as soon as there was any overt act of neglect, and it was not necessary to wait until the school had been pronounced inefficient. As regards question 4, no steps were necessary beyond those enumerated, but with reference to question 5, the Law Officers added 'that questions of general policy of very great gravity are raised by this case, and that the circumstances of each case ought to be carefully considered before any action is taken'.[2]

The copy of the Opinion given to the National Society contained a full statement of the position of Carmarthenshire prepared for the Society as a basis for legal action under section 16 of the Act of 1902 with particular reference to voluntary schools. The case had to be considered under two heads:[3]

1. As to the default of the local education authority and the means of compelling it to carry out its duties.
2. As to the position created by such default for the managers of voluntary schools conducted as public elementary schools.

Counsel stated that these questions chiefly existed in the Principality of Wales and were caused by the manifest reluctance, and in some cases declared intention, of the local education authorities not to carry out the Act.[4] With reference to the default of the local education authority, its responsibilities were stated quite clearly in the Act, viz. as from the date on which the Act comes into operation (section 27, which must be

[1] PRO Ed 111/254, Index to Documents, op. cit., Document XI.
[2] Ibid., Document XII.
[3] Ibid., Index to Further Papers, op. cit., p. 1 (b).
[4] PRO Ed 111/254, Index to Further Papers, op. cit.

The Carmarthenshire Inquiry

on the 26 March 1903 or such other date, not being more than 18 months later as the Board of Education may appoint, the Board having license to appoint different dates for different purposes, and in Wales, 31 March 1904 has usually been appointed) is responsible for, and is to have control of all secular instruction in its district even in public elementary schools not provided by it, i.e. voluntary schools. In addition, the local education authority was required to follow other recommendations of Part III, notably sections 6 and 7.

To be able to discharge such duties by the appointed day it would be clearly necessary that the local education authority should be well prepared with information and funds. In other words, before taking over, the local education authority should be in possession of all the facts and figures regarding all the schools within its area before the appointed day. In England, and in all places where the Act was being worked properly, very detailed information had been required by the local education authority from the managers long before the appointed day, as regards their teachers, their salaries and qualifications, and the condition of the schools. In the light of this information, the local education authority was able to forecast the funds required to meet its probable expenditure.[1] In order to assist the local authorities an Act was passed in 1903 which provided 'that the local education authority may, with the consent of the Local Government Board, borrow under section 19 of the Education Act of 1902, or in such other manner as the Local Government Board may approve, such sums as in the opinion of that Board are required to provide working balances for carrying the 1902 Act into effect'.[2] In this way, therefore, pending a rate or receipt of parliamentary grants, the local authority had the power to obtain a working balance so as to be ready with all that was required for school expenditure on the appointed day.

Carmarthenshire had done none of these things and the National Society was deeply concerned because many voluntary schools in the county (which were in union with the Society) had written to complain about their plight. Many pages of the case were occupied with the attitude of Carmarthenshire towards these schools and the letters received from the school Correspondents by the Society ended usually with the question 'is there no power to make the local education authority do its duty'?[3]

---

[1] PRO Ed 24/578, op. cit.: On 4 June, 1903 Merioneth County Council (which imitated Carmarthenshire) having received a recommendation from its Finance Committee for the levying of a rate of 10d. in the £ to meet the requirements of the 1902 Act, including the probable cost of carrying on the voluntary schools for the half-year ending 31 March 1904, resolved that the rate should only be 8½d., the 1½d. in the £ being the estimated cost of voluntary schools in the county.

[2] 3 Edw. VIII, c. 10: *The Education (Provision of Working Balances) Act*, 1903.

[3] PRO Ed 111/254, ibid supra.

The Carmarthenshire Inquiry

For the second part of the subject, i.e. the position created by this default for the manager of a voluntary school carried on as a public elementary school both before and after the appointed day. The managers of such a school, then, would meet the appointed day, carrying on everything up to midnight of the previous day, with all the expenditure required by the government, in order to earn parliamentary grants and all the machinery of the school in full working order. In Carmarthenshire, it was the case that the local education authority had not enquired after nor approved the staff, or nominated managers to act with the foundation managers. Important questions arose regarding the liability of the old managers with reference to the employment of teachers and their salaries.[1]

After dealing with this aspect in considerable detail, and assuming that the local education authority had not appointed managers to act with foundation managers, Counsel advised, among other things, (a) that foundation managers could act as a full body of managers under the Act, (b) managers could spend money on coal and other requisites without the consent of the council, and (c) teachers' salaries should be paid by the new statutory bodies of managers out of the funds of the local authority. The Board of Education were advised that no remedy existed to compel a local education authority to do their duty except: firstly, the Board made an inquiry under section 16; secondly, an Order that the local education authority do so and so; and thirdly, if necessary the Order be enforced by *mandamus*.[2] Finally, on requesting as to the best way of raising a test case on the points suggested, with a view of clearing up the working of the Act, the National Society were advised that 'any proceedings which might be instituted must relate to a school which complied with the conditions of section 7, and if any doubt was raised as to such compliance by the local education authority, such doubt should be cleared up by a decision under section 7(3), and, if by any means possible before any proceedings under section 16 are instituted.[3]

Fortified with all this imposing array of preliminary legal opinion from all parties concerned, the Board of Education received an additional document from the National Society which contained further advice on the evidence for the inquiry (after considering the Opinion of their learned counsel) and it was sent to the Treasury solicitor on Anson's instructions.[4] The Society impressed upon the Board to make quite

---

[1] PRO Ed 111/254, Index to Further Papers, op. cit.
[2] Ibid.
[3] Ibid., 'If any question arises under this section between the local education authority and the managers of a school not provided by the authority, that question shall be determined by the Board of Education.'
[4] Ibid., National Society to Board of Education, 11 February; Board of Education to Treasury Solicitor, 13 February.

The Carmarthenshire Inquiry

certain 'that the circular from the county council refusing to carry the Act into effect generally had been received by the whole of the schools in Carmarthenshire'. Canon Brownrigg was prepared to give evidence on the state of the accounts in the various voluntary schools 'so as to show that the grants will not exceed the local education authority expenses in the first year after the appointed day in as many cases as possible, and to give corresponding figures in respect of the remaining schools'. He also requested that as many managers as possible of voluntary schools should be prepared to vouch for the figures in respect of each of their schools. The same applied to teachers' salaries and individual cases of schools where the refusal of the local education authority to perform its duty had prejudicially affected the efficiency of such schools, and also if the local authority's surveyor had told the managers that certain repairs were necessary, and the managers had complied with such instructions—evidence to that effect should be available.[1]

The Board of Education's next step was to determine the form of the inquiry and they proceeded to explain, in a lengthy memorandum, the state of affairs which they desired to deal with, by the procedure made available under section 16 and in particular by an inquiry held under that section.[2] The Board set out the official terms of reference and the complete sources of evidence for their case. They said that certain local authorities in Wales, constituted local education authorities by the 1902 Act, were not administering the Act in its integrity, their default taking the form of a refusal to recognise in full the claims of a class of schools known popularly as voluntary schools. Different local authorities adopted different methods of default, but the only authority to which the inquiry immediately contemplated referred was the county council of Carmarthenshire. The full details of the legal aspect had been conveyed in the Opinion of the Law Officers of the Crown. The clearest evidence of illegalities by this county council were available in the facts accumulated in (a) the General Chronological Summary,[3] (b) the Minute to Sir William Anson,[4] (c) the Reports of HM Inspector of schools,[5] and (d) the Correspondence.[6]

But there were preliminary procedural difficulties. No departmental precedent, which was at all relevant, existed for a guide as to the form which this inquiry might take. Section 73 of the Elementary Education

---

[1] PRO Ed 111/254, Preliminary Advice on Evidence for Inquiry, National Society.
[2] Ibid., Index to Documents, op. cit., Document 1.
[3] Ibid., Document IX.
[4] Ibid., Document X.
[5] Ibid., Documents V, VI, VII: Instructions to A. G. Legard, HMI, and Reports on Pembrey and Llangennech National Schools.
[6] Ibid., Documents III, IV: Correspondence relating to above schools.

152

The Carmarthenshire Inquiry

Act, 1870, laid down certain provisions as to an Inquiry, but beyond this the Board had no direction. For practical purposes, all stages of the proceedings under section 16 were so mutually interdependent—for example, the formalities of Inquiry, the instructions to be given to persons holding the Inquiry, the Report of the Inquirer, the Order based on the Report, and the *mandamus* proceedings, if necessary—that the settlement of one involved the consideration of all. But the practical objects of the Inquiry were:

1. To get a report from a competent Inquirer, sitting in a more or less judicial position, both sides having been heard, which would serve to put the matter before the public, and, if necessary, before Parliament, in a clear light.
2. To bring legal pressure to bear by means of an Order made under section 16, and perhaps by *mandamus* proceedings, so that the determination by the local education authority to persist might be tested; further, to show the moderate party among the opponents of the Education Act that the action of Carmarthenshire county council was really illegal, and to detach the law-abiding from the law-breaking party.
3. To exhaust, or at any rate to make a test of the remedy provided in the Act before seeking new ones outside it.[1]

The extent of the Order intended to be made depended upon whether the Board wished to call upon the local education authority to do certain things with reference to a certain school, or to obey the law regarding all voluntary schools in their area. On the other hand, a few specific instances of schools being improperly treated could be brought to the notice of the Inquiry or a general rush of complaints from numerous schools so that a fair numerical average would be represented by the Report. A third course might lie in getting a report on the general conduct of the local education authority by inference from a few specific instances. It was not possible to settle the form of the Notice of Inquiry until these questions had been considered. The form of the early proceedings as, for example, the Notice of the Inquiry was important 'because it has been assumed that when once the form was settled, the conduct of the matter would be out of the hands of the Board. The Board do not see how they can appear by counsel before their own Inquirer'.[2] But there was no doubt that the National Society would take care of any complaining school at the Inquiry by employing leading Counsel to act on their behalf.

[1] PRO Ed 111/254, Index of Documents, op. cit., Document I.
[2] Ibid.

The memorandum then stated that the Education Acts from 1870 to 1902 contained practically the whole law on public education and explained the difference between Provided or Council schools, and the Non-Provided, National or Voluntary school. The former were practically the same as the old Board schools (and the older British schools) but the Board schools were owned and solely controlled by the local education authority, whilst the latter (voluntary) schools were vested in Trustees and the property of private persons, managed by a body of managers constituted by statute and 'given genuine power which the local education authority could not abrogate' and were responsible for part of the upkeep of the school, for example, the repair of the school building.[1] Before the Act of 1902, voluntary schools were in the nature of private institutions, subsidized by parliamentary grants paid direct to the managers and the deficit on the maintenance of such schools was met by voluntary contributions. Under the Act of 1902 the new situation arose whereby, although voluntary schools were to enjoy their role as distinctive institutions within the new local education authorities—a denominational role—yet they looked to public funds for financial support. In reality, section 7 of the 1902 Act was the charter of voluntary schools, and the Law Officers had already given the legal situation at some length, but the words 'maintain and keep efficient' were the crucial ones which imposed or defined the duty which lay on the local education authority towards voluntary schools.[2]

It was in the context of the words 'maintain and keep efficient' that the Carmarthenshire county council had shown breach of duty towards its voluntary schools. The illegalities of the council were enumerated to them in a letter from the Board of Education on 1 February 1904. This was followed up, on Anson's instructions, by the confidential reports of Mr. A. G. Legard, HM Inspector, on the two voluntary schools at Pembrey and Llangennech.[3] These schools were selected and would probably be investigated at the Inquiry, subject to the advice which the Board might receive from the solicitor to the Treasury, because they afforded examples of three heads of illegality (a) failure by the council to provide funds for the current necessities of the schools, (b) failure to give necessary directions for secular instruction under the control of the council, and in particular, failure to sanction the appointment of teachers (section 7(1) (a) and (c) of the Act, and (c) failure to appoint managers (section 6(2). This last head, universal in Carmarthenshire, obviously

---

[1] Ibid.
[2] PRO Ed 111/254, Index of Documents, op. cit., Document I, ibid.
[3] Ibid., Documents V, VI, VII.

The Carmarthenshire Inquiry

illegal, did not appeal so much to the public. The second head, the refusal to appoint teachers, a more flagrant illegality, was less common. But the first head, to provide funds, was the most common, and in public estimation in Wales, the most important.[1]

The centre of the whole question in Carmarthenshire was the failure to provide funds for the necessary existence of voluntary schools. But the council made a public claim that they were adequately performing their duty towards such schools by attempting to use a certain device. They paid the parliamentary grants to voluntary schools, but no money from the rates, and argued that if all the incomes in all the voluntary schools *before the Act of 1902 were added together* 'the total would be the same as the grants which the schools earned under the Act, and that the county council were adequately performing their duty if they provided the same aggregate sum for the maintenance of the schools as was provided from all sources in the last previous years'.[2] But the employment of this device by the council was politically rather than legally valid. On the surface, the argument put forward by the local education authority might sound quite feasible and within the law, but in practice it was illegal and caused financial embarrassment and lack of efficiency in many voluntary schools. This was due to the fact that the system of parliamentary grant payments had changed under the Act of 1902. Before the Act, there were three grants payable to voluntary schools under the Voluntary Schools Act of 1897. Of these (the Annual grant, Fee grant and Aid grant)[3] the Annual grant was not paid until the end of the school year, and the practice followed by managers of voluntary schools was to conduct the schools out of their own pockets (often by pre-arranged bank overdrafts) until the grants arrived and thus practically all schools were a year in arrears.[4]

The passing of the Act of 1902 changed all this, since the appointed day fell in the middle of the school year of any voluntary school, and it was necessary 'to make arrangements for the apportionment between the local education authority and the managers, of the annual grant and fee grant when they came to be paid'.[5] In fairness it should be mentioned that the Board of Education came to the rescue of the local authorities by sending the parliamentary grants as quickly as possible after the appointed day. But there was a more important aspect to the financial

---

[1] Ibid., Document I.
[2] Ibid., Under the 1902 Act, the Aid grant disappeared and the grant specified in section 10 was substituted.
[3] 60 & 61 Vict. c. 5.
[4] PRO Ed ibid. supra.
[5] PRO Ed 111/254, Document I, ibid.

side so far as Carmarthenshire county council was concerned, and which considerably strengthened their contention of working, in what they called, within the law. The grants payable under section 10 of the 1902 Act[1] were, in the aggregate, in the case of every local education authority greatly in excess of the amounts which would have been received by all the managers of voluntary schools in their area under the Voluntary Schools Act, i.e. the Aid grant. Indeed, they in fact, in many cases amounted *to nearly as much as the total sum of all grants payable to managers in the area under that Act plus all voluntary subscriptions received.* Thus, in the case of Carmarthenshire, the old aid grant payable in respect of all voluntary schools in the county in the last completed twelve months was £1,037, and the voluntary subscriptions £1,526, while the section 10 grant payable to the local education authority for the first twelve months after the Act came into operation would be £2,498. Thus Carmarthenshire and every local education authority in Wales could say that voluntary schools could be maintained without recourse to rates.[2]

But the plausibility of this argument rested on aggregate sums and not the position of individual voluntary schools. In Carmarthenshire, 23 schools benefited and 37 lost by the change in the 1902 Act, and it was the duty of the council to see that all schools were maintained and kept efficient. The Board were aware that the agitation against rate aid was very widespread in Wales, and that 'it had good organizations and leaders. A special feature of it was the pretence made of legal knowledge. The agitation against the Act had been marked by much legal quibble, which was ardently taken up by the laymen on the various county councils. Probably, however, the leaders and many of the rank and file were quite aware of the illegality of their position, and were content to make a show of obeying the law, while, in fact, resting upon the practical strength of their position'.[3]

---

[1] Section 10, 1. In lieu of the grants under the Voluntary Schools Act, 1897, and under section 97 of the Elementary Education Act, 1870, as amended by the Elementary Education Act, 1897 (60 and 61 Vict. c. 16), there shall be annually paid to every local education authority, out of moneys provided by parliament—
  (a) a sum equal to four shillings per scholar: and
  (b) an additional sum of three halfpence per scholar for every complete twopence per scholar by which the amount which would be produced by a penny rate on the area of the authority falls short of ten shillings a scholar; provided that, in estimating the produce of a penny rate in the area of a local education authority not being a county borough, the rate shall be calculated upon the county rate basis, which, in cases where part only of a parish is situated in the area of the local education authority, shall be apportioned in such manner as the Board of Education think just. But if in any year the total amount of parliamentary grants payable to a LEA would make the amount payable out of other sources by that authority on account of their expenses under this part of this act less than the amount which would be produced by a rate of 3*d.* in the £, the parliamentary grants shall be decreased, and the amount payable out of other sources shall be increased by a sum equal in each case to half the difference.
  2. For the purposes of this section the number of scholars shall be taken to be the number of scholars in average attendance, as computed by the Board of Education, in public elementary schools maintained by the authority.

[2] PRO Ed, ibid supra.

[3] PRO Ed 111/254, Document I, ibid.

The Carmarthenshire Inquiry

The Board of Education were not unmindful of the fact that the proposed Inquiry might be ignored by the county council, but at the same time were quite convinced that probably the council would appear in force and be represented by distinguished counsel who would take up all possible points.[1] In order to prepare a rock-bottom case, the Board had to be particularly careful to fulfil the following conditions in their search for examples, especially those under the first head of illegality, namely, failure to provide funds for current necessities: (a) the school buildings selected for the Inquiry should be good, in order to avoid accusations of being in bad repair and which required attention before the council assumed responsibility for it—a good clerical witness was essential, and also a school 'having a numerous Church of England and Roman Catholic population was desirable in order to avoid comment of a political character';[2] (b) a school which gained under the new financial arrangements was to be avoided, for it would be less easy to claim rate aid for such a school; (c) one of the important aspects on the financial side was to select cases of schools which had deficits, and this question was complex. It had to be carefully shown that certain schools suffered financially because grants were insufficient to meet their needs, and very often some school managers were not too careful in keeping their accounts, and again some teachers were paid monthly and some annually. But the chief point the Board wished to stress and prove in the two schools chosen for the Inquiry was that the county council 'refused to recognize for voluntary schools the standard of efficiency which they set for themselves in their council schools. It was quite clear that non-provided schools were being treated ignominiously by the council. A rate was being raised for the council schools, and proofs of preferential treatment could be supplied. Teachers and cleaners in such schools received salaries at a higher rate, apparatus was more abundant, and all funds were promptly supplied'.[3]

With regard to this inequality of treatment, Anson's reply to Griffith-Boscawen in the House of Commons should be noted—'that the standard of efficiency at which all public elementary schools are maintained must be alike, unless special educational reasons can be shown for a distinction'. The important question which the Board had to decide was 'how far this inequality of treatment could be regarded as a definite illegality in breach

---

[1] Ibid., At the Public Inquiry, neither the Clerk nor any other member of the county council appeared to give evidence.

[2] Ibid.

[3] Ibid.

of section 7(1) of the Act, and how far it goes only to evidence'.[1] It has been seen that under the Act of 1902 the system of grant payments had been fundamentally changed, the local education authority held the parliamentary grants received from Whitehall, they were no longer earmarked for individual schools but were merged into the county fund for educational purposes. Out of this fund all the proper expenses of education had to be met. The duty of the local education authority towards any public elementary school within its area depended in no way upon the amount of grant received by any particular school. In fact, it was not primarily a claim by a school for maintenance which the local education authority had to face, but a positive duty upon themselves to take active steps to maintain and keep efficient, and to seek out and remedy any deficiency.[2]

In its search for cases to place before the Inquirer, the Board of Education asked several managers for estimates for the current six months between the appointed day and the end of the financial year. Apart from the fact that such estimates were *exparte*, they had to be treated with great care, because managers had very vague ideas as to the law, of their own financial position. Thus, when asked as to the deficiency of funds, managers attempted to include as assets, balances in hand before the appointed day, or grants paid on the appointed day but earned in respect of the period before it. The Board assumed that all accounts ought to start with a clean sheet as from the appointed day, all debts previously incurred being disregarded by the local education authority, and all balances being managers' assets for managers' purposes. The accounts sent by the Pembrey managers were a typical instance of the inclusion of items on either side of the accounts, which belonged to the period before the appointed day, and was also an easy case because the beginning of the school year coincided with the appointed day. The Board added, parenthetically that 'if an Inquiry and the Order failed to provide a suitable basis for *mandamus* proceedings owing to any of the technical difficulties mentioned, the measures taken would, nevertheless be useful as showing the impossibility of relying upon the procedure under section 16 as a means of coercing recalcitrant local education authorities to carry out the Act. By such means the remedies provided by the Act would have been exhausted, and one object of the Inquiry contemplated would have been fulfilled'.[3]

[1] PRO Ed 111/254, Document I, ibid.
[2] Ibid. In some areas the LEA asserted the failure upon the part of the managers to comply with section 1 (d) of the 1902 Act (repairs, improvements, etc.,) as a ground for refusal to maintain schools but this plea was not used by Carmarthenshire county council.
[3] Ibid.

The Carmarthenshire Inquiry

Anson's instructions for an inspectorial survey of the situation in two selected voluntary schools—Pembrey and Llangennech—as evidence in the proposed Inquiry produced fruitful results. Legard was sent to the two schools and was required to answer specific questions gleaned from the managers.[1] Before his visits, the headteachers of the schools had been refused permission by the county council to appoint additional and necessary members of staff, and to acquire other materials for the efficient maintenance of the schools. Legard also observed that the county council discriminated between council and voluntary schools.[2] When the school Correspondents wrote to the county council about their difficulties, they received the same reply 'that this council has decided that it will not for the present interfere at all in the management of voluntary schools'.[3] Accordingly, the Board of Education wrote a comprehensive letter to the county council pointing out the illegalities and intimated that they contemplated the necessity of an Inquiry.[4] It only remained for the Board to issue the following preliminary Recital of Notice of Inquiry:

> 'WHEREAS complain has been made that the local education authority of Carmarthenshire have failed in their duty to maintain and keep efficient all the Public Elementary Schools within their area as required by the Education Act, 1902, and in particular have failed to supply the funds and exercise the control of secular instruction necessary for the efficiency of Pembrey National School and Llangennech Church School or to give such directions as from time to time may be required for the supply of necessaries and the appointment of teachers, or to appoint managers as directed by section 6 (a) of the Education Act, 1902, or to perform the duties of a School Attendance Committee'.[5]

On 29 February 1904 this was confirmed by the solicitor to the Treasury[6] and on 8 March the procedure for making and enforcing an Order under section 16 of the Education Act, 1902 had been sent 'for information to the Board of Education'.[7] On 9 March all the necessary papers and documents were seen by Anson who passed them on to the President.[8]

IV THE INQUIRY AND RESULT

The Public Inquiry (held under Sections 16 and 23 of the Education Act, 1902, and Section 73 of the Elementary Education Act, 1870) was held at the Assembly Rooms, Carmarthen, on 24 and 25 March 1904,

---

[1] Ibid., Documents V, VI, VII, ibid.
[2] PRO Ed. 111/254, Documents VI, VII.
[3] Ibid., Document IX.
[4] Ibid.
[5] PRO Ed 111/255.
[6] Ibid., Treasury to Board of Education, 29 February.
[7] Ibid., Treasury to Board of Education, 8 March.
[8] Ibid., Minute from Pease to Lindsell, 9 March.

The Carmarthenshire Inquiry

before the Commissioner, Mr. A. T. Lawrence, KC, appointed by the solicitor to the Treasury on behalf of the Board of Education[1]. The non-provided schools, forty-eight in number, upon whose behalf complaints had been made to the Board of Education, were represented by Mr. John Rawlinson, KC, and Mr. Edwardes Jones (instructed by Messrs. Crawley, Arnold and Co)., on behalf of the National Society.[2] The Carmarthenshire county council was represented by Mr. Abel Thomas, MP, KC, and Mr. Llewelyn Williams (instructed by Mr. H. W. Thomas, Carmarthen, and Mr. William Howell, Llanelli).[3] Mr. Claude Schuster and Mr. R. P. Hills attended on behalf of the Board of Education, and supplied the parties and the Court with such information as was from time to time required.[4] The Inquiry was largely attended, but no other parties were represented.

At the beginning of the formal proceedings, Mr. Abel Thomas, for the county council, lodged an application for an adjournment (which had already been made to the Board of Education) but this was opposed by Rawlinson and Schuster. The grounds for an adjournment were that the Inquiry had been instituted at short notice, that the county council could prove (if sufficient time were given) that the school buildings of the schools in question were not in a proper state of repair, and on an alleged statement by Sir William Anson in answer to questions asked by Mr. Lloyd George in the House of Commons to the effect that the Inquiry should be as full and as complete as possible.[5] After a prolonged argument, the Commissioner felt bound to refuse the application, because (a) the fact that an Inquiry would be held must have been apparent for some months, (b) that the state of the school buildings was not the cause of the attitude adopted by the county council, and was a matter to be considered *after* the local education authority assumed control of the schools, and not before it did so, (c) that the points on which the county

---

[1] Ibid., *Official Notice of Inquiry and Schedule of Schools.*

[2] PRO Ed 111/255, Part 1B.

[3] Ibid.

[4] PRO Ed 111/255, *Minutes of Proceedings in Re the Education Acts*, 1870–1902, *Administrative County of the County Council of Carmarthenshire, in an Inquiry held before A. T. Lawrence, K.C.*, from the shorthand notes of James Towell, 33 Chancery Lane and 26 Castle Street, Cardiff. Two Volumes, Vol. I, first day of Inquiry, 24 March, 1904, pp. 138; Vol. II, second day of Inquiry, 25 March, pp. 98.
ibid., *Report of a Public Inquiry held under Sections 16 and 23 of the Education Act*, 1902, *and Section 73 of the Elementary Education Act*, 1870, by A. T. Lawrence, K.C., 18 April, 1904, presented to both Houses of Parliament, HMSO, London.

[5] PRO Ed ibid. supra, Vol. I, Discussion of adjournment by Thomas, Rawlinson, and Schuster pp. 4–33.

Parl. Deb., 4th ser., vol. cxxxi, cs. 1024, ff: On 14 March, 1904, Lloyd George asked Anson 'whether the hon. gentleman could give instructions that the Inquiry should cover all the circumstances and conditions and not be subject to technical restrictions'. Anson replied 'that he had every reason to hope that the Inquiry would be full and complete'. In answer to a further question that 'the Inquiry should be full and complete', Anson replied 'he thought the Board of Education would impress upon Mr. Lawrence that the Inquiry should take as complete a form as possible regarding everything that might affect the judgement of the Board in making the Order which might have to be made as the result of the Inquiry'

council required time to collect evidence were not relevant to the subject-matter of the Inquiry, and (d) that as the interests of some 8,000 children were in jeopardy, the matter should be finalised as soon as possible.[1] The Commissioner emphasized that on all matters relevant to the Inquiry directed, he was anxious to make it as full and complete as possible. The Inquiry then proceeded.

Rawlinson, on behalf of the non-provided schools made four charges (mentioned in the Notice of Inquiry) against the county council as local education authority, failure to control secular instruction in such schools, failure to appoint managers to such schools, failure to maintain and keep efficient such schools or to control the expenditure required for that purpose, and failure to give consent to the appointment of teachers on other than educational grounds. He gave a detailed historical background of the attitude of the county council from October 1902 and the actions they had taken to keep their hands off the non-provided schools.[2] In his opinion, the position therefore was that the county council duly administered the Act in the case of provided schools; it appointed managers, it provided funds for their needs, and school attendance officers. But in the case of non-provided schools the county council took no notice of them apart from sending to each school such portion of parliamentary grants earned by the school. The council appointed no managers, and the attendance officers were dismissed, although the 'minor education authority'—Carmarthen borough—had duly appointed managers. The managers of the voluntary schools had asked the county council for advice and assistance, but they were merely referred to the council's circular letter of 29 October 1903.[3] The minute books of the forty-eight schools handed in as evidence of the course of events since 30 September 1903 were objected to on behalf of the county council on the ground of surprise, and after some discussion, the Commissioner thought it unreasonable that they should be examined in detail, and did not refer to them.[4]

Rawlinson then selected six non-provided schools (Llangennech was not included) as examples of the effect on those schools of the attitude of the local education authority, supported by the Correspondent manager as witness in each case. The schools were Capel Mair, St. Clears, Mothfai (Myddfai), Pembrey, Abergwili, and Llanfihangel ar Arth.[5] These schools

[1] PRO Ed, ibid. supra, Vol. I, A. T. Lawrence rules on adjournment, pp.33–35.
[2] This account is dealt with in Part I of this study. PRO Ed 111/255, Vol. I, op. cit., pp. 35–62.
[3] PRO Ed 111/252, *Report of a Public Inquiry*, op. cit.
[4] Ibid.
[5] PRO Ed 111/255, Vol. II, op. cit., pp. 1–64.

had asked for school materials, funds for teachers' salaries, permission to appoint additional teachers (on the recommendation of HM Inspector) and Abergwili required a new headteacher. Capel Mair and St. Clears were in debt to the tune of £33 and £97 respectively. But when the managers of Myddfai, Pembrey, and Abergwili were cross-examined it seemed that a case could be made out that the schools were as well off as they were before the 1902 Act.[1] More than one witness maintained that if the managers had not pledged their credit, the schools could not have carried on, and very often the vicar had to collect money for such things as coal, firewood and books, and sometimes salaries.[2] For the county council, it was argued that these schools were selected cases, but counsel admitted that the county council had dealt with the whole forty-eight schools in accordance with the resolutions passed in favour of non-interference with voluntary schools.[3]

The Rev. Canon Brown, secretary of the St. Davids Diocesan Association of Church schools (of which the forty-eight schools were part) stated that no applications had come before him for the repair of any of the schools from the county council, except a surveyor's report which had come to him a fortnight previously. He also stated that in many of the parishes, Nonconformists had contributed to the building fund of voluntary schools and that in the majority of such schools more Nonconformist than church children attended.[4]

The local education authority declined to call any member of the county council or its clerk to appear, to explain the grounds on which they had acted, Thomas maintaining (on losing the plea for an adjournment) that the council was unable to answer the case made without detailed particulars, and an adjournment.[5] The Commissioner thought this an extremely flimsy excuse in the circumstances, and was at a loss to know why the council should be unable to give their reasons for an attitude adopted in September and October 1903, and adhered to since that time.[6] It was admitted that in not appointing managers and attendance officers for the voluntary schools, the county council had acted contrary to the provisions of the Act. But in other respects it was submitted that in refusing financial or other assistance, except transmitting parliamentary grants when received, the council had not acted illegally because they were

[1] Ibid., Evidence of respective clergy as Correspondent managers.
[2] Ibid., Evidence of Rev. C. F. Owen, St. Clears, pp. 54–64. 36 of the 91 children in this school were Nonconformist.
[3] PRO Ed 111/252, *Report* ibid. supra.
[4] PRO Ed 111/255, Vol. I, op. cit., pp. 85–106; Vol. II, pp. 52–54.
[5] Ibid., Vol. I, pp. 108–138.
[6] Ibid.

only concerned with secular instruction, and also, that since the schools had, in fact, been efficiently maintained by others, the county council had not made default in maintaining them. Llewelyn Williams, in his summing up for the county council made great play of the fact (in excuse for the conduct of the council) that its members came to the administration of the Act with a tradition of injustice of thirty or forty years behind them, in that Nonconformists had contributed liberally to build and support many voluntary schools and Nonconformist children attended them, but in the past they had had no adequate representation in the management of the schools.[1]

The Commissioner was not convinced by any of these arguments, either on the issue of finance or management, since the council had declined to afford any assistance to the Board of Education, especially in framing its orders constituting Foundation Managers. Moreover, he was quite satisfied that 'he could detect no act of sectarian narrowness on the part of any of the managers, who were remarkable for their open-minded and liberal disposition towards their Nonconformist scholars'. To him, the most serious matter, whereby the action of the council in using the powers of the Act to levy rates upon churchmen and Nonconformists alike, and then refusing to apply this money to any but provided schools, was neither legal nor excusable, and was, in his opinion, a grave abuse of the powers confided to them by the Act.[2]

Summarizing the main points for both sides in the Inquiry, Rawlinson's case on behalf of the voluntary schools showed (a) that the county council as the local education authority had passed resolutions explicitly providing for the dismissal of all attendance officers who looked after voluntary schools; had withheld all money from such schools except parliamentary grants; confined the loan under the Working Balances Act to provided schools, and refused to appoint managers to voluntary schools; (b) that the County Clerk had been authorized to write to the voluntary schools repudiating the duty of the council to those schools; and (c) this action had considerably impaired the efficiency of the majority of the voluntary schools.[3]

The county council, on the other hand, had some justification in looking upon the Inquiry as premature. Their case was, firstly, that the scope of the Inquiry ought to have been enlarged, and counsel for the county council wished to go into the educational question as a whole. They

[1] Ibid., Vol. II, pp. 72–97.
[2] PRO Ed 111/252, *Report*, op. cit.
[3] PRO Ed 111/255, Vol. II, op. cit., pp. 67–71.

The Carmarthenshire Inquiry

wished to give evidence as to the number of Nonconformist children in voluntary schools, the part played by Nonconformists in building the schools, the composition of the bodies of managers in the schools, and the state of the school buildings. On all these points they quoted Anson's reply to Lloyd George in the House of Commons. Secondly, it was strongly urged that the Inquiry should be adjourned (if enlarged as demanded) in order to have more time for investigation, and because the council ought to have details in advance of the charges made by counsel on behalf of the voluntary schools, against them. Thirdly, it was contended that voluntary schools were in fact being maintained and kept efficient, and did not suffer from the action of the council. Fourthly, the council maintained that many voluntary school buildings were 'inefficient', and as a condition precedent to maintenance, the managers should repair and improve them. Fifthly, there was no legal duty upon the local education authority to pay for religious instruction in voluntary schools.[1] But it was admitted, in the end, after some demur, that the failure of the council to provide attendance officers and representative managers was illegal.[2]

Schuster, on behalf of the Board of Education, had stated that there were special means, apart from the Inquiry, by which the county council might make representations to the Board as to Foundation Managers, and also as to schools being out of repair.[3] The Commissioner had taken both these points, and further, on the question of adjournment, had held that the county council must be presumed to have duly considered their reasons at the time of passing their resolutions. In any case, he had maintained that the matter was urgent and could not be postponed, and that, according to *Hansard*, Anson had not said 'what the local education authority's counsel said he did, and that Section 7(1)(d)—repairs to schools, etc.,—involved a condition subsequent and not a condition precedent'.[4]

Rawlinson, in reply to the council's demand for an adjournment, had argued *inter alia* that there were provisions in the Act to meet Nonconformists' grievances, and that as the local education authority were recalcitrant, they could not properly ask for an adjournment. The points most emphasized for the voluntary schools were the illegal resolutions and less emphasis was placed on the actual hardships imposed upon the voluntary schools or their managers by the action of the local education authority.

---

[1] Ibid., Vol. II, pp. 65–7. Discussion as to liability of the county council to pay for religious instruction.
[2] Ibid., Vol. I, op. cit., pp. 108–125.
[3] Ibid., p. 72.
[4] Ibid., Summary of Proceedings at Carmarthenshire Inquiry.

The Carmarthenshire Inquiry

The main points for the council appeared to be the demand for adjournment in view of the March county council elections, and to have particulars of the charges, and the contention that failure to maintain and keep efficient was not proved. Minor points of interest in the case of the non-provided schools were that the county council had made no demands for repairs, had called no evidence, and so admitted the case against them, and the failure of counsel to emphasise difficulties schools must be placed in, by the long intervals between the payments of parliamentary grants by the council. In the case of the county council, it was argued that it did not matter who maintained the schools, provided they *were* maintained.[1]

In his Report, the Commissioner felt constrained, with great regret, to say that the county council of Carmarthenshire, as the Local Education Authority, had failed to fulfil their duties under the Education Act of 1902, towards forty-eight Public Elementary Schools within their area mentioned in the Schedule[2] in that:—

1. They have failed to be responsible for, or to control the secular instruction to be given in such schools.
2. They have failed to appoint a manager or managers for such schools respectively.
3. They have failed to maintain and keep efficient such schools, or to control the expenditure required for that purpose.
4. They have withheld their consent to the appointment of teachers on other than educational grounds.[3]

The Carmarthenshire county council had been found guilty on all four counts. What action did the Board of Education propose to take? They could now proceed to make an Order, enforceable by *mandamus* under Section 16 of the Education Act of 1902, as to the duties of the local education authority, and also an Order under Section 73(4) of the Elementary Education Act, 1870, as to the costs of the Inquiry. What was the reaction of the county council, and how did they propose to act as a result of the Inquiry? The answers to these questions were dictated by two events in Wales and Westminster during the time of the Inquiry, and after the publication of the result, and, further, were determined by the policy which the Board of Education had adopted before the institution of the Inquiry.

---

[1] PRO Ed 111/255, Summary of Proceedings, ibid.

[2] Ibid., *Schedule of schools in Report*, p. 11.

[3] Ibid., *Report*, op. cit., p. 10.

The Carmarthenshire Inquiry

In Wales, the county council elections in March were unquestionably a personal triumph for Lloyd George and a clear endorsement of his policy to defy the government in the working of the 1902 Act. This was reinforced, after the passing of the Default Act in August 1904, by the resolution adopted at a national convention in Cardiff on 6 October that when the Default Act was applied, authorities would refuse to maintain any elementary schools, and Nonconformist parents of children at non-provided schools would then withdraw them and they would be educated out of voluntary effort, in chapels and vestries.[1] At Westminster, the Default Bill had been introduced on 26 April, just a week after the publication of the Report of the Inquiry, and was a measure designed to authorize the Board of Education to administer the 1902 Act where a local education authority was in default. Even before the Inquiry, the attitude of the Welsh councils had stiffened because their policy appeared to be progressing satisfactorily, and the county council elections in March had given popular support to it.[2] By the end of June, of twenty-nine local education authorities, only some Part III Authorities such as the borough councils of Carmarthen, Pembroke and Neath, and the urban districts of Ebbw Vale, Barry and Abertillery refused to carry out Lloyd George's policy.[3] The Welsh situation was causing grave embarrassment to the government, for by this time it was apparent that it could be proved that most of the Welsh authorities were in default.[4]

The policy followed by the Board of Education after receiving complaints from voluntary schools from November 1903 onwards was based on the advice which they received from the Law Officers of the Crown, namely, that no legal action could be taken by the Board merely upon a 'no rate' resolution which was rather a declaration of intention to disobey the law than an actual disobedience of it. They also pointed

---

[1] *The Manchester Guardian*, 8 October 1904. A '*Cronfa'r Revolt*' (Revolt Fund) was started at many places to open '*Ysgol Revolt*' (Revolt school), in the Welsh chapels. One of these was in operation at Glanrafon, Merioneth, in 1905. D. Tecwyn Lloyd (ed.), *Ysgol Llawrybetws, 1908–1958*, Gwasg y Bala, 1958, p. 9.

[2] PRO Ed 24/577, *Confidential Memorandum*, op. cit., p. 4.

[3] PRO Ed 24/578, *The educational situation in Wales*, op. cit., pp. 10–11. Wrexham Borough (appointed day 30 September 1903) began by administering the Act . . . the expenses of the schools being met out of a loan on the rates, but when at the end of March a question of levying a rate arose, it was expected that pressure would be brought on the voluntary schools to accept a compromise. The question of levying a rate arose on 20 April, when the Finance Committee of the Town Council decided to levy a rate for the council schools but deferred the case of the voluntary schools for six months.

[4] PRO Ed 24/577, ibid supra, p. 21:—Question of Illegality: 'Sometimes it is said by the Welsh leaders that there has been no breach of the law in Wales, and other times they say that Carmarthenshire is the only county which has broken the law. Mr. Lloyd George, for instance, said that Carmarthenshire was the only council which the Board of Education had been able to "declare in default". This expression is really quite meaningless. We could have held public inquiries about other councils in Wales and obtained a Report nearly as strong as that of Lawrence. In fact, in Merioneth, the deficiency of funds has been much worse than in Carmarthenshire; but Carmarthenshire was settled upon for the Inquiry only because the council when committing an illegality generally did it in solemn form by resolution, and such resolutions were easily proved in evidence'. (In 1905, Merioneth, Montgomery, Barry, Mountain Ash and Glamorgan were all found in default and had their grants withheld by the Board of Education).

out that under the Act of 1902, in no circumstances could parliamentary grants be paid to managers directly but to the local education authority. Further, *mandamus*, preceded by a public inquiry and an Order was the only legal remedy for a failure to maintain and keep efficient a particular school. But the Board had decided that *mandamus* proceedings, ending in the imprisonment of members of a Welsh council for contempt would be a mistaken policy. However it was decided to proceed legally up to the point of a public inquiry under section 16, and, if necessary, up to an Order made under that section against some council whose case appeared favourable in order (a) that the facts should be clearly proved to parliament and the public by a semi-judicial inquiry, both sides having been heard and witnesses being cross-examined in public (b) that the length and the *futility* of the remedies in the Act for dealing with the Welsh situation might be demonstrated, and *the necessity of further powers proved* (c) *to gain time and protract the matter* until parliament were in a position to interfere and provide increased or improved powers.[1] Hence, Carmarthenshire was selected for a Public Inquiry as affording the clearest evidence of illegal resolutions in order to strengthen the government's case that legislative action in the form of a Default Act was the only effective means of dealing with the Welsh councils.

Subsequent events, both on the part of the Board of Education and the Carmarthenshire county council bear out this argument. The answers to the two questions raised earlier were simple enough. The Board of Education had no intention, and was indeed apprehensive, of invoking *mandamus* in Carmarthenshire. In the explosive situation which existed in Wales during 1904–05, which coincided with the Welsh religious revival, was it conceivable that the government would imprison any local education authority officials? It contented itself with having proved the Carmarthenshire case in order to justify its Default Bill, and in the event, merely issued an Order against the council for the costs of the Inquiry. The county council, for its part, took cognisance of the result of the Inquiry, eventually climbed down, and more or less followed the Caernarvonshire policy.

The remaining relationships between the Board of Education and Carmarthenshire county council up to the passing of the Default Act in August 1904 showed that the Board allowed the council plenty of time to lick its wounds, and come to terms with the situation. The result of the Inquiry caused some concern to Bromley at the Treasury. On 28 March, in a Minute to Morant, he stated that grants had been paid to the county

---

[1] PRO Ed 24/577, *Confidential Memorandum*, op. cit., pp. 3–4.

council since the appointed day on the assumption that the council were complying with the terms of the 1902 Act. Bromley now proposed the further payments of grants be suspended until assurance was forthcoming that the statutory obligations were being carried out, and expressed the hope that Morant concurred. But Morant, in cautious mood, not yet having received a copy of the Report of the Inquiry, immediately sent Bromley's request to the President, saying 'that your authority is needed to continue paying these grants for the present', to which Londonderry gave his consent 'to continue payment till further instructions'.[1]

The Commissioner had completed his Report on 18 April. On 20 April, the Board sent a letter and two copies of the Report to the county council, with the request that in accordance with the provisions of Section 73 of the Elementary Education Act, 1870, one copy should be deposited at the County Offices and that this fact should be advertised. The Board drew the council's 'most serious attention to the very grave nature of the statements contained in the Report with reference to the manner in which your council have carried out their duties as local education authority in their area, and before proceeding to make any Order under Section 16 as to the duties of the council, or under Section 73(4) of the Elementary Education Act, 1870, as to the costs of the Inquiry, the Board would be glad to receive any observations which the council had to offer with reference to the matters alleged'.[2] Nicholas replied on 28 April stating that he had placed the letter, together with the Report, before the council, and the following resolution was passed 'that the letter from the Board of Education be referred to the education committee for early consideration and report, and that meanwhile it be an instruction to that committee to appoint a special sub-committee to confer with the national executive committee of the Welsh County Councils created at the Llandrindod national conference'. He also requested sufficient copies of the Report for distribution to each member of the council.[3]

Henceforward, the county council began to recant. During early May, 'a delegation of the Nonconformist party on the county council were in conference with the Welsh MPs'. The outcome of the deliberations was a decision to imitate the Caernarvonshire policy. As a result, the county council, on 21 May rescinded their 'no rate' resolution together with the resolutions as to the non-appointment of managers and attendance

[1] PRO Ed 111/252, Minute from Bromley to Morant, 28 March, 1904. Minute from Morant to President, 28 March; Minute from President to Morant, 28 March.
[2] PRO Ed 111/252, Board of Education to Carmarthenshire County Council, 20 April.
[3] Ibid., Carmarthenshire County Council to Board of Education, 28 April. The national executive committee of the Welsh county councils had been elected at the 1904 Easter Conference at Llandrindod, with Lloyd George as chairman.

officers. By the beginning of June, 'these had been appointed, and measures were taken to pool the grants earned by voluntary schools so that such schools would be maintained out of the central fund'.[1] Such were the initial steps taken by the council to meet the challenge of an Order from the Board of Education after the Inquiry. The next stage was the matter of teachers' salaries. Canon Brown had written to the Board of Education on 4 June complaining that the teachers in the voluntary schools were not being paid their salaries according to the scale adopted by the local education authority for the teachers in their council schools, and the council gave 'no definite educational reasons for the discrimination between the two classes of schools and between the teacher—a discrimination which Mr. Balfour declared to be impossible under the 1902 Education Act, and which Sir William Anson in answer to Mr. Griffith-Boscawen, MP, officially stated in the House of Commons to be in contravention of the Act'.[2] Brown was prepared to supply the Board with many examples of schools where such treatment had led to much suffering.

Apparently, nothing further was heard about this matter for almost a year. In fact, there seems to have been very little communication between the county council and the Board of Education from June 1904 to May 1905, apart from some complaint from the Correspondent of Newcastle Emlyn national school about arrears of payment, and a quick reply from Nicholas saying that the entire staff of his office were dealing with such claims as soon as possible.[3] There was also a request for repairs to a schoolroom which showed that the council were now demanding certain standards in school buildings.[4] In May 1905 the local education authority decided to revise the salaries of teachers in council and voluntary schools and in order to carry this out, Nicholas had served notices on the teachers in council schools terminating the existing contracts between them. He wrote in similar terms to the teachers in the voluntary schools enclosing copies of the circular and notice which had been served to teachers in the council schools.[5] One example was that of Llanddarog national school which was the subject of a mass of correspondence between Nicholas and the Board, Canon Brown and the Bishop of St. Davids, and the school Correspondent, the Rev. T. Jones, vicar of Llanddarog.[6]

[1] PRO Ed 24/578. *The Educational Situation in Wales*, op. cit., p. 4.
[2] PRO Ed 111/252, Brown to Board of Education, 4 June 1904.
[3] Ibid., Board of Education to Carmarthenshire County Council, 4 August; Carmarthenshire county council to Board of Education, 5 August.
[4] Ibid., Carmarthenshire County Council to Board of Education, 28 February, 1905; Board of Education to Carmarthenshire County Council, 7 March.
[5] PRO Ed 111/252, Nicholas to Rev. T. Jones, Vicar of Llanddarog, 27 May.
[6] Ibid., Jones to Nicholas, 30 May.

The Carmarthenshire Inquiry

The managers of the voluntary schools were deeply concerned about two matters (a) on what educational grounds (Section 6 (a) of the Education Act, 1902) the local education authority were pleading in dismissing the teachers, and (b) whether the salaries of some teachers were to be raised and others reduced. On the first point, Nicholas stated that the fixing of salaries of the teachers in voluntary schools was an educational ground[1] and this was questioned by Canon Brown and the Rev. Jones.[2] Eventually, the advice of the Board of Education was sought, but their answer was evasive. They avoided committing themselves especially in answer to an attempt on the part of a Welsh local education authority to get the Board to assist them in carrying out their 'no rate' policy. Nevertheless, they ventured the opinion that the 'refusal of managers to carry out general directions of the character of those now in question, to dismiss teachers in their schools, does not appear unreasonable or to interfere with a proper exercise of the control over expenditure in voluntary schools given to the local education authority by the Act'.[3] The Bishop of St. Davids intervened and the council withdrew this demand, Schuster remarking that 'they had climbed down' and were in a compromising mood for further mutual discussion.[4] With this, the correspondence ended abruptly without any indication as to the ultimate result.

There remained the bill for the Inquiry. This was the only Order served by the Board of Education on Carmarthenshire county council. But the framing of such an Order raised much discussion as to its format and content, since it was the first of its kind to be issued, for 'no doubt there is a distinction between an Inquiry held under Section 73 of the Act of 1870 alone, and one which is also governed by Section 16 of the 1902 Act. The essence of an Inquiry of the latter kind is a breach of the law, whereas Inquiries held only under the Act of 1870 contemplate no such breach'.[5] The Board had to determine whether the costs at the Carmarthenshire Inquiry were those of the Board only, or should also include costs incurred by any other party appearing as witnesses.[6] After consultations between Hills and Lindsell, and observations by Morant and Anson, it was decided that the Order should be made for the payments of the costs of the Board only, which amounted to £520.14.11.[7] A letter

[1] Ibid. Nicholas to Jones, 31 May.
[2] Ibid., Brown to Board of Education, 2 June; Brown to Bishop of St. Davids, 3 June.
[3] Ibid., Minute from Hills to Kingsford, 21 June.
[4] Ibid., Minute from Schuster to Hills; Minute from Hills to Kingsford, 22 June.
[5] PRO Ed 111/255, Statement prepared by Hills, 17 June; Minute from Schuster to Lindsell, 18 June; Minute from Lindsell to Morant, 20 June; Minute from Morant to Anson, 20 June.
[6] Ibid., Statement by Hills, ibid. supra.
[7] PRO Ed 111/255, Minute from Hills to Bromley, 27 June 1904.

The Carmarthenshire Inquiry

together with the formal Order was sent to Carmarthenshire county council on 6 July[1] and a cheque was sent to the Board of Education on 5 August.[2]

In a Confidential Memorandum sent to Morant on 25 June, Hills made the following comment: 'The fact that the Welsh councils are now falling back on the Caernarvonshire policy in practice and in argument is an admission that the Carmarthenshire policy will not keep sufficient Voluntary schools, in spite of the claim of Carmarthenshire county council at the Inquiry. The Carmarthenshire change of front is no doubt prudent, but for a council to have to revise their minute book and solemnly reverse resolutions as solemnly passed is undignified. Further, the fact that Carmarthenshire and other councils are now to follow a policy less hurtful to voluntary schools is, after all, a first fruit of the Carmarthenshire Inquiry and the introduction of the Defaulting Authorities Bill'.[3]

The Inquiry and its results were looked upon with scorn by the Carmarthenshire Nonconformists. To them, the Inquiry resembled a police-court session where the county council was brought to justice for misbehaving on technical points. It demonstrated that the bitterness of religious controversy could not be assuaged by litigation, especially when it was alleged that the prosecuting party—the Board of Education—'was fast becoming an Anglican outpost'.[4] Indeed, Nonconformist commentators in England lent sympathetic support to the Welsh Revolt and the struggle waged by Welsh Dissent—'the Battle of Nonconformity'. They denounced the passage of the Education (Local Authority Default) Act, saying that coercion by the State confirmed the suspicion that its policy was essentially sectarian.[5]

But the Carmarthenshire county councillors were infuriated that the Adjournment was dismissed, and the opportunity missed to give 'the full and complete story' of the attitude of Carmarthenshire without being subject to the technical restrictions. Anson dishonoured his reply to Lloyd George in the House of Commons, and hence the county council took no part in the Inquiry. Anson and Morant probably did not want the Inquiry to know what part the Nonconformists had played in the

---

[1] Ibid., Board of Education to Carmarthenshire County Council, 6 July.
[2] Ibid., Treasurer, Carmarthen County Council to Board of Education, 5 August.
[3] PRO Ed 24/577, *Confidential Memorandum*, op. cit., p. 19.
[4] Benjamin Sacks, *The Religious Issue in the State Schools of England and Wales*, 1902–1914, University of New Mexico Press, Albuquerque, 1961, p. 54.
[5] Ibid. The editor of the *Baptist Times* (13 November 1903) termed the dismissal in 1903 of Sir George Kekewich, Secretary since 1890 of the Board of Education and Edward R. Robson, architect since 1884, to be the result of clerical objection to the efforts of these men *to administer honestly* the Act of 1902 with regard to state of buildings of Welsh voluntary schools, i.e. they were not prepared to pass school buildings which did not reach the desired standard.

building of Church schools in rural Carmarthenshire before 1902 or even pre-1870. In any case, from 1903-5 they were more than deeply enmeshed with Lloyd George and the Welsh county councils in trying to establish a Welsh National Council of Education. It was very strange that Carmarthenshire, once again, upheld its independence and did not participate with the rest of the Welsh councils in joining the Welsh Council.

APPENDICES

I COPY OF INSTRUCTIONS TO A. G. LEGARD, HMI, TO VISIT PEMBREY AND LLANGENNECH NATIONAL SCHOOLS

II CONFIDENTIAL REPORTS ON PEMBREY AND LLANGENNECH NATIONAL SCHOOLS

III FINANCIAL STATEMENTS ON PEMBREY AND LLANGENNECH NATIONAL SCHOOLS

IV PUBLIC INQUIRY NOTICE

V CONCLUDING PARAGRAPH OF THE PUBLIC INQUIRY AND THE SCHEDULE OF SCHOOLS

The Carmarthenshire Inquiry

APPENDIX I

Copy of Instructions to Mr. Legard, H.M. Inspector
to visit Pembrey & Llangennech National Schools.

Paper A

Sir W. Anson's confidential instructions given to me February 1st 1904.

I. Is supply of necessaries refused, or is it inadequate?
If not

1. Are the Schools maintained to any and what extent out of private benefactions, or contributions of any Society?

2. Are the Managers using for purpose of maintenance

    (a) Balance in hand at appointed day.

    (b) Stores in hand at appointed day.

II. Has there been a refusal to sanction appointment of necessary teachers, or reduction of a salary increased or settled between 1902 and 1903?

III. Is there any difference of treatment in Voluntary and Council Schools?

    (a) As to supply of coal, stationery &c.

    (b) As to salary of teachers.

    (c) As to staffing and appointment of teachers.

    (d) As to access of Pupil Teachers to Centres.

PRO Ed. 111/254.

The Carmarthenshire Inquiry

APPENDIX II

CONFIDENTIAL REPORT ON PEMBREY NATIONAL SCHOOL,
County of Carmarthen

I visited this School on Tuesday February 2nd.

Pembrey Village until recently formed part of the large School Board District of Pembrey and Burry Port, in which there are several Board Schools.

The Village of Pembrey is at some little distance from the populous place called Burry Port, and in the village itself there is one Council School and one National School.

The National School comprised two Departments, one mixed the other Infant.

The Mixed Department is divided from the Infant Department by a wooden partition.

In the former there are 83 children on the books.

In the latter there are 36 children on the books.

Total—119.

The attendance is regular and 104 were present on the day of my visit.

The staff consists of a certificated master and his wife also certificated, and of a Pupil Teacher, First year, who is absent at the Pupil Teacher Centre two days in the week.

This is absolutely inadequate as the Master has to teach practically all the standards by himself.

The Managers have been anxious to appoint an assistant but on application to the County Council no sanction was given to their request (see correspondence in Pembrey National file).

(Today a confidential letter was received from the Secretary of the National Society, saying that the National Society will take steps to appoint an assistant.)

Apparatus &c.

A fair supply of this has been obtained by the Managers since the appointed day but there is a lack of reading books.

On the appointed day there was no store of coals, but loads of coal have been since ordered by the Managers as they were required.

FINANCES:

On September 30th the end of the Financial Year there was an overdrawn balance of £60. 9. 2.

Since then the Managers have received—

Annual Grant from the Board of Education	£101 9 7
Balance of Fee Grant from the Board of Education	11 17 4
Parliamentary Grants from County Council forwarded in November	25 14 1
Parliamentary Fee Grant from County Council in January	12 1 0

Out of this amount the Teachers' salaries due quarterly were paid up to the end of December 1903, and various School requisites were procured.

The Carmarthenshire Inquiry

APPENDIX II—(cont.)

(There seems now to be an overdrawn balance at the bank of about £12, but I hope to forward shortly exact figures as to this.)

(I understand that the Council School in the Village is well staffed, there being on the staff with an average attendance of about 94 in the Mixed Department, 1 certificated Master, one Assistant Mistress, one sewing Mistress and three Pupil Teachers. I hope to send exact figures on this matter also very shortly.)

I met the Manager Correspondent, Rev. D. Jones, and talked to him about the condition of the School.

He tells me that no difficulties are raised as to religious instruction, and that the number of Churchmen in his Parish is considerable.

He has a very large Parish and employs three Curates, but Pembrey National School is the only National School in the Parish.

ANSWER TO PAPER 'A'.
(Sir W. ANSON'S MEMORANDUM).

I. Supply inadequate
  1. Out of funds provided by Managers.
  2. (a) no balance in hand on appointed day but some balance remained after receipt of Government grant due on appointed day, not paid till some weeks later.
     (b) stores in hand were used.

II. Yes, sanction could not be obtained to appointment of Assistant.

III. (a) Yes.
   (b)
   (c) Yes, Council School in village well staffed.
   (d) Pupil Teachers went to centre before appointed day and still attend centre.

A. G. Legard,

February 2nd 1904.

The Carmarthenshire Inquiry

APPENDIX II—(cont.)

CONFIDENTIAL REPORT on LLANGENNECH NATIONAL SCHOOL, COUNTY OF CARMARTHEN

I visited this School on February 2nd.

Llangennech is a village near Llanelly with a population rather exceeding 2,000.

It contains two elementary Schools, one National and the other British.

The latter was a few days ago transferred to the County Council and is now a provided School.

There is no feeling in the village against the National School which is at some little distance from the British one, and parents select the one or the other simply on account of convenience of access.

The Master of the National School has been at his post some 25 years, and is much respected.

The Vicar whom I met, seemed to be a good man of business, and is a member of the Local District Council, Board of Guardians &c.

The National School consists of two Departments, Mixed and Infants.

In the former 110 children were on the books.

In the latter 58 children were on the books.

Of these 94 were present in the Mixed Department on the day of my visit; 50 in the Infant Department.

The staff is woefully deficient.

In the Mixed Department there is one Headmaster, certificated, and three girls who sat for the candidates examination last April and failed.

In the Infant Department there is one teacher, qualified Article 68, and one girl who failed in the candidates examination.

In the last report just received the Board of Education append the following warning:—

"The staff should be at once strengthened to meet the requirements of Article 73 which are not at present satisfied."

Since these remarks were made two male teachers in the School, who sat for the King's Scholarship last December, have left and their places have not been filled.

(In the file of Llangennech National correspondence on this subject will be seen.)

Apparatus &c.

The apparatus is very deficient, nothing practically has been procured since the appointed day, and much is wanted. On the appointed day about one load of coals was in stock, and since the day, about three loads have been procured from the Managers' resources.

Finance.

The Annual Grant (Financial Year ended Septr. 20th 1902) amounting to £128. 14. 0 has just been paid by the Board of Education to the Managers, but as there was

APPENDIX II—(cont.)

an adverse balance against the Managers at the end of the year of £122. 7. 6 this Grant will be practically absorbed.

The Managers have only received from the County Council the sum of £37 (Parliamentary Grant) since the appointed day. Quarterly payment of salaries due December 31st 1903 has just been made, viz:—

Principal Teacher	£30. 0. 0
Assistants	12. 0. 0
Pupil Teachers	12. 0. 0
	£54. 0. 0

I paid a short visit to Llangennech Council School which was a British School until a few days ago. In this School a good stock of apparatus has just been received from the County Council.

The staff is not a strong one but it is decidedly better than in the National School.

ANSWER TO PAPER A. (SIR W. ANSON'S MEMORANDUM).

I. Supply totally inadequate.
   1. Schools maintained from private resources of Managers.
   2. (a) no balance in hand.
      (b) stores in hand used.

II. Yes, sanction could not be obtained to appointment of Assistant.

III. (a) Yes, supply much better in Council School.
    (b)
    (c) Yes, staff better in Council School.
    (d) Candidates for Pupil Teachers do not attend centre.

A. G. Legard.

February 2nd 1904

PRO Ed. 111/254

The Carmarthenshire Inquiry

APPENDIX III

FINANCIAL STATEMENT AS TO SCHOOLS

1. PEMBREY NATIONAL SCHOOL:—

The accounts sent to the Board by the Managers are not forwarded herewith, as they are of a very confused character.

On the appointed day the School presumably started with a clean sheet of account. The grants accruing between the appointed day the 31st March 1904 (presumably the only legitimate source of income for current expenses of the School, outside Managers' expenses), were:—

November	Annual Grant	5. 5
	Fee Grant	2. 8
	Sec: 10 Grant	24. 2. 8
January	Fee Grant	12. 0. 0
	Total	£36.10. 9

EXPENDITURE:

The following items would seem to be the absolutely necessary expenditure for the same period:—

Head Teachers salary Quarter ending 31.12.'03	£22. 10. 0
Assistant ,, ,, ,, ,, ,, ,, ,,	13. 5. 0
Other ,, ,, ,, ,, ,, ,, ,,	6. 0. 0
Books &c. Apparatus &c. Fuel, Postage (½ year)	25. 7. 10
Salaries of Teachers Quarter ending 31.3.'04	41. 15. 0
Total	£108. 17. 10

Thus it will be seen that the grants accruing to the School for the 6 months would not suffice to pay the teachers' salaries for the quarter ending 31st December, 1903. By 31st March 1904, there should be a deficit of at least £72. 7. 1. It is very difficult, however, to be certain, as matters of evidence, of this kind of calculation, and it is understood that the advisers of managers who appear at the Inquiry will be very careful to investigate these accounts thoroughly.

2. Llangennech National School:

The case of financial deficit for the purpose of an Inquiry is not so clear here. The grants paid since Septr. 30th and accruing before April 1st. are as follows:—

		£ s. d.
November	S 10 Grant	39. 4. 4
January	Annual Grant	25. 18. 6
	Fee Grant	12. 14. 2
March	Fee Grant	19. 10. 0
	Total	£97. 7. 0

Thus the income to be applied by the County Council for the upkeep of the School for the period from 31st December to 31st March 1904, is £97. 7. 0

APPENDIX III—(cont.)

The necessary items of expenditure for the first quarter of this period are:—

	£	s.	d.
Quarters salaries to 31 Decr. 1903	54.	0.	0
Books, Coals, apparatus, &c., ,,	12.	10.	0
	66.	10.	0
Similar items for 2nd. Quarter up to 31st March 1904	66.	10.	0
Total	£133.	0.	0

Thus there should be a deficiency on 31st. March of £35.

The Llangennech accounts are rather less certain than those of Pembrey, and it is to be noted that if the Inquiry were held before the end of March, as the current quarter's salaries would not have fallen due, the £97 would probably have been sufficient to wipe off any arrears which had been outstanding on the 31st. December. So although the Managers could say before the Inquirer that they had been in arrears, and would be in arrears, it is not certain that they would be able to tell the Inquirer that they actually were in arrears.

PRO Ed. 111/254

The Carmarthenshire Inquiry

APPENDIX IV

EDUCATION ACTS, 1870—1902.

Administrative County of the County Council of Carmarthenshire

WHEREAS representations have been made to the Board of Education that the Local Education Authority of the Administrative County of Carmarthenshire as regards some or all of the Public Elementary Schools within their area named in the schedule hereto annexed, being Schools not provided by the said Local Education Authority have failed to fulfil their duties under the Sections hereinafter mentioned of the Education Act, 1902, with respect thereto and in particular—

(1) Have failed to be responsible for or to control the Secular Instruction to be given in such Schools (Section 5);

(2) Have failed to appoint a Manager or Managers for such Schools respectively (Section 6(2));

(3) Have failed to maintain and keep efficient such Schools or to control the expenditure required for that purpose (Section 7(1));

(4) Have withheld their consent to the appointment of Teachers on other than educational grounds (Section 7 (1) (c)).

AND WHEREAS the Board of Education have determined to hold a Public Inquiry with respect to such failure as aforesaid under Sections 16 and 23 (10) of the said Act and have appointed A. T. Lawrence, Esq., one of His Majesty's Counsel, to hold such Inquiry.

NOW THEREFORE the Board of Education HEREBY GIVE NOTICE that the said A. T. Lawrence. Esq., one of His Majesty's Counsel, will hold a sitting at the Assembly Rooms in King Street, in the Borough of Carmarthen, on Thursday, the twenty-fourth day of March, 1904, at 11 o'clock in the forenoon, and will thereat hear receive and examine any evidence and information offered, and hear and inquire into any objections or representations made respecting the subject of the Inquiry with power from time to time to adjourn any sitting.

H. M. LINDSELL,
Principal Assistant Secretary.

The Carmarthenshire Inquiry

APPENDIX V

CONCLUDING PARAGRAPH OF THE PUBLIC INQUIRY AND THE SCHEDULE OF SCHOOLS

In conclusion, I feel constrained, with great regret, to report that the County Council of Carmarthenshire, as the Local Education Authority, have failed to fulfil their duties under the Education Act of 1902, towards the 48 Public Elementary Schools within their area mentioned in the Schedule hereunder, in that:—

(1) They have failed to be responsible for or to control the secular instruction to be given in such schools;

(2) They have failed to appoint a Manager or Managers for such schools respectively;

(3) They have failed to maintain and keep efficient such schools, or to control the expenditure required for that purpose;

(4) They have withheld their consent to the appointment of Teachers on other than Educational grounds.

A. T. LAWRENCE

3, Paper Buildings, Temple,
    April 18th, 1904.

SCHEDULE.

Abergwilly National School.
Llanvihangeluwchgwili National School.
Yspytty National School.
Abernant National School.
Berrisbrook National School.
Cil-y-cwm Church School.
Tremoilet Memorial School.
Kidwelly National School.
Brook National School.
Laugharne National School.
Golden Grove National School.
Llanarthney National School.
Llanddarog National School.
Llandebie National School.
Llandefeilog National School.
Cwm Amman National School.
Llandilofawr National School.
Trapp National School.
Llandovery National School.
Llandowror National School.
Hendy National School.
Old Llanedy National School.
Tycroes National School.
Llanegwad National School.

Felinfoel Trinity National School.
Capel Cynfab National School.
Rhandyrmwyn National School.
Llanfihangel-ar-Arth National School.
Llanfynydd National School.
Capel Mair National School.
Llangeler National School.
Llangennech National School.
Llangunnock Vaughan's Charity School.
Llangunnor National School.
Llanllwni National School.
Llannon National School.
Llanstephan National School.
Llanbri National School.
Merthyr National School.
Cwmdwr Church School.
Mothfai National School.
Newcastle Emlyn National School.
Newchurch National School.
Pembrey National School.
Pemboyr National School.
St. Clears National School.
Ferryside St. Thomas' Parochial School.
Llansaint National School.

A.T.L.

IV

THE GENESIS OF THE WELSH DEPARTMENT BOARD OF EDUCATION

INTRODUCTION 184

I ABORTIVE ATTEMPTS TO ESTABLISH A WELSH NATIONAL COUNCIL FOR EDUCATION 186

II THE CREATION OF THE WELSH DEPARTMENT, BOARD OF EDUCATION 213

APPENDICES 231

The Genesis of the Welsh Department, Board of Education

A WELSH National Council for Education, if it had come into being, would have consummated the highest aspirations of Welsh political and educational leaders in the opening years of the twentieth century. Politically, in the re-awakened Welsh national consciousness of that period, such a Council would have gone a long way towards satisfying a growing demand for Welsh administrative recognition. On the educational side it envisaged the co-ordination of all branches of Welsh education. Indeed, had Lloyd George been successful in his quest for the fulfilment of the National Council between 1903 and 1906, it would have given Wales a substantial measure of educational autonomy and there would have been no occasion to discuss the Welsh Department of the Board of Education.

But long before 1903 there had been a strong desire to secure for Wales a National Council for Education. In the late eighties, two ardent Welshmen were in the forefront in demanding autonomy for Welsh affairs including home rule, which of course included educational autonomy— Tom Ellis, MP for Merioneth and J. Herbert Lewis who was elected to Parliament for Flint District in 1892. Lewis, who was the first chairman of Flintshire county council, in his enthusiasm for a measure of self-government for Wales, spoke at a Liberal conference at Newtown in 1888 which passed a resolution in favour of combining the Welsh county councils under Section 81 of the Local Government Act of that year to form a Welsh National Council. In another oration at Rhewl, Mostyn, soon afterwards, he detailed his plan: 'I also look forward to the constitution of a General Council for the whole of Wales . . . upon the powers given in the 82nd [sic] Section of the Local Government Act . . . when it will become possible to combine the Welsh county councils in order that in future they may be able to give attention to matters peculiar to Wales alone . . . I contend that we may begin by the medium of these councils in regard to education, Crown lands, administration, and establish Schools of Forestry and Agriculture'.[1]

---

[1] K. Idwal Jones, (ed.), *Syr Herbert Lewis*, 1858–1933, Cardiff, 1958, pp. 47, ff. K. Viriamu Jones, *Life of J. Viriamu Jones*, London, 1921, p. 211, footnote: In 1875, A. C. Humphreys-Owen had proposed a Central Body for Wales, and in 1887 Owen Owen had put forward a proposal for a Welsh Education Department at Whitehall.

The Genesis of The Welsh Department, Board of Education

On 3 July 1891, a meeting of the 'National United Council' was held at Shrewsbury which included representatives from Carmarthenshire, Caernarvonshire, Denbighshire, Flintshire, Glamorgan, Merioneth, Montgomeryshire, Pembrokeshire, Radnor, Cardiff and Newport. Caernarvonshire was represented by Alderman D. Lloyd George. The meeting decided to form an association of the Welsh county councils under the title 'National Council of Wales and Monmouthshire'. Later, two further meetings of the association were held at Llandrindod and Shrewsbury respectively when it was resolved to establish a Welsh National Council. But the project came to nought because the Local Government Board advised that there would be constitutional difficulties with regard to the expenditure of public money for such a purpose.[1]

Tom Ellis together with Stuart Rendel, MP for Montgomeryshire (who piloted the Welsh Intermediate Education Bill of 1889 through the Commons) had included in the Bill, but subsequently deleted, a National Council of Education for Wales.[2] In 1891 and 1892, Alfred Thomas, MP for Glamorgan East, brought forward his National Institutions (Wales) Bills, supported by most of the Welsh Members. The substance of the Bills included the appointment of a Secretary of State for Wales, a Welsh Education Department, further provision for Local Government and the creation of a National Council, but both Bills were dropped.[3] The nearest approach to a National Council for Education arose out of the necessity of creating a body for the implementation of the Welsh Intermediate Education Act when in September 1890, A. H. D. Acland, chairman of the Joint Education Committees set up under the Act, suggested a central educational body for Wales. This produced the Central Welsh Board which received Royal Assent on 13 May 1896, a body solely concerned with Welsh intermediate schools.[4] These sporadic attempts, up to 1903, to secure a Welsh National Council for Education—the phase of ways and means—ends the first part of the story. Henceforward, it was to develop into a major political issue led by Lloyd George and aided (up to the end of 1905) by his indefatigable assistant, Evan R. Davies, secretary to the Caernarvonshire education committee.

---

[1] K. Idwal Jones, op. cit.

[2] *Parl. Deb.*, 3rd series, vol. cccxxxvi, c. 147, ff. In the debate, Ellis traced back the idea of such a Council to the Schools Inquiry Commission of the sixties when he referred to a Board of Education for Wales.

[3] *Parl. Deb.*, 3rd series, vol. ccclv, c. 1327; ibid., vol. ccclvi.

[4] *Report of Proceedings. Joint Education Committees of Wales and Monmouthshire*, 1890; *The Welsh Intermediate Education Act: Its Origin and Working*, W. N. Bruce, Education Department, Vol. I, pp. 10, ff.

I ABORTIVE ATTEMPTS TO ESTABLISH A WELSH NATIONAL COUNCIL FOR EDUCATION

Two main attempts to translate the idea of this Council into practical reality are of particular relevance to the creation of the Welsh Department. The first, conducted mainly by Lloyd George and Davies, was an external negotiation phase, from April 1903 to November 1905.[1] A primary requirement of the 1902 Education Act was that provisional education committees had to be set up by the county councils to prepare county schemes for submission to Whitehall. By the end of April 1903, with the exception of Carmarthenshire which had passed its scheme, all the Welsh county councils including Monmouthshire had succeeded in deferring 'the appointed day' under the Act until 30 September with a view to adopting *uniform schemes* for the constitution of a Joint Board for Wales for educational purposes under section 17 (5) of the Act. The Welsh County Councils Association appointed T. Mansel Franklen, clerk to Glamorgan county council and Evan R. Davies to prepare a draft scheme for a Welsh Joint Board, which, if approved by all the Welsh councils would be sent to the Board of Education.[2] It contemplated a limited measure of educational autonomy by delegating to the Joint Board matters relating to the training of teachers, the examination and inspection of schools, and 'any further matters to be decided from time to time'.[3]

Accordingly, at the beginning of May, the draft scheme was sent by Franklen on behalf of the provisional education committee of Glamorgan to the Board of Education for their consideration. By 17 June, the Board of Education in a reply to Franklen, made certain observations and also proposed important amendments, especially with regard to the clause constituting the Joint Board. Bruce emphasized that the Board of Education raised no objection to the principle of a Joint Board for the whole of the Principality, but were concerned that the personnel of the Joint Board might not include persons 'with the necessary technical knowledge and educational experience' essential to enable them to successfully administer matters appertaining to any larger area of which their county council might from part.[4]

No doubt the Board of Education had sound reasons for imposing its conditions and safeguards, for it was not slow to recognize the important

---

[1] Leslie Wynne Evans, 'A Welsh National Council for Education, 1903–6', *Welsh History Review*, Vol. 6, No. 1, 1972. This deals in detail with the external negotiating phase.

[2] *Western Mail*, 4 May 1903.

[3] PRO Ed 91/10: Welsh Draft Scheme.

[4] PRO Ed 91/11: Bruce to Franklen, 17 June. William Napier Bruce, second son of Henry Austin Bruce first Lord Aberdare. After a long spell as Commissioner under the Charity Commission became Principal Assistant Secretary at the Board of Education in 1903.

place that such a Welsh Joint Board might ultimately occupy in the Welsh educational system. It might, if constituted on the lines approved by the Board of Education become endowed with wider powers, for example, in Bruce's words 'it might take over the powers of inspection and examination now possessed by the Central Welsh Board of intermediate education'. Furthermore, the Board of Education realized that the proposal contained in the clause might produce the germ of one education authority for the whole of the Principality in respect of both primary and secondary education, notwithstanding the separatist policy of the Carmarthenshire county council.[1]

But Glamorgan proved intransigent and returned the scheme unaltered to the Board of Education, Alderman T. J. Hughes, Bridgend, maintaining that 'if the Board of Education deemed wise to reject it, then it became the duty of the county authorities throughout Wales to strive unitedly . . . for the attainment of what had long been the ideal of true Welsh educationists—the unification in one national system of the primary and secondary systems of the Principality'.[2] Further meetings and correspondence ended in a complete deadlock, and the county councils were advised by Whitehall to submit their county schemes without more delay because 'it would take a long time to settle the Joint Board question'.[3] But Lloyd George's advice to the county councils was 'to stick to their guns on the question of a Welsh Joint Board to supersede the existing Central Welsh Board and really forming the nucleus of a future Welsh Education Department'.[4]

At this juncture, the guiding hand of Sir William Anson, Parliamentary Secretary to the Board of Education provided a solution to the problem. Having consulted his legal adviser at the Board, Anson believed 'that what the Welsh counties want will be best affected by a *Joint Committee* for the special purposes contemplated and not by the introduction of delegation of certain powers into the scheme of each council . . . In the case of a Joint Committee we might more readily ensure a sufficient supply of expert opinion without requiring that each county and county borough should provide one or more experts'.[5] Indeed, he was prepared to go much further. He made a definite promise on behalf of the Board of Education, to submit counter-proposals in the form of a draft scheme for the consti-

---

[1] *South Wales Daily News*, 19 June 1903.
[2] *South Wales Daily News*, 19 June 1903.
[3] PRO Ed 91/10: Draft letter from Bruce to Davies, 14 July 1903.
[4] PRO Ed 91/W49, Ref. 11, Minutes of emergency meeting at the House of Commons. Note from Bruce to Morant re 'Welsh County Schemes', recording observations made by Lloyd George. ibid., Bruce to Glamorgan and Welsh County Councils, 20 July.
[5] PRO Ed 91/10, Minute from Anson to Morant, 12 July, passed to Bruce, 15 July.

The Genesis of The Welsh Department, Board of Education

tution of the Joint Committee which he hoped would be acceptable to his Board and to the Glamorgan and other Welsh county councils.[1] In a press interview on 30 July, Lloyd George disclosed that he hoped the new proposals would eventually lead to the co-ordination of all grades of Welsh education including the training of teachers. He also remarked that representation should be based on population and that in the meantime the Welsh councils should postpone their schemes until they saw the government plan.[2]

Anson's proposal consisted of two outline draft schemes A and B, which were considered at a conference of the Welsh county councils at Swansea on 1 October 1903.[3] The main difference between the two schemes centred on the co-option of outside experts and the number of representatives to be elected on the Joint Committee. Scheme B was adopted with certain reservations, for example, clause 2 was amended by Ald. Hughes, to read 'provided that the councils in appointing members of the Joint Committee shall make provision for the co-option of persons having educational knowledge, etc'.[4] Lloyd George, who took a prominent part in the discussions (when an equality of voting arose regarding the number of representatives to be elected, whether 51 or 60) gave his casting vote as chairman, in favour of 60: 51 elected, seven selected, and two women.[5] Moreover, the scheme was to be re-drafted by the drafting committee on the lines agreed upon.

At the Board of Education in November, Bruce and Morant were negotiating with the Local Government Board in smoothing out certain financial difficulties in the way of the constitution of the Joint Committee. The Local Government Board agreed to co-operate on the understanding that the financial arrangements were to be set out in an Agreement to be drawn up between each combining council composing the Joint Committee.[6] On 25 April 1904, Claude Schuster, an eminent parliamentary draughtsman and counsel to the Board of Education, saw Lloyd George, Herbert Lewis, Frank Edwards, T. J. Hughes and Evan R. Davies at the House of Commons, and for two days they were engaged in discussing the topics of re-drafting referred to them by the Swansea conference. They

---

[1] Ibid., Minutes of House of Commons meeting when Anson and Bruce met T. J. Hughes, Lloyd George and the Welsh Members, 30 July. *Manchester Guardian*, 31 July 1903.

[2] *Western Mail*, 31 July 1903.

[3] PRO Ed 91/10, Bruce to Welsh county councils, 3 August 1903.

[4] PRO Ed 91/10, Hughes to Bruce, 31 July: clause to be included in Board of Education scheme that if experts be co-opted that they should be co-opted by a vote of the Joint Committee itself and not by the votes of constituent councils.

[5] *Manchester Guardian*, 2 October 1903.

[6] PRO Ed 91/10, Minutes from Bruce to Morant, 6 November 1903; from Morant to Schuster, 21 February 1904; from Schuster to Morant, 22 February 1904.

The Genesis of The Welsh Department, Board of Education

were the perennial questions of co-option, larger representation for rural areas, the position of autonomous districts and the problem of the Central Welsh Board. But although the scheme was again to be re-drafted, was incomplete, and in an imperfect condition, Schuster had to announce 'that it had been accepted in that form by all the parties'.[1]

But the new scheme was hailed with tremendous enthusiasm in Wales, the Welsh members and Lloyd George 'expressing themselves in terms of high appreciation as to the manner in which the Board of Education have met the wishes of the Principality in this matter by pursuing a very liberal and sympathetic policy throughout'.[2] The national executive committee of the Welsh county councils which had been elected at the recent Easter conference at Llandrindod with Lloyd George as chairman, was quite satisfied that as soon as the draft scheme and agreement was adopted by the county councils and finally sanctioned by the Board of Education, the Welsh Education Council would be operative throughout Wales within six months.[3] The *Manchester Guardian* proclaimed that 'Wales will have for the first time in its history a directly elected national body in full touch with the aims and aspirations of the overwhelming mass of the electorate ... the goal to be aimed at is the creation of an official government department for Wales'.[4]

Indeed, had Providence smiled during the following weeks, such prophetic utterances might have been translated into actuality. Towards the end of June, Balfour, the Prime Minister, in a report of Cabinet proceedings to the King, had inserted a tiny paragraph—sandwiched between problems of State involving Abyssinia and 'the old and difficult question of the King's Statutory Declaration against Transubstantiation'— stating that 'Lord Londonderry, President of the Board of Education has brought before the Cabinet a proposal for establishing a Welsh Branch of the Education Department in the Principality'. This was referred for report to a Cabinet committee, but it apparently lapsed.[5] But the final draft scheme together with an accompanying draft agreement, became, for over eighteen months, until the fall of the Unionist government in December 1905, the subject of prolonged correspondence between Davies and the Board of Education.

The trend of events both in parliament and in Wales during the summer of 1904 had made Welsh education a real problem and an embarrassment

---

[1] Ibid., Minute from Schuster to Sykes and Bruce on the Welsh Joint Scheme, 7 May 1904.
[2] *South Wales Daily News*, 12 May, 1904.
[3] Ibid.
[4] *Manchester Guardian*, 9 May, 1904.
[5] PRO, PM Cabinet Letters to the Sovereign, Cab. 41, Vol. 29, No. 21, Balfour, 29 June, 1904.

to the government. Led by a defiant Lloyd George—infuriated by the debates on the Education (Default) Authorities Bill passed in August 1904—the Welsh county councils were refusing to implement the Act of 1902 on the question of rate-aid for voluntary schools. It could be argued, from the evidence, that the government had decided to devise retaliatory measures in such a manner as not to incur undue hostility towards the Welsh people and Lloyd George. There remained no better scapegoat than the Welsh Education Council. To be obstructive towards its realization seemed to be the policy of the Board of Education which explains their change of attitude in subsequent negotiations.

On 7 November, Davies, on behalf of the Welsh National Executive, sent copies of the draft Agreement and Scheme for the constitution of a Welsh Education Council to the Board of Education, stating that 'they have been adopted by nearly all the constituent authorities . . . and am directed to ask that formal approval be given by your Board in order that the scheme may be published officially, with a view to its final sanction by your Board'.[1] The reaction of the Board was immediate and opposed to this request. They maintained that the scheme was merely a draft, and that words like 'formal sanction' and 'approval' were inappropriate at this stage. Also, that in the case of a joint scheme, the Board required 'a proper and authentic resolution from each local education authority'.[2] Morant categorically confirmed that 'Sir William Anson fully agrees that the letter is absurdly impertinent in what it pretends to expect us to do'.[3] Bruce was directed to reply to Davies 'that practical effect could only be given to *identical schemes* for a Joint Committee submitted by *individual* local education authorities'.[4]

More letters on this subject were exchanged up to mid-February 1905, when Davies submitted an Agreement and Scheme in respect of Caernarvonshire county council, with the request that 'it now be approved and published'.[5] At this point, Morant thought it expedient to ask Lloyd George for an interview with Anson and other officials of the Board, to consider further amendments regarding the training of teachers and the apportionment of expenditure by several autonomous districts.[6] It was decided that no action could be taken for the approval of the scheme until Davies had heard from the Welsh councils whether or not they were in

[1] PRO Ed 24/579, Davies to Board of Education, enclosing draft Agreement and Scheme, 7 November 1904.
[2] Ibid., Minute from Bruce to Morant, 14 November.
[3] Ibid., Minute from Morant to Bruce, 16 November.
[4] PRO Ed 91/11, Bruce to Davies, 28 November.
[5] Ibid., Davies to Board of Education, 9 February 1905.
[6] Ibid., Morant to Lloyd George, 15 February.

opposition to the scheme. Davies informed the Board on the 9 March that few councils, to date, had adopted the scheme for a Welsh Education Council.[1]

It became obvious from the ever accumulating mass of correspondence relating to all the technical details, amendments and the insistence of the Board that every council should participate in the scheme, that negotiations were reaching a stage where unanimity seemed remote, if not impossible. Even Sykes (the superb drafter of official letters at the Board) had to confess that he found it extremely difficult to draft replies which 'had to be worded in such a way as not to leave us exposed to a complaint ... that we are making conditions which we must know to be impracticable, and which we might have made as well at an earlier stage'.[2] However, by 10 April, the Board of Education had decided to send a circular to all Welsh councils setting out the position and the proposals in detail for the establishment of a Joint Committee to be designated the 'Welsh Education Council'. This circular contained copies of all the correspondence between Davies and the Board from November 1904, with additional copies of the draft Agreement and Scheme. It was disclosed that only eight county councils and four urban district councils had furnished the Board with resolutions, and that this lack of unanimity on the part of the Welsh councils was insufficient to justify the Board's approval of the scheme, and the Board invited the councils to submit their views on the proposals.[3]

Some councils corresponded with the Board and requested additional copies of the circular and enclosures for consideration by their committees. By the end of August, most had replied in favour of the scheme, although even at this stage autonomous districts, for example, Wrexham and Pontypridd were still wavering. At the end of September, Carmarthenshire was the only dissentient.[4] A deputation from this county, headed by its clerk, J. W. Nicholas, met the Welsh National Executive at Shrewsbury on 29 September, and pressed for larger representation on the proposed National Council. T. J. Hughes made an impassioned plea, strongly endorsed by Lloyd George, that the county should join, and not wreck a scheme which had cost so much labour and which provided a scaffolding for a future Welsh Education Department. But the deputation refused to make any pledge and retired. The Executive had no alternative but to

---

[1] PRO Ed 91/11, Bruce to Davies, 7 March; Davies to Board of Education, 9 March.
[2] Ibid., Minute from Sykes to Bruce, 17 March 1905.
[3] PRO Ed 91/11, *Circular to Local Education Authorities, whether for Parts II and III or for Part III only, of the Education Act, 1902, in Wales and Monmouthshire*, 10 April 1905.
[4] Ibid., Nicholas to Bruce, 2 October 1905.

The Genesis of The Welsh Department, Board of Education

resolve to ask the Board of Education to sanction the scheme excluding Carmarthenshire, and a deputation was appointed to wait upon the Board.[1] Accordingly, on 20 October, Morant asked Bruce to see Anson to fix an appointment to meet the deputation on 22 November, stating that 'Sir William Anson will doubtless explain to them very definitely the impossibility of complying with their wish'.[2]

But there were other ominous under-currents, with Morant at the centre, working against the implementation of the National Council. On 16 October, Lord Cawdor wrote to the President of the Board stating that 'the Welsh National Education scheme which Lloyd George is pushing ... has been strongly opposed by the Carmarthenshire county council and also by Pembrokeshire ... I am told that Anson is rather inclined to give way to Lloyd George on certain points, but I hope you will prevent this for I feel sure the wise thing to do is to let the scheme die'.[3] On 21 October, Morant received a short note from Anson saying 'the President, Lord Londonderry, writes "show this to Morant and tell him that I am writing Cawdor I agree with him" '.[4] On the same day, Morant had written to Cawdor saying 'Lord Londonderry has already written you in regard to the Welsh Education Council ... there is not the faintest likelihood of our sanctioning the scheme ... as we hope to entangle Lloyd George and his friends into admissions of hopeless disagreement among themselves ... there is no doubt the deputation will depart wholly discomfited ... we should not now definitely say that we wholly reject the scheme, but we should practically squelch it in other ways. You may feel assured that this latter will be done'.[5] It was well done, squelched, unsanctioned, and the scheme was put away forever. Less than a month after the visit of the deputation to the Board, the Unionist government had collapsed.

In the Book of Proverbs it is recorded 'In the multitude of counsellors there is safety'. Perhaps it would be equally correct to say that in the multitude of councils there is much confusion. This might help to explain some of the reasons for the failure of the first attempt to establish a Joint Committee or Welsh Education Council which clearly emerged during the course of the long negotiations. Morant and Bruce had summed up some of the Welsh defects as hopeless disagreement among Lloyd George and his followers and 'the inadequacy of consideration given to points of

---

[1] Ibid., Davies to Board of Education, 12 October. *Manchester Guardian*, 30 September, 1905.
[2] PRO Ed 91/11, Minute to Bruce from Morant, 20 October.
[3] PRO Ed 24/579, Cawdor (from Cawdor Castle, Nairn) to Londonderry, 16 October.
[4] PRO Ed 91/11, Minute from Anson to Morant, 21 October.
[5] PRO Ed 24/579, Morant to Cawdor, 21 October 1905.

The Genesis of The Welsh Department, Board of Education

much importance'.[1] But there were other important factors which spelled the doom of the National Council at this stage. In the first place, the indecision and diffidence displayed by the Welsh county councils. Secondly, the smaller autonomous districts along with the sparsely populated rural counties were dissatisfied with their proposed representation along with certain financial considerations, and feared that they might be engulfed or out-voted (on matters that might arise affecting them) by their more powerful neighbours.[2] Thirdly, from the outset, Carmarthenshire had affirmed its detachment, not only by approving its county scheme before the 'appointed day' and being the most hostile council in the working of the Education Act of 1902 on religious grounds, but also by believing that the proposed Education Council would merely be another version of the Central Welsh Board which had failed to foster the Welsh language.[3] Also, the county had failed to secure on the Council, increased representation which would give it a clear majority over its autonomous districts. This led in the final event, to its refusal to enter the combination.[4] Fourthly, Glamorgan, the largest and most important county council, uncompromising and evasive in the initial stages, later consented to join, although a few of its autonomous districts eventually conceded only with some hesitancy. Such tardiness and prevarication on the part of the Welsh councils as a whole demonstrated that such unanimity as existed was purely nominal and superficial. Finally, the external negotiation phase coincided with the period immediately following the Education Act of 1902 which gave LEAs considerable powers and opportunities to develop their own schemes. It was too early to expect them at that stage, before they had settled down to grapple with their administrative responsibilities, to surrender any part of their local sovereignty for national unity.

The Liberal landslide in the general election of January 1906 produced the new Administration with Sir Henry Campbell-Bannerman as Prime Minister. This initiated the second attempt to establish a Welsh National Council for Education—the parliamentary phase of 1906—when Lloyd George, as President of the Board of Trade, had a seat in the Cabinet. Augustine Birrell, the new President of the Board of Education, introduced his Education Bill in the Commons on 9 April, which sought to amend the Education Act of 1902 in line with Nonconformist demands on the religious issue, and also included in Part IV of the Bill a provision relating

[1] PRO Ed 91/11, Bruce to LEAs, 10 April 1905.
[2] Herbert Lewis's Diary, 28 April, 1, 2, May 1904; 16, 17 February 1905, Penucha MSS.
[3] *South Wales Daily News*, 5 August 1903.
[4] *The Manchester Guardian*, 30 September 1905: Carmarthenshire would not accept any proposal which did not give an administrative county a clear majority over its autonomous areas.

The Genesis of The Welsh Department, Board of Education

exclusively to the administration of education in Wales in the form of a National Council for Education, to be established by Order in Council. It was an opportunity for Lloyd George to try to secure by parliamentary legislation what external negotiation had failed to achieve. In so far as it envisaged the control of all levels of education in the Principality, (apart from grants in aid of the University and University Colleges) in the words of Morant, 'effective and complete educational autonomy', this Council was a much more elaborate version of Anson's Joint Committee proposal under the Act of 1902.[1] But, in the event, the meagre reward for all the efforts of Lloyd George was the Welsh Department of the Board of Education.

The origin of Part IV of the Bill, as Balfour said 'came from the inventive ingenuity of the President of the Board of Trade'.[2] Several preliminary drafts of the proposed clause and schedule had been scrutinized before final submission to the Cabinet on 20 March.[3] Even before the drafts for the Cabinet document had been contemplated, a long memorandum had been prepared by Lloyd George for a proposed Welsh Education Council.[4] This Council was to include all the Welsh MPs in order to strengthen it for the purposes of devolution. There were to be 130 members made up of 96 representatives of counties, county boroughs, and autonomous areas and 34 MPs. Three committees were to be established for primary, secondary education, and finance, and each committee was to be sufficiently large to render it possible to provide for the representation of each of the contributory authorities. A consultative committee would be formed consisting of 11 members who would represent the views of the teaching profession and who would prepare reports for the committees of the Council on any subject or subjects referred to them by the Education Council. The Council was to be invested with all the powers and functions of the Board of Education in respect of education in Wales and such other powers and functions as might be from time to time determined by the Imperial Parliament.[5]

This memorandum was mentioned in Morant's letter to Lloyd George on 28 February 1906. Bearing in mind the extremely contemptuous manner in which Morant had written former letters about the new Cabinet

---

[1] PRO Ed 24/579, Morant to Lloyd George, 28 February 1906.

[2] *Par . Deb.*, 4th series, vol. clvii, cs. 461, ff.

[3] PRO Ed 24/579; 24/110–126, Minutes of Cabinet meetings. PRO Ed 118, (1906), Drafts of Cabinet Memoranda: *Proposed clause and schedule providing for the establishment by Order in Council of a Welsh National Council for Education.*

[4] Lloyd George Papers, A/3/6/1, Beaverbrook Library: Draft Memorandum for a Welsh National Council, its Constitution, Consultative Committee, power, functions and funds.

[5] Lloyd George Papers, A/3/6/1, ibid.

minister to members of the previous government it is strange to read the mellifluous words which he employed on this occasion. Referring to the Welsh National Council for Education he said that 'he was sorry to have been so obstructive the other night as to the Welsh Council, *I am, and have long been, as anxious as you are to bring about (so far as my Chief will go) effective and complete educational autonomy.* But we have had great difficulty in discovering how far the local authorities were prepared to hand over their powers to the new Council in respect of various items of education. And until we know as to these things we could not get a clear scheme for consideration. Hence my plying you with one point after another in order to get a clear notion of what is contemplated . . . I think the simplest thing is for me to set out in a memorandum what we now understand to be the intention of the proposal, and this I will do with Mr. Birrell's permission . . . it would be a great help if you could let me have the typewritten memorandum which you had in your hand that evening which set out the main points which we were discussing'.[1]

By 5 March Morant had completed his memorandum.[2] He passed it on to Bromley at the Treasury for his comments on the financial implications and then on to Lloyd George. Bromley went into the matter thoroughly, was evidently impressed with the idea of a Welsh Education Council and saw no undue difficulties from the financial standpoint. Saying that the Board could not accept responsibility for finance if they were divested of control, he went on to explain that the Education Council could, as suggested in paragraph 8 of the memorandum, draw its funds from the Treasury as in the case of universities and colleges, or the Board of Education might include in its estimates a grant in aid for the Welsh Education Council and disburse it in quarterly instalments as required. He pointed out that the weakness of grants in aid was the loss of control by Parliament over the detailed expenditure upon which such grants were expended. But there was no reason why the grant in aid to the Welsh Education Council *should not be treated exceptionally.*[3] Morant had obviously spent a great deal of time working out the details of the machinery for the establishment of the Council, and it is a matter of speculation whether Lloyd George took the trouble to read it properly, as apart from the fact that he was attracted by the 'Minister responsible to Parliament' idea, subsequent events in Parliament showed that he had not worked out any concrete scheme based on the memorandum and

---

[1] PRO Ed 24/579, Morant to Lloyd George, ibid., 28 February.
[2] Ibid., Confidential Memorandum on the proposed Welsh National Council for Education, R. L. Morant, 5 March 1906.
[3] Ibid., Minute from Bromley to Mr. Richmond (for Morant) 6 March.

seemed, in the debate on the Committee stage of the Education Bill in the Commons, to be completely unknowledgeable as to the administrative basis of the Welsh National Council for Education.

Morant had consulted Bromley because the question of finance and its allocation, disbursement and control was a matter of major importance not only to the establishment of a National Council but in the financial relationships between the National Council and the Board of Education on the one hand, and the Board of Education and Parliament on the other. What was really important was to secure that powers over education in Wales that would be taken over by the National Council were absorbed in such a way as not to involve the Board of Education or the government —any government irrespective of party—in responsibilities for the exercise of which they would be unable 'to secure adequate means or safeguards without trenching on the powers and responsibility of the National Council under the scheme'.[1] The National Council, to have any real power for influencing educational policy throughout Wales and for helping the development of education in Wales, should be in a position to frame regulations for the carrying on of educational work by the various local authorities and for distributing money to those authorities on the basis of the regulations which it made. There was also the possibility that the amount of money provided in the estimates might not, at the end of the year, be sufficient to work the regulations and therefore the National Council should be in a position to make up any deficiency and to pay to any individual authority what it would have earned, so to speak, under the Council's regulations, although the total in the Council's hands would not cover this. Therefore, the money for meeting this contingency would have to be found by the National Council out of its ordinary funds. It could not be found by the Board of Education since this would mean that the Board would be in any year liable to the necessity of a supplementary estimate owing to the working by the National Council of the Council's regulations. This would involve intervention by the Board of Education in the Council's work, the very thing that the new plan was intended to abolish, and it was therefore essential that the Board of Education should be distinctly relieved from this responsibility.[2]

It was necessary to be quite clear on constitutional grounds what was to be the amount and nature of responsibility which the National Council should have on the one hand and the Board of Education on the other. Morant advised that 'in the abstract it would probably be best if the

[1] PRO Ed 24/579 : Confidential Memorandum, ibid., p. 1.
[2] Ibid.

The Genesis of The Welsh Department, Board of Education

National Council was to have really large powers over educational policy in Wales, that it should draw its funds direct from the Treasury, and that the Board of Education should not be interposed between. This would be on the analogy of funds which Parliament gave, for example, to the British Museum or to University Colleges'.[1] If however, as was probable, Parliament would hardly go this length in regard to the large exchequer grants in respect of education in Wales, and it was necessary that some Minister (not merely the Treasury) should be responsible in some degree in Parliament for the educational effects in Wales of the exchequer grants, no doubt the President of the Board of Education would have to answer for the educational vote for Wales, but his responsibility must be extremely general. To suggest that the National Council's regulations for educational expenditure in Wales should be submitted for the approval of the Board of Education and that the President was to be responsible to Parliament for those regulations—though possibly desirable towards enabling Parliament to secure detailed control—was intrinsically impossible as being inconsistent with the responsibility which the National Council was *ex hypothesi* necessarily to possess. The body which was to work the regulations and watch the daily work of the schools was the only body which could be responsible for the regulations. The President of the Board should not be responsible, but would be required only to exercise a very general supervision over the progress of education in Wales, so that he would be able to assure the House in each year's debate on the estimates as to how things were going on in Wales.[2]

Morant suggested that the exchequer grants for education in Wales should be given to the National Council in the shape of a lump sum each year to be allocated between elementary, secondary and technical education and also to the individual local authorities. In this way, the National Council could exercise real guidance on Welsh educational policy and not be subject to any intervention 'by the English Board of Education'. The National Council would be given practically all the powers and duties in regard to educational expenditure which the Board of Education exercised and would act for all those purposes as the central authority towards the individual local authorities in Wales. Some basis therefore would have to be designed for fixing each year the aggregate amount of the exchequer grants for Wales and for allocating money to each local authority. Finally, the scheme necessitated that every authority in Wales and Monmouthshire should be included within it and *included*

---

[1] PRO Ed 24/579 : Confidential Memorandum, ibid., p. 2.
[2] Ibid.

permanently, and that the most important point to be settled was the respective spheres of the responsibility of the Board of Education on the one hand and of the Welsh National Council for Education on the other.[1] Lloyd George and also perhaps Birrell might have saved themselves a great deal of embarrassment in the debate at the Committee stage of the Bill had they given heed in some depth to the detailed proposals worked out by Morant and the Treasury. These proposals were the solid flesh which was so necessary to clothe the 'skeleton' of the National Council—a skeleton referred to more than once by Balfour in his speeches for the opposition.

The preliminary stages of discussion over, the memorandum prepared and the financial difficulties settled, all was set for the first public announcement. On 3 March in a speech to the Cardiff Cymmrodorion Society, Lloyd George proposed the idea of a Welsh National Council for Education and called for a national conference to discuss the proposal. On 9 March in a message to a Liberal rally at Colwyn Bay where the Education Bill was to be the main feature of the occasion, Lloyd George said 'If Wales agrees to it, provision will be made in the coming Education Bill for setting up a Council of Education for Wales. To that Council would be delegated powers with regard to the training of teachers and matters of kindred character and powers now vested in the Board of Education for examining and inspecting secondary schools. Such a Council would have been set up by the late government, but one out of 16 counties disagreed and the whole thing fell through. I warn you that unless Wales is united a similar fate will overtake this scheme. I think that a national conference should be held composed of men of all shades of opinion, to discuss the scheme in detail and arrive at unanimity'.[2]

The conference was held in Cardiff on 23 March. Lloyd George succeeded in persuading the Bishops of Llandaff, St. Asaph and St. Davids and the Roman Catholic Bishop of Menevia to attend, together with representatives of the Nonconformist denominations and of the Welsh county councils. The case for a National Council for Education was ably presented by D. Brynmor Jones, MP, and the proposal was carried overwhelmingly. Later, in parliamentary debates this apparent unanimity of approval was to be challenged more than once. To this Council were to be delegated the powers of the Board of Education in Wales, the educational functions of the Board of Agriculture and Fisheries, and the

[1] Ibid., pp. 3–4.
[2] Lloyd George Papers, B/2/9/1, Telegram to Liberal Rally, Colwyn Bay, 9 March 1906, Beaverbrook Library.

powers of the Central Welsh Board.[1] On 20 March Lloyd George had already circulated a confidential memorandum to the Cabinet containing the 'First Draft of a Clause proposed to be inserted in the Education Bill for establishing by Order in Council a Welsh National Council for all educational purposes in Wales'.[2]

The Clause provided for the establishment by the King by Order in Council, of a central education authority in Wales to be called the National Council for Education, composed of members drawn from each of the counties, county boroughs, boroughs, and urban districts with a population of over 25,000. The Council was empowered to supply and to aid the supply of education of all kinds in Wales. The powers and duties, as far as they were related to Wales were, by Order in Council to be transferred to the Council, namely, those of the Board of Education, Board of Agriculture and Fisheries (relating to instruction connected with agriculture and forestry) and the Central Welsh Board. The Council would administer the Parliamentary grant in respect of education, science and art in Wales, with the exception of money granted in aid of the university and university colleges. The Council would be granted, by Order in Council powers to raise funds by means of contributions from the member-appointing authorities, for the borrowing of money and the acquisition of land, and for any other matters for which it was necessary or expedient to make provision for the purpose of enabling the Council to perform its duties or exercise its powers. The draft of any Order in Council was to be laid before each House of Parliament for four weeks before submission to the King.[3]

The Education Bill was introduced in the House of Commons by Augustine Birrell, President of the Board of Education on 9 April. Speaking of Part IV of the Bill relating to a National Council of Education for Wales Birrell said that singular unanimity upon the subject prevailed 'not only among Welsh MPs but amongst the Welsh counties themselves' and if on investigation it was found that England could hand over to Wales whatever her share might be of money allocated to education and 'leave her to distribute it in her own way, Whitehall would have no occasion to regret her departure'.[4] Anson was chiefly concerned about the necessity for retaining the influence which the Board of Education exercised in assisting local authorities to discharge their functions and was particularly worried about the rights of the *minority* (the Anglican church)

---

[1] *South Wales Daily News*, 24 March, 1906.
[2] PRO Ed 24/579: Confidential Memorandum circulated to the Cabinet at the request of Lloyd George
[3] PRO Ed 24/117, 24/118: various drafts of Clause 37.
[4] *Parl. Deb.*, 4th series, vol. clv, cs. 1039, ff.

in Wales 'which though in large numbers is wholly unrepresented in this House'.[1] Sir Alfred Thomas, member for East Glamorgan, arose on behalf of the Welsh members to thank the President of the Board of Education for having taken power to set up the Council, for in this matter Wales was worthy of Home Rule in educational affairs while the principle of such a Council had been unanimously acclaimed at the national conference in Cardiff.[2]

In the debate on the second reading which began on 7 May, Lloyd George, in a long speech on the origin of the clause relating to the National Council, referred to the severe criticism which had been levelled by Balfour against this clause, at a meeting in the Albert Hall at the end of April. Lloyd George accused Balfour of 'assuming that it was simply a conspiracy on the part of the Nonconformists of Wales to secure the control of education, to be independent altogether of the Imperial Parliament and to trample on the rights of churchmen'.[3] Lloyd George went on to say that the clause was merely to establish a central education authority for Wales for the administration of education—primary, secondary and university and that there was not the 'smallest power to legislate on the smallest detail' to be vested in the Council. On the whole, Welsh opinion was unanimously in favour of the Council, but there might be differences of detail about it—not among the Welsh members but on the opposition side. Lloyd George referred to the question which had been raised of the unfairness of handing over to a Welsh Council the administration of trusts relating to voluntary schools and, if the opposition considered that the guarantees in the Clause were not satisfactory in that respect, the government would have no hesitation in accepting amendments. If guarantees were required he did not demand that the matter should be left to an Order in Council, but amendments could be made at the Committee stage. He realised that it would not be fair after the bitter controversy in Wales to hand over to a body representing the Welsh county councils matters that were in controversy at that moment.

Lloyd George emphasized that all he required was that Wales should secure the co-ordination of all branches of education, since it already had 'complete control of secondary and higher education, but primary education was controlled from Whitehall, so far as administration was concerned. It was most important that they should all fit in and for the adequate reason that Wales was a country where 4/5ths of the children

---

[1] Ibid., cs. 1041, ff. The opposite was true of the House of Lords—the *majority* (Nonconformist) was wholly unrepresented and Part IV or Clause 37 was rejected.

[2] *Parl. Deb.*, ibid. supra, c. 1077.

[3] Ibid., vol. clvi, c. 1174, ff.

in the secondary schools came straight from the primary schools. To talk about the disruption of the Empire because of this proposal was simply part of that gross and futile exaggeration which had gone on about the whole of this Bill'.[1] But Anson was concerned about who was going to be responsible for the action of the Council and the money handed over to it (something in the region of £800,000) and moreover, there was nothing that could be done by this Council which could not have been done under Section 17(5) of the 1902 Act by means of the Joint Committee of the various local authorities. Llewelyn Williams, MP for Carmarthen District, drew Anson's attention to the fact that the late government had offered to Wales the same sort of Council 'with much the same sort of powers which this Bill conferred'. However, Anson insisted that what was proposed by the previous government was a Joint Committee which was an absolutely different thing from this Council 'for which no one was going to be responsible to the House'. Williams replied that he would find the answer to that when the Order in Council was made. It was not suggested that the whole constitution of the Council was provided for in this Bill, and after all, the Rt. Hon. gentleman in his Joint Committee offer 'trusted the Welsh county councils and allowed them to enter into committees and gave them powers'.[2]

Balfour interposed at this stage to answer criticisms made by Lloyd George and said that 'he had been read a moral lecture by that fairest of all controversialists, the President of the Board of Trade, upon the misrepresentation which he alleges I have committed with regard to that clause in the Bill for which he publicly claims paternity'. He did not feel disposed to withdraw a single word which he had uttered about it and re-iterated that so far as education was concerned the clause meant Home Rule for Wales in educational matters and was one which did establish administrative autonomy for Wales, but he was at a loss to know 'how the fleshless skeleton of the clause was to be clothed'.[3] The second reading was passed by 410 to 204.

On 21 May, Stuart Wortley, Unionist MP for the Hallam division of Sheffield, sought special consideration and legislation for Part IV of the Bill. He rose to move that it be an Instruction to the Committee 'that they have power to deal separately with Part IV (Council for Wales) and to report the same to the House as a separate Bill'. He said that 'the appearance of this Instruction upon the Paper would create little surprise amongst

---
[1] *Parl. Deb.*, 4th series, vol. clvi, cs. 1175, ff.
[2] Ibid., cs. 1575, ff.
[3] *Parl. Deb.*, 4th series, vol. clvi, cs. 1589, ff.

those acquainted with the provisions of the Bill'. Like Anson, he was worried about the large and influential minority in Wales totally unrepresented in the House and, in a large majority of instances practically excluded from a semblance of power upon any of the elected local authorities. The Instruction was submitted upon grounds which need not excite any of the animosities which might possibly arise upon other parts of the Bill. He moved it because he was convinced that the clause ought not to have its fate tied up with 'the rest of this self-contained, but nevertheless quite sufficiently extensive measure'. He also had other reasons including the desire to diminish bitter controversies, and moreover the clause might be regarded 'as the beginning of an organic or structural change in our system so great and far-reaching as to deserve the name of a constitutional change'. Wortley thought they all agreed to the abstract idea of a Welsh Council but they did not intend to do anything to oust the only independent external authority which could at present arbitrate between disputing authorities. It was clear that the power of the purse was about to be conferred on the Welsh Council 'by the Imperial grant being handed over to that body for distribution to the local education authorities ... the Welsh Council in Wales would practically be judges in their own cause ... and it was not a clause which the Bill ought to carry, for it really was a constitutional change which should be discussed under other conditions and at another time'.[1]

Birrell's reply was concise and clear. He said the government could not accept this proposal and firmly supported administrative devolution for Wales. The Welsh people wanted to do for elementary education what they had so successfully done for intermediate education. The Welsh Council embodied this desire and anyone who knew anything about the administration of education at Whitehall realised that Welsh subjects and Welsh questions formed a part by themselves and did not apply to other parts of the country. If wise counsels prevailed and wise methods devised, he saw no objection to handing over public money for elementary education in Wales.[2] Vigorous support for Birrell's reply came from the Irish MP for Waterford, Mr. John Redmond who said he would vote against the Instruction if only in gratitude for the support of Welsh members over a period of many years to the Irish nationalists and, moreover, he regarded this Instruction as a hostile movement towards this measure of Home Rule for Wales! Balfour complained that this part of the Bill had never been discussed—not even by the government, and certainly not by

[1] Ibid., vol. clvii, cs. 961, ff.
[2] *Parl. Deb.*, vol. clvii, ibid., cs. 963, ff.

the House of Commons—it was a mere sketch. The only defence of the Minister of Education of this part of the Bill in the second reading debate was that 'if the Education Department could get rid of the President of the Board of Trade and Wales, they would be delighted if they could do so by means of this clause, and if Wales could get rid of the Board of Education, Wales also would be delighted. It was the case of a mutual desire to separate—a mutual repulsion with which they all had a natural sympathy'.[1] The Instruction was overwhelmingly defeated by 388 to 102.[2]

On 1 June a conference of the Welsh National Council for Education was held at Llandrindod to consider draft resolutions, to express approval of Part IV of the Education (England and Wales) Bill 1906 and 'to urge upon the government to secure its passing into law'.[3] The Council was to consist of 100 members, was to elect officers, an executive committee and a consultative committee to decide the powers of the Council and consider rating powers. The resolutions were proposed by D. Brynmor Jones MP and seconded by J. Herbert Roberts MP. At this conference the conservative chairman of the Cardiff education committee, Lewis Morgan, expressed his gratitude to D. Brynmor Jones for his motion which was passed regarding the position of voluntary schools 'that in case any appeal should be allowed by the trustees and managers of the non-provided schools against any decision or act of the local education authority to the Board of Education, such appeal in the case of Wales as in England shall lie to the Board of Education and not to the National Council'. Lloyd George seconded Morgan's resolution and said 'this is a body to deal with educational matters. At the present moment, and having regard to the events of the last few years, it would be unreasonable to expect one party to trust the other party to adjudicate upon an appeal in a purely controversial matter. As it is important to work without friction and to secure the co-operation of all parties I heartily support the motion of Mr. Lewis Morgan that in these matters, which will have to be decided between voluntary schools and Council, that the appeal should lie to an independent body. In the first few years things will be complicated and embarrassing. The National Council should devote itself to purely educational matters and not be hampered by controversial matters'.[4]

---

[1] Ibid., cs. 966, ff.

[2] Ibid., cs. 1496, ff. A similar motion was moved by Bridgeman on 18 June supported by F. E. Smith, Anson, Lord Robert Cecil and Walter Long.

[3] PRO Ed 24/579: National Council of Education for Wales, Draft Resolutions Llandrindod Conference, 1 June 1906. Also: Herbert Lewis's Diary, 5 June 1906, Penucha MSS.

[4] PRO Ed 24/579: Draft Resolutions and discussions, Llandrindod Conference, ibid. Also: Herbert Lewis's Diary, 11 June. Penucha MSS: Education Bill in Committee: L.G. and I spoke for Clause 37 which sets up a National Council—at 1.30 a.m. Carried! 9 July: Obstructive debate on Education Bill, 11 Divisions.

The Genesis of The Welsh Department, Board of Education

Morant had to have a finger in this pie. On 9 June he wrote a cordial letter to Evan R. Davies—who was presumably still *persona grata* and secretary to the executive committee—requesting a copy of the resolution defining the power of the Council because 'this is precisely what, as an Office, we are most anxious to get at, particularly as respects the differentiation between the powers of this Board and the powers of the Council, and this, quite apart from the question of any appeal from the managers or trustees of voluntary schools'.[1] The resolution passed with regard to the powers of the Council stated: Firstly, there should be transferred to the Council the powers and duties of the Board of Education so far as they related to Wales except (a) any power or duty of the Charity Commission transferred from the Commission to the Board by the Board of Education Act 1899; (b) the powers proposed to be conferred on the Board of Education by Part II of the Education Bill 1906; (c) the power of deciding certain questions proposed to be conferred on the Board of Education by the Education Bill 1906 S.33; the powers conferred on the Board by the Education Act 1902 S.13 and the powers proposed to be conferred on the Board by the Education Bill 1906 S.39. Secondly, there should be transferred to the Council the powers and duties of the Welsh Central Board for Intermediate Education, and also the powers and duties, so far as they related to Wales, of the Board of Agriculture and Fisheries with regard to instruction in Agriculture and Forestry.[2] Again it is strange to reflect that Morant *was not conversant with the 'essential details' of the powers* of the proposed Welsh National Council for Education just before the important committee stage of the Education Bill in July!

The Education Bill came up for debate at the Committee stage on 17 July and this debate proved to be not only animated but also highly contentious in the several altercations between Lloyd George, Anson and Balfour in particular.[3] Other leading members of the Opposition including F. E. Smith, MP for the Walton division of Liverpool, took a leading part, especially with regard to Clause 37 (the Welsh Education Council). Smith moved an amendment 'that His Majesty may, by Order in Council, establish a Consultative Committee under the Board of Education to be called the Welsh Central Committee, consisting of members appointed by the councils of counties, county boroughs, and of boroughs, provided

[1] Ibid. : Morant to Davies 9 June 1906.
[2] Ibid. : Draft Resolutions, ibid. supra, Section 3. See Appendix 2.
[3] Herbert Lewis's Diary, 17 July, 1906, Penucha MSS: 'Welsh Clause under debate. Today Balfour came down to the House prepared to beat the Home Rule Drum with all his might. But when he found that L.G. had put his foot through the Home Rule Drum by the concessions which he was prepared to make in order to carry the Welsh Clause through the House of Lords, his annoyance was obvious'.

that the President of the Board of Education shall be responsible to Parliament for any act of the Welsh Central Committee done in the exercise of any of the powers of the Board of Education delegated to the Committee under this section and shall have full control over the Committee in respect of the exercise of such powers'. Smith objected to the fact that Clause 37 came before the House in a skeleton shape, that not sufficient time would be given to discuss it, and that this was a slip-shod method of legislation. He very much questioned the unanimity which existed in Wales in regard to this Council and even Lloyd George had said at the Cardiff conference that so long as they talked about general principles it was very easy to get agreement, but as soon as they tried to form a practical plan they found everyone criticizing them from every point of view. The Anglican bishops at that conference desired more details of the scheme before committing themselves, and it was on the strength of the amendment put forward by Lewis Morgan at the Llandrindod conference that 'such unanimity as was forthcoming was later obtained'.[1]

Smith was especially concerned regarding the details of administering the scheme and he had been driven to the conclusion that the government, and indeed Lloyd George himself had not made the investigation of which Birrell spoke when introducing the Bill, and Lloyd George had not satisfied himself as to the feasability of working any details in practice. Smith demanded to know 'where was the administrative responsibility to be assigned for the acts of the Welsh Council' and was very apprehensive about the position of voluntary schools if they came under the jurisdiction of the Welsh county councils.[2] Lloyd George in reply repeated the old story of unanimity and emphasized the reasonable manner in which the conservative representatives had dealt with the religious difficulties at the June conference and the approval of the amendment which gave the right of appeal in matters relating to voluntary schools to the Board of Education and not to the Council.[3] Lloyd George stated in plain terms that he could not accept the amendment proposed by Smith to set up a Consultative Committee because it reduced the Welsh Central Committee to a minor body, but was prepared to accept its principle, viz. 'that the President of the Board of Education shall be responsible to Parliament for any act of the Welsh Central Committee done in the exercise of any of the powers of the Board of Education delegated to the Committee under

[1] *Parl. Deb.*, 4th series, vol. clxi, cs. 41, ff.
[2] Ibid.
[3] Ibid.

this section, and shall have full control over the Committee in respect of the exercise of such powers'.[1] But Lloyd George did not think that the responsible Minister should be the President of the Board of Education. Out of the blue he made the astonishing proposal that a special Minister with a special staff should be appointed 'who might be a member of the present Ministry holding the office of junior Lord of the Treasury or some other office and he would have the power of the purse ... in other words, what he contemplated was that the Minister should have financial responsibility and financial control'.[2]

Balfour was in a militant mood particularly with regard to the new Minister's proposal. A little earlier, he had denounced Lloyd George for causing trouble in Wales over the working of the 1902 Act and was extremely suspicious of a proposal which handed over to a Welsh Central Body powers to do legally that which 'those gentlemen had endeavoured to do illegally'.[3] Balfour maintained that it was a constitutional change of the utmost gravity to appoint a new Minister, a new office, a new occupant of the Treasury bench and the creation of a new staff—all these suggestions were a sudden development.[4] Asquith accused Balfour of being involved in 'an artificially engendered passion' and mocked him for using such phrases as 'gigantic constitutional changes sprung on the House of Commons'.[5] Asquith suggested that the proposal was merely to modify the plan of the government which had been before the House since the second reading. Anson strongly defended Balfour's charges and said the proposal of clause 37 was to transfer the whole duties of the Board of Education so far as Wales was concerned to a Council for which no one would be responsible to the House and for whose expenditure no one was responsible. He said they were now discussing something quite different, for it was proposed that the Council for Wales should be advised by a new inspectorate and be represented in the House of Commons by a Minister. Another matter which he wanted to refer to was the extremely conciliatory speech which the President of the Board of Trade made adverting to the religious difficulties. But what did he urge the Welsh councils to do when the Default Act first came into operation? That the whole of the children in Wales should be turned into the streets and that elementary education should be brought to a standstill. How could the Committee have any confidence in this clause or in the assurances

[1] Ibid.
[2] *Parl. Deb.*, 4th series, vol. clxi, cs. 50, ff.
[3] Ibid.
[4] Ibid., cs. 56–65.
   Ibid.

of the Rt. Hon. gentleman when those assurances could only be made effective by a crude scheme such as this involving a complete constitutional change in the administration of Welsh education, a scheme which was not even now set down on the Order Paper for their consideration?[1]

At this stage, Sir Edward Carson, MP for Dublin University, endeavoured to sum up what had been discussed to date. He understood that three important points emerged. Firstly, they were to have a new Minister in the House with a new department; secondly, they were to have a recasting of Clause 37 with a view to allocating certain matters to the new Minister of the new department; and thirdly, to retaining certain matters, as far as he understood, in the Board of Education as they at present existed, or in the Board of Education in conjunction with the new Council. The clause itself was a clause of devolution 'but the proposals now made however, if devolution at all, were in a modified form and were to be under a department in connection with this House'.[2] Lloyd George denied that he had a new department in mind—all he had said was that they had accepted in substance the amendment of the hon. member for the Walton division of Liverpool and the hon. member for Blackpool. The substance in his opinion was *parliamentary control*. Lloyd George proceeded to show the way in which he proposed to deal with the amendment—'by amending the amendment and to make it read "the Order in Council shall provide for the appointment by His Majesty, of a member of Parliament, whether holding office under the Crown or not, who shall be responsible for any act of the Welsh Council done in the exercise of any of the powers of the Board of Education delegated to the Council under this section, and shall have full control over the Council in respect of the exercise of such powers" '.[3] Lloyd George emphasized that it was not proposed to create a new staff, no new officials would be appointed and there would be no additional expense.[4]

This was a crucial and, indeed, a critical stage in the fortunes of the Welsh National Council. It also involved a personal rebuff to the reputation of Lloyd George which might have threatened his political career. It was evident that Lloyd George and the government had not given serious thought beforehand to the Minister proposal and this was only one aspect of the haphazard manner in which he completely mis-handled the debate on clause 37 in the Commons. Lloyd George had to pay dearly for his

---

[1] Ibid.
[2] *Parl. Deb.*, vol. clxi, cs. 65, ff.
[3] Ibid., cs. 78, ff. PRO Ed 24/117: Council for Wales, Draft proposal for Committee stage amendment. *Parl. Deb.*, ibid. supra, c. 86.

rash action regarding the Minister proposal. During that week he found himself in dire 'trouble in high quarters' and also with the Prime Minister, Campbell-Bannerman, whom he had not consulted regarding the proposal. The King had expressed his annoyance with the Prime Minister 'at not being given prior notice of the proposal for a new Minister'.[1] On 19 July Lloyd George sent the Prime Minister an extremely apologetic letter—probably one of the longest letters he ever wrote—expressing his sorrow 'if through inexperience I have transgressed constitutional propriety. But I still think I am innocent and that the King's rebuke is due to a misunderstanding of what really happened'. He assured the Prime Minister that 'no new Minister had been created and there was no idea of setting up such a Ministry, but the Opposition claimed that there should be some Minister in the House responsible for the deeds or misdeeds of the new Council who could answer questions as to its doings'. Birrell thought it would be better that this task should be entrusted to someone who would be in contact with the Council and Asquith who was in charge in the Prime Minister's absence agreed. Lloyd George regretted that 'he could not get the Prime Minister's assent to his proposition for it was decided at a midnight meeting', and said 'that if he had sinned it was purely through inadvertence and inexperience'.[2]

In the resumed debate on the new Minister proposal Balfour and Anson still continued to press their points and wanted to know if there was any precedent for the creation of a new Minister of the Crown by Order in Council. Balfour had come to the conclusion that the government had not given five minutes' thought to this proposal and that the Minister in charge of this part of the Bill (Lloyd George) had thought of the scheme for the first time at ten minutes past three on 17 July! The proposal of the government was to transfer certain officials of the Board of Education and constitute them a separate department under a new minister—that was not denied.[3] Sir William Robson, Solicitor-General retorted that although it was not usual to appoint a Minister by Order in Council they could do this by Act of Parliament and they were merely proceeding in the ordinary way by creating powers and indicating how an appointment was to be carried out, namely, by Order in Council.[4] F. E. Smith decided that after the discussion which had taken place earlier and the assurances which had been given he would withdraw his amendment. Anson had also

---

[1] J. A. Spender, *The life of the Rt. Hon. Sir Henry Campbell-Bannerman*, London, 1923, p. 313, ff.
[2] Lloyd George to Campbell-Bannerman, 19 July 1906. B.M., Add. MSS, 41239, f. 96.
[3] *Parl. Deb.*, vol. clxi, ibid., cs. 80, ff. This was similar to Lord Londonderry's previous suggestion in June 1904, but this remark by Balfour clearly envisaged a future Welsh Department—but without the Minister!
[4] *Parl. Deb.*, ibid. supra, c. 83.

submitted an amendment in which he sought to make the Council correspond to the Joint Committee proposed by the late government, but this was subsequently withdrawn.[1]

Birrell admitted certain shortcomings in Clause 37 and conceded that there was no indication in the Clause (Part IV) as it stood in the Bill during the past weeks of what parliamentary control there would be over the Welsh Council, or of what his position as President of the Board of Education would be with regard to the money that was to be allocated. It was most unfortunate that it was left to the amendments on the Paper to bring out the concessions which the government proposed to make. He thought the speeches made by the President of the Board of Trade must have satisfied those who listened to them and he agreed that Wales was justified in the demand it made to have control in a larger degree than any other part of the country over its education. But he was not happy with Part IV because it left the Board of Education in an improper and dangerous position and he had tried to find how proper parliamentary control could be achieved. It could not rest on him and no one could run the two systems of education at the same time and it was absolutely necessary that there should be a separation of offices. Welsh control in education had been in the air for many years and the Opposition knew this and his Office was not afraid of being shorn of some of its authority.[2] The Minister proposal was carried in the Commons by 279 to 50.[3]

By 23 July, Birrell had evidently given more thought to the question of parliamentary control and in spite of the fact that the Minister proposal had been passed overwhelmingly, Birrell was mindful of the constitutional objection urged by the Opposition, with the result that 'the embryonic Welsh Minister—the embarrassed phantom' never appeared. Instead, Birrell now proposed to make the Council responsible solely to the Treasury with a public audit of accounts, and which would provide a spokesman in the Commons answerable for its actions.[4] Lloyd George was to sum up the real facts by noting the amendments accepted by the government and in which considerably modified form the Welsh National Council proposal was incorporated in the Bill. He said that the government

---

[1] Ibid., c. 73.

[2] *Parl. Deb.*, vol. clxi, ibid., cs. 92–95. Also, Herbert Lewis's Diary, 20 July, 1906, Penucha MSS: 'Went to the Board of Trade to settle the form of the Welsh Clause and The Education Bill. Met by LL.G., Morant, Thring the official draughtsman. At our previous meeting at The Board of Education, Morant *had raised every* conceivable difficulty with a view to defeating the Establishment of the Council—originally he, had urged LL.G. to introduce it in a form which he must have known would have caused the House of Lords to reject it. Fortunately, Thring took the view that it was possible to raise innumerable differences in connection with the Parliamentary wording of almost any department. LL.G. dealt with the situation with great skill and moderation'.

[3] Ibid. c. 100.

[4] Ibid. cs. 741, ff.

had put down a motion on the Paper which would, if carried, have set up autonomy in Welsh education and created a Welsh Council, but they had accepted five amendments which, he had to admit, had transformed the Clause. The first, was parliamentary representation and control; the second, was representation of minorities. As a general principle he admitted that would be undesirable, but Wales was an exceptional case, the majorities on the county councils being overwhelming. The third demand was that all questions dealing with religion should be reserved to the Board of Education. The fourth, was that estimates should be tabled by somebody representing the government, and the fifth, that there should be an audit by the Auditor and Comptroller-General. Lloyd George thought the amendments fair and reasonable and stated that the government proposed to stand by their proposals claiming that the major criticism, centred on the lack of effective parliamentary control and supervision had been met.[1] The Bill with the Welsh Council as Clause 26 passed its third reading on 30 July by 369 to 177, the 28 Welsh members present voting in support.

Thus, so many modifications were introduced into Part IV of the Bill that the Welsh National Council for Education to which the House of Commons gave its final sanction was a vastly different structure from that which was foreshadowed in the first draft. The powers originally conferred upon it were so comprehensive that many who believed in the soundness of the principle that Wales should achieve some degree of autonomy in educational matters were inclined to withhold their support of the government's proposals. They were subjected to such fierce criticism in Wales especially by Church leaders that Lloyd George realized the impossibility of expecting anything like unanimity in their favour. This was undoubtedly the reason for his conciliatory attitude in the debate in Committee. Provided he could secure a fair measure of united opinion on his side he was prepared to concede much to the 'minority'. His prime object was to mould this part of the Bill in such a way that the Lords might not reject it *in toto*. He realized that it was better to get an inferior machine with limited powers which the majority of Welsh people would countenance without suspicion than a more sophisticated one which a large body of the population would regard with mistrust.[2]

The resounding support accorded the Bill by the House of Commons was by no means reflected in the Lords. On 1 August when it arrived in the Upper Chamber it had few supporters—the Welsh Council being the

[1] Ibid. cs. 751, ff.
[2] *Journal of Education*, August 1906 p. 558.

subject of considerable antagonism. The Lord President—the Earl of Crewe—had to undertake its defence almost singlehanded. Lords Cawdor, Londonderry, and the Bishop of St. Asaph stoutly denied the unanimity claimed for the National Council in Wales. Londonderry echoed practically everything which Balfour had said in the Commons whilst the Bishop of St. Asaph 'came with an open mind'. He confessed that 'he should be tampering with accuracy if he led the House to believe that churchmen in Wales were unanimously in favour of such a Council' though he admitted that in his talks with the President of the Board of Trade regarding an attempt to bring about an educational concordat in the diocese of St. Asaph he found the President to be a man whose word he trusted and always showed a readiness to reciprocate a spirit of concession and generosity, but he could not say the same of his followers.[1]

Lord Cawdor's speech overflowed with sarcasm and bitterness towards Part III (the Welsh National Council). He jeered at the government in the way they had handled this clause in the Commons and said that it meant giving over to the Council £800,000 a year of Imperial funds for grants without any check or control. He showed little mercy in his bitter attacks on Lloyd George and magnified the whole concept of the Council 'based on evidence he had carefully collected' into nothing less than complete Home Rule for Wales. He maintained that Lloyd George, in a speech at Caernarvon in January 1906 had shown what he really wanted for Wales —'once the Council is set up delegation will follow ... we will not stop with education for there are powers under the Local Government Board which I hope to see delegated and also powers under the Board of Trade and the Home Office'.[2] On 21 November Cawdor almost repeated his previous arguments against the Council when he moved an amendment to omit clause 26 (the Welsh Council) from the Bill.[3] Lord Rendel, in his maiden speech in the Lords supported the government and resented Cawdor's attacks on Lloyd George and 'had urged it as a reason for turning this clause ignominiously out of doors'. The clause merely provided for an Order in Council for the establishment of such a scheme and the House would have an opportunity of considering the scheme when it was laid before them. The Bishop of St. Davids, one of Cawdor's closest friends, whilst commending Rendel for his speech, re-iterated the lack of unanimity in Wales and condemned the Welsh county councils for

[1] *Parl. Deb.*, ibid., vol. clxii, cs. 1287, ff.
[2] Ibid., cs. 1279, ff.
[3] *Parl. Deb.*, op. cit., vol. clxv, cs. 779, ff.

The Genesis of The Welsh Department, Board of Education

not considering the proposals seriously.[1] The Earls of Dunraven and Crewe together with the Bishop of Hereford supporting the clause claimed that all the necessary safeguards had been accommodated.[2] But Cawdor's amendment to delete the clause was carried by 109 to 44, the Bishops of Bangor and St. Davids voting with the majority.[3]

The rejection of the National Council by the House of Lords on 21 November and the return of the Bill to the House of Commons 'with clouds of amendments' was a bitter blow to Birrell, Lloyd George and the Welsh members. According to Birrell, the Cabinet 'acted perhaps unwisely, refused to consider the amendments one by one, but advised the House to reject them *en bloc*. An impasse was thus created and the Bill perished'.[4] The withdrawal of the Bill was announced by Campbell-Bannerman in the House of Commons on 20 December.

A large measure of blame for the failure of Part IV of the Education Bill must rest fairly and squarely on the shoulders of Lloyd George who completely bungled the issue at the Committee stage in July. Birrell was also at fault. As a trained lawyer and Queen's Counsel, he apparently failed to master or appreciate Morant's detailed memorandum on the proposed National Council. Neither Birrell nor Lloyd George could have studied it in any depth, if at all. Had they done so, they could have replied with more insight, knowledge and authority to many of the straightforward questions asked by Balfour and Anson regarding the matters of parliamentary responsibility and finance. Moreover, Lloyd George had not heeded the advice offered by Morant in his letter of 28 February 'that the important thing in framing a scheme of this kind *is to be sure that no serious difficulty has been overlooked*, which when raised afterwards by some opponent, would cause us difficulty *through not having prepared ourselves for it*, or having failed to obviate it in casting the scheme'.[5]

Thus ended the second attempt to acquire administrative decentralization for Welsh education. Lloyd George's dream was shattered. But the demise of the National Council did not mean *total* capitulation. Though the main battle was lost, and the Council never materialized, it produced an important practical by-product in the form of departmental re-

---

[1] Ibid. Also, Eluned E. Owen, *The Later Life of Bishop Owen*, Llandysul, 1961, p. 53, ff.
[2] *Parl. Deb.* supra.
[3] Ibid.
[4] Augustine Birrell, *Things Past Redress*, London, 1937, p. 191. Also, Lloyd George (to his wife, Margaret), from Hotel Continental, Biarritz, 29 December, 1906, where he was staying with Herbert Lewis: 'Robson and Emmoll are both staying here. Had a chat with Robson this morning. He has a poor opinion of Birrell's fighting qualities. He saw a good deal of him during the Education Bill—he is no fighter' *N.L.W. Letters, Lloyd George MSS*, 20427C, *Letter* 1236.
[5] PRO Ed 24/579, Morant to Lloyd George, 28 February 1906.

II THE CREATION OF THE WELSH DEPARTMENT, BOARD OF EDUCATION

The substitution of the word 'department' for National Council was a feature of parliamentary discussions of Birrell's Education Bill as early as July, 1906. From a close scrutiny of the statements expressed by MPs who took part in the debates, several conclusions may be drawn. In the first place, apart from the official announcement, there was nothing sudden about the establishment of the Welsh Department, notwithstanding the remark made by Lloyd George when he met A. T. Davies on the station platform at Criccieth late on the night of 19 January 1907, that 'the Cabinet had just reached a very important decision'.[1] In fact, the Welsh Department had gone through a long period of gestation since 1902. Secondly, there was nothing novel regarding its title. It had been on the lips of MPs more than once after the introduction of Birrell's Bill. Thirdly, there were strong grounds for believing that the government had a premonition several months before November, that Clause 37 had no chance of survival in the House of Lords,[2] and there was very little doubt that by 20 December, 1906, the Cabinet had decided to do something administratively in lieu of what they had not been permitted to do legislatively, i.e. to separate the administration of education in Wales from that of England. It was a determined act by the government and not a charitable gesture to mollify anyone in particular, and certainly not (as has so often been advanced) a sop to Lloyd George. Fourthly, this decision was made by Birrell and Lloyd George with the approval of the Cabinet.[3]

In the debate at the committee stage of the Bill in July 1906, erosive processes in the form of successive amendments were whittling down the stature of the National Council, and Members of Parliament tended to discard the term Welsh National Council in favour of the word 'department'. F. E. Smith, the Member for the Walton Division of Liverpool, who had proposed a Consultative Committee in place of a National

---

[1] A. T. Davies, *The Lloyd George I Knew*, London, 1948, pp. 51, ff.

[2] Herbert Lewis's Diary, 21 October, 1906 Penucha MSS: 'Had a long chat with L.G. on many things. Morant is known at The Board of Education as "The Serpent"; L.G. is sure the House of Lords will throw out the proposal to create a Council of Wales, but we think he can yet find a way to circumvent it. The Welsh County Councils can be called together and can put forward a joint scheme which will go before Parliament in the usual way'.

[3] A. T. Davies, op. cit.

Council, quoted a Welsh MP as saying 'it will be necessary to create, in some form, a Welsh Department'.[1] Lloyd George mentioned a 'special department', and Balfour, 'a new department'. Sir William Anson declared that 'the Government proposed to create another Department—a Welsh Department—and they proposed to transfer to that Department the duties and officers of the present Board of Education. Could they do that without Statutory Authority'?[2] Birrell was convinced that there should be a 'separation of offices'. But the key phrase was coined by Sir William Robson when he said 'that this was a question very largely of *departmental reorganization* and not new work ... the clerks were there ... and looking at this humble and modest measure of departmental reorganization, it did not strike him personally as going quite so deep down to the foundations of our Constitution'.[3] Lord Balcarres, who elaborated upon Robson's suggestion, was to provide the final solution to the problem, when he confessed that 'he really could not understand why Wales should not be content with the President of the Board of Education. The Solicitor-General had said that Clause 37 was a humble measure of departmental reorganization. Did that coincide with the views of the Welsh representatives? If it was merely the grouping of officials in Wales, who were to be placed in a corner of the building in Whitehall, and the responsibility towards Parliament was to remain, he could not understand why Welsh Members were not content that the President of the Board of Education should found his own Welsh Department within the great Department, and himself be the responsible Minister to the House'.[4]

In December, during the closing stages of the debate on the Bill which had been sent back to the Commons by the Lords, the Welsh Members were infuriated at the deletion of Clause 37. Lloyd George, speaking at a Liberal demonstration in the Shire Hall, Gloucester, bitterly denounced the action of the House of Lords, and in particular Lord Cawdor, whom he described as 'a Scotchman to whom, for our sins, Providence has allotted a Welsh estate ... I am not so sure that he does not regard this great enthusiasm for education in Wales in the same spirit as he regards an outbreak of swine fever—something to be ruthlessly suppressed ... the Lords have wrecked an education scheme. The Bill as it came back is perfectly worthless—it is destroyed'.[5]

[1] *Parl. Deb.*, 4th series, vol. clxi, c. 45.
[2] Ibid., c. 89.
[3] Ibid., c. 88, ff.
[4] Ibid., c. 99.
[5] *Gloucester Citizen*, 26 November 1906.

The Genesis of The Welsh Department, Board of Education

In the House of Commons, several Welsh MPs, clinging to the last supplicatory straw, were still hoping that some kind of administrative differentiation be accorded to Welsh educational matters. On 12 December, Herbert Roberts, the Member for Denbighshire West, said that Part IV of the Bill was designed to set up an Education Council for Wales, and hoped that it might be possible to bring about some arrangement which would meet the wisespread desires of the people of Wales to have granted to them educational autonomy.[1] On the same day, Llewelyn Williams, MP for Carmarthen District, concentrated his attack on Lord Cawdor, who had said in the House of Lords, that the proposal was part of a scheme for promoting Welsh Home Rule. Williams maintained that it was merely a small measure of reform in educational machinery. He hoped that 'if the Right Hon. Gentleman found it impossible to secure the passing of this Bill with Part IV in it, at all events he would see that the principle that they admitted was a right principle, and should be carried out by an administrative act which would not require the sanction of the House of Lords. If the Government said it was impossible to get Part IV through this House and the other House, they could, at all events, assist Wales by establishing a subordinate branch of the Board of Education in Wales with permanent officials to deal with Welsh education. If that were done, he did not much care what became of Part IV. All he was anxious for was that the separate and distinct case of Wales should be recognized in some tangible form by the Government, and if that were done he cared not very much what became of the Bill at all'.[2]

Exactly a week later, on 19 December, the first correct parliamentary reference to the Welsh Department was made by Sir Alfred Thomas, MP for East Glamorgan, who understood that 'the Minister of Education was about to reorganize the Office and to set up a Welsh Department in the Board of Education. Of course, he and his friends would very much have preferred to have a Council chosen by the Welsh people, but they recognized that what was now proposed was a great advance towards securing autonomy in educational matters in Wales'.[3]

The following day, Campbell-Bannerman announced the withdrawal of the Bill.[4] The birth of the Welsh Department was imminent. Everything was ready, and those entitled to attend were present at the accouchment. One matter was overlooked in the excitement—the official registration

---

[1] *Parl. Deb.*, 4th series, vol. clxvii, c. 433, ff.
[2] Ibid., c. 449, ff.
[3] Ibid., c. 1755.
[4] Herbert Lewis's Diary, 31 July, 1906, Penucha MSS: 'C.B. (Campbell-Bannerman)—What a wonderful hold he has obtained over the House of Commons. He has been away for most of the session owing to Lady C.B.'s critical state and has taken little part in the debates, but his influence is simply unbounded—and the whole Liberal party swears by him, and he is the greatest asset we possess'.

The Genesis of The Welsh Department, Board of Education

of the date of birth! But of one thing, nothing is more certain, if the calendar of day to day events is followed closely, namely, that the Welsh Department came into being before the end of December 1906.[1] After his announcement, Campbell-Bannerman almost immediately summoned Birrell to his private room in the House of Commons and offered him the post of Chief Secretary for Ireland.[2] Later, he wrote to confirm this to Birrell, who had gone to spend Christmas at Sheringham, Norfolk, and Birrell replied on 23 December accepting it. He told the Prime Minister 'our conclusion is to do whatever we are bidden to. A wise old Tory once gave me this advice: "never ask for anything; never refuse anything; never resign anything", and hitherto I have followed it to the letter. If therefore you still want me to go to Ireland, I will go ... I feel obliged to add that I think there are good reasons for my leaving the Board of Education at this moment, though I shall say goodbye to Morant with some sorrow. I am sure he has served us faithfully'.[3]

Before the end of December, Birrell, in consultation with Lloyd George, had plans well in hand for filling the chief posts in the new Welsh Department. Professor Henry Jones of Glasgow University was called to London to see Birrell, who seemingly offered him the chief administrative post—that of Assistant Secretary.[4] Jones, however, was uncertain of what was involved, but was 'inclined to accept at least tentatively for a few months of his long vacation', hesitating about a longer commitment because he doubted his congruity with a government department.[5]

No final decision was reached before Birrell left the Board, but he wrote to Jones expressing his regret that he would not himself witness Jones's educational experiments in Wales.[6] But Jones, in his reply on 13 January 1907 (the day before Reginald McKenna succeeded Birrell) had evidently withdrawn, when he said 'Of course I shall not mention the matter to the University Court, but let it drift into the past—*all*, save one thing, namely, the memory of our interview and the exceeding generosity of your confidence in me. Your successor takes up his problem absolutely without respect to what took place between *us*, and if he finds a stronger hand than mine for my dear little distracted country, I shall be more than happy'.[7]

---

[1] The Press announcement on 12 February 1907 stated 'In pursuance of the intention of the Government at the close of last Session, a distinct Department of the Board would be set up to deal with all grades of education in Wales'.

[2] Augustine Birrell, op. cit., p. 194.

[3] Birrell to Campbell-Bannerman, 23 December 1906. B.M., Add. MSS., 41239, f. 192.

[4] This was the original designation of the post before A. T. Davies's appointment. Davies insisted on the title 'Permanent Secretary'.

[5] H. J. W. Hetherington, *Life and Letters of Sir Henry Jones*, London, 1924, p. 99 ff.

[6] Ibid.

[7] PRO Ed 24/581, Jones to Birrell, 13 January 1907.

The Genesis of The Welsh Department, Board of Education

Many other names were mentioned and considered at the beginning of January. One of the earliest was that of D. Lleufer Thomas, of whose qualities Morant had enquired of W. N. Bruce, who wrote, saying 'he has plenty of brains and I have always found him sensible and straightforward . . . he is a man I have always liked to meet, and wished to know better'.[1] By the 14 January, Lloyd George had written to J. Herbert Lewis enclosing what might be termed the official short list for the two posts.[2] This list was remarkable for the omission of three names, two of which were so prominent in the negotiating phase of the National Council with Lloyd George, namely, W. N. Bruce and Evan R. Davies. The third should surely have been that of Dr. William Edwards, HMI. Here, indeed, was a man. Inconspicuous perhaps in the Welsh public eye, and never a seeker of high places, he was one of the most able, dedicated, and efficient Welsh educationists of his time.

In his letter, Lloyd George told Herbert Lewis that he sought 'a man of fresh ideas and high national ideals'. Lewis, in a draft letter in reply, commented on Lloyd George's nominations: 'Isambard (Owen) may not be the ideal man . . . but in my opinion he is the best available man. In all, but language, he is a Welshman. He is no partisan of the clergy—they don't like him. He is a terrific worker. I am sure he would impress the county councils . . . where is there a better man than Isambard? I wish I had more confidence in O. M. (Edwards) for this particular job. My admiration of him as a Welsh writer is unbounded, but I don't think he would run the Department well. But he is the best I know of for the headship outside Isambard'. Lewis then referred to 'the second' and said that Lloyd George had three admirable men of choice in the list which he sent: 'Lleufer is hardworking, painstaking and capable, and the same may be said of T. J. (Hughes) and Alfred (A. T. Davies), both of whom add strength to capacity and have proved their administrative power by work on the Denbighshire and Glamorgan county councils. A. T. Davies is not conciliatory . . . It is hardly just to lay stress because he couldn't have done licensing work in Liverpool without it. I don't think he would accept. Would you like me to sound him? T. J. is more influential with the big authorities in south Wales'.[3]

---

[1] Ibid., Bruce to Morant, 3 January 1907.

[2] Lloyd George to J. Herbert Lewis, 11 January, 1907, Penucha MSS.

[3] Draft letter from Lewis to Lloyd George, 14 January, Penucha MSS. Ald. T. J. Hughes, Glamorgan County Council and Solicitor, Bridgend. Hughes and Evan R. Davies were Joint Secretaries of the Welsh County Councils Consultative Committee, and drafted the Welsh Model Scheme for the Welsh National Council of Education. Lloyd George said of Hughes, 'he knows more about the Education Act and its workings than probably any other man in Wales', (*South Wales Daily News*, 12 May, 1904).

A little later, but perhaps too late in the day, around 25 January, a new young star appeared in the educational (and later, the political) firmament of Whitehall, another T. J. from Rhymney, Monmouthshire, who was to exercise not a little control over affairs in high political places, and who was to prove to be a bulwark of counsel and strength to more than one British Prime Minister. Lloyd George had sent a letter to Morant, including 'a fresh name' together with an immensely glowing testimonial from Henry Jones, expounding the excellence of Thomas Jones, a young lecturer in the University of Glasgow. But by that time the chief administrative post had been filled.[1] Lloyd George, acting with the knowledge of the President of the Board of Education, McKenna, had offered the appointment to A. T. Davies, a Liverpool solicitor in partnership with J. Herbert Lewis, and a member of the Denbighshire County Council.

On the day of his secret meeting with Lloyd George in Criccieth, Davies was invited to London for an interview with Morant.[2] Immediately after the interview, Davies wrote a letter to his wife, describing all that happened:

> 'Just walked across from the Board of Education to the Welsh Club, Whitehall Court, S.W. where I have had one and a half hours with the great Mr. Morant... We discussed things thoroughly from top to bottom and I think we thoroughly understand each other. His idea is a Head who shall be responsible for the whole of Welsh education—elementary, secondary, and, when the new buildings at Whitehall are finished, technical as well—who shall be absolutely at the top and next to the President, with, what is *most* important from an official point of view, direct access to the President.
>
> His title would be Assistant Secretary or Secretary[3] with rank and salary equal to the existing heads of departments now, but with what they have not, viz., the right of access. Rooms would be on the "swagger" first floor, opposite the President's, and below this 'Head' would be two or three examiners as they call them, and a full staff of clerks. Also, of course, the whole of the Inspectorial Staff in Wales. If Morant has his way, there will be no Henry Jones or other academic chief. I should be my own Chief. Morant wants a man with a good legal brain and administrative abilities—not academic qualifications.
>
> Verily, the thing looks very tempting, although it would be anything but a "soft job". Delicate, difficult and laborious are mild terms to apply to it, and I almost begin to doubt my powers, as I should have, next to Morant, the position of greatest responsibility in the Education Office... I was to assume nothing, of course, from the interview... for Lloyd George or the President might have their own views as to the person to be appointed... salary probably would be

[1] PRO Ed 24/581, Lloyd George to Morant, 25 January 1907. Also, Jones to Lloyd George, addressed from the National Liberal Club (undated).

[2] Ibid., Morant to Davies, 19 January 1907. A. T. Davies, op. cit., pp. 51, ff.

[3] A. T. Davies, op. cit., Davies said that he managed to convince Morant that the title Assistant Secretary would not be acceptable to the Welsh people, and subsequently it was changed to that of Permanent Secretary.

The Genesis of The Welsh Department, Board of Education

£850 to £1,000, but Morant would have to go to the Treasury ... and not being dealt with by the Permanent officials, but by the Chancellor of the Exchequer—Asquith—direct. On the question as to whether he (Morant) is to be over me or not, we are, he tells me, in absolute agreement, but the President may, and probably will, insist, that at least in regard to certain items, e.g. grants, Code, etc., (which would be clearly specified in writing) he should be the titular Chief. As regards the general administration of the elementary and secondary schools, he frankly says he wants to have nothing to do with me or them ... but even on matters of grants, etc., I could have the right to lay my views before the President equally with Morant.

The official leave is 42 days in the year "if you can get them", and office hours 10 to 5 or 11 to 6. Holidays, "if I was away when Parliament was sitting, the President would have my head off"! All this, etc., Morant said to me, and was *very* frank and outspoken in regard to Anson, Lloyd George, Henry Jones and others ... Certainly it is all very strange and perplexing to find oneself asked tentatively to undertake the management of a great branch of the Civil Service, and to be practically at the head of educational affairs in Wales ... It humbles me to think of being in such a place to which I should never have aspired ... I shall need a good deal of grace to keep my head and do my duty'.[1]

On 1 February, Morant invited Owen M. Edwards, of Lincoln College, Oxford, (on the direction of Lloyd George and McKenna) to London, 'to confer in regard to certain matters arising out of the Government's decision to handle Welsh education by means of a Special Department of this Board'.[2] After discussing various aspects of the work, Edwards returned to Oxford, and on 8 February, was offered the post of Chief Inspector of Education for Wales.[3] On 11 February, Edwards replied, 'I feel it is my duty to accept it gratefully ... the more I think about it, the more the work appeals to me'.[4]

A third Welshman was also appointed to the post of Junior Examiner in the new Department, T. G. Roberts, of Towyn, assistant clerk to the Merioneth education committee, described by Morant as 'Haydn Jones's young man, and it may be useful to you to be able to name his appointment when talking to friends about the Welsh Department that you will have a Welshman under you with some real knowledge, and with a real Welsh point of view, instead of merely English officials'.[5]

On the administrative side, the separation from England of Welsh educational affairs demanded careful reorganization of the Board's Office with the least possible interruption and friction. Many complicated

---

[1] Davies to his wife, 5.45 p.m., 23 January, 1907, Very Confidential. A. T. Davies Papers, Wilton, Connecticut, USA.

[2] PRO Ed 24/581, Morant to Edwards, 1 February 1907.

[3] Ibid., Morant to Edwards, 8 February.

[4] Ibid. Edwards to Morant, 11 February. PRO Ed 23/242, Official notice of appointments by McKenna, 22 February.

[5] PRO Ed 24/581, Morant to Davies, 13 February; Davies to Morant, 14 Feb.
PRO Ed 23/242, Treasury to Board of Education, 22 February.

The Genesis of The Welsh Department, Board of Education

administrative and statistical details had to be sorted out before Morant could produce his *Memorandum on Office Organization* towards the end of January. Already, at the beginning of the month, there was a considerable flurry of administrative activity between Morant and his minions. By 10 January, he was busily employed in matters of re-allocation of staff and working out details of the establishment of the Welsh Department 'with every desire to avoid raising the question of promotion more than is absolutely necessary'.[1] It is too tempting to refrain from quoting a superb example of civil service phraseology with reference to the new Department: 'If it may be assumed that the Department for Wales is not an Inferno (Lasciate opui speranta, etc.,) but a Purgatorio, and that officers transferred to it may at some future time recover their lost Paradiso, it is immaterial whether promotions thus rendered necessary are made, at the outset, into the Department for Wales, or, subsequently, in the English Department'.[2]

On a population basis—Wales having a population of just over 2 millions against a total population for England and Wales of about 32½ millions—the Department for Wales was entitled to 1/16th of the Board's total staff, i.e. 1/16th of about 80, giving Wales 1 Assistant Secretary, 1 Senior Examiner, and 3 Junior Examiners. This was later revised to 1 Assistant Secretary, 1½ Senior Examiners and 4 Junior Examiners.[3] Finally, in a note on comparative statistics of England and Wales, a rough estimate of the relative amount of educational work was:

	England	*Wales*
Public elementary schools	92½%	7½%
Secondary schools	90%	10%
Pupil teachers	92%	8%
Technical, etc.,	96%	4%

Before the end of January, Morant had issued a strictly confidential Memorandum on Office Organization which announced and described the Welsh Department in the following terms:

> The Government has decided to establish a separate Department for the Welsh work of the Board of Education, the degree of separation having not yet been precisely determined. For the present, as from 4 February, Mr. Kingsford will act as Assistant Secretary for the Welsh Department, with Messrs. Casson and Talbot as Senior Examiners, and Messrs. C. Sykes and Eaton, Junior Examiners. This Department will take charge of all the work of the Board in respect of Wales, with

---

[1] PRO Ed 24/581, Minute from Sykes to Morant, 10 January 1907.
[2] Ibid.
[3] PRO Ed 23/216F, Strictly Confidential Memorandum on Office Organization, January 1907, p. 6, para. 22.

the exception of (for the present) Training Colleges, Training Schools for Domestic Subjects, Teachers' Pensions, the work at present done at South Kensington, and such other matters as may be named hereafter. It is probable that other officials, probably Welshmen, will shortly be appointed to this Branch.[1]

The chief posts having been filled and the basic details of reorganization settled to accommodate the Welsh Department within the Board of Education, it now remained to make the fact known to the world. In this connection, between 20 December 1906 and 12 February 1907, an uncanny secrecy had been observed by all concerned. At Westminster, the Members of the Welsh Party were not even consulted, and very few, if any, other MPs knew what was going on.[2] There were occasional rumblings in the Welsh Press before the public announcement on 12 February. In January, the *Journal of Education* reported 'now that the Welsh National Council for Education is defunct, there has been a revival of the rumour that a separate branch of the Board of Education will be created, whose sole function will be the administration of Welsh education ... perhaps nothing more serious is contemplated than that certain officials of the Board will be chosen to deal exclusively with Wales and its difficulties. That an independent Department of Education for Wales will be established forthwith does not appear likely'.[3] Even in February, the same *Journal* was convinced that 'only a slight re-arrangement of the present staff of the Board of Education is implied'.[4]

Two days before the Press announcement, A. T. Davies had kept Morant waiting for his 'biographical notes', the compiling of which he found 'so distasteful that he had to turn the work over to an old friend'. He was also most concerned that the *Western Mail* and the *South Wales Daily News* would be 'gluttonous for information'.[5] He particularly requested that Morant should send him a telegram as soon as possible 'saying definitely when the official announcement would be made by the Board, of both his and Edwards's appointment, for he attached the greatest importance to both barrels being let off at the same time'.[6] Morant assured him that this would be done and said that he 'took special steps in regard to the two Welsh papers and the *Manchester Guardian*'.[7]

The establishment of the Welsh Department was duly announced in the Press on 12 February:

[1] Ibid.
[2] J. Vyrnwy Morgan, *Welsh Political and Educational Leaders in the Victorian Era*, London, 1908, p. 85.
[3] *Journal of Education*, January 1907, p. 52.
[4] Ibid., February 1907, p. 130.
[5] PRO Ed 24/581, Davies to Morant, 11 February 1907.
[6] Ibid. Davies to Morant, 12 February.
[7] Ibid. Morant to Davies, 13 February.

The Genesis of The Welsh Department, Board of Education

> In pursuance of the intention of the Government at the close of last Session to consider the possibility of creating some organization in Whitehall for dealing with Welsh education, Mr. McKenna, President of the Board of Education, has decided to make arrangements for establishing a distinct Department of the Board *to deal with all grades of education in Wales and Monmouthshire.*[1] As a first step, Mr. McKenna has decided to appoint a *Permanent Secretary* of this Welsh Education Department, and a Chief Inspector for Welsh Education. These appointments have been offered to, and have been accepted by Mr. A. T. Davies and Mr. O. M. Edwards, respectively, both of whom will be directly responsible to the President. These gentlemen will not be able to take up their duties until the beginning of April. In the meantime steps are being taken by the President *gradually* to separate the work relating to education in Wales from the rest of the Board's work, in order that the new Department may be in a position to undertake by that date the various functions assigned to it except such as are necessarily dealt with at South Kensington pending the concentration of all branches of the Board's work in the new premises next Christmas.[2]

The reception given to this announcement caused great satisfaction to both Davies and Edwards, as expressed in their letters to McKenna and Morant. Davies was particularly jubilant because 'two of the staunchest Conservatives and churchmen of Liverpool, who had hitherto been political opponents, and also the Denbighshire County Council had sent him congratulations.[3] Edwards, in a long letter to McKenna, for which he apologized by saying 'I am afraid my first duty will be to learn to write shorter letters to Cabinet Ministers, but I hope that you are satisfied with the way in which my appointment has been received in Wales, especially in Glamorgan and Monmouthshire. I am better known in these counties, I believe, than in north Wales. They know at Cardiff and Swansea, at any rate, that I have given all my spare time and all my surplus income to the cause of Welsh education during the last 20 years'.[4] His reference to south Wales was 'not so surprising when it is remembered that his popular publications such as *Cymru, Cymru'r Plant*, and *Cyfres y Fil*, were avidly read by thousands of the working classes in the industrial valleys of south Wales'.[5]

No doubt anxious to acquaint himself with his new work before taking up his appointment, Davies had pestered Morant with questions regarding lists of staff at the Board of Education, the relationship of the staff to the new Welsh Department, and requests for the Board's official publications.

---

[1] The italics are mine. This statement and others in this announcement are most relevant to Study No. 6, when Davies insisted on the transference of responsibilities to the Welsh Department.

[2] PRO Ed 24/581, copy of Press release.

[3] Ibid., Davies to Morant, 14 February 1907. Education Office, Ruthin, Denbighshire, to Morant, 2 March 1907.

[4] PRO Ed 24/581, Edwards to McKenna, 19 February 1907.

[5] Sir Ben Bowen Thomas, 'The Welsh Department, Ministry of Education', *Trans. Cymm. Soc.*, 1958 (Session 1957), p. 23.

He even went so far as to ask for a supply of official notepaper, which, to Morant, was a bold infringement of civil service propriety—especially since Davies had not assumed duties, and was not yet even a civil servant! Morant sent Davies a rather sharp reply, with the approval of McKenna, who agreed with Morant that it was not 'too rude'. At the same time Morant said that the President was rather involved in many matters, 'amongst other things he is being rained upon with Questions in the House and otherwise, in regard to the establishment, staff, and so forth, of the new Welsh Department of this Board'.[1]

It was no surprise that the President was being subjected to such rigid cross-examination in the Commons between 21 February and 13 March. Members knew very little about the Welsh Department, and it was from the answers supplied by McKenna that details were forthcoming regarding its role and responsibilities. It was disclosed that the President had no intention of introducing a Bill to establish a National Council of Education for Wales, because many of the purposes that such a Council might serve would be effectively secured by the new Welsh Department.[2] This Department and its new officials would not control public elementary education or any form of education, but would carry out the administration and inspection of education of *all grades* in Wales under the control of the Board of Education.[3] In reality, it became immediately responsible for the administration of elementary and secondary education in Wales, and the relations of the new Department to the Central Welsh Board would be those of the Board of Education to that Board.[4] The Department was to be located in Whitehall, and both Davies and Edwards would have their headquarters in London, but the latter would spend a considerable proportion of each month in Wales.[5] The total administrative staff would consist of six—the Permanent Secretary, Chief Inspector, two Senior and two Junior Examiners. There was no intention of assigning any clerical staff exclusively to the Department—its clerical work was to be done by the clerical sections of the Board generally.[6]

The new Department was self-contained only in the sense that the Permanent Secretary had control of the administrative staff assigned to his Department—in other respects the personnel of the Department were eligible for promotion within the Board, and also could be transferred

---

[1] PRO Ed 24/581, Morant to Davies, 13 February; Davies to Morant, 5 March; Morant to Davies. 6 March 1907.
[2] Question, House of Commons, 4 March 1907 by D. A. Thomas, MP.
[3] Question, House of Commons, 11 March by Samuel Roberts, MP.
[4] Question, House of Commons, 28 February by Llewelyn Williams, MP.
[5] Ibid.
[6] Ibid. 13 March by Evelyn Cecil, MP.

freely as required.[1] In addition, the special Departments of the Board, such as for example, the legal, medical, and architectural branches were outside the purview of the Welsh Department, but could be used by it as, and when, required. The Department was to have a separately organized Welsh inspectorate, and the expenditure of the whole Department would be accounted for by the Accountant-General of the Boards.[2] In short, the Welsh Department, although it dealt exclusively with Welsh education, was dependent on other sections of the Board for the exercise of its functions. The two chief officials were to receive £1,200 p.a. each, and their ranking was equivalent to that of Principal Assistant Secretary, while their pensions and conditions of service were governed by the rules of the Civil Service.[3] In the case of both Davies and Edwards, special arrangements had to be made to accommodate them as established civil servants.[4]

An important prerogative attached to the posts of the two chief officials was that they were responsible directly to the President.[5] Indeed, the Welsh Permanent Secretary had the right of 'direct access', i.e. he could approach the President directly, on any matter, without the agency of the Permanent Secretary of the Board—R. L. Morant—but in practice this procedure was reserved for the more important matters of policy and administration.[6] Finally, in the sphere of policy formation, it was the responsibility of the Welsh Permanent Secretary to keep the President of the Board of Education informed about the particular Welsh aspects of education and the general impact in Wales of the policies and decisions undertaken by the Board.

In the Education debate on 13 March 1907 the Conservative Opposition opened fire on the Welsh Department and the new appointments. Lord Robert Cecil, Anson and Bridgeman were concerned that Davies, a member of the Denbighshire County Council, who had been active as a 'passive resister' to the Act of 1902, could not be impartial towards the Welsh voluntary schools.[7] Edwards came off lightly and was merely accused of having been a Liberal MP,[8] but Lord Robert Cecil strongly

[1] Ibid.
[2] Ibid. 12 March by Mr. Cavendish, MP. Also, PRO Ed 24/581, Minute from Sykes to Morant, 10 January 1907.
[3] PRO Ed 23/242, Bromley to the Treasury, 15 February;
    Ibid., Treasury to Board of Education, 22 February 1907.
[4] PRO Ed 23/242, G. H. Murray, Treasury Chambers to Board of Education, 21 June 1907; ibid., Treasury Minute re Superannuation, 17 June.
[5] Question, House of Commons, 28 February 1907 by Llewelyn Williams, MP.
[6] A. T. Davies, op. cit., p. 131.
[7] *Parl. Deb.*, 4th series, vol. 171, 1907, cs. 87–126.
[8] Ibid.

protested against the creation of the Welsh Department 'at a very considerable expense, and under the circumstances it would certainly be regarded by the country and by Wales as a mere means of rewarding the political associates of the Government'.[1] But McKenna warmly supported both appointments and said that Edwards's whole career had been apart from controversial topics, and his whole desire was to improve education in Wales. The duties of the Chief Inspectors in England were confined respectively to the elementary, secondary and technical grades. In Wales it would not be so. There would be one Chief Inspector of all the three grades together, and Edwards desired to preserve that unity. McKenna added that Davies was a man of great capacity, industry and integrity, and he did not think or anticipate that the unhappy controversial period in Wales would last very long. The Welsh Department had been devised for the organizing of Welsh education, not merely now, but for the future, in order to establish Welsh education upon a basis better fitted for the people of Wales. Those were the only grounds upon which the appointments had been made.[2]

When Davies and Edwards started their work on 9 April, the President was able to re-assure them that the House was quite satisfied with their appointments, and 'criticism in the House is something to which we all learn to become very callous'.[3] Edwards had already planned his programme for the initial period and mentioned to McKenna 'when you are quite free, I should be very grateful if I could see you. I know most of the Welsh inspectors, I have watched the growth of the system, and I have thought a good deal about (a) the second language question (b) the better training of teachers, and (c) the unity of the whole Welsh system. Other subjects like that of Evening Continuation schools will also demand fairly immediate attention. But, as there is a whole year to think about the New Code, perhaps I had better not trouble you until I have made myself at home in my new Office'.[4]

Davies and Edwards had not only to initiate developments *de novo* in the administration of Welsh education, but also, quite early, had to encounter a series of personal resentments by Morant and other officials at the Board who apparently had formed strong opinions of departments with disruptive tendencies, for they did not take kindly to the establishment of the Welsh Department. After all, the fact had to be faced that whatever qualifications the new chief officials possessed, they had had no experience

[1] Ibid. A. T. Davies had been Election Agent to Lloyd George on more than one occasion.
[2] *Parl. Deb.*, ibid. supra.
[3] PRO Ed 24/581, McKenna to Davies, 15 March, 1907.
[4] Ibid. Edwards to McKenna, 19 February 1907.

of the administration of a government department, let alone a new Welsh Department, and as McKenna had pointed out in the debate, 'it was not easy to find any men outside and take them into the Civil Service and expect them to get an immediate grasp of the whole business of that Service'.[1] This fact undoubtedly hardened the attitude of Morant and his officials towards the new and older entrants into a Service in which such officials had spent so much of their lives. In addition, the privilege bestowed upon the 'new boys' of being responsible directly to the President undermined not only Morant's overall authority as Permanent Secretary to the Board, but other high officials such as E. B. Phipps, Chief Clerk of the Board, E. K. Chambers of the Technical Branch and Dr. Heath of DSIR, displayed open antagonism to the intrusion of the Welsh Department in Whitehall.

In addition to the administrative grades, about 1,800 men, women and youths were employed by the Board for clerical and miscellaneous duties, and the Chief Clerk was responsible for their overall efficiency and organization. His duty was to ensure that the whole of the Office worked smoothly.[2] Phipps complained that the pressure of work at his Office had increased, and that there was no need for two Senior Examiners in the Welsh Department. He told Morant 'it must be remembered that all work on procedure and forms in the clerical section is done for the Welsh Department which only has to walk on the roads made by the English, at such a pace and carrying such weight as may please it ... the new Welsh Department alone is responsible for additions to (my) work, so unnecessary and so troublesome that I cannot trust myself to write of them'.[3] Friction arose between Chambers, of the Technical Branch (part of whose Department was to be handed over to the Welsh Department) and Davies, due to an irresponsible action, grossly exaggerated, of a Junior Examiner in trespassing on grounds outside the Welsh Department.[4] Dr. Heath and another official at the Department of Special Inquiries and Reports, poured contempt on Davies's request that the Board should publish some pamphlets, including his own, dealing with aspects of Welsh education, and his letter was dismissed as being 'a very absurd bid for self-advertisement'.[5]

[1] *Parl. Deb.*, 4th series, vol. 171, 1907, c. 102.

[2] P. H. J. H. Gosden, *The Development of Educational Administration in England and Wales*, Blackwell, Oxford, 1966, p. 108.

[3] PRO Ed 23/216 C, Chief Clerk's Report on the duties of his post, 11 September 1908.

[4] PRO Ed 24/586, Minute from Morant to Davies, 13 December 1910.

[5] PRO Ed 24/585, Davies to Runciman, 2 December 1909; DSIR to Runciman, 3 December. See Study No. 6.

The Genesis of The Welsh Department, Board of Education

A more disturbing lack of concern and sympathy for the work of the Welsh Department was shown by Walter Runciman, the new President of the Board and Morant, in July 1908, relating to the Board's Annual *Report*. Davies had appreciated that because the Welsh Department was newly created at the end of 1906, that the Board's *Report* for the year 1906-7 should combine both that of the Board of Education and the Welsh Department. But when this procedure was repeated in the *Report* for 1907-8, Davies sent a long Minute to the President requesting a separate *Report* and volume for the Welsh Department. To make matters worse, the joint *Report* carried Morant's signature.[1] Davies, supported by Edwards, stated brusquely but cogently that a separate Department with different problems demanded a separate *Report* and that it was incongruous not only that Morant's name appeared under the Welsh matter of the *Report*, but also represented unfairly the relative positions and responsibility of himself and Morant. Runciman did not concede a separate volume, but from 1908 onwards, the Board's *Report* contained a separate section for Wales, but Morant's signature remained.

So much for obstructiveness within the Board of Education. Unfortunately for the two new officials, suspicious and malevolent minds working in Wales made their task no easier. One particular instance may be quoted. Mr. John Rowland, of the Welsh Board of Health, and one of the conveners of the National Conference to set up a National Council of Education for Wales in 1906, had written a highly indignant letter to Davies, criticizing the work and policy of the Welsh Department. Edwards wrote to, and discussed the contents of this letter in some detail with J. Herbert Lewis, adding that Lewis was at liberty to show Rowland 'as much or as little of the letter as he liked'. Edwards said that if the Welsh public and the Press misunderstood their work, opportunities, and their difficulties as thoroughly as Rowland, very grave injustice would be done to the Welsh Department. He went on to say that they had been attacked most unmercifully and unfairly by the *Western Mail* and the *Manchester Guardian;* that the Welsh Department had been regarded as having been established to supplant the Central Welsh Board, or to stave off a Welsh National Council for Education, and that Davies and himself, in spite of their past services and well-known views, were regarded as anti-national. Rowland maintained, among other things, that they ignored the Welsh University and the Central Welsh Board, that they were an "*achos rhwyg*" (disruptive influence) rather than a power for national unity, and that they

---

[1] PRO Ed 91/1, Wales: General Files, 'Contributions of the Welsh Department to the Board of Education's Annual Report for 1908', 8 July 1908.

The Genesis of The Welsh Department, Board of Education

had no policy. With reference to the Central Welsh Board, Edwards said that they were using them in every possible way, because that was the direction he received from McKenna when he first came to Whitehall. Edwards contended that he had attended all their meetings and was on the most amicable terms with Owen Owen, their Chief Inspector. But the Central Welsh Board looked upon the Welsh Department as a rival, and 'no assurance by the President could satisfy them ... and the officials of that Board, instead of conferring with the Welsh Department, rushed into print and to the lobbies of the House of Commons'.[1] But in spite of all opposition,—from the Board of Education's officials or from Wales—Davies was determined to build up and enhance the separate identity of the Welsh Department, and Edwards was constrained to say in 1909 'nid ydynt wedi sylweddoli eto mor deyrngarol ac anhunangar, mor dryloew ac unplyg yw ei gariad at Gymru'.[2]

If the work of Davies, ensconced in his office in Whitehall, was arduous and, at times frustrating, that of Edwards, travelling the length and breadth of Wales, was doubly so. Indeed, as he himself confessed, 'in two and a half years at Whitehall, I have not had more than two and a half weeks away from my work'.[3] Whether, in this connection, he meant *Neuadd Wen*, (Whitehall) Llanuwchllyn, or the London location is not quite apparent, but one could hazard a guess!

The bosom friend and confidant of Edwards was J. Herbert Lewis, MP, who, although at that time was at the Local Government Board, was always consulted on educational matters. Very often, Edwards wrote Lewis two or three lengthy letters every week. Writing in October 1907, he said 'the duties of my new office are exceedingly heavy, but I think I can go on with my publishing, as I have now disciples who will do the work for me. I hope to be able to turn out ... at least six volumes in Welsh every year ... the demand exists, and if we do not supply it, our young folk must depend upon the literature of the railway bookstalls. I look forward to the future with the keenest delight. I feel less old after coming into closer touch with Wales again'.[4] A year later, Edwards described his work as 'absolutely engrossing. There is much to do, and everywhere I find my countrymen so responsive. If I live for ten years, I shall have done

---

[1] Edwards to Lewis, 10 April 1909, Penucha MSS.

[2] Ibid. 'They have not yet realized how loyal and unselfish, how sincere and guileless is his love for Wales'.

[3] PRO Ed 24/584, Notes on the work of the Welsh Department, 29 November 1909; Minute from Edwards to the President, 27 November 1909.

[4] Edwards to Lewis, 9 October 1907, Penucha MSS.

more than I ever dreamt of being able to do, or I shall have grossly neglected my opportunities'.[1]

Describing the policy of the Welsh Department, he said that the chief aim was to carry out more efficiently and expeditiously than before, under the direction of the President, the work of the Board of Education in Wales, which included: 1. Forming the Regulations of the Board where the special and exceptional interests of Wales should be considered; 2. Giving the Welsh language its right place in the system of Welsh education; 3. Improving the inspectorate; 4. Developing the technological aspects of education, especially in the industrial parts of north Wales; 5. Development of school libraries and making the school a centre of intellectual life in rural districts; 6. More punctual payments of grants. Moreover, he hoped to get something definite done every year, and had drawn up a three-year plan: First Year: Autonomy for Wales in secondary education, which the Central Welsh Board had rejected. Here, he divulged for the first time, part of the private correspondence he had with McKenna before he accepted the post of Chief Inspector: 'it was Mr. McKenna's offer to give us this, that tempted me to leave Oxford. The idea was, give Wales a yearly lump sum, 1/12th of the whole grant for England and Wales, and let her do what she liked with it. If we had been allowed by the Central Welsh Board to accept this offer, Wales could have made her own experiments and lead England'.[2] This was the first of his great disappointments, 'an offer rejected by Wales, misled by men who ought to have known better'.[3] The second disappointment was the hostility of the Central Welsh Board, and especially the 'revolt' in Parliament. Much of his private correspondence at this period revealed that he went to great lengths to conciliate that Board. This might well be sufficient grounds to dispel the allegation made in some quarters that Edwards was antagonistic to that body for rejecting his application for the post of Chief Inspector in 1896. Edwards emphasized that they were aiming at getting as much power for the Central Welsh Board as was consistent with the thorough efficiency of the Welsh system of education.

Second Year: A complete system of Training Colleges for Wales, unsectarian, efficient, and answering to the needs of the country. The system was complete and practically sanctioned.

Third Year: A review of the provision for the education of Blind, Deaf

---

[1] Ibid. 14 October 1908, Penucha MSS.
Owen Edwards died in May 1920.
[2] Edwards to Lewis, 17 April 1909, Penucha MSS.
[3] Ibid.

and Dumb, and defective children, because they were not provided for at all.[1]

Other aspects of Welsh education were taken over by the Welsh Department in subsequent years, including Training Colleges which Edwards examined and inspected, and technical education. When Davies took up his appointment he was offered responsibility for technical education, but he preferred to wait (perhaps a little too long) until this Branch of the Board's work was transferred from South Kensington to Whitehall. After considerable negotiation and unsuspected difficulties this was accomplished in January 1912.[2]

The young Welsh Department had become an integral part of the whole Department of Education and Science. The words of Sir Gilbert Flemming, a former Permanent Secretary of the Ministry of Education, sent, in a message to celebrate the fiftieth anniversary of the Welsh Department in 1957 are, perhaps, appropriate:

> 'We appreciate what the Department, by its unique constitution and traditions has contributed to the development of Welsh education, both in its uniqueness and as a valuable element in the common life of England and Wales ... As an addition to the old slogan "remember Wales", so well established in Whitehall and Curzon Street (and now partly, in Elizabeth House, Waterloo) I feel like saying for the benefit of my English colleagues: "Wales and the Welsh Department have been very good to you" '.[3]

* * * * *

Fourteen years later, in November 1971 the responsibility for Welsh primary and secondary education was transferred to the Welsh Office in Cardiff.

[1] Ibid.
[2] See Study No. 6.
[3] *Trans. Cymm. Soc.*, op. cit., p. 26.

APPENDICES

I JOINT EDUCATION COMMITTEE, SCHEME B

II NATIONAL COUNCIL OF EDUCATION FOR WALES, DRAFT RESOLUTIONS

APPENDIX I

JOINT EDUCATION COMMITTEE, SCHEME B

WHEREAS by Section 17 of the Education Act, 1902, (hereinafter referred to as "the Act"), it is amongst other things enacted that any Council having powers under the Act shall establish an Education Committee or Education Committees constituted in accordance with a scheme made by the Council and approved by the Board of Education, and that any such scheme may for all or any purposes of the Act provide for the constitution of a Joint Education Committee for any area formed by a combination of counties, boroughs, or urban districts, or of parts thereof.

AND WHEREAS the Councils of the Counties and County Boroughs named in the Schedule to this Scheme (hereinafter called "the Combining Councils") have respectively made schemes for the establishment of Education Committees and those schemes have been approved by the Board of Education.

AND WHEREAS the Combining Councils have agreed to establish a Joint Education Committee for the area formed by a combination of the said administrative Counties and County Boroughs for the purpose of dealing with matters relating to the training of teachers and the examination and inspection of schools throughout their area, IT IS HEREBY PROVIDED AS FOLLOWS:—

1. There shall be established a Joint Education Committee for the Combining Councils, to be called the Welsh Joint Committee (hereinafter referred to as "the Joint Committee").

2. The Joint Committee shall, save as hereinafter provided, consist of x members, $\frac{x}{y}$ of whom (hereinafter referred to as "the Conciliar Members") shall be elected by the Combining Councils respectively in the numbers set opposite to their names in the second column of the said Schedule, and shall be persons who at the time of their election are members of some one of the Combining Councils. The remaining members (hereinafter referred to as "the selected Members") shall be persons of experience in education and acquainted with the needs of the various kinds of schools in the combined area and shall be appointed as hereinafter provided.

Provided that there shall always be upon the Joint Committee persons of experience in respect of the training of teachers and of the examination and inspection of the various kinds of schools in the combined area, at least two of whom shall be women.

3. In the selection of members of the Joint Committee by each Council due regard shall be had to the inclusion of persons who are members of the Education Committee of the Council making the appointment.

4. The members of the Joint Committee shall be appointed annually for a term of office ending upon the 15th day of April in the year succeeding that in which the election is made. The appointment of the Conciliar Members shall be made in the case of a County Council at the meeting at which the Chairman of the Council is ordinarily elected, and in the case of a County Borough Council at a meeting to be held on the 16th day of March in every year, or on such other day, within ten days of that date, as the Council concerned may from time to time fix.

Provided that the members first to be appointed shall be appointed as soon as conveniently may be after the approval of this Scheme by the Board of Education for a term of office ending upon the 15th day of April 1905.

5. Within three days of the election by each Council of the Conciliar Members, the Clerk of the Council shall notify to the Convening Officer the names of the persons appointed by the Council concerned. The Convening Officer shall, as soon as conveniently may be, summon a preliminary meeting of the Conciliar Members to be held on the seventh day, excluding Sunday, after the day on which he has received notification that all the Conciliar Members have been appointed, and for that purpose shall, on the day next after that on which he has received such notification, send by post a notice specifying the day, hour and place at which the meeting will be held.

6. The Conciliar Members shall at the preliminary meeting, or at any adjournment thereof held before the 10th day of April, nominate the selected members and at a meeting of the Council selected for the purpose by agreement by the Combining Councils, held as soon as conveniently may be after the said nomination, that Council shall appoint the members so nominated.

7. The Convening Officer shall be in the case of the Committee first appointed under this Scheme such person as the Combining Councils shall in the agreement for combination appoint, and in subsequent years the Secretary of the Joint Committee.

8. Any vacancy arising upon the Joint Committee owing to death, resignation or otherwise, shall be filled up by the Council by whom the dead or retiring member was appointed at the first available meeting of the said Council after the vacancy has been notified to them.

9. The matters to stand referred to the Joint Committee shall be such matters relating to the exercise by the Combining Councils of their powers under the Act as relate to the training of teachers and the examination and inspection of schools, together with other such matters relating to the exercise of the said powers as the Combining Councils may, with the sanction of the Board of Education, from time to time determine, and, save as hereinafter provided, such matters shall not stand referred to the Committees established by the schemes for the establishment of Education Committees made by the Combining Councils and approved by the Board of Education as hereinbefore recited.

If any difference shall arise as to whether any matter stands referred under this Scheme to the Joint Committee, any of the Combining County Councils or the Joint Committee may refer the question to the Board of Education whose decision shall be final.

10. If the Council of any County or County Borough in Wales or Monmouthshire which is not a party to the said agreement for combination shall at any future time give to the Combining Councils notice of their desire to enter the combination, the Combining Councils may by resolution admit the said Council. In that event

(a) the said Council shall appoint such number of members upon the Joint Committee as shall be agreed upon between the said Council and the Combining Councils, and the number of Conciliar Members and of Selected Members upon the Joint Committee shall be enlarged accordingly so that the proportion between Conciliar and Selected Members in Clause 2 of the Scheme provided shall be observed;

(b) The provisions of this Scheme shall have effect as if the name of the said Council had appeared in the Schedule to this Scheme.

11. In the event of any of the Combining Councils giving to the remaining Councils not less than six months' notice, expiring on the 15th April then next ensuing, of their intention to retire from the combination,

(a) At the date of the expiration of the said notice the members appointed upon the Joint Committee by the said Council shall cease to hold office, and the number of Conciliar and of Selected Members upon the Joint Committee shall be reduced accordingly so that the proportion between Conciliar and Selected Members in Clause 2 of the Scheme provided shall be observed;

(b) The provisions of this Scheme shall have effect as if the name of the retiring Council were omitted from the Schedule;

(c) The matters relating to the exercise by the said Council of their powers under the Act which under this Scheme or any agreement made thereunder would have stood referred to the Joint Committee shall, subject to the provisions of any future Scheme made and approved in accordance with the provisions of the Act, thenceforth stand referred to the Committee established under the hereinbefore mentioned Scheme for the establishment of an Education Committee for that Council.

If at any time the number of Councils in the combination shall fall below six, the Joint Committee shall be dissolved, and the provisions of sub-Clause (c) of this section shall have effect in the case of each of the Councils which formed part of the combination at the date of the dissolution.

12. In the appointment of any executive committee by the Joint Committee due regard shall be had to the inclusion of persons specially experienced in respect of the training of teachers and of the examination and inspection of the various kinds of schools in the combined area.

Provided further that in the event of any question arising as to the terms on which any Council is to retire as aforesaid, that question shall be determined by the Board of Education, whose decision shall be final.

L.G.B. Clause

SCHEDULE

Name of Authority	Number of Conciliar Members.
Anglesey	2
Brecknockshire	2
Cardiganshire	2
Carmarthenshire	1
Carmarthen B.	1
Llanelli U.D.	1
Carnarvonshire	3
Denbighshire	2
Wrexham B.	1
Flintshire	2
Glamorganshire	5
Neath B.	1
Rhondda U.D.	2
Mountain Ash U.D.	1
Aberdare U.D.	1
Pontypridd U.D.	1
Merthyr Tydfil U.D.	1
Barry U.D.	1
Merionethshire	2
Montgomeryshire	2
Monmouthshire	3
Abertillery U.D.	1
Ebbw Vale U.D.	1
Pembrokeshire	1
Pembroke B.	1
Radnorshire	2
Cardiff C.B.	4
Newport C.B.	2
Swansea C.B.	2
	51

PRO Ed. 91/10

The Genesis of The Welsh Department, Board of Education

APPENDIX II
NATIONAL COUNCIL OF EDUCATION FOR WALES

DRAFT RESOLUTIONS

*To be submitted to the Conference at LLANDRINDOD,
on Friday, June 1st, 1906.*

1. That this Conference expresses its approval of Part IV. of the Education (England and Wales) Bill, 1906, and urges the Government to secure its passing into law.

2. That the Council shall consist of not more than 100 members appointed by the Councils of Welsh Counties and of County Boroughs and Welsh Borough and Urban Districts having a population of over 25,000 according to the census of 1901, in the following proportions:—

COUNTY AND COUNTY BOROUGHS

	Population	Necessary Members	Additional Members
Anglesey	50,606	2	
Brecknockshire	54,213	2	
Cardiganshire	61,078	2	
Carmarthenshire	109,711	2	
Carnarvonshire	125,649	2	
Denbighshire	131,582	2	
Flintshire	81,485	2	
Glamorganshire	284,294	2	
Merionethshire	48,852	2	
Montgomeryshire	54,901	2	
Monmouthshire	230,806	2	
Pembrokeshire	87,894	2	
Radnorshire	23,281	2	
Cardiff	164,333	2	
Newport	67,270	2	
Swansea	94,537	2	
		32	

BOROUGHS AND URBAN DISTRICTS OF OVER 25,000

CARMARTHEN

Llanelli	25,617	1	

GLAMORGAN

Rhondda	113,735	1	
Aberdare	43,365	1	
Mountain Ash	31,093	1	
Merthyr Tydfil	69,228	1	
Barry	27,030	1	
Pontypridd	32,316	1	

The Genesis of The Welsh Department, Board of Education

OFFICERS

The Council shall have power to appoint a President, a Secretary, a Treasurer, Inspectors, and such other officers and servants as they think fit, and may grant them such remuneration (if any) as they think reasonable.

EXECUTIVE COMMITTEE

The Council shall have power to appoint an Executive Committee, and may delegate to the Executive Committee any of their powers or duties except the power of raising money by means of precepts and the power of borrowing money.

CONSULTATIVE COMMITTEE

The Council shall have power to appoint a Consultative Committee which shall report to the Council on any matter referred to it by the Council, and which shall have power to advise the Council on any educational questions. The Consultative Committee shall consist of such a number of Members of the Council as the Council thinks fit and of
- (*a*) Two persons appointed by the University of Wales.
- (*b*) One person appointed by the University College of Wales, Aberystwyth.
- (*c*) One person appointed by the University College of North Wales.
- (*d*) One person appointed by the University College of South Wales and Monmouthshire.
- (*e*) Two Head Teachers in Secondary Schools in Wales appointed by the Council.
- (*f*) Two Head Teachers in Public Elementary Schools in Wales appointed by the Council.
- (*g*) One person appointed by the Council of the National Museum of Wales.
- (*h*) One person appointed by the Council of the National Library of Wales.
- (*i*) Such a number of persons of experience in education and acquainted with the needs of the Colleges, Schools, and other educational institutions in Wales, as the Council may think fit provided that at least two of such persons shall be women.

POWERS OF COUNCIL

3 (1) That there shall be transferred to the Council the powers and duties of the Board of Education so far as they relate to Wales except:—
- (i) Any power or duty of the Charity Commission transferred from the Commission to the Board by the Board of Education Act, 1899;
- (ii) the powers proposed to be conferred on the Board of Education by Part II of the Education Bill 1906;
- (iii) the power of deciding certain questions proposed to be conferred on the Board of Education by the Education Bill 1906, s. 33;
- (iv) the powers conferred on the Board by the Education Act 1902 s. 13 and the powers proposed to be conferred on the Board by the Education Bill 1906 s. 39.

(2) There shall be transferred to the Council the powers and duties of the Welsh Central Board for Intermediate Education; and also the powers and duties, so far as they relate to Wales, of the Board of Agriculture and Fisheries with regard to instruction in Agriculture and Forestry.

RATING POWERS

4. The Council shall have power by means of a precept to demand from the local authorities appointing members of the Council and the local authorities respectively on the receipt of such demand shall pay such further sums as may be required by the Council in addition to the Parliamentary grant for Wales for the purposes:—

    (*a*) Of making further grants for supplying or aiding the supply of Education in Wales; and

    (*b*) of providing for the Council's expenses, including the expenses of administration and inspection.

Provided that the amount raised in any one year by the Council for the purpose of any year out of rates levied by the Council shall not exceed the amount which would be produced by a rate of two pence in the pound.

To be Proposed by D. BRYNMOR JONES, Esq., M.P.,

and Seconded by J. HERBERT ROBERTS, Esq., M.P.

V

THE EXPLOSIVE REPORT

INTRODUCTION	240
I BACKGROUND OF THE 1909 REPORT	243
II THE 1909 REPORT	248
III REACTIONS TO THE REPORT	255
IV REPLY BY OWEN EDWARDS	264
V THE AFTERMATH	278
APPENDICES	303

The Explosive Report

In 1910, the twenty-first anniversary of the Welsh Intermediate Education Act was to be celebrated in a manner very different from that contemplated by the Central Welsh Board, the body responsible for the administration of the Act. In their annual *Report* for the year 1908–9 the Board of Education stated that 'by the Welsh Act the secondary education problem was most effectively handled, representative authorities for secondary and technical education being created, and rating powers given for working out organized schemes of secondary education for each county and county borough in the Principality, and for establishing new secondary schools where needed'.[1] In the same *Report* the Board of Education paid further tribute to the Welsh educational pioneers of the last two decades of the nineteenth century, and to the work of the Central Welsh Board— 'no review of the present position and condition of the work done as a result of their labours ... would be complete without warm recognition of the selfdenying and persistent labours of those upon whom has devolved the responsibility, to which they have applied themselves with equal ardour, of working the educational machine, the component parts of which, so far as regards secondary education, are to be found today in the ninety-six intermediate schools scattered throughout the length and breadth of the land—

> "O Lanandras i Dyddewi
> O Gaergybi i Gaerdydd".[2]

Yet, notwithstanding this glowing tribute, the publication of the Board of Education's 1909 *Report*[3] on the administration of the Welsh intermediate schools caused a national conflagration, for the reception given to it by many people in Wales, including the Central Welsh Board, could be described as nothing less than bitter hostility. It brought into open warfare the already existing strained relationships between the Central Welsh Board and the Welsh Department of the Board of Education. The main target of this deplorable outcry was Owen Edwards, His Majesty's Chief Inspector of Education for Wales, at the Welsh Department.

---

[1] *Report of the Board of Education (Welsh Department) under the Welsh Intermediate Education Act, or the year 1909*, HMSO, p. 3.

[2] Ibid., From Presteigne to St. Davids
   From Holyhead to Cardiff'.
In Wales, 1895–6 there were 47 intermediate schools with 3,367 pupils, 1908–9 96 intermediate schools with 13,760 pupils.

[3] Published 18 July 1910 (sometimes referred to wrongly as the 1910 Report).

The Explosive Report

The emergence of this Department in December 1906 had created a completely new situation within the administrative structure of Welsh education. From 1907 onwards, the Department was delegated over-all responsibility for the administration of Welsh elementary education and all Welsh secondary schools established *after* the Education Act of 1902, while the Central Welsh Board merely retained statutory authority for the administration of Welsh *intermediate schools* established by Scheme under the Act of 1889. But in accordance with a specific directive contained in the latter Act, the Board of Education (which had acquired the powers of the Charity Commissioners over endowments regulated by schemes under the Welsh Act) were required to prepare and present an annual report to parliament on the work of the Welsh intermediate schools.

An earlier Study has revealed the suspicion and resentment which the Central Welsh Board harboured against the Welsh Department. The appearance of the 1909 *Report*, the usual normal procedure of the Board of Education, produced a wholly unexpected and hostile reaction which ignited the fuse for the explosion. The blast yielded a two-fold result. In the first place it exposed to the world the defects of the Central Welsh Board system of secondary education. Secondly, it provided a unique opportunity for HMCI for Wales to compile one of the most important educational documents which appeared in the Principality in the first quarter of the twentieth century—Edwards's scathing, though considered rejoinder to his opponents.[1] In his own urbane, but forthright manner, Edwards, the author of the offending *Report*, confessed that 'the storm was entirely of his own brewing', since Edgar Jones had seen fit 'to set the Welsh heather on fire'.[2] Indeed, the Chief Inspector had landed himself in the dual role of villain of the piece and the victim!

The *Report* was an important landmark in the history of Welsh education for at least three reasons. First, it discussed the weaknesses and problems of Welsh secondary education at the end of its first experimental period, the decennium 1897–1907. Second, Edwards's reply to Jones's criticisms, prepared for the President of the Board of Education, refuted the allegation made at that time that 'a tyrannical bureaucracy at Whitehall was trying to throttle a democratic national institution—the Central Welsh Board'.[3] Third, the reply set out in detail, clearly and comprehensively, Edwards's policy, ideas and ideals regarding the content and

---

[1] PRO Ed 24/588, *Report* by Owen Edwards to the President on Edgar Jones's criticism of the Board of Education's Report to Parliament under the Welsh Act, 1909: 18 November 1910.
[2] Ibid.
[3] Ibid *Reply to the Report on Intermediate Education issued by the Welsh Department of the Board of Education*, 1909, by Edgar Jones. Cardiff, n.d. p. 1. (Presidential Address to the Welsh County Schools Association, Shrewsbury, 28–29 October 1910).

purpose of Welsh secondary education appropriate for *all* pupils, related to their native environment. He knew (and this theme was elaborated in his official report for 1912) that it was the intention of those who designed the initial Welsh county schemes, that intermediate or secondary education 'while embracing all the subjects usually taught in a secondary school, should have a definite reference to the needs of the school districts'.[1]

Although it was said that Edwards had been influenced by Ruskin and others for this view, there is no doubt that Edwards must have been well-versed in the recommendations of the Schools Inquiry Commission and later, the Bryce Report of 1895, where it was stated that the curricula of schools should be differentiated in accordance with their environment. He wanted to see individual pupils developing as human beings within their communities. Edwards suggested those industries which should be considered when courses of instruction were being prepared for each school.[2] Agriculture and Rural Science were appropriate for rural counties; schools situated in the ports and towns of the Welsh coastline should cater for Navigation. In smelting and mining areas such as Swansea, Llanelli, Glamorgan and Merioneth attention should be given to Metallurgy and Mining. In some schemes, Woodwork and Craftmaking in iron and tin were compulsory, and in others, optional. But in course of time, dominance of examinations and uniformity of curricula in the intermediate schools had led to the exclusion of the more desirable practical and quasi-vocational subjects. He complained that Governing Bodies of schools paid insufficient attention to possible differentiation and even neglected such essential subjects as Physical Training, Music, Drawing and Domestic Science.[3] This was the special danger to which the intermediate schools were exposed. They were inspected and examined by their own *ad hoc* body which made them excessively assimilated in type to each other.

For many years Edwards had discussed with school governors and heads alike, the necessity for adaptation in accord with the many avenues of occupations open to pupils in their neighbourhoods. He urged less dependence on old academic courses and deplored schools which always anticipated examination demands. To him, Welsh secondary education was something far more fundamental than an academic interlude between elementary school and university. He saw 'Wales as a democracy, the democracy of the "werin"—gwerin yr Ysgol Sabothol, yr Eisteddfodau

[1] PRO Ed 24/588, Minute from Edwards to Maurice, 8 November 1910. Board of Education (Welsh Department) *Report*, 1907, p. 5.

[2] PRO Ed 24/588, Minute from Edwards to Maurice, 8 November 1910.

[3] *Report of the Board of Education, Welsh Department*, 1912, p. 9.

The Explosive Report

a'r Cyfarfodydd Llenyddol'.[1] An important function of higher education should be to sustain and enrich such heritage by preparing the youth of Wales 'to reflect the life, language and literature of the community they served'.[2] Not that he feared nor despised the emergence of an intellectual *élite*. This was inevitable in a nation which, having secured a secondary school system, passionately believed in opportunities for academic excellence and advancement. With all its faults, the Central Welsh Board precisely supplied this desirable need. In the eyes of the Welsh working classes it not only had prestige but also a subtle aura of romance. Countless tales could be related of Welsh parents in rural and industrial Wales who had been only too prepared at great sacrifice to send at least one of their offspring to university—through the much maligned examination machine of the Central Welsh Board. Edwards was aware of this. He came from a similar background. Had he been born later he might have been part of the story. His deep concern was that the Central Welsh Board system might be made *sufficiently flexible to serve Wales* as well as its university. This was the theme of the explosive Report.

I BACKGROUND OF THE 1909 REPORT

Section 15 of the Welsh Intermediate Education Act 1889 stated that 'the Charity Commissioners shall in every year cause to be laid before both Houses of Parliament, a Report of the Proceedings under this Act during the preceding year'. Parliament did not exact any such Report from England, since that country did not receive the Treasury grant.[3] In the Board of Education's *Report* for 1901 under the Act, it was stated that 'under the Board of Education Act 1899 and the Board of Education (Powers) Order in Council 1900, the powers of the Charity Commissioners over endowments regulated by schemes under the Welsh Act were, with some minor exceptions, transferred on 1 November 1900 to the Board of Education, and that it had become the duty of the Board to make, in respect of these endowments, the annual *Report* required by the Act'.[4] The explosive *Report* was therefore the ninth issued under these regulations.

Briefly, each *Report* up to 1909 contained sections dealing with: administration of intermediate schools; the inspection and examinations

---

[1] PRO Ed 24/584, Memorandum I from Edwards to the President, 27 November 1909. "Werin"—ordinary people (is a difficult word to translate) 'the Welsh people of the Sunday school, the Eisteddfod and the Literary Meetings'. P. T. J. Morgan, 'Gwerin Cymru—y Ffaith a'r Ddelfryd'. *Trans. Cymm. Soc.*, Session 1967, Part I. This paper deals fully with this term.

[2] *Pioneers of Welsh Education*, op. cit.

[3] This is explained in Study No. 1. The Treasury grant was made under Section 9 of the Act.

[4] *Report of the Board of Education on the Administration of Schools under the Welsh Intermediate Education Act* 1889, 1902. p. 1.

The Explosive Report

of such schools; a statement showing the numbers of schools (recommended by the Board of Education on consideration of the *Report*) qualifying for a grant under the Act (Treasury Regulation No. 3); statistics of staff and pupils in the schools; comments on material supplied by Owen Owen, CI of the Central Welsh Board on curricula and examiners' reports. The inspection and examination of the schools were conducted under the direction of the Central Welsh Board. Two forms of inspection had been adopted i. a complete administrative and educational inspection held triennially in each school, and ii. a subsidiary inspection held annually in each school which was not undergoing the complete inspection. For example, during 1906, thirty-three schools in the counties of Brecon, Carmarthen, Denbigh and Merioneth, and in the county boroughs of Cardiff, Newport and Swansea were visited for the purposes of the complete inspection, and the remaining sixty-three schools were visited for the subsidiary one.[1]

Before 1907 the Board of Education's *Annual Reports* which dealt with Welsh education were compiled by the Board's officials, based on information selected from the annual report drawn up by the Chief Inspector of the Central Welsh Board, for that Board. But when the Welsh Department began to function, the situation changed dramatically. Henceforth, Welsh educational administration, including the Central Welsh Board (for Treasury grant purposes), came under the jurisdiction of that Department, and was responsible, through the President of the Board of Education, to the central government. In other words, the Welsh Department was now interposed between the Central Welsh Board and the Board of Education. The *Report* of the Board of Education on the Central Welsh Board's activities was, from 1907, *seen for the first time* through the eyes of a Welsh chief official—Owen Edwards, who entertained very definite views on Welsh secondary education, and in the 1907–8 *Report* had begun to set out quite clearly his observations on the administration, inspection and examinations of the Central Welsh Board.

It is not surprising that Edwards in this, his first *Report*, comments on certain aspects of the work of the Central Welsh Board of which he was fully aware, first, as a Welshman, and secondly, as a person who brought to the Board of Education a pretty thorough knowledge of the Central Welsh Board from its beginning. He had taken a large part in the movement which produced that Board, and could confer with inspectors who had inspected the Welsh intermediate schools for years before the Welsh Department was created. He had inspected the very first of the Welsh

---

[1] *Report of the Board of Education on the Administration of Schools*, op. cit., 1905–6, p. 4.

The Explosive Report

intermediate schools, before the Central Welsh Board came into existence to do the work. For three and a half years he had conducted full inspections of several of the early schools, in addition to the Welsh secondary schools outside the 1889 Act, i.e. the municipal secondary schools established after the 1902 Act. He had visited every intermediate school in Wales, and had brought the matter contained in the Board of Education's *Reports* to the attention of every headmaster and headmistress in Wales. In short, he could claim that, with forty years' experience of Welsh schools, his knowledge of them was almost unique.[1]

A perusal of the *Board of Education's Report* for 1907-8 on the work of the Central Welsh Board contains nothing to which exception might be taken, or, indeed, anything which could excite the mildest form of acrimony. In fact, Edwards merely dilates on matters raised by the Chief Inspector of the Central Welsh Board, seasoned with kindly advice and judicious criticism in extreme moderation. Yet, this *Report* did not flutter the dove-cotes of the Central Welsh Board, although it differed very little in content from the offending *Report* of 1909. In order to be quite fair, it would not be amiss to recapitulate what Edwards had to say in 1908 in order to make a comparison with 1909, and consider if the fracas of 1910 was really necessary.

Owen, in his annual report to the Central Welsh Board had called attention to the course of instruction and the need of adapting the curricula of the schools, and the examinations of the Central Welsh Board to the requirements of those who desired to become elementary school teachers. With reference to the first, he advocated an eight years' course of instruction from the age of eleven to nineteen, so that 'over-pressure would cease, and immature work would disappear'.[2] But Edwards held that with regard to the relations between elementary and secondary education, the contions in Wales were different from those in England. He doubted whether Welsh children should leave the higher forms of elementary schools, 'where they got the teaching best adapted to their age and environment, before reaching the age of twelve'. In the intermediate schools, many children needed a course which should not exceed three years, comprising a curriculum of further teaching in elementary school subjects, to which could be added other subjects of importance relating to their district, such as Agriculture, Biology, or a Modern language, which a higher elementary school did not provide.[3]

---

[1] PRO Ed 24/588 *Report* by Owen Edwards to the President, op. cit., p. 5.
[2] *Report of the Board of Education (Welsh Department)*, op. cit., 1908 pp. 5-6.
[3] Ibid.

The Explosive Report

The topic of examinations figured quite prominently in the 1908 *Report* and Edwards pointed out emphatically that the Welsh Board's 'highly centralized system' was detrimental to any differentiation of curricula or even to provide suitable courses for intending teachers. Moreover it was quite possible for a school to have poor examination results, and yet be one of the best schools in the country. He hoped that the Central Welsh Board were fully alive to the danger of debasing, into a craving for examination results, 'that pure and unselfish love of knowledge that was, happily, one of the chief characteristics of modern Wales'.[1]

His criticisms embraced other matters as well. He deprecated the poor provision of school libraries which resulted in lack of individual effort and general reading on the part of pupils; that there was no reference to physical training and its proper place in intermediate schools; the tendency in some of the best schools to waste too much time and the energy of teaching staff on the higher forms where pupils could be directed to do more work on their own. It was not surprising that pupils left school *in a degree of mental helplessness* without a desire to go on learning more.[2] He was ashamed of the place given to Welsh and his remarks on this subject are worth recording in their entirety: 'the neglect of Welsh—in many cases, the long neglect of it—is the weakest spot in the Welsh system of secondary education. Now, that the secondary school has become, in a greater degree than ever, the training-ground for the elementary schoolteacher of the future, there are very few, if any, such schools in Wales where the omission of Welsh is justifiable on educational grounds. There is more prominence now given to this important subject by the Central Welsh Board, and their dissatisfaction with regard to its place in the schools is amply justified. In not many more than one-half of the intermediate schools in Wales is Welsh taught at all, and, even where it is taught, its place in the curriculum must be regarded as unsatisfactory when it is made alternative to such subjects as English literature, Latin, Scripture or Music. It cannot be said that the almost unique educational value for Wales, of Welsh and Welsh literature has yet been rightly appreciated. The neglect of the subject entails a break in the course of the children who come from the elementary schools; the best opportunity of teaching a second language well is neglected; many of the advantages of directly connecting school education with home education and home influences are lost, and the future usefulness of the pupils who intend to enter the teaching profession is seriously impaired'.[3]

[1] *Report of the Board of Education (Welsh Department)*, 1908, op. cit.
[2] Ibid., p. 6 ff.
[3] Ibid., p. 8.

The Explosive Report

The *Report* for 1909 was different, mainly because it was more comprehensive than the previous one, and appeared later than usual. It was the aim of the Welsh Department to make all its *Reports* much fuller than hitherto, in order to be of greater service to LEAs, governing bodies of schools and school heads. Moreover, the Welsh Department's reports on elementary schools were to be fuller, and Edwards was on the point of issuing full Area Reports as well.[1] He gave other reasons why the 1909 Report had appeared so much later—in July 1910—since Jones had made 'a most unworthy imputation that it had appeared during the holiday season, when the schools had ceased work, and the parliamentary session was drawing to its close'.[2] But the truth was that the Welsh Department did their utmost to get the *Report* out in time for the meeting of the Central Welsh Board in May, for it was thought then that the Board were going to celebrate their twenty-first anniversary, and the Welsh Department considered it would be helpful if they pointed out the dangers of the future. This became impossible on account of the long and careful consideration given to the *Report* by a great number of the officers of the Board of Education. Its quotations were carefully verified, and its suggestions were submitted to experts. Edwards stressed that all the points criticized so vehemently by Jones, were also included in the previous year's *Report*.[3] In the circumstances, it was not unnatural for Edwards to ask the question 'Why should the storm arise this year, and not last year'? The answer he gave was that the Welsh Department, in 1908 'dragged the name of the Central Welsh Board into the *Report* of that year, whenever they could, and expressed a pious opinion that they would set everything right. This year (1909) we prepared a *Report* on the same lines; but it was thought that we had better not connect our praise or criticism with the name of the Central Welsh Board, because (a) others were implicated, for example, ourselves, the LEAs, and school governors; (b) we were anxious to avoid even the appearance of criticizing or condemning the Central Welsh Board'.[4] With reference to the latter reason, specific criticism of the Central Welsh Board system was made only in the last two brief sections of the *Report*. But this could be narrowed down to one short sentence, which probably caused more offence than anything else in the *Report*, and was the spark which set alight the explosion, viz. 'That the Central Welsh Board should now consider to what extent their rigid examination system may be the cause of the *wooden and unintelligent*

---

[1] PRO Ed 24/588 *Report* by Owen Edwards to the President, op. cit., pp. 3–4.
[2] PRO Ed 24/588 *Reply to the Report on Intermediate Education issued by the Welsh Department of the Board of Education*, 1909, by Edgar Jones. op. cit.
[3] PRO Ed, ibid. supra, *Report* by Owen Edwards to the President, op. cit., p. 3.
[4] Ibid., Minute from Edwards to the President, 16 November 1910.

type of mind of which their Examiners complain'.[1] This, according to Edwards, was merely another way of saying 'a degree of mental helplessness' which he had used in the previous year's *Report*, but which had gone unheeded.

II THE 1909 REPORT

Were the observations embodied in this *Report*, covering a whole range of topics relating to Welsh secondary education, the mellowed reflections and conclusions of a man sequestered for the major part of his life in an Oxford College, and seemingly far removed from events in the educational life of Wales? Nothing could be further from the truth. Edwards was in more intimate touch with Welsh educational affairs than most of his contemporaries in the Principality. His knowledge and experience of Welsh secondary education have already been quoted from his own words. When he arrived at the Welsh Department, he had fully made up his mind that his work, henceforth, lay in the one direction of overhauling the whole machinery of the Welsh secondary system which was controlled, in the main, by the Central Welsh Board. The fact that the content of his *Report*, disclosing the shortcomings of that system, together with the remedial measures proposed, could arouse so much enmity, was positive proof of the susceptibility and complacency of the Welsh Board.

The *Report* contained twenty-seven sections, sixteen of which dealt with the usual routine administrative matters. Sections seventeen to twenty-six covered Edwards's observations, which might be called the offending part of the Report. His criticisms covered four main topics:

(a) The Central Welsh Board examination system and its effects on the intermediate schools.

(b) Curricula and teaching methods.

(c) The neglect of practical subjects.

(d) The effects of indifferent teaching on pupils.

From the latter part of section 26 to the end of the *Report*, certain remedial measures were recommended.

(a) Edwards noted that 4,668 pupils were presented for the written examinations of the Central Welsh Board in 1909, and was pleased that fewer papers had been set in the Junior Examination, although the fact remained that 'it was possible to lessen the burden of examinations still

---

[1] *Report of the Board of Education (Welsh Department)*, 1909, p. 19.

further at this stage'.[1] Owen had supplied a brief explanation of the examination system which was the most characteristic, as well as the most dominating feature of modern secondary education in Wales at that time. It was explained that 'the standard maintained at the Senior Certificate was determined by the requirements of those public bodies from whose examination the Senior Certificate secured exemption'.[2] The substitution of one external examination for many, simplified school organization, but alternative papers still had to be set to suit the requirements of the various public bodies who recognized the Certificate. The disadvantages of this system caused concern to Edwards, for several reasons: i. Since the Senior examination was the school-leaving one, and required four years of preparation, overpressure was inevitable for those pupils who stayed on for a less period of time; ii. Examinations should test the average of classes which were not specially drilled for them, but the Senior Certificate 'became the difficult goal to attain, which produced competition between schools for certificates'. The test of a good school seemed to be this prime consideration, for the Central Welsh Board frequently commented 'the Board will expect better examination results next year'—a statement which appeared no less than *fifteen times* in their reports from 1906–8; iii. All schools became uniform in type when their energies were directed towards one examination, and differentiation of courses was either impossible or ignored, but certainly sacrificed for academic results. Most important still, any originality on the part of headmasters and headmistresses found no scope.[3]

The dangerous consequences of this examination mania had been pointed out to the Central Welsh Board, both by its Chief Inspector, Owen Owen, and the Charity Commissioners as far back as 1899. They had warned the Board that sound educational methods could not flourish under conditions which produced pupil-fodder for examinations. Worse still, the certificates were being mis-used as a short cut to a complete education. Indeed, in some cases, even 'where the instruction appeared to be of inferior quality, a very respectable percentage of certificates were obtained'.[4] This was a shameful and unprofessional admission. Lists of scholastic achievements should never be used to advertise a school, for such a list was no conclusive evidence of the value of a school as a place of moral and intellectual training. Such an examination system further retarded the principle of differentiation in two ways. In the first place,

---

[1] *Report of the Board of Education (Welsh Department)*, 1909, op. cit., p. 11.
[2] Ibid.
[3] *Report of the Board of Education, (Welsh Department)*, op. cit., p. 12.
[4] Ibid. p. 13.

there was a tendency to find the easiest mark-getting subjects, for example, those who intended to become elementary schoolteachers found it easier to pass in French than in Welsh. Secondly, it was difficult to frame one syllabus that was equally adapted to all schools. The teaching of Agriculture and Cookery, for example, had suffered much from an unsuitable and rigid examination syllabus. The examiner in Cookery reported 'that in many districts, particularly country districts, the syllabus was not adapted to the peculiar needs of those districts'. There was a better aim than rigid uniformity of school organization—it was the natural and useful development obtained by examining *each* school upon its own work.[1]

(b) Edwards exposed one of the greatest weaknesses of the Welsh intermediate schools—the inability of pupils to express themselves in good English. Examiners reported lack of appreciation of literary points, and the Welsh examiner deplored the inefficient attention paid to the English idiom. Edwards claimed that too much time was devoted to formal grammar, phonetics, historical grammar and Anglo-Saxon. Again, the pressure of examinations made general reading of good English literature impossible, and the school library had not been given its due place in any of the schools. The place given to Welsh naturally concerned him, and although its teaching had improved since 1904 (for example in November 1908, the number of schools taking Welsh had risen to seventy-eight, and the number of pupils to 4,844) he was far from satisfied. He reflected on the strange circumstance, that the teaching of this subject, which should be the most important feature of Welsh secondary schools, was, until 1908, the most neglected of all. He blamed 'timid and inexperienced teaching, inadequate time, and the avoidance of the direct method by the teacher, who was conscious that pupils might criticize his pronounciation—he avoided speaking fairly good Welsh, and gladly took the opportunity of speaking very bad French'![2]

In Welsh teaching, formal grammar again took first place, and no attempts were made to arouse the pupils' interest in Welsh literature, and very often Welsh was taught through the medium of English![3] School libraries, where they existed, were singularly deficient in Welsh books of any quality or quantity, and if there were any at all, made no appeal to pupils, although, at the request of many headmasters, Edwards had compiled useful lists in Welsh literature.[4] Moreover, it was strange that

---
[1] Ibid.
[2] *Report of the Board of Education (Welsh Department)*, op. cit., p. 15.
[3] Ibid. PRO Ed 24/588 *Report* by Owen Edwards to the President, op. cit.
[4] Ibid. A useful list suitable for secondary school pupils was difficult to compile at that time.

the standard of examinations in Welsh were so high, especially when compared with the exceedingly low standard in French, which, in the majority of schools, was an alternative to Welsh. He stated that 'though many English-speaking children wished to take the examination in Welsh, the standard was that of a mother tongue, and a very high one at that ... In the Higher Honours Stage in French ... 100 per cent passed. In Welsh, the home language of most of the children, only 64.3 passed'.[1] It was little wonder that French was more popular than Welsh, and that the Board, at that time, was often described as the Central French Board!

The remaining subjects in the curriculum did not escape Edwards's attention. The examination results of the teaching of Latin showed 'much inequality of attainments, partly due to inequality of opportunities'. He strongly advocated the study of Latin in the lower Forms, and also Greek, because it was useful. To Edwards, 'in a country like Wales, where the great majority of children educated in secondary schools became Sunday school teachers or scholars, and quite a considerable number annually entered universities and denominational Theological Colleges, where Greek was necessary, it is difficult to understand why such facilities are not available. Welsh-speaking boys should start Latin at twelve and Greek at fourteen, and should be introduced to an easy author at the end of one year, for example, Xenophon and Andocides'.[2] German was taught effectively; only one pupil took Italian, whilst no one was examined in Spanish, 'perhaps the most important commercial language for Wales'.[3]

On the Science side, Edwards was equally forthright. Whilst the teaching of Mathematics was, on the whole, favourable, there was 'much inaccuracy and some lack of intelligence among the Junior pupils'. The general standard in Elementary Experimental Science had improved, and although the level of work in Physics in different schools was very even and fairly good, many pupils were presented for examination when they were too young. In Chemistry, teachers tended to overlook 'the peculiar value of essay-writing, in their anxiety to cover the detailed subject matter of the

---

[1] *The Welsh Intermediate Education Act*, 1889, *Its Origin, etc. op. cit.*, Appendix G: The number of schools taking French in the first examination conducted by the Central Welsh Board in 1897 was 79, i.e. all the Intermediate Schools at that time, but the number of schools taking Welsh was 31. Total *scripts* marked in French: 6,539; in Welsh, 988. Total number of pupils examined in all Intermediate Schools in 1897: 5,634.
Note: The fact that Welsh was taught with a strong philological bias in the schools, and very often through the medium of English, merely reflected the demands and the practice of the University of Wales, where philology took precedence over Welsh literature, and the Welsh professors lectured to the Welsh students right up to Honours, through the medium of English!

[2] *Report of the Board of Education*, supra, p. 16. *Education in Wales, Report of the Board of Education, Welsh Department*, 1924, p. 12 ff Special Report on Greek.

[3] Ibid.

syllabus'. The chief defect in the teaching of Botany and Geography, a very serious one, was 'a want of knowledge of Nature itself'.[1]

(c) Edwards condemned those schools and teachers who did not fully see and appreciate the educational value of practical subjects, for example, Manual work for boys, which embraced woodwork, metalwork in iron and tin, and modelling, and for girls, Needlework, Cookery and Laundrywork. Manipulative skills were equally important for future surgeons, mechanics and skilled artisans. Other subjects, such as Drawing, Music, and Physical Training should, with advantage, be included in every school programme for the full development of every pupil.[2] He did not reserve these comments for his official reports only, but prosecuted the same theme whenever he had the opportunity, especially at the meetings of the Central Welsh Board.[3] It was his desire to make practical subjects an integral part of each schools' curriculum, and to offer every pupil a variety of concrete interests as opposed to pure examinations and bookwork, which, in most cases merely produced half-educated mushroom mediocrities and not educated individuals. But again, it was the examination system which interfered with such salutary and practical pursuits—it was difficult to give Manual Work, whether for boys or girls, its proper place in the curriculum. As soon as pupils got near the examination stage, such activities were neglected. It was suggested that Manual Work and Drawing might be examinable subjects, but 'there was little hope of any of the subjects involving hand and eye training, attaining to their proper place until each school was examined, as it was inspected, on its own curriculum, and that curriculum was framed to meet the needs of the pupils and not those of any external bodies'.[4]

(d) The last part of the *Report* caused the greatest outcry of all, when reference was made to the over-all impact of the Central Welsh Board system of education on school pupils. Nearly all the examiners, 'with painful monotony, complained of a general lack of intelligence in the examination papers'. It was stated that the minds of the pupils were very mechanical, their memory overburdened where reasoning power should have been developed, and there was a depressing want of originality and a general inability to apply their knowledge to anything that was new to them. Examiners in English and Welsh complained of 'mechanical answers', and the examiner in History called attention to the 'repeated attempts to reproduce dictated notes'. In Science, pupils showed a lack of

[1] Board of Education Report (*Welsh Department*), op. cit., p. 16 ff.
[2] Ibid., p. 17.
[3] Minutes of the Central Welsh Board, 1908–1915, op. cit.
[4] Board of Education Report, supra ibid.

The Explosive Report

clear thinking at the expense of masses of factual material, for example, in Botany, 'the pupils seemed to have a knowledge of numerous facts, but had not been able to pin them together to form a concrete whole'.[1]

Edwards concluded, from all the evidence in the examiners' reports, that 'efforts to apply ordinary common sense were seldom made by pupils'. This 'was tantamount to saying that the highest aim of education had been missed. The criticism was very disquieting, in fact, it was the most serious criticism that could be made'.[2] Lack of intellectual curiosity, originality, and readiness of resource on the part of pupils was a real danger to Welsh education, and he suggested, for 'early and earnest consideration' important remedial measures. Teachers should be encouraged to attend Summer Courses to undergo training to teach their subjects more effectively; for example, History teachers who dictated notes did not make a study of their pupils and teach them. In the elementary schools, pupils received good teaching, and passed on to the intermediate schools 'with alert minds and deft hands'. Therefore the best teaching available should be given to the lower Forms, for 'unskilful and unsympathetic teaching during the first year of a secondary school effectually stopped the development of interest and reasoning power, and substituted the mechanical memorizing of facts. The belief was far too prevalent in Wales that the duty of a teacher was to see that the pupil learned, with a near or distant examination in view, all the facts in a crammed text-book'.[3] Pupils in the higher Forms should be given opportunities for independent work, carefully supervised, instead of being overloaded with formal teaching, which could be better used in the lower Forms. County Exhibitions should not be awarded on marks obtained in examinations which tested work done over a period of five or six years. The University should award such prizes 'in such a way that promise for

---

[1] *Board of Education Report (Welsh Department)*, op. cit., p. 17 ff. Also, R. Brinley Jones, (ed.), *Anatomy of Wales*, Gwerin Publications, Peterston-super-Ely, Glam., 1972, pp. 196, ff: Mr. Roland Mathias in his Study X comments on the lack of creativity and independence of mind in Welsh intermediate schools: 'It lay in the nature of the education offered by the new secondary schools. In English as it was, it nevertheless partook very fully (because of the teachers who transmitted it) of the virtues and vices of that Education in Welsh which had evolved from the Circulating Schools to the all-age Sunday Schools, and from these into the British and National Schools of the late nineteenth century. All the Education of the first two had been in the Bible, and excellence in that education had been measured, particularly from the days of Thomas Charles, by examination—sometimes written but more often oral. This system put a heavy premium on *memorisation and accuracy rather than analysis and interpretation*, and through all the changes of syllabus and emphasis that followed, teachers continued to stress these elements *because it had been by these means that they themselves had been taught.*'

Owen Edwards with his Oxford training was now criticizing the rigid examination system of the Central Welsh Board—where creativity and independence of mind were undervalued in such an educational structure. To be successful academically it was necessary to remain in a stage of arrested development. 'This was a chicken and egg situation—a cycle remarkably difficult to break. This predilection for caution and accuracy, for memorisation as the key to success in Examinations brought back into the system teachers—they had to be teachers for lack, economically, of other opportunity—*who had themselves succeeded by means of it, and wished for nothing more than the similar success of those whom they taught.*'

[2] Ibid.

[3] Ibid.

the future rather than performance in the past' should be the criterion of selection.[1]

Edwards reserved for the last, his most damning phrase of all, which incensed his enemies more than anything else. He enjoined the Central Welsh Board 'to consider to what extent their rigid examination system might be the cause of the wooden and unintelligent type of mind of which their examiners complained ... and they would be well advised to rely less upon examination and more upon inspection in carrying out the functions entrusted to them'. The system of Welsh intermediate schools, which had been operating since 1897 was in danger of becoming stereotyped and ineffective unless constant vigilance was excercised. The Welsh system 'with its virgin soil and freedom from any traditional fetters was more simple, more elastic, and more progressive than any system could be in England, but ... with the greater freedom for development obtainable in England, Wales may be in danger of falling behind'.[2]

Such was the document which caused the explosion and earned for itself—from its enemies—the inglorious title of the 'Wooden Report'. It condemned:

i. a system of secondary education which was a prototype of the traditional English Grammar School.

ii. a system which catered for 'a fraction of the children of Wales who required or could afford secondary education'.

iii. a system which was examination-centred, prevented differentiation, and induced fierce competition for certificates, upon which the success or otherwise of a school and its head depended.

iv. a system where most roads led to university and ignored the majority of Welsh children.

v. a system wherein the language and literature of Wales was relegated to less than second place.

Edwards was no visionary idealist harbouring illusions of a perfect system of secondary education. Rather, he was intensely pre-occupied with the stark realities of the defects of a system, which if properly orientated to the needs of Wales and the Welsh child, could be as near perfection as possible. As a chief official of the Welsh Department, he was, for the first time, able to disclose his educational views in an official report, since, as a civil servant, he was precluded from giving public utterance to his opinions. He was merely unloading his mind of matters—

[1] Ibid., p. 19.
[2] Ibid.

The Explosive Report

accumulated through many years of observation and experience before coming to Whitehall—which bothered him and had to be said. But far more fundamental was the delicate situation of relationships between the two Boards. McKenna had made it quite clear to Edwards, when he came to the Welsh Department in 1907, that the Department should make full use of the Central Welsh Board, build up, and maintain harmonious partnership. In such circumstances it could be argued that Edwards perhaps acted unwisely and somewhat precipitately with regard to the timing and content of the *Report*, and that it might have been more diplomatic had he waited a little longer and revealed the defects in smaller doses, and in a less spectacular manner. In the event, Edwards preferred immediate action to indefinite postponement, and total disclosure to moderate censure.

III REACTIONS TO THE REPORT

The *Report* was attacked from three directions and by the same persons: i. The President of the Welsh County Schools Association, Mr. Edgar Jones, MA, headmaster of Barry County School, who was also a member of the executive committee of the Central Welsh Board; ii. By the Denbighshire Local Education Authority, led by J. E. Powell, also a member of the Central Welsh Board, and 'its eloquent champion at all times and on all matters'; iii. By the Central Welsh Board, whose manifesto or Statement was ascribed to Lord Sheffield, its vice chairman. In addition, there were other vigorous and vilifying protestations from the provinces in the form of letters, leaflets and Press cuttings which were sent to Runciman, President of the Board of Education. November 1910 was a stirring and exciting month for Welsh education which revealed the conflict that was emerging between the Central Welsh Board and Whitehall.

The first attack was launched in Shrewsbury on 28 October 1910 at the annual meeting of the Welsh County Schools Association. The President, chose as the subject of his address, a *Reply to the Report on Intermediate Education, issued by the Welsh Department of the Board of Education, for the year* 1909. The address was printed and circulated to all headmasters and the Welsh Press. At the outset, Jones said that since the Report had appeared during the summer vacation, no one had had a chance of replying to the 'amazing document, professing to be a report by the Welsh Department on the intermediate schools of Wales'.[1] In addition, the *Report* had appeared very late, the Association had been deprived of

---

[1] *Reply to the Report, by Edgar Jones,* op. cit., p. 1.

any opportunity to issue an official reply, and he had the chance, as President, to devote his address to a full inquiry 'into this calumny on our schools'. The Welsh Department 'with its few years' experience had brought charges against the Welsh education system in its entirety— against the Central Welsh Board, the schools (including Heads and Assistant Staff), and even against the intelligence of the Welsh pupils'. This had not happened before the Welsh Department came into existence, for previous reports were based on careful inquiry and accurate investigation of fact. Moreover, the *Report* had been circulated in the English and Welsh Press, the prestige of the Welsh schools had been damaged, and it was little wonder that a spirit of indignation had arisen in the minds of all Welsh secondary schoolteachers. He maintained that many believed the *Report* 'to be part of a fixed and settled policy of the Welsh Department to destroy confidence in the Central Welsh Board, and instead of a democratic body representative of all phases of educational thought in Wales, to establish a bureaucracy at Whitehall'.[1]

His main criticisms included the following: that the *Report* was based on the Central Welsh Board's examiners' reports, and not as a result of detailed inspection by the Welsh Department; that it ignored the well-organized scheme of inspection of the Central Welsh Board, and deliberately selected all the unfavourable criticisms made by examiners most of them completely out of context, in order 'to saddle on the Central Welsh Board the responsibility of retarding differentiation in the schools —whereas the Board of Education themselves had been mainly responsible for the curricula of the schools through the Regulations of that Board'.[2] But the cardinal aberration in the *Report*, that the schools produced 'wooden and unintelligent pupils' was not only untrue, but *was nowhere to be found in the reports of the examiners*. The Welsh Department were obviously ignorant of the aim and intention of examiners in writing reports, wherein, usually, more criticism than praise was the normal feature, for example, the reports on the Oxford Local Examinations bristled with criticisms far more severe than those which appeared in the report of the Central Welsh Board.[3]

Jones protested that the *Report* was unjust, especially with reference to the teaching of English and History, when adverse comments by examiners had been lifted out of their context, for example, English in the schools was 'bald and poor', whereas, in reality, at the Senior Stage,

---

[1] Ibid. p. 2.
[2] Ibid. p. 3.
[3] *Reply to the Report*, by Edgar Jones, op. cit., p. 4.

The Explosive Report

'serious attempts were being made to study literature as literature, and the old confusion of the literature with the grammar lesson is now a thing of the past'. This did not tally with the assertion of the Welsh Department that 'the duty of the teacher is to see that the pupil gets up, with a near or distant examination in view, all the facts in a crammed text-book'.[1] Equally distorted and unjust was the reference to the teaching of History at the Junior Stage, where 'repeated attempts were made to reproduce dictated notes in class, especially in answer to questions on Welsh history'. No reference was made to the laudatory summaries of the History examiner on work done at the Higher Stages'.[2] The imputation of a general lack of intelligence deserved the severest censure, particularly the phrase 'wooden and unintelligent type of mind'. This accusation was refuted by none other than Principal E. H. Griffiths, University College, Cardiff, who, from experience of dealing with pupils after they left the Welsh intermediate schools, stated that 'they were not wooden . . . if anything they were too alert. To say that they are wooden is about the most incorrect criticism one could make. I say this, after an exceptional experience as a coach in Cambridge, and as Principal of Cardiff College, so that I have had an opportunity of comparing the products of English Public Schools and our Welsh schools'.[3]

The remainder of the address was devoted to alleged inaccurate statements regarding the achievements of the Welsh schools, their teachers and methods, differentiation of curricula, school activities and general influence. The references to the exceedingly low standard of the examinations in French, the lack of school libraries, that English was sacrificed to formal grammar, phonetics, and Anglo-Saxon—were all vigorously denied by Jones. He mounted an impressive account of the record of ex-pupils' careers, which compared favourably with those from English schools, and wondered how 'they would all welcome the term "wooden" '. To suggest that teachers should attend Summer Courses was, to Jones's mind, 'a work of supererogation', since most of the teachers had already availed themselves of such courses. He especially resented the suggestion that heads of schools competed with one another for the highest number of school-leaving certificates and also directed their pupils to take the easiest mark-getting subjects. Regarding differentiation, Jones was emphatic 'that the present character of the schools has not been determined by the Central Welsh Board—it only examines and

[1] Ibid. p. 6.
[2] Ibid.
[3] Ibid. p. 7 ff.

inspects, but does not control the curriculum. That was the concern of the Board of Education which had fixed, by Regulations, the exact subjects each school should teach, and the University of Wales, which demanded certain requirements for its matriculation examination. Apart from this, a considerable variety of subjects were taught, including Agriculture and Metalwork, and in the matter of training intending teachers for elementary schools, the widest differences existed.[1]

The address concluded with a lengthy eulogy on the wide influence of the Welsh intermediate schools in the field of Welsh general culture and intellectual interests—they fostered the 'gifts of art' as well as the 'gains of science'. Before the assembly dispersed, the following resolution was passed (in the heat of the moment) unanimously:

> 'That the Welsh County Schools Association protests strongly against the *Report of the Board of Education on the Intermediate Schools of Wales for the year* 1909 as unjust, and directly contrary to the tenour of the reports of the examiners of the Central Welsh Board, on which it claims to be based; and that, as the *Report* gives a distorted and misleading view of the state of intermediate education in Wales, the Association calls upon the Board of Education *to withdraw the Report*'.[2]

While the guns were flashing in Shrewsbury, Edwards was in south Wales conducting a full inspection of Mountain Ash secondary school. He told Maurice to warn Runciman that the Central Welsh Board 'were on the war-path again ... they are at their old trick ... combining to write to the Welsh MPs to make a difficulty in Parliament (I sincerely hope the Welsh Members will not be caught this time). Last time they objected to our inspecting Welsh schools ... this time they resent our *Report* on the working of the Welsh Act. Please assure the President that, in case of a Question, there is a complete and crushing answer'.[3] But Maurice was already in touch, for the Press kept the Board of Education fully informed of the activities of the Central Welsh Board. He told Edwards 'I think that Runciman ... though he may not know that they are stirring up the Welsh Members, expects to hear something about our *Report* when the House meets again ... you might as well prepare a reply, point by point against the attack when it comes'.[4]

On 4 November, Edwards received a copy of the Shrewsbury Address together with a request from Runciman for 'ammunition in a compact,

---

[1] *Reply to the Report*, by Edgar Jones, op. cit., p. 16. The subject of the training of elementary schoolteachers has been discussed in Study No. 2.
[2] Ibid. p. 19.
[3] PRO Ed 24/589, Edwards to Maurice 31 October 1910.
[4] Ibid. Maurice to Edwards 1 November.

form' in case a Question should be asked in Parliament. Maurice had been considerably 'impressed by Jones's allegations', which he described as (on the face of it) 'rather overwhelming ... and looked forward to what Edwards had to say'.[1] In the meantime, Edwards had begun to 'pulverise the outrageous and mischievous Address', and on 8 November had completed a 'hasty outline of an ammunition reply'—with a covering Minute to Maurice: 'I am rather glad you find it "rather overwhelming"; this will help you realize how easy it has been for it to mislead the newspapers and the country ... could you let A. T. Davies see this refutation some time? Of course, he is not concerned—his contributions were cut out ... but I know that Davies is anxious'.[2]

The second attack came from Denbighshire LEA on 2 November. Acknowledging the *Report*, the authority wrote to the Board of Education stating that a resolution had been passed at a meeting of the education committee on 9 September in the following terms: 'That in view of what appears to be an unfair and unwarranted attack upon the system of intermediate education in Wales by the Board of Education, a copy of the last General Report of the Central Welsh Board upon the work of the schools in the whole of Wales be procured for the use of each member, in order that they may have an opportunity of judging for themselves as to the partiality or otherwise of the Board of Education's *Report*, and that both *Reports* be referred to the chairman, vice chairman and Mr. James Darlington for consideration and report'.[3] A report of censure duly appeared, was approved by the education committee on 28 October, and a copy was sent to the Board of Education.[4] The other two members responsible for the report of censure were Messrs. J. E. Powell and W. G. Dodd, well-known to Edwards from experience. He described Powell as 'a man of strong convictions and very stormy eloquence ... and was above all others, the champion of the Central Welsh Board—which he considered to be perfect ... and any criticism of Welsh intermediate education was treason ... it was quite impossible to convince him that it was not the chief aim of the Welsh Department to destroy the Central Welsh Board; Dodd was not so impetuous, but was labouring under the same impressions ... Mr. Darlington, I regret, is unknown to me'.[5]

---

[1] PRO Ed 24/588 Maurice to Edwards 4 November.

[2] PRO Ed 24/589 Minutes from Edwards to Maurice, 6 November; Maurice to Edwards, 7 November (A. T. Davies had suggested that Edwards should draft a detailed reply); Edwards to Maurice, 8 November.

[3] Ibid. Denbighshire LEA to Runciman, 2 November.

[4] Ibid.

[5] Ibid. Edwards to Maurice, 14 November.

The Explosive Report

Edwards, naturally, had to deal with this document. He said that Denbighshire was always strongly represented on the Central Welsh Board executive, but their report of censure, which had been widely circulated, obtained unanimous approval under two misapprehensions, (a) that the Board of Education's *Report* was an aimless attack on the whole Welsh secondary system, its governing bodies, heads and teachers, and not a *Report* to parliament made necessary by Statute; (b) that it was based entirely on the reports of the examiners of the Central Welsh Board. His answer was brief—that the conclusions arrived at in the 1909 *Report* were based on the Welsh Department's independent knowledge.[1] In basic essentials, the Denbighshire criticisms contained nothing not referred to by Jones, and were made 'mainly to raise a popular cry in favour of the Central Welsh Board by grossly misrepresenting the Board of Education *Report*'. Messrs. Powell and Dodd were angry because the Welsh Department had not consulted the Central Welsh Board before publishing the *Report*, and maintained that many of the difficulties might have been solved by discussion. Edwards again had his answer, that all points raised by the Welsh Department had already been discussed on innumerable occasions by Casson and himself at the meetings of the Central Welsh Board. If the important points, now criticized by Denbighshire, had not been thrashed out by the body against which the indictment was brought, then it was entirely the fault of that body.[2]

The third attack came from the Central Welsh Board at their meeting on 18 November which Edwards and Casson attended. Agendum 5 was the consideration of a long draft Statement of twenty-nine pages on the subject of the 1909 *Report*[3]. Edwards had only a 'vague idea' of the line the meeting would take, but promised Maurice his answer after the meeting.[4] Having previously conferred with Edwards, Maurice had carefully instructed Casson (who had received the Agenda and papers for the meeting, but not a copy of the Statement) how to conduct himself. If the omission to send the draft Statement was not accidental, and if it was not supplied at the meeting, Casson was to request that this fact be entered in the Minutes. Another situation might also arise—Edwards and Casson might be requested to retire, together with the Press and general public, during the discussion of the Statement. Should Edwards and Casson not be requested to leave, then Edwards, as the person

---

[1] Ibid. Edwards to the President, 16 November. Reply by Edwards to the Denbighshire criticism of the Board of Education *Report* under the Welsh Act.
[2] PRO Ed 24/588 Reply by Edwards to the Denbighshire criticism, op. cit.
[3] Ibid. *Draft Statement of the Central Welsh Board on the Report of the Board of Education for 1909 under the Welsh Intermediate Education Act, 1889. Private and Confidential.*
[4] Ibid. Minute from Edwards to Maurice, 16 November.

The Explosive Report

mainly responsible for the *Report*, should intervene and say that the two representatives of the Board of Education were desirous not to hamper in any way the proceedings of the meeting, and since statements might be made with which the representatives could not find themselves in agreement, it would be undesirable that the Board of Education's officers should allow them to pass *sub silentio* or should intervene in a debate *coram publico*, and that therefore they should propose to retire voluntarily.[1] Whether or not the document concerned was made available to Edwards and Casson is not known, but both retired voluntarily from the meeting.[2]

The draft Statement of the Central Welsh Board repeated the worst of the misrepresentations of the headmaster's address in an aggravating form, but contained nothing new. The introductory passage of the Statement said:

'The Central Welsh Board are anxious that the work done in the schools placed under their supervision should be as good as possible, and would welcome all helpful criticisms from the Board of Education, but they regret to have to say that this *Report* contains what appear to them to be grave mis-statements and serious insinuations. They must therefore examine it in some detail in order to vindicate the work done for secondary education in the Welsh County Schools; to re-assure the people of Wales, whose money is being spent on these schools and whose children are being educated in them; and to prevent friends of education in the United Kingdom generally from supposing that serious allegations made by a responsible Department of State are presumably true and are justified by the evidence alleged. The charges contained in the Board of Education's *Report* are so serious and sweeping, that, in the eyes of the general public and of all who do not know the true state of affairs, the Welsh County Schools must needs appear condemned as utter failures, unworthy of the confidence of the nation'.[3]

Denuded of verbal fantasy, the Statement in reality was a critical comment on the five suggestions proposed by Edwards. His reference to Summer Courses was referred to as being superfluous since a large number of teachers had already availed themselves of such facilities by attending courses at Oxford, the Welsh Summer Schools, and on the continent. The second suggestion, that the best teaching was not available in the lower Forms, was quite untrue, for the specialist system, under which each subject was taught in every Form by specialist teachers, gave all Forms the best teaching possible. The Central Welsh Board held the view that the smaller Forms in the Upper School received too little teaching.

---

[1] PRO Ed 24/589 Maurice to Casson, 16 November.
[2] Minutes of the Central Welsh Board, op. cit., 21 October, 5 and 18 November 1910. *Manchester Guardian*, 19 November, 1910.
[3] PRO Ed 24/588 *Draft Statement of the Central Welsh Board*, op. cit., p. 1, ff.

The Explosive Report

County exhibitions were awarded as a result of work tested over a period of five or six years, and the Board desired no better testimonial for its examinations. As to the fact that their examination system was too rigid, the Board were of the opinion that their examinations were 'the last system in the world to deserve that description. In every subject at every stage, a school was examined either on a syllabus provided by the Central Welsh Board, or, on a syllabus provided by the school and accepted by the Board'.[1] As to the phrase "wooden and unintelligent type of mind" nowhere found in the examiners' reports, 'the Central Welsh Board, the teachers and pupils in the Welsh schools, and the Welsh people might reasonably complain that unsupported charges should be made by a Government Department, which had undertaken the task, that Burke pronounced impossible, of framing an indictment against a nation'.[2] The Central Welsh Board called upon the Board of Education to cancel those statements in their *Report* 'which this reply, now submitted to them, shows to be without justification or foundation'.

Repercussions from other directions, mainly correspondents and the Welsh Press, joined forces in support of Jones's address. A Mr. Arthur D. Sanderson had sent Runciman excerpts from numerous letters, which had been passed on to Maurice, purporting to be 'a reflection in some way of part of public Welsh opinion'.[3] One stated that 'the Welsh Department are determined to damage the Central Welsh Board ... we are glad that Mr. Runciman cannot be charged with having any part in it'. Another said 'A. T. Davies has made allegations which do not exist in the examiners' reports ... public opinion protests against the grossly unfair and dishonest use of such reports, and against the juggling and hocussing by a Government Department'. Other choice examples included such phrases: 'the Welsh Department had acted in a vicious spirit ... Principal Griffiths of Cardiff University College, a man of world wide reputation ... the whole of the secondary schoolmasters, *The Manchester Guardian*, and the Denbighshire education committee had all united in denouncing the *Report*. Lord Sheffield ventured to say that the *Report* was twenty pages of falsehood; never in the history of the Board of Education had such a dishonest report been issued, which would be very injurious to the Central Welsh Board; the best people in Wales are angry ... and Mr. Jones's address ... will astonish people that a Government Department can stoop to such mean tactics'.[4] *The Schoolmaster* and *The Times Educational*

[1] Ibid. p. 21 ff.
[2] Ibid.
[3] PRO Ed 24/589 Sanderson, of Doxford, Chathill, Northumberland, to Maurice, 10 November 1910.
[4] PRO Ed 24/589 Sanderson to Maurice, ibid.

The Explosive Report

Supplement demanded an answer to the charges against the Welsh Department and expressed a hope that the President and the Chief Inspector for Wales would do so without delay.[1]

But the level headed Maurice, cool, and unruffled by the spate of malicious correspondence, and equally loyal to both Runciman and Edwards, was able to re-assure Sanderson 'that Runciman was absolutely responsible for the *Report* and has no reason whatever . . . to shirk the responsibility . . . and after reading Edwards's reply to Mr. Edgar Jones, I see that he pulverises Jones very successfully. The thing to remember is that Owen Edwards, edited by me, is the author of every line of that part of the *Report* which is complained of, and no one alive, in all probability, can speak with such authority on the subject of Welsh education, and that Welsh education never had, and probably never will have again, a friend so entirely and enthusiastically devoted to its services'.[2]

The Welsh Press reacted quickly to the address. The *Western Mail* considered that, although some further action seemed imperative, to call for a withdrawal of the *Report* would—if acted upon by the Board of Education—'declare that the author or authors were unqualified or disqualified for their offices . . . When so good a nationalist and educationist as Mr. Jenkyn Thomas declares the *Report* to be "infamous", one may be pretty sure that the grievance is a real and serious one . . . Mr. Thomas recalls the case of the notorious *Brâd y Llyfrau Gleision* . . . it is due to Wales to know who is responsible for this sweeping condemnation, which so many capable judges in Wales resent as unjustifiable in fact, and peevish in spirit'.[3]

Edwards knew that the Welsh headmasters were by no means unanimous at the Shrewsbury meeting, and this caused him a great deal of disappointment. He complained that 'not one of the really strong headmasters spoke', and regretted the lead they had chosen to follow.[4] Several wrote to him, defending the *Report*, and more than one said 'you make a mistake in referring to the Central Welsh Board examiners' reports—we never pay any attention to them'.[5] Edwards referred to a spirited letter, praising his *Report*, in the *South Wales Daily News*, 'by an assistant master in one of the most important intermediate schools . . . they will realize, gradually, that we are fighting for liberty for them, to adapt their curriculum, etc. . . . *Brâd y Llyfrau Gleision* (The Treachery of the Blue

---

[1] *The Times Educational Supplement*, 25 November.
[2] PRO Ed supra, Maurice to Sanderson, 12 November.
[3] *Western Mail*, 30 October.
[4] PRO Ed 24/588 Minute from Edwards to Maurice 14 November.
[5] Ibid.

The Explosive Report

Books) refers to Lord Lingen's *Report on the State of Elementary Education in Wales* in 1847. It aroused a storm of indignation, but it produced much good, and is now generally felt to have been a national boon. Mr. W. Jenkyn Thomas was at one time headmaster of an intermediate school in Wales—Aberdare, I believe. I know him well. He has no tact nor judgement—every headmaster in Wales knows that'.[1]

In the midst of all the gloom produced by relentless criticism from almost every quarter, at least one MP emerged to defend the *Report*. H. Haydn Jones, MP for Merioneth, and a member of the Central Welsh Board, assured the President that 'as a person who had taken an active part in Welsh intermediate education since 1889 (he had been Secretary to the Merioneth Education Committee) I am qualified to express an unbiased opinion on the Board of Education *Report*, and can without reserve, support the *Report* in its entirety . . . and unpleasant though it may be to the official and interested persons of Wales, I am thankful the Board of Education had the courage to publish it'.[2] He further begged the President not to modify nor withdraw anything, because the Board of Education had rendered a valuable service to Wales, and he was sure that all the Welsh Members would support it without reserve, and also in the House of Commons. Acknowledging the letter, Runciman expressed his appreciation of such support should a Question arise, but until he had received the rejoinder of the Central Welsh Board, he did not propose to offer any reply.[3] From now onwards, the stage was to be occupied by Owen Edwards.

IV REPLY BY OWEN EDWARDS

Edwards prefaced his Reply with a brief personal memorandum to the President of the Board of Education, setting out the main issues of the controversy.[4] He said that the Central Welsh Board were 'moving again', and, as usual 'were trying to create difficulties in Parliament'. They appealed to the country and to MPs on two grounds. First, that the

---

[1] PRO Ed 24/588 Minute from Edwards to Maurice, 14 November.
Ibid. 'Edgar Jones's criticism will be, or is rather, widely distributed. It will give the following their *only* impressions of our *Report*—the newspapers, the LEAs, many MPs. The *Report* itself will not be seen. The parents will not see it. I doubt whether many headmasters have read it. On Thursday night, the headmaster of Ruabon school—probably one of the class of the ablest headmasters in Wales, and a thoroughly honest man, travelled with me from Newport to Shrewsbury. He had been *denouncing* the *Report*, he explained, in addressing the boys at the Newport Intermediate school. I found that he had entirely ignored the bulk and the tone of our *Report*, and had drawn all his conclusions from two half pages. I simply pointed my finger to the passages, and, after reading them, he confessed he ought to have seen them. If a headmaster of independent mind is so misled by Mr. Edgar Jones, though he has the *Report* in his possession, what of the County Councillor who has never seen it, or the MP who has no time to read it? It is on this account, and on this account alone, that we have to pay serious attention to the document i.e. the Address'.
[2] PRO Ed 24/589 Jones to Runciman, 23 November.
[3] Runciman to Jones, 24 November.
[4] PRO Ed 24/588 Edwards to the President, 16 November.

Board of Education had taken the condemnatory portions of the Central Welsh Board examiners' reports, shut their eyes to the laudatory parts and condemned the whole system of Welsh secondary education. The *Report* was said to be 'admittedly based' on the reports of the examiners of the Central Welsh Board, and was drawn up by 'selecting every bit of condemnation and rejecting every bit of praise'. Edwards vigorously repudiated this assertion, on the grounds that although the Welsh Board's examiners' reports fully bore out his conclusions, he had independent information about each intermediate school in Wales because he had, himself, inspected the teaching which he criticized, and had, moreover, discussed with all the headmasters and headmistresses—'except one or two of the 96'—the main points of his criticism.[1] Second, that the Board of Education had libelled the Welsh child by calling him wooden and unintelligent.

In his 'suggested outline of an answer' to such allegations, Edwards proposed to include certain aspects which he deemed essential to emphasize (a) from his own experience of the Central Welsh Board system, and (b) that which might be important to include in any parliamentary reply to a Question, should it arise. In the first place, the *Report* was an appeal to all concerned with the working of the Welsh Act: to give the headmaster all possible freedom to adapt the curriculum of the school to the needs of the neighbourhood; to give every teacher the right to teach his subject in the way he could teach it best, and to give each child the education that would best develop his mind, and serve him best in after-school life. Secondly, the *Report* criticized the Welsh system with regard to two points only, the disappointing results of the teaching of the English subjects, and the tendency of a system that was too examination-ridden to burden the memory rather than develop the reasoning power of the child. Regarding all other points, the *Report* mingled praise with blame, or praised unreservedly. The criticisms had not been made without a strong sense of responsibility, or before making the most exhaustive inquiries. The most regrettable feature was, that the Central Welsh Board's criticism of the *Report* was based merely on two sections of it, to the exclusion of the rest.[2] Thirdly, with regard to the suggested remedies, Edwards was convinced that if they were expedited, would lead to a 'strengthening of the intermediate schools where we consider them weak, and place them in a better relation to the elementary schools below them, and to the University above them'—but these suggestions had not even been considered by the Central Welsh Board. In spite of this, the *Report*

[1] PRO Ed 24/588 Edwards to the President, 16 November.
[2] Ibid.

The Explosive Report

had recommended the Treasury to pay the grants in full, with one insignificant exception. Furthermore, it should be made clear in any public debate on this matter, that the *Report* made the fullest acknowledgement of all good work done—'it begins with a generous tribute to the creators of the Welsh system; it criticizes the work of the schools favourably except in two important points; it ends with the highest compliment, though delicately put, that the Board of Education have ever paid to Welsh education'.[1]

Edwards placed before the President his personal reflections on the situation. He felt disappointed and hurt, because the *Report* ought to have been received gratefully by all, as in the case of Merioneth and Caernarvonshire, and its suggestions should have been carefully considered. But the President of the Headmasters' Association had delivered a speech which ignored 19/20th's of the *Report*; the Denbighshire LEA had sent a most misleading circular, and a most unjust form of resolution to the other Welsh Authorities, and the Central Welsh Board would pose again as the national champion of Wales against their calumniators. The latter body should have been the first to improve the efficiency of the schools, but their sole thought was given to their own prestige.[2] Edwards now regretted that his *Report* was not fuller, but promised that in future they would be so—with proofs and answers if necessary. This would please the Welsh Members and afford little consolation to the Central Welsh Board. At the end of this personal note to Runciman, Edwards said 'I am sorry for the trouble. But, if the matter comes before Parliament, and if the Central Welsh Board is beaten again (as it inevitably will), we shall have taught Wales to look forward to an annual report from the Board of Education, and this will be a long step towards increasing the efficiency of the Welsh intermediate system of education'.[3]

The Reply which Edwards submitted to the President consisted of two lengthy documents. One was in manuscript, and dealt, seriatim, with the allegations in Jones's address. This was provided for the information of the President, in case the matter should be raised in the House of Commons.[4] The other was issued on the instructions of the President, in

---

[1] PRO Ed 24/588 Edwards to the President, ibid.
[2] Ibid.
[3] Ibid. *Report* by Owen Edwards to the President, op. cit., p. 3.
[4] Ibid. This Report consists of approximately 10,000 words in MS. In his introduction, Edwards commented on the Address and its author: 'Mr. Jones . . . delivered an Address which, for reckless disregard to sober and dispassionate consideration, I have never seen equalled. Mr. Jones himself is a thoroughly honest and a most amiable man; I bear no resentment towards him, even after this most unfair attack upon us. But he is the last to whom 'sober' and 'dispassionate' can be applied. His convictions are strong, his speech intemperate, and his statements exaggerated. Yesterday, at the executive meeting of the Central Welsh Board, he referred contemptuously to the most conscientious headmaster in Wales as a humbug. I know he would repent within a short time. He will, I am certain, feel ashamed of this most unjust and most mischievous Address'. (It should be noted that Jones had referred to his predecessors in the Presidential office as having been 'sober and dispassionate in speech' when discussing matters).

The Explosive Report

printed form, as the official reply of the Board of Education 'upon the Statement in which the Central Welsh Board commented upon the *Report of the Board of Education* for the year 1909'.[1] This comprised 7 sections: Preliminary observations; salient characteristics of the *Report of the Board of Education*, 1909; domination of examinations over the curriculum and teaching in the schools; differentiation of curricula; teaching of the English subjects; remedial measures proposed; conclusion.

In his preliminary remarks, Edwards showed clearly the fundamental errors upon which the Central Welsh Board had issued their Statement. In the first place, they had read the *Report* under a misapprehension, both as to the data on which it was founded, and the purpose with which it was written—saying that it was a *Report* 'on their work', but in fact it was a *Report* of the proceedings under the Welsh Intermediate Act, 1889 made to Parliament under Section 15 of that Act. There were certain matters, such as the appointment of teachers, and the provision of supplementary education and training for them, for which the Central Welsh Board were only indirectly, or, if at all, responsible, and it could not be said that 'the *Report* attempted to hold the Central Welsh Board responsible for any defects which were not attributable to them, or which they had no direct means of remedying'.[2] Secondly, the Central Welsh Board had incorrectly maintained that the criticism contained in the *Report* rested 'almost exclusively' on the evidence furnished by the reports of their examiners—but such reports were quoted by the Board of Education because they clinched the independent conclusions reached by the inspectors of that Board and by Edwards. Thirdly, it was not the intention of the *Report* to make a 'sweeping accusation against the Welsh intermediate schools as a whole'. It merely contained certain criticisms intended to lead up to a series of suggestions which the Board of Education hoped would prove useful and salutary, but unfortunately the Central Welsh Board had construed the *Report* as an attack upon some persons or bodies. But the Board of Education did attack certain conditions and methods of instruction which they believed were having, and would continue to have a serious effect upon the intelligence of the pupils who passed through the schools, and ultimately on the Welsh nation. These defects had been brought to the notice of the Central Welsh Board at all their meetings by the representatives of the Board of Education, without avail, and the only new feature in the *Report* which was now maligned, was the series of suggestions drawn up after a careful study of the intermediate schools of

---

[1] Ibid. *A Report made by the Chief Inspector for Wales*, op. cit., p. 2.
[2] PRO Ed 24/588 *Central Welsh Board Draft Statement*, op. cit., p. 1.

Wales, and 'offered as a contribution to the remedying of defects which the Board of Education regarded as both apparent and serious'.[1]

Finally, Edwards regretted that the Central Welsh Board had, by concentrating their attention on only a part of the *Report*, created the impression in the minds of the Welsh people that it was 'defamatory and unsympathetic'. This was far from the truth, since due recognition had been given to the work done in the schools and by the LEAs, and severe criticism had been employed where necessary in order to draw attention to urgently needed reforms. In this respect, Wales was not different from England, and he confidently anticipated 'that all interested in the working of the Welsh Act would give the criticisms and suggestions their fullest consideration in spite of the passing feeling of irritation they had caused'.[2] All the misconceptions referred to had led the Central Welsh Board to put forward certain arguments which were completely irrelevant, especially those parts of their Statement where they replied 'to a supposed attack upon the intelligence of Welsh children, and those pages at the conclusion of the same document in which they adduced evidence of the enthusiasm of the Welsh nation for education—neither of which was called in question'.[3]

The salient characteristics of the *Report* set forth in the Statement of the Central Welsh Board included: unfavourable criticisms 'which appeared to rest exclusively on the evidence furnished by the reports of the examiners of the Central Welsh Board'; that the 'full and complete scheme of inspection organized by that Board ... was almost entirely ignored'; that 'unfavourable criticisms which were made by the Board's examiners on parts of the work were selected for the purpose of the *Report*, while those summaries of a favourable character were omitted', and that the Board of Education had not realized 'the usual aim and intention of examiners in writing a report'.[4] To each and all of these assertions, Edwards gave a full and detailed answer, based on his own experience of the Welsh schools. The unfavourable criticisms made by him were fully substantiated by the Central Welsh Board's examiners reports. He had been disappointed by the limited general reading of Training College students who had been in the intermediate schools, and as a result had made a study of the teaching of English in those schools by

---

[1] Ibid. *A Report made by the Chief Inspector for Wales*, op. cit., p. 2.
[2] PRO Ed 24/588 *A Report by the Chief Inspector for Wales*, op. cit., p. 3.
[3] Ibid.
[4] PRO Ed supra: *Central Welsh Board Draft Statement*, op. cit., p. 2 ff.

The Explosive Report

visiting every one of them.[1] He was worried about the influence of examinations on the teaching of the other English subjects, notably History and Geography. The methods of teaching these subjects were 'antiquated and barren', notes being dictated, and pupils made to learn them.[2] In other words, pupils were crammed with information in order to pass examinations, and teachers were unable to have the freedom to teach in the way they desired. He wanted the intermediate schools to make a determined effort to make the teaching of the English subjects—English literature, History and Geography—more modern in type and more efficient.[3]

The 'full and complete scheme of inspection organized by the Central Welsh Board' was not 'almost entirely ignored' but was criticized, and in some directions, praised.[4] Edwards had repeatedly tried to get them to extend it by having 12 specialists to inspect for one month instead of one temporary inspector throughout the year. This would have obviated the greatest defect of their inspection system, i.e. the schools had no specialist to visit them. The Board of Education had never suggested any criticism of the two Central Welsh Board inspectors—since they were overworked and extremely conscientious. But two men were not sufficient to advise on every subject taught in a secondary school.[5] The other matters, such as selecting unfavourable examiners' comments out of context and the 'intentions of examiners' in writing reports have already been discussed. The Central Welsh Board 'could not accuse the Board of Education as having stated that the Welsh schools "were utter failures" or inefficient. This was sheer nonsense, since the Board of Education had paid up all the grants for efficiency, with the exception of Whitland intermediate school'.[6]

---

[1] PRO Ed supra: *A Report*, etc. op. cit., : 'I must often compare notes with Principals of Training Colleges, Masters of Method, etc., about the students who come from the intermediate schools, e.g. a fortnight ago, I was at Bangor. Principal Harris, while warmly congratulating the Board of Education on having issued a helpful *Report*, said he had just come from a class of men who had passed the Central Welsh Board examinations, and who were absolutely ignorant of the great English books which boys generally know—they had done no general reading'. Again, Edwards referred to the schools: 'I discussed with almost every Head, problems of organization and the influence of examinations on teaching ... I listened to the teaching of some of the English subjects ... made careful inquiries about school libraries ... dictating of notes and home-lessons took the place of teaching, and the learning of notes took the children away from the real study of their books. These defects could not be blamed on the want of capacity in the school staffs. I was compelled to seek the cause elsewhere ... and found it in the examination system as applied to the schools'.

[2] Ibid.

[3] PRO Ed 24/588 *A Report by the Chief Inspector for Wales*, op. cit., 'This danger to education was laid by me before small conferences of experts at each of the University Colleges, and at a conference representative of, among others, the Central Welsh Board, and the headmasters and headmistresses of the intermediate schools of Wales. In the last Report of the Board of Education the pressure of examinations and the lack of modern methods of teaching were placed, not for the first time, before all the authorities concerned with the working of the Welsh Act. The action taken by the University Colleges and the University was prompt, and it has been attended already with excellent effects'.

[4] *Report of the Board of Education (Welsh Department)*, 1909, op. cit., p. 10.

[5] PRO Ed supra, Report by Owen Edwards to the President, op. cit., p. 7. ff.

[6] *Report of the Board of Education (Welsh Department)*, supra.

The Explosive Report

The third section of Edwards's Reply dealt with the assertion made by the Central Welsh Board 'that the Board of Education were in error with regard to the question of overpressure on pupils in the schools, and the domination of examinations over the curriculum and teaching'. He could not regard three years as the ordinary, or four years as the ideal course of preparation for the Senior Certificate, and tended to agree with the Chief Inspector of the Central Welsh Board 'that in three cases out of four, pupils ought to get at least three years' training before their entry for the Junior Certificate'. The governors of one school had asked the Central Welsh Board to insist upon the three years in every case. Two more years would be required by most pupils before they were fit to take the Senior Certificate. In stating these conclusions, Edwards was guided by long experience and by intimate acquaintance with Welsh schools and Welsh children, and instances of mental and physical suffering among pupils had come under his personal observation, for which he was convinced the overpressure of the examination system was directly responsible.[1]

At this point, Edwards made his attitude towards examinations quite clear. He was of the opinion that, apart from the question of adequate time for preparation for the examinations, the examination 'spirit' was too dominant in the schools. His experience, which was also the experience of many others, went to show that teachers handled their subjects with an eye on examination results. This was not a reflection on the teachers but on human nature. The teacher would not be human if, when called upon to prepare his pupils for an examination common to all schools of the same class in the country, he did not adapt his teaching, however reluctantly, to the purpose of securing the highest percentage of passes, and the best record of distinction. Few persons with experience of the subject would be found to deny that this purpose was best achieved by the method of 'cramming', the acquisition of material for replies to questions rather than developing the faculties of the pupils by what he termed 'more disinterested and more educational methods'. He did not wish to condemn school examinations as a whole, and he did not contend that examinations were, in their nature, vicious. But he was convinced that repeated examinations which gave the pupils no breathing space, and kept them always 'on the stretch', defeated their own ends and might work incalculable harm. In short, what the Board of Education complained of was a system of examinations which tended to become the *raison d'être* of school work and vitiated its results: 'It is no answer to this—to

[1] PRO Ed supra, *A Report by the Chief Inspector*, op. cit. p. 6.

The Explosive Report

point to a list of successes. The list quoted by the Central Welsh Board could be amplified. But we must look at the effect of the teaching on the average pupil, and through the average pupil, on the nation. The Board of Education have only repeated the warning which the Chief Inspector of the Central Welsh Board found it necessary to give as long ago as 1899—"there is grave danger that sound educational methods should be sacrificed to the pressure for immediate results" '.[1]

The craze for examination results and certificates was nation-wide and had its humorous side. Edwards had condemned the system in the interests of the headmasters and headmistresses, who had complained bitterly to him that they were expected to get 'as many certificates as the neighbouring schools', and parents had been taught to expect them. The vice-chairman of the executive committee of the Central Welsh Board had related that 'a farmer's daughter in Cardiganshire lost her certificate in the train, and her father said that she had thereby lost the result of two years' money spent upon her education! It is to free headmasters from this intolerable tyranny that we are trying'.[2]

Edwards then dealt with the subject of differentiation of curricula, regarding which, the Board of Education was also said to be 'in error'. He was sure that the Central Welsh Board had not really comprehended the meaning of his criticism. There had to be, of necessity, a large measure of uniformity in the general education of the junior classes, and pupils had to be prepared for examinations which opened doors to the earlier stages of professions. But the Board of Education were not satisfied that the differentiation necessary in Wales, and possible under their Regulations, had been attained. The rigid system of examination made it difficult for schools 'to take a classical or a mathematical or a science bent according to the genius and influence of the teachers, or a bias towards Agriculture or Geology or Navigation according to the needs of the neighbourhood. It also made it difficult to give children differing in ability, and with their faces set on different vocations, an examination suited to their needs'.[3] He argued that the schools should provide a suitable curriculum for the average pupil which gave him a broad general education, leading eventually to a kind of examination which would be accepted for entry to Training Colleges. But the Central Welsh Board compelled intending teachers to take the Senior Certificate which was too difficult.

---

[1] PRO Ed 24/588 *A Report by the Chief Inspector for Wales*, op. cit., p. 6 ff.
[2] Ibid. Report by Owen Edwards to the President, op. cit., p. 10. Edwards to Lewis, 18 December 1910, Penucha MSS.
[3] PRO Ed 24/588 *A Report by the Chief Inspector*, op. cit., p. 7.

As a result, many good potential teachers were refused admission to the Training Colleges.[1]

It was in the final section of his Reply that Edwards, in great detail, made his most penetrating criticism of the Central Welsh Board system—the methods employed in teaching the English subjects. This was a matter to which he had paid the closest attention. Referring in particular to the teaching of English, History and Geography, he called attention to the remarks of the Central Welsh Board examiners on the unintelligent character of some of the work presented by pupils in the examinations. In many schools, 'the teaching of English and English literature was conducted by methods which did not tend to awaken the mind or to develop an appreciation for literature; the teaching of History in the great majority of schools was neither skilful nor inspiring, being almost exclusively confined to narrative Political History; the teaching of Geography, though improving, was very rarely in the hands of teachers who had any special knowledge of the subject'.[2] The pressure of examinations, and the absence of, or poor provision of books in school libraries was reflected in the limited character of general reading by pupils. In 1908, although the Board of Education, in an attempt to remedy the lack of school libraries, had offered a special grant under their Regulations for Secondary Schools for that purpose, only 3 out of the 92 recognised intermediate schools even applied for the grant.[3] The library had not been given its due place in the life of the schools, and after discussing this matter with the heads of all the intermediate schools, Edwards had succeeded in getting the Central Welsh Board to appoint a committee to draw up a list of suitable books, but the committee had never met.[4]

The large number of untrained teachers employed, and unskilful teaching in the English subjects upon which the majority of the pupils depended for the awakening of their minds, and for incentive to future reading, naturally led to unintelligent study.[5] Edwards was struck by the fact that in several schools, the Senior pupils were less self-reliant than

[1] Edward to Lewis, 10 April 1909, Penucha MSS. Also see Study No. 2.

[2] PRO Ed supra, p. 8. Geography was not available as a degree subject in the University of Wales at that time.

[3] Ibid.

[4] Minutes of the Central Welsh Board, op. cit., 16 December 1910.

[5] PRO Ed 24/588: MS Draft of *A Report by the Chief Inspector for Wales:* A suggested form of answer to the Statement by the Central Welsh Board: 'Ten years ago, a group of 70 Boys' Secondary Schools in England, many of which had the same characteristics and difficulties as intermediate schools in Wales, were selected for an inspection of the teaching of the literary subjects. The report was an exceedingly severe one, the very first elements of good work were declared absent, textbooks overburdened with notes, and verbal minutiae were declared to be of no educational value, and it was stated that the system must have a most harmful influence on the intellect and character of the nation. Last year, the Board of Education were able to state that, as a result of that report, and subsequent action, English was becoming a factor of increasing value in secondary school education; and that the improvement was most noticeable in the class of schools criticized so severely ten years before'.

The Explosive Report

the new ones. After a full inspection of Mountain Ash secondary school, he 'put it to the teachers, and then to the governing body, that the children just entered from the elementary schools were more thoughtful and more able to apply their knowledge than the pupils at the top of the school ... and it was freely admitted that this fact was true'.[1]

His criticisms on the teaching of the English subjects, and on the tendency to unintelligence was borne out by certain facts, all well-known to the executive committee of the Central Welsh Board. Nine of their chief examiners in the most important and widely taught subjects, commented on the unintelligent nature of the work at the Senior and Honours Stages. For example, the general report of the chief examiner in English said that the essays submitted at the Senior Stage 'contained matter which was hackneyed, conventional and obvious to a degree'. There was a total 'want of original effort'.[2] It was most significant that the current reports by the inspectors of the Central Welsh Board on the five intermediate schools of Cardiganshire: Aberystwyth, Aberaeron, Tregaron, Llandysul and Cardigan—schools in which the natural ability of the children and the conscientiousness of the teaching were second to none in Wales, practically repeated the criticisms—whilst a manifesto issued in 1910 by the Welsh County Schools Association, discussing the one fixed syllabus of the Central Welsh Board in English, which enabled a teacher to teach English through modern methods, was described as uneducational![3]

With reference to the teaching of History, his own subject, Edwards could speak from wide experience and with authority. Generally, the teaching of History was unsatisfactory in the Welsh schools, and, except in a few, 'the teaching was of an unskilful and barren kind; the pupils got up laboriously a bewildering mass of the disconnected facts of Political History, and the great clear issues of History were not placed before them by textbook or teacher; the industrial and social aspects of History were rarely touched upon, and the study of the subject did not lead to an explanation of modern institutions and ideas'.[4] Although references to the teaching of History were slight in the *Report*, Jones attacked it vehemently because Edwards had said that 'while many of the teachers can dictate notes on History, they cannot teach'.[5] In his Reply to Jones, Edwards was able to go fully into the subject. He had taught History for twenty-five years, and had examined every type of school pupil

[1] PRO Ed supra Report by Owen Edwards to the President, op. cit., p. 9.
[2] PRO Ed supra MS Draft of *A Report*, op. cit.
[3] Ibid.
[4] PRO Ed 24/588 : *A Report by the Chief Inspector for Wales*, op. cit., pp. 9–10.
[5] *Report* by Owen Edwards to the President, op. cit., p. 12.

The Explosive Report

from the lowest Forms of almost one-half of the schools in England, to the crowds of boys and girls who came to the university scholarship examinations. He had also stood along-side almost every History teacher in the Welsh intermediate schools, heard them teach, tested their pupils, and conferred with them about their work. He further remarked—'the Central Welsh Board examiner, even if he differed from me, which he does not, has probably not heard one'.[1] In the past, teachers of History in Wales could not know their subject. They read their English History in school, but in the university (with some exception of courses at Bangor) they took foreign History only, and if they took Honours, studied a very short period of English and Welsh mediaeval history. When they returned to the schools, they had only their own schooldays' History to teach. They were also often untrained, and the only method was dictating of notes and the setting of home-lessons.[2] History teachers in Wales were of three types: (a) the effective minority who taught in the right way, in spite of examination results, for example, at Friars' School, Bangor, Tregaron, Ruabon, etc.; (b) those who had reluctantly given up good teaching in order to be 'crammers' for examinations; (c) the remainder, which comprised over fifty per cent, 'who made their pupils get up a textbook—that of the examiner in most cases—and depend almost entirely on their memories'.[3] The teachers could not be blamed, because their pupils had to pass examinations, and rightly or wrongly, the most effective way of achieving this end was to make the pupils learn the textbook, but 'interest in great movements, a knowledge of economic history, even a most elementary knowledge of modern institutions, one does not get'.[4] Many of the headmasters in Wales had been told that History—'of the utmost importance to every citizen as well as to every teacher, had no educative value as taught in their schools, and that nothing would be lost by substituting a book of railway time-tables for the textbook'.[5]

Geography, at this time, was a new subject in the Welsh secondary schools, 'was least known and worst taught'. It was not taught really satisfactorily in more than about half a dozen schools. Here again, the learning of facts came before a broad treatment of the subject, and far too little was done 'to familiarise the pupils' eyes with the processes of geographical change going on around them, or with the evidence of past change which their neighbourhoods might show'.[6] This was not surprising,

[1] Ibid.
[2] Ibid.
[3] Ibid. p. 13
[4] Ibid.
[5] Ibid.
[6] *Report of the Board of Education (Welsh Department), for* 1909, op. cit., p. 17.

The Explosive Report

since few professors were available who had the proper insight into a subject which had not yet been recognized as a discipline by any university. But the teaching of this subject 'had been revolutionized recently' by Herbert J. Fleure at the University College of Wales, Aberystwyth,[1] who was in close contact with the pioneers of the subject, for example, Professors Herbertson, Roxby, Myres, Haddon and Peake.[2]

Although Welsh was taught in almost every intermediate school in Wales, the teaching was often ineffective and poor.[3] At the Federal Education Conference held in London in 1907, it was stated that the Languages sub-committee looked to Wales, with its keen interest in education, for a solution of the problems of language teaching which faced so many parts of the Empire. But the occasional teaching of Welsh to children whose home language was Welsh, by means of the English alphabet, and the common practice of teaching Welsh to Welsh-speaking children in English, showed that the elements of language teaching had not been mastered in many of the Welsh secondary schools.[4] If the conference met again, Edwards said that his report would have to be a humiliating one. The problems of bilingual teaching had not yet been faced seriously in Wales, and there was not a single school in the country known to him where language teaching was carried out on scientific lines. His impressions were confirmed by the director of education for Mauritius, who saw some of the Welsh elementary schools, after seeing the schools of Belgium and Switzerland.[5]

One of the accusations made by Jones was that the *Report* contained statements which were incorrect, for example, the almost casual reference to the 'exceedingly low standard of the examinations in French'.[6] No extended reference is made to this charge in the official, printed Reply by Edwards, but the comments in his written report to the President were extremely valid. The Central Welsh Board's chief examiner in French had reported that, 'in an Honours paper' "*tout l'est de la ville*" was translated by nearly half the candidates by "the whole town", and 95.3 per cent of the candidates, i.e. very nearly all obtained Honours'. Edwards called the attention of the executive committee of the Central Welsh Board to this amazing fact. It was considered so strange that a special committee was

---

[1] PRO Ed 24/588: Report by Owen Edwards to the President, op. cit., p. 23.
[2] *Royal Commission on University Education in Wales: Appendix to First Report: Minutes of evidence, October* 1916–*November* 1916 (*The Haldane Commission*), p. 288. HMSO, 1917. Sir Owen Edwards was one of the members.
[3] PRO Ed supra ibid.
[4] Ibid. *A Report by the Chief Inspector for Wales*, op. cit., p. 10.
[5] Ibid. Report by Owen Edwards to the President, op. cit., p. 25.
Report of the Board of Education, supra ibid., p. 15.

275

appointed to inquire into the matter, but that committee never reported, and in fact, never met! Later, a letter was read from Professor Kastner of Aberystwyth stating that students came to that College after passing the Central Welsh Board Honours in French, who could not read or write or speak French.[1] Jones had nothing but praise for the methods employed by teachers, especially teaching languages by the direct method, but Edwards maintained that teaching French by that method 'had been a failure and a waste of time in Wales. It was a waste of time because the vocabulary obtained was small, out of all proportion to the time spent. A method and books adapted to children of seven and eight were used in the case of children of twelve and thirteen'.[2]

The chief aim of the *Report* was to offer suggestions which would help to make the *teaching* in Welsh intermediate schools more efficient. Far from being 'a libel on teachers', as Jones suggested, the criticisms were the outcome of 'the deep sympathy of an old teacher for them'.[3] The suggestions, practical and sympathetic, had been made in the hope that the more enlightened teachers would follow them.[4] On 31 January 1909, out of 631 assistant teachers on the regular staff of Welsh intermediate schools, only 74 had been trained for secondary school teaching. Three more had been trained for Kindergarten work, and 153 for elementary schools, while 401 had received no recognised training at all. Thirteen intermediate schools did not appear to have had on their regular staff a single teacher with any training recognised by the Board of Education.[5] The first suggestion was that teachers should be encouraged and urged to avail themselves of opportunities offered for training. For such a purpose, excellent Summer Schools were provided by the University Colleges, LEAs and the Welsh Language Society.[6]

Summer Schools in Welsh, Welsh Literature and History had been operating for many years, assisted by grants from the Board of Education.

---

[1] PRO Ed 24/588: Report by Owen Edwards to the President, op. cit., p. 25. At the school, at the invitation of the Headmistress, Edwards took a small Honours class of 3, preparing for County Exhibitions in History. He found one girl 'evidently overworking ... I warned the Headmistress and the girl's mother, but in vain: the girl soon afterwards broke down, paralysed. She was taking History, French, and a few other subjects. I gave her a list of French books written in a beautiful style, in which she could read her History, so as to strengthen both subjects at the same time, and ease the strain which was evidently telling on her. She answered simply, that she could not read even easy French without difficulty and without a dictionary: that she was taking French on the off-chance of getting marks. When I learned that *all* candidates had taken Honours, I had the curiosity, to look up my little friend's marks: she had got more marks in French than in anything else'!

[2] Ibid.

[3] Ibid. p. 23: 'Take what I find in many schools: a young girl who has just passed or failed in her degree examination, who has never had any practice in teaching, who has never been trained, is placed before a Form of thirty children. She does not teach them, and she cannot be expected to do so: she dictates notes, sets home-lessons, and asks pupils how much of the cram book they have made an effort to remember'.

[4] Ibid.

[5] *Statistics of Public Education*, Part 1, 1910, p. 350. Cd. 5355.

[6] PRO Ed supra. *A Report*, op. cit., p. 9.

The Explosive Report

Many distinguished Welsh scholars took part, including Professors Edward Anwyl (chairman of the Central Welsh Board), John Morris Jones—'a most inspiring teacher'—J. Edward Lloyd, 'the highest living authority on Welsh History', and Mr. Samuel J. Evans, headmaster of Llangefni intermediate school, (and author of many books on Welsh language teaching)—'in which the successful teaching of Welsh was one of the most prominent features'.[1] Every year, these courses, where intermediate school teachers required training were very badly attended, for example, in 1908, no history teacher attended the Summer School at Aberystwyth, where special courses were provided in Welsh History, Colonial History, and modern development, and the lectures were not delivered. The attendances at the Welsh Summer Courses were: Rhyl, 1907, nil; Bangor, 1908, two; Swansea, 1909, two. In 1910, the Summer School in Geography at Aberystwyth, where Dr. Fleure, 'who had made the subject his own, and had been appointed by the University College to teach it to teachers . . . was most successful . . . the lectures were excellent, and after each lecture many teachers stayed for the whole morning to ask questions. While inspecting this School, I saw crowds of elementary school teachers, but to the best of my knowledge, the number of secondary teachers did not exceed five'.[2] In view of these striking facts as to courses available, and the poor response by the secondary school teachers, Edwards remarked that 'the Central Welsh Board had incurred a grave responsibility in calling the advice to attend such courses "a work of supererogation" '.[3]

The second suggestion was that the best teaching available should be given to the large lower Forms in order to maintain and develop further the keen minds of the new pupils who came from the elementary schools. Although good teaching was also necessary in the upper Forms, more opportunities should be given for individual work, and possibly less teaching. Younger teachers should not be allowed to take too many subjects, in order that they might gradually obtain enough experience and knowledge for their work. Although the Central Welsh Board stated that 'the system commonly in operation in Wales was the "specialist system", only sixty-two teachers out of 668 could be regarded as teaching one subject. Many took three, four, five, or more, subjects'.[4]

Finally, the Board of Education suggested greater freedom for the teacher, and more efficiency in their teaching by a more thorough inspec-

---
[1] Ibid., p. 10.
[2] PRO Ed 24/588 : *A Report by the Chief Inspector for Wales*, op. cit., p. 10.
[3] Ibid.
[4] Ibid. p. 11.

tion system and a less elaborate examination machine. The schools had their own terminal examinations, and issued their own reports on individual pupils, but the Central Welsh Board had, in addition, four external examinations during the course. The desire of the Board of Education was to secure for each headmaster and headmistress in Wales, the same freedom for the adaptation of the curriculum to the needs of the neighbourhood, and for each teacher the same right of teaching his subject in the way he could teach it best—as were already possessed by heads and teachers in schools of the same type in England.[1]

The concluding paragraph of the Reply summarized the whole unpleasant episode in the relationships between the Board of Education and the Central Welsh Board. Edwards profoundly regretted that the *1909 Report* had been received in the spirit which marked the *Statement*, the publication of which had done injustice to both Boards, producing tension and hostility. It was the policy of the Board of Education to co-operate as fully as possible with the Central Welsh Board in order to improve the schools under their charge, by frequent conferences, in order to smooth out educational problems, and to strengthen the hands of that Board, in order to carry out reforms which they had already begun to implement. Had the executive committee of the Central Welsh Board taken the representatives of the Board of Education into their confidence when drafting their Statement, many misconceptions might have disappeared. Both Boards had one common object, 'the furtherance of efficiency in Welsh secondary education, attainable only by joint and harmonious co-operation. Above all, past misunderstandings should not be allowed to permanently interfere in any relationships'.[2]

V THE AFTERMATH

On 3 January 1911 Edwards sent his 'suggested answer' to the Statement of the Central Welsh Board to Maurice, saying that he had 'made it as short, as relevant, and as studiously moderate in tone and language' as he could. He had abstained from answering anything irrelevant, or 'imitating the occasionally rude tone of the Statement, or answering any condemnation by the Central Welsh Board of the policy or the work of the Board of Education'.[3] The vital issues had been properly emphasized, particularly the teaching of the English subjects by antiquated and barren methods leading to unintelligence, and it was hoped that the refutation

---

[1] Ibid.
[2] PRO Ed 24/588: MS Draft of *A Report by the Chief Inspector for Wales*.
[3] Ibid. Minute from Edwards to Maurice, 3 January 1911.

of every attack on their *Report* would be found convincing. He was willing and anxious to take the whole responsibility—'If I cannot get the suggestions carried out in Wales, I am quite willing to resign my place to a stronger man'.[1]

On submitting the draft to the President, it fell to Maurice to suggest ways and means of effecting the precise format of the Reply 'to the Celtic oration of Jones, and the fulminations and hysterical statements of the Central Welsh Board'. But it was a more delicate task than he had imagined, and several procedures were possible. Consideration was given to a printed letter for circulation to the Welsh press; a Memorandum to the Board of Education, signed by Edwards; a personal letter from the President to a Welsh MP, or a letter from the Board of Education to the Central Welsh Board, acknowledging the Statement, but stating that they were not prepared to withdraw any part of the *Report*.[2] Eventually it was decided to re-draft the Reply 'with an attitude of friendliness, but regretting that the Central Welsh Board had apparently attempted to force a quarrel with the Board of Education, which was not of their own seeking'. Runciman proposed that the re-drafted Reply should be in the form of a Minute addressed to himself from Edwards, and 'every appearance of prejudice in phraseology against the Central Welsh Board had better be avoided . . . without sacrificing any essential points'.[3]

While Maurice and Edwards were pre-occupied with the re-drafting, Trevelyan, Private Secretary to the President, suggested addressing a 'short manifesto to Wales'.[4] But Maurice ignored this proposal, for he felt that Jones and the Central Welsh Board had deliberately misled Welsh opinion 'by shouting too rudely and loudly . . . if the address had been uttered by an Englishman, one would have put the man down to be either mad or else the most reckless liar in the country. As it is, one can be content to regard that strange document as no more than the outpourings of the fervid imagination of a Celt'.[5] Also, the Statement 'was a contemptible production', and therefore the only course open to the Board of Education was to prepare an official Reply, addressed to the

---

[1] Ibid.: Edwards included in the Minute the story of the three stages in the development of the Central Welsh Board Statement: i. Edgar Jones's speech, published in pamphlet form and 'scattered broadcast over Wales. It is the most reckless and dishonest publication in the long history of Welsh education. The people who speak and vote and sign petitions have only seen *this* pamphlet—they do not see our *Report*. This became the basis for ii. The rough Draft prepared by the executive committee of the CWB. In this Draft, much of the inaccuracy and offensiveness has been jettisoned. This again was altered into iii. The Statement submitted to us. It has been modified all the way through, and if the minority on the CWB had been able to get the matter postponed for another month, the 1909 *Report* would have been tacitly accepted'.

[2] PRO Ed supra: Minute from Maurice to the President, 5 January.
[3] PRO Ed 24/588 : Minute from the President to Maurice, 7 January, 1911.
[4]   Ibid.   : Minute from Trevelyan to the President, 18 January.
[5]   Ibid.   : Minute from Maurice to Trevelyan, 21 January.

President—'a real one, worth reading'. Maurice sent the new Draft to Bruce and Sir Robert Morant, who were satisfied that 'whilst all essentials were included, the Reply was also both temperate and dignified'.[1] After the President had approved, the Draft eventually appeared as the printed *Report by the Chief Inspector for Wales*. Later, Maurice informed Edwards that the President had decided not to publish the Reply until a Question was addressed to him in the House, thus preserving 'the traditional attitude of the Board of Education of not replying except on Questions addressed to the Minister, to attacks made upon us in the country ... we strengthen our position by sitting tight and keeping our batteries masked—we shall be all the more effective when eventually we open fire'.[2] Maurice, at this stage, even envied Edwards, did not sympathise with him, and did not entertain the smallest doubt that he was bound to come out on top.

Meanwhile, in Wales, a strong reaction was setting in. All events pointed to a glorious victory for Edwards, the Welsh Department and the Board of Education. Public speeches by Frank Morgan, Keble College, Oxford, at Llandysul, and Llewelyn Williams, MP at Carmarthen, gave full support for the Board of Education, and Edwards was able to say that 'the more thoughtful monthlies are taking our side, and the newspapers are changing their tone'.[3] Haydn Jones, MP, assured Edwards that 'the Central Welsh Board and Edgar Jones would be sorry that they had spoken',[4] and writing to Herbert Lewis on 16 January, Edwards said that 'in reality, while protesting to save their faces, the Central Welsh Board are diligently carrying out our policy ... their Statement reveals a sorry attempt at struggling against what they know to be the best educational course ... in their Reports for the last term, their inspectors say exactly what we say'.[5]

In February, additional support arrived from Wales which gave the Board of Education and Edwards much heart, and proved that the latter was more secure than ever in the affections of Welsh educationists. The Merioneth LEA 'the most efficient and independent authority in Wales', which had a very powerful voice in the House of Commons, passed a resolution at Bala on 13 February (a copy of which was sent to the President and other chief officials at the Board) welcoming the *Report* of the Board of Education on the intermediate schools of Wales 'which it

[1] Ibid. : Ibid.
[2] Ibid. : Minute from Maurice to Edwards, 26 January.
[3] Edwards to Lewis, 10 January 1911, Penucha MSS.
[4] PRO Ed supra: Jones to Edwards, 5 January.
[5] Edwards to Lewis, 16 January, Penucha MSS.

The Explosive Report

regards as the most suggestive and helpful review of Welsh secondary education since the passing of the Welsh Act of 1889, and, believing that frank and sympathetic criticism is more needed and more useful than mere eulogy, trusts that the Board will continue to give Wales each year the benefit of the expert advice now at the disposal of the Welsh Department'.[1]

A few days before, the Barmouth intermediate school governors had passed a similar resolution. The Welsh Society at Cambridge did likewise, and the director of education for Cambridgeshire (an old student of the University College of Wales, Aberystwyth), explained at the meeting that the 1909 *Report* 'laid down the true lines of progress for Welsh education'.[2] The Principals of two Welsh Training Colleges, Parry, of Trinity College, Carmarthen, and Harris, of Bangor Normal College, added their tributes and admiration, and by this time Edwards believed that 'the great mass of the people of Wales are with us . . . but the malcontents are very active'.[3] He could now say of the Central Welsh Board that it was thoroughly awakened, 'it has made more progress since the publication of our *Report* than during the previous ten years. I really think we can make it into quite a useful body . . . the *Report* will have established our position as the guide, philosopher and friend of this unprogressive, but not hopeless, Central Welsh Board'.[4]

At the end of March, a private unofficial deputation (described inaccurately in the press as sent by the Central Welsh Board and the Welsh county authorities) comprising a few members of the Welsh Board —Lord Sheffield, Dr. T. H. Morris (Glamorgan), and Principal Griffiths of Cardiff, waited on the Welsh Members to protest against the *Report*, and to demand absolute autonomy for the Central Welsh Board.[5] But the Chairman, Ellis Griffith, MP (Anglesey), promptly ruled this out, and said 'that a deputation should merely state what it had to say'. The only notable feature of this meeting was an intemperate speech made by Lord Sheffield, backed by his colleagues, which consisted of a most cowardly attack on Edwards, 'attributing the most ignoble motives'. The malcontents were certainly extremely active behind Edwards's back, but he was not too concerned about the behaviour of the noble Lord—'fe dyf

---

[1] PRO Ed 24/589: Minute from Edwards to Maurice, 14 February. Merioneth LEA to the Board of Education, 13 February.

[2] Ibid., Minute from Edwards to Maurice, ibid.

[3] Ibid., Edwards to Maurice, 18 February.

[4] Ibid.

[5] Edwards to Lewis (undated), Penucha MSS: 'Anwyl took pains to assure me that the Executive Committee of the C.W.B. had nothing to do with the Deputation . . . It was, as far as I can see, a number of private persons'.

The Explosive Report

y draen a'i flaen arno',[1] but he was hurt that Principal Griffiths and Dr. Morris 'should have spoken as they did—as five minutes' perusal of documents in their possession would have given them the truth. I am quite sure that, in spite of the very badly informed misrepresentations of one Member, Sidney Robinson, MP, (Brecon and Radnor), the Welsh Members will do what is right'.[2] For the time being, the Welsh Members agreed not to commit themselves until they had read the reply, a copy of which was sent to each one at the request of Robinson and Haydn Jones, the latter being quite convinced that the majority of his fellow members would give unqualified support.[3] Herbert Lewis was able to inform Edwards at the end of April that the Welsh Members were in accord with the *Report*.[4] This victory was a most valuable one for Edwards—it meant that the Welsh Department had 'established the right to criticise where we grant the money entrusted to us by Parliament'.[5] Greatly relieved of the tension of the previous months, Edwards confided to Lewis that the matter had caused him much anxiety—'on the one hand I am very loth to bring Runciman or A. T. Davies into trouble; on the other hand, there is the supreme importance of doing justice to Welsh children'.[6]

On 15 April, Hobhouse, Private Secretary to Maurice, sent a letter to the Central Welsh Board, along with some copies of the Reply, under the imposing title *A Report made by the Chief Inspector for Wales of the Board of Education to the President of the Board on the Statement of the Central Welsh Board with Reference to the Report of the Board of Education made in Pursuance of Section* 15 *of the Welsh Intermediate Education Act,* 1889, *on the Proceedings under that Act in the year* 1909.[7] The letter was read at a special meeting of the Central Welsh Board on 21 April, and Anwyl, in a floundering manner, and obviously ill at ease, confessed that since the document was marked 'Private and Confidential', he 'did not know what to do with them . . . he proposed to write to the President and ascertain what use he was permitted to make of them'![8]

---

[1] Edwards to Lewis, 20 April, Penucha MSS: 'the bramble grows with its prickle on it'. Edwards to Maurice, 6 April.
[2] Edwards to Lewis, 20 April, Penucha MSS; Maurice to Edwards, 10 April: 'I do not think that Lord Sheffield's venom will hurt you or the Board of Education. You will have heard from Hobhouse that your Reply is to be sent to the Central Welsh Board. I doubt if they will ask to have it laid as a Parliamentary Paper when they have seen it! Meanwhile, all we have to do, I think, is to sit tight'.
[3] PRO Ed 24/589: Jones to Edwards, 12 April.
[4] Lewis to Edwards, 30 April, Penucha MSS.
[5] Edwards to Maurice, 11 April: Edwards added in his letter: 'I had a tempting offer to come up to town today to see the embalmed head of Oliver Cromwell (there is no doubt whatever about it). Is it not a pity that it cannot be put back in the empty grave in Westminster Abbey'? Maurice, in his reply to Edwards (12 April) said: 'The President agreed to send a copy of your Reply to the Welsh Members, and that it would soon be in the hands of the CWB—I have seen in the papers a good deal about Oliver Cromwell's head . . . I am afraid that my attention has been entirely concentrated lately upon the head of the President . . . which had, at times, appeared to be in some jeopardy'!
[6] Edwards to Lewis, 3 May, Penucha MSS.
[7] PRO Ed 24/588: Board of Education to Central Welsh Board, 15 April.
[8] Minutes, CWB, op. cit., 21 April.

The Explosive Report

The President's reply was read at the May meeting, in which he said 'that the document was marked in the particular way, solely out of consideration for the susceptibilities of the Central Welsh Board, and with a view to their convenience, and that he had no objection whatever to its publication, or to its further distribution to any extent which the Central Welsh Board might desire, and, furthermore, desired to know how many copies they should like'.[1] Lord Sheffield immediately told the meeting that the document should neither be private nor confidential, and before Anwyl had time to speak, the meeting approved, 'with Edgar Jones ejaculating "then we can fight" '.[2] Then followed a dramatic scene when Anwyl, in his innocence, proposed that 100 unmarked copies be requested from the Board of Education. He was promptly interrupted by Lord Sheffield who said that they had already arrived! The crafty Lord had, long beforehand managed to get hold of Maurice's letter from the clerk to the Central Welsh Board, and had instructed him to send for the unmarked copies.[3] These were distributed for consideration at the next meeting on 19 May. This meeting, quietly dreaded by Edwards, proved to be a complete anticlimax. When the matter of the Reply was brought up—at the end of the meeting, when only eight or nine members were present—there was no discussion 'due to lack of time', and it was merely decided to confirm a resolution made by the executive earlier in the day, that 'a reply should be drawn up'![4] The brave threats of more fighting, made in the heat of the moment, as on so many occasions in the past, dissolved into thin air, as the Central Welsh Board realized that further temporizing would lead nowhere, and that the realities of the situation would have to be faced—in the words of Edwards, he hoped 'that reading his Minute (Reply) would bring them into better mind, and that they would withdraw their Statement'.[5]

However, the meeting was the swell after the storm. Yet it produced the first major move in the direction of reform. It has been noted in an earlier study[6] that J. H. Davies, Registrar of the University College of Wales, Aberystwyth, had proposed the appointment of an independent

---

[1] PRO Ed 24/589: Maurice to the Central Welsh Board, 30 April.
[2] Minutes of the Central Welsh Board, op. cit., Executive Committee, 11 May.
[3] Ibid. Casson, of the Board of Education, made detailed notes of this meeting.
[4] Ibid., Meetings of executive committee and full CWB, 19 May.
[5] Edwards to Lewis, 20 April, Penucha MSS: 'What pains me is that they make it a personal matter. They think I bear malice owing to what happened long ago; but, quite honestly, I have never harboured the slightest resentment. They bring Davies in; and you know how absolutely guileless and straightforward he is. They really dislike me because I am a reformer. I have always been one; at Oxford I have been through this same fight for efficiency; but I have never brought personal feeling into a struggle; and I have never, until now, aroused such a feeling. They began with a suspicion; and, though I have done everything within my power to gain their confidence, even the many ways—in which we have helped them to extend their power and utility—are looked at askance'.
[6] Study No. 2.

The Explosive Report

committee to inquire into the curricula, organization, and work of the intermediate schools, and the whole Central Welsh Board system.[1] In the event, this action proved to be far too drastic, for the tardy Central Welsh Board preferred to move in a much less spectacular manner. At the November meeting, the motion was defeated by 40 to 2, because most of the influential members argued that such an inquiry would 'amount to nothing less than a censure on the Board'.[2] But the motion, though unsuccessful, produced results in another way. These were substantial measures of reform, adopted piecemeal at subsequent meetings of the Board from November onwards. Emotional eloquence on matters of importance (which usually prevailed at most meetings of the Board) at last succumbed to practical measures which eventually had a revitalizing influence on the Welsh secondary schools. In retrospect, the headmaster's condemnatory address, intended to protect and preserve a traditional and stagnating school system, proved to be merely an ephemeral melodramatic convulsion. Nevertheless, it had initiated a process of constructive change, which, under Edwards's direction, was to infuse a regenerating and lasting influence on Welsh secondary education for many decades to come.

Before dealing with the reforms adopted by the Central Welsh Board from 1911 onwards, attention should be given to their second Statement[3] produced by Anwyl, Lord Sheffield and Charles Lloyd, and described by Edwards as 'the useless parting shot of a defeated enemy in the pamphlet war'.[4] This was drawn up during the summer of 1911 and sent to the Board of Education on 17 August.[5] To all concerned at Whitehall, it appeared to be a very tame rejoinder which did not attempt to combat the point made by Edwards that they 'wilfully misrepresented the 1909 Report'.[6] It was 'not only weak and spiteful, but grossly and recklessly inaccurate' and Edwards remarked that 'probably they will stop here, as they know they will get no support from the Welsh Members'.[7] His reply to the President was brief, for they merely repeated what had

---

[1] *The Manchester Guardian*, 20 May.

[2] Minutes of CWB, op. cit., 17 November, additional entry by Edwards. *The Manchester Guardian*, 18 *November:* 'The motion was strongly opposed by the Rev. Dr. Aaron Davies as being a vote of censure on themselves, the schoolteachers, the inspectors, and the whole scheme from the beginning, and he hoped there would be an unmistakable vote against it'.

[3] PRO Ed 24/588: *Statement of the Central Welsh Board with reference to the Reply of Mr. O. M. Edwards, HMCI, to the Statement issued by the Central Welsh Board on the subject of the Board of Education Report for* 1909–10, 2 August, 1911.

[4] Ibid: Minute from Edwards to Maurice 19 August. Memorandum on the *Statement of the Central Welsh Board with reference to the Reply of Mr. O. M. Edwards, HMCI*, supra: by Owen Edwards, 19 August.

[5] Ibid.: Central Welsh Board to the President, 17 August. Minute from Maurice to the President, 18 August.

[6] Minute from Maurice to Edwards, 18 August.

[7] Minute from Edwards to Maurice, 19 August.

The Explosive Report

been said before, in a hasty manner. They defended their examination system, were annoyed that the Board of Education had not withdrawn their criticisms, and included two incorrect statements on the old question of dual inspection.[1] But Edwards felt keenly the personal attack made upon him in their last paragraph[2] and ended by saying: i. That the *Report* of 1909 embodied modern, progressive educational ideas; ii. that every English educationist would agree with the educational policy recommended to the Central Welsh Board, which was in keeping with the considered policy of the Scotch Department; iii. that the Merioneth LEA had embraced the *Report* in question as the most helpful since the passing of the Welsh Act; iv. the Caernarvonshire LEA, having had a separate inspection of their own 'confirmed ours'; v. the Welsh University Colleges, 'to the annoyance of the Central Welsh Board, evidently, ... have met our views'; vi. The Central Welsh Board attacks had alienated the Welsh MPs—'if it is known that the controversy is to be continued, I have no doubt the Welsh Members will censure that Board ... it might be well, in our next year's report, to give a sketch of a suggested examination syllabus for Wales'.[3]

In addition to the Minutes taken by Casson at the November meeting of the Central Welsh Board, Edwards had also appended a personal minute to A. T. Davies: 'The Central Welsh Board was concerned mainly with measures for self-reform. It rejected the motion to appoint a committee of inquiry ... as it would be a dreadful vote of censure on itself ... a number of far-reaching suggestions for reform were adopted by the executive'.[4] Most of the reforms envisaged by Edwards were implemented during the years 1911–15, an abundant harvest which resulted from the explosive *Report*. This was the major achievement, on the academic side, of Edwards's tenure of the Chief Inspectorship for Wales at the Welsh Department, and by 1915 over one-half of the brief period of his stewardship had expired.[5] One thing is quite clear, his relationships with the Central Welsh Board were far more significant for Welsh education, and far less inimical and provocative than Professor R. T. Jenkins would have us believe, and it is difficult to follow his argument that Edwards was

---

[1] Memorandum by Owen Edwards, supra.

[2] Ibid.: The first incorrect statement was 'that they did not know how long my visits were, or how thorough my inspection ... they knew perfectly well because they had addressed inquiries to all the Heads in Wales, and had thought of publishing the results of the inquiries in the papers ... but the answers they received, no doubt, put an end to that ... and they therefore invoke the old grievance of dual inspection'. Secondly, the Central Welsh Board had tried to interfere with Edwards's inspections of intermediate schools. Edwards maintained he had a right to inspect, and 'if any attempt were made to curtail my freedom ... I must immediately go to the President and say that my work could not be done'.

[3] This was done in the *Board of Education Report (Welsh Department)*, 1912, p. 6, ff.

[4] Minutes, Central Welsh Board, op. cit., personal Minute from Edwards to Davies, 18 November.

[5] Sir Owen M. Edwards died on 15 May 1920, aged 62.

too concerned with details which might have been best evaded, and that he was unfortunate in his dealings with that Board. With reference to the latter statement, the reverse would be nearer the truth.[1]

There was a long list of changes awaiting attention. They were referred to in the Minutes, and discussed in some detail in the Board of Education's annual *Reports* after 1910. Indeed, having 'established the right to criticize', the *Reports* of 1911 and 1912 were much bolder in spirit and content, and more penetrating—but no subsequent explosions took place! In his *Report* for 1910, Edwards stated that so far as the provision of schools was concerned, the system of intermediate education in Wales was complete, but whether that system was the best adapted to the needs of the people, and whether it was progressing in the right direction, was a matter of deep concern. The important matters needing immediate attention were an extension of the system of inspection, and a reconsideration and overhaul of the examination system with a view to greater efficiency in the teaching, and to a greater flexibility and adaptation both of curricula and syllabi. So far as it went, the Central Welsh Board inspection system was good. There were two permanent inspectors, the chief inspector responsible mainly for the literary side, and the assistant, for science and technology. Temporary women inspectors assisted in the girls' and mixed schools, and other temporary ones were occasionally employed. But this arrangement was not satisfactory, and Edwards suggested several ways of useful extension. He recommended that the triennal full inspections should be fuller and more thorough, for invariably, such inspections, irrespective of the size of the school, had been the work of three inspectors for one day only.[2]

Again, the inspection should be more specialist in character, and he considered that there should be more correlation between inspection and examination. The simple and most effective solution would be to appoint the chief examiners as temporary inspectors, since many of these were also teachers of wide experience, and if they were invited to inspect selected schools, especially unsatisfactory ones, the reports of methods of teaching could be of the greatest value to new teachers.[3] In 1911, the Welsh Department was able to state that the inspections and reports were fuller, and that more inspectors took part, notably chief examiners. It was contended that an extension of this practice, where specialist

---

[1] Y Bywgraffiadur Cymreig, op. cit., pp. 179–180: Syr Owen Morgan Edwards, 1858–1920, gan R. T. Jenkins: 'Ni bu lawn mor ffodus yn ei ymwneud â'r Bwrdd Canol; dan rym ei deimlad greddfol fod yr ysgolion canolradd yn Seisnigaidd eu naws, arweiniwyd ef i ddadleuon ar fanion y buasai'n well eu hosgoi, ac felly cymylwyd y ddadl sylfaenol'.

[2] *Report of the Board of Education, Welsh Department*, 1910 (1 *August* 1911), pp. 5–6.

[3] Ibid.

The Explosive Report

advice was available, enabled the examiners to make the examinations fairer tests of the schools.[1] It was also important that specialists should be employed to inspect those subjects, of which, because of their novelty or recent development, the ordinary inspector could not have a thorough knowledge, for example, Geography and Physical Training.[2] In the case of Geography, the exertions of its inspiring chief examiner, Dr. Fleure, had made the subject interesting and more human; he attracted large numbers of teachers to study human geography at his Summer School at Aberystwyth, and also paid informal visits to schools by invitation.[3]

But the teaching and inspection of Physical Training was most pathetic, and was not even on the time-table of many schools, and although a committee had been set up to deal with this matter, Owen, the chief inspector, 'did not see the need for action'.[4] In order to bestir the Central Welsh Board, the Board of Education had sent some of their own inspectors from the Medical Branch to Cardiff, but 'this caused some bitterness to the Central Welsh Board who now promised to report fully on the matter of Physical Training in schools'. Some improvement was made in 1914, when it was reported that Physical Training was included in a selected number of Welsh intermediate schools,[5] but this subject, which touched so closely the health of the pupils, should be one of the most important activities of every school.[6] In 1913 the Central Welsh Board decided to engage an inspector with specialist knowledge.[7]

Closely connected with inspection, 'the multiplicity and rigidity of the examination system' of the Central Welsh Board was the sharpest thorn in Edwards's flesh. The right path towards reform and simplification lay in modifying the external nature of the examination system. This had been started in two ways: by showing much greater willingness to accept alternative schemes; by placing the examiners in a position which enabled them to know more definitely what the work of each of the schools entailed. Edwards urged the abandonment of the Junior Examination as an external examination, for he thought that it was possible for a more educative and more reliable internal examination to be substituted.

---

[1] Ibid. for 1911 (10 June 1912), p. 5.

[2] The teaching of Physical Training and Music is referred to in Study No. 2.

[3] *Report of the Board of Education, Welsh Department*, 1911, supra.

[4] Minutes, Central Welsh Board, op. cit., Minute by Owen Edwards, 17 December 1911; ibid., 22 December: 'Mr. Owen Owen, CI, was asked to make a statement at the next meeting as to these two subjects (Physical Training and Vocal Music) which are to a certain extent crowded into a corner by the multiplicity of subjects'; ibid., 3 May 1912.

[5] Ibid., 2 November 1914: 'Miss Davies, who made reports on the subject in the schools at Aberystwyth, Caernarvon, Holyhead, Brecon, Newport, Pontypool, Rhyl, Tenby, Swansea and Wrexham, attended the meeting'.

[6] *Report of the Board of Education, Welsh Department*, 1912 (16 June 1913), p. 13.

[7] Ibid., for 1913 (10 July 1914), p. 12.

Every school should be allowed to examine itself and tested on its own work, and if the inspectors of the Central Welsh Board so wished, the papers could be sent to an examiner. The Senior Examination presented more difficulty, because in any change in its character, a number of examining bodies, by whom it had been accepted as an equivalent to their own examination, would have to be consulted. But here again, the two main aims should be: to make the examination an examination of the work of the school; and to associate the teachers with the examiners in the work of examination to an increasing extent. The value of two advanced examinations such as the Higher and Honours was questionable, since the aim, from the standpoint of the school was to test ability, and that of the university to discover promise, but whether the two aims could be achieved by the same examination was open to grave doubt.[1]

In the Board of Education's *Report* for 1912, Edwards had sketched the outline of an examination system which would test the schools more thoroughly without interfering with any adaptations relating to the needs of localities. In his report for 1911-12, the Chief Inspector of the Central Welsh Board described their examinations: the Higher and Honours were geared for scholarships to the universities; the Senior was determined by the requirements of Public Bodies; the Junior examination provided the Central Welsh Board with the best means of expressing its own educational ideals and policy. Edwards acknowledged that 'in the cautious care and indefatigable watchfulness bestowed upon it, the Central Welsh Board examination system was as perfect as any system could be, but after such a rigid discipline during a period of growth . . . it should now be considered whether, in order to give the schools more freedom to meet the growing demand for adaptation, the external examination should not make fewer demands upon the time and the course of instruction of a school'.[2] The simple solution was to adopt an internal examination instead of the Junior, the freeing of the Senior examination from dependence on the examinations of other bodies, and to let the university supplant the Honours.[3] For a more modern and efficient system of Welsh secondary education, to which the Central Welsh Board were giving serious attention, Edwards proposed: (a) that the two examinations above the Senior stage should be combined, and called the Higher examination, for pupils of 17 or 18, which would be of such a character that the university could regard it as an equivalent for

---

[1] Ibid., for 1911, op. cit., pp. 6-7.
[2] *Report of the Board of Education, Welsh Department*, 1912, op. cit., p. 7 ff.
[3] Ibid., p. 12.

The Explosive Report

intermediate or first year courses; (b) the existing Senior or School Leaving Certificate, for pupils around the age of 16. Both examinations would be external. The Junior examination should be discontinued as an external examination, and conducted entirely by the school staff, and the pass mark, if necessary, could be decided by the Central Welsh Board inspectors.[1]

In connection with such reforms, Edwards made a few well-calculated suggestions. He was very mindful, that in Wales, parents were avid for certificates of proficiency, and since many pupils left school after only three years, there would be no record of their work. He suggested the substitution of a school record book for examinations, which would be acceptable to parents and prospective employers, with the history of the pupil in all his aspects of school work—academic, athletic and social. In the same way, perhaps the Senior examination could become partly an internal examination, and a representative of the teachers in each subject could be added to the external examiners, as was the practice in the universities. But the abolition of the Junior examination, although effected many years later, was to be the subject of long controversy within the fold of the Central Welsh Board and the governing bodies of the intermediate schools. By 1921, the new examination structure devised by Edwards had come into being—the Higher and Senior examinations, with the abolition of the Junior—but Edwards had died before he saw the new system at work.[2]

From 1910 onwards serious consideration was given to improved methods of teaching, particularly the teaching of the literary and humane subjects 'upon which, especially in the lower Forms, the mental development of the child mostly depends ... the Welsh child has a natural sense of literary style, especially when he is bilingual'.[3] Distinct progress was being made in the teaching of English, History and Geography, because the Central Welsh Board and their inspectors were showing increasing sympathy with improved methods, and the response of the teachers to newer and more modern methodology 'had been ready and almost universal'.[4] It was realized that English should be taught as a living language, more prominence was given to the reading of literature 'which aroused appreciation of the thought of the text than at committing

---

[1] Ibid., for 1913, p. 11. Minutes, Central Welsh Board, op. cit., 2 November, 1914.

[2] Ibid., p. 12. Minutes Central Welsh Board, op. cit., 20 November. *Western Mail*, 21 November, 1914. Study No. 2 deals with subjects and examinations appropriate for intending teachers. *Reports of the Board of Education for 1920 and 1921*: for 1921, pp. 11–12.

[3] *Report of the Board of Education, Welsh Department*, 1910, op. cit., p. 13.

[4] *Report of the Board of Education, Welsh Department*, 1911, op. cit., pp. 10–11.

explanatory notes to memory... and less stress was laid on formal grammar'.[1] In the teaching of History, both teaching and content had been overhauled, more stress was laid in the upper Forms on the history of more recent times, in such a way as to enable the pupil to see the main outlines of the development of modern institutions. Geography teaching had been revolutionized, more schools taught the subject 'in the new and better way... very soon, this subject will combine the human interest of History with a thoroughly scientific training in observation and experiment'.[2]

But the teaching of Welsh in some schools was less satisfactory, due to inefficient teaching 'especially the deadening of interest by attempting to load the memory of the pupil with rules and exceptions instead of teaching him to speak, and leading him as soon as possible to some simple lyric, or to some terse and clear prose-work. The vivacity, the readiness to speak that should characterize language teaching, is unfortunately often absent from the Welsh classroom'.[3] Edwards condemned a Welsh secondary system which gave Welsh an inferior place in the curriculum, and less time for its study as compared, for example, with French. A syllabus based on the direct method had been drawn up for Monmouthshire schools, and this could be applied to other parts of Wales so that English-speaking children could be taught and examined in such a way that their desire to learn Welsh should not 'imperil their chances of passing their examination as a whole'. He appealed to the governing bodies of schools and the Central Welsh Board, *which professed to be national in character*, to pay more attention to its national language and culture, and, incidentally, Music, which in 1910 occupied 'a most unsatisfactory position in many of the schools'.[4] This subject should be given as much attention in the intermediate schools as it received in the elementary schools and Training Colleges, especially for those pupils who were pupil-teachers or Bursars. He advocated proper facilities for the teaching of singing and the reading of music, the formation of school choirs and orchestras, and large-scale schools music festivals.[5]

The Board of Education had initiated a system of grants to schools which had a certain percentage of intending teachers. This had been of

[1] Ibid.
[2] Ibid.
[3] Ibid.
[4] Ibid. for 1910, p. 15.
[5] Minutes, Central Welsh Board, op. cit., 15 December 1911, additional Minute by Edwards, 17 December: 'I obtained a discussion on the teaching of Music in secondary schools. Though Owen Owen, the Chief Inspector of the Central Welsh Board was to have called the attention of the Headmasters to the subject, I believe nothing has been done. I was backed up by Principal Griffiths (Cardiff) and Principal Roberts (Aberystwyth), but Mr. Owen's sympathy is with inaction. The Principals had been greatly influenced by our Reports on the inability of Training College students to teach Music'.

The Explosive Report

great help, especially to the smaller schools which were doing excellent work in the face of many financial difficulties, but due to the 'alarming decrease in the number of intending elementary schoolteachers, many schools had found it impossible to qualify for the grant'.[1] But by 1911 the responsibility for the education of intending teachers had a good influence on the schools, especially in teaching method. It had made the teaching of languages more modern, and History more real. The serious study of Geography had been introduced, Arithmetic was more practical, and those subjects necessary for the education of every Welsh child had been brought into some prominence, such as Penmanship, Music, and Physical Training.[2]

Such improvements in teaching method, becoming evident in 1911, were maintained and developed further in subsequent years, and the *Reports* on this aspect of school work were much more favourable in 1912 and 1913. While much remained to be done, the teaching of English, History, Geography, and, by this time, Welsh, had improved considerably. But one thing still hampered quicker progress, (and would continue to do so until the examination system was revised) teachers did not have that freedom to teach their subjects 'in the way they could teach them best', for example, History could only 'be taught by modern methods at the certain cost of poor examination results'. After a visit to an English school, a teacher of English in one of the Welsh schools said 'I have seen how education can be taken as a whole, when an organizer having culture and a powerful personality is not thwarted by minor public examinations' —a view held by many teachers in Wales.[3]

By 1912 there were more hopeful signs in the teaching of Welsh. There was better teaching and better teachers, especially in the context of teaching Welsh as a foreign tongue, and by the direct method. But still, in too many schools, where Welsh was taught to pupils who could not speak it, (here it is worth quoting one of the most important observations made by Edwards on the teaching of Welsh)

> 'there is a great contrast between the bright teaching of French on modern lines and the dreary teaching of Welsh on ancient lines; in the one case interest is aroused by pictures and vivacious talking, in the other it is killed by a paradigm of initial mutations and a selection of irregular forms. Where Welsh is taught to children who already know it, the contrast between the teaching of English and the teaching of Welsh, though they ought to be based on exactly the same principles, is disconcerting. English is taught by means of itself, and in such a way

[1] *Board of Education Report, Welsh Department*, 1911, op. cit., p. 11.
[2] Ibid.
[3] Ibid. for 1912, op. cit., p. 15.

The Explosive Report

as to develop some interest in its great writers; *Welsh is often taught in English*, though to the pupil the vehicle of instruction is the language less perfectly known, and its classics are treated too often as a storehouse of illustrations of grammar and philology.[1] While rejoicing in the excellent and increasingly efficient work that is being done in many intermediate schools, it is very important that the Welsh school Governors should remember that much remains to be done. Welsh children can be taught to read French and German, to enter upon the great literature enshrined in each of these languages, to speak the languages with fair facility, and to compose in them with commendable accuracy; but the schools of Wales are not called upon to exert an influence on the development of the literature of France or of Germany. With regard to Wales, their power is infinitely greater, their mission far more definite; they are called upon to do more than teach a language; they can profoundly affect the development of a literature, and it is to them that Wales looks for a generation of writers that are equal to those of the present day, and not unworthy of those of the past'.[2]

Regarding the question of differentiation and the greater adaptation of school courses to the needs of their localities, together with the value of a sound general education for those pupils who left school at sixteen, there was room for considerable planning and reform. In the past, the Central Welsh Board always argued that there were difficulties surrounding the differentiation of schools due to pressure of examinations, and because parents and pupils found it difficult to decide upon the question of a career. J. H. Davies, when introducing his motion to appoint a committee to inquire into the work of the Central Welsh Board had deplored the academic courses emphasized by that system. He was very doubtful as to whether the intermediate schools were doing their duty to the communities in which they were situated. The great majority of pupils came from the elementary schools, were the children of working class people, and would have to fend for themselves on leaving school. Two thousand children left the intermediate schools every year, but only fifteen per cent went in for higher education. Of the remaining 1,700 who sat for the Central Welsh Board examination, seventy-five per cent took Latin, and eighty per cent French. He was told by commercial men that they did not get what they required, because the whole Central Welsh Board system was governed by the idea of the Welsh University at the top. Scotland was solving this problem, whilst Wales was merely turning out teachers and preachers![3]

---

[1] This state of affairs was not peculiar to the Welsh intermediate schools. At the Welsh University Colleges, distinguished professors of Welsh lectured on their subject in English, and often, students were expected to answer their examination papers in English. (*Royal Commission on University Education in Wales, Appendix to Final Report, Minutes of Evidence, March–June*, p. 101 ff. Cd. 8993, 1918. Also, Owen Edwards, a member of the Commission, questions the Rev. D. H. Williams, Vice Chairman of the Central Welsh Board. Minutes 12830–12849.

[2] *Report of the Board of Education*, (*Welsh Department*), 1912, op. cit., pp. 16–17.

[3] *The Manchester Guardian*, 20 May 1911.

The Explosive Report

As far back as 1895 the Charity Commissioners had suggested the right lines of development when they said that the intermediate schools should include a special branch of vocational study in addition to the ordinary school course, in order that pupils with a sound general education, who did not wish to proceed to university, could take subjects which would be useful for them in their after-school life.[1] In 1911 Edwards stated that differentiation was, at last, a practical question, since a certain amount already existed between intermediate and municipal secondary schools, the former being more academic in bias and the latter more industrial, and, being self-examining, were more free to give a bias to their curriculum, such as geology or metallurgy. By this time, even the Chief Inspector of the Central Welsh Board was beginning to realize its importance, but foresaw financial and other difficulties, including extra staffing. For whilst Owen envisaged differentiation as a major exercise, Edwards showed that a school could take a good trade, commerce, or technical bias along with a sound course of general education.[2]

At Rhyl, it was intended to give the school a strong commercial bias.[3] At Porth (Rhondda), elaborate preparations had been made towards an engineering bias, and at Welshpool a promising attempt was being made towards an agricultural bias.[4] With the elimination of external examinations below Senior level, it would be possible to elaborate in such directions, but for pupils who left school before attaining the age of 16, they should be allowed to drop other subjects and concentrate on the particular bias, causing little departure from the normal curriculum.[5] School

---

[1] *Report of the Board of Education (Welsh Department)*, 1910, p. 11. The Commissioners stated that agriculture had been included at Botwnnog (Caernarvonshire), Llandeilo, Dolgellau and Carmarthen. Other places should follow suit, e.g. navigation should be taught at Fishguard, Cardigan, Aberaeron, Aberystwyth, Towyn and Porthmadog; the principles of mining at Blaenau Festiniog; metallurgy at Llanelli, and mechanics at Pembroke Dock. Edwards also suggested mining and metallurgy at Swansea, Cardiff, and Rhondda Valleys. (Owen Edwards, Report to the President, op. cit.)

[2] *Report of the Board of Education (Welsh Department)*, 1911, p. 10.

[3] Edwards to Lewis, 20 April 1911, Penucha MSS: 'The two points in dispute are: i. *To adapt education to needs*. The intermediate schools are getting out of date and stagnating. The Central Welsh Board are still pressing on them the old discarded policy of the Board of Education; whether on principle or in ignorance, I do not know. The result is—private secondary schools are rising or reviving everywhere. At Carmarthen, there is one of between 100 and 200 pupils; at Caernarvon, an old private school is reviving, while the intermediate school has to dismiss two of its teachers owing to reduced numbers; at Holyhead, a new private school is being established. The outlook is disquieting, and I want the Central Welsh Board to awake to the fact. Take one example. Rhyl school is not what it should be, as everybody in Rhyl will tell you. The Governors thought the Board of Education barred all progress. I was asked to meet them, and I showed them four ways of giving their school the useful and the commercial bias they all wanted. They declared any one of them would do: but the headmaster promptly said that none of them would be possible under the Central Welsh Board regulations. ii. To get the humane subjects, notably English and Welsh literature and History taught by modern methods. Wales is about fifteen years behind England in this matter'.

[4] Minutes, Central Welsh Board, op. cit., 19 May 1911; 17 November 1911; 11 June 1915. Professors William Phillips (Cardiff) and Bryner Jones (Aberystwyth) had proposed setting up Special Committees of the Central Welsh Board to consider the teaching of Agriculture. Jones suggested the awarding of county scholarships for pupils who had followed an Agricultural course in the intermediate schools, to go to the University College of Wales, Aberystwyth, to a Diploma in Agriculture or Husbandry. But the Central Welsh Board hated such committees, were very slow to convene them, and were still discussing these propositions in 1915!

[5] *Report of the Board of Education (Welsh Department)*, 1911, p. 11.

The Explosive Report

governors were slowly awaking to the importance of adaptation, and were asking headmasters to submit courses bearing more definitely on the life of the district, and to place less reliance on old model academic courses or on anticipation of examination demands.[1]

This prompted Edwards, as another necessary reform, to address himself to the governing bodies of the Welsh intermediate schools. Part of their duties was responsibility for the nature and scope of the courses taught in their schools—subject to the provisions of their County Schemes—in close consultation with the headmasters and county councils. Although the newer Schemes did not prescribe what should be taught, governing bodies were given as much latitude as possible in devising academic and vocational courses. Edwards discovered, to his surprise 'that in one school the governors admitted that they had never regarded the drawing up of school courses as part of their duties, and had left this in the hands of the headmaster, whose natural tendency was to disregard the adaptation of education in favour of the demands of examinations, and a good haul of certificates'.[2]

The remaining matters which called for serious attention and reform were: school libraries; the fees charged for examination certificates; the rising expense of secondary education; the stereotyped kind of representation on the executive committee of the Central Welsh Board, and the comfort and health of school pupils. The Minutes of the Central Welsh Board, taken down by Casson for the Board of Education, bristle with the futile pleas made by Edwards at their meetings for the provision of good school libraries, extending over a period of four years from 1910 to 1914. The long delay was due to 'the dogged conservatism of Owen Owen', and the fact that although committees were always appointed, they never met.[3] Edwards, in his *Report* for 1912, while he was able to say that 'great progress had been made', envisaged a more elaborate scheme such as a Schools' Circulating Library in conjunction with the newly established National Library of Wales, 'which could serve 1,200 teachers and 17,000 pupils ... in the secondary schools scattered over Wales', and this in turn could forge a strong link between two national institutions, the National Library and the Central Welsh Board. The diffusion of knowledge thus brought about would permeate from the schools to the homes 'across which the shadow of the examination room

---

[1] Ibid. 1912, p. 9.

[2] *Report of the Board of Education, Welsh Department*, 1912, op. cit., p. 9: New Schemes in Cardiganshire, Anglesey, and Montgomeryshire had stated that the Natural Science courses should bear on the trades and industries of those areas, including Agriculture.

[3] Minutes, Central Welsh Board, op. cit., 28 July 1911; 3 May 1912. On 15 November 1912 Edwards asked if the Library Committee appointed on 16 December, 1910 had met!

The Explosive Report

does not lie'.[1] National institutions should inspire national anniversaries, and he pleaded for the proper celebration of St. David's Day in the secondary schools—a practice which was so commendable and successful in the elementary schools.

Fees were charged by the Central Welsh Board for entry to their examinations—whether or not the candidate was successful—and these varied from 7/6 to 10/-. One of the Welsh county councils had made a complaint that many parents could ill-afford such payments. Edwards noted that the Central Welsh Board received so much money from this source that they did not always levy the full amount of contributions from the county councils, which the Schemes permitted, and they often had a balance in hand of over £2,000. He strongly deprecated this practice and advised the Central Welsh Board to reduce their fees and levy the full contributions from the local authorities.[2] There was another matter on the financial side which demanded radical change due to the rising cost of secondary education. Many intermediate schools provided preparatory classes for children under twelve, and also post-matriculation and university intermediate courses. Edwards ruled that greater economy could be effected by the prevention of unnecessary overlapping in the system of elementary schools, secondary schools, and university colleges.[3]

In the *Board of Education Report* for 1910 attention was called to the health of school pupils. It was suggested that proper feeding arrangements should be available in schools, and, since a large number of pupils had to travel by rail, and many had to be accommodated in lodgings, proper supervision was necessary. For example, the two Welsh counties with the largest numbers of pupil-lodgers were Cardiganshire and Carmarthenshire, with 169 and 175 respectively. The main factors accounting for the presence of young lodgers were a scattered population, the absence of convenient facilities for travelling, and the poverty of many parents that made it impossible for them to pay boarding fees. It was essential that such lodgers should go to approved lodging-houses, and that they should be properly supervised by the schools. In the same way, co-operation between Heads and staffs of schools (and the appointment of train prefects and monitors) the servants of the railway companies, and the travelling public, could be invaluable in ensuring the safety and good behaviour of school pupils.[4]

---

[1] *Report of the Board of Education, Welsh Department*, 1913, op. cit., pp. 9-10. Minutes of Central Welsh Board, op. cit., 18 December 1914.
[2] Minutes of Central Welsh Board, ibid.: 3 May 1912; 16 May, 1912: 'It appears to me that the Central Welsh Board are being paid twice for the same work—the second time by the children's fees. (Minute by Owen Edwards).
[3] *Report of the Board of Education, Welsh Department*, 1912, op. cit., pp. 13-14.
[4] Ibid. for 1910, op. cit., p. 22; ibid. for 1913, pp. 13 ff.

The Explosive Report

Finally, Edwards, from bitter experience, ventured to allude to some of the disadvantages under which the executive committee of the Central Welsh Board laboured. The committee's 'honorary offices had almost become offices for life' and there was a tendency 'to a stereotyped kind of representation which excluded some LEAs and nearly all the schools from what would be a very educative participation in its work'. From the beginning, not more than four schools had ever been represented on the executive committee. One of the curious and characteristic features of this committee was the fact that although it referred important matters to sub-committees, most of them never met. But most serious of all was the Board's lack of interest in educational matters beyond the Principality, tending to make it rather parochial in outlook. If, as a body, it were made acquainted with reports and publications which described educational activities elsewhere, its horizon would be considerably widened and it could learn much.[1]

Edwards was always careful—in order to guide the Central Welsh Board into a new order of things, and to move them to implement his suggestions for change—to crown his Reports with the adroit use of a little flattery and words of encouragement along with the recognition of any activities in the direction of reform. In the *Report* for 1910, immediately following the explosive one, he made two observations in order 'to prevent misconceptions': first, although the Reports of the Central Welsh Board were used, the *Report of the Board of Education*, as in former years, was based on information supplied by their own inspectors, and 'the responsibility for the accuracy of the facts and for the justice of the conclusions' was entirely that of the Board of Education; second, the Board of Education had 'purposely called attention to defects rather than to excellences', and they also believed that criticism was more useful than praise, and suggestions for future development were more valuable than praise of the past.[2] In the *Reports* for 1911 and 1912 the executive committee of the Central Welsh Board was commended for the energy and determination displayed in overcoming the initial difficulties of new developments, and the governors of schools were praised for their willingness to try new experiments 'in the modern demand for reconstruction'.[3] In this connection, it was significant that between 1911 and 1913 the number of copies of the Board of Education's annual *Report* had increased in circulation from 300 to 1,800.[4]

[1] Ibid. for 1912, op. cit., p. 13.
[2] *Report of the Board of Education, Welsh Department*, op. cit., 1910, p. 23.
[3] Ibid. for 1911, p. 13; for 1912, p. 17.
[4] Ibid. for 1913, p. 23.

The Explosive Report

The explosive *Report* blew many cobwebs away from the Central Welsh Board system and initiated reforms that sought to create a more modern and streamlined institution. Criticism and censure were not solely responsible for the conflict between the Welsh Department of the Board of Education and the Central Welsh Board. There were other, more permanent factors, of much deeper consequence, involved. It seems clear, from the evidence, that varying degrees of incompatibility existed between two personalities, two ideologies, and two administrative bodies. In their official roles, Edwards and Owen had few things in common—both were meticulously efficient and conscientious inspectors and neither excelled in administration; but in all things else they differed. Edwards, pre-occupied with the reform of a secondary school system, involved in every problem of Welsh education at national level, and an incessant traveller in his calling, was no office man, and had no use for telephones nor private secretaries.[1] Owen was the servant of the fractious Central Welsh Board—his duty to ensure that the Board functioned as a well-lubricated machine. He was happy in his office, had an eye for detail, but a slow worker 'with a tremendous capacity for working, but not for work'.[2] Overwhelmed with administrative minutiae and with a small office staff, he could not maintain a high standard of administrative efficiency.[3] To many people, his appointment as Chief Inspector of the Central Welsh Board was disastrous. He was set in his ways, and encouraged the tendency that existing staffs and possibly social pressures were bringing about, to turn the new intermediate schools into socially-exclusive and even Anglicised bodies. To him educationally, Wales meant a system of well run intermediate schools. The inadequate financing of the Central Welsh Board led Owen towards a multiplication of examinations so as to gain fees—so that the new schools began very quickly to turn into 'cram-schools' dominated by external examinations.[4]

---

[1] G. Arthur Jones, *Bywyd a Gwaith Owen Morgan Edwards*, Aberystwyth, 1958, p. 77. Edwards attended to his vast burden of secretarial work personally, mostly at Neuadd Wen (Whitehall), Llanuwchllyn, Merioneth. He had no use for typists or typewriters. He wrote practically everything—even at his office at the Board of Education—in beautiful, tiny, but very legible writing. All the masses of documents and Reports in the official files were written likewise. This must be unique in Civil Service administration.

[2] Percy E. Watkins, *A Welshman Remembers: An Autobiography*, Cardiff, 1944, p. 6. Watkins, early in his career, was the first Clerk to the Central Welsh Board and was in daily touch with Owen.

[3] See Study No. 5, the Jolliffe Case.

[4] A. C. Impey, one of my M.Ed. students, has given information on education in Cardiff in 'The development of State-Provided Education in Cardiff, 1870–1939'. (Unpublished, University of Wales, M.Ed. dissertation, 1973).
C. Carr, *The Spinning Wheel: History of Cardiff School for Girls*, Cardiff, 1955, p. 42. For example, in Cardiff, the Girls' School opened in 1895 was run by Miss Mary Collin. Educated at Bedford College; taught in the Channel Isles, and then in a small private school in Cardiff. She organized the school closely modelled on the Schools of Girls' Public Day School Trust, even insisting on calling her school a 'High School'. There was no school in the afternoons; she kept the number of scholarships to a minimum and recruited pupils mainly from the private schools of Cardiff.
The Boys' School, opened in 1898 under J. J. Findlay, operated a House System, prefects, compulsory games, etc. In neither school did Welsh occupy an important position.

Edwards, as His Majesty's Chief Inspector of Education for Wales, was the servant, not only of the Board of Education, but also of Wales. Wales was his parish, the Welsh people his parishioners, and the constant theme of his pastoral letters—the annual *Reports* of the Welsh Department of the Board of Education—was the creation of a viable national system of education, embracing all institutions of learning. He was universally respected as a national figure, who was at home in the Welsh elementary and secondary schools, in the Training Colleges, the University Colleges, at the meetings of the Central Welsh Board, in the farm-houses of rural Wales and the terraced dwelling houses of the mining valleys and industrial areas. More important still, he was known, through his writings and periodicals—which were eagerly bought—to all the Welsh people and their children. He maintained that Welsh children were the brightest and ablest of all children he had seen in any country, and 'urged on by men like T. E. Ellis, A. H. D. Acland, R. A. Jones (Emrys ap Iwan), and Herbert Lewis, had provided them with literature for over 25 years', although this had meant spending every penny he earned together with the sacrifice of all his leisure. It was generally known in Wales that he 'stifled every ambition for rising in the study of (his) subject in order to write books for the education of the children and peasantry of Wales'.[1]

Both men had different ideologies. Owen, although born and nurtured in the rural Lleyn peninsula (Caernarvonshire), was educated at Oxford; ex-headmaster of an English boarding school, steeped in the traditional aura of the older grammar schools, and conservative to a high degree in matters academic. In short, a worthy and sincere traditionalist. To him, the Central Welsh Board was the perfect vehicle to convey pupils to university. In this respect he was Anwyl's lapdog, to be 'driven unmercifully', for Anwyl demanded the highest standards in the Central Welsh Board examinations, especially in Latin and Greek. Edwards was a practical visionary and educational reformer, born in the heart of rural Merioneth, educated at Bala Theological College, the University College of Wales, Aberystwyth, Glasgow University (where he studied under Professor Edward Caird) and at Oxford, and had travelled extensively on the continent. His dream was the creation of a truly Welsh system of secondary education which should cater for all types of children.

He firmly believed that the role of the school in the community was as important as its role within the Central Welsh Board—a joint involvement, where the educational process was symbiotic—the latter enriching the former by providing appropriate intellectual stimuli for academic pupils,

---

[1] PRO Ed 24/588: Report by Owen Edwards to the President, op. cit., p. 14.

and the fullest degree of differentiation in curricula for the vast majority who returned to their homes and occupations in their neighbourhoods. But there were Jeremiahs both within and without the Central Welsh Board who considered that the principle of adaptation or differentiation, if extended substantially would be incompatible with the juggernaut of the examination system and certificates, and in their reluctance to depart from that system, suspected that Edwards might be flinging bridges hastily constructed which would, perhaps, later on, have to be as hastily abandoned.

Then there remained the discontent between the Central Welsh Board and the Welsh Department of the Board of Education, for which, the historical background was mainly responsible. Ten years before the creation of the latter, the former had already planned its system of secondary education for Wales by its network of intermediate schools. The original county schemes, carefully thought out by the early pioneers, incorporated progressive educational ideas, which had, unfortunately, been allowed to lapse in favour of a narrow, traditional curriculum, intensely academic in content. The Central Welsh Board had never anticipated a rival administrative body within the Board of Education (although they had hoped to inherit the functions of the abortive Welsh National Council for Education) and the unexpected creation of the Welsh Department, with responsibility for administering the Act of 1902 for Wales, meant that the new Department had three roles to play in the field of Welsh secondary education: (a) responsibility for the new municipal secondary schools; (b) the right of access to inspect the older intermediate schools; (c) from 1907, was required to report to Parliament on the work of the Central Welsh Board. These were the reasons for the unsteady and bitter relationships between the two administrative bodies. Several attempts on the part of the Central Welsh Board to acquire the newer schools and to be solely responsible for the inspection of all secondary schools, on legislative grounds, proved to be insoluble. But the most mortifying and embarrassing situation, which produced the deepest cleavage, was the appointment of Edwards as HMCI, who, in his fulfilment of the three roles, not only had to report on the work of the Central Welsh Board, but also presumed to reform what he considered to be an obsolescent system.

But all the blame for their blunderings and indiscretions could not be laid at the door of the Central Welsh Board. Their lack of imagination and planning for a more comprehensive system of education was hindered and blocked by other considerations. As an institution performing its basic functions of inspecting and examining, it was, in Edwards's words 'as perfect as any system of that kind could be'.[1] But the Board had to contend, not only with the Welsh Department of the Board of Education, but also with the governing bodies of schools, the LEAs and the University of Wales, which at that time was badly in need of reform both from the administrative and academic aspects. Distinguished scholarship is not always commensurate with, or a qualification for good leadership and administration, and Anwyl was hardly an exception to this criterion. His henchman, Lord Sheffield, seemed on many occasions to be considerably hampered by his own pomposity, coupled with deep resentment towards the Welsh Department, in his frequent deliberations at the meetings of the executive committee of the Central Welsh Board.

Before the creation of the Welsh Department, the Board of Education could not be absolved from some measure of stricture, for, as far back as 1901 the Board complained 'there are not wanting indications of a tendency to assimilate Welsh intermediate schools to a single type by softening down differences of curriculum ... the broad principle of differentiation of schools is, in their opinion, matter for the serious consideration of the Central Welsh Board as an inspecting authority'.[2] In subsequent *Reports*, the same theme was repeated, punctuated by unfavourable comments by examiners of the Central Welsh Board on the poor teaching of the English subjects and Science. Yet the Board of Education were as inactive on these matters as the Welsh Board. After 1907, action was not delayed, for the Board of Education, through the Welsh Department, sent Edwards and Casson to every meeting of the executive committee and full meetings of the Welsh Board, where minutes were taken, and Edwards was able to bring up important matters and get them discussed. No more dust could be swept under the carpet—Edwards lifted it up as a preliminary to a thorough spring-cleaning of the whole system—hence the resentment of the Central Welsh Board, and the consternation of the Board of Education when their *Report* caused such a disturbance.

The LEAs and governing bodies of schools were not alive to their responsibilities under each county scheme, were slow to adopt measures which could make the schools more adaptable, but always looked forward to the publication of examination results. Tremendous interest was always displayed when questions of finance arose. For example, when

---

[1] Report of the Board of Education, Welsh Department, for 1910, op. cit., p. 6.

[2] *Report of the Board of Education on thr Administration of Schools, under the Welsh Intermediate Education Act* 1889, for 1901, pp. 6–7, Report by W. de W. Abney.

The Explosive Report

Bursars, who were in receipt of grants from the LEAs failed their Senior examination (because it was too difficult), there were vigorous protests from the larger LEAs like Denbighshire, Glamorgan and Carmarthenshire.[1] In most schools, the highlight of the school year for governing bodies was the annual Speech or Prize Day, when the headmaster could announce an impressive list of examination successes. They also appointed the heads and school staff, and conscientious governors and heads always concerned themselves with the teaching efficiency of school staffs. But others, less interested in this matter gave little encouragement to teachers to attend courses in order to better themselves and improve their class teaching. In all these matters, the Central Welsh Board had little control and could not be blamed.

Finally, the University of Wales (at that time composed of three constituent Colleges at Aberystwyth, Cardiff and Bangor) had intimate relationships with the Central Welsh Board, the secondary schools, and the Welsh Department.[2] But, apart from the fact that the examinations of the Central Welsh Board were geared to the University, and that Edwards was involved indirectly with the Day Training Departments of those Colleges, one of the really crucial matters with reference to the *Report* was the Welsh language which was so badly taught in the schools. This could be attributed very largely to the kind of Welsh teaching provided in the University—and it should be remembered that the Professor of Welsh at Aberystwyth was Edward Anwyl, chairman of the Central Welsh Board. Edwards pointed out the absurd situation where 'a lecturer who *knows* the language, and you have students who *know* the language, and Welsh is taught, not by means of that language, but by means of a foreign language—English'.[3] The University courses in Welsh 'were too narrow in character, too much restricted to the history and philology of the Welsh language, *and too little concerned with the literature, history, and civilization of the Welsh people*'.[4] The graduates in Welsh left the Colleges to teach in the secondary schools, and it was little wonder that the

---

[1] Minutes, Central Welsh Board, op. cit., 27 October, 1911; 15 December, 1912.

[2] Edwards to Lewis, 10 April 1909, Penucha MSS: 'We cannot, of course, interfere with the University of Wales. Such interference would be resented at once. But ... the relations between the Welsh Department and the University are closer and more cordial ... than those between the Board of Education and any other University. I have had long and exceedingly harmonious conferences with the Day Training Committees of each of the Colleges ... and with small committees of the professors ... the result will be a very important modification in the interest of intending teachers, in the degree courses of the University'.

[3] *Royal Commission on University Education in Wales*, op. cit., *Appendix to Final Report*, 1918, Minute 12,834, p. 108.

[4] ibid.: pp. 55–56. Principal J. H. Davies said that 'Sir John Rhys, Professor of Celtic at Oxford, and late Principal of Jesus College ... taught most of the University teachers of Welsh, including J. Morris Jones and Edward Anwyl. Their main interests were philological, to the neglect of Welsh literature. Young students who came to the Welsh Colleges were full of zeal for Welsh literature or Welsh history, desiring to take Honours in Welsh, after having a fair training in Latin ... the teaching of Latin in the Welsh schools, especially the rural ones from which we get our Welsh scholars, is not of a very high standard. They are thrown into the midst of the philological whirlpool, and of course they lose all interest'.

The Explosive Report

unfortunate pupils were taught so much formal grammar, and little, if any, literature. Again, for this state of affairs, the Central Welsh Board could not be censured, neither could they be held responsible for the poor teaching of the subject, for the University Training Departments, which had no facilities for proper instruction in Welsh methodology, sent ill-equipped teachers to the schools, and this had been the rule for twenty-one years.[1]

But the effective teaching of Welsh, and its place in the schools of Wales was to be a very long-term problem. Although Edwards showed the way, the question was only tackled peripherally during his lifetime and still remains to be solved. It became the subject of more than one major report, from 1927[2] to the Gittins Report forty years later.[3]

[1] *Royal Commission on University Education in Wales*, op. cit., Minute 12,844, p. 109.
[2] *Welsh in Education and Life*, (*Y Gymraeg Mewn Addysg a Bywyd*), Board of Education, HMSO, 1927
[3] *Primary Education in Wales, A Report of the Central Advisory Council for Education (Wales)*, HMSO, 1967.

APPENDICES

I   EDWARDS'S SUMMARY OF JONES'S CRITICISMS: Facsimile

II   FACSIMILE PAGE OF OWEN EDWARDS'S WAY OF WRITING MINUTES: Facsimile

The Explosive Report

APPENDIX I

Edwards's Summary of Jones's Criticisms

Board of Education.   MINUTE PAPER.   31.

Regd. No.

P. 24.

"To all this, as to any other good feature in our schools, the Welsh Department of the Board of Education is deliberately blind."

This summary of the most mischievous and most misleading speech delivered in Wales within living memory is got at by —

i/. Taking two sections out of twenty-four, and thereby giving the Report the meaning which, of all meanings, we are most anxious to avoid.

ii/. Saying that we quote the most condemnatory parts of the C.W.B. Report on one subject, and denying by silence the fact that we quote the most laudatory passages about all the rest.

iii/. Assuming that our Report is based on that of the C.W.B. for last year, while the fact is that all the statements are made on our own responsibility and from our own knowledge. We do, of course, as far as possible, quote the C.W.B. examiners; and we say so when we differ from them.

iv/. Ignoring the fact that, with one insignificant exception, we have recommended the Treasury to pay all grants in full.

v/. Ignoring the fact that in last year's Report we made exactly the same accusations. This year we said that the system tends to make children "wooden and unintelligent"; last year we said it tended to produce "mental helplessness".

vi/. Ignoring the fact that the whole of the Report has been written with a view to recommending remedies. These suggestions are not even considered.

vii/. Wilfully shutting eyes to the delicately-put compliment in the last line of the Report, the highest compliment that the Board of Education or anybody else has ever paid to the Intermediate School system in Wales.

O. Edwards.
18.XI.10.

PRO Ed. 24/588

APPENDIX II

Page of Owen Edwards's Method of Writing Minutes

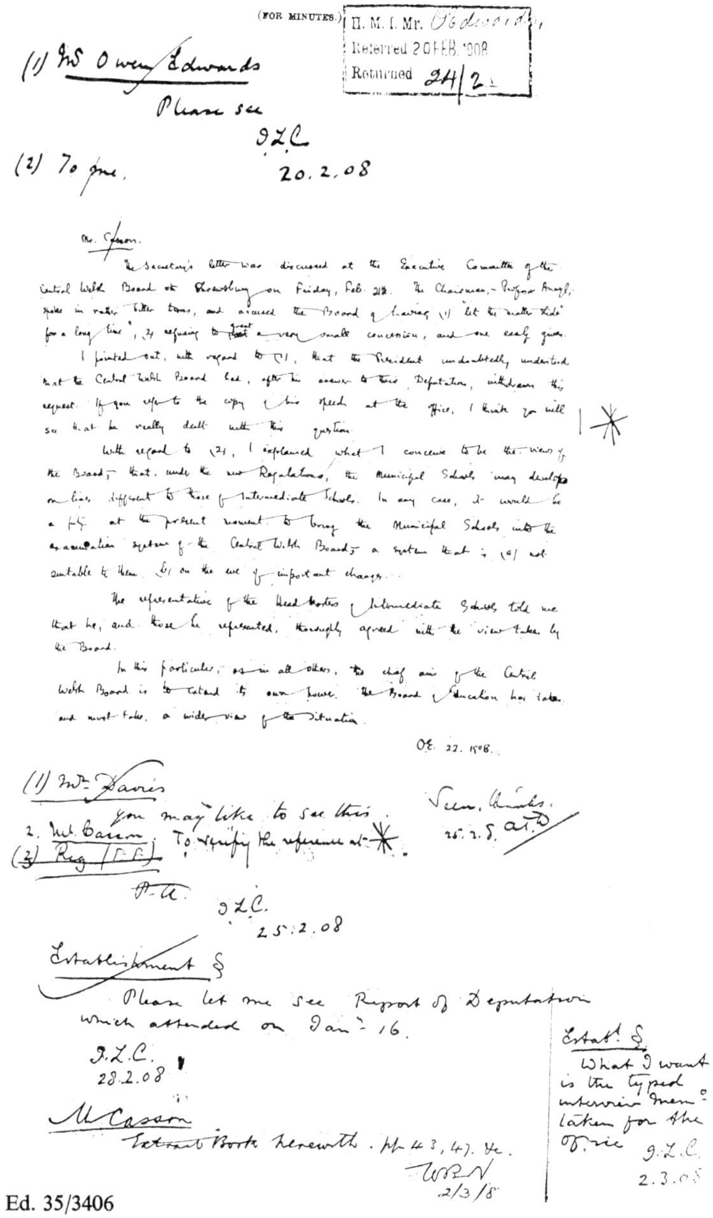

(FOR MINUTES.) H. M. I. Mr. O'Edwards,
Referred 20 FEB. 1908
Returned 24/2.

(1) Mr. Owen Edwards
Please see
I.Z.C.
(2) To me.
20.2.08

Mr. Gasson.

The Secretary's letter was discussed at the Executive Committee of the Central Welsh Board at Shrewsbury on Friday, Feb. 21st. The Chairman, – Professor Angel, spoke in rather bitter terms, and accused the Board of having (1) "let the matter slide" for a long time", (2) refusing to grant a very small concession, and one easily given.

I pointed out, with regard to (1), that the President undoubtedly understood that the Central Welsh Board had, after his answer to their Deputation, withdrawn this request. If you refer to the copy of his speech at the Office, I think you will see that he really dealt with this question.

With regard to (2), I explained what I conceive to be the views of the Board; that, under the new Regulations, the Municipal Schools may develop on lines different to those of Intermediate Schools. In any case, it would be a pity at the present moment to bring the Municipal Schools into the examination system of the Central Welsh Board; a system that is (a) not suitable to them, (b) on the eve of important changes.

The representative of the Head Masters of Intermediate Schools told me that he, and those he represented, thoroughly agreed with the view taken by the Board.

In this particular, as in all others, the chief aim of the Central Welsh Board is to extend its own power. The Board of Education has taken, and must take, a wider view of the situation.

O.E. 22. 1908.

(1) Mr. Davies
You may like to see this.
2. Mr. Gasson. To verify the reference at ✳.
(3) Reg. (E.B.)
A.C.
I.Z.C.
25.2.08

Seen, thanks.
26.2.8. A.T.D.

Establishment §
Please let me see Report of Deputation which attended on Jan. 16.
I.Z.C.
28.2.08

M Casson
Extract Book herewith. pp 43, 47. &c.
W.B.N.
2/3/8

Estab. §
What I want is the typed interview mem. taken for the Office
I.Z.C.
2.3.08

PRO Ed. 35/3406

VI

THE WELSH DEPARTMENT, BOARD OF EDUCATION 1907–1925

INTRODUCTION 308

I ADJUSTMENT AND GENERAL OBJECTIVES 310

II EXTENSION OF RESPONSIBILITIES 324

III GROWTH AND RE-ORGANIZATION OF THE WELSH INSPECTORATE 337

APPENDICES 367

The Welsh Department, Board of Education, 1907-1925

THE main task which confronted Davies and Edwards at the Board of Education was to ensure that the new Department should not only function as an integral part of the Board, but also contribute to the enrichment of Welsh national life and culture. The assumption of responsibilities by the two men at that particular time brought them face to face with many delicate problems and situations, most of which have already been discussed in the foregoing studies.

It has been said that men appear in history in complementary, yet contrasting pairs. Such a pair were Davies and Edwards. Before his appointment, Davies, who had on his own admission a lucrative legal practice in Liverpool, was unknown in Wales apart from his membership of the Denbighshire county council from 1904 to 1907. He had acted more than once as Liberal agent for Lloyd George at the hustings. A typical late Victorian and Edwardian figure, whose word on the household hearth was law, he never really established a close bond between himself and his children.[1] On the administrative side he had considerable ability and his memoranda and reports were concise and always couched in polished legal phraseology. He relished his role as a senior civil servant and all that went with it. But his partner in his former legal practice opined that Davies's brashness and egotism could make him a most difficult person to work with.[2]

Much more is known about Edwards.[3] His was already a national name. When he assumed office as Chief Inspector of education for Wales and was released from Oxford, he forthwith returned to his native heath at Llanuwchllyn which became his official headquarters for his work in the Principality.[4] According to one of his successors, 'he was not, by nature, expert or adroit in committees and such gatherings',[5] an observation which requires some qualification. Indeed, when occupied with

---

[1] I am indebted to Mr. A. Mervyn Davies, Wilton, Connecticut, USA, for a frank, personal discussion relating to his late father.

[2] Herbert Lewis's Diary, 21 January 1907, Penucha MSS.

[3] A great deal is revealed in these Studies. Also, *Pioneers of Welsh Education*, op. cit., Bibliographical notes by Wynne Ll. Lloyd.

[4] During his latter years, after an illness, more time was spent in London: 'I mean, during the coming winter, to spend alternate weeks at the Board . . . I really live in London, it should be my official centre.' Edwards to Lewis, 27 September 1918, Penucha MSS.

[5] *Pioneers of Welsh Education*, op. cit., p. 98.

The Welsh Department

important national committees, for example, the Royal Commission on University Education in Wales, he was extremely patient and astute. His role on the Commission in listening to, and examining and cross-examining large numbers of witnesses, together with his balanced and mature judgement on the evidence, revealed that he possessed considerable skill in negotiating an argument. But in the realm of routine administration perhaps he was less at home; if, at committees of lesser ilk, for example, the Central Welsh Board, where so often, mundane and trivial matters were discussed, signs of impatience and intolerance appeared, he could be forgiven. Nevertheless, if the by-products of such committees as recorded in his official papers in the form of minutes, reports and memoranda are consulted, they remain fascinating and absorbing reading in their incisive turn of phrase and brilliant verbal repartee.[1]

No attempt is made in this study to make a full assessment of Edwards's personality and character. Others have been made in the past but none of them satisfactory, apart from W. J. Gruffydd's volume which deals with his early life.[2] It would be superfluous to repeat what has already been examined in his papers. Therein lies an interpretation of important aspects of his work in later life—in truth—a large part of his biography.

The outbreak of the first world war, when the financial and administrative resources of the country were diverted to the prosecution of the war made the work of the two chief officials difficult. During the first period of its existence up to 1915, the Welsh Department encountered inevitable teething troubles associated with administrative complications within the Board of Education, the struggle with the Central Welsh Board, and the acquisition of such new responsibilities as technical education and the structuring of a new Welsh inspectorate. The second period after 1918 saw further adjustments, such as reforms in the examination system of the Central Welsh Board, and the complete re-organization of the Welsh inspectorate and inspectorial terrain. By 1925, a broad, sound basis of co-operation had been achieved between the Board of Education and the Welsh Department, for the latter had learned to use the resources of the former in administrative and specialized expertise, which, however, in some instances was only placed at their disposal with some reluctance by the Board. Moreover, at the end of the war, the LEAs which had become more important with increasing responsibilities, especially after the Education Act of 1918, and the Central Welsh Board, which was becoming

---

[1] See Appendix I. His additional comments on the Board of Education's Minutes of the Central Welsh Board afford excellent examples.

[2] W. J. Gruffydd, *Owen Morgan Edwards: Cofiant, Cyfrol I*, 1858–1883, Aberystwyth, 1937.

a more flexible body, began to realize that it was to their advantage to work in closer harmony with Whitehall. Perhaps the matter of greatest educational significance in the period 1907–1925 and afterwards, was the stubborn refusal of the Welsh Department and the Central Welsh Board to abdicate their individual responsibility in the field of Welsh secondary education especially regarding the awkward relationship of dual inspection of schools.

This and other controversial matters during this period have been discussed. This study is concerned with the preliminary problems of the Welsh Department on the administrative side in the development of its work in Wales and the extension of its sphere of responsibility in its formative years.

I ADJUSTMENT AND GENERAL OBJECTIVES

In his attempts to adjust, consolidate and develop the separate identity of the Welsh Department, which meant nothing less than 'the gradual transference to the Welsh Department of the administration of *all* branches of education in Wales',[1] Davies met with obstruction and resentment from many officials at the Board of Education. It has been seen how Phipps, chief clerk to the Board, had complained of additional work in his department, which the creation of the Welsh Department had entailed; his displeasure that extra staff would be necessary for that Department; and the President's refusal to accede to Davies's request (strongly backed by Edwards) for a separate annual report for Wales, etc.

But there were other matters which gave rise to some disquiet and friction. The biting and hurtful rebuff which Davies suffered at the hands of the Board's S.I.R. (Publications) Department,[2] including Dr. Heath, was undoubtedly the result of Davies's inexperience as a civil servant. In all good faith Davies had suggested to the President (in a letter which was, unfortunately, not too carefully worded and rather pompous) reasons for initiating a series of educational publications which might furnish the Welsh people with some 'ocular evidence' of what the Welsh Department was doing to justify its existence. He was of the opinion that the literary output from the 'English side' of the Board had little or no application to Wales and was practically useless for Welsh purposes. He proceeded to criticize rather recklessly the 'stiff and very official-looking documents ... issuing from the Board to Wales'. He suggested publications with 'more of the human element' which would show that the Welsh

[1] PRO Ed 23/244, Minute from Davies to Heath, 5 March 1914.
[2] Special Inquiries and Reports Department.

The Welsh Department

Department could be helpful in a thoroughly practical way to the LEAs and teachers of Wales, and would also demonstrate that the central authority in London 'knew how to recognize and make use of, such expert opinion as was to be found in Wales, and to turn it to good account'.[1] Davies further presumed to enlighten the President as to the course of action, mentioning that he had received complaints from a leading Welsh publisher and 'other mutterings to the same effect' that the Board were not publishing (as had been the practice in the past) extracts from HMIs reports which 'gave a graphic description of the state of elementary education in both countries'. He was quite convinced—and thought that Edwards felt the same—'that unless something was done, it was quite possible that these sentiments would find expression in Parliament' and that the President might have 'a bad quarter of an hour in the House' on account of a Department, which, although it was endeavouring to do good and effective work from the administrative point of view, had not yet given 'in accustomed directions those evidences of it which the public were wont to look for and to expect, if not demand'. He proffered advice to the President as to how the problem might be solved. A most useful purpose would be served if the Welsh Department brought out 'in the red garb which is now the familiar badge of the Department' a series of handy pamphlets dealing with a number of practical subjects 'in regard to which there was a need in Wales for the dissemination of useful information'.[2] Whilst acknowledging the great experience and scholarship of Edwards 'in the fields of authorship and publishing', Davies could not forbear from impressing upon the President that he himself knew 'what it is to write and to publish books and pamphlets which, in every case have speedily found a market and run through several large editions, ... so that, between us ... the Welsh Department ought to be able to turn out some educational booklets which would be interesting, practical and useful ... especially designed to meet the particular needs of Wales'.[3]

The President, naturally, passed on the letter and the proposed scheme to Dr. Heath, Director of S.I.R., for his consideration and report. It is a matter for conjecture whether or not Davies had access to the reply sent to the President on the next day, 3 December. No reply could have been made so expeditiously, treated with such urgency and with utter contempt for the whole project. One thing was clear, that no action was taken to

[1] PRO Ed 24/585, Davies to the President, 2 December 1909.
[2] Ibid.
[3] Ibid.

The Welsh Department

implement Davies's proposals on that occasion. But several years later and in a more leisurely manner, the Welsh Department published a useful series of St. David's Day pamphlets for the encouragement of the teaching and study of Welsh literature and history[1] and in 1916, a volume entitled *A Nation and Its Books* was issued containing 'lists of Welsh books and books relating to Wales and other information respecting libraries, books and home reading'.[2]

The occasion of the reply and the form which it embodied, demonstrated very clearly the attitude of certain officials of the Board towards the Welsh Department. Davies could be excused for his ignorance of official procedure as practised by experienced and unemotional civil servants, but his tactless act of criticizing S.I.R. and his lack of modesty in the publishing field provoked an extremely unpleasant and sarcastic response. With every desire to be sympathetic, the S.I.R. official who studied and discussed the proposals with Dr. Heath, dismissed Davies's scheme as 'a very absurd bid for self-advertisement', did not consider them germane to the interests of the Welsh Department, and objected to the whole principle involved, on five counts, each one directly aimed to undermine the individuality of the Welsh Department in its desire to serve specific Welsh needs.[3]

The first was the 'constitutional objection', for S.I.R. which was part of the central staff of the Board—acting for the Board as a whole, including the Welsh Department—was unwilling that a separate publication department should be set up for Wales. It was 'extremely necessary that there should be only one Publications Department ... in order that the Board's policy with regard to publications might be consistent, and to secure their being controlled by *expert minds*'. Secondly, it was affirmed that Davies's proposal was based on 'a huge educational fallacy', namely, that all school subjects required special treatment in Wales, or for Wales, which was an 'absurd proposition'. Thereafter, the topics of Davies's scheme for proposed publications were mauled about unmercifully by the S.I.R. For example, 'was the place of Music and the teaching of Home-making in a Welsh school so different from an English school?; school gardens—do flowers and vegetables ... grow differently in a Welsh school garden?; regarding rural schools, is the problem different in Wales, and what does Mr. Davies know about it? But the most delicious of all the proposed pamphlets would be No. 11, "*The Civil Service as a Career for Welsh Boys*" ... I should like to discuss the possibilities of this pamphlet,

---

[1] *Report of the Board of Education (Welsh Department), The Patriotic Publications of the Welsh Department (illustrated)*, 1917, p. 18.
[2] Ibid., for 1916, p. 8.
[3] PRO Ed 24/585, D.S.I.R. to the President, 3 December 1909.

but I won't.'[1] Thirdly, it was stated that many questions dealt with in the proposed pamphlets were those that could be best handled by HMIs, and could be produced, if needed, by LEAs or by publishing firms if they thought that there was a market for them. Fourthly, it was the policy of the Board to publish pamphlets on educational developments and problems, i.e. 'S.I.R. published to meet each occasion ... but Davies desired to manufacture occasions for publishing'.[2]

Finally, Davies's attention was drawn to certain important points regarding proper procedure should the Welsh Department require guidance. He was reminded that since his scheme involved the services of the higher officers of the Board who were not attached to the Welsh Department, 'he, with apparent intention, omitted all reference to the Central Publication Department ... which was possessed of expert knowledge in such matters'.[3] Furthermore, should any problem specially affecting education in Wales creating the need for special guidance to Welsh LEAs arise, the proper course would be for the Welsh Department to approach S.I.R., who, after consultation with, and having received the approval of the Heads of the Office, would proceed to produce the necessary pamphlet or other publication, to see that it should be cast in such form as to meet the special needs of Wales. The last paragraph of this memorandum was revealing in its contempt both for Davies and the Welsh Department: 'it might even be arranged that any such (Welsh) publications should be bound in red covers; but that appears, after all, to be the matter to which Mr. Davies attaches most importance'.[4]

Since Davies and Edwards were not established civil servants when they assumed their appointments, special adjustments were necessary in formal matters such as pension rights and ceremonial dress. Edwards, as Chief Inspector came under clause IV of the Superannuation Act, 1859, receiving the 'addition of years' of an inspector of schools, viz. 5 years or less according to his age. But in the case of Davies it appeared doubtful whether the Treasury would acknowledge the office of Secretary to the Welsh Department as one coming under the same clause of the Superannuation Act. Furthermore, he had not, apparently, received his appointment directly from the Crown nor had he entered the service with a certificate from the Civil Service Commission. If that was so, Section 17 of the Superannuation Act would not have been complied with, and Davies's

---

[1] PRO Ed 24/585, D.S.I.R. to the President, 3 December 1909.
[2] Ibid.
[3] Ibid.
[4] Ibid.

The Welsh Department

pension prospects seemed to be endangered.[1] Phipps, on enquiring whether this matter had been considered when the appointment was made, was informed in the negative,[2] and McKenna himself had to confirm that Davies 'certainly was promised, and must have the usual pension, but not any addition of years'[3] and this was confirmed by the Treasury on 21 June 1907.[4]

The status or standing of the new Welsh Department in relation to State ceremonial occasions or 'pomp and circumstance' had to be considered. Whether or not Davies had requested parity of treatment with other government departments in the matter of ceremonial dress is not clear (although he had certainly raised the question of dress), but McKenna had conveyed to Morant 'that as the Board of Trade, Office of Works, Post Office, Local Government Board and Agriculture have only got third class uniforms for their Permanent and Parliamentary Secretaries, he could not see his way clear to pressing for a second class for the Secretary of a small Department of this Board'.[5]

The 'Milne incident' was yet another example of an unfortunate misunderstanding which arose between the Welsh Department and the Technical Branch of the Board during the initial stages of adjustment, due to ignorance about matters of procedure and lack of co-ordination.[6] Milne, a Junior Examiner (or administrative assistant), who had been allocated to the Welsh Department by Morant, had committed an administrative indiscretion, which not only aroused the anger of his former master, but also produced a delicate situation between the Welsh Department and the Board on a matter relating to the education of defective children in Swansea. On 21 September 1910, Milne, in reply to a minute from Davies, who sought his opinion, quite openly volunteered his own views on the situation by suggesting that the Welsh Department

---

[1] PRO Ed 23/242, Minute from Staff Records Department to Phipps, 14 May 1907.

[2] Ibid. Minute from Phipps to Richmond, 15 May.

[3] Ibid. Morant to Phipps, 30 May.

[4] Ibid. Treasury to Board of Education, 21 June: 'I am directed by the Lords Commissioners of His Majesty's Treasury to transmit, for the information of the Board of Education, copy of a Minute which They are causing to be laid before Parliament, bringing the office of Permanent Secretary to the Welsh Department of the Board of Education under the operation of Section 4 of the Superannuation Act, 1859', G. H. Murray.
Treasury Minute dated 17 June 1907: 'My Lords read Section 4 of the Superannuation Act, 1859. After consideration of a representation on the subject from the Board of Education, Their Lordships are pleased to declare that, for the due and efficient discharge of the duties of the office of Permanent Secretary to the Welsh Department of the Board of Education, professional or other peculiar qualifications, not ordinarily to be acquired in the Public Service, are required, and that it is for the interest of the Public that persons should be appointed thereto at an age exceeding that at which Public Service ordinarily begins. Their Lordships are, at the same time, pleased to direct that any holder of the aforesaid office may be entitled to Superannuation, but without any addition of years, although he may not hold his appointment directly from the Crown, and may not have entered the Service with a certificate from the Civil Service Commissioners'. (7/1324 Y.).

[5] Ibid. Morant to Phipps, 30 May 1907 (extracted from original on Levee File).

[6] PRO Ed 24/586, Documents relating to distribution of work between the T. Branch and the Welsh Department.

should provide grants for the post-elementary education of blind children at the Swansea institution under Secondary Regulations, should the Technical Branch (which controlled such education) fail to do so.[1] This aroused an angry response from Morant and E. K. Chambers, Head of the Technical Branch.[2] The latter protested against 'a serious interference by the Welsh Department with the work of T. Branch'.[3]

Before this incident, Chambers had already pointed out to Davies, on 15 September, 'that confusion had already arisen owing to the post-elementary work of the Swansea institution becoming the subject of concurrent correspondence with both Branches'.[4] Chambers could see many arguments 'both for the transference of all Welsh T. work to the Welsh Department, and for the transference of all post-elementary work for defectives, both in England and Wales, to those officers who dealt with the elementary work. But if a change was to be brought about, it ought to be as the result of a definite decision altering the arrangements established by the printed documents and not in contravention of those documents'.[5] Unfortunately, Davies, after three months delay, had re-opened the matter confessing that he 'found a difficulty in understanding the precise position',[6] to which Chambers retorted 'that this was very natural since it was a matter over which Davies had no administrative control'.[7] But at a subsequent conference with Morant,[8] Davies had intimated to Chambers 'his full acquiescence to the transference of the case to the Welsh Department with reference to the minute of 15 September',[9] and, furthermore, in a mild form of rebuke to Morant, urged 'that there should be more closeness of touch and more consultation between T. Branch and the Welsh Department, which is as essential to effective and smooth working as are other parts of the office machinery to which attention has been directed in this discussion.'[10] He reminded Morant that the problem had arisen in a similar case, (Rhondda), in March 1910, when Milne had understood from Maudsley—another official—that discussions were going on between T, E, L and Medical Branches respecting such children.[11] But the unfortunate Milne, the scapegoat, was made to

---

[1] PRO Ed 24/586, Minute from Milne to Davies, 21 September 1910.
[2] Ibid., Minute from Chambers to Morant, 8 December. Morant asked, in a marginal note 'Why this three months interval?'
[3] Ibid.
[4] Ibid., Minute from Chambers to Davies and Simpkinson, 15 September.
[5] Ibid.
[6] Ibid. Minute from Davies to Chambers, 6 December.
[7] Ibid. Minute from Chambers to Morant, 8 December.
[8] Ibid. Minute from Morant to Davies, 13 December.
[9] Ibid. Minute from Morant to Chambers, 31 December.
[10] Ibid. Minute from Davies to Morant, 19 December.
[11] Ibid.

apologize for an action which had occurred due to lack of co-operation between his masters—Morant and Davies.[1] Such an incident was necessary, apparently, to produce the adjustment.

One of Edwards's first acts after his appointment was to write to the President to ask for a discussion concerning his new work. He already knew most of the Welsh inspectors and had 'watched the growth of the (Welsh) system'. He had also thought a good deal about the second language question, the better training of teachers and the unity of the training system. Other subjects also required fairly immediate attention such as evening continuation schools, the drawing up of the Welsh edition of the Code and school libraries. Another matter brought to the President's attention, which had always concerned Edwards, was his connection with literature: 'For many years, all school books in Wales have been written by myself or by men I have brought up; books on Welsh history, nature study, folklore, nursery rhymes, etc., . . . I ought to explain that such work is not remunerative in the ordinary sense; it costs me a good deal every year. My own view is that I ought to continue it, provided it does not impair my efficiency or affect the independence of the teachers in Wales'.[2] Edwards was also anxious that his new office should not debar him from maintaining the closest touch with distinctively Welsh institutions, for instance his membership of the councils and courts of the University Colleges.

By October 1907 Edwards had developed his ideas on what he called the 'library movement'. His immediate objective was to secure good school libraries which might serve the remote Welsh rural areas.[3] His longer-term policy was to negotiate with John Ballinger, librarian of the new National Library at Aberystwyth, to link up the resources of the library with other academic institutions.[4] Just six months after his appointment, the library movement 'had extended as far as Penllyn, so far as country villages were concerned'—but he was disappointed. He found that school libraries, elementary and secondary, were exceedingly poor. His idea was to make the school—in country districts—the home of the library. This had been done at Llanuwchllyn, where 'the children are the bearers of books from the school to the home and back. In this way, parents realize the value of the school as a fountain of good literature, and the children are taught to become life-long students'.[5]

[1] Ibid. Minutes from Davies to Milne, Milne to Davies, 16 December.
[2] PRO Ed 24/581, Edwards to McKenna, 19 February 1907.
[3] Edwards to Lewis, 9 October 1907, Penucha MSS.
[4] Edwards to Lewis, 10 April 1909, Penucha MSS.
[5] Edwards to Lewis, 9 October 1907, Penucha MSS.

The Welsh Department

Wherever he went, Edwards drew his inspiration and ideas from among the ordinary Welsh people whom he sought to serve. He made the 'higher standard' children tell him what they had read during their leisure hours and where they procured their books. He was determined to 'place good literature within the reach of children and before their eyes, for the older books, which trained thought and style are neglected, and school children descend to the level of "Ally Sloper" and indecent postcards'.[1] He envisaged libraries (other than those in village schools) where established, should be managed by the parish councils, 'for people will not read books unless they feel that they have a right to them'. He called the attention of the best men of the districts to this 'crying need'; he told the children to demand a library and tried 'to arouse schoolmasters out of their apathy. ... On the whole, I think it is in this direction that I can do most good'.[2]

At the beginning of April 1909, just two years after the Welsh Department had started its work, Rowland's letter had appeared with its criticisms. Above all he accused the new Department of ignoring the Welsh University and the Central Welsh Board, and of being a disruptive influence rather than a power for national unity.[3] He further alleged that the Welsh Department favoured the claim of the Glamorgan and Monmouthshire LEAs to have Two Year Training Colleges of their own, and that the Welsh Department had no policy. Before the appearance of the explosive report of 1909 and the strained relationships with the Central Welsh Board after 1910, Edwards had paid a great deal of attention to that Body. Replying to Rowland's attack, and bearing in mind that the offending report for 1909 had not yet appeared, Edwards was able to say that the policy of the Central Welsh Board was often wrong and that, in one important direction at least, 'they had caused irreparable mischief to Welsh education ... but I state my views, not to the Press, but to the Chief Inspector of the Central Welsh Board, for whose devotion and pluck I have the most profound admiration; I try to influence his Board through him, and the relations between us have always been everything I could desire'.[4]

Edwards described the charge that the Welsh Department was a disruptive influence as a 'very unjust one' and maintained that they were rapidly becoming the unifying force in Wales: 'We see all the forces, while they (the LEAs, Central Welsh Board, and University) do not see each other, and we can get them to work harmoniously'. He admitted that

[1] Ibid.
[2] Edwards to Lewis, 9 October 1907, Penucha MSS.
[3] See Study No. IV, p.227.
[4] Edwards to Lewis, 10 April 1909, Penucha MSS.

there were many difficulties, especially with regard to the training of teachers 'where the LEAs and the University Colleges did not see eye to eye'. But the Welsh Department was able to bring together at a conference in Shrewsbury, representatives of the University Senate, the Central Welsh Board and the Headmasters' Association for the purpose of discussing this all-important matter: 'the air was cleared and now they are all co-operating heartily with us concerning the aims we placed before them ... and our ablest helper on this occasion was Principal Griffiths of Cardiff University College'.[1] The Welsh Department had nothing to do with the administration side of the Welsh Training Colleges so the Department could not favour the claims of one LEA against another. But Edwards did inspect the Training Colleges and since 1907 had been in constant touch with the LEAs while the long and constant deliberations were proceeding on this matter. Although Edwards (as he thought) had evolved 'as ideal a system as was possible at that time', and while 'North and Mid-Wales had got all that they wanted, the great LEAs of South Wales must fight the University and Tom John, over their long-laboured decisions and half-bought sites'.[2]

Rowland's further accusation that the Welsh Department had no policy, was, in one respect, true, since it was their business to implement policies which the Board of Education took from Parliament. Davies and Edwards could easily employ all their time in routine work—'Davies is overwhelmed with cases to advise about and schemes to amend ... I am doing the ordinary work done by two inspectors before my appointment ... but Davies and I have very definite *aims*, of which we never lose sight'.[3] A great deal of what Edwards had to say about his work is not recorded in the files of the Welsh Department; but much is revealed in his voluminous private correspondence with Lewis. One of his immediate aims was 'the place and teaching of Welsh—and giving the Welsh language its right place in the system of Welsh education'.[4] Edwards gave this a prominent place in the new Welsh edition of the Code, in the elementary and secondary schools, and in the Training Colleges: 'Welsh-speaking infants are now taught exclusively in Welsh; the direct method is becoming universal (and, when tested, is applied to the teaching of English to English, as well as to Welsh children); the educational advantages of teaching two languages are realized ... All our elementary school inspectors are now

---

[1] Ibid.
[2] Edwards to Lewis, 10 April 1909, Penucha MSS.
[3] Ibid. See also Study No. IV, p.227.
[4] PRO Ed 24/584, Edwards to the President, 27 November 1909.

fully alive to the importance of this question'.[1] Edwards claimed that when he came to the Welsh Department 'only about one-half of the secondary schools, though they were even then designed to take the place of Pupil Teacher Centres, taught Welsh. Now, owing to the new Secondary Regulations and our constant pressure, they nearly all provide teaching in Welsh'.[2] In 1907 nearly all intending teachers took French instead of Welsh, but in 1909 nearly 300 Pupil Teachers and Bursars took Welsh (an optional subject) in the Preliminary Examination for the Teachers' Certificate. In the same year Edwards was able to state that all the Training Colleges taught and provided training in Welsh, and that 'a way had been devised to provide grants to the Ysgol Haf [Summer School] and to evening classes in Welsh'.[3]

His other immediate aims were to strengthen and improve the Welsh inspectorate 'in order to get greater efficiency with more economy; more information for the Board, and more help for the LEAs and all types of schools'; providing education for defective children, and a complete system of Welsh Training Colleges. He intended to review the facilities for the education of blind, deaf and dumb children: 'I am afraid that many are not provided for at all. When they are, the poor little things are sent away to schools in England and taught to read and write English. When they come back, their parents do not understand them; their education stops, and they are no better off than they were before'.[4]

For the second year of his three-year plan, he had sketched a detailed scheme for a Welsh system of Training Colleges, unsectarian, and in keeping with the needs of Wales: 'The system is complete and practically sanctioned... but the University Colleges are raising a belated cry against it'.[5] He described the system as it then was, and the complete system as envisaged, together with his reasons and comments:

I The Welsh system of Training Colleges, 1909.

'There are now two types: (i) The Day Training Colleges attached to a University College. Of these, there are three, Aberystwyth, Bangor, Cardiff.

[1] Edwards to Lewis, 17 April 1909, Penucha MSS.
[2] Ibid.
[3] Ibid.
[4] Edwards to Lewis, 17 April 1909, Penucha MSS.
[5] Ibid. Also: Herbert Lewis's Diary, 18 February 1909, Penucha MSS: 'Had a long interview with Owen Edwards with reference to his Training Colleges in Wales. It is proposed to establish three, at Swansea, Barry and Caerleon. He explained the difficulties in the way of establishing the colleges at Cardiff. The LEAs who have to pay 25 per cent of the cost are insisting that they shall be in their own spheres respectively. Those interested in the University College have not been alive to the situation, and the preparations are now so far advanced that it will be difficult to alter them'.

Characteristics: (a) Students take three years, (b) Students take a degree course as well as their professional training.

(ii) Residential Colleges, independent. Of these, there are four, Bangor Normal, (Men); Bangor, N. Wales, (Women); Carmarthen, (Men); Swansea, (Women).

Characteristics: (a) Students take two years (b) Students specialize in elementary school subjects.

Why more?

(i) There are not enough trained teachers.

(ii) There are not enough places for those who wish to be trained. The hardship of the Nonconformist intending teacher is great; there is only one undenominational college for men, and one for women, in the whole of Wales. Church teachers have an additional college of their own, for women at St. Mary's, Bangor, and for men at Trinity College, Carmarthen. According to our calculation, the new provision will just meet the demand.

Why not the University College type alone?

1. Comparatively few students can take a degree except at the sacrifice of their professional training.
2. A large number of intending elementary teachers will make it impossible for the University Colleges to do their proper work.
3. The university courses are not at all well suited to elementary teachers; they leave college without the knowledge requisite for teaching in an elementary school.
4. Intending teachers, girls especially, are forced to read for their degrees, though degrees are useless to them, and unattainable by them, and though the third year entails a great sacrifice to them.
5. Additional rooms, professors, and equipment will probably cost the University Colleges more than they can afford.

My experience, after inspecting for two years, is that, under present conditions, between one-half and two-thirds of the Normal Students in the Day Training Colleges ought not to be in them. It would be better, in their own interests, and in those of the University Colleges, if they were in colleges of their own.

II The proposed Welsh system of Training Colleges.

There are to be Day Training Colleges and Residential Colleges in each district, side by side, all undenominational, so that students may enter the one college or the other as he chooses, and migrate from the one college to the other, if that is seen to be the best:

The Welsh Department

DISTRICTS	COLLEGES	
	Three Year	Two Year
1. *North Wales:* Caernarvon, Anglesey, Flint, Denbigh	1. University College of North Wales Day Training College	1. Normal College, Bangor 2. Diocesan College, Bangor
2. *Mid Wales:* Cardigan, Merioneth, Montgomery, Pembroke, Radnor, Brecon, Carmarthen	1. University College of Wales, Aberystwyth	1. *Either* a Two Year Section of the University College of Wales, or a Residential College at Aberystwyth: the committee of the seven counties is now deliberating. 2. Carmarthen
3. *South Wales* Glamorgan, Swansea, Merthyr, Monmouth, Newport (Cardiff is wavering).	1. University College of South Wales and Monmouthshire. Cardiff	1. Training College, Swansea (Women) 2. Caerleon College (Men) 3. Barry College (Women)

It is with regard to Barry and Caerleon that controversy arises: it is true the two colleges are not so near the Day Training Colleges as in North Wales—still, they are not very far away. *As far as possible*, I am entirely in favour of elementary schoolmasters being taught in University Colleges'.[1]

The first official interim account of his work as Chief Inspector and the work of the Welsh Department was submitted to the President by Edwards in November, 1909.[2] He described his own work as: (a) seeing that the

---

[1] Edwards to Lewis, 17 April 1909, Penucha MSS. The above schemes regarding Training Colleges have been extracted from this correspondence. Edwards ended his long letter, saying: 'If you have any suggestion or warning, I should be very grateful ... Gydag amynedd a pheidio mynnu bawb ei ffordd ei hun, daw popeth i'w le yn araf deg' (with patience, and provided that everyone worked together, everything should work out properly in the end).

For a full discussion of the University of Wales and the Training Colleges for Teachers some years later (1916–18), see *Royal Commission on University Education in Wales*, op. cit., II, pp. 118, ff., and Final Report of same, Part II, pp. 52, ff. Principal Harris, Normal College, Bangor, had drawn up a comprehensive scheme for the training of teachers, and even at that time envisaged a Faculty of Education within the University in which training colleges should be recognized as Schools of the University. In his constituted Faculty, Harris proposed (a) that the two-year course in the training college should be organized by the Faculty, on whose authority the teacher's certificate would be awarded and be recognized by the Board of Education; (b) that a student who had satisfactorily completed the two-year course at a training college should be permitted to proceed to a University College where his two-year course would be recognized as one year in the University for the purposes of reading for a degree; (c) in addition to the two-year course the training college should offer a three-year course for a better kind of teacher for the 'higher tops' of elementary schools and Continuation Schools; (d) that the professional training of all teachers, graduate and non-graduate should be undertaken at training colleges; (e) that the training colleges, should, as Schools of the University, undertake courses for a degree in the history, theory and practice of education—similar to the present day B.Ed. degree. In brief, Harris made the Faculty of Education the mainspring of the whole organization for the training of teachers. It should also be noted that at this time, the LEAs of Glamorgan and Monmouthshire had 'deliberately decided' to train their teachers in residential colleges at Barry and Caerleon in preference to either the use of the existing Day Training Department at University College, Cardiff, or the establishment of a residential college in that city. (Final Report, op. cit., p. 53).

[2] PRO Ed 24/584, Memorandum I, from Edwards to the President, 27 November 1909.

The Welsh Department

reforms introduced by the Board were carried out in Wales, and suggesting, where necessary, changes or adaptations; (b) bringing the special needs of Wales before the Board, as chairman of the Welsh Code and Secondary Regulations Committee, as a member of the Training Colleges and examinations committees, or in matters of extreme importance, by right of personal access to the President; (c) keeping up, and guiding enthusiasm for education in Wales, and guiding and encouraging LEAs; (d) preventing the love for education from being satisfied by mere examination results. To date, Edwards was satisfied that the views of his Department had not clashed with the general policy of the Board, but was convinced that 'Wales could move faster and was an excellent ground for experiments'. He also emphasized 'I know that our work is not seen by friends outside, and many of them think—because I feel it my duty to decline all invitations to speak in public—that I am doing nothing . . . the Welsh Department does not issue a yearly report about education in Wales. If it did, no one would ask what it is doing. So far, we have not issued any circular, but we are at work on two, one on bilingual teaching and the other on the teaching of Welsh history . . . the Central Welsh Board issue big volumes; possibly we are misjudged because we issue nothing. I think it would be well to publish a report every summer'.[1]

His report on the function and work of the Welsh Department was a model of conciseness and clarity, punctuated with his own inimitable comments.[2] The Department administered and inspected elementary and secondary education in Wales, and inspected Welsh technological education and training colleges. In elementary education it was responsible for the Welsh edition of the Code, and in its administration endeavoured to deal wisely and efficiently with the distinct problem of Welsh education—the bilingual one. It was also important that education should be related to the everyday life of the child, and attention was being given to the Pupil-Teacher and Bursar System. In secondary education, the Welsh Department drew up Regulations for Wales, and in its administration and inspection care was taken to establish the right connection between the elementary and secondary schools by attempting to secure that the curriculum of the secondary school should be both a continuation of, and something different from that of the elementary school. It was most important to secure differentiation of type, for the worst feature of Welsh schools was their uniformity in terms of curricula and organization, in spite of great diversity of needs and aims. The Welsh Department was

[1] Ibid. pp. 1, ff.
[2] See Appendix 2 to this Study.

The Welsh Department

working as closely as possible with the Central Welsh Board in the matter of inspection and advice.[1]

In technological and further education Wales was very backward. Only five per cent of elementary school children were able to proceed to secondary schools for which there was ample provision. In this direction there was considerable room for improvement by developing a voluntary system of further education for all young persons between the school-leaving age and eighteen. Regarding training college education, Wales had, in the making, a complete system, and it would be possible to turn out sufficient trained teachers to supply the wants of its schools. Future plans in the Welsh Department included negotiations by its inspectors to secure the adaptation of the degree courses of the University of Wales to the needs of intending teachers; the advising of students to pursue courses best adapted for their profession, and attempts to establish well-equipped and well-staffed demonstration and practising schools.[2]

The President had also called upon Davies for a report on the administrative aspect—'What the Welsh Department has done for Wales'.[3] Compared with the memoranda prepared by Edwards, this was a cumbersome and uneven effort, and he

> 'found it difficult to state in concise terms what the Department had done for Wales because, from the nature of the case, the Welsh Department is not expected or intended to do more for Wales than the Board of Education is expected or intended to do for England. In short, the excuse for the existence of the Welsh Department is that the central administration may have the advantage in dealing with Welsh questions, of the advice of a body of men conversant with Welsh sentiments, familiar with conditions affecting educational problems in Wales, and sympathetic towards Welsh ideals. Consequently, if it can truly be said that the administrative work of the Welsh Department has shown a proper understanding of Welsh problems, and has displayed rational sympathy with Welsh ideals, it may be said that the Department has fulfilled the function for the performance of which it was specially created'[4].

The rest of the document was a loyal endorsement of the topics discussed by Edwards, such as the recognition of the Welsh language in the Code,[5] and the appointment of Welsh-speaking inspectors of schools; the publication of separate statistics for Welsh education, and references to minor

---

[1] PRO Ed 24/584, Memorandum II, from Edwards to the President, 27 November 1909.
[2] Ibid.
[3] PRO Ed 24/584, Memorandum from Davies to the President, 29 November 1909.
[4] Ibid.
[5] *Report of the Board of Education*, 1906–7, Cd. 3862, p. 8: 'The outstanding feature of the year in connection with the work of the Board in Wales has been the definite recognition of the Welsh language and literature in the curriculum of the elementary, secondary schools, and training colleges of the Principality. The Welsh language had for some years past formed a subject of instruction and, in a greater degree, a medium of instruction, in some, at least of the elementary schools in almost every county in Wales and Mon., whilst it also received some, but more scanty, recognition in the secondary schools. In the Code for 1907, as also in the Regulations for secondary schools and for training colleges in Wales for that year (see p. 73), the teaching of Welsh was fully and definitely recognized'.

details such as 'the publication of reproductions of good pictures specially suitable for Welsh schools, notably Sir E. Poynter's cartoon in mosaic of "St. David" in the central lobby of the House of Commons, and a Summer School of Temperance and Hygiene at Rhyl in August 1909. But one important measure had been accomplished. Special attention had been given to cases where application had been made for building grants to enable Council Schools to be built in districts where parents had no alternative but to send their children to denominational schools. As a result, 'some 29 Council Schools, accommodating nearly 4,000 scholars had been erected in the Principality within the last two years'.[1]

II EXTENSION OF RESPONSIBILITIES

It was stated in the *Report of the Board of Education* for 1906–7 that since the work 'covered a period of twelve months, during eight of which the educational interests of Wales were dealt with under the administrative conditions which prevailed prior to the creation of the Welsh Department, it had been found convenient to treat of the work in Wales conjointly with that in England, instead of as a separate branch of the Board's operations'. The transfer to the Welsh Department of major responsibilities concerned with Welsh education was a gradual process extending between 1911 and 1915, because one administrative branch dealing with a part of the Board's work in Wales—relating to technology and higher education in Science and Art, including evening schools—was located at South Kensington. Davies, although T. work was offered him when he took office, preferred to wait until this section was moved into new buildings at Whitehall.[2] Transference of other sections of the work of the Board relating to Wales was neither easy nor quick because intricate administrative and sometimes legal details required careful disentanglement and re-arrangement. Consequently the Board of Education showed little enthusiasm and were extremely reluctant to devolve administrative responsibilities which demanded major re-adjustments of traditional routine to meet the requirements of the small Welsh Department.

Four years or more were to elapse before any action took place, and only then because of the impatience and at the instigation of Haydn Jones, MP, who proposed to ask a question in the House. On 19 July 1911, in a letter to the President, he wrote 'as a friend, to acquaint him with what was in the air'. There were some matters in connection with Welsh education which were causing him 'not a little uneasiness' and his

---

[1] PRO Ed 24/584, Memorandum from Davies to the President, op. cit.
[2] PRO Ed 24/582, Minute from Davies to the President: 'Observations of the Permanent Secretary of the Welsh Department on Haydn Jones's Question for 25 July 1911', 22 July 1911.

feelings 'were shared by other Welsh Members—so much so that steps were likely to be taken to give expression to the prevailing dissatisfaction'. In the circumstances, he advised the President to adopt prompt administrative action to avoid 'that public criticism of the Board and its President, of which there had been more than enough of late'. The supporters of the government felt that the Board of Education had not, to date, redeemed their pledges to develop and strengthen the Welsh Department of the Board which was created for the *administration of education* in Wales. Important aspects of Welsh education were still retained by the Board, notably technical and other continuation classes which had been promised early transfer as far back as 1907, and 'the present condition of things was absurd in the extreme, involving as it did such essentially Welsh concerns as courses in the Welsh language being under the control of the Technical and not the Welsh Department of the Board ... There were other anomalies equally indefensible'.[1]

The Welsh Members were still awaiting a pronouncement as to when other work, such as Training Colleges would be transferred, since the location of the new colleges and the building grants in respect of them had been settled, and there seemed no reason why the administration of the Board's Regulations should not, forthwith, be entrusted to the Welsh Department. Jones was anxious that this should be accomplished by voluntary action on the part of the President and not by any outside pressures which were building up, which might give rise to more conflicts and unpleasant situations. Another matter of urgent importance was that Welsh interests should be represented in the projected composition of the newly formed Joint Committee formed by the Board of Agriculture and the Board of Education to deal with agricultural education. Wales was entitled to be directly represented on this important body, especially as it had to do with primary and secondary schools. Jones warned that all such matters, unless attended to, might well become the subject of resolution at the meetings of the Welsh Party. He begged the President *'to extend the usefulness of the chief officials at the Welsh Department* ... apart altogether from a desire to prevent the political atmosphere becoming again disturbed ... and unless you take action, others will do so in a spirit hostile to the Board. This has induced me to put down some questions for Tuesday next, in the hope that the answers you will give may tend to peace and to a more sensible system of administration of Welsh education than obtains at the present moment'.[2]

[1] PRO Ed 24/582, Jones to Runciman, 19 July 1911.
[2] Question Paper No. 57, House of Commons, 25 July 1911: Mr. Haydn Jones 'To ask the President of the Board of Education when he proposes to transfer to the Welsh Department that portion of the Board's work in Wales that relates to technology and higher education in Science and in Art, including evening schools, as outlined in the Board's Report for 1906-7'.

The Welsh Department

This letter produced immediate results—both in the few days before the Question was put in the House of Commons, and subsequently. On 21 July, Runciman pressed Davies for his observations on the proposed Question by 24 July.[1] On 22 July Davies had completed his memorandum 'on the matter in all its aspects',[2] which was, he said, 'an opportunity to unburden my mind of what has been causing me considerable anxiety lately'.[3] The old arrangements which had operated until Haydn Jones's initiative meant that technological work in Wales was under Edwards and his staff for inspectorial purposes, but was administered by the Board of Education. Davies rightly emphasized the confusion which often occurred on the inspectorial side not only on account of lack of co-ordination at the Board but also due to the geographical difficulties in a country like Wales which made the work awkward when two branches of the Board might send urgent messages on simultaneous matters which necessitated visits to places in their areas which were miles apart. In addition, the organization of T. work in Wales differed from that in England. There was comparatively little in Wales of the higher technological work such as was carried on in Manchester, Liverpool and other large centres possessing well-equipped Technical Institutes. T. work in Wales consisted mainly of evening continuation classes organized in public elementary school buildings, taught by elementary school teachers who had themselves learned their technological subjects in similar classes by taking the external examinations of the Science and Art Department and the City and Guilds.[4]

The matter raised by the Question had also received some attention in parliamentary quarters. According to the Press, the Welsh Party 'were giving it their attention, though in a fitful sort of way: it would appear to have been crowded out at their meetings by their recent discussions on our Report (i.e. the 1909 one), the Insurance Bill, and other more urgent matters'.[5] Two Welsh MPs, Sir Herbert Roberts (Denbigh West) and Edgar Jones (Merthyr Tydfil), the small minority of two of the Welsh Members who fought the battle of the Central Welsh Board,

---

[1] PRO Ed 24/582, Minute from the President to Davies, 21 July.
[2] Ibid., Minute from Davies to the President, 22 July.
[3] Ibid., Davies to Runciman, 23 July.
[4] PRO Ed 24/582, Davies to the President, 22 July. Also Leslie Wynne Evans, *Education in Industrial Wales*, 1700–1900, Cardiff, 1971, p. 261, ff.
[5] PRO Ed 24/582, Davies to Runciman, 22 July.
The events leading up to the transference of the administration of technical education were the result of previous official pronouncements—the Board's Report for 1906–7, and answers given by McKenna in the House. On 4 March 1907 it was revealed that the Welsh Department 'would assume many of the purposes which a Welsh National Council for Education might have effected' and that Davies had had experience of Technical education in Lancashire. On 11 March, the House was informed that the 'new officials would carry out the *administration of all grades* in Wales under the control of the President'. (*Parl. Deb.*, 4th ser., vol. clxx, C.S. 454,492,1261.)

The Welsh Department

could be really hostile to the Board of Education 'though happily, neither carried much weight with their colleagues'. But Davies 'had learned of late', which caused him some concern 'that these two Members and the Central Welsh Board were pointing to the present arrangements at Whitehall, and to the limited jurisdiction of the Welsh Department as a reason for claiming more autonomy for Wales, which, in plain English, means according to them, extending the powers of the Central Welsh Board. ... I should not be surprised if the next move of one or other of the above minority was not an astute one in the direction of seeking to take advantage of what they refer to as an anomalous and unsatisfactory position. It was quite conceivable therefore that Haydn Jones's initiative might be inspired by the desire to forestall some move on the part of these champions of the Central Welsh Board'.[1]

The process of transference was set in motion quickly. Runciman was able to announce in the House on 11 August 1911 that he hoped 'to complete arrangements very soon for the transfer to the Welsh Department of the administration of technical education in Wales',[2] and an additional Senior Examiner was allocated to the Welsh Department who had previously undertaken the Welsh work in the Technical Branch.[3] On 24 October, Joseph A. Pease, who had succeeded Runciman as President, asked Chambers to prepare a 'careful Office Memorandum' on T work in Wales.[4] This would explain the complicated arrangements under which T grants were controlled and passed for payment by Chambers and Pullinger, upon the recommendations of HMIs. With regard to the conduct of the Science and Art examinations, and the award of scholarships, no change was made, nor was the work under the Choice of Employment Act, for this 'entailed special relations with the Board of Trade, but the local knowledge possessed by the Welsh Department would be put at the disposal of the Technological Branch'.[5] On 28 December a circular issued by Davies from his Department was addressed to all the Welsh LEAs stating that as from 1 January 1912 the following branches of the Board's work would be transferred to the Welsh Department: (a) The administration of all grants to Wales and Monmouthshire under Part I of the Regulations for technical schools, schools of Art, and other forms of provision of further education, except grants to University Colleges; (b) the administration of the new regulations governing the distribution

---

[1] PRO Ed 24/582, Davies to the President, 22 July, 1911.
[2] *Parl. Deb.*, 5th ser., *vol. xxix*, c. 950.
[3] F. E. Douglas, who was to consult Chambers on all technical matters.
[4] PRO Ed 24/582, Memorandum on T. work in Wales by E. K. Chambers to the President. Ibid.

of grants to be made by the Board out of the Development Fund for Agricultural education in Wales and Monmouthshire; (c) the administration of the endowments in Wales and Monmouthshire which were applicable to further education.[1]

It was also revealed that the Welsh Department proposed to arrange for the issue of triennial Area Reports[2] on the work of each LEA in Wales. The first instalment of such reports, dealing with approximately one-third of the total number of authorities in the Principality were almost ready, and the remainder would be taken in rotation in 1912 and 1913.[3] The earlier reports 'were necessarily of a somewhat experimental character, and in view of the special organization of secondary education in Wales, and of the transfer of the responsibility for the work of technological education only taking effect in the New Year, would deal mainly with elementary education'.[4] The intention was to develop the reports scheme in the future so that ultimately they would include references to the multifarious educational activities of LEAs under review and might be distributed to teachers as well. The inspectors' reports on individual schools would continue and would not be superseded by the Area Reports which, in effect, would be summaries of the former reports. Finally, Davies welcomed any suggestions from the LEAs which might improve the arrangement and increase the usefulness of Area Reports.[5]

Press comments on the transfer were enthusiastic. The *Daily Telegraph* called it 'an important devolution scheme' and the *Manchester Guardian* welcomed the announcement 'as a sound administrative reform and an important extension of powers ... that elementary and secondary education in Wales should have been administered by an entirely different set of officials from those who administered Welsh technical education was an anomalous condition of things which proved unsatisfactory on many occasions'.[6]

Further transfer of responsibility was contemplated in March 1914, that of the Welsh work of the Universities Branch (formed in 1910), which covered the training and examination of elementary and secondary school teachers and the administration of Training Colleges. This was achieved

---

[1] PRO Ed 23/244, *Office Memorandum No. 43*, 1911 (*Revised and printed* 29 *January* 1912), circulated 22 December 1911 by E. B. Phipps, signed by A. T. Davies.
[2] PRO Ed 23/145, Edwards to Davies, 31 March 1912.
[3] Ibid.
[4] PRO Ed 23/244, *Circular to all Welsh LEAs* by A. T. Davies, 28 December, 1911.
[5] Ibid. Also *Manchester Guardian*, 29 December 1911 and 2 April 1925 (on Davies's retirement): 'Space forbids more than the mere mention of the comprehensive series of Area Reports (28 in number) issued by the two colleagues, Davies and Edwards, in which, for the first time, the educational system of Wales was surveyed, county by county, in a manner and on a scale never before attempted in this country'.
[6] *Daily Telegraph*, 29 December 1911; *Manchester Guardian*, 5 and 29 December.

The Welsh Department

despite another altercation between Davies and Heath, who was unwilling and antagonistic to the proposal.[1] Negotiations began when Davies stated that the President was wishful to be in a position to take, at an early date, a further step in the direction of giving effect to the original intention of the government when it formed the Welsh Department, that the latter should ultimately be responsible for the administration of all branches of education in Wales. Davies was directed by the President to obtain the necessary information and to bring proposals to him 'with a view to the transfer to the Welsh Department of (*inter alia*) work in Wales which was being administered by U Branch'.[2] After discussion with the Chief Clerk, Davies was advised to ask Heath for (a) the scope and volume of the work done in Wales by U Branch, (b) an evaluation of it from the point of view of staff.[3] This request annoyed Heath, for it involved the preparation of a lengthy and detailed memorandum by Beresford, together with schedules and statistical tables, setting out the relative amount of work performed by U Branch for England and Wales respectively, and the number of senior staff employed.[4]

As in the case of the transfer of technical work, the matters involved, were, if anything, much more complicated. At that time it appeared that Training Colleges were not self-examining, but were examined and controlled by the Board's examiners and examination committees. This also applied to colleges of Domestic Subjects. Also, University Departments of education trained elementary school teachers who were admitted as two or three-year students and some such Departments were not self-examining, as also were similar Departments who admitted four-year students for training as secondary school teachers. Again, no less than seven schedules dealt with the main divisions of work carried out by U Branch in respect of the Board's educational responsibilities in Wales. Administrative work under Schedule A (which came under the heading 'The Statement') was concerned with the Engineering Department of University College, Cardiff; evening classes under T Regulations, and two separate sets of regulations dealing with Royal Scholarships, Free Studentships, Whitworth Scholarships and Exhibitions.[5] Schedule B

---

[1] PRO Ed 23/244, Minute from Davies to Heath, 5 March 1914.
[2] Ibid.
[3] Ibid.
Note: In various Minutes to the President, Davies, foreseeing more difficulties ahead in further negotiations, made his own personal position very clear in a series of forthright views, e.g. he entrusted the President to redeem the Board's pledges, 'It was on this assumption that I consented to accept the office I now hold ... and the promises made to me by McKenna regarding the jurisdiction of the Welsh Department weighed with me to relinquish my public work in Liverpool and Wales ... to become the administrative head of a Department for the administration of education in Wales'.
[4] PRO Ed 23/244, Memorandum from Beresford to Heath, 26 March 1914.
[5] Ibid. Schedule A.

administered the Regulations for the training of teachers in elementary schools, University Training Departments admitting two or three-year students, University Training Departments admitting four-year students, and the regulations for the training of teachers in secondary schools.[1] Schedule C had to do with Regulations for the training of teachers in Domestic Subjects,[2] and Schedules D, E, and F provided the syllabi and examination machinery for the Board of Education's Teachers Certificate and Preliminary Examination.[3] Schedule G recorded the number of students examined in each year.[4]

In addition to the Schedules, certain general matters with regard to teachers came under the jurisdiction of U Branch, for example, the determination of equivalent qualifications for the purposes of Schedules I A and I C of the Code; the emigration of teachers to the Colonies, and all questions arising on the admission to, or the results of the Board's examinations referred to in Schedules D, E, and F. Where possible, Beresford, had prepared a series of mathematical calculations from the Schedules to indicate approximately the amount of Welsh work (W) in proportion to the whole, dealt with by U Branch, in order to have some idea (in the event of the work being taken over by the Welsh Department) whether additional staff would be justifiable. With some justification he maintained that the percentages might not be an exact estimate, since for example, 'a greater amount of labour was entailed in the case of the admission of students to Welsh Training Colleges than was entailed by an equivalent number of English Colleges'.[5] This was largely due to the complexity of the regulations of the Central Welsh Board's examinations. But with regard to 'forms, statistics, and endowments' Beresford had to confess that 'no mathematical calculation could be made of the amount of work which Wales involved'.[6] The preliminary training of Welsh teachers was already controlled by the Welsh Department.[7]

A formidable and complex arrangement existed for the large volume of administrative work connected with the Board's examinations for teachers, due mainly to the fact that the Training Colleges were not self-examining.[8] This was administered by U Branch in consultation with the Examinations

[1] Ibid. Schedule B.
[2] Ibid. Schedule C.
[3] Ibid. Schedules D, E, and F.
[4] Ibid. Schedule G, E, and F.
[5] PRO Ed 23/244, Memorandum from Beresford, op. cit.
[6] Ibid.
[7] Ibid.
[8] Schedules D, E, F.

The Welsh Department

Committee, which was divided into five sub-committees, and, for the Final Examination, into seven sub-committees.[1] The Assistant Secretary of U Branch chaired the sub-committees and 16 chief examiners made arrangements for setting and marking papers in their respective subjects. Beresford was of the opinion that 'if the responsibility for the examination of Welsh candidates were entirely undertaken by the Welsh Department and their own Examinations Committee, the labour saved to the existing Examinations Committee and the higher staff would obviously be negligible. To the clerical section some labour would be saved in the case of the approved Final Examinations of the Welsh University Elementary Training Departments'.[2]

In spite of all his mathematical calculations Beresford revealed that the amount of Welsh work in U Branch was almost negligible as compared with England, and it was clear at this stage in the negotiations that it would be difficult to justify the allocation of extra staff to the Welsh Department, should the Welsh work be transferred. Schedule B, for example, showed the following percentages:[3]

Training Colleges, Elementary 1913–14	England and Wales	Wales	Percentage of Wales to Total
1. Recognized Training Colleges:			
(a) University Training Colleges			
Number	20	3	15.00
Accommodation	3466	544	15.70
(b) Council Training Colleges			
Number	20	2	10.00
Accommodation	3918	400	10.21
(c) Voluntary Training Colleges			
Number	47	2	4.26
Accommodation	5709	189	3.31
Total Number	87	7	8.05
Accommodation	13093	1133	8.65
Council Training Colleges in course of provision with aid of Building Grant			
Number	7	2	28.57
Accommodation	1284	250	19.47

[1] Ibid. List 20.
[2] Ibid., Memorandum from Beresford, op. cit.
[3] Ibid., Schedule B.

The Welsh Department

2. Training Colleges, Secondary 1913–14	England and Wales	Wales	Percentage of Wales to Total
(a) University Training Colleges			
Number	12	2	16.67
No. of students	109	12	11.01
(b) Voluntary Training Colleges			
Number	10	—	—
No. of students	104	—	—
Total Number	22	2	9.09
No. of students	213	12	5.63[1]

Heath (not unmindful that any transfer of work might undermine the status of his Branch and also the loss of some of his staff) drew Davies's attention to the fact that U Branch had a smaller proportion of Assistant Secretaries and Senior Examiners to Junior Examiners than any Branch of the Board. Of the eight Junior Examiners, two were engaged on full-time work for England only, two were occupied on examination and kindred work, and the transfer of examination work to Wales would afford no relief to them. Another was engaged on special work, and the Welsh work performed by the remaining three was nothing like a tenth of the whole of their work, and its transference would, therefore, not render any transfer of staff possible.[2]

Davies appreciated, in such circumstances, that it would be impracticable to transfer the examination work, but thought it desirable to follow the analogy of *Office Memorandum No. 43, 1911*, which set out the conditions of transfer of T work to the Welsh Department. This specially excluded examination work, etc., from that Branch to Wales.[3] But, not to be out-done, Davies noted that although it was not possible to transfer to the Welsh Department any of the officers engaged in the work, he hoped that U Branch would help as much as possible towards bringing about the proposed transfer and requested Heath to suggest what divisions of work done by U Branch were capable of being transferred to the Welsh Department so that definite recommendations might be forwarded to the President.[4] Heath, however, now faced with the question of supplying definite proposals, conceived an easy way to allocate as little as possible of the work of U Branch to Wales. Proceeding on Davies's assumption

---

[1] Schedule B, op. cit.
[2] PRO Ed 23/244, Minute from Heath to Davies, 28 March 1914.
[3] Ibid. Minute from Davies to Heath, 6 April 1914.
[4] Ibid.

that it was impossible to transfer the examination work to the Welsh Department, certain conclusions seemed necessarily to follow. Since the responsibility for examinations and awards in teacher-training carried with it the approval of courses leading up to those examinations, this meant that the Board of Education should retain administrative responsibility for the courses of instruction in the four (later six) non-university Training Colleges in Wales, for it scarcely seemed possible that 'one Department of the Board should be responsible for educational matters and another for all other matters in the same Institute'.[1] Heath reminded Davies that the responsibility for the inspection of Welsh Training Colleges was already in the hands of Edwards 'so that the closest possible touch with Welsh needs was already ensured between the Welsh Department and U Branch'.[2]

With regard to the three Departments for the training of elementary school teachers attached to the Welsh University Colleges, there was no unity of administration. The examinations of those students at Bangor and Cardiff were conducted by the college authorities, with Edwards acting as the Board's assessor. But the Aberystwyth students took the Board's examination in professional subjects, and therefore would be administered by the Board of Education. Heath saw no reason why Cardiff and Bangor should not be transferred to 'W', but he was sure that the President would take into account 'the anomaly which would arise if the students of these two Colleges were to receive *a certificate different in form from that issued to all other teachers in England and Wales*'.[3] There were also two Departments for the training of secondary school teachers at Aberystwyth and Cardiff. Since the training of these teachers was largely in the hands of the same tutors as those responsible for elementary school teachers, it would not be easy for them to be administered 'by a Department other than that responsible for the elementary department', i.e. the Board of Education. The Board were also considering new regulations for Schools which trained teachers of Domestic Subjects, and included the examination and the award of diplomas to such students by the Board of Education, so that the School at Cardiff would again, under Davies's assumption, be administered by the Board of Education.[4]

The remainder of the work connected with the Welsh University Colleges was concerned with the academic side, certain small classes

[1] PRO Ed 23/244, Minute from Heath to Davies, 8 April 1914.
[2] Ibid.
[3] Ibid.
[4] Ibid.

under the T regulations, and Welsh endowments. The academic work was in the hands of the Advisory Committee of the Board, which acted, in respect of the Welsh colleges, for the Chancellor of the Exchequer and not for the President. The annual reports made to Parliament by the Welsh colleges were included in the two volumes issued by the Board for the whole of university work in England and Wales. Heath conceded, that if on general grounds it was thought desirable, there would be no practical difficulty in publishing separately for Wales all the summary tables containing the financial and educational facts, but the work under T and the endowments should remain in U Branch.[1] He was most anxious to reiterate that he had attempted to show how far a transfer of the work done by U Branch for Wales was administratively possible on the assumption made by Davies, adding that 'the question of the desirability of transfer on general grounds is a matter for the President, upon which, I gather, you do not ask for my opinion'.[2]

Understandably, Heath's observations were unpalatable, and Davies, in belligerent mood, conveyed his feelings to the President in no uncertain terms on the subject of his recent instructions to him: 'until the considerations and difficulties raised by Dr. Heath in his last minute have been the subject of definite decision by you (and possibly also ... by the Chancellor of the Exchequer) and that decision has been duly communicated to the Branch concerned, it will be hardly possible for me ... to carry this matter further, still less to submit to you proposals for the transfer to the Welsh Department of any of the work now done in Wales by U Branch'.[3] In further protest, Davies, at the great risk of gravely embarrassing the President, made it clear that he did not deem it necessary to discuss the important questions which Heath raised, because he had always regarded them 'as matters which the Board had already decided in principle, but to which ... they had simply thought fit to postpone'.[4] Indeed, he felt it was not only right, but essential, that it should be placed on record 'that at no time during the very full discussions which took place when the formation of the Welsh Department had been decided upon, and when it was being organized (and to many of these, with the then Heads of the Office, I was a party) was it ever stated or suggested (a) that any portion of the Board's work in Wales was to be excepted from the decision at which the government arrived in 1907, (b) that there would be any special difficulty about transferring the Training

[1] Ibid.
[2] PRO Ed 23/244, Minute from Heath to Davies, 8 April 1914.
[3] Ibid. Minute from Davies to the President, 16 May 1914.
[4] PRO Ed 24/585, Confidential Memorandum from Davies to the President, 21 November 1913, paras. 2–8.

The Welsh Department

College (or, indeed, the University College) work, though the latter was, perhaps, not specially discussed, (c) that (except for purely temporary purposes) any difference would be made in the respective jurisdictions to be exercised in Wales by the administrative and inspectorial sides of the Welsh Department'.[1] The President was requested to make an early decision on the administrative question 'raised in these minutes ... because that decision must vitally affect—both now, and for years to come—everything that was contemplated by, or is involved in, the original intentions of the government in establishing the Welsh Department'.[2]

Although the President gave the matter his immediate attention, he tended to agree with Heath that certain administrative difficulties might arise in the Training College sector. He could not understand how Davies proposed to accept the responsibility for administering through W (the Welsh Department) 'the courses leading up to examinations and awards, when these are admittedly to be left with U Branch, and how it is proposed to avoid any distinction in the certificate for teachers, if Training Colleges and their work are transferred to W'.[3]

But, in the meantime, Davies had called upon another authority for guidance and advice. He had asked Edwards for his educational views on the problems raised by Heath, and almost endorsed by the President. Edwards made only three comments. In the first place, he foresaw no difficulties in transferring the administrative work, while leaving the examinations, especially the fixing of the pass standard as they were. There was nothing inconsistent in W approving courses, and U examining, since the colleges selected the courses from their knowledge of the needs of students, the Board of Education approved on his advice—advice which was given according to his knowledge of what the elementary schools needed. Secondly, if there were difficulties, it would be perfectly feasible for England and Wales to examine separately, and still have the same certificate. It only meant 'that our inspectors would mark the Welsh papers and the English inspectors the English papers, instead, as is the case now, of mixing the papers and dividing them among all'.[4] The number of failures in Wales was so small (nine out of 396) that they could be referred to the English chief examiners so that the pass mark would still be the same. Thirdly, the Welsh Training Colleges were rapidly becoming self-examining: 'Cardiff and Bangor were so already, and

[1] PRO Ed 23/244, Minute from Davies to the President, 16 May 1914.
[2] Ibid. Comment by the President on Davies's Minute of 16 May, sent to Trevelyan.
[3] PRO Ed 23/244, Minute from Edwards to Davies, 3 June, 1914.
[4] Ibid.

The Welsh Department

Aberystwyth would soon be. In these cases, the colleges, with myself as the Board's assessor, simply place the results before the Board, and the Board act on these results'.[1] Finally, Edwards declared that 'the time has come, in Wales, for *all* Training Colleges to be self-examining. They are so now in the professional subjects; they can easily be so in the academic subjects. Our examinations are the best external examinations I know; but I am quite sure that the Colleges themselves would do the work better. But, without making any change, I think W could decide on courses, and U examine without any practical difficulty'.[2]

Armed with such a superb analysis of the situation, and determined to scotch any further delaying tactics, Davies proceeded to enlighten the President as to how the problem might be solved, on the lines suggested by Edwards. He felt bound 'to dissent strongly from Dr. Heath's assumption that the responsibility for examinations and the awards arising therefrom, need or should, carry with it the approval of courses leading up to those examinations, and that there need not necessarily be any distinction in the value of the certificate for teachers in the two countries'.[3] If difficulties arose, they should be overcome, for it was unsound educationally and administratively that the final training of teachers should be separated from that of their preliminary training—the latter being already an important part of the work of the Welsh Department. Moreover, the Board of Education already had some experience to guide them. When the administration of the work under the Regulations for technical schools, etc., was transferred to the Welsh Department, the examination work remained with T Branch. Davies stressed that no difficulty had resulted from that arrangement, and he apprehended none with reference to U work, provided that his Department was properly staffed for its new commitments and also enjoyed the co-operation of the Branch which did the like work for England.[4]

This evoked a reply from the President on the same day in the form of brief minutes to Davies, Heath and Trevelyan. Davies was asked to state his requirements as to extra staff, should the transference occur; Heath

---

[1] Ibid.
[2] PRO Ed 23/244, Minute from Edwards to Davies, 3 June 1914.
    With reference to examinations for intending teachers, the Board of Education conducted the old Queen's Scholarship (later King's Scholarship), and later still, the Preliminary Examination for student teachers who wished to enter Training Colleges; the Acting Teacher's Examination for those who wished to become certificated teachers without going to college; and the Final Examination for teachers in Training Colleges after two years' study. The papers for all examinations were set and marked by HMIs. The Preliminary Examination and the Acting Teacher's Examination were eventually discontinued, and the Training Colleges conducted the Final Examination with HMIs acting as assessors.
    LEAs also had the Labour Proficiency Examination which allowed children who passed it to leave school at 12, and was merely a test of proficiency in the Three R's which was assessed by HMIs.
[3] PRO Ed 23/244, Minute from Davies to the President, 16 June.
[4] Ibid.

The Welsh Department

was asked to comment on the minutes supplied by Davies and Edwards, and Trevelyan had the task of advising the President as to what course he should pursue.[1] But all the activity was suddenly halted, the projected scheme of transfer was not realized, and the ideas advanced, together with the lines of procedure were forgotten in the events leading up to the outbreak of war on 4 August. When Davies re-opened negotiations in April 1915, he displayed far less zeal for the cause of a Welsh U Branch, and was merely content to ask Barlow for his views on any proposed increase of staff which the President had requested ten months before.[2] But if the former difficulties had seemed insurmountable, there was now scant prospect of a solution. The plain and sober fact remained—that the Welsh Department was too small to warrant any change. The unsuccessful attempt merely showed that in many administrative aspects, the Welsh Department would necessarily have to utilize the office facilities of the Board as a whole. Barlow, having thoroughly discussed the matter with Davies, Edwards and Casson, reluctantly had to report that the transfer of Welsh U work would inevitably be wasteful of staff. It could not be accomplished except by an increase in the establishment, or, by the transference of another Junior Examiner post from England to Wales—but no case could be made for adding another official, such as a Senior Examiner or an Assistant Secretary post to W.[3] Heath had won the day.

III GROWTH AND REORGANIZATION OF THE WELSH INSPECTORATE

One of the immediate tasks—perhaps the most important and major one—which faced Edwards as Chief Inspector of Education for Wales was the creation of an inspectorate composed of persons who had a real knowledge of Wales, her educational needs and the Welsh language. But long before 1907 the inspectorate working in Wales boasted such distinguished Welshmen as Dan Isaac Davies, Dr. William Edwards and

---

[1] Ibid. Minutes from the President to Davies, Heath and Trevelyan, 16 June.

[2] PRO Ed 23/244, Minute from Davies to Barlow, 13 April 1915. Minutes from Barlow to Davies, 22 April, 28 May.

[3] PRO Ed 23/244, Minute from Barlow to Heath, 28 May. Barlow said 'that the chief difficulty in regard to the transfer of work seems to me likely to arise at the Assistant Secretary stage. It seems to me impossible to expect any one Assistant Secretary, in addition to dealing with the S, E, and possibly T work, and keeping abreast of developments in those Branches, to make himself familiar also with Training Colleges, "Statement" work, Training Schools of Domestic Subjects, and to keep abreast of the changes in the Regulations regarding them. One practical difficulty is that the bulk of Welsh work in the various categories dealt with by U Branch is so small that it would be very difficult for any man dealing with it alone to become properly acquainted with the work, however closely he tried to keep in touch with U Branch. This is, of course, a difficulty which necessarily arises out of the smallness of the Welsh Department'.

The Welsh Department

Thomas Darlington.[1] Edwards himself, already deeply immersed in this craft, had no intention, when he took up his appointment, of being an office man, but along with his other inspectorial colleagues took more than his share of incessant travelling in the work of inspecting schools and Training Colleges. He had definite ideas regarding the responsibilities of inspectors of schools. 'His view of the function of the inspector was well in advance of his time, in the emphasis it placed on guidance and advice, and the insistence on the establishment of a body of inspectors in Wales who would "in qualifications, training and experience be able to meet general educational requirements and to discharge a particular responsibility for the traditional language and culture of Wales" '.[2]

In May 1907, Phipps sent Edwards the list of inspectors who would be working under his direction in Wales.[3] For elementary schools: Messrs. A. G. Legard (Divisional Inspector), John Bancroft, Thomas Darlington, William Edwards, Robert Edward Hughes, Henry Price, Edward Roberts and Lewis Jones Roberts. For secondary schools and technology, Messrs. David Evan Jones and Benjamin Beck Skirrow. There was also a Junior Inspector, William Cecil Rees Johns, and the following sub-inspectors: Mr. Wakeford, responsible to Legard; J. B. Williams and Mr. James to Bancroft; T. H. Johnson and D. Thomas to Darlington; Mr. Holliday, Mr. G. Jones and Mr. Evans to William Edwards; Mr. Copus and Mr. Bowen to Hughes; Mr. Hooson to Price; Mr. Matthews to E. Roberts, and Messrs. Morris and Rhydderch to L. J. Roberts. Messrs. Shaw, Dufton and Boothroyd (Junior Inspectors) were also allocated to Wales until 31 July 1907. This was the revised list given to Edwards by Morant,[4] and Phipps was instructed to send a minute to each inspector stating that they were now under the control of Edwards.[5]

In June 1907, Legard, who since 1896 had acted as Divisional Inspector of elementary education for Wales, retired after thirty-six years service on reaching the usual age limit. Further changes occurred in the Welsh

---

[1] Dan Isaac Davies, (1839–87), one of the pioneers of Welsh *teaching* in schools. In 1866 he succeeded in getting Welsh acknowledged as a grant-earning subject, and also prefaced a memorandum on bilingualism for the Royal Commission on Elementary Education in 1866, and in 1888 most of his recommendations were adopted.
Thomas Darlington (1864–1908) a distinguished linguist, who learnt Welsh as a boy in school, was unsuccessful in his application for the post of Principal at the University College of Wales, Aberystwyth in 1891. (*Y Bywgraffiadur Cymreig hyd* 1840), pp. 103 and 98.
[2] *Pioneers of Welsh Education*, op. cit., p. 90.
[3] PRO Ed 23/144, Minute from Phipps to Edwards, 1 May 1907.
[4] Ibid. Minute from Edwards to Phipps, 8 May.
[5] Ibid. Minute from Phipps to Bray, 5 May: 'Mr. . . . I am directed to inform you that the President has appointed Mr. O. M. Edwards to be Chief Inspector of the Welsh Department. Mr. Edwards took up his duties on 1 April 1907. Mr. Legard, Divisional Inspector for elementary schools in Wales retires on 31 May. After that date any references which would have been made to Mr. Legard as Divisional Inspector will be made to Mr. O. M. Edwards. Also, Mr. Shaw, late Divisional Inspector for Wales in the Technological Branch, has been transferred to England. Any references which would have been made to Mr. Shaw . . . should be made direct to Mr. O. M. Edwards'.
Note: On 17 May, Edwards, after seeing this minute, crossed out his initials 'O.M.' and substituted 'Owen' From that date onwards he was to be referred to as Owen Edwards.

The Welsh Department

inspectorate during the year 1907-8. In February 1908, the Board sustained a severe loss by the death, at an early age, of Thomas Darlington 'whose brilliant gifts had always been ungrudgingly employed to further the best interests of education in Wales'.[1] In May, Edward Roberts retired after thirty-seven years service. These vacancies gave the Board an opportunity to re-arrange the Welsh inspectorial districts and to re-group the counties for this purpose. William Williams, D.Sc., late superintendent of education to the Swansea Borough Council was appointed HMI, and was placed in charge of Denbighshire, Flintshire and Montgomeryshire.[2]

Inspectors employed by the Board of Education were appointed by the President and organized in two grades. The first grade was composed of 'full' or His Majesty's Inspectors, selected either from the second grade or from outside the inspectorate. The second grade consisted of Sub-inspectors and Junior inspectors. The recruiting of Sub-inspectors ceased in 1900, and of Junior inspectors in 1913. In 1914, a new grade, that of Assistant inspector (Men) was created, to fill vacancies occurring in the second grade of the inspectorate by the retirement or promotion of either Sub-inspectors or Junior inspectors.[3] Under the old system, therefore, appointments to the inspectorate and subsequent advancement of an inspector was based on a graduated apprenticeship. New entrants were Sub-inspectors, proceeding to Junior inspectors, and finally to HMI. Groups of two or three Sub-inspectors might be allocated to HMI, or one Junior inspector became attached to HMI and given more responsibility. Up to 1913, the inspectorial pattern and territorial distribution of the Welsh inspectorate was as follows:[4]

A. Up to 31 May 1907, A. G. Legard, Divisional Inspector for elementary education in Wales.
B. Owen Edwards, Chief Inspector, Wales. Assistant: Abel John Jones, Junior inspector, South Wales.
C. John Bancroft, HMI: elementary schools in Cardiganshire, Carmarthenshire, and Pembrokeshire.
D. William Edwards, HMI; Ivor Thomas, Junior inspector: elementary schools in Glamorgan, including Neath B; Aberdare UD; Mountain Ash UD; Merthyr Tydfil CB and Swansea CB.
E. Robert Edward Hughes, HMI; Caleb Rees, Junior inspector: elementary schools, Monmouthshire.
F. Henry Price, HMI: elementary schools in Breconshire; Barry UD; Pontypridd UD; Rhondda UD; Cardiff CB and Radnorshire.
G. Lewis Jones Roberts, HMI; Griffith Prys Williams and William Cecil Rees Johns, Junior inspectors: elementary, secondary, evening schools, technical instruction and PT centres in Anglesey, Caernarvonshire and Merioneth.

[1] *Report of the Board of Education*, 1907-8, op. cit., p. 12.
[2] Ibid.
[3] PRO Ed 23/147, *Board of Education, Office Rules* 12, *Assistant Inspectors (Men)*, May 1914.
[4] Board of Education, *List 6 and Establishment List*.

H. Benjamin Beck Skirrow, HMI: secondary and evening schools, PT centres, and technical instruction in Cardiganshire, Carmarthenshire, Neath B; Aberdare UD; Mountain Ash UD; Merthyr Tydfil CB; Swansea CB, and Pembrokeshire.

I. William Williams, HMI; T. H. Johnson, Assistant inspector: secondary, technical, evening schools and PT Centres in Anglesey, Denbighshire, Flintshire, Montgomeryshire and Merioneth.

J. David Evan Jones, HMI: Technical instruction, evening schools, secondary schools and PT centres in Breconshire, Radnorshire, Monmouthshire, Pontypridd UD; Rhondda UD; Cardiff CB.

In March 1912 Davies had asked Edwards for a review of his work generally, with particular reference to the inspectorate over the past five years. He said 'on the side of our work entrusted to me ... and after a rather searching examination, it gave me results that made me quite happy'.[1] Bruce had told him, when he came to the Welsh Department, that there was a 'flagging interest in education', but that had been revived, and a prominent MP had stated that the new Area Reports had brought new life to Welsh education. Edwards had endeavoured to place his ideals, especially in secondary education and in his dealings with the Central Welsh Board clearly before the country, and was happy that he enjoyed the growing confidence of the Welsh MPs on both sides of the House, in the work of the Welsh Department. The Area Reports had brought the Department into intimate contact with LEAs, and relationships with them 'not excepting Denbighshire' were most cordial.[2] With regard to the inspectorate, they had an excellent nursery of Junior inspectors whom 'we can hope to see equalling the older HMI ... there were five of them who were ready to do HMIs work, and would, in point of ability, education and experience, probably be the best inspectors Wales has seen ... If anything happens to me, my work will go on without any break. This is a consolation: it is also a salutory reminder that should lead to humility. I have not had a day's illness to incapacitate me for work since I came to the office, but I take no risks ... and my work is so congenial that it makes me well if some short vacation has made me ill'.[3]

One of Edwards's chief attributes—his dedicated conscientiousness—was, paradoxically as it may seem, his greatest weakness in his dealings with his colleagues. Time and again, on reading his official papers and memoranda—not only those in connection with the inspectorate—the inescapable question arises whether it was possible that he could bring himself to entrust to others any responsibilities, for he undertook so

[1] PRO Ed 23/145, Memorandum from Edwards to Davies, 31 March 1912.
[2] Ibid.
[3] Ibid.: 'The week before last, I had a bad cold, but could do O (office) work all through. When I got up to meet Denbighshire, my doctor (a most worthy man) saw me hurrying to the station ... "look at that devil" he said, "trying to catch a train ... when I told him to stay in bed" '.

The Welsh Department

much—indeed, too much—himself. But the smooth working and efficiency of the inspectorial machine of the Welsh Department, together with the limitations of his physical and mental resources demanded the delegation of a greater measure of responsibility to his minions, in the expectation that they would emulate his example. He openly confessed that his 'inspecting work would always remain hard, but not half as hard as it had been. I had, of course, to bring myself into close contact with every aspect of Welsh education. In order to do this, I have done all the work of inspecting and examining in every aspect of it. By doing so, I have brought my own knowledge up to date, and in so doing, I have given my colleagues my own ideas, which they will loyally materialize'.[1] Edwards, indeed, had a superabundance of faith in human nature! Nothing seemed to have escaped his meticulous attention, and what he professed to have achieved is beyond the bounds of credibility. For example, in 1912, *he saw every student in every Training College*, but he was going to use 'the Juniors next year'. The same applied to secondary school Full Reports and conferences with governors, but 'now that every school has been reported upon once, I am going to entrust *some* this year to my colleagues, and to D. Evan Jones, to put him on his mettle'. Again, 'Higher Elementary Full Reports have all been done by me so far. This year, William Edwards and H. Price take them'.[2] All inspectors' Diaries were 'always carefully examined . . . if there is much O (office), I insist on having a minute description . . . there was some difficulty with T work, but now, with Douglas at hand, I can pull his rein tight also when necessary. Most of the inspectors are very conscientious'.[3] It probably never occurred to Edwards that paper or office routine work played such an important and integral part in the life of an inspector of schools. He himself was able to spend so much time at his country home near Bala, was fond of travelling a great deal in Wales, and London saw little of him. No wonder he could claim 'I seem to get through so little work in a day at the office (London), and through so much when working in the country, (Llanuwchllyn)'.

---

[1] PRO Ed 23/145, Memorandum from Edwards to Davies, 31 March 1912. At this time Edwards was planning future promotions within his team, for in 1915, William Edwards and John Bancroft were due to retire. From the comments which he made on the 'possibles', some names were favoured more than others. He was quite certain that G. Prys Williams and Abel J. Jones 'could step into their places at once, and failing them, Caleb Rees could do the work now; also W. Roberts and Ivor Thomas were ready'. He expressed more concern for Johns 'whose promotion was long overdue . . . , he is a most amiable and conscientious man, but he lacks the grip and ability of the others'. D. Evan Jones he found somewhat a problem—'D. E. Jones will always be D. E. Jones. I have calculated on that from the beginning. Shall the leopard lose his spots? As far as he is concerned, no new work will be entrusted to him'. These remarks were very odd—for after 1912, Jones was doing very conspicuous work as HMI for technical schools-evening schools, secondary schools and PT centres, in Breconshire, Radnorshire, Monmouthshire, Ponty, pridd UD; Rhondda UD, and Cardiff CB.

[2] Ibid.

[3] Ibid.

The Welsh Department

At this time, the main weaknesses in the Welsh inspectorate were the lack of women inspectors and specialists. Wales had only one woman inspector, and Edwards received help on this side from the English staff. Johnson was due to retire and Edwards proposed to ask Miss Lawrence, C.I. (England) to recommend a woman inspector in his place. Edwards argued that Wales was too small to appoint specialist inspectors and deplored the fact that Fred Pullinger, C.I. for Technology and Evening Schools in England, was allowed to offer higher salaries in order to tempt them into the English inspectorate. Edwards preferred occasional outside help, and in that way he maintained that he was able 'to get the very ablest men of the day'.[1] He was also unduly concerned about another matter, the question of Staff Inspectors: 'being so small, we cannot have them—not even Divisional Inspectors. Wales falls into three parts. There are six inspectors: you could not make one of them the superior of the other. There is no room between the C.I. and six HMI's for an intermediate officer'.[2] He added, 'If we retain W. Edwards, we must retain Bancroft: we probably shall retain both. If I went now, Edwards would take my mantle by seniority. But for the University, Central Welsh Board, and the *whole* of my work, William Williams is the man, out out. He could now carry my work on to the finish. What a pity! If I went now, the Department's work would go on all the same'.[3]

But, in June 1913, Edwards realized that more inspectors were necessary. He conferred with Sir Lewis Amherst Selby-Bigge, Secretary to the Board,[4] making out a strong case for strengthening the Welsh inspectorate. It was pointed out that Morant, in 1907, had fixed upon the number of inspectors in Wales for all branches, giving Wales its due in comparison with England. Since then, the work had increased, especially on the T and S sides, but the number of inspectors had remained the same. The chief difficulty was that Wales had only one woman inspector, Miss Menai J. Rowlands, whose programme of work was unduly heavy—responsible for the whole of the Domestic Subjects work in elementary schools, taking part in the full inspection of all girls' secondary schools, a certain amount of T work, the inspection of Poor Law schools, and advising LEAs and governors about the education of girls—to which was added the difficulties of travelling. A second, less pressing difficulty, according

---

[1] The establishment showed 8 HMIs, apart from Juniors and occasional inspectors, e.g. Fred Pullinger, borrowed from England for T inspection.

[2] This was not true. Edwards, bent on economy, was begging the question. One inspector who worked with him closely, referred to his parsimony, i.e. that no more inspectors were employed than was necessary to account for the work. Promotions, of course, involved more money. See p. 354 of this Study.

[3] PRO Ed 23/145, Memorandum. op. cit.

[4] Selby-Bigge succeeded Morant on 30 December 1911.

The Welsh Department

to Edwards, was that he had only two men to cover the whole of S and T work.[1] Two results of this were, first, that it was difficult to get specialist inspection of some subjects, and secondly, Edwards actually complained that he practically did all the secondary school work, 'my time is so occupied in inspecting that it is difficult to get any opportunity for work at the office, except committee work and consultation with examiners. The existence of the Central Welsh Board has, so far, been a hindrance rather than a help. I have had practically no vacation for six years, and the President, quite rightly, has reproved me for the arrangement which keeps me constantly at work'.[2] Edwards suggested that he should occasionally use the services of an inspector from England—'an eminent specialist from outside'—and that a second woman inspector be appointed.[3]

Selby-Bigge instructed his Assistant Secretary, A. H. Sidgwick, to invite the opinions of the four English C.I's: Miss M. A. Lawrence (Women), F. H. Dale, (Elementary schools), W. C. Fletcher (Secondary schools) and Fred Pullinger (Technology and Evening schools).[4] Miss Lawrence confirmed that a second woman inspector was long overdue in Wales, who might combine the inspection of Domestic Subjects with elementary schools, just as Miss Rowlands did for Domestic Subjects, secondary schools, and Poor Law schools.[5] Dale could not help, since Edwards required assistance for T and S work.[6] Fletcher's staff, both men and women, was already worked to its full capacity, and he could only promise slight help in very special cases.[7] Pullinger had for some years, given excellent services in *ad hoc* cases, for example, the provision of an Agricultural inspector to deal with the Farm Institute at Madryn Castle, and he himself, together with an Engineering and Building inspector, had visited Cardiff to advise on a new Technical School. Pullinger was prepared to continue on this basis, but could promise no staff to be involved in general and routine work in Wales. He had kept records for five years, showing the amount of work done by his staff, which showed that T inspectors worked on the average between 50 and 51 hours per week. He warned the Permanent Secretary to the Board that any work done in Wales would have to be met by a corresponding reduction of work in

[1] But the establishment list for this time showed that more HMIs were involved in S and T work: W. Williams, assisted by Johnson; L. J. Roberts by G. Prys Williams; D. E. Jones and B. B. Skirrow.
[2] PRO Ed 23/146, Minute from Edwards to Selby-Bigge, 19 June 1913.
[3] Ibid.
[4] Ibid., Minute from Selby-Bigge to Sidgwick, 24 June. Minutes from Sidgwick to C.Is, 24 June.
[5] Ibid. Minute from Lawrence to Permanent Secretary, 1 July.
[6] Ibid. Minute from Dale to Fletcher, 10 July.
[7] Ibid. Minute from Fletcher to Permanent Secretary, 15 July.

The Welsh Department

England. He agreed with Edwards that T work difficulties could be surmounted by the employment of occasional inspectors, if Edwards was allotted £100 or £150 'out of Vote B.I.'.[1]

Selby-Bigge was satisfied that Edwards had made his case for additional inspectors, and advised the President to proceed on the lines suggested by the English Chief Inspectors, that an additional woman inspector be appointed at once to Wales, irrespective of any vacancy arising.[2] Also Edwards had agreed to Pullinger's plan that money might be allocated to Wales under Vote B.I. for occasional inspectors. The President approved on 13 August.[3] But these arrangements were merely a prelude to a complete reorganization and overhaul of the Welsh inspectorate. The proposed scheme was the result of extensive deliberations between Davies and Edwards on the whole question of the status, remuneration and future expansion of the inspectorate. Also, an early approach to this matter was rendered necessary by two events: in 1913, the E inspectorate for England had been reorganized, and a new class of Assistant inspector established[4] and the retirement of three inspectors in Wales was impending.

Davies had been considering the question of following England's example of appointing Assistant inspectors instead of Junior, and Edwards advised this change, because (a) the same names should be used in England and Wales; (b) it had been taken for granted by teachers 'that it was easier for acting teachers to get an Assistant inspectorship than a Junior one. Indeed, the Treasury also seem to take for granted that it is so generally'; (c) financially, the Assistant grade was better, for example, the maximum salary might be £500, and there might also be a higher initial salary; (d) since Assistant inspectors were called upon to perform general duties, this would be admirable in a small country like Wales, with a small inspectorate—indeed, 'this condition was imperative'.[5] Davies laid his case before the President, saying that 'when the E inspectorate for England was reorganized, and the new class of Assistant established the new arrangements were not applied to Wales because the subject was

---

[1] PRO Ed 23/146, Minute from Pullinger to Selby-Bigge, 16 July: 'Mr. Orange informs me that out of Vote B.I., £1,830 is allotted to occasional inspection. If Mr. Edwards were to have £100 or £150 . . . out of this Vote he could do everything necessary for specialist inspection in Wales'. Minute from H. W. Orange to Pullinger, re Vote B.I., 12 August: 'Do we spend it all? We saved £600 of the £1,830 last year, and we shall no doubt be able to let Mr. O. Edwards have £100 to £150 this year'. Vote B.I. referred to the annual Parliamentary vote for Educational purposes of which B.I. would be a sub-division.

[2] PRO Ed 23/146, Minute from the Permanent Secretary to the President, 12 August 1913.

[3] Ibid., Minute from the President to the Permanent Secretary, 13 August, seen by Edwards, 18 September.

[4] PRO Ed 23/147, Treasury to Board of Education, Sir Thomas Heath's letter of 21 December 1912 (21166/12).

[5] PRO Ed 23/147, Minute from Edwards to Davies, 2 April 1914.

344

The Welsh Department

not then pressing in that country, and it was deemed better to await developments and judge as to what was desirable in the light of them'.[1] He now felt that the time had arrived for the President to approve a similar principle for Wales.

The President readily assented, and proposed, in consultation with Davies to appoint a selection committee (for the appointment of Assistant inspectors) constituted on similar lines to the English one, and requested Davies to consult Orange about a draft letter to the Treasury.[1] Eventually, Casson was entrusted to make preliminary arrangements with the Establishment Section to supply information as to 'the existing arrangements within the Welsh inspectorate ... and to send some officer who has this knowledge ... who would discuss this matter with me'.[2] After this was done, the draft letter was sent to Davies on 8 October 1914,[3] and passed on to Edwards for his comments. Davies also suggested the composition of the Welsh selection committee: Chief Inspector for Wales (chairman), the Permanent Secretary of the Welsh Department, a representative of the Civil Service Commission, and a representative of the Establishment Section of the Office—the Chief Clerk.[4] Edwards agreed on all points and reminded Davies that 'at least three vacancies would have to be filled by August 1915'.[5] The letter to the Treasury was issued by Orange on 26 October.[6] It was a comprehensive statement incorporating the following points. First, the Board of Education referred to Sir Thomas Heath's letter of the 21 December 1912, which sanctioned the institution of the new class of Assistant inspector for service in England, and stated that 'the Board now desire sanction for the institution of a similar class for service in Wales. The first year's experience of the new class of subordinate inspector in England has proved satisfactory, and although the work of the Welsh inspectorate is arranged on somewhat different lines from ... the English side, no substantial reason exists for maintaining a different system of recruitment; secondly, at that time, the staff of the Welsh inspectorate numbered twenty-nine: one C.I. at £1,200; eight HMI's on the scale £400 x £20 to £800; two women inspectors on

---

[1] Ibid. Minute from Davies to the President, 3 April. In addition to the reasons given by Edwards, Davies added another: 'that in the mind of the public, or at any rate a certain section of it the non-application to Wales of the new arrangements would almost certainly be construed as an effort to prevent the class of men from whom the ranks of the Assistant Inspectorates are mainly recruited, from obtaining posts on the Welsh inspectorial staff. This would not, of course, be true, but it would not be wise for such an impression to get abroad and be fostered by any differentiation in this matter between the two countries'.

[2] PRO Ed 23/147, Minute from Orange (on behalf of the President) to Davies, 14 May 1914. Minute from Casson to Establishment Section, 29 September. Minute from RHC to Casson, 7 October.

[3] Ibid, Minute from Casson to Davies, 8 October.

[4] Ibid, Minute from Davies to Edwards, 13 October.

[5] Ibid, Minute from Edwards to Davies, 21 and 29 October.

[6] Ibid. Board of Education to the Treasury, 26 October.

The Welsh Department

the scale £200 x £15 to £400; two Sub-inspectors on a scale rising to £520; nine Sub-inspectors on a scale rising to £440; seven Junior inspectors on the scale £200 x £15 to £400'.[1] Vacancies on the subordinate staff were filled by the appointment either of Junior inspectors (men) or of women inspectors, the recruitment of Sub-inspectors having been entirely abandoned.

Unlike the English inspectorate, the Welsh side was not organized into separate Branches corresponding to different types of work, for example, elementary, secondary, technical, or teacher training, but was entrusted with the duty of inspecting and reporting on all types of education administered by the Welsh Department. It would be necessary therefore, to look for candidates with more varied kinds of experience for work in Wales, and Edwards was confident that they would be able to obtain a sufficient supply of suitable applicants, provided they were offered similar terms as regards salary, pension and prospects as were offered to their counterparts in England.[2] This structural unity of the Welsh inspectorate was achieved in Edwards's time. 'It was not until almost forty years later, after the 1944 Act, that the inspectorate in England was so unified. He saw the work of the Welsh Department, through its inspectors especially, as generally surveying "practically the whole of Welsh education", and aimed "at guiding and advising so that each part performed its proper work"—functions not usually associated with the work of inspecting in the early part of the century—and to (him) must be given credit, in Wales at least, for emphasizing this approach'.[3]

Formal approval was given by the Treasury in November 1914, to the appointments and salaries of the new class of Assistant inspector for Wales. Entries above the age of thirty-five were reserved for specific classes of candidates, for example, headmasters of schools, specialists in Drawing and other subjects, and those holding administrative or inspecting posts under LEAs, in which cases appointments would be made exceptionally, even beyond the age of forty-five.[4]

These changes in the structure of the Board's English and Welsh inspectorate demanded a new set of regulations and conditions of employment of Assistant inspectors[5] which were additional to the already existing elaborate details contained in a memorandum, *Miscellaneous*

---

[1] Ibid.
[2] PRO Ed 23/147, Minutes from Edwards to Davies, 27 and 29 October.
[3] *Pioneers of Welsh Education*, op. cit., p. 90.
[4] Ibid. Treasury to the Board of Education, 6 November.
[5] Board of Education, *Office Rules* 12 (England only), *Conditions of employment, etc., of Assistant Inspectors (Men), May* 1914.

346

The Welsh Department

Regulations and Instructions, (*T Inspection, No. 12*). This was designed to afford a convenient index to some of the more important regulations which concerned inspectors of all branches as well as T inspectors.[1] These were the iron laws which governed the day to day (and almost minute to minute) working life of HMI. But the choicest piece of all was found in an observation made by Morant as early as 1904—is worth recording for posterity—and should be of particular interest to the present day Women's Liberation Society! The regulations for inspectors of schools, and Morant's views on femininity deserve attention, if it were only for the sake of enlightening the unitiated and an ignorant public, of the demands made by the State upon its dedicated officials.

Morant, when confronted with the problem of filling a new post of Chief Woman Inspector, found it extremely difficult 'to give any precise or definite description' of what he was looking for. He had to confess that the work of the women inspectors of the Board had been mis-handled 'not only—perhaps not so much—by the women themselves, as by the methods adopted by the men under whom they have been placed; and this to such an extent that the Inspectorate generally pray that no more women inspectors be appointed, and to be quit altogether of those they have. The schools too, and the school authorities, have begun to feel very much in this way'. But in spite of his cynicism, he was apparently successful in his quest, and was moved to appoint Miss M. A. Lawrence, who evidently measured up to his chief requirement, that he 'must get a woman who will give prestige to the work of women inspectors'.[2]

Inevitably, a considerable amount of an inspector's work was routine, monotonous, time-consuming and demanded a high degree of continuous mental effort and physical energy—not forgetting such rare gifts as tact and diplomacy. But, surprisingly, there was no lack of enthusiasts waiting to assume the inspectorial yoke. In September 1914 there were vacancies impending in the Welsh inspectorate, and the President gave close attention to the question of promotion from the Junior staff. The vacancies arose because Mathews, a Sub-inspector, was being transferred to England in January 1915, and both William Edwards,[3] and J. Bancroft were due to retire in September and October 1915 respectively. It was necessary to

---

[1] Board of Education, *Memorandum, T Inspection, No.* 12. This superseded instructions in *Memoranda to Inspectors T, Nos.* 18, 63, 83, 194 *and* 224.

[2] PRO Ed 23/152 B, Note by Morant, December 1904.

[3] William Edwards, M.A., LL.D., (1851–1940). Appointed inspector of schools in 1877, and for 38 years was HMI for elementary schools in Glamorgan. On retirement in 1915, was prevailed upon to succeed Owen Owen as Chief Inspector of the Central Welsh Board, a position he held until 1926. Published a novel pamphlet *'Cynllun Newydd'* (A New Plan), in 1929, setting out a case that *every* pupil should receive a 'School Certificate' containing details of the pupil's performance in school examinations. (*Y Bywgraffiadur Cymreig op. cit., p.* 187).

The Welsh Department

promote two from the Junior staff, and of the four Sub-inspectors interviewed, Messrs. Gomer Jones, J. Evans, J. Bowen, and D. Thomas, along with three Junior inspectors, Messrs. Johns, G. P. Williams and A. A. Jones, only G. Prys Williams was promoted. With regard to the appointment of three new Assistant inspectors, the appointing committee was composed of Owen Edwards (chairman), Stanley Leathes (Civil Service Commission), A. T. Davies, the Chief Clerk to the Board, and T. G. Roberts (Secretary). The posts, widely advertised, attracted 300 applicants, and interviews were conducted at Bangor, Cardiff, Shrewsbury and London. Finally, four appeared before the President, and were appointed: J. Elias Jones, S. G. Jones, R. Rhydderch and W. J. Williams, the latter becoming Chief Inspector some years later.[1]

The remaining years of Edwards's work at the Welsh Department, from 1916 to his death in May, 1920 (he was knighted in 1916), covered the most crucial years of the war—1916 to 1918. With heavy routine office work, he also had to contend with depletion of inspectorial staff due to several inspectors being away in the armed Forces, and the deaths of two others Gomer Jones and Wakeford in 1916 and 1917 respectively. It would appear that this was more than enough for one, considerably overworked man. But again, during this period, he inevitably became heavily involved in other major responsibilities which placed a severe strain upon his physical and mental resources, and hastened his end at the comparatively early age of sixty-one.[2] These additional commitments had repercussions in one way or another upon the Welsh inspectorate, which, at the end of the war again needed review and further reorganization. In addition, the long-standing issue of the awkward dual inspection of schools by the Central Welsh Board and the Welsh Department demanded attention and re-consideration, and, if possible, final adjustment acceptable to both sides. The time-consuming tasks for which Edwards was destined, included his membership of the Royal Commission on University Education in Wales, the drafting of the Education Bill of 1918, and his work on the Bruce Committee for the reorganization of Welsh secondary education in 1919, whose Report appeared after his death in 1920.

But Edwards, though saddled with such demands upon his time and energy, was comforted and fortified by the arrival of a trusted friend and confidant. In May, 1915, J. Herbert Lewis, one of the most able and articulate of the Welsh Members, was transferred from the Local Govern-

---

[1] PRO Ed 23/148, Minutes from Edwards to Parliamentary Secretary and the President, 9 July and 9 September 1915.

[2] Owen Edwards, born 26 December 1858, died 15 May 1920.

The Welsh Department

ment Board to the Board of Education as Parliamentary Secretary, a position which he held until 1922. Lewis came among old friends, and after six months in his new post he wrote 'Maudslay, my Secretary is excellent, able, hardworking and willing to the last degree . . . Selby-Bigge, the Permanent Secretary, a very able head of office. Morant has, I think, very distinctly left his stamp on him and on Phipps, a man of remarkable personality—tall, very handsome, with beautiful white teeth, a perpetual smile . . . My old friend Bruce is the head of the Secondary Branch. It is now 25 years since I began to work with him in Intermediate education. What a curious fact it is, that after so many years, A. T. Davies and I, who were partners together in Liverpool, are now once more in harness together . . . Owen Edwards is the C.I. for Wales. The greatest honour I have at the Board of Education is that of being, at any rate the nominal "Chief" of the greatest living benefactor to Welsh literature. I often say that when those of us who are now working for Wales are forgotten dust, two names will survive—those of Lloyd George and Owen Edwards. Ceir gweled. [We shall see]'.[1]

Edwards and Lewis were now able to work in close harmony together. One of Lewis's first acts was to see that Edwards had a hand in reforming the Welsh University. The financial condition of the University Colleges was causing concern to the Principals and University officials. They appealed to Lewis for advice. It was decided to set up a Royal Commission to inquire into University education in Wales, with Lewis mainly responsible for choosing the members of the Commission. Among them were Sir Henry Jones and W. N. Bruce; Edwards was an 'obvious must'. But surprisingly, a strong current of opposition was mounting against Edwards. Lewis told the President 'I feel we *must* have on the Commission a man who, without being specially connected with any particular college, knows every branch of Welsh education thoroughly, and from the inside . . . Owen Edwards. His great services to the children of Wales . . . his Welsh enthusiasm (pooh-poohed by the educationists of the old-fashioned type who regard Welsh as a sentimental fad) and his reforming zeal make him in my judgement indispensable . . . But I am bound to tell you that to the three Principals and those who follow them, he is anathema, and they will be intensely dissatisfied if he is appointed. Judging from letters I have received, this exclusion is their chief anxiety. They solemnly predict a Minority Report as if that were the last calamity that could befall Welsh education'.[2] Edwards was appointed and Lord Haldane was persuaded to

---

[1] J. Herbert Lewis's Diary, 29 November 1915, Penucha MSS.
[2] Lewis to the President, 4 January 1916, Penucha MSS.

act as chairman.[1] When the Report of the Commission was published, it revealed Edwards's views on modern university studies and administration from his examination of the witnesses (including his own brother, Professor Edward Edwards), his zeal for Welsh studies, modern methods of teaching, and the emphasis he placed on the education of the *Welsh* student.

In 1917–18, the new President, the historian H. A. L. Fisher, together with Lewis and Edwards were drafting the new Education Bill which became the Education Act of 1918. Edwards, anticipating the changes rendered necessary by the Act in Wales—which included, among other provisions, Lewis's cherished scheme of adolescent education between the ages of 14 and 18, the raising of the school leaving age to 14, and day continuation classes—had to await the new schemes which had to be submitted to the Board by the LEAs, but which were never implemented due to the economic depression at the end of hostilities.[2]

The reorganization of the Welsh inspectorial districts and the inspectorate was Edwards's next immediate task at the end of the war, but he only lived long enough to sketch his ideas before he died in 1920. The complete scheme was designed by others, took over six years to materialize, with considerable modification of his suggestions. He started his grand survey in February, 1918, in a hand-written questionnaire to each of his HMIs—R. E. Hughes, B. B. Skirrow, G. Prys Williams, D. Evan Jones, H. Price, W. Williams and L. J. Roberts.[3] He asked for detailed information on the distribution of inspection work in each Welsh inspectorial district.

An analysis of the replies showed that a large amount of time and effort was expended by inspectors on War Savings work, for example, G. Prys Williams in the south west Wales area and D. E. Jones in Radnor, Barry and Mountain Ash.[4] Also Dr. W. Williams (for north Wales and Montgomeryshire), L. J. Roberts (Glamorgan and Merthyr), H. Price (Breconshire, Cardiff, Pontypridd and Rhondda), and R. E. Hughes (Monmouthshire, Newport, Ebbw Vale, and Abertillery), complained of insufficient staff to carry on 'even the ordinary work of school inspection'.[5] Insufficient inspectors meant that HMIs were arranging among themselves

---

[1] K. Idwal Jones, (ed.), *Syr Herbert Lewis*, op. cit., p. 83.

[2] Edwards to Lewis, 23 July 1917, Penucha MSS: Departmental Committee for Juvenile Education in relation to employment after the war, (the Lewis Report). Edwards made an interesting observation on further education: 'Nothing ought to be settled until the Report of the University Commission is before the country. The new University Court, a thoroughly democratic body, will, I hope, take the guidance, if not the control of the whole nation's education in the case of persons over 18. If it works well, it might, in time, guide the education of children and youths as well'.

[3] PRO Ed 23/149: Questionnaire to all HMIs, 15 February 1918.

[4] Ibid., Williams to Edwards, 18 February; Jones to Edwards, 17 February.

[5] PRO Ed 23/149, W. Williams to Edwards, 21 February 1918; Roberts to Edwards, 23 February; Price to Edwards, 19 February; Hughes to Edwards, 16 February.

certain distribution of work between their respective territories.[1] All HMIs stressed that they were overworked and advised Edwards to appoint additional inspectors.[2] G. Prys Williams (a favourite of Edwards), in answer to question 2, (which asked for suggestions for a better distribution of inspection districts) proceeded to unfold his ideas on the complete reorganization of the Welsh inspectorate, and included a long memorandum on a suggested redistribution of inspectors' districts in Wales, with detailed comments. His plan gave the complete picture of E, S, and T schools in Wales in 1918.[3] In the introduction to his observations on the plan, Williams—an ever-ready purveyor of unsolicited advice, though always sensible and relevant—made certain suggestions: 'Assuming that the number of HMIs is to remain what it is now, I would suggest that the Chief Inspector should be relieved of the detail work incidental to having charge of a district, however small—reserving for himself the duties of generalissimo, and for the broader phases of educational policy'.[4] Then he explained the district arrangements, basing his statistics on those given in the *Directory* for 1915, which would do away with the great disparity that existed between one district and another, for example, Dr. William Williams's district had 698 E Departments, while D. E. Jones and Skirrow had only 114 and 122 respectively. Secondly, under his proposed arrangement, each HMI would have sole charge of E, S, and T work in his area. It was pointed out that 'under the proposed Bill, the Part III Authorities, in consultation, of course, and in collaboration with the major Authorities, would have more to say than hitherto, to the administration of education other than E. Thirdly, nearly all the proposed districts would be composed of areas, each of which would have educational and administrative problems to solve 'that were analogous with those of the other component parts'.[5] This would help to give more congruity to the work of the HMI—a result that was, from some points of view desirable, though HMI himself might prefer variety. Thus District No. 1 would be composed entirely of county boroughs; District No. 2, of Glamorgan urban districts; District No. 5, of areas that were partly rural and partly industrial, i.e. the counties on the fringe of the south Wales coalfield.[6]

Williams believed that his plan would go some way towards restoring the balance in favour of rural Welsh Wales. Its interests, in so far as

[1] Ibid.
[2] Ibid.
[3] Ibid., G. Prys Williams to Edwards, 18 February 1918. See Appendix 3.
[4] PRO Ed 23/149, G. Prys Williams to Edwards, 18 February 1918.
[5] Ibid.
[6] Ibid.

The Welsh Department

school inspection and all it signified were concerned, were in some danger of being sacrificed to the industrial and somewhat cosmopolitan population of Glamorgan. The table failed to show what T work, other than that of the larger institutions, was being done under the conditions prevailing at that time. He emphasized that the passage of the Education Bill into law would inevitably put a different complexion upon the administration of T work. The last column of the table—the population in thousands—was inserted to give some sort of rough indication of how the Districts would compare in the number of young persons who would be under instruction, either full time up to 16, or part time up to 18, and accordingly columns I and IV should be considered together. Finally, in the matter of accessibility from any H.Q., the two north Wales Districts would be difficult. The remedies were obvious, (but the expenses would escalate) a more extensive use of the telephone between HMIs headquarters and the LEA offices, and a motor car for each HMI 'to render himself as independent as possible of the railways, where those were awkward'.[1] Two days after he received this reply and memorandum, Edwards sent G. Prys Williams his own scheme for the reorganization of the Welsh inspectorate.[2]

At this juncture, before referring to his scheme, it would appear to be relevant to reflect on the statement that Edwards's involvement in time-consuming committee work of a national character, tended to have repercussions within the Welsh inspectorate, and, perhaps, on his own duties as Chief Inspector. He had set about collecting information on the work of his inspectors in a rather strange manner, i.e. in the form of a questionnaire to them. It is hardly credible that due to his pre-occupation with other important matters, he was so out of touch, so isolated, and unaware of the precise duties and problems of his colleagues, when it is known that he was still travelling around the schools. Yet, this is the unmistakable impression left upon the mind after reading the replies. Meticulous records had to be kept and transmitted to the Welsh Department for the Board of Education, and all the statistics and other information which he required were readily available, but it was apparent that he had neither the time nor the inclination to assemble them. As Chief Inspector it was his responsibility to ensure that the distribution of work was equitable and satisfactory, and it would seem to be an easy matter to get his staff together to discuss mutual problems. Was it not his business to see that the schools were inspected regularly and according to a fixed schedule? Did he not know what E, S, and T work were inspected, and

[1] PRO Ed 23/149, Prys Williams to Edwards, 18 February 1918.
[2] PRO Ed 23/152 A, Edwards to Prys Williams, 20 February 1918.

how? On the other hand, it was possible that Edwards framed his questions in such a way so that his inspectors could convey to him the difficulties and problems which confronted them, so that he could muster his ideas quicker about reorganization and the number of extra staff required.

It was evident that Edwards had given some thought to this matter before circulating the questionnaire, for enclosed with a 'private and confidential' letter to G. Prys Williams, was a half-sheet of note paper on which was written his plan in Welsh:[1]

'Y cynllun yr wyf fi wedi bod yn cyfeirio'n araf ato yw hwn:—

I. Rhannu Cymru'n dair—
(a) Gogledd (b) De-Orllewin: Ceredigion, Dyfed, Deheubarth, a hwyrach Brycheiniog a Maesyfed. (c) De Ddwyrain—Morgannwg a Mynwy.

II. Rhoi Divisional HMI ym mhob un, hynny yw, codi tri uwchlaw'r lleill.

III. Rhoi HMI neu Assistant I. danynt, un ymhob sir.
Y mae'r Gogledd yn gyflawn, fel y gwelwch, y De-Orllewin yn agos a bod,—ond y De-Dwyrain!

(i) Ar hyn o bryd y mae cyflogau'r holl HMIs yr un.

(ii) Y mae pum HMI cyfartal ar y gwastadeddau—Skirrow, Roberts, Price, D. E. Jones, R. E. Hughes. Pwy rhoddid yn ben? Ai'r hynaf?

Ar hyn o bryd, rhaid i mi fodloni ar geisio rhannu Morgannwg yn wastatach— rhoi mwy i Skirrow a Jones.

Rhaid i ni gyfarfod gynted a medrwn wedi i'r Bil basio'.[2]

In the light of later events, Edwards's plan was never implemented, for in terms of seniority according to age, Skirrow and D. E. Jones were the obvious candidates for consideration as Divisional HMIs, and according to seniority of appointment to the inspectorate, L. J. Roberts and Jones.[3] But none achieved that rank. In fact, Edwards vacillated to the point of inaction regarding promotion, which provoked frustration among his colleagues. This was more then substantiated by one of his ablest inspectors

---

[1] Ibid. As late as May 1920, Prys Williams enclosed this half-sheet in a letter to A. T. Davies, saying 'I should be glad . . . if you would kindly let me have the original back. Everything written by him is precious'. This was a few days before Edwards died.

[2] The plan for which I have been slowly working is this: I. Divide Wales into three (Divisions)
(a) North (b) South West: Cardigan, Pembroke, Carmarthen, and perhaps Brecknock and Radnor (c) South East: Glamorgan and Monmouth.

II. Put a Divisional Inspector in each, i.e. raise three above the others.

III. Put an HMI or AI under them in each county. The North is, as you will see, complete: the South West is nearly so; but the South East!

i. At present the HMIs are all on the same scale of salaries.

ii. There are five HMIs of equal rank on the plains—Skirrow, Roberts, Price, D. E. Jones, and R. E. Hughes. Who is to be made head? The senior?

At present I must be content with trying to divide Glamorgan more evenly—giving more to Skirrow and Jones. We must meet as soon as possible after the passage of the Bill'.

[3] Dates of birth: B. B. Skirrow, 5.10. 1863; L. J. Roberts, 29.5.1866; H. Price, 22.3.1872; D. E. Jones, 21.12.1863; R. E. Hughes, 19.6.1866. The senior HMI was, according to age, Skirrow. According to appointment to the inspectorate, L. J. Roberts, 10.2.1894, and D. E. Jones, 7.3.1894.

The Welsh Department

who worked closely with him for over five years. Abel J. Jones, perhaps, had an axe to grind, but his observations on his Chief Inspector are more than revealing. He has recorded 'When I say he (Edwards) was the greatest chief I ever worked under, I mean that he was the greatest man I ever worked under. Whether he was a great Chief Inspector is open to argument . . . he had very little idea of delegation of duties. He would take upon himself a great load of the most important work'.[1] Jones went much further, and attributed the weak *structure* of the Welsh inspectorate to Edwards's mania for economizing. It was said that when the Welsh Department was formed, and the two chief officials appointed at a salary of £1,250 each, that this £2,500 had to be saved in some other way! Edwards tried to solve this problem by making HMIs districts larger, and the proportion of Assistant inspectors higher—a procedure which considerably retarded the promotion of Assistant inspectors. Jones remarked that 'during Edwards's tenure of the post of Chief Inspector from 1907 to 1920, only one Assistant inspector was promoted. Within five years of his death, there were ten promotions'.[2] The composition of the Welsh inspectorate on 25 March 1920 was: 1 Chief Inspector; 8 HMIs; 5 Sub-inspectors; 5 Junior inspectors, and 8 Assistant inspectors.[3]

Reorganization of the Welsh inspectorate was in abeyance for a period of over two years, and shifted from Edwards to A. T. Davies in the years 1919–20, when Edwards had been weighed down with personal setbacks, including the death of Lady Edwards in April 1919. Prys Williams was not slow to acquaint Davies of the plan which Edwards had sent him in February, 1918, no doubt since Davies had proceeded to consider the reorganization of the inspectorate during Edwards's indisposition in May, 1920. Important preliminary discussions had been initiated between Davies, Dr. W. Williams and Prys Williams during the very week of Edwards's death. Definite action was impending, when Davies, after a meeting at W. Williams's home in Wrexham, asked him to review the position of the Welsh inspectorate as compared with the English side. As a result of a further meeting with Davies at Dolywern (Glynceiriog), his country retreat, in the same month, W. Williams had prepared a memorandum on the statistics of the inspectorate in England and Wales, which, he stated 'presented the case very clearly' for overhauling the Welsh one.[4]

[1] Abel J. Jones, '*I was Privileged.*' Cardiff, 1943, pp. 67–72.
[2] Ibid.
[3] See Appendix **4** to this Study. This was two months before the death of Edwards.
[4] PRO Ed 23/152 A. W. Williams to Davies, 15 May 1920.

The Welsh Department

Inspectorial Staff	England	Wales	
Chief Inspectors	5	1	
Inspectors of Senior or Divisional Rank	31	0	MEN
Ordinary Inspectors (HMI)	128	7	
Subordinate Staff	105	19	
TOTAL	269	27	
Chief Inspectors	1	0	
Inspectors of Senior or Divisional Rank	5	0	WOMEN
Ordinary Inspectors (HMI)	48	2*	
TOTAL	54	2	
GRAND TOTAL	323	29	

*lent from England

The latest returns showed:

	England	Wales	Ratio
No. of school pupils on books	5,499,892	466,321	11.8:1
No. of school pupils in average attendance	4,782,597	401,623	11.9:1

In his analysis, Williams stated that, taking the ratio as 12 : 1, it measured the relative amounts of work to be dealt within the two countries. Secondary education (in schools receiving grants from the Board of Education) was, relatively and numerically, more advanced in Wales than in England, while T work at all grades was also, relatively, about the same. Again, tested by the ratio 12:1, the standard of the inspectorial staff in Wales fell far short of that of England. For Wales, the number of inspectors of senior and Divisional rank was much too low, since Wales should have three—a senior and two Divisionals—and not one. Also, the number of inspectors of ordinary rank, HMIs, was too low—Wales should have ten or eleven, and not seven. It was very strange that while the Subordinate staff in England was only 7/11 of that of full inspectors—in Wales it was otherwise, the Subordinate staff being $2\frac{1}{2}$ times that of full inspectors.[1] Indeed, Edwards had been completely out of touch with his own needs, and the needs of Wales and its inspectors, and had never bothered to investigate the bare figures of comparison between the two countries.

W. Williams made three observations on this state of affairs. First, the differences in the inspectorial staff of Wales as compared with England made it impossible to secure the same efficiency in the standard of the

[1] PRO Ed 23/152 A, W. Williams to Davies, 15 May 1920.

work in the two cases. Second, the Chief Inspector for Wales must have been grossly overworked, and help could have been given him by HMIs only at the expense of adding to the responsibilities and difficulties of the latter, who were also overworked—responsible as they were for E, S, and T work. Again, HMIs had to contend with the work of Divisional inspectors, and the Subordinate staff had to help in the work of HMIs. Third, inadequate staff of full and senior inspectors, which caused so much borrowing from one grade to another and obviously temporary in effect, with no long-term policy and depth of knowledge of strange inspectorial terrain, could but seriously impair the efficiency of the Welsh inspectorate. Williams rightly emphasized that inspectors should be able 'to concentrate upon, and give time (clear and fresh) to the real work of education (*ysbryd y peth byw*—in the schools and with the pupil teachers —that for which all else exists) ... It is most desirable that they should be enabled to do this as their highest and most inspiring duties'.[1] The remedy seemed clear. The staff in Wales was adequate in quality and calibre, but required re-adjustment as to grades and standing, so as to share, and distribute, the higher responsibilities of the work. Such adjustment would merely bring it just to the standard of the English inspectorate. Additionally, and most important of all perhaps, other excellent inspectors needed re-grading and a number of new appointments absolutely necessary.[2]

In his dispassionate analysis, Williams had revealed the truth underlying the weaknesses of the Welsh inspectorate—too few trying to do too much—inspectors who were denied the status and remuneration which their English counterparts enjoyed, with considerably less strain and more congenial prospects of advancement. It was both ironical and tragic that such a clear indictment of Edwards's shortcomings as an administrator should have emanated from one of his most loyal colleagues.

Suggesting a scheme of reorganization, Williams proposed the promotion of three HMIs to senior and Divisional rank in accordance with the English standard. One would be in charge of the whole of north Wales for E, S, and T work, 'with Aberystwyth added, and such part of mid-Wales as might be considered naturally allied to the bulk of north Wales'.[3] The second would be responsible 'for E and Training College work in the rest of south Wales (as English E Divisionals inspect Training Colleges),

[1] Ibid.
[2] Ibid.
[3] PRO Ed 23/152 A, W. Williams to Davies, 15 May 1920.

The Welsh Department

and as Mr. Legard acted in Wales'.[1] The third would be concerned 'for S and T work in the rest of Wales, as Capt. Shaw acted'.[2] If three HMIs were promoted, the staff needed ten HMIs, and six of the Subordinate staff should be promoted, and according to the English standard, Wales was also entitled to two additional women HMIs. Williams maintained that this scheme was a very moderate statement of the case for Wales, and urged that 'the present seems the opportunity to get the adjustment made on the general lines we discussed'.[3] Judging from other matters raised in his memorandum, Williams, obviously *persona grata* with Davies, asked (perhaps with visions of eventually assuming Edwards's mantle) if he might 'occasionally, be allowed to visit the office in London to discuss matters connected with our work', and, 'if the HMI staff in Wales were on the scale of that in England . . . and the due proportion of them assigned to north Wales . . . there would be no difficulty for me, if desired, to attend the Central Welsh Board'.[4] Sir Owen Edwards died the very day Williams sent his memorandum to Davies.

After Edwards's death, Davies was left alone to face the reorganization of the inspectorate and the all-important matter of the role of the Central Welsh Board inspectorial staff in relation to it. It was the old, old story repeated yet again, but with mounting crescendo—the existence of two inspecting bodies, the Board's inspectorate charged with responsibility for *all* types of secondary education in Wales, and the Central Welsh Board's inspectors, possessing certain defined, but limited functions respecting *intermediate schools* only. In the past, certain steps had been taken to effect some kind of integration between the two bodies in the form of an interim arrangement mainly for consultations, conferences and joint visits to schools. But, from 1918 onwards, the intermediate schools required increasing financial assistance from the LEAs (which received additional grants in aid from the Board of Education) which meant that the latter had the unavoidable duty of satisfying themselves that the expenditure by the LEAs was both properly and economically disbursed. Greater financial assistance from public funds through the LEAs to supplement the slender income of the Central Welsh Board implied greater control and supervision by the Board of Education through the Welsh Department.

---

[1] Ibid.
[2] Ibid.
[3] Ibid.
[4] Ibid. In a post-script to the Memorandum, W. Williams's reference to the Central Welsh Board meant that he would like to fill Edwards's place at their meetings. Williams also proceeded, in the manner of a testimonial to himself, to say 'this, I would on other grounds, like, as I am fond of creative and organizing work. As you know, I have had to do with difficult public bodies—both before and after coming under the Board—one of them regarded by Sir Owen (Edwards) as very awkward—but have never had a difficulty —nor failed to get what was desired through, and usually carried out successfully. But this, and other matters relating to S work you will be able to . . . discuss more in detail if I can see you on Thursday'?

During 1923, the Central Welsh Board, who faced a yet greater expenditure, had to make further overtures to the LEAs for voluntary aid. In December of the same year, Sir Alfred T. Davies (he had been knighted in 1918) submitted, informally, proposals to the Central Welsh Board for a unified inspectorate of education in Wales. Almost identical proposals, with the acquiescence of two successive Presidents of the Board of Education were, subsequently, submitted officially, with the object of helping the Central Welsh Board to overcome their financial difficulties, and to bring about a fusion of the two inspectorates—a question which formed such an important part of the recommendations of the *Departmental Committee on the Organization of Secondary Education in Wales*. The proposals submitted to the Central Welsh Board were under consideration by that body from early January until 25 July 1924 without any definite outcome.[1]

Charles Trevelyan, President of the Board in the first Labour government, had sent the proposals to the Central Welsh Board on 8 July for consideration at their meeting on 25 July. He explained the reasons which prompted the Board of Education to attempt to arrive at a solution of serious administrative difficulties connected with the organization of secondary education in Wales. The jurisdiction of the Central Welsh Board should be extended to include the inspection of all grant-aided secondary schools in Wales. The inspectorates of the Central Welsh Board and the Board of Education should be fused by the appointment as HMIs of the inspectors of the Central Welsh Board. A panel of the unified inspectorate should be assigned to the Central Welsh Board to report to them on all schools exactly as their own inspectors had done hitherto. As a measure of compensation for the surrender of their inspectors, the Central Welsh Board should be given an equal voice with the Welsh Department in all future appointments to the Welsh inspectorate; while, in return for the Board of Education taking over the cost of the Central Welsh Board's inspectors, the Treasury Grant of £1,200 payable to that Board should be surrendered, resulting in a net saving to the latter about £1,000 *per annum*.[2]

The President recalled the circumstances under which these proposals were made—the inadequate finances of the Central Welsh Board which made it difficult for them to fulfil their duties, and the unofficial proposals put before their representatives by Sir Alfred T. Davies. That Board's representatives were so impressed that they unanimously resolved, that

[1] *Report of the Board of Education (Welsh Department)*, 1924, pp. 6–7.
[2] Ibid. Appendix 1, p. 18.

The Welsh Department

if they were put forward officially, that they would request their Board to give them sympathetic consideration. After these proposals were submitted officially, they became the subject of prolonged discussion in Welsh educational circles. The main objection arose from a fear that the 'autonomy' of the Central Welsh Board, enjoyed for thirty years, would be diminished. The President emphasized that he had no desire to impair this 'autonomy'. He was anxious to maintain its position, and to assist its work more efficiently, for it was 'in that spirit that he had consented to endorse proposals which had already received the approval of (his) predecessor'.[1]

The Departmental Committee on the *Organization of Secondary Education in Wales* had been concerned with the establishment of a national system of public education in the Principality. Administratively, secondary education was becoming more complicated after the war. The President was aware that 101 intermediate schools were inspected by the Central Welsh Board, and a further thirty-four secondary schools, continually increasing in number, together with all elementary schools, Training Colleges, and institutions for further education were inspected solely by the Board of Education.[2] It seemed to him inconsistent with the idea of a national system of education that the intermediate schools should be separate. For the unification of Welsh education the proposals envisaged were a necessary preliminary to that end. Dual inspection would disappear, and the Central Welsh Board would have at their disposal, at least fourteen inspectors who would report to them in exactly the same way as their own three inspectors did. The financial straits in which that body found themselves could be re-considered by the Board of Education as soon as it was known whether the proposals were acceptable. But the President knew that the cautious Central Welsh Board were clinging resolutely to a condition of acceptance that was totally inadmissible. He stated 'that at the recent conference in London with the Parliamentary Secretary, it would appear that the acceptance of these proposals was made *contingent upon an entirely new consideration,* viz., that I should definitely pledge myself to the establishment of a National Council of Education for Wales . . . I have endeavoured . . . to make absolutely clear my own position, which is, that I am in favour of the principle of devolution, whether in education or in any other field of local government. But that is a wider question of general national policy which involves many other considerations. I can only say that there is nothing in these proposals

[1] Ibid.
[2] The number of pupils in Welsh intermediate schools in 1895–96: 3,367; in 1923–24: 23,276.

The Welsh Department

which would form any obstacle to any further measures of devolution of which Parliament might subsequently approve'.[1]

Meanwhile, in the absence of any agreement by the Central Welsh Board, together with the prospect of either no acceptance or further interminable delay, the Welsh Department proceeded to reorganize the Welsh inspectorate. None of the schemes outlined by Sir Owen Edwards or the two Welsh HMIs—G. Prys Williams and W. Williams—was, in the event, adopted. In October 1924, Sir Alfred Davies issued a *Circular* to the Welsh LEAs and other governing bodies of schools, on the *Reorganization of the Board's Welsh Inspectorate*.[2] The regrading and redistribution of the entire staff of twenty-seven inspectors of all grades made it possible for the Board of Education, without impairing in any way the rights or functions of the Central Welsh Board, to meet the growing demand for supervision of the secondary schools in Wales of all types. *Circular 153* gave the authorized establishment and the motives for the reorganization:

> 'The rapid expansion of the Board's work in Wales, as evidenced by the increase in the number of educational institutions of all kinds which has taken place since the Welsh Department was set up in 1907, has rendered necessary a re-grading, re-organization, and re-distribution of the Board's inspectorial staff in Wales with a view to effecting that co-ordination of different types of education which it was one of the aims of the Education Act of 1902 to bring about, and which the Education Act of 1918 has made still more necessary'.[3]

The number of inspectors was reduced from twenty-nine because the increase in the number of full inspectors authorized to assume complete responsibility 'greatly facilitated the despatch of public business. The increased use of motor cars and motor bicycles has also enabled the inspectorate largely to overcome the difficulties of the train services and of geographical conditions, with the result that inspectors can now cover a much wider area with much less fatigue and inconvenience than was previously possible'.[4]

The composition of the new Welsh inspectorate was:

Divisional Inspectors	2
H M Inspectors	12
H M Inspectors (Women)	2
Assistant Inspectors	11
Total	27

[1] *Report of the Board of Education* (*Welsh Department*), 1924, Appendix 1, p. 19.
[2] *Board of Education, Welsh Department, Circular* 153, October 1924.
[3] Ibid. p. 2.
[4] *Report of the Board of Education* (*Welsh Department*), 1924, p. 7.

The Welsh Department

As was expected, the President appointed Dr. W. Williams and Dr. G. Prys Williams, HMIs,[1] to the new posts of Divisional Inspectors, both of whom, in the capacity of Supervising Inspectors, had actively assisted in carrying out the duties of Chief Inspector, a post which had been taken over by Sir Alfred Davies (in addition to his post of Permanent Secretary) in 1920, on the death of Sir Owen Edwards. Dr. W. Williams became responsible for the whole of north Wales, in addition to the counties of Montgomeryshire, Radnor, Brecon and Monmouth, including the county borough of Newport. Dr. G. Prys Williams was assigned the rest of south and west Wales. Promoted to the new posts of HMI, and to vacancies in the same grade were: Messrs. W. C. R. Johns, Caleb Rees, John Thomas, J. Elias Jones, W. J. Williams (later to become the third Chief Inspector), Tom Owen and A. G. Prys-Jones, who were formerly Assistant inspectors. The two women HMIs were Miss Menai J. Rowlands and Miss M. E. Ellis.[2]

Inspectorate Staff (Wales), October 1924

Area A: Divisional Inspector, Dr. William Williams, HMI., with headquarters in north Wales (Llandudno).

Area B: Divisional Inspector, Dr. G. Prys Williams, HMI., with headquarters in south Wales (Llanelli).

HM Inspectors

W. R. C. Johns; Dr. Abel J. Jones, O.B.E.; J. Elias Jones; Tom Owen, M.C.; H. Price; A. G. Prys-Jones; Caleb Rees; R. Rhydderch; W. Roberts; B. B. Skirrow; John Thomas; W. J. Williams; Miss M. J. Rowlands; Miss M. E. Ellis.

Assistant Inspectors

C. P. Clayton, M.C.; D. T. Davies; M. H. Davies, M.C.; W. H. Evans; J. E. Hooson; T. Jones; J. W. Lewis; P. A. Lewis; A. Taylor; David Thomas, O.B.E.; T. H. Lewis, who took up appointment 1 April 1925.

In charge, University Tutorial Classes, Area A: W. Roberts, HMI.
In charge, University Tutorial Classes, Area B: W. J. Williams, HMI.

For Training Colleges and University Training Departments, the following English inspectors assisted: W. K. Spencer, HMI (Science); W. Scutt, HMI (Drawing); Dr. A. Somervell, and G. T. Shaw, HMI (Music); A. S. Bright, HMI (Handicraft.)

In the interim period, pending the result of negotiations between the Central Welsh Board and the Board of Education, it was stated that, as hitherto, the Board of Education would rely on the reports of the Central

---

[1] G. Prys Williams was appointed Chief Inspector, 22 November 1928. Died, 27 October 1933. He was the second Chief Inspector after Sir Owen Edwards—a gap of 8 years. The Board paid the following tribute to Williams: 'In him, a profound and liberal scholarship combined with native gentleness of character to produce a personality of uncommon charm. The loss of his wise and inspiring influence will be felt in every branch of Welsh education, but nowhere more than in the little country schools for which he had so warm an affection'. (*Board of Education (Welsh Department) Report*, 1933, p. 11.

[2] *Circular* 153, op. cit.

Welsh Board for information as to the conditions and progress of intermediate schools. Regarding the financial side, the Education Act of 1918 had inaugurated a new system of paying grants which had considerably increased the responsibilities and duties of the Board of Education, whereby the latter had to undertake a detailed scrutiny of the expenditure of LEAs in order to satisfy themselves, through their inspectors, 'that all schools and institutions on which public money was expended, were conducted in such a way as to comply in all respects with the Board's grant regulations'.[1]

But the 1924 proposals did not meet with acceptance at the hands of the Central Welsh Board or of the LEAs. That unity in administration and inspection, so dearly sought by Sir Alfred Davies and the Board of Education, remained unresolved; he had the mortification of having to retire from his post without having accomplished his cherished desire of bringing the Central Welsh Board to a far less truculent attitude than they had displayed for eighteen years.[2] It fell to the lot of his successor, Percy Watkins, during the next few months, to open fresh discussions with representatives of the Central Welsh Board 'with a view to devising proposals which, while aiming to achieve the same objects as the 1924 proposals had in view, *should leave unimpaired, the appointment by the Central Welsh Board of their own inspectorate*',[3] and '*certain adjustments in the existing scheme for the administration of the Central Welsh Education Fund*'.[4]

The new proposals were approved by the Central Welsh Board on 17 July 1925 and subsequently confirmed by the LEAs. But still the old story had not come to an end, dichotomy remained in diluted form, because the proposals were framed in such a manner 'as to avoid the placing of any barriers in the way of any future measure of devolution for Wales, and did not aim at any immediate alteration of a fundamental character in the existing powers either of the Central Welsh Board or of the Board of Education'.[5] But in fact they did—they certainly enhanced the individuality and prestige of the former, both administratively and financially.

---

[1] *Circular* 153, op. cit., p. 3.

[2] A. T. Davies Papers, op. cit., G. Prys Williams to Davies, 26 November 1923: 'It is pitiful—tragic—to think that your endeavour to bring about co-operation and a thorough collaboration with the Central Welsh Board should, so far at least, not have gone through. It seems to me that the good seed you have sown must ultimately produce a good harvest ... The very stress, financial and other, which all educational bodies have now to bear, from the University downwards, should weld them all into one'.

[3] *Board of Education (Welsh Department) Report*, 1925, p. 4.

[4] Ibid., p. 6, Appendix 1.

[5] Ibid.

The Welsh Department

The proposals were in two parts, Proposals A—for co-operation between the Central Welsh Board and the Board of Education in the matter of inspection of schools, and Proposals B—for a change in the method of providing income for the Central Welsh Board.[1] Proposals A were to be regarded as provisional arrangements pending the framing of a practical scheme of devolution in the form of a National Council of Education for Wales, on the lines recommended by the Departmental Committee. They were: (i) *two sets of inspectorates would continue*, subject to the general control of their own Boards, but the inspections themselves would be joint and unified inspections; (ii) *the Central Welsh Board should, forthwith, appoint a Chief Inspector*, and the Scheme of the Board be amended to enable them to offer a salary with a higher maximum than the £800 permitted under the old Scheme;[2] (iii) the Chief Inspector of the Central Welsh Board should continue to take charge of the inspection of intermediate schools, but, by agreement, could also use on his panel, the inspectors of the Board of Education; (iv) in the case of a full inspection of intermediate schools, the Chief Inspector of the Central Welsh Board would be in charge of the joint panel, and he or one of his colleagues, selected by him, should be the reporting inspector; (v) in the case of a subsidiary inspection, it would be undertaken either by an inspector of the Central Welsh Board or by an inspector of the Board of Education, to be arranged between the Chief Inspector of the Central Welsh Board and the Divisional Inspector in Wales of the Board of Education.[3]

With regard to the inspection of non-intermediate schools, the Divisional Inspectors of the Board of Education for north or south Wales would continue to take charge, but could, by arrangement, use the inspectors of the Central Welsh Board. In the case of full and subsidiary inspections, the Welsh Divisional Inspectors of the Board of Education would act precisely in the same way as the Chief Inspector of the Central Welsh Board in (iv) and (v) above.[4] Further methods of co-operation were set out in great detail, in a list, which included:

That the Board of Education should consult the executive committee of the Central Welsh Board with reference to
(a) the consideration of schemes of LEAs.
(b) the consideration of programmes of expenditure of LEAs

---

[1] *Report of the Board of Education (Welsh Department)*, 1925, Appendix I, pp. 6, ff.

[2] Mr. D. Vaughan Johnston, M.A., Headmaster of Lewis School, Pengam, was appointed on 21 January 1926, on the retirement of Dr. William Edwards (former HMI), who had 'temporarily' held the post since 1915.

[3] *Report of the Board of Education (Welsh Department)*, 1925, Appendix I, pp. 7-8.

[4] Ibid., Appendix I, p. 8.

The Welsh Department

    (c) the nomination of teachers for admission to vacation courses organized by the Board of Education

    (d) periodic consultations between the Welsh Divisional Inspectors and the Chief Inspector of the Central Welsh Board

    (e) joint consultation by inspectors of both Boards with LEAs on matters affecting intermediate schools

    (f) that opportunities be afforded to Central Welsh Board inspectors to accompany the Divisional Welsh Inspectors on visits to elementary schools, Central Schools, Junior Technical schools and Training Colleges, not for inspecting purposes, but in order to get first hand information on the work of such institutions.

    (g) that the Scheme of the Central Welsh Board should be amended in order to enable that Board to give effect to the proposals.[1]

Proposals B had been prepared by the Permanent Secretary of the Welsh Department in his personal capacity, for the purposes of discussion. If accepted by the Central Welsh Board and approved by the LEAs, he was prepared to recommend their adoption to the Board of Education and to the Treasury.[1] For historical reasons, any proposed scheme of providing additional income for the Central Welsh Board on a statutory basis might prove complicated and difficult.[2] Actually, all they were entitled to, under Treasury regulations and the Scheme of the Central Welsh Board, was £1,200 *per annum*, which was fixed in 1904 by protracted negotiation. By 1924, growth of schools and administrative commitments had greatly increased, and the Welsh Board could only approach the LEAs for voluntary supplemental contributions or raise the certificate fees for pupils examined. The amounts received from the LEAs between 1920–24 were £4,000, £2,000, £1,500, and £2,000 respectively. Such a method was extremely unsatisfactory, for the applications to the LEAs were variable and recurring. It also rendered the financial position of the Welsh Board dependent, year by year, on obtaining the consent of seventeen separate Authorities. It was evident that some action was necessary to guarantee the finances of the Board.[3] A device was eventually formulated 'that in lieu of the contributions made by the Board of Education to the LEAs (amounting to 50 per cent of the total contributions made by the Authorities to the Central Welsh Board) there shall be paid, as from 1 April 1926 a direct annual Treasury grant to the Central Welsh Board of an amount equivalent to the total amount of the Statutory Contributions made in each year by the LEAs of Wales and Monmouthshire, under Section 42 of the Education Act, 1918, such direct Treasury grant to be in addition to the existing fixed annual grant of £1,200'.[4]

[1] *Report of the Board of Education (Welsh Department)*, 1925, Appendix I, pp. 7–9.
[2] See Study No. 2, Section 1.
[3] *Report of the Board of Education (Welsh Department)*, 1925, Appendix II, p. 9.
[4] Ibid., p. 10.

The Welsh Department

The President accepted the proposals in the following terms:

> 'I am authorized . . . to inform the Central Welsh Board of my approval of the proposals for ensuring better co-ordination and co-operation in the inspection of Intermediate and Secondary Education in Wales. Such proposals are regarded not merely as a series of administrative arrangements for governing future procedure, valuable as these may be . . . the chief merit of the arrangements lies in the fact that they afford an agreed basis upon which the Board of Education and the Central Welsh Board may, with due regard to their respective responsibilities, work together with mutual trust and esteem, in furthering the interests of education in Wales'.[1]

It remains to record that the proposals were approved by the Board of Education and HM Treasury. At the end of 1926 the system of joint and unified inspection of secondary schools by the two Boards was brought into operation. Effect was given to the new financial scheme by the publication, in January 1927, of draft regulations for the payment of grants to the Central Welsh Board under Section 118 of the Education Act, 1921.[2]

[1] Ibid., pp. 4–5.
[2] *Report of the Board of Education (Welsh Department)*, 1926, p. 6.

APPENDICES

I REPORTS ON SCHOOLS TO THE PARLIAMENTARY SECRETARY J. HERBERT LEWIS BY OWEN EDWARDS 15 MARCH 1918

II THE WORK OF THE WELSH DEPARTMENT 27 NOVEMBER 1909 BY OWEN EDWARDS

III SUGGESTED RE-DISTRIBUTION OF INSPECTORS' DISTRICTS IN WALES

IV THE WELSH INSPECTORATE 1920

V COST OF STAFF, WELSH DEPARTMENT

The Welsh Department

APPENDIX I

Reports on Schools to the Parliamentary Secretary, J. Herbert Lewis by Owen Edwards, 15 March 1918

Parliamentary Secretary

There are three things in Secondary Schools that give us concern at present:—
  i. The arranging of the curriculum at the top of the school according to examination requirements, working every subject to the same level regardless of its comparative importance; and so forming an aimless incoherent course. The Advanced Course grants are to go to the schools which form the best advanced courses,—a connected, coherent course, with subjects divided into principal and subsidiary, according to their importance.
  ii. The neglect of music in Secondary Schools. The evidence given by the Music experts of the University Colleges before the Royal Commission was to the effect that the rising generation of teachers know no music, and become apathetic towards it. What will become of "Cymru, gwlad y gân?" Still Dr. Hadow said that he knows of no country which has so much musical *promise* as Wales.
  iii. The neglect of Greek, especially in the case of children who finish their education in the Secondary School. Rightly or wrongly they choose the New Testament as the book of their lives, but a little elementary knowledge of Greek would make their Sunday School work more profitable.

Mold.

As in my report, quoted in Mr. Roberts' minute.

The Headmaster is conscientious, vigorous, believing strongly in his teachers and in his school. But he breathes and thinks in examination terms, of the sterile old Oxford and Cambridge Locals type. The teaching is not what is most likely to draw the children out. Little attention is,—or was,—paid to local history. I wish you would tell them something about *Mold*, one of the most interesting and (to me at any rate) one of the most beautiful places in Wales.

  i. In mediaeval times it was the Alsace-Lorraine, the Strasburg or the Metz of Wales. When Owen Gwynedd, the most thoughtful of Welsh princes, was inconsolable for the loss of his son Rhun, the taking of Mold Castle made him take heart again to do his work. It was for the sake of this beloved part of Wales that Llywelyn the Last put the fate of Wales to the ordeal of battle.
  ii. Mold has much to appeal to the young mind, e.g.—
      a. The grave of Richard Wilson (near the church wall in the churchyard)— the "father of British landscape painting", the discoverer of that *wild* beauty of nature which found its poet in Wordsworth and its final painter in Turner.
      b. The house of John Blackwell,—(Alun),—one of the poorest of the children of Mold; whose great anxiety during his Oxford course was that his old father and mother at Mold should have a pig to keep. Afterwards vicar of Manor Deifi, editor of *Y Cylchgrawn Cymraeg;* author of "Marwnad Heber", "Cathl yr Eos", "Cân Gwraig y Pysgotwr",—the sweetest of all Welsh poets.
      c. The statue of Daniel Owen, who has made the life of Mold immortal, by the greatest of Welsh sculptors.

The Welsh Department

  d. The home of Roger Edwards, the pioneer of Welsh journalism. He edited the first Welsh newspaper with a political message in 1838.

The influence of the H.M. is entirely for good, and his staff is a hard-working one.

Hawarden

Headmaster an aggressive, loud-voiced, opinionated man; thinking the thoughts of Bernard Shaw. But his bark is much worse than his bite, and he has most excellent qualities. The teachers are rather dwarfed by the Headmaster! The war has caused difficulties here as elsewhere. He can be praised without stint for many things,—

  i. His care for the physical welfare of the children under his charge. His school dinners show that he is a thoroughly good business man,—an excellent thing in a Headmaster.
  ii. The School garden is excellent,—the result of long and laborious work by the Headmaster and the children. They have turned a desert into a garden.
  iii. The Headmaster is an excellent musician. I heard Elgar's *Snowflakes* at the school once; and the rendering was so fine that I shall never forget it.
  iv. Welsh has been introduced into the school, especially for intending teachers. *All* Intermediate Schools in North Wales teach Welsh now.
  v. The school will be needed, and more than ever, with its humane character, whatever Technical Institute is built in its neighbourhood.

O.E. 15.111.18.

The Welsh Department

APPENDIX II

THE WORK OF THE WELSH DEPARTMENT

The Welsh Department administers and inspects:—
  i. Elementary Education in Wales.
  ii. Secondary Education in Wales.

The Inspectors inspect:—
  i. Technological Education in Wales.
  ii. Training Colleges in Wales.

Generally:—
  i. It keeps the Board of Education in closer and more immediate touch with Wales; more sympathy naturally arises when knowledge is more intimate.
  ii. It can deal more speedily with Welsh Schemes and with Welsh educational problems generally.
  iii. It surveys practically the whole of Welsh education, and aims at guiding and advising so that each part performs its proper work, and so that there is no over-lapping or unnecessary competition.

In Elementary Education:—
  i. It draws up the Welsh edition of the Code; recommendations are submitted to the President by a Committee of Welsh Officers and Inspectors.
  ii. In administering the Code, it has some special aims, such as
     A. To deal wisely and efficiently with the distinct problem of Welsh Education, —the bilingual problem. It has changed a "bilingual difficulty" into a bilingual opportunity. In most Elementary Schools children get the educational advantage that comes from a knowledge of two languages. The utilization of Welsh dates much further back than the establishing of the Welsh Department; but it was the Department that made universal, where Local Education Authorities desire it, an efficient and logical system of bilingual teaching, varying according to whether the district is Welsh-speaking, bilingual or English-speaking. The problem is important to other parts of the Empire; and the experience of the Welsh Department has been of much value to such parts as Mauritius and Cape Colony.
     B. To connect education with the every-day life of the children, by introducing education by means of Manual Work wherever possible, e.g. Carpentry, Metal Work, Gardening, Cookery, House-wifery, and by giving Nature Study a strong bias towards Agriculture, or Geography towards Navigation. An attempt is being made, e.g. to utilise Carpentry as a means of training boys' hands:-
        a. Where possible, the Elementary School has a Manual Work Room,—built by the Local Education Authority, or by private generosity.
        b. The Elementary School children use the Manual Work Room of a neighbouring Secondary School.
        c. Where no room is available, the village carpenter's shop is used; the children draw the article in school, and make it, under supervision, in the carpenter's shop.

The Welsh Department

    C. To secure a better education for intending Elementary Teachers:—
        a. The Pupil Teacher System is giving place gradually to the Bursar System. We are not pressing the Local Education Authorities to force the change on; but simply advising them where necessary.
        b. The Student Teacher System is becoming almost universal. We have taken a good deal of trouble to get this system adopted and to get uniform Schemes, almost every Local Education Authority has a good scheme now. It has been recognised already that the new system is much better than the old.

New System	*Old System*
3 years at Secondary School	
1 year as Bursar at Secondary School	Pupil Teacher
1 year as Student Teacher:—	2 years at College
a. Learning how to teach	
b. Reading good Literature	
2 or 3 years at College	

In Secondary Education:—
    i. The Welsh Department draws up Regulations for Wales. The rate of grant per child being the same, the conditions of grant must be the same in England and Wales.
    ii. In administering and inspecting it has, among other aims:—
        a. Establishing the right connection between the Elementary and the Secondary Schools; e.g. it attempts to secure that—
            i. The curriculum of the Secondary School should be both a continuation of and something different from that of the Elementary School, e.g.

	In Elementary School	*In Secondary School*
English Literature	Easy separate poems: a good anthology	A complete work, the unity of which the child must try to grasp.
English History	Stories or narrative outlines.	A definite period beginning with the Roman Period; while beginning Latin Grammar.

            ii. That every child of real promise should have a chance of continuing its education at a Secondary School. In Wales, *with only one* exception, all the schools give 25 per cent free places.
        b. Having the right number of Secondary Schools, with a view to the supply of other schools, such as Higher Elementary Schools. With the exception of the Industrial Schools of Glamorgan and Monmouth, where a few more Schools are being built, the Schools are numerous enough, and the system is complete. It is the work of one generation only.
        c. Getting the Schools to form their curriculum, not by finding out what the easiest examinations are, but by carefully considering the needs of the neighbourhood. So far, such subjects are History, Geography, Geology and Navigation are sacrificed to such subjects as oral French, of very doubtful

The Welsh Department

educative value and practically useless. The Department, after incessant watching and continued advice, are getting such subjects as Welsh, Geology, and Agricultural Chemistry into their right places in the School Time Table.

d. To secure differentiation of type. The worst fault of Welsh Schools is that they all propose the same subjects for the same examinations, in spite of great diversity of needs and aims. There is little place in the system for a Headmaster of strong personality, and there is not enough opportunity for individual development. A strong re-action is, however, setting in against this uniformity.

Most of the Welsh Secondary Schools 96 out of 108 are inspected by the Central Welsh Board. The Welsh Department is in close and constant touch with the Central Welsh Board, utilising the information obtained from its examinations and inspections, and giving it all the help and sympathy it can.

In Technological Education:—

It is strongly felt that Further Education has been neglected in Wales. Of the children who leave the Elementary Schools, about 5 per cent can go on to Secondary Schools. For these there is ample provision; Wales is covered by a system of new Secondary Schools, and the Central Welsh Board is continually urging willing Managers to spend more money upon them.

For the remaining 95 per cent there is little provision; and the time of youths between 14 and 18 is generally spent in loafing. The Inspectors of the Welsh Department, with the consent of the Board, aim at

  i. Gradually developing a voluntary system of Further Education for all young people between the school-leaving age and 18. There are at present:—
     a. Schools provided by Local Education Authorities.
     b. Schools provided by voluntary organisations,—School Committees for separate districts.
     c. Individual Voluntary Schools.
  ii. Beginning with popular subjects,—e.g. Welsh Literature, Music,—or subjects once popular in Welsh homes, e.g. Wood Carving,—and extending the education to other literary and scientific subjects.

A universal voluntary system would prepare the way for giving to Local Education Authorities compulsory power.

In Training College Education:—

Wales has now in the making a complete system:—
  a. When the old Colleges have been extended and the two new ones built, Wales can turn out enough trained Teachers to supply the wants of its Schools.
  b. There will be a choice between a three year degree course at a University College and a two-year course at a Residential College for each student.

The Inspectors are now trying to get:—
  A. The adaptation of the degree courses of the University of Wales to the needs of intending Teachers. After a conference the University has agreed to
     i. Give courses in English Literature as distinguished from English Language.
     ii. Give courses in English History as well as in Foreign History.

The Welsh Department

    iii. Introduce Physical Geography into the Geology course.
- B. The advising of Students to take the courses best adapted for their profession.
- C. The securing of well-equipped and well-staffed Demonstration and Practising Schools.

I feel that there is an increased activity all through the system. The introduction of Welsh to Elementary Schools, Secondary Schools, and Training Colleges has already begun to re-act on, and give new vigour to the three great educational institutions that stand outside the Board's purview,—the Sunday School, the Literary Meeting and the Eisteddfod.

O. Edwards.
27th November, 1909

I ought to add that, whenever I am asked I put everything aside to meet Local Education Authorities. I have met those of Glamorgan, Cardiff, Merthyr Tydfil, Swansea, Monmouth, Pembrokeshire, Flintshire, Merioneth, Brecknockshire, Carmarthenshire,—some of them several times.

I have attended all the Central Welsh Board meetings, about once a month, except one; in this case they changed the date at very short notice, and put the meeting on a day appointed for me to meet a committee of the Haberdashers at Monmouth.

The Welsh Department

APPENDIX III

Suggested redistribution of inspectors' districts in Wales

Name of LEA	No. of E Depts.	Sec. Schools Inter.	Sec. Schools Non Inter.	T	Popn. in thousands 1911 Census
DISTRICT No. 1					
County Boroughs:					
Cardiff	98	2	6	Tech. Sch.	182
Swansea	62	2	2	Tech. Coll.	114
Merthyr	56	1	2	Treforest	80
Total	216	5	10	3	376
DISTRICT No. 2					
Pontypridd	34	2	–	–	43
Rhondda	103	4	–	–	153
Mountain Ash	37	1	–	–	42
Barry	23	2	–	–	34
Aberdare	49	2	–	–	51
Neath Borough	11	1	–	–	18
Total	257	12	–	–	341
DISTRICT No. 3					
Glamorgan A.C.	422	10	1	–	402
DISTRICT No. 4					
Monmouth A.C.	232	6	4	–	312
Newport	47	2	–	Tech. Sch.	83
Total	279	8	4	1	395
DISTRICT No. 5					
Carmarthen A.C.	190				
Carmarthen Borough	12	8	–	–	160
Llanelli Borough	26				
Pembroke A.C.	146	8	–	–	90
Pembroke Borough	15				
Brecknock A.C.	107	5	–	–	60
Total	496	21	–	–	310
DISTRICT No. 6					
Denbigh A.C.	180	8	1	–	145
Wrexham	11				
Flint A.C.	133	5	1	–	93
Montgomery A C.	112	8	1	–	53
Radnor A.C.	54	2		–	23
Total	490	23	3	–	314
DISTRICT No. 7					
Anglesey A.C.	78	3		–	51
Caernarvon A.C.	184	10		–	125
Merioneth A.C.	91	7		–	45
Cardigan A.C.	115	5	1	–	60
Total	468	25	1	–	281

The Welsh Department

APPENDIX IV

WELSH INSPECTORATE (25.3.20)

Name	Grade	Age yrs. mos.	Salary £	War Bonus £
Edwards, Sir O.	Chief Inspr.	61 . 2	1200	420
Roberts, L. J.	Inspr.	53 . 9	800 + 50†	315
Jones, D. E.	,,	56 . 3	800	300
Hughes, R. E.	,,	53 . 8	800 + 50†	315
Skirrow, B. B.	,,	56 . 5	741	282—6/–
Price, H.	,,	47 . 11	700	270
Williams, W.	,,	56 . 3	620—9/–	246-2-8
Williams, G. P.	,,	45 . 8	481—15/–	204-10-6
Vacancy	,,	—	—	—
Taylor, A.	Sub.-Inspr.	54 . 5	520	216
Evans, J.	,,	61 . 9	425	187—10/–
Thomas, D.	,,	54 . 1	415	184—10/–
Rhydderch, R.	,,	55 . 8	375	172—10/–
Hooson, J. E.	,,	50 . 11	395	178—10/–
Bowen, J.	,,	56 . 0	355	166—10/–
Johns, W. C. R.	Junr.-Inspr.	45 . 11	400	180
Jones, A. J.	,,	41 . 9	350	165
Roberts, W.	,,	43 . 5	320	156
Rees, C.	,,	36 . 7	305	151—10/–
Thomas, J.	,,	39 . 8	275	142—10/–
Jones, J. E.	Asst.-Isnpr.	41 . 9	270	141
Williams, W. J.	,,	41 . 6	280	144
Evans, W. H.	,,	32 . 10	200	120
Owen, T.	,,	31 . 0	200	120
Davies, D. T.	,,	43 . 6	280	144
Clayton, C. P.	,,	34 . 11	200	120
Davies, M. H.	,,	34 . 1	200	120
Prys-Jones, A. G.*	,,	32 . 0	200	120

†Messrs. Roberts and Hughes are also eligible for an honorarium of £25 for evening school inspection with 30% War Bonus added.

*Overstrength.

APPENDIX V

WELSH DEPARTMENT, 1920

Cost of Staff

	£
Higher Staff—	
1 Perm. Sec. at £1,500	1,500
War Bonus	500
1 Asst. Sec. at £1,000–50–1,200	1,100
War Bonus	390
2 Principals at £700–25–900	1,600
War Bonus	943
2 Asst. Principals at £200–20–500	700
War Bonus	522
Inspectorate—	
1 C.I. at £1,200	1,200
War Bonus	420
8 Inspectors at £400–25–800	4,800
War Bonus	3,023
18 Asst. Inspectors at £200–15–400 (one-fourth may proceed exceptionally to maximum of £500)	5,600
War Bonus	4,372
2 Women Inspectors at £300–20–500	800
War Bonus	569
Travelling Expenses	4,000
	32,039

PRO Ed. 23/152A

EPILOGUE

Epilogue

(i) *Retirement of Sir Alfred T. Davies*

SIR ALFRED was not to surrender his seals of office in the orthodox way. He attempted one last powerful swim against the rising tide of his retirement. The circumstances surrounding the termination of his appointment were both unfortunate and unpleasant, and might have created an extremely delicate situation at Whitehall and in Wales. It would appear that he had been invited, at the age of sixty-one, by the new President of the Board, the Hon. Edward Wood (1st Earl of Halifax), on 6 December 1922, to discuss this matter.[1] Sir Alfred's reaction in the views he expressed to the President was hostile and forthright.[2] It appeared that since the death of Sir Owen Edwards in 1920, Sir Alfred had been asked to assume the dual role of Permanent Secretary and Chief Inspector. At their discussion, the President had informed him that the new government had decided to dispense with the separate post of Chief Inspector, and that the two posts should be combined—a proposition, which, in the general interests of the service, had Sir Alfred's support.[3] Indeed, during October 1923, when the announcement of his retirement was impending the *South Wales News* predicted a great deal of controversy in Wales regarding the future of the Welsh Department, believing that 'the end of the Department was at hand .. it has few friends in Whitehall, and fewer still in the present government ... the Tories regard it as in the nature of a luxury ... while the official mind is hostile to any arrangement which adds to the internal complications of administration ... we believe that the present government would seize a pretext ... to abolish the Department'.[4]

Sir Alfred raised four main points in his letter to the President. First, the Treasury claimed to be entitled to alter at will, the status, duties and conditions of service of the office of Permanent Secretary to the Welsh Department, to which he was appointed, and that he should also be responsible' and perform many of the duties of another office of equal rank, but of a different nature, namely, that of Chief Inspector of Education for Wales ... but it was not proposed to grant any additional remuneration'.[5]

---

[1] President to Davies, 5 December 1922. A. T. Davies Papers, op. cit.
[2] Davies to the President, 11 December, ibid.
[3] President to Davies, 8 January 1923, ibid.
[4] *South Wales News*, 15 October 1923.
[5] Davies to the President, 11 December.

Epilogue

Second, he had been asked to retire at an early date—not later than early in 1924 'before reaching the age of sixty-five with a view to my place being filled by a gentleman un-named, but who, I did not gather, had had any *administrative* experience in the field of education, either in England or Wales'. Sir Alfred was annoyed because the President had put his proposals immediately on taking office and without bothering to acquaint himself 'with the nature, extent, or complexity of Welsh education ... or with the personnel of the staff under his command ... who naturally looked to him to defend their interests should they be assailed'. Third, he thought it proper to be frank, and state how he regarded the President's suggestions, and 'if they were adopted, what would be their resultant effect and the judgement of Wales upon them ... indeed, it was his bounden duty not to leave the President in ignorance on those aspects of the matter'. Fourth, Sir Alfred feared that the action of the Treasury would be considered by Welsh opinion generally, as but another in a series of efforts on their part in late years which had tended—and would tend still further—to lower the status of the Welsh Department, to curtail its usefulness, and to impair its efficiency. A comparative statement of strikingly differential treatment by the Treasury brought this home clearly:[1]

England	Wales
A. Salary or Bonus (or both) of Secretary to the Board raised three times in the past four years:	A. Treasury have refused, since 1919, when salary was raised from £1,200 to £1,500 to make any corresponding re-adjustment in the *salary* of the Secretary to the Welsh Department.[2]
1. November 1918, from £1,800 to £2,000 with £300 Bonus.	
2. November 1919, Bonus increased to £500.	
3. March 1920, from £2,000 to £3,000 with £500 Bonus (since discontinued). And this in addition to the relief afforded to him by B (infra).	
B. A new post of Second Secretary to the Board created in April 1920, at a salary of £2,000 plus £500 Bonus (latter discontinued in August 1921).	B. Treasury in 1920 put forward and insisted on their contention at (1) ante.

[1] Davies to the President, 11 December 1922, A. T. Davies Papers, op. cit.
[2] It was stated by the Treasury that Davies's salary was £1,500 plus £500 War Bonus.

Epilogue

England	Wales
C. An additional allowance of £300 p.a. over and above his salary of £1,500 was paid for many years, to the Board's Chief Medical Officer for also acting as Medical Assessor. His salary (now paid by the Ministry of Health) has been raised to £2,000. In addition, the special allowance of £300 from the Board of Education was continued to him.	C. Treasury refused in 1920 and since, to permit *any* additional allowance to the Secretary of the Welsh Department, for also acting temporarily as C.I. for Wales.
	D. Treasury refused in 1920, and since, to allow a Welsh HMI acting as Supervising Inspector, and, so doing (but to a larger extent) the work of a Divisional Inspector, to receive the Salary regularly attached to that rank, thus penalised him by over £100 p.a.

He also reminded the President that he had sacrificed a lucrative legal practice in 1906 'on the unsolicited invitation of the government' in order to accept the office which was 'pressed' upon him, and he absolutely declined to be an assenting party to the proposals which he had been asked to consider. He maintained that his services were most essential at this juncture because (i) of the number and nature of special Welsh questions which demanded attention; (ii) a promising scheme (of his own devising) for co-operation with the Central Welsh Board had just been launched and accepted by that body[1] which would need careful steering; (iii) two vacancies (actual in the one case, impending in the other) were to be filled—the office of Chief Inspector for Wales, and Chief Inspector to the Central Welsh Board; (iv) the long experience of Welsh intermediate education possessed by J. L. Casson, the late Assistant Secretary to the Welsh Department had ceased to be at the disposal of the Board.

The last part of his letter gave the reasons why he should stay at Whitehall, and his stubborn refusal to consider retirement:

'To create, needlessly, a fourth vacancy (and that in the most important office of all, viz., the Permanent Secretary to the Welsh Department), and to do so at such a juncture, and, further, to fill the two posts which it is desired to merge into one by the appointment thereto of anyone, however able, who has not hitherto had practical experience of the actual work of administration of education, whether in England or in Wales, would, in my judgement, be a step which could only be justified by

---

[1] Sir Alfred was premature in his statement, for a modified scheme was accepted by the Central Welsh Board in July 1925. Most of the credit for this conciliation has been wrongly attributed to Sir Percy E. Watkins by Sir Wynn Wheldon. (*Y Bywgraffiadur Cymreig*), 1941–1950, London, 1970, p. 59.

Epilogue

overwhelming necessity. As to whether that necessity exists I am bound to advise you that public opinion in Wales, and not improbably also among the Welsh members in the House of Commons, will not be either slow or restrained in expressing itself.

You are, of course, the judge as to all this . . . As to myself I have, as I informed you, no desire to retire from the Board's service at the present time, nor even in the very near future. My health and vigour, as everyone knows, are in no degree impaired; my capacity for hard and exacting work remains undiminished. I am not blocking promotion in the Department, and no complaint has ever been made to the Board as to the way in which I have discharged my duties . . . Moreover, I shall not, until March 1926, reach the age at which I must, in any case, retire from the public service . . . If I am retired as proposed, my prospective pension on 1 April 1923 will actually amount to less than £350; if on the same date in 1924, to but little more'.[1]

Sir Alfred, anticipating the worst, should the President or the government adhere to the several intimations conveyed to him, was prepared to bow to the decision. But he reserved the right to be at liberty, having 'his character and reputation' to consider, to make known the circumstances under which it was brought about, and to explain why his connection with the Welsh Department had been severed at a time when it was never more necessary that his departmental and other special experience should continue to be available for the Board and for Wales. On the other hand, if the contents of his letter modified in any way the President's views, he asked that the question raised regarding his contract of service be resolved, at latest, by the end of the year.[2]

But the President was intransigent. His letter in reply to Sir Alfred, in January 1923 was, in effect, fourteen months notice for him to terminate his joint appointment as Permanent Secretary and Chief Inspector on 31 March 1924, beyond which date the President 'should not feel able to retain' his services.[3] His claim for additional remuneration was brushed aside; the constitutional position was, that since Sir Alfred had passed the age of 60, the President was free, if he thought right, to call on him to retire at any time in the public interest; the post of Chief Inspector for Wales would not be filled, and the salary for the combined posts should be £1,500. Moreover, the President, reciprocating the frankness displayed by Sir Alfred, and having 'regard to the exigencies of the public service' felt bound to make provision for the future, and expressed concern about the difficulty of finding men suitable to fill administrative posts for Wales. He stated that 'Wales is a small country and the field of choice is small. If therefore, I see my way now to secure the services of a man well

[1] Davies to the President, 11 December 1922, A. T. Davies Papers, op. cit.
[2] Davies to the President, 11 December 1922. A. T. Davies Papers, op. cit.
[3] President to Davies, 8 January 1923. The President hoped that Davies 'could see (his) way to perform the functions of C.I. as well as those of Permanent Secretary up to that date'. A. T. Davies Papers, op. cit.

Epilogue

qualified to succeed you, and if, by delay, my chance of doing so is imperilled, I do not think I should be justified in allowing myself to be deterred from doing so by the consideration that such an arrangenent involves your retirement at an earlier age than you would yourself desire'.[1] Heeding the warning as to the effect of the proposed arrangements on public opinion in Wales, and its possible expression in Parliament, the President, taking no exception to Sir Alfred's remarks, added that 'it is indeed as much the duty of the Civil Servant to warn his Minister candidly of any consequences he may foresee, as it is to abide loyally by his Minister's decision when finally given', and he stressed that there was no question of Sir Alfred's devotion to his duties or of his zeal for advancing the cause of education in Wales, and he would leave the Board with the record of a man who had given them loyal service.[2]

Sir Alfred was not to be so easily deflected from his argument that the Welsh Department had been treated so shabbily as regards remuneration —a matter which the President had ignored. In his reply, Sir Alfred demanded extra remuneration for his duties as Chief Inspector, if he was required to hold this office until March 1924. With typical legal adroitness he invoked the clause 'special services requiring special reward' under Section 9 of the Superannuation Act of 1859. He argued that 'at the risk of being summarily retired or ejected from office', (should he not comply with the request) he was expected 'to perform for a further fifteen months duties which the Treasury had no right to expect'.[3] He added that should nothing be done about this matter, it would be '[his] invidious duty to call public attention to the differential treatment meted out to the officers of the Welsh Department as compared with that which those on the English side of the office [had] long enjoyed'.[4]

This letter remained unanswered. The attempt to force the President's hand had failed and apparently the remuneration issue was never resolved. In the meanwhile, presuming to remain in office until March 1924, Sir Alfred had seemingly capitulated, and was pre-occupied with plans for his retirement. An invitation from a 'barrister friend' to visit Egypt in the early part of 1924 made it necessary for him to request 'a little special leave' from the President, which meant his leaving the Welsh Department in the last week of February. 'I hope to leave the Welsh Department and Welsh educational affairs in such a peaceful condition that Talbot and the rest of the efficient staff ought to have no difficulty in carrying on

[1] Ibid.
[2] Ibid.
[3] Draft letter from Davies to President (undated), A. T. Davies Papers, op. cit.
[4] Ibid.

Epilogue

during the three weeks, which is all (beyond what I could strictly claim) that would be involved by the concession'.[1] In October and November 1923 announcements of his impending retirement, together with appropriate tributes, appeared in the *South Wales News, Western Mail, Liverpool Daily Post and Mercury, The Manchester Guardian, The Times, The Journal of Education and the School World,* and *The Schoolmaster.* All were unanimous that he had performed a difficult task with conspicuous success.

But all the tumult was premature. Subsequent events took a dramatic turn. Early in January 1924, Haydn Jones, MP, had had a conversation with the President (whether Sir Alfred had any hand in this manoeuvre will never be known) with the result that Sir Alfred was invited to remain in office until March 1925.[2] Jones, no doubt, impressed by the efforts made by Sir Alfred to come to terms with the Central Welsh Board, had prevailed upon the President to extend his tenure of office in order to consummate his plans.[3] In a 'gratified' mood, Sir Alfred conveyed his acceptance to the President, but, alas, with another plea for extra remuneration.[4] The negotiations with the Central Welsh Board, and the proposals submitted to them, which had met with 'the warm approval' of the President, together with the efforts made by Sir Alfred to settle what he called 'undoubtedly the most difficult and controversial problem in the field of Welsh education ... which promise eventually to have a successful result'—were unacceptable to the Central Welsh Board.[5] But although a compromised settlement was reached, four months after his retirement, the main credit for success must be assigned to Sir Alfred.

The President had asked Sir Alfred to continue in office for another year 'without inconvenience to himself'[6]—which gave him another opportunity to advance his case for extra remuneration. His reasons were two-fold—personal and 'extra onerous duties'. On the personal side he had already made 'a number of dispositions, e.g. his town house and cottage in the country ... personal and family movements and affairs generally 'which had to be entirely altered, and that, at short notice and not a little expense'. On the official side, the entire reorganization of the Welsh inspectorate, the pending changes in the Central Welsh Board and

---

[1] Davies to President, 17 October 1923; President to Davies, 22 October: 'I will gladly do whatever I can to meet your wishes in the matter of granting you special leave pending your retirement'. A. T. Davies Papers, op. cit.

[2] President to Jones, 23 January 1924, A. T. Davies Papers, op. cit.

[3] President to Davies, 17 January 1924, ibid.

[4] Draft letter from Davies to President, 18 January 1924, A. T. Davies Papers, op. cit.

[5] Ibid.

[6] President to Davies, 17 January 1924, A. T. Davies Papers.

Epilogue

the reform of its administrative systems of finance—'a very ticklish business'. He ventured to add his hope that the President 'would find it possible to adjust this little matter with the Chancellor of the Exchequer or the Treasury before any change of government took place'.[1] Whether or not this plea went unheeded is a matter of conjecture.

The usual official announcement of his retirement appeared in the *Report of the Board of Education (Welsh Department), 1925*. Tributes were paid in all national newspapers and the educational press. *The Manchester Guardian* coupled the name of Sir Owen Edwards in a glowing tribute to both men, with a summary of their difficulties and achievements, adding that 'Governments set up departments, but it is the men whom they place at the head who really make them ... the Welsh Department was an experiment which might easily have failed: happily, after 18 years of trial, it has proved a conspicuous success'.[2] *The Times Educational Supplement* proclaimed that Sir Alfred Davies 'had been successful in making permanent what was at first considered as a somewhat hazardous, if not ill-advised, experiment'.[3] Thus ended the first chapter in the history of the Welsh Department of the Board of Education, and the end of the Davies and Edwards partnership. It was a period, which—for drama, controversy, personalities and excitement—has had no parallel in the evolution of the educational system of modern Wales.

(ii) *Conclusion*

One of the most striking features in the evolution of modern Welsh educational structure and administration was the implacable hostility which prevailed between two distinct institutions, fated to be at complete variance with one another—the Central Welsh Board and the Welsh Department of the Board of Education. For eighteen years, from 1907 to 1925, there was constant recrimination. Although in 1925 a certain measure of conciliation was achieved, the main problems stood unresolved until after the end of world war II.[4]

It has already been shown that the main obstacle in the way of effective cooperation between the Central Welsh Board and the Welsh Department rested on the word *autonomy*. In December 1923 it appeared that Sir Alfred Davies had submitted proposals for a unified inspectorate in Wales.

---

[1] Draft letter from Davies to the President, 18 January 1924, A. T. Davies Papers.
[2] *The Manchester Guardian*, 2 April 1925.
[3] *The Times Educational Supplement*, 4 April 1925.
[4] The report of the Working Party on *The Administration of Education in Wales, HMSO*, 1947, led to the creation of a Welsh democratic body, the Welsh Joint Education Committee (WJEC) in 1948, which incorporated the Central Welsh Board, the two Advisory Councils on Technical Education and the Federation of Welsh Education Committees. Wales at last achieved a national organization which could both consider educational policy and discuss its educational affairs.

Epilogue

But fourteen months subsequently, the proposals—which had been freely discussed at conferences, meetings of LEAs, as well as in the press—were finally rejected. National newspapers became impatient and sought to inquire the cause. But the most obvious reason for inconclusiveness and rejection arose, as so many times in the past, 'from the employment of loose and inexact terminology, *the autonomy of the Central Welsh Board*, the constant and indiscriminate use of which vitiated argument and darkened counsel'.[1] It has been shown that the powers and functions of this Board were extremely limited.[2] What sort of autonomy could an inspecting and examining body claim, when their only function as such was to report to the Charity Commissioners initially, and later, to the Board of Education; were dependent on the Welsh Department to act as their intermediary, and did not have the means of providing themselves with sufficient income? It was never meant that the Central Welsh Board should have autonomy, and it was quite futile to argue that the proposals for a unified inspectorate would impair it.

It could not be denied that the Central Welsh Board were casting avaricious eyes on the future pattern of Welsh educational administration. In spite of all their faults this body was the only truly *national* educational institution, wholly Welsh, with its prominent members convinced that the only way to secure complete educational devolution for Wales lay in the hope for a National Council of Education on the lines suggested by the Departmental Committee, in which the prominent members of the Central Welsh Board might play a leading part.[3] This was another reason for countering any moves by the Welsh Department for closer partnership. After the Board of Education reorganized the Welsh inspectorate at the end of 1924, to deal more effectively with all types of schools and other institutions in Wales, the new proposals of July 1925, discussed at a meeting of the Central Welsh Board, were accepted on the motion of Ald. William George, supported by Ald. D. H. Williams, chairman. Their adoption secured certain advantages and dispersed much of the administrative confusion then existing, and brought within the purview of that body the *whole field* of Welsh secondary education, elementary schools and Training Colleges. Moreover, they also enabled them to establish direct contact with LEAs on educational matters instead of merely having to deal with local school governors.

But the successful new proposals, attributed to Watkins, were regarded by the press as a surrender to Whitehall. *The Liverpool Courier* described

[1] *The Manchester Guardian*, 18 May 1925.
[2] See Study No. 1.
[3] *Wales Today and Tomorrow*, Central Welsh Board.

the scheme as 'tickling the trout into the basket'. Watkins was credited with the ability of handling certain members of the Central Welsh Board, and his proposals distinctly showed that 'under the guise of goodwill on the part of the Board of Education, they involved schemes which must ultimately undermine the authority and vitality, if not indeed, the existence of the Welsh Board'. The hollowness of the proposals were laid bare, for on the financial side no concession whatever was made to Wales. The Treasury would give no extra money, but merely transferred to the Central Welsh Board the sum which they granted to the LEAs. Dual inspection remained, but the line of demarcation, for all practical purposes was eliminated—'the lion and the lamb were to make peace on the clear understanding that they were allowed to wander over each others' preserves'.[1] The two worthy aldermen, together with their supporters on the Central Welsh Board, who had previously bitterly opposed Sir Alfred's scheme, and had now capitulated to Watkins, were described by J. C. Davies, Director of Education for Denbighshire, as 'a strange spectacle, the like of which he had never seen before'.[2] The same correspondent professed to diagnose the change of front. He ventured to suggest that the two aldermen, so obsessed with eagerness to establish a National Council of Education, had tempted Watkins 'to skilfully play upon that obsession, with the result that when he assured them that he, too, shared their enthusiasm for the same Council . . . they were ready to accept his gift-horse from Whitehall without troubling to take the wise precaution of first looking it in the mouth'.[3]

The other institution, the Welsh Department, along with its personalities, created many problems. For the Board of Education it became an administrative embarrassment, to the Central Welsh Board, a hated rival. For ten years that body had pursued the even tenour of its way, in an unmolested and unruffled fulfilment of its duties. But in the tenth year a fresh and complicating factor was introduced into the situation by the appearance of the Welsh Department. To many Welsh educationists, this innocent offspring of the rejected National Council for Education, became an unpopular alien Department in far-away London, a little Welsh compound under the roof of the Board of Education, where Davies and Edwards were regarded as bureaucrats of the government and servants of the President of the Board. It fell to Davies's lot, to have unfortunate relations with the Board of Education and the Central Welsh

---

[1] *Liverpool Courier*, 27 July 1925.
[2] Ibid.
[3] Ibid.

Epilogue

Board. With the former, because he insisted, quite rightly, upon the transference of spheres of Welsh work to his Department, which, not unnaturally, involved delicate re-adjustments to the traditional office machinery. This, in turn, upset most of the permanent officials of the Board—as tending to undermine their status and prestige. With the latter, because he always favoured resistance to their requests for extension of power. Moreover, he had also disclosed the flaws in their administrative system, procedure, and their methods of conducting written examinations, for example, the Jolliffe case. It was, therefore, not surprising that no compromise was possible with the Central Welsh Board so long as Davies was at the helm of the Welsh Department.

Davies was not an expert educationist when appointed to his Permanent Secretaryship, but a successful lawyer who had specialized with some distinction in licensing cases. Nevertheless, it is open to question whether anyone else could have served Wales more faithfully, having due regard to the restrictions, limitations, and frequent frustrations under which he was compelled to work, especially in building up a new Department. The fact that he was not a Minister, but a subordinate official, meant that his power and opportunity of initiating changes and innovations was always subject to the President of the Board. Had he been a greater authority on education, it was quite possible that he would have succeeded in satisfying his critics, in spite of the limitations of the position.

The appointment of Edwards, on the other hand, was, in every way, for Lloyd George, the master stroke. Not only one of the most brilliant, but also the most popular Welshman of the day, he immediately captivated the imagination of the Welsh nation. His acceptance of the Chief Inspectorship of Education for Wales was acclaimed on every hand. Even the most phlegmatic reacted to the confident anticipation that under his guidance Welsh education would be in safe hands. At that time it was fully expected by Welsh educationists in general, and Lloyd George in particular, that, as the two institutions—the Central Welsh Board and the Welsh Department—had each its own sphere of interest and of action, there was no possibility of conflict between them. This dream never came true.

During his early years at the Welsh Department many people in Wales were led to believe that Edwards harboured a past grudge against the Central Welsh Board for rejecting him as their first Chief Inspector—an allegation which he vigorously refuted more than once. But even if this could have been established, it was as an idealist and educational reformer that he came into conflict with the Welsh Board. He was a ruthless critic

Epilogue

of that system and his chief mission was to reform it in accordance with his belief in what Welsh secondary education should be. Perhaps one of the greatest contributions the experimental years of the Welsh Department made to Welsh education and to Wales *was the tremendous reforming influence it brought to the Central Welsh Board* through constant pressure from Edwards.

As Chief Inspector of Education for Wales, Edwards brought a new inspiration and the idealism of a dedicated life to the service of Welsh education, especially to the children in the schools. This has been perpetuated to this day through the work of his illustrious son, the late Sir Ifan ab Owen Edwards—founder of *Urdd Gobaith Cymru* (Welsh League of Youth), and the *Ysgolion Cymraeg* (the 'Welsh' schools)—who was destined to put his father's educational ideals into practice[1]:

> 'Ond odid mai datblygiad arall o holl ddatblygiadau yr Urdd a roddai fwyaf o bleser i'm tad, sef sefydlu'r Ysgol Gymraeg, canys dyna yn syml ydoedd yr ysgol Gymraeg gyntaf yn Aberystwyth—ysgol wedi ei sefydlu ar ddelfrydau addysg fy nhad. Erbyn heddiw, lledaenodd yr ysgolion Cymraeg i bob rhan o Gymru gan gadw at eu hegwyddorion a'u delfrydau sylfaenol ac ysprydoli to ar ôl to o blant â theyrngarwch i Gymru, i gyd-ddyn, ac i Grist. *Ni adawodd fy nhad gyfundrefn addysg ar ei ol, eithr delfrydau.* Pwy a wyr na ddatblyga'r ysgolion Cymraeg hyn yn gyfundrefn seiliedig ar ei ddelfrydau ef?'[2]

The first eighteen years of the Welsh Department would have proved difficult for anyone else appointed to the chief posts. The process of construction and stabilization was complicated and fraught with delicate problems unforeseen by any government or Ministers of the Crown. Perhaps in other hands many difficulties would not have arisen and the Department might have achieved more popularity in Wales. It is possible to be certain of at least one thing. *The problems which confronted Davies and Edwards existed as a result of legislation by past governments.* The Welsh Intermediate Education Act, 1889, gave Wales a system of intermediate schools under a strange and inflexible scheme, which, unless repealed could not be altered. The Board of Education Act, 1899, created the Board of Education, and the Education Act of 1902 a new type of secondary school controlled by the LEAs, all of which involved administrative participation by the Board of Education, which, so far as Wales was concerned, had to be shouldered by the Welsh Department—the

---

[1] 'The 'Welsh Schools' or *Ysgolion Cymraeg* is a term used to distinguish them from the Welsh primary school in the Welsh-speaking areas. They are essentially bilingual-medium schools in which Welsh is the main medium of instruction at the outset and English is introduced at the junior stage, and thereafter used increasingly as a medium of instruction. There are now 39 LEA Welsh Schools with about 3,000 pupils. This without doubt is the most outstanding development in bilingual education in Wales today'. (*Primary Education in Wales*, Gittins Report, op. cit. p. 221 and p. 7.)

[2] *Trans. Hon. Soc. Cymm.*, Session 1956, p. 15. Sir Ifan said '*that his father created no educational system—but bequeathed his ideals*'. In recent years similar secondary Welsh schools have been established.

Epilogue

latter a result of an abortive legislative measure in 1906. Davies and Edwards had emerged at an unfortunate period. If the events that were to follow could have been predicted, no Welshman would have relished any senior post in the Welsh Department.

Since 1925, neither the Welsh Department of the Board of Education,[1] nor its successive chief officials, whether Permanent Secretaries or Chief Inspectors have been implicated in any major disturbance or controversy in the educational life of the Principality. Theirs have been halcyon days compared with the stormy years of 1907—1925. The Welsh Department have been fortunate enough to be able to devote their energies to constructive work, since 'the Education Act of 1944 and subsequent Acts were able to bring prevailing opinion and statutory requirements into harmonious relationship, and over the years, better ways of managing administrative and constitutional difficulties have been devised'.[2] It is to be hoped that the Department will continue to maintain the individuality and distinctiveness of Wales in the field of education in close co-operation with the Welsh Joint Education Committee or any other major machinery —perhaps of a more truly national character in the form of complete devolution—in the years that lie ahead

[1] After 1944, the Ministry of Education; since 1 April 1964, the Department of Education and Science.
[2] *Trans. Hon. Cymm. Soc.*, 1957, op. cit., p. 34.

BIBLIOGRAPHY

A. Manuscript Collections

B. Official Papers

C. Periodicals, Pamphlets, and Reports

D. Works of Reference

E. Biographies

F. Other Works

Bibliography

A. MANUSCRIPT COLLECTIONS

1. *In Libraries, Museums, and Record Offices*

Bangor, University College of North Wales

Bangor MSS., 6159–6162; 6193.

The Hon. Soc. of Cymmrodorion Inquiry as to the introduction of Welsh into elementary education in Wales; letters from W. Hart Dyke to Sir John Puleston, MP.

Beaverbrook Library, London

The private papers of Lloyd George consist of a collection of 1,041 transfer cases of documents which are not numerous for the period before 1916. The card indexes show a political and personal series, and the list of persons who have special files in each series reflects Lloyd George's changing interests and growing influence. In the political series, the papers covering his educational activities include:

A. MP up to 1905 (13 boxes)
B. President of the Board of Trade 1905–8 (5 boxes)

Papers: A/1/3/1, 2, 3, 5; A 3/6/1, 2; A 11/2/22, 49, 53; A/12/1/48, 49, 51; A/12/2/5; B/2/9/1, 2; B/2/6/2; B/Box 3; B/4/2/4; B/4/2/37.

Mainly correspondence between Evan R. Davies and Lloyd George with reference to the Welsh National Council for Education; memorandum drawn up by Lloyd George on the Welsh National Council and its draft constitution, also with detailed notes regarding a Joint Education Council (a term often used by Lloyd George for the former); comments on Wales 'Coercion Bill' and draws up the National Manifesto; First draft of Clause to be inserted in Part IV of the Education Bill, 1906, or Order in Council 'to establish a Welsh National Council for all education in Wales', March 20, 1906, also printed for use of the Cabinet (Confidential) and circulated at the request of Lloyd George. Notes of public meetings addressed in north Wales, Cardiff, and Carmarthenshire.

Bodleian Library, Oxford

Fisher MSS., Fisher Diary 1918.

Bibliography

British Museum
Campbell-Bannerman Papers (Add. MSS., 41, 239–41, 242). Vol. XXXIV, f. 96; f. 192; f. 199; f. 200.

Caernarvonshire County Record Office
Education Department Letter Books
Education Committee Minute Books

Department of Education and Science Library, Curzon Street, W1
Indexes of Education Files (Wales) transferred to the Public Record Office. After 1968 the Departmental Records were moved to Elizabeth House, Waterloo, SE1.

National Library of Wales, Aberystwyth
  Deposited Collections
  MS 88B: Minutes of the Central Welsh Board (taken for the Board of Education) by J. L. Casson and Owen Edwards, HMCI, 5 October 1908–22 October 1915.
T. E. Ellis Papers
Glansevern Collection (papers of A. C. Humphreys-Owen)
Lloyd George MSS., 20424C–20429C: Letters 1044–1087; 1088–1139; 1190–1237; 1238–1280; 1281–1349.
Thomas Jones MSS., (under restriction): Class J., Vol. iv, f. 67; f. 76. By courtesy of Lady Eirene White and Mr. Tristan Jones.
Herbert Lewis Papers
Stuart Rendel Papers

Public Record Office, London
PM Cabinet Letters to the Sovereign (Cab. 41, XXIX, No. 21, Balfour, 29 June 1904).

Ed. 10/14	Miscellaneous papers, Welsh Department, Board of Education, 1903–12.
Ed. 10/122	Regarding appointment of Minister of Welsh Affairs and the Welsh National Council for Education.
Ed. 16/393	Elementary Education, Cardiff, 1870–1910.
Ed. 16/394	do., Cardiff, 1910–1921.
Ed. 21/22563	Cardiff Higher Grade Council School.
Ed. 23/144	Staffing of Welsh Department, HMIs; HMIs in 1907.
Ed. 23/145	Memorandum from Owen Edwards to A. T. Davies on the Welsh inspectorate, 1912. Edwards also reviews six years' work as HMCI for Wales.

Bibliography

Ed. 23/146	Methods of procedure to increase the Welsh inspectorate, 1913.
Ed. 23/147	Correspondence between the Welsh Department and the Board of Education to initiate new grade of assistant inspector in lieu of junior inspector, 1915.
Ed. 23/148	Owen Edwards: correspondence regarding appointment of Welsh inspectors.
Ed. 23/149	Owen Edwards corresponds with his HMIs.
Ed. 23/150	Suggestions from Welsh HMIs to Edwards.
Ed. 23/152	Organizational matters at the Board of Education and the Welsh Department.
Ed. 23/152A	Re-organization of the Welsh inspectorate; correspondence between Owen Edwards, A. T. Davies and G. Prys Williams.
Ed. 23/152B	Morant: re appointment of woman inspector.
Ed. 23/216C	Chief Clerk's Report (Board of Education) on the duties of his post.
Ed. 23/216F	Confidential Memorandum on Office Organization, No. 3, 1907, by R. L. Morant.
Ed. 23/216G	Setting up the Welsh Department, procedure and preliminaries.
Ed. 23/218.49	T Inspection, No. 12 regarding HM Inspectors of schools.
Ed. 23/220	Miscellaneous Papers, Welsh Department.
Ed. 23/242	Details and circumstances of appointments of A. T. Davies and Owen Edwards to the Welsh Department, Board of Education.
Ed. 23/244	Procedures and difficulties of the transfer of work and responsibilities from the Board of Education to the Welsh Department. Correspondence between A. T. Davies, Dr. Heath and the President of the Board of Education.
Ed. 23/245	Office Memorandum, No. 43, 1911. Revised, January 1912.

Class Cab. 37, Cabinet Office Papers dealing with the 1906 Education Bill, Ed. 24/110–126:

Ed. 24/110	1906–7 Box A
Ed. 24/111	1905–7 Box B
Ed. 24/112	1906 Box C
Ed. 24/113	1906 Box D

Bibliography

Ed. 24/114	1906 Box E
Ed. 24/115	Index to Boxes A to E
Ed. 24/116	1906, Box H, Minutes of Cabinet meetings.
Ed. 24/117	1906, Box J: Amendments, Draft Bills; Mr. Thring's notes on Amendments; Draft Clauses 26 or 37.
Ed. 24/118	1906, Box K, Welsh National Council for Education: Drafts of Cabinet Memoranda on Clause 37.
Ed. 24/119	1906, Box L. Marshalled list of Amendments to be moved in the House of Lords.
Ed. 24/120	Box M. Mr. Eaton's history of the 1906 Education Bill, etc.
Ed. 24/121	1906, Memoranda Nos. 1–30, Indexed.
Ed. 24/122	1906, Cabinet Memoranda Nos. 31–46, Indexed.
Ed. 24/123	1906, Cabinet Memoranda, Nos. 47–66, Indexed.
Ed. 24/124	1906, Education Bill in its various stages.
Ed. 24/125	1906, Education Bill, Amendments at various stages, Clause 37.
Ed. 24/126	1906, Correspondence, Notes, and Amendments at various stages.
Ed. 24/127	Relating to clauses on the delegation of powers and duties of county councils.
Ed. 24/576	*Proposals Towards an Interim Concordat in Wales*, Confidential.
Ed. 24/577	*Confidential Memorandum on The Defaulting Authorities Bill* from R. P. Hills to R. L. Morant, 25 June 1904.
Ed. 24/578	Education Act of 1902: *The Educational Situation in Wales* (*Revised*) 27 *June* 1904.
Ed. 24/579	Proposed Welsh National Council for Education.
Ed. 24/579C	Confidential Memorandum on same by Morant; correspondence and other material.
Ed. 24/580	Appointments of A. T. Davies and Owen Edwards; other candidates; Questions and Answers, House of Commons on same.
Ed. 24/581	Welsh Department: correspondence re appointments of Davies and Edwards and staffing of the new Department.
Ed. 24/582	Criticism of the Welsh Department by Haydn Jones, MP.
Ed. 24/583	Correspondence, Haydn Jones and Welsh Department.
Ed. 24/584	Notes for the President of the Board of Education on the work of the Welsh Department, by Owen Edwards and A. T. Davies, 27 November 1909.

Bibliography

Ed. 24/585	A. T. Davies and publications of the Welsh Department.
Ed. 24/586	Friction between the Welsh Department and the Board of Education.
Ed. 24/587	Towyn case: closure of Church of England school.
Ed. 24/588	*Controversy between the Welsh Department and the Central Welsh Board;* Edgar Jones (Barry) denounces the Board of Education (Welsh Department) Report of 1909; *Reply by Owen Edwards and his criticisms of the Central Welsh Board system:* deterioration of relationships between the Welsh Department and the Central Welsh Board.
Ed. 24/589	Re-action to the 1909 Report from various quarters.
Ed. 24/590	Defaulting Authorities: campaign in Caernarvonshire, Moriah, Caernarvon; correspondence, Sir Harry Reichel, Bishops.
Ed. 24/2027	Memorandum by Sir A. T. Davies on the University of Wales.
Ed. 31/5	Draft Bills, Welsh Intermediate Education, 1884–87.
Ed. 31/6	Bill for promotion of Technical Instruction, 1886.
Ed. 31/7	Technical Instruction: Parliamentary counsel instructed to prepare Bill to provide for transfer of Schools of Art or Schools of Science and Art to Local (Education) Authorities, 2 April 1891.
Ed. 35/3225–29	Cardiff Municipal Secondary Schools 1907–1923.
Ed. 35/3230–36	Intermediate and Technical Education Fund, Cardiff.
Ed. 35/3406	The Central Welsh Board seeks increase of powers; request to amend Scheme; dual inspection of schools.
Ed. 35/3407	Deputations and correspondence from the Central Welsh Board to the Board of Education re increase of grants.
Ed. 35/3408	Deputations from Central Welsh Board to Board of Education re inspection of all secondary schools and other matters including dual inspection; the Jolliffe case.
Ed. 35/3409	Central Welsh Board seeks amendment of Scheme and extension of powers.
Ed. 35/3410	Defalcation of Central Welsh Board office staff; re-organization of the Welsh Board; retirement of Owen Owen.
Ed. 35/3411	Inquiry and trial of Central Welsh Board office staff.
Ed. 35/3412–14	Central Welsh Board reports and curricula.
Ed. 35/3415A	Central Welsh Board, 1921.

Bibliography

Ed. 35/3415B	Deputations from Central Welsh Board to Board of Education; dual inspection; overhaul of administrative procedures between Board of Education and Central Welsh Board.
Ed. 35/3415C	Regulations, reports and curricula, Central Welsh Board.
Ed. 35/3415–18	Central Welsh Board reports, statistics, and reports to Board of Education.
Ed. 35/3419	Central Welsh Board meetings, 1901.
Ed. 35/3420	Central Welsh Board meetings, 1902, 1903.
Ed. 35/3421	Central Welsh Board meetings; correspondence with Board of Education; accounts; reports of inspection of schools, 1905.
Ed. 35/3422	Central Welsh Board, 1904–7; inspection of schools.
Ed. 35/3423	Central Welsh Board, Minutes of meetings, 1908–9.
Ed. 35/3424	Central Welsh Board meetings, 1907
Ed. 35/3425	Central Welsh Board Reports, 1911–12.
Ed. 35/3426	Ibid. 1913–14.
Ed. 35/3427	Ibid. 1914–16.
Ed. 35/3428	Ibid. 1917.
Ed. 35/3429	Reports Triennial and Subsidiary, 1918–22.
Ed. 35/3432	Welsh Department, Board of Education, Subsidiary Reports, 1920–21.
Ed. 35/3433	Welsh Department, Board of Education, Inspectors Reports.
Ed. 35/3435	Welsh Department, Board of Education, Triennial Reports, 1921–22.
Ed. 35/3436	Report on the Welsh Intermediate Education Act, 1889 (Annual Report of the Board of Education for 1907 required amending in line with the setting up of the Welsh Department) with observations by Owen Edwards. Minute Paper 3436/WS4, comments by A. T. Davies, 7 April 1908.
Ed. 35/3437	Grants for Intermediate education, 1900. Correspondence re county rates from Welsh counties.
Ed. 91/1	Contributions of the Welsh Department to the Board of Education annual report for 1908, 8 July 1908.
Ed. 91/5	Area Reports, Cardiff, 1911.
Ed. 91/8	Six Files: Preliminaries to the Departmental Committee of 1880 on Higher and Intermediate Education in Wales.

Bibliography

Ed. 91/9	Functions of the Welsh Department and its Officers: Questions and Answers, House of Commons, March 1907.
Ed. 91/10	Initiation of external negotiations for the Welsh National Council for Education; correspondence and discussions between Board of Education, Anson, Morant, Bruce, etc., with Lloyd George, Evan R. Davies, etc., Draft Model Schemes of Joint Council, Joint Board, etc., correspondence between Welsh County Councils and Board of Education, etc.
Ed. 91/11	Evan R. Davies, *Caernarvonshire Draft Scheme for National Council and Agreement;* position of Welsh County Councils and Carmarthenshire County Council; failure of National Council: end of external negotiations.
Ed. 91/14	Memorials concerning the establishment of a University College for South Wales at Cardiff, 1882–4.
Ed. 91/39	Area Reports, Cardiff, 1914.
Ed. 91/W49	Ref. 11: Minutes of Emergency Meeting at the House of Commons: Memorandum from Bruce to Morant recording observations made by Lloyd George regarding proposed Joint Education Board for Wales.
Ed. 111/250	Caernarvonshire, working of the Education Act of 1902.
Ed. 111/251	Appointment of Officers for Inquiry.
Ed. 111/252	Carmarthenshire and the working of the Education Act of 1902; correspondence with Board of Education and fears of illegalities by certain members of county council; position of voluntary schools and disputes; refusal of Carmarthenshire to recognize rights of voluntary schools under the Act; Welsh County policies in regard to the Act.
Ed. 111/254	Preliminaries to the Inquiry by the Law Officers of the Crown for the Board of Education; Index to Documents referred to in Instructions.
Ed. 111/255	*The Public Inquiry and result; Report by A. T. Lawrence, K. C. Aftermath.*
Ed. 111/256	Statistics of schools.
Ed. WS 3328	Memorandum on application for extension of jurisdiction by the Central Welsh Board, from A. T. Davies to the President, 26 October 1911.

Bibliography

2. *Privately Owned*

Sir Alfred T. Davies Papers. By courtesy of A. Mervyn Davies, Esq., Wilton, Connecticut, USA.

Penucha MSS: i. *Diaries, Letters, and Speeches of Sir J. Herbert Lewis.* ii. *Correspondence between Lewis and Sir Owen Edwards.* By courtesy of Mrs. K. Idwal Jones, Plas Penucha, Caerwys, Flintshire.

Bibliography

B   OFFICIAL PAPERS

Hansard's *Parliamentary Debates*, Third Series.

Parliamentary Debates (Authorized Edition and Official Reports), Fourth and Fifth Series.

Report of the Commissioners Appointed to Inquire into the State of Education in Wales, 1847. 3 vols., (C. 870; 871; 872), XXVII.

Report of the Royal Commission (known as the Schools Inquiry Commission), 1868. Vol. I, 1867–68. (C. 3966), XXVIII; Vol. VIII.

Report of the Committee appointed to Inquire into the condition of Higher Education in Wales (C. 3407, H.C. (1881). XXXIII. 1.

Report of the Royal Commission on Technical Education, 1882–84. 1881–82, (C. 3171), XXVII; 1884, (C. 3981), XXIX.

Second Report of the Commissioners appointed to Inquire into the Elementary Education Acts (C. 5056), H.C. (1887). XXIX. 1.

Final Report of the Commissioners appointed to Inquire into the Elementary Education Acts (C. 5485), H.C. (1888). XXXV. 1.

Report of the Royal Commission on Secondary Education, (C. 7862), H.C. (1895). XLIII. 1.

The Welsh Intermediate Education Act: Its Origin and Working, (W. N. Bruce), Special Reports of Educational Subjects, Education Department, Committee of Council, Vol. II, 1898.

Report of the Board of Education on the Administration of Schools under the Welsh Intermediate Education Act, 1889, 1902.

Report of the Board of Education for the Year, 1902–3. (Cd. 1763, XX).

Report of a Public Inquiry held under Sections 16 and 23 of the Education Act, 1902, and Section 73 of the Elementary Education Act, 1870, by A. T. Lawrence, K.C., at Carmarthen on the 24th and 25th March, 1904 Presented to both Houses of Parliament, 18 April 1904. (Cd. 2041), LXXV.

Statistics of Public Elementary Schools, Pupil Teacher Centres, and Training Colleges with Schedules. (Cd. 2000), LXXV, 1904.

Board of Education: Précis of Debates in the House of Commons and House of Lords on the Education Bill, 1906, together with Index.

Codes of Regulations For Public Elementary Schools with Schedules, 1906. (Cd. 3043), LXXXV.

List of Public Elementary Schools in Wales on 1 August 1906 (Cd. 3640), H.C. (1907). LXIII.

British Museum, State Papers Department:

Parliamentary Debates on the Education Bill, 1906:

Bibliography

    Introduction and Second Reading (vol. 1), Cs. 1174–1191 (inclusive): Cs. 1575–1578 (inclusive); Cs. 1589–1590 (inclusive); C. 1077.
    i. *In Committee, Instructions Clauses 1 and 2.*
    ii. *Procedure Resolution* (vol. II), Cs. 961–970 (inclusive).
    Report and Third Reading. (vol. VI), Cs. 741–760 (inclusive).
    House of Lords Committee, Clause 5 to end. (vol. IX), Cs. 779–805 (inclusive); Cs. 941–998 (inclusive).
Statistics of Public Education (Cmd. 5355), Part I, 1910.
A Report made by the Chief Inspector for Wales of the Board of Education to the President of the Board on the Statement of the Central Welsh Board with Reference to the Report of the Board of Education made in pursuance of Section 15 of the Welsh Intermediate Education Act, 1889, on the Proceedings under that Act in the year 1909. (Owen Edwards, 3 January 1911).
Final Report of the Departmental Committee on Juvenile Education in Relation to Employment after the War. (Cd. 8512), Vol. 1, 1917.
Royal Commission on University Education in Wales: Three Volumes, 1916–1918, (Cd. 8507, 8993, 8991), 1918.
Report by the Juvenile Organizations Committee of the Board of Education on Juvenile Delinquency, HMSO, 1920.
Report of the Departmental Committee on the Organization of Secondary Education in Wales. (Cmd. 967), H.C. (1920). XV. 1.
Report of the Departmental Committee appointed ... to Inquire into the position of the Welsh Language and to advise as to its promotion in the Educational System of Wales: 'Welsh in Education and Life' (Y Gymraeg mewn Addysg a Bywyd, translated by G. J. Williams). HMSO, 1927.
The Administration of Education in Wales. Bilingual. HMSO, 1947.
The Future of Secondary Education in Wales: Report of the Central Advisory Council for Education (Wales). Bilingual. HMSO, 1949.
Education, 1900–1951: Ministry of Education, HMSO, 1951.
Primary Education in Wales. A Report of the Advisory Council for Education (Wales), Department of Education and Science, HMSO, 1967.
Annual Reports of the Board of Education (after 1899).
Annual Reports of the Welsh Department, Board of Education (after 1907).

Bibliography

C PERIODICALS, PAMPHLETS, AND REPORTS

1. *Newspapers*

(a) English
Daily Chronicle
Daily News
Daily Telegraph
Gloucester Citizen
Liverpool Courier
Liverpool Daily Post and Mercury
Liverpool Post
Manchester Guardian
Morning Post
Standard
The Baptist Times
The Times
Yorkshire Post

(b) Welsh
Aberdare Times
Baner ac Amserau Cymru
Cambria Daily Leader
Cardiff Times
Y Goleuad
Yr Herald Cymraeg
Merthyr Express
North Wales Observer and Express
Seren Cymru
South Wales Daily News (*South Wales News* from 1919)
Y Tyst a'r Dydd
Western Mail

2. *Other Periodicals*

(a) English
British Quarterly Review
British Weekly
Church Times
Journal of Education
Liberal Magazine
Review of Reviews
School World
School Board Chronicle
The Schoolmaster
Times Educational Supplement
Westminster Gazette

(b) Welsh
Cymru
Cymru Fydd
Y Diwygiwr
Efrydiau Athronyddol
Yr Haul
Y Llenor
National Library of Wales Journal
Wales (1894–7, ed. by Owen M. Edwards)
Wales (1911–14, ed. by J. Hugh Edwards)
Welsh Outlook
Welsh History Review
Welsh Secondary Schools Review
Transactions Caernarvonshire Historical Society
Trafodion Cymdeithas Hanes Bedyddwyr Cymru
Transactions, Honourable Society of Cymmrodorion
Young Wales

Bibliography

3. *Pamphlets*

Aaron, Richard I., *The Central Welsh Board as an examining and servicing agency for primary, secondary, and further education in Wales.* Jubilee Pamphlet, May 1896–May 1946.

Alderley, Lord Stanley of: *The Relations of the Welsh Elementary School System with Higher Education.* London, 1910.

Anon: *The Failure of the Central Welsh Board System.* Cardiff, 1912.

Draft Statement of the Central Welsh Board on the Report of the Board of Education for 1909, under the Welsh Intermediate Education Act, 1889. Private and Confidential. Shrewsbury meeting, 18 November 1910, Agendum 5.

Edwards, William, *Cynllun Newydd*, Caerdydd, 1929.

Jones, Edgar, *Reply to the Report on Intermediate Education issued by the Welsh Department of the Board of Education, 1909.* Presidential Address to the Welsh County Schools Association, Shrewsbury, 1910, Cardiff, n.d.

Lloyd, Bishop D. Lewis, *The Missing Link in Education in Wales*, Bangor, 1876.

Pryce, Rev. R., *The Working of the Education Act, 1902: Its failure and future*, London, 1902.

Statement of the Central Welsh Board with reference to the Reply of Mr. Owen Edwards, HMCI, to the Statement issued by the Central Welsh Board on the subject of the Board of Education Report for 1909–10. 1911.

Williams, W. Moses, *A Case for the Central Welsh Board.* (Welsh version by Evans, Elsbeth Owen): 'Gair Dros y Bwrdd Canol', Cardiff, 1947.

Williams, T. Marchant, *The Educational Wants of Wales*, London, 1877.

4. *Reports*

Annual Reports of the Central Welsh Board (1897 to 1947).

Report of the Association of Welsh Clergy in the West Riding, 1854.

Reports of the Conferences of the Joint Education Committees of North Wales. Wrexham, 1890.

Reports of the Conferences (General) of the Joint Education Committees of Wales and Monmouthshire. Wrexham, 1890–3.

D. WORKS OF REFERENCE

Burke's Landed Gentry.
Burke's Peerage, Baronetage, and Knightage.
Y Bywgraffiadur Cymreig hyd 1940. Llundain, 1953.
Y Bywgraffiadur Cymreig, 1941–1950. Llundain, 1970.
Dictionary of National Biography.
Dictionary of Welsh Biography, 1959.
Ellis, Thomas Edward, and Griffith, Ellis Jones, *Intermediate and Technical Education (Wales). An Explanation of the 1889 Act.* The National Association for the promotion of Technical and Secondary education. London, 1889.
Gosden, Peter H. J. H., *The Development of Educational Administration in England and Wales.* Blackwell, 1966.
Hughes, T., *The Law Relating to Welsh Intermediate Schools.* Cardiff, 1898.
Hughes, Thomas, *Great Welshmen of Modern Days.* Cardiff, 1931.
Jenkins, R. T., and Rees, William, (ed.): *A Bibliography of the History of Wales,* Cardiff, 1931. Second Edition, Cardiff, 1962. Supplements to same published in the *Bulletin of the Board of Celtic Studies* (vol. xx, 126–64 for the years 1959–62; vol. xxii, 49–70 for the years 1963–5; vol. xxiii, 263–83 for the years 1966–68; vol. xxv, 75–90 for the years 1969–1972).
Newspapers Press Directory and Advertisers Guide.
Rees, T. Mardy, *Notable Welshmen (1700–1900),* Caernarvon, 1908.
Roberts, T. R., *A Dictionary of Eminent Welshmen,* Cardiff, 1908.
Statesmen's Year Book.
Who's Who in Wales (first ed., 1920; second ed., 1933; third ed., 1937).
Who was Who
Williams, T. Marchant, *The Welsh Members of Parliament,* Cardiff, 1894.

E. BIOGRAPHIES

Birrell, Augustine, *Things Past Redress*, London, 1937.

Campbell-Bannerman, Rt. Hon. Sir Henry, *The Life of the Rt. Hon. Sir Henry Campbell-Bannerman*, by J. A. Spender, London, 1923.

Davies, John Humphreys, *John Humphreys Davies*, by T. I. Ellis, Liverpool, 1963.

Edwards, Archbishop Alfred George, *Memories*, London, 1927.

—— *Alfred George Edwards, Archbishop of Wales*, by George G. Lerry, Oswestry, 1940.

Edwards, Ifan ab Owen, 1895–1970 by Norah Isaac, Cardiff, 1972.

Edwards, Owen M., *O. M., A Memoir*, by Alfred T. Davies (ed.), London, 1946.

—— *Owen Morgan Edwards, Cofiant. Cyf. I, 1858–1883*, gan W. J. Gruffydd, Caerdydd, 1937.

—— *Bywyd a Gwaith Owen Morgan Edwards*, gan G. Arthur Jones, Aberystwyth, 1958.

—— *Owen M. Edwards, (1858–1920)*, by Wynne Ll. Lloyd, in *Pioneers of Welsh Education*, Swansea, 1962.

Edwards, Thomas Charles, *Letters of Thomas Charles Edwards*, 3 vols., edited by T. Iorwerth Ellis, Aberystwyth, 1952–3.

Ellis, Thomas Edward, *Speeches and Addresses*, Wrexham, 1912.

—— *Thomas Edward Ellis*, by T. Iorwerth Ellis, 2 vols., Liverpool, 1944–8.

—— *Thomas Edward Ellis*, by Wyn Griffith, Llandybie, 1959.

The Forerunner, by Neville C. Mastermann, Christopher Davies, Llandybie, 1972.

Fisher, H. A. L., *An Unfinished Autobiography*, London, 1940.

Gee, Thomas, *Cofiant Thomas Gee*, gan Thomas Gwynn Jones, Dinbych, 1913.

Humphreys, E. Morgan, *Gwŷr Enwog Gynt*, Aberystwyth, 1950.

—— *Gwŷr Enwog Gynt: Yr Ail Gyfres*, Aberystwyth, 1953.

Jenkins, R. T., *Edrych yn Ol*, Llyfrau Clwb Cymraeg, Llundain, 1968.

Jones, Sir Henry, *Old Memories*, London, 1924.

—— *Life and Letters of Sir Henry Jones*, by H. J. W. Hetherington, 2 vols., 1924.

Jones, J. Viriamu, *Life of J. Viriamu Jones*, by Katherine Viriamu Jones, London, 1915.

—— *J. Viriamu Jones, 1856–1901: Pioneer of the Modern University: An Appreciation*, by Neville C. Masterman, Llandybie, 1957.

—— *John Viriamu Jones and other Oxford memories*, by E. B. Poulton, London, 1911.

Bibliography

Lewis, J. Herbert, *Syr Herbert Lewis, 1858–1933*, gol. gan Kitty Idwal Jones, Aberystwyth, 1958.

—— 'Sir John Herbert Lewis', by Ben Bowen Thomas, in *Flints. Hist. Soc. Pubns.*, *XVIII*, 1960.

Ysgol Llawrybetws 1908–1958. Casgliad o Ysgrifau, gol. gan D. Tecwyn Lloyd, Y Bala, 1958.

Lloyd George, David, 1st Earl, *The Lloyd George I Knew*, by Alfred T. Davies, London, 1948.

—— *David Lloyd George. The Official Biography*, by Malcolm Thomson, London, 1948.

McKenna, Reginald, *Reginald McKenna*, by Stephen McKenna, London, 1948.

Morant, Robert Louis, *Life of Sir Robert Morant*, by B. M. Allen, London, 1934.

Mundella, A. J., *A. J. Mundella, 1825–1897. The Liberal Background to the Labour Movement*, by W. H. G. Armytage, London, 1951.

Owen, Bishop John, *The Early Life of Bishop Owen*, by Eluned E. Owen, Llandysul, 1958.

—— *The Later Life of Bishop Owen*, by Eluned E. Owen, Llandysul, 1961.

Reichel, Harry R., *Sir Harry Reichel*, ed. by John Edward Lloyd, Cardiff, 1934.

Rendel, Stuart, 1st Lord, *Personal Papers of Lord Rendel*, ed. by F. E. Hamer, London, 1931.

Roberts, Thomas Francis, *Thomas Francis Roberts, 1860–1919*, by David Williams, Cardiff, 1961.

Watkins, Percy E., *A Welshman Remembers: An Autobiography*, Cardiff, 1944.

Bibliography

F. OTHER WORKS

Archdall, Henry K., *St. David's College, Lampeter, Its Past, Present, and Future*. Lampeter, 1952.

Carr, C., *The Spinning Wheel: History of Cardiff School for Girls*. Cardiff, 1955.

Claridge, S. A., 'The First of the County Schools. (Caernarvon)'. *Transactions Caernarvonshire Historical Society*, XIX, 1958.

Davies, W. Cadwaladr, and Jones, W. Lewis, *The University of Wales and its Colleges*. London, 1905.

Ellis, E. L., 'Some Aspects of the Early History of the University College of Wales', *Transactions Honourable Society of Cymmrodorion*, 1967,
—— *The University College of Wales, Aberystwyth, 1872–1972*, Cardiff, 1972.

Ellis, T. Iorwerth, *The Development of Higher Education in Wales*, Wrexham, 1935.

—— 'The Development of Modern Welsh Secondary Education', *Transactions Honourable Society of Cymmrodorion*, 1932–33.

Evans, D. Emrys; Wheeler, Olive A.; and Williams, W. M.: 'The Welsh Intermediate Education Act, 1889.' Addresses. *Transactions Honourable Society of Cymmrodorion*, 1939.

Evans, D. Emrys, *The University of Wales. A Historical Sketch*. Cardiff, 1953.

Evans, Eric, 'Datblygiad Syniadau Addysgiadol yng Nghymru'. *Efrydiau Athronyddol*, XXIII, 1960.

Evans, Leslie Wynne, *Education in Industrial Wales*, 1700–1900. Cardiff, 1971.

—— 'The Evolution of Welsh Educational Structure and Administration, 1881–1921'. *Studies in the Government and Control of Education since 1860*. (History of Education Society), London, 1970.

—— 'The Genesis of the Welsh Department, Board of Education, 1906–7', *Transactions Honourable Society of Cymmrodorion*, Session 1969, Part II, 1970.

—— 'The Welsh National Council for Education, 1903–6'. *Welsh History Review*, vol. vi, no. 1, (June 1972).

George, William, *Cymru Fydd: Hanes y Mudiad Cenedlaethol Cyntaf*, Lerpwl, 1945.

Gosden, P. H. J. H., *How They Were Taught*, Blackwell, Oxon, 1969.

Griffith, R. E.: *Urdd Gobaith Cymru, Cyfrol* 1, 1922–1945.
——*Urdd Gobaith Cymru, Cyfrol* 2, 1946–1960. Gwasg Gomer, Llandysul, 1971 and 1972.

Bibliography

Gruffydd, W. J., 'Rhagarweiniad i'r Bedwaredd Ganrif ar Bymtheg', II, *Y Llenor*, Hydref, 1935.

Howells, A., 'The Development of Secondary Education in Merthyr Tydfil', (unpublished University of Wales M. Ed., 1971).

Impey, A. C., 'The Development of State-Provided Education in Cardiff, 1870–1939, (unpublished University of Wales M. Ed., 1973).

Jones, Abel J., *I was Privileged*, Cardiff, 1943.

—— *From an Inspector's Bag*, Cardiff, 1944.

Jones, Iorwerth, *David Rees: y Cynhyrfwr*. Gwasg John Penry, Abertawe, 1971.

Jones, John Viriamu, 'The University of Wales', *Transactions Liverpool Welsh Nat. Society*, 1895–6.

Jones, R. Brinley, (ed.), *Anatomy of Wales*, Gwerin Publications, Peterston-Super-Ely, Glam., 1972.

Jones, R. Tudur, *Hanes Annibynwyr Cymru*, Gwasg John Penry, Abertawe, 1966.

Jones, Thomas, *Leeks and Daffodils*, Newtown, 1942.

Jones, W. R., *Bilingualism in Welsh Education*, Cardiff, 1966.

Lloyd, J. E., (ed.) History of Carmarthenshire, Vol. II, 1939, Cardiff.

McCann, J. E., *Thomas Howell and the School at Llandaff, 1860–1890*, Cowbridge, 1972.

Morgan, Iwan J., (ed.) *The College by the Sea*, Aberystwyth, 1928.

Morgan, Rev. J. Vyrnwy (ed.), *Welsh Religious Leaders in the Nineteenth Century*, London, 1908.

—— *Welsh Political and Educational Leaders in the Nineteenth Century*, London, 1908.

Morgan, Kenneth O., *Wales in British Politics*, 1868–1922, (Second Edition), Cardiff, 1970.

Morgan, P. T. J., 'Gwerin Cymru—Y Ffaith a'r Ddelfryd', *Transactions Honourable Society of Cymmrodorion*, Session 1967, Part I.

Owen, Geraint Dyfnallt, *Ysgolion a Cholegau yr Annibynwyr*, Abertawe, 1939.

Owen, Prys Eifion, 'The Beginnings of the County Schools in Caernarvonshire', *Transactions Caernarvonshire Historical Society*, 1957.

Pioneers of Welsh Education, (Faculty of Education, University College of Swansea), 1962.

Randall, Peter J., 'The Development of Administrative decentralization in Wales from the establishment of the Welsh Department of Education in 1907 to the creation of the post of Secretary of State for Wales in October 1964'. (Unpublished University of Wales M.Sc.(Econ.), 1969).

Reichel, Harry R., 'Patriotism, True and False', *Welsh Outlook*, 1921.

Bibliography

—— *The University in Wales*, Newtown, 1920.
Roberts, Brynley F., 'Syr Edward Anwyl (1866–1914)', *Transactions Honourable Society of Cymmrodorion, Session* 1968, Part II.
Sacks, Benjamin, *The Religious Issue in the State Schools of England and Wales, 1902–14*, Albuquerque, University of New Mexico, 1961.
Selby-Bigge, L. Amherst, *The Board of Education*, London, 1927.
Thomas, Sir Ben Bowen, 'Agwedd ar Wleidyddiaeth Cymru, 1900–14', *Y Llenor*, 1948.
—— 'Perthynas Crefydd ac Addysg yng Nghymru, 1883–1919, trwy lygaid Thomas Francis Roberts'. *Trafodion Cymdeithas Hanes Bedyddwyr Cymru*, 1961.
—— 'Establishment of the Aberdare Departmental Committee, 1880. Some notes and letters', *Bulletin of the Board of Celtic Studies*, May, 1962.
Tropp, Asher, *The School Teachers*, London, 1957.
Trow, A. H., and Brown, D. J. A., *A Short History of the University College of South Wales and Monmouthshire, Cardiff, 1883–1933*, Cardiff, 1933.
Webster, J. R., 'The Welsh Intermediate Education Act of 1889'. *Welsh History Review*, Vol. 4, 1968.
Wheldon, Sir Wynn, and Thomas, Sir Ben Bowen, Addresses: 'The Welsh Department, Ministry of Education, 1907–1957'. *Transactions Honourable Society of Cymrodorion*, 1957.
Williams, Gwyn A., 'Twf Hanesyddol y Syniad o Genedl yng Nghymru', *Efrydiau Athronyddol, cyf. xxiv* (1961).

INDEX

Index

Aberaeron, 273.
Aberdare: Intermediate School, 264; 1902 Act in operation, 141; 'no rate' resolution, 141.
Aberdare Departmental Committee on Higher Education, 9, 10, 11, 12, 13; Report on, 13, 14, 36.
Aberdare, Henry Austin Bruce, 1st Baron; and Gladstone, 6; and Welsh Higher Education, 9, 10, 13, 40.
Abergavenny, 8, 20n; 76.
Abergele, 95.
Abergwili, 121, 161.
Abertillery, 141, 141n, 147n, 166.
Aberystwyth, University College of Wales, 9, 10, 12, 13, 28, 68, 273, 277.
Abney, W. de W, 300n.
Abyssinia, 189.
Academies, 8, 120.
Academic Board, 33.
Accounts, Central Welsh Board, 50–57, 362–65.
Acland, Arthur Hart Dyke, 9, 17, 18, 25, 27, 185, 298.
Acting Teachers' Examination, 336n.
Acts, *see* Education.
Adaptation, 21; in schools, 242–243, 245; of curriculum, 278; school courses, 292, 300.
Adolescent education, 350.
Additional donation or endowment, 57.
Advanced Elementary Schools, 42n.
Advisory Councils, Technical Education, 36.
Agreement, 188; Joint Committee, Scheme, Caernarvonshire County Council, 190.
Agriculture: Board of Agriculture and Fisheries, 198, 325; agricultural education, 325, 328; teaching of, 67, 94, 242, 271; Diploma in, 293n; and Husbandry, 293n.
Aid grants, 126, 155, 156.
Albert Hall, 200.
Alderley, Lord Stanley of: *See* Stanley.
Amending Scheme, Central Welsh Board, 58, 61, 71, 72, 104.
Ammanford, 130, 131, 132.
Andocides, 251.
Angell, Lewis, 40.
Anglesey, 93, 141.
Anglo-Saxon, 250, 257.
Annual grant, 155.
Anson, Sir William: and the Education (Local Authority) Default Bill, 29; and joint Board of Welsh County Councils, 29, 37; and Minute of 'State of Wales' 143, 151, 154, 157, 159, 160, 164, 169, 170; and his joint Committee, 187; and Agreement, 190, 192, 199; compares joint Committee with Welsh National Council for Education, 201; Committee stage Education Bill 1906, 204; and Minister proposal, 206, 208, 212, 224.
Anwyl, Sir Edward: 52, 52n; and Municipal Schools and their Inspections, 58–69, 65, 70, 76; Dual Inspection, 78, 85, 88, 89, 97, 99, 101, 102, 122, 128, 132, 135, 276, 284, 300.
Appointed Day, 121n, 141n, 166n.
Architectural Branch, Board of Education, 224.
Area Reports, 247, 340.
Armstrong College, Newcastle upon Tyne, 27n.
Assistant Inspectors, 344; 345n.
Assizes, Glamorgan, 50, 102.
Asquith, Herbert Henry, (1st Earl of Oxford and Asquith), Minister Proposal, 205, 208.
Atkin, Mr. Justice, James Richard, 102.
Atkins, Professor J. W. H., 90n.
Auditor and Comptroller-General, 120.
Autonomy, 7, 23, 28, 30, 36, 58–61, 184, 186, 384.
Autonomous districts, 189, 191, 193, 229, 359, 384.

Bala, 280, 298, 341.
Balcarres, Lord, 214.
Balfour, Arthur James (1st Earl of Balfour): 9, 29, 189, 194, 198, 200; calls Welsh National Council for Education, 'Home Rule for Wales', 201; 'How fleshless skeleton can be clothed', 201, 202, 212; Committee stage Education Bill 1906, 204, 204n; and new 'Minister' proposal, 206–208; and 'a new department', 214.
Ballinger, Sir John, 316.
Bancroft, John, HMI, 338.
Bangor, Bishop of, 40, 212.
Bangor, borough, 139.
Bangor, Normal College, 8, 269n, 281, 321, 321n.
Bangor, St. Mary's College, 8n, 320, 321.
Bangor, University College of North Wales, 7, 15, 321.
Baptist, 119, 124.
Barlow, Mr., 337, 337n.
Barmouth, 281.
Barnett, Mr., 91.
Barry, 141, 166, 321, 321n.
Beavan, F. J., 76, 78.
Beaverbrook Library, 3.
B.Ed., degree, 321n.
Belgium, 275.
Beresford, Mr., 329, 330, 331.
Betton Charity, 42.
Bias in curriculum, 242, 271, 293, 293n.
Biblical instruction, 28.

412

Index

Bilingualism, 370.
Bilingual teaching, 26, 31, 289.
Birkenhead, 1st Earl of, *see* Smith, Frederick Edwin.
Birrell, Augustine, 9; his Education Bill, 29, 193, 199, 195; supports administrative devolution for Wales, 202; and parliamentary control over Welsh National Council for Education, 209; and public audit of accounts, 209, 212, 212n, 214, 216, 217.
Bishop, Lewis, 129, 130, 131.
Blaenau Festiniog, 293n.
Blind (children), 229.
Board of Celtic Studies, 33.
Board of Education: Central Welsh Board Amending Scheme, 58, 66, 67, 82; Board of Education preliminary examination for teachers, 90; examination committee, 91, 104; consultative committee on examinations in Secondary schools, 105; institutes Inquiry, 119, 121, 122, 125; machinery for Inquiry, 136; and Welsh County Councils, 138; advised by law Officers of the Crown, 148; determines form of Inquiry, 152; parliamentary grants, 155, 164; Glamorgan draft scheme, 186; safeguards for Joint Board, 186; and local Government Board, 188; and Welsh National Council for Education, 196; Board of Education Act 1899, 204; its Welsh Inspectorate, 224; Accountant-General, 224; Report 1908-9, 240; Board of Education (Powers) Order in Council 1900, and Powers of the Charity Commissioners over endowments, 243; 280; its Annual Report, 296; criticism of, 300; and A. T. Davies at his new post, 310; and Central Welsh Board, 386.
Boards, School, 154.
Bompas, H. M., 8n.
Boothroyd, Mr., Junior Inspector, 338.
Borough Road Training College, 8.
Botwnnog, 50n, 293.
Bowen, J., Mr., Sub-Inspector, 338.
Brâd y Llyfrau Gleision, 7, 263-4.
Bramwell, Sir Frederick, 15.
Braybrooke, Lord, 126.
Brecon, Christ's College, 8, 20.
Brecon, Normal School, 8.
Brecon, Voluntary Schools, 140.
Brecknockshire, 93.
Bridgend, 14, 76.
Bridgeman, William Clive (1st Viscount Bridgeman), 224.
Bright, A. S., HMI, (Handicraft), 361.
Bristol, university, 27n.

British Museum, Parliamentary Funds, 197.
British Schools, 28.
British and Foreign School Society, 120.
Bromley, John, 167, 168, 195.
Brown, Canon, 162, 169, 170.
Brown, Charles Gilbert, Trinity College, Carmarthen, 136.
Brownrigg, Canon, 136, 152.
Bruce, Henry Austin, *see* Aberdare, 1st Baron.
Bruce, Hon. William Napier, 6, 10, 16n, 18, 18n, 25, 34, 51, 53, 54, 55, 57, 87, 106, 186, 186n, 192, 349.
Bruce, Professor Herbert, 90n.
Brunel, Isambard Kingdom, 27n.
Bryce, James, (1st Viscount Bryce), 9, 13, 242.
Builth Wells, 68.
Bürger-Schulen of Prussia, 20, 20n.
Burgess, Bishop Thomas, 11, 120.
Bursars, 64, 301, 371.
Bursars, failure of, 95-97.
BI Vote, 344, 344n.

Cabinet, 189, 194, 199.
Caerleon, 52, 319, 321n.
Caernarvon, 4, 68.
Caernarvonshire, 21, 25, LEA, 68; 139, 142, LEA, 285.
Caernarvon Training College, 8.
Caird, Professor Sir Edward, 298.
Cambridge, Corpus Christi College, 98.
Cambridgeshire County Council, 126-7, 126n, 128; Cambridgeshire Case and Opinion, 144-6.
Cambridge Welsh Society, 281.
Campbell-Bannerman, Sir Henry, 30, 193, 212, 215, 215n, 216.
Canton Boys and Girls Secondary Schools, Cardiff, 61n, 74, 113.
Cape Colony, 32, 370.
Capel Als, Llanelli, 119, 121.
Capel Mair, Carmarthenshire, 161.
Capitation fees, 52.
Carbutt, E. H., MP, 40.
Cardiff, 11, 14, 15, 16, 18, 50; LEA, 74; 75, 77, 107, 123, 141, 222, 240n.
Cardiff Technical Institute Committee & School, 26, 343.
Cardigan, 273.
Cardiganshire, LEA, 68, 89, 141, 141n.
Carlingford, Chichester Samuel-. Fortesque, 1st Baron, 15.
Carmarthen Borough Town Council, 142.
Carmarthen District, 280.
Carmarthenshire, 93, 119.
Carmarthenshire Dissenting Schools, 120.

413

Index

Carmarthenshire Inquiry, 2, 118–182; objects of Inquiry, 153; Carmarthenshire Education Committee, 122.
Carmarthenshire Voluntaryist Schools, 120; and managers of Voluntary Schools, 133; failure to provide services to Voluntary Schools, 135; proceeding in illegal manner, 134, 139, 142; Institution of the Inquiry, 143–159; evidence of illegalities, 152; General Chronological Summary, 152; notice of Inquiry, 153; funds for Voluntary Schools, 155.
Carson, Sir Edward Henry, 146; and Clause 37, 207.
Casson, J. L., 51, 56, 57; and Inspections of the Central Welsh Board, 62, 65, 71, 72; observations on Intermediate and Municipal Secondary Schools, 74; discovers irregularities, 79; his memorandum on office procedure, 80, 84, 88, 100, 220, 260, 285, 300, 345, 380.
Cavendish, Mr., MP, 224n.
Cawdor, 3rd Earl of. *See* Emlyn, Viscount.
Cawdor Castle, Nairn, 192n.
Cecil, Lord Robert, (1st Viscount Cecil of Chelwood), 224.
Celtic Studies, 33.
Cenarth, 127.
Central Publication Department, Board of Education, 313.
Central French Board, 27, 251.
Central Welsh Board, 6, 16, 21; its establishment, 22; constitution of, 22; funds of, 22; functions of, 23; examinations, 24–25; Central Welsh Board and Welsh department, 32, 34; finances, 34n; and Welsh Joint Education Committee, 36, 37; and its Intermediate Schools, 37–38; its relations with Welsh Department, 48, 49, 50; its headquarters in Cardiff, 49; deputations to Whitehall, 50; Junior certificate, 51; Honours certificate, 51; Treasury Regulations, 51; its cost up to 1907–8, 51; its growth, 52; salaries for review, 52–56; examination fees, 52; increase of grant, 54; Dual Inspection, 58; 'Practical Autonomy', 58; extension of powers, 61–62; demand for complete autonomy, 64; deputation, 65; its inclusion in Board of Education reports, 68; and Municipal Secondary Schools, 71; not to inspect and examine Municipal Secondary Schools, 71; 'Thus far' meeting, 72; Deputation to Whitehall, 1913, 74, 74n; irregular letters to Merthyr Tydfil, 80; curricula and Elementary School teachers, 90; inflexibility of Senior certificate, 91; superannuation fund, 104; reorganizing committee, 104; Owen appointed Clerk and Superintendent of examinations, 104; and Welsh National Council for Education, 199; hostility to Welsh department and the 'revolt' in Parliament, 229, 241; defects of its Secondary education, 241; and Welsh working classes, 243; its inflexibility to serve Wales, 243; its Reports, before and after 1907, 244; attacks 1909 Report, 260; its Statement, 260; Senior Certificate, 271; weaknesses in inspection, 280; stereotyped report on it, 294; its merits, 299; struggle with Welsh department, 309; and financial aid from Local Education Authorities, 358; approved new proposals confirmed by local Education Authorities, 362; Proposals A (Inspection) and proposals B (providing income), 363; methods of further co-operation with Board of Education, 363; financial changes with Board of Education, and Local Education Authorities, 364.
Central Welsh Education Fund, 362.
Central Schools, 364.
Centres, pupil teacher, 90.
Certificates, C.W.B. Honours, Senior, Junior, 52, 249, 256–257, 270–71, 289.
Chambers, E. K., 91, 226, 315, 327.
Chancellor of the Exchequer, 22.
Charity Commissioners, 9, 17, 22, 204, 241, 293.
Charter, University of Wales, 33.
Chester, King's School, 52n.
Chester, Bishop of. *See* Jayne, Francis.
Chemistry, teaching of, 251.
Chief Inspector of Schools, Central Welsh Board, 22, 297.
Chief Inspector of Education, Wales, 22, 22n; 219, 222.
Chief Medical Officer, Board of Education, 224.
Chief Woman Inspector, Board of Education, 343.
Choice of Employment Act, 327.
Christ's College, Brecon, 8, 20.
Church of England, 157.
Church rates, 119.
Church Schools, 9, 28.
Cilycwm, 135.
Circular to LEAs, 191; Circular 11, Wales, 88; Circular 153, 360.
City and Guilds, 326.
Civil Service, 224.
Civil Service Commission, 313, 345.
Clarke, Sir Edward, 144.
Clayton, C.P., Assistant Inspector, 361.

414

Index

Code, Welsh, 316; Schools and Training Colleges, 318, 370.
Coercion of Wales Bill. *See* Education (Local Authority) Default Bill.
Colonial Compromise, 29, 29n, 138.
Colonies, emigration of teachers, 330.
Colonial history, 277.
Coltman-Rogers, Mr. & Mrs., 94, 96.
Collin, Mary, 65, 297n.
Colwyn Bay, 78.
Commissioner (Carmarthenshire Inquiry), 160, 162, 164.
Complete inspection, demand for, 58–70.
Concordat, 138.
Confidential memorandum on Welsh National Council, 194; Order in Council, 199.
Conservative and Liberal Unionist Association, Carmarthen, 121.
Consultative Committee & Welsh Central Committee, 204.
Cookery, 252.
Co-optive principle, 188.
Co-option, 189.
Copus, Mr., Sub-Inspector, 338.
Corpus Christi College, Oxford, 98.
Costs of Inquiry, 167.
County Governing Bodies, 25, 242, 270, 290, 294.
County Schemes, 21, 34, 38, 63, 294, 294n, 299, 300.
Court of Petty Sessions, Carmarthenshire, 125.
Coventry, 120.
Cowbridge, Boys' Grammar School, 8, 20.
Cowbridge, Girls' Intermediate School, 71, 74, 76.
Cowper-Temple Clause, 28.
Cramming and examinations, 270, 276n, 297.
Crawley, Arnold and Co., 160.
Craftmaking, 242.
Creation of Welsh Department, Board of Education, 213–237.
Crewe, Robert Offley Crewe-Miles, Marquess of: and Welsh National Council for Education, 211.
Criccieth, 213, 218.
Crichton-Stuart, Lord Ninian, 103.
Crimean War, 11.
Cromwell, Oliver, 282n.
Cross Commission, 27.
Crown Lands, 184.
Crown, Law Officers of, 143–181.
Cunliffe, Sir Robert, Bart., 40.
Curricula, 24, 38, 371.
Cwmamman, 135.
Cymmrodorion, Honourable Society of, 33.

Cyfarthfa Castle Secondary School, 75.
Cyfarfodydd Llenyddol, 243.
Cyfres y Fil, 222.
Cymru, 222.
Cymru'r Plant, 222.

Dale, F. I., CI, Elementary Schools, England, 343.
Danckwerts, W.O., 144.
Darlington, Thomas, HMI, 9, 25, 338, 338n, 339.
Darlington, James, 259.
David, George, 102.
Davies, Dr. Aaron, 94.
Davies, Sir Alfred T., 30, 49; and Inspection 62; relations between Welsh Department and the Central Welsh Board, 63, 65; Dual Inspection, 66; his view of Central Welsh Board inspection, 68; and education, 69; and administrative, 69, 70; Memorandum prepared by, 74; Casson's memorandum on office procedure, 80; and Jolliffe, 97; and Jolliffe's complaints, 100; and Central Welsh Boards examinations, 101, 106; and dissenting 'quasi secondary' schools, 120; 213, 217, 218, 218n, 221, 222, 223, 224, 225n, 226, 227, 259, 262, 282, 285, 308; Liberal Agent, 308; practice in Liverpool, 308; his publications, 310–315; and Chambers. 315; his administrative report, 323; Memorandum on Technical Education and other work, 326; and U branch, 334, 336, 348; and re-organization of Inspectorate, 357; and Central Welsh Board for unified Inspectorate of Education, 358; absence of agreement by Central Welsh Board, 360; reorganizes Welsh Inspectorate in a *Circular* to the Welsh Local Education Authorities, 360; and non-acceptance of changes by Central Welsh Board, or by Local Education Authorities, 362; his retirement, 378; offered Chief Inspector's post, 378.
Davies, A. Mervyn, 3, 308.
Davies, Dan Isaac, HMI, 27, 337, 338n.
Davies, D. T., Assistant Inspector, 361.
Davies, Ellis, 65.
Davies, Evan R., 185, 186, 188, 189, 190, 204, 217.
Davies, J. C., 386.
Davies, J. Humphreys, 94, 283, 292.
Davies, M. H., Assistant Inspector, 361.
Davies, Richard, 12, 40.
Day Continuation Classes, 350.
Day Training Departments, University Colleges, 301, 333.
Deaf and dumb children, 229.

Index

Defaulting authorities, 9, 29, 119, 139, 166, 166n, 167, 171.
Defective children, Swansea, 314; Rhondda, 315.
Defalcation, 102–3.
Demonstration and practising schools, 373.
Denbigh, Howells School, 8, 68, 141.
Denbighshire, LEA 74; County Council, 218, 222, 224; LEA 255, 259, 301.
Denominational right of entry, 29n.
Denominational Theological Colleges, 251.
Department of Education and Science, 3, 389.
Departmental Committee, 1880, 6, 13–15; 1919, 106.
Department of Science and Art, 24, 326.
D.S.I.R., Board of Education, 310–13.
Deputations, 58–60, 64–67, 73–79, 85–86, 87–89.
Development fund, agricultural education, 328.
Diaries, Inspectors, 341.
Differentiation, 242, 271, 292, 293, 293n, 297, 298, 299, 372.
Diploma in Agriculture or Husbandry, 293n.
Direct Access, 224.
Direct Method, 276, 290; Monmouthshire, 291.
Directory for 1915, 351.
Discussion of Adjournment, 160–1, 171.
Dismissal of teachers, 19, 169.
Disraeli, Benjamin (1st Earl of Beaconsfield), 9.
Dissenting schools, 120.
District Auditor, 134.
Districts, inspectors, 337–40.
Divisional inspectors, 342, 353.
Diwygiwr, Y, 119.
Dodd, W. G., 259.
Dolgellau, Dr. Williams School, 8.
Dolywern, 354.
Domestic science, 242.
Douglas, F. E., 327.
Draft scheme, Welsh Joint Board, 186; Schemes A and B, 188.
Drawing, 242, 252.
Dual inspection, 32, 34, 58–79.
Dufton, Mr., Junior Inspector, 338.
D u n r a v e n, W y n d h a m T h o m a s Wyndham-Quin, (4th Earl of.), 212.
Durham Act, 27n.
Durham Colleges, 27n.
Dynevor, Arthur de Cardonnell Rice, 6th Baron, 40, 129, 130, 132.
Dynevor Castle Estate, 129.

Eaton, Mr., (Welsh Department), 220.
Ebbw Vale, 41, 166.
Edinburgh Academy, 8.
Education: Blue Books, 1847, 7; Schools Inquiry Commission, 1867, 18; Act of 1870, 9, 28, 130, 152, 168. Endowed Schools Act, 1874, 18; Education (Scotland) Act of 1878, 24n; Welsh Intermediate Education Act, 1889, 37, 38, 65, 89; Technical Instruction Act, 1889, 17, 18; Voluntary Schools Act, 1897, 156n; Elementary Education Act, 1897, 156n; Board of Education Act, 1899, 36; Act of 1902, 9, 34, 36, 49, 58, 66, 118, 121, 122; Part III of the Act, 125, 130, 135, 136; Clauses, 137, 143, 146, 150; Order under Section 16, 159, 169, 186, 193; Education (Provision of Working Balances) Act, 1903, 163; 1904, Education (Local Authority) Default or 'Coercion' Act, 9, 29, 119, 166, 167, 190; Education Bill, 1906, 30, 37, 58n; Part IV, Welsh National Council for Education, 194, 199, S33, S13, S39, 204; passed its 3rd reading, 210; Act of 1918, 33, 34, 148, 309; new system of paying grants, 362.
Edwards, Alfred George, 1st Archbishop of Wales, Bishop of St. Asaph, 211.
Edward, Clement, MP, 64n.
Edwards, Dean of Bangor, 12.
Edwards, Professor Edward, 90.
Edwards, Sir Frank, 65, 188.
Edwards, Sir Ifan ab Owen, 388, 388n.
Edwards, John Hugh, 76.
Edwards, Sir Owen (Morgan): In, 22, 30; his initial work at the Welsh Department, 31; Welsh teaching and bilingual policy, 31, 32; and Training Colleges, 31; criticizing the Central Welsh Board, 38, 49, 50, 58; arranges inspections with Anwyl, 60, 64, 65; discusses Board of Education and Central Welsh Board inspectors, 66; brevity of reports, 70; rebukes Tom John, 73; and Municipal Schools, 73; and Local Education Authorities, 73n, 74; memorandum prepared by, 74, 75, 88; and Welsh Training Colleges, 90; and University Colleges, 90; and curricula of Welsh Intermediate Schools and intending teachers, 90; his subjects for Elementary school teachers, 92; and Jolliffe, 97; his views on Central Welsh Board's methods of conducting examinations 98; criticism of Central Welsh Board's examination administration, 99; and Jolliffe's letter, 100; meets officials of the Central Welsh Board, 101, 106,

Index

217, 219, 222; Liberal MP, 224; and McKenna 228; criticizes Central Welsh Board, 228; describes his work to Lewis, 228; a target for the Central Welsh Board, 240; his attack on the Central Welsh Board, 241; 1909 Report an important landmark in Welsh Education, 241; educational ideas, 243; his experience in Intermediate Schools, 244; his views on Elementary and Secondary education, 245; and Central Welsh Board examinations, 246; school libraries, 246; his views on the teaching of Welsh, 246; and Edgar Jones's criticisms, 247; and disadvantages of Central Welsh Board examinations, 248; and practical subjects, 252; and 'mechanical answers' especially in history, etc., 252; concern about lack of intellectual curiosity and originality, 253, 253n; his famous phrase, 'wooden and unintelligent type of mind' 254; and the 'Wooden Report' 1909, 254; his condemnation of the Central Welsh Board's Secondary Educational System, 254; and Denbighshire criticism, 260; Edgar Jones's criticism, 264n; his reply to criticism, 264; MS report, 266n; pressure of examinations, 269n, 270; on History teaching, 273; teaching in Welsh Intermediate Schools, 276, 276n; and statement of Central Welsh Board, 279n; his victory, 280; and Lord Sheffield, 282n; and 'embalmed' head of Oliver Cromwell, 282; his reforms of Central Welsh Board, 285; his new examination system, 288; honorary offices in the Central Welsh Board, 296; as an Official, 298; his background, 298; summary of Jones's criticism, 304; his way of writing Minutes, 305; Llanuwchllyn, 308; Royal Commission on University Education in Wales, 309; and early Welsh inspectors, 316; interim account of his work in 1909, 321; on Training College Examinations, and University branch, 335; reviews his inspectors 1912, 340; memorandum to Davies on Welsh inspectorate 1912, 34n; as an Inspector, 341; and occasional inspectors 342; his parsimony, 342n; and Royal Commission on University Education, 348; and Education Bill of 1918, 348; and re-organization of Welsh Secondary Education in 1919, 348; reforming Welsh University, 349; opposition to him on University Commission, 349; his scheme for the re-organization of Welsh Inspectorate, 1918, 352; repercussions of outside work on his duties as Chief Inspector, 352; his inspectorate plan, 353.

Edwards, Dr. William, HMI, 105, 217, 337, 338, 347n.
Eglwys Lloegr, 119.
Egypt, 382.
Eisteddfod, 31.
Elementary Experimental Science, 251.
Elementary Branch, Board of Education, 370–1.
E. S. and T. work, Board of Education, 351, 352, 356.
Ellis, Thomas Edward, 9, 17, 184, 185n, 298.
Ellis, Miss M. E., 361.
Emlyn, Frederick Archibald Vaughan, Viscount (3rd Earl of Cawdor), 37, 123, 124, 192, 211, 212, 214.
Endowment, educational, 19, 42.
Endowed schools, 8, 9, 12, 14.
Endowed Schools and Charitable Trust Acts, 100; *See* Education.
England, 1902 Act Working correctly, 150.
English Subjects, 278.
English, teaching of, 250, 272, 272n, 278, 289.
English inspectors, 342–348.
Established Church in Wales, 14, 119.
Establishment section, Board of Education, 345.
Examiners, 248.
Examinations, 270.
Examinations Committee, Board of Education, 91.
Expenditure, Central Welsh Board, 110, 364.
Explosive Report, 50, 239–305; 240, 243, 248, 255, 264, 278.
Extension of Powers, Central Welsh Board, 58–97.
Extension of responsibilities, Welsh Department, 324–337.
Evans, Ben, 122.
Evans, David, 104.
Evans, Rev. D., 40.
Evans, Gwilym, 124.
Evans, Myrddin, 104, 105.
Evans, Samuel J., 277.
Evans, Stephen, 40.
Evans, W. H., Sub-Inspector, 338, 361.
Evening Continuation Schools, 225.

Faculty of Education, 321n.
Fawkes, W. H., 104n.
Fearon, D. R., 25.
Federal Education Conference, 275.
Federation of Welsh Education Committees, 36.

417

Index

Feeding, schools, 295.
Fees, examination certificates, 294–5; 295n.
Fee Grant, 155.
Ferndale (Rhondda), 74, 76, 77.
Ferryside, National School, 50–51.
Final Examination for Teachers in Training Colleges, 336n.
Finances, Central Welsh Board, 50–54.
Findlay, J. J., 297n.
Finlay, R. B., 146.
Firth College, Sheffield, 15.
Fisher, H.A.L., 106; and Education Act, 1918, 350.
Fishguard, 293n.
Flemming, Sir Gilbert, 230.
Fletcher, W. C., CI, Secondary Schools, England, 343.
Fleure, Professor H. J., 275; Summer Schools, 277, 287.
Flint District, representation of, 184.
Flintshire, 141, County Council, 184.
Formal grammar, 257, 290.
Forms, teaching in higher, 253–4, 261, 262; lower forms, 277.
Form of Notice of Inquiry, Carmarthenshire, 159.
Formalities, of Inquiry, Carmarthenshire, 159–160.
Forster, W. E., 9; Forster Bill, 28.
Forestry, 184.
Foundation managers, 163, 164.
Franklen, T. Mansel, 71, 78, 186.
Freedom of teaching, 265, 277–8.
Free studentships, 329; free places, 371.
Friars School, Bangor, 8, 12, 274.
French, 27, 250, 275.
French, teaching of, 275–6, 291–2.

Gee, Thomas, 28.
General Council, Wales, 184.
General elections, 6, 9, 193.
Genesis of the Welsh Department, Board of Education, 184–212.
George, David Lloyd, *see* Lloyd George, David.
George, William, 34, 105, 106, 385.
Geography, teaching of, 99, 252, 269, 274–5, 289.
Geology, 271, 293.
German, 251.
Germany, 19.
Girls secondary schools, education, 8.
Gittins report, 302.
Gladstone, William Ewart, 6, 9, 10, 11n, 13, 15, 17, 28.
Glamorgan East, 185.
Glasgow University, 218.
Gloucester, 214.
Glynceiriog, 354.

Golden Grove National School, 135.
Governors, and school curriculum, 24; 25, 281.
Goschen fund, 16.
Goschen, Sir John, 22.
Governing Bodies, 242, 270, 290, 294.
Grants, 66; Grant payments Act, 1902, 158; to Voluntary schools, 158; to schools and intending teachers, 290–291.
Great Western Hotel, Paddington, 16.
Greek, teaching of, 24, 99, 251, 368.
Grey, Sir Edward, 1st Viscount Grey of Fallodon, 102.
Griffiths, Ven. Archdeacon, 40.
Griffiths, Principal E. H., 257, 262, 281, 318.
Griffiths, Ellis (Jones), 64n, 65, 86, 281.
Griffith-Boscawen, Arthur S. T., 122, 157, 169.
Griffiths, W. Crynant, 88, 101, 102.
Gruffydd, Professor W. J., 309.
Guest, Ivor, 64n.
Guildhall, Carmarthen, 124.
Gwerin, 242–3, 243n.
Gwynedd, Owen, 368.

Hadow, Dr. W. H., 368.
Haldane, Richard, Burton (Viscount Haldane of Cloan) 33, 349.
Hardie, James Keir, 64n.
Harris, Principal D. R., 269n, 281.
Hart-Dyke, Sir William, 9, 17, 17n.
Haul, Yr, 119.
Hawarden, 369.
Headlam, J. W., 25.
Heath, Dr. (D.S.I.R.), 226, 310; and Davies's so-called 'Publications', 310; and U branch, 329; and Training Colleges, 332, 336.
Health, school pupils, 294.
Hemmerde, Edward, 64n.
Herbertson, Professor, 275.
Hendy, Carmarthenshire, 127.
Henllan Amgoed Independent Church, 120.
Higher Elementary, full Reports, 341; Schools, 371.
Higher Grade department, 20.
Higher Grade schools, 20n.
Higher School certificate, 21; and Honours, 288.
Hills, R. P., 132, 132n, 160, 170; Confidential memorandum to Morant, on Defaulting Authority Bill, 171.
History, teaching of, 269, 273; poor teaching of, 273, 289.
HMIs, insufficient staff, 350; overworked, 351.
Hobhouse, Mr., 88, 282.
Holliday Mr., Sub-inspector, 338.

418

Index

Holyhead, 240n.
Homework, 94.
Honorary offices, Central Welsh Board, 296.
Honours certificate, Central Welsh Board, 52, 249, 256–7, 270–71, 289.
Hooson, J. E., Sub-inspector, 338, 361.
Howard Gardens School, Cardiff, 61n, 74.
Howell Charity, 42.
Howell, William, 160.
Howells School, Llandaff, 8, 20, 76; Denbigh, 8, 20, 76.
Hughes, Gwynne, 124.
Hughes, R. E., HMI, 338.
Hughes, T. J., 187, 188, 188n; and Carmarthenshire, 191, 217.
Hume, Joseph, 120.
Humphreys-Owen, Arthur C., 18, 21, 52, 53, 90n, 184n.

Idris, Howell, 64n.
Illegality, question of, 118; Carmarthenshire, 123, 130, 166n.
Implementation, Part III, Education Act, 1902, 351.
Imprisonment, members of County Council, 167.
Independents, in West Wales, 119; Carmarthenshire; 119–120.
Industrial Schools, 371.
Inspectors' Diaries, 341.
Inspectorate, England and Wales, 354–357.
Inspectorial Districts (Welsh) distribution of inspectorial work, 350, 352; redistribution of, 374.
Inspectors, Elementary Schools, 338; and Secondary Schools, 338.
Inspectors, grades of, 339.
Inspection, Central Welsh Board, 23, 24, 62, 69.
Inspection, dual, 32, 34, 69.
Inspection of Municipal Secondary Schools, 61, 69.
Inspection, views of Owen Edwards, 60–61, 62, 69, 340, 341, 342, 346, 350–4.
Inspectorate staff, Wales, 1924, 361.
Inspectorate unified, 35, 363–5.
Institutions for Further Education, 359.
Instruction to the Committee, on Part IV of Education Bill 1906, 201; defeated, 203, 203n.
Italian, 251.
Intermediate schools, 9, 19; number of, 21, 24, 32, 48n, 89; getting out of date and stagnating, 293n; classes for children under 12, 295; Post-matriculation courses, and University Intermediate courses, 295.

Ireland, 30.

James, Mr., Sub-Inspector, 338.
Jayne, Francis, Bishop of Chester, 11n.
Jenkins, Professor R. T., 285, 286n.
Jersey, Rt. Hon. Earl of, 40.
Jesus College, Oxford, 12, 13, 14.
John, Tom, 65, 72, 75, 78, 85, 96, 318.
Johns, Rev. Thomas, 121, 122, 123, 124.
Johns, W. R. C., HMI, 338, 361.
Johnston, D. Vaughan, 363.
Johnson, T. H., Sub-Inspector, 338.
Joint Board of Welsh County Councils, 186.
Joint Committee of Welsh County Councils, 186, 187.
Joint Education Committees, 18, 19, 21.
Jolliffe, A. E., 97–102.
Jolliffe case, 50, 97.
Jones, A. A., Junior Inspector, 348.
Jones, Abel J., his reflections on Owen Edwards, 354, 361.
Jones, Professor C. Bryner, 94, 293n.
Jones, Sir D. Brynmor Jones, 65, 198, 203.
Jones, Rev. D. Eleazar, 122, 124.
Jones, David Evan, HMI, 338, 340, 341n, 350, 353, 353n.
Jones, Edgar (Barry), 92, 255; his address, 255; teaching of English and History, 256; Board of Education asked to withdraw Report, 258; 280.
Jones, Edgar, M.P., 326.
Jones, Edwardes G., 144, 160.
Jones Foundation Schools, 20n.
Jones, Gomer, Sub-Inspector, 338, 348.
Jones, Griffith, Rev., 119.
Jones, H. Haydn, MP, 264, 280, 282, 324, and Technical Education, 325n; 327, 383.
Jones, Sir Henry, 216, 218, 349.
Jones, Rev. H. Longueville, 26.
Jones, J. Elias, Assistant Inspector, 348, 361.
Jones, Sir John Morris, 277.
Jones, Rev. J. Towyn, 124.
Jones, J. Viriamu, 10n, 15, 16, 26, 27.
Jones, K. Idwal, 3.
Jones, R. A. (Emrys ap Iwan), 298.
Jones, S. G. Assistant Inspector, 348.
Jones, S. N., 76.
Jones, Dr. Thomas, 218.
Jones, T., Assistant Inspector, 361.
Jones, T., Rev., 169, 170.
Jones, William, 65.
Journal of Education, 221, 383.
Junior Certificate examination, 105, 289.
Junior Technical schools, 364.
Junior Examiner, 314.
Juvenile employment, 350n.

Index

Kastner, Professor, 276.
Kay-Shuttleworth, Sir James, 8, 26.
Keble College, Oxford, 280.
Keighley Institute, 25.
Kensington, Lord, 40.
Kekewich, Sir George, 171n.
Kingsford, Mr., Welsh Department, 220.
King's Bench Division, High Court of Justice, 118n.
King Henry Grammar School, Abergavenny, 76.
King's School, Chester, 52n.
King's Scholarship, 336n.
King's Statutory Declaration against Transubstantiation, 189.

Labour Proficiency Examination, 336n.
Lampeter, 8, 11.
Lampeter, St. Davids College, 11n, 13.
Lands Clauses Act, 130, 132.
Latin, teaching of, 24, 99, 251, 298.
Laugharne, 127.
Laundrywork, 252.
Law Officers of the Crown, 121; Their Opinion, 144, 152, 166.
Lawrence, A. T., 160.
Lawrence, Miss M. A., CI, England (Women), 342, 343, 347.
Leathes, Stanley, 348.
Legal Branch, Board of Education, 71, 224.
Legard, A. G., HMI, 9, 25, 154, 159, 174, 175, 176, 338.
Lefroy, Mr., 70.
Lewes, Col. W., 121, 125, 126, 136.
Lewis, Charles P., 125, 126.
Lewis, Sir J. Herbert, 6, 65, 184, 188, 218, 227, 280, 282, 298; becomes Parliamentary Secretary to Board of Education, 349; and A. T. Davies, 349; and Lloyd George, 349; and Owen Edwards, 349; Royal Commission on University Education in Wales, 349; his scheme of adolescent education, 350; Lewis Report, 350n; reports on Schools by Owen Edwards, 1918, 368.
Lewis, J. W., Assistant Inspector, 361.
Lewis, Rev. Joshua, 120.
Lewis, P. A., Assistant Inspector, 361.
Lewis Report, 350n.
Lewis, T. H., Assistant Inspector, 361.
Lewis School, Pengam, 363n.
Liberal Conference, 184.
Liberal landslide, 193.
Liberal MPs, 9.
Liberal nonconformity, 119, 120.
Liberal Rally, Colwyn Bay, 198.
Library movement, 316.
Lincoln College, Oxford, 22, 219.
Lingen, Lord, 264.

Lindsell, Henry Martin, 128, 130, 132, 134, 170, 181.
Literary meetings, 31.
Littledale, Professor Harold, 90n.
Liverpool, 10, 308.
Liverpool Courier, 385.
Liverpool Daily Post and Mercury, 383.
Llandaff, 8.
Llanddarog, Carmarthenshire, 169.
Llanddeusant National School, 135.
Llanddowror National School, 135.
Llandefeilog, Carmarthenshire, 127.
Llandeilo, 68, 129.
Llandingat, Carmarthenshire, 125.
Llandovery, 125.
Llandovery Collegiate School, 8, 20.
Llandrindod Wells, 34, 203, 205, 236.
Llandybie, United District School Board, 130, 131.
Llandysul, 68, 273, 280.
Llanedi, Carmarthenshire, 127.
Llanelli, 68, 141, 141n, 361.
Llanfihangel ar Arth, 161.
Llanfynydd, 127.
Llangefni, 82, 277.
Llangennech National School, 135, 154, 159.
Llanllwni National School, 127, 135.
Llanpumsaint, 120.
Llansaint National School, 135.
Llanuwchllyn, 238, 316, 341.
Llanybri, Carmarthenshire, 127.
Lleyn, 298.
Lloyd, Charles, 65, 88, 284.
Lloyd George, David (1st Earl Lloyd-George of Dwyfor), 7, 9; and Welsh Parliamentary Party, 9; and religious instruction, 28; and Welsh Local Authorities, 29; and Joint Education Committee, 29; and public control of Voluntary Schools, 29; and 'Colonial Compromise', 29; and his 'No control, no cash', 29, 122; in the Cabinet, 29; and National Council for Education, 37; and external negotiations, 37; his manifesto, 118; and Carmarthenshire Council, 123; and 'Colonial Compromise', 138; Caernarvonshire policy, 140; and Carmarthenshire Inquiry, 160; asks for complete inquiry, 160n, 164; defying 1902 Act, 166; and Welsh Education Department, 187; and the training of teachers, 188; Scheme B, Joint Committee, 188, Llandrindod Wells Conference, 189; autonomous districts, 190; President of the Board of Trade, 193; Memorandum on Welsh Educational Council, 194; Cardiff Cymmrodorion Society, 198; at Colwyn Bay, 198; Cardiff Conference 198; Clause for Welsh

420

Index

National Council for Education, 199; describes Central Education Authority for Wales, 200; Llandrindod Conference, 203; Education Bill, 1906, Committee stage, 204; argues with F. E. Smith, 205; 'Minister' proposal, 206; and parliamentary control over Welsh National Council for Education, 207; in trouble with Campbell-Bannerman and the King, 208; summarises amendments to Clause 37, 210; and A. T. Davies, 213; and 'Special Department', 214; and appointments to Welsh Department, 217; and Edwards, 387.
Lloyd, Bishop D. Lewis, 12, 12n.
Lloyd, Sir John Edward, 8n, 277.
Lloyd, John, 124.
Lloyd, M., 40.
Local Government Act, 1888, 17, 121, 184.
Local Government Board, 124, 134, 150, 185.
Local Taxation (Customs and Excise) Act, 1890, 16, 18.
Lodgings, school pupils, 20n, 20n, 295.
London, 11, 12, 219, 223, 228, 275, 341.
Londonderry, Charles Stewart Vane-Tempest Stewart, 6th Marquess of, 129, 132, 168, 189, 192, 211.
London school leaving examination, 93.
London University, 9, 12.
Lords, House of, 210, 211, 212.

Mackail, John William, 126, 127.
McKenna, Reginald, 49, 58; deputation from C.W.B., 59; obstacles to Practical Autonomy for C.W.B., 60, 64, 70, 216, 218–19, 222, 223, 225, 229.
Macmorran, A., 126n; Opinion, 144.
Madryn Castle, Farm Institute, 343.
Maesteg Secondary School, 72, 73, 74, 76, 78.
Magistrates, 126.
Maitland, W. Fuller, 40.
Manchester, 10.
Manchester Guardian, 189, 221, 227, 262, 328, 383.
Manchester Welsh Society, 7.
Mandamus, proceedings, 118, 118n, 121, 148, 148n, 151, 153, 158, 165, 167.
Mansfield College, Oxford, 52n.
Mathematics, teaching of, 251.
Mathias, R., 253n.
Mathews, Mr., Sub-Inspector, 338.
Maurice, Henry Gascoyen, 258, 259, 260, 262, 263, 278; and Edgar Jones, 279, 280, 283.
Mauritius, 32, 275.
Manual work, 67, 99.
Mayor, R. J. G., 91.

Medical Branch, Board of Education, 224, 315.
Memorandum on Curricula for Primary Teachers, 1909, 91–93.
Memorandum on T work in Wales, 327.
Memorandum on Office Organisation, Morant, 220.
Memorandum on Welsh Intermediate education, J. L. Casson, 66n.
Memorandum on the Welsh Inspectorate, Dr. W. Williams, 354–7.
Memorial to the Lord President of the Council on Welsh Education, 41–43.
Menevia, Bishop of, 198.
Merioneth, 139, 142, LEA 280, 285.
Merthyr Tydfil, 71, 72, 74; Cyfarthfa Castle, 74, 75, 77, 95, 107.
Metallurgy, 26, 242, 293.
Methods of teaching: Literary and Humane subjects, English, History, Geography, Welsh, Music, Chemistry, etc., 272–9.
Meyrick Endowment, 42.
Midlothian campaign, 6.
Milne incident, Board of Education, 314–16.
Mining, 26, 242.
Ministry of Education, 389.
Miscellaneous Regulations and Instructions T Inspection, No. 12, 346–7.
Model Schemes, 29.
Monmouth, Jones Foundation School, 76.
Monmouthshire, LEA 74; 141.
Mold, 368.
Montgomeryshire, LEA 68: 140.
Morant, Sir Robert Louis, 18n, 24n, 25; and his confidential memorandum on office administration, 30; 37, 53, 54, 57, 122, 123, 127, 130, 132, 167, 168, 170; and Agreement, 190; 192, 194; and Welsh Educational Council, 194; Finances of Welsh Educational Council, 196; and Exchequer grants for Welsh education, 197, 204, 212, 213n, 216–24; his authority undermined, 226; 227, 280, 314, 315, 342; and Women Inspectors, 347; 349.
Morgan, Frank, 280.
Morgan, Sir George Osborne, 10, 40.
Morgan, Hopkin, 73, 78.
Morgan, John, 87.
Morgan, J. Lloyd, 65.
Morgan, Lewis, 60, 61n, 203, 205.
Morrell, Enoch, 80n.
Morris, Lewis, 40.
Morris, Mr., Sub-Inspector, 338.
Morris, Dr. T. H., 76, 281.
Morris-Jones, Sir John, 277.
Mostyn, 184.

Index

Mothfai (Myddfai) National School, 135, 161.
Mountain Ash, 63, 73, 76, 141, 142, 258.
Mundella, A. J., 9, 13, 15, 15n, 16, 17, 18, 40.
Municipal Secondary Schools, 37, 73.
Murray, G. H., 65.
Murray, H. J. R., 53, 58.
Music, teaching of, 67, 94, 99, 242, 252, 290, 290n.
Myers, J. L., 275.

National Council of Education for Wales, Draft resolutions, Llandrindod Conference 1906, 236.
National Council for Wales and Monmouthshire, 185.
National Council of Music, 33.
National Exchequer, 54.
National Institutions (Wales) Bills, 185.
National Library of Wales, 6, 33, 294, 316.
National Museum of Wales, 6, 33.
National Society, 136; Case and Opinion, 144, 148; National United Council, 185.
Navigation, 271.
Neath, 141, 166.
Needlework, 252.
Neuadd Wen (Whitehall), Llanuwchllyn, 228.
Newcastle Emlyn, 127, 169.
Newport, 18, 141.
Newport, Technical School, 374.
New Code (Edwards), 225.
Newtown Intermediate School, 19, 184.
Nicholas, J. W., 122, 124–7, 135, 168, 169, 170, 191.
Night Schools, Young Colliers, 26.
Nonconformist Academies, 8.
Nonconformist Voluntaryist Schools, 120.
Nonconformity, 9, 199; and Voluntary Schools, 162, 163; grievances, 164; non-provided (National or Voluntary Schools), 154, 200.
'No rate' movement (Wales) 139; resolutions, 141n; rescinded by Carmarthenshire, 168.
Northamptonshire Education Society, 25.
Norris, C.M., 129n, 130n, 133n, 135n.
North Wales, inspectorial districts, 352.

Office Memorandum, No, 43, 1911, T Education, Wales, 327.
Old Llanedi, Carmarthenshire, 127.
Oral examinations, Central Welsh Board, 51.
Orange, H. W., 344n, 345.

Order (Carmarthenshire Inquiry), 153, 158, 165, 167.
Order for Costs, Carmarthenshire Inquiry, 170.
Order in Council, Welsh National Council for Education, 194, 199.
Oriel College, Oxford, 52n.
Ormsby-Gore, Hon. William G.A., (4th Baron Harlech), 103.
Oswestry High School, 12, 22.
Overseers, parishes, 125, 126.
Owen, Rev. C. F., 162n.
Owen Daniel, 368.
Owen, David (Brutus), 119.
Owen, Sir Hugh, 7, 10, 11, 13.
Owen, Hugh, K.C., his Opinion, 143–144.
Owen, Sir H. Isambard, 27, 27n, 33, 217.
Owen, John, Bishop of St. Davids, 50n, 122, 123, 126, 127, 169, 170, 211, 212.
Owen, J. Trefor, 76n.
Owen, Owen, 12, 12n, 22n, 49, 50, 50n, 55, 60, 63, 65, 85, 88, 89, 94, 101, 102, 104, 184n, 228, and examinations, 288; as an official, 297; his background, 298.
Owen, Tom, HMI, 361.
Oxford University Commissioners, 42.
Oxford Senior Locals, 93; 256.
Oxford University, 12.

Parry, Rev. A. W., Trinity College, Carmarthen, 281.
Part III Authorities, 141, 166.
Peake, Professor Harold, 275.
Pease, J. A., 74, 103, 327.
Pelham, 91.
Pembrey, 135, 154, 159, 161.
Pembroke, 93, 141, 142, 166.
Pembrokeshire, 93, 141, 192.
Penllyn, 316.
Penrhyn, Lord, George Sholto Douglas-Pennant, 2nd Baron, 40.
Permanent Secretaries, Welsh Department, 222.
Phillips, Professor William, 293n.
Philology, 301n.
Phipps, E. B., 226, 310, 314; list of Inspectors, 338, 349.
Physical Training, 67, 94, 99; teaching of, 242, 252, 287.
Physics, teaching of, 251.
Pistol Bill, 123.
Political History, 272, 273.
Pontypool, Jones Foundation School, 76.
Pontypridd, 141, 142, 191.
Pontywaun, 68.
Poor Law Schools, 342, 343.
Population, Wales, 10, 220.
Porth, Engineering bias, 293.

422

Index

Portmadoc, inspection of school, 67.
Port Talbot, Intermediate School, 76.
Powell, J. E., 60, 65, 76–78, 88, 255, 259.
Powell, W. R. H., 40.
Poynter, E., 324.
Practical autonomy, Central Welsh Board, 58.
Practical subjects, 252.
Prefatory Memorandum to Secondary Schools regulations, 70.
Preliminary examinations for student teachers, 84, 84n, 90n, 91, 92.
Preliminary examination for teachers certificate, 319.
Preparatory classes, 295.
Presbyterian College, Carmarthen, 124.
Presbyterian and Congregational fund Boards in London, 8.
Presteigne, 240, 240n.
Price, Henry, HMI, 338., 361.
Prize day, 301.
Prys-Jones, A. G., HMI, 361.
Procedural irregularities, Central Welsh Board, 79.
Professors of Welsh, 292n, 301n.
Progressives, 138.
Proposals 'A' inspection of schools, 363.
Proposals 'B' income for Central Welsh Board, 364.
Proposed Welsh system of Training Colleges, 320–21.
Provisional Education Committee, 186.
Proprietary Schools, 106.
Provided Council Schools, 154.
Private secondary Schools, 293n.
Prussia, 9, 20.
Pullinger, Fred, 344, CI for Technology and evening schools (England), 327, 342–343.
Pupil lodgers, 295.
Pupil Teachers Registration Committee, 91.
Pupil Teachers and Centres, 64, 81–84, 86, and Bursars, 89, 93, 319, 322.
Pugh, L. P., 40.

Quarter (of school), 20n.
Quasi-representative Authorities, 17.
Queen's Colleges, Ireland, 9, 11.
Queen Elizabeth Grammar School, Carmarthen, 8, 82.
Queen's Scholarship, 336n.
Quinquennium, first, Central Welsh Board, 50.
Questionnaire to inspectors from Owen Edwards, 352-3.

Radnorshire, 140.
Rail travel, pupils, 295.
Rate Book, poor rates, 125.
Rathbone, William, 40.

Ratio of inspectorial staff, 355.
Raven Hotel, Shrewsbury, 16.
Rawlinson, John, 160, 161; summarizing the Inquiry, 163, 164.
Real-schulen of Prussia, 9, 20, 20n.
Rebecca, 119.
Recital, Notice of Inquiry, 159.
Redmond, John, 202.
Rees, Caleb, HMI, 361.
Rees, Rev. David, 119, 121.
Reform Act, 1867, 9.
Regulation for Secondary Schools (England), 1904, 24n.
Regulations for Secondary Schools, (Wales) 1908, 31, 66, 322.
Regulations for Technical Schools and Art Schools, 327.
Reichel, Sir H. R., 7, 15, 19, 21, 94.
Religious census, 1851, 119n.
Re-organization of Board of Education's Welsh Inspectorate, 360–361.
Report by Chief Inspector for Wales, 280, 282.
Report of the departmental committee, 1920, 34–35.
Residential Training Colleges, 320.
Rendel, Stuart, 1st Baron, 11n, 17, 17n, 27, 40, 185, 211.
'Revolt' Fund, 166n.
'Revolt' in parliament, 64, 64n.
'Revolt' School, 166n.
Rhewl, 184.
Result fees, 12n.
Rhandirmwyn National School, 135.
Rhondda, 93, 95, 141, 142; defective children, 315.
Rhydderch, R., Sub-Inspector, 338, 348, 361.
Rhyl Intermediate School, 82; Commercial class, 293, 324.
Rhymney, Mon, 218.
Rhys, Professor Sir John, 65, 301n.
Richard, Henry, 10, 40.
Richards, Thomas, 64n.
Roberts, Edward, HMI, 338, 339.
Roberts, John Herbert (1st Baron Clwyd) 65; and Central Welsh Board inspections 68n; 88, 203, 215, 326.
Roberts, L. J., HMI, 338.
Roberts, Principal T. Francis, 73, 90, 94.
Roberts, T. G., 219, 348.
Roberts, W., HMI, 361.
Robinson, Sidney, 65, 282.
Robinson, W. Hammond, 49, 70, 88, 95, 97, 101.
Robson,Edward, R., 171n.
Robson, Sir William, 208, 214.
Roxby, Professor, 275.
Roch, Walter, 64n.
Roman Catholic, 157.

Index

Rowland, Sir John, 227; and Central Welsh Board, 227; and Welsh Department, 317.
Rowlands, Miss Menai, J., HMI, 342, 361.
Royal Commission, University Education, Wales, 34, 38, 309.
Royal Scholarships, 329.
Runciman, Walter, 65; discusses arrangements for inspection, 65; Practical Autonomy denied to Central Welsh Board, 70; 227, 255, 258, 262, 264, 266, 282, 326, 327.
Ruabon, 274.
Rural Science, 242.
Ruskin, John, 242.
Ruthin School, 8, 20.

St. Clears National School, 135, 161.
St. Davids, 240n.
St. Davids Day pamphlets, 312.
St. Davids Day celebrations, 295.
St. Davids Diocesan Association of schools, 136, 162.
St. Mary's Training College, Bangor, 8, 320–21.
Salaries, Inspectors, Wales, 379.
Salaries, Inspectors, differential treatment, England and Wales, 379.
Salaries, teachers, 127, 169.
Sanderson, Arthur, D., 262, 263.
Sandford, H., 42n.
Scheme, Central Welsh Board, 22–24, 364.
Schemes of scholarships, 13.
Science teaching, 251.
Science and Art Department, 24, 114, 326, 327.
School Board, 28.
Schools Inquiry Commission, 8, 20, 242.
School of Medicine, 33.
Schools of Forestry and Agriculture, 184.
School Libraries, 229, 250, 272, 294; Schools Circulating Library, 294, 316.
Schuster, Claude, 133, 134, 144, 146; and LEAs 147; 160, 164, 188.
Scotland, 13, 24n, 292.
Scottish Department, 285.
Scott, Sir Walter, 8.
Scripture, 246.
Scutt, W., HMI (Drawing), 361.
Secondary Schools Examination Council, 24.
Secretary of State for Wales, 185.
Senior Certificate, 288.
Secundar-schulen of Zurich, 20, 20n.
Senior Examiner, T. Branch, 327.
Selby-Bigge, Sir Lewis Amherst, Bart., 342, 343, 349.
Seymour, Charles W., 102.

Shaw, G. T. Capt., Divisional Inspector for Wales in Technological Branch, 338n.
Sheffield, Hallam Parliamentary Division, 201.
Sheffield, Lord, 72, 95, 104, 255, 262, 281, 283, 284, 300.
Sheringham, 216.
Shrewsbury, 16, 191, 255, 258, 263, 318.
Shire Hall, Gloucester, 214.
Simner, Abel, 40.
Sidgwick, A. H., 343.
Skirrow, Benjamin Beck, HMI, 338, 361.
Smith, Frederick Edwin (1st Earl of Birkenhead), 204–214.
Smith, Dr. Vance, 12.
Somervell, A., HMI (Music), 361.
South Kensington, 49, 221, 230, 324.
South Wales (Daily) News, 103, 221, 263, 378, 383.
Spanish, 251.
Spencer, Lord, John Poyntz, 5th Earl, 9, 13.
Spencer, W. K., HMI (Science), 361.
S. Regulations, 85.
Stanley of Alderley, Henry Edward John, 3rd Baron, 60, 65, 85.
Staff Inspectors, 342.
Statement of the Central Welsh Board, 261.
Statutory Authority, 214.
Statutory contributions, 364.
Staff, Welsh Department, 220, 223.
Stephens, Mr. 80.
Staff, Welsh Intermediate Schools, 276.
Stuart-Wortley, C. B., 201–203.
Student Teachers, 371.
Summer Schools, 257, 261, 276.
Sunday Schools, 8, 31; teachers, 251.
Superannuation Act, 1859, 313, 314n, 382.
Supervising inspectors, 361.
Swansea, 14, 18, 74, 75, 77, 78, 93–5, 102, 103, 104, 107, 141, 222.
Swansea Grammar school, 76n.
Swansea Technical College, 374.
Swansea Institution (Blind), 315.
Swansea University College, 33.
Sykes, John C. G., 79, 191.
Switzerland, 19, 275.

Talbot, Mr. (Welsh Department), 220.
Taylor, A., Assistant Inspector, 361.
T Branch, Board of Education, 315.
Teaching in Welsh, 292n, 301n.
Teachers Training Colleges (Elementary) England and Wales, 1913–14, 331–2.
Technical classes, Wales, 26.
Technical education, 25, 26, 230, 309, 323, its administration, 326n, 372.

Index

Technical Instruction Act, 1889, 17, 18.
Technical Institutes, Manchester; Liverpool, 326.
Technical Instruction Committee, Cardiff, 26.
The Education (Provision of Working Balances) Act, 1903, 163.
Theological Colleges, 8, 298.
The Schoolmaster, 262, 383.
The School World, 383.
The Times Educational Supplement, 262.
The Times, 383, 384.
The Welsh Outlook, 7.
Thomas, Abel, 160, 162.
Thomas, Sir Alfred, 29, 30, 58, 185, 200, 215.
Thomas, D. A., 65.
Thomas, David, Sub-Inspector, 338, 361.
Thomas, D. Lleufer, 217.
Thomas, Edward ('Cochfarf'), 85.
Thomas, H. W., 160.
Thomas, Ivor, Junior Inspector, 339.
Thomas, John, HMI, 361.
Thomas, Jenkyn, 263, 264.
Thomas, Morgan, 105.
Thomas, Dr. R. L., 124.
Thomas, T. J., 40.
Thomas, William, Rev., 124.
Towyn, 219.
Training Colleges in Wales, 229, 319–321, 321n, 372.
Training of Elementary school teachers, 291, 330, Schedule B, 331; 371.
Training Schools of Domestic subjects, 329, 333.
Treachery of the Blue Books (Brâd y Llyfrau Gleision), 7.
Treforest, Technical College, 374.
Tregaron Intermediate School, 273, 274.
Tremoilet Memorial National School, 135.
Trevelyan, Charles, 279, 336; and Central Welsh Board Secondary Education and Inspectorate, 358.
Triennial Area Reports, 328, 328n.
Triennial inspection, 65.
Trinity College, Carmarthen, 8, 136.
Trustees (Voluntary Schools), 154.
T work in Wales, 324, 325, and England, 326.
Tycroes, 127.

U Branch, administrative and examinations, 329; 'The Statement' and Schedules, 329–30.
U Branch, Board of Education, 328.
Uniformity of curricula in Intermediate Schools, 242.
Uniform Schemes (Joint Board for Wales), 186.
Unified inspectorate in Wales, 365.
Unification of Welsh education, 200.
Union of Welsh Independents, 124.
Unitarian, 119.
University College of Wales, Aberystwyth, Treasury Grant, 44–5.
University College, Cardiff, 11, 14, 15 26.
University Colleges, and Central Welsh Board, 269n.
University Colleges, financial state of, 349.
University College of Medicine, 33.
University College of Wales, Students at, 16; Parliamentary funds, 197, 301, 321n, 330, 333–5.
University Sunday, 10.
University Training Departments, teachers (secondary), 318, 319, 320–22, 321n.
University Tutorial classes, 361.
University of Wales, Welsh teaching in, 301–2.
University Council, 33.
University Court, 216.
University Senate, 33, 318.
University of Wales, 9, 10, 27, 33; Royal Commission, 1916–18, 33, 309.
Untrained Teachers, 272.
Urdd Gobaith Cymru, (Welsh League of Youth), 388.

Verney, Capt. R.N., 40.
Victoria University, Manchester, 12.
Vivian, Sir H. Hussey, (1st Baron Swansea,) 13, 14, 40.
Vocal music, 290.
Voluntaryists, 120.
Voluntaryist schools, Carmarthenshire, 120.
Voluntaryist movement, West Wales, 120.
Voluntary schools, 28; Carmarthenshire, 124, 128; difficulties of, Carmarthenshire, 129, 154; Managers, 170.
Voluntary schools Act, 1897, 155, 156n.
Voluntary societies, 7.
Voluntary supplemental contributions, 364.
Voluntary Training Colleges, 8.
Vote. B.I., 344, 344n.

Wakeford, Mr., Sub-Inspector, 338, 348.
Wales (National Institutions) Bills, 185.
Walton Parliamentary Division Liverpool, 204.
Warry, W. T., 9.
War Savings in schools, 350.
Waterford, 202.
Watkins, Sir Percy E., 22n, 25n, 362, 386.

Index

Wells Charity, Cardiff, 42.
Welsh Central Board, 19.
Welsh Central Committee, 204, 205.
Welsh County Councils and University, 33, 122; administering the 1902 Act, 139–143.
Welsh County Councils Association, 168, 184, 186; and Swansea Conference, 188; indecisions re W.N.C.E., 193.
Welsh Circulating Schools, 119.
Welsh County Policies (Act of 1902), 137, 141, 141n.
Welsh County Schools Association, 105, 255; manifesto on English teaching, 273.
Welsh Clergy, West Riding, 11, 11n.
Welsh Department, Board of Education, 22, 28, 30; its functions, 30, 34, 103, 104, 215, 216, 280, 281, 300, 307–376; Introduction, 308; adjustment and general objectives, 310; extension of responsibilities, 324; growth and reorganization of Welsh inspectorate, 337; administrative complications, 309; attitude of certain officials of the Board, 312; its aims, 318; transfer of Technical Education, 327; 1920, 376; reforming influence by Edwards, 388.
Welsh defaulting authorities, *see* Defaulting Authorities.
Welsh Educational Charter, 13.
Welsh Education Department, 185.
Welsh Education Inquiry, 120.
Welsh elections, 6.
Welsh Grammar Schools, 13; endowments of, 13.
Welsh headmasters' Association, 90, 95, 318.
Welsh MPs, 264, 282, 285, 325, 340.
Welsh history, teaching of, 274, 277.
Welsh home rule, 201, 211.
Welsh Intermediate Education Act, 1889, 14, 18, 185, 240, 243, 281; *see* Education Welsh Inspectorate, 31; compared with England, 346.
Welsh inspectorate, 1913, 339.
Welsh Intermediate Schools, 240n.
Welsh Joint Education Committee (W.J.E.C.), 36.
Welsh language, 26, 27, 323n.
Welsh Language Society, 276.
Welsh Literature, 14.
Welsh Model Scheme, 29.
Welsh National Council for Education, 17, 28, 34, its functions under departmental Committee of 1920, 35, 58; abortive attempts to establish it, 183; its meaning, 184; Lloyd George and, 184; external negotiating phase, 186; its parliamentary phase of 1906, 193; and Wales, 196; Llandrindod Conference 1906, 203; draft resolutions considered, 203; Powers of Council, 204; Powers and duties of Central Welsh Board for Intermediate education, 204; Powers and duties of Board of Agriculture and Fisheries, 204; eroded form, 210.
Welsh methodology, 302.
Welsh Nonconformists: chapels, 10, 14; and Welsh literature, 14.
Welsh Parliamentary Party, 103, 139, 258, 326.
Welshpool, 95, 93.
Welsh press, 263.
Welsh public Elementary Schools, 20n.
'Welsh Revolt', 28, 118.
Welsh religious revival, 167.
Welsh School Boards, 28.
Welsh Selection committees for inspectors, 345.
Welsh Society, Cambridge, 281.
Welsh-speaking inspectors, 337.
Welsh Sunday Closing Act, 1881, 15.
Welsh Sunday School, 8, 9.
Welsh system of Training Colleges, 319, 319n, 320; Barry, and Caerleon, 321, 321n.
Welsh and French, 291, 301, 318.
Welsh, teaching of, 250; formal grammar, 250, 275, 290, 325.
West Wales Dissent, 119.
Welsh work, Universities Branch, Board of Education, 330, 337n.
Western Mail, 221, 227, 263, 383.
Westminster, Hugh Grosvenor, 1st Duke of, 40.
Westminster, 9.
West Monmouth Grammar School, 76.
West Riding, 25n.
Wheldon, Sir Wynn P., 380.
Whitehall, 18, 218, 202, 222, 223, 226, 228, 230, 255, 386.
Whitland County School, 269.
Whisky money, 16, 23.
Whitworth scholarships and Exhibitions, 329.
Williams, Benjamin T., 11.
Williams, David, 102.
Williams, D. H., 71, 72, 73, 75, 76, 78, 87, 104, 385.
Williams, G. Prys, 348; his ideas on inspectorate; suggests re-distribution of inspectorial districts; his plan of E.S.T. schools in Wales in 1918, 351; and A. T. Davies regarding inspectorate, 354; appointed Divisional Inspector, 361, 361n, 362.
Williams, J. B., Sub-Inspector, 338.
Williams, John, 65.

Index

Williams, John, Venerable, 8.
Williams, W. J., HMI, 348, 361.
Williams, W. Llewelyn, 30, 103, 160, 163, 201, 215.
Williams, William, 120.
Williams, William, HMI, 339, 354; Memorandum on Inspectorate in England and Wales, 354; compares Inspectorate in England and Wales, 355; shows weaknesses of Welsh inspectorate, 356; and C.W.B., 357n; promoted Divisional Inspector, 361.
Willow Street Academy, Oswestry, 12.
Women Inspectors, 347.
Women's Liberation Society, 347.
Wood, Hon. Edward (1st Earl of Halifax), 378.
Woodwork, 242.
Working Balances Act, 163.
Works elementary school system, 7.
Wortley, Stuart, 201.
Wrexham, 141, 166n, 191.

Xenophon, 251.

'Y Mesur Gormes', 123n, *see* 'Coercion of Wales' Bill.
Yorkshire, 25, 25n.
Ysgolion Cymraeg (Welsh Schools), 388, 388n.
Ysgol Haf, 319.
Ysgol Llawr y Betws, 166n.
Ysgol Sabothol, 242.

Zurich, 20, 20n.

Printed by
CSP PRINTING - FAIRWATER - CARDIFF